THE VICTORIA HISTORY
OF THE
COUNTIES OF ENGLAND

A HISTORY OF
SOMERSET

VOLUME V

THE VICTORIA HISTORY
OF THE
COUNTIES OF ENGLAND

EDITED BY C. R. ELRINGTON

THE UNIVERSITY OF LONDON
INSTITUTE OF
HISTORICAL RESEARCH

Oxford University Press, Walton Street, Oxford OX2 6DP
London   New York   Toronto
Delhi   Bombay   Calcutta   Madras   Karachi
Kuala Lumpur   Singapore   Hong Kong   Tokyo
Nairobi   Dar es Salaam   Cape Town
Melbourne   Auckland

and associated companies in
Beirut   Berlin   Ibadan   Mexico City   Nicosia

Oxford is a trade mark of Oxford University Press

Published in the United States by
Oxford University Press, New York

© University of London 1985

ISBN 0 19 722764 3

Printed in Great Britain
by Bigwood & Staple Ltd, Bridgwater, Somerset

INSCRIBED TO THE
MEMORY OF HER LATE MAJESTY
QUEEN VICTORIA
WHO GRACIOUSLY GAVE THE TITLE
AND ACCEPTED THE DEDICATION
OF THIS HISTORY

WATCHET FROM THE EAST

On the left can be seen two sections of the West Somerset Railway, the further one crossing the track of the mineral railway beside which stands Wansbrough Paper Mill; Daw's Castle is beyond the houses at the west end of the town

A HISTORY OF THE
COUNTY OF
SOMERSET

EDITED BY R. W. DUNNING

VOLUME V

PUBLISHED FOR
THE INSTITUTE OF HISTORICAL RESEARCH
BY
OXFORD UNIVERSITY PRESS
1985

Distributed by Oxford University Press until 1 January 1988
thereafter by Dawsons of Pall Mall

CONTENTS OF VOLUME FIVE

LIST OF ILLUSTRATIONS

Thanks are rendered to the following for permission to reproduce material in their possession: Cambridge University Collection of Aerial Photography, Lady Gass, the National Monuments Record of the Royal Commission on Historical Monuments (England) (marked N.M.R.), Somerset Archaeological and Natural History Society (marked S.A.S.), Somerset County Council, Somerset County Library, Somerset Health Authority, and the executors of the late Mr. G. C. Wyndham.

LIST OF MAPS AND PLANS

The maps and street plans were drawn by Millicent B. Thompson of the Somerset County Planning Office from drafts by R. W. Dunning and M. C. Siraut, the three street plans being based on the Ordnance Survey with the sanction of the Controller of H.M. Stationery Office, Crown Copyright reserved. The plans on pages 42, 99, 114, 123, 132, 154, and 167 were drawn by A. P. Baggs.

EDITORIAL NOTE

THIS IS the third volume to be produced as a result of the partnership between the Somerset County Council and the University of London Institute of Historical Research. That partnership is described in the Editorial Note to Volume III, which was published in 1974. The County Council's responsibility for the *Victoria History of Somerset* has, during the compilation of the present volume, been borne by the Libraries, Museums and Records Committee (until 1978 the Libraries and Museums Sub-Committee of the Education and Cultural Services Committee) under the successive chairmanship of Dr. A. W. G. Court (until 1977), the late Mr. G. C. Wyndham (1977–8), the late Sir Michael Gass, K.C.M.G. (1978–81), and Mrs. D. S. Prettejohn (from 1981). The University here records its most sincere thanks for the generosity with which the County Council has met and continues to meet the expense of compiling the *History*.

Mr. R. J. E. Bush, B.A., resigned as Assistant Editor in March 1978 and was succeeded in September of the same year by Miss Mary C. Siraut, B.A., M.Litt.

Many people have given valuable help in the preparation of this volume. Those who were concerned with particular parishes are named in the footnotes to those parishes; they are thanked most warmly. For more extensive help particular thanks are rendered to Lt.-Col. G. W. F. Luttrell, M.C., Lord-Lieutenant for the County of Somerset; the late Sir Michael Gass; Lady Gass; the late Mr. G. C. Wyndham; Dr. Katherine Wyndham; Mrs. R. Brayne-Baker; Dr. A. W. G. Court; Mr. W. Hancock; Mrs. Anna Pawlyn; and Mr. A. F. Tyler. Among the public libraries and record offices to whose librarians or archivists and their staff the thanks of the *History* are offered for their sympathetic and patient co-operation, special mention must be made of the Somerset Record Office.

The structure and aims of the *History* as a whole are outlined in the *General Introduction* (1970).

LIST OF CLASSES OF DOCUMENTS
IN THE PUBLIC RECORD OFFICE
USED IN THIS VOLUME
WITH THEIR CLASS NUMBERS

Chancery

		Proceedings
C	1	Early
C	2	Series I
C	3	Series II
C	54	Close Rolls
C	66	Patent Rolls
C	131	Extents for Debts
		Inquisitions post mortem
C	133	Series I, Edw. I
C	135	Edw. III
C	136	Ric. II
C	137	Hen. IV
C	138	Hen. V
C	139	Hen. VI
C	140	Edw. IV and V
C	142	Series II
C	143	Inquisitions ad quod damnum
C	149	Modern Deeds

Court of Common Pleas

CP 25(2)	Feet of Fines, Series II
CP 43	Recovery Rolls

Exchequer, King's Remembrancer

E 117	Church Goods
E 122	Customs Accounts
E 134	Depositions taken by Commission
E 142	Ancient Extents
E 150	Inquisitions post mortem, Series II
E 179	Subsidy Rolls
E 190	Port Books
	Ancient Deeds
E 210	Series D
E 211	Series DD

Exchequer, Augmentation Office

E 315	Miscellaneous Books
E 317	Parliamentary Surveys, Commonwealth
E 318	Particulars for Grants

Exchequer, First Fruits and Tenths Office

E 331	Bishops' Certificates of Institution

Home Office

HO 107	Census Papers, 1851 Census
HO 129	Census Papers, 1851 Census; Ecclesiastical Returns

Exchequer, Office of the Auditors of Land Revenue

LR 2	Miscellaneous Books
LR 6	Receivers' Accounts, Series I

Registrar General

RG 10	Census Returns, 1871

Court of Requests

REQ 2	Proceedings

Special Collections

SC 2	Court Rolls
SC 6	Ministers' Accounts
	Rentals and Surveys
SC 11	Rolls
SC 12	Portfolios

State Paper Office

SP 14	State Papers Domestic, Jas. I

Court of Star Chamber

	Proceedings
STAC 1	Hen. VII
STAC 2	Hen. VIII
STAC 3	Edw. VI
STAC 4	Mary

War Office

WO 30	Miscellaneous

Court of Wards and Liveries

WARD 7	Inquisitions post mortem
WARD 9	Miscellaneous Books

SELECT LIST OF ACCUMULATIONS
IN THE SOMERSET RECORD OFFICE

Deposited Collections

DD/AB	Marquess of Ailesbury
AH	Acland-Hood family of Fairfield
AS	Lord Ashburton
BW	Bridgwater Borough Council
CC	Church Commissioners
CCH	Couch of Stogumber (solicitors)
CCHg	Couch (additional deposit)
CH	Channer, Channer, and Ligertwood of Taunton (solicitors)
CN	Clarke, Lukin, and Newton of Chard (solicitors)
CPL	Capel of Chipstable
DP	Dodson and Pulman of Taunton (solicitors)
DR	Miss J. E. Deering of Aldburgh
DT	Dorset Natural History and Archaeological Society
DV	H. G. E. Dunsterville
EDS	Department of Education and Science
FS	Foster of Wells (solicitors)
GB	Gibbs family of Barrow Gurney
GC	Capt. Graham-Clarke (Hestercombe MSS.)
HB	Hodges of Weston-super-Mare (solicitors)
HC	Hancock family MSS.
HLM	Helyar family of Poundisford
HWD	Howard family of Creech St. Michael
JL	Mme Jullien of Gotton (Musgrave MSS.)
KW	King, Wilkinson, and Co. of Taunton
L	Luttrell family of Dunster
MDW	J. Meadow (St. Albyn of Alfoxton MSS.)
MGR	Moger, Campbell, and Trounson of Bath (solicitors)
MY	Revd. H. C. B. Mynors (Halliday MSS.)
NA	National Trust
NW	Nantes and Wylde of Bridport (solicitors)
PD	Capt. Picton-Davies of Weston-super-Mare
PLE	Poole and Co. of South Petherton (solicitors)
RI	Risdon and Co. of Williton (solicitors)
RR	Rutter and Rutter of Wincanton (solicitors)
SAS	Somerset Archaeological and Natural History Society
SF	Sanford family of Nynehead
SFR(w)	Society of Friends (West Somerset Division)
SH	Lord Strachie of Sutton Court
SL	Slade family of Maunsel
SOG	Society of Genealogists
SP	Sheppard family of Taunton
SX	Sussex Archaeological Society
TB	Trollope-Bellew family of Crowcombe
TK	Throckmorton family of Coughton Court, Alcester
V	Vernacular Architecture Group
WG	Waldegrave family of Chewton Mendip
WI	Somerset Federation of Women's Institutes
WO	Trevelyan family of Nettlecombe
WOA	Wood and Awdry of Chippenham (solicitors)
WY	Wyndham family of Orchard Wyndham
S/SH	Col. H. R. H. Southam
WH	Lord Wharton (Halswell MSS.)

X/BOA	Miss E. R. Broadmead (W. Gresswell's papers)
BOU	H. B. Boucher of Portugal
CG	Miss E. Commings of Taunton
CNN	Wm. Cunnington and son, Devizes
ET	Exeter City Library
FRC	R. S. France (Bluett MSS.)
GV	F. R. Govett
HEA	G. V. M. Heap (Lord Taunton's papers)
HU	C. R. Hudleston
HUX	Mrs. M. Huxtable
HYA	Mrs. W. Hayward
LGV	Longueville of Oswestry (solicitors)
LOV	E. Lovett of Bristol
LY	J. W. & D. R. Maxwell-Lyte (Lyte MSS.)
MMN	P. W. H. Mossman
PLY	Plymouth City Archivist
PRD	Mrs. E. W. Paradine of Taunton
PSE	A. A. Pearse of Watchet
SU	Miss V. Sully
TYL	A. F. Tyler of Nether Stowey
VZ	Vizard and Co. of Monmouth (solicitors)
WD	J. D. Wood and Co.
BR/ely	Peirs Ellis and Jackson Young (Bouverie, Pym, and Hale MSS.)
fc	Frere, Cholmeley, and Nicholsons of London (solicitors)
fr	Farrer and Co. of London
gd	Goldsmiths Company (Warre MSS.)
gm	Glyn, Mills, and Co. of London
lw	Robson Lowe of London
nf	Norfolk Record Society
nsb	Nisbet and Co. of London (solicitors)
py	Perry of Brighton (solicitors)
vi	Vizards of London
D/P/	Parish Collections
D/R/wil	Williton Rural District Council
D/U/wa	Watchet Urban District Council

Diocesan Records

D/D/B reg	bishops' registers
B returns	benefice returns
Bg	exchanges of glebe
Bi	commissions to institute
Bo	ordination papers
Bp	presentation deeds
Br	resignations
Ca	act books
Cd	deposition books
Cf	faculty papers
Ol	licence books
Pd	deans' peculiar papers
Ppb	prebendal peculiar papers
Rg	glebe terriers
Rm	meeting house licences
Rr	bishops' transcripts of parish registers
V	diocesan books
Vc	visitation acts
V returns	visitation returns

SOMERSET RECORD OFFICE ACCUMULATIONS

Quarter Sessions Records

Q/RDe	inclosure awards
RE	parliamentary elections
REl	land tax assessments
REr	electoral registers
RL	victuallers' recognizances
RR	recusants' lands, meeting house licences
RSf	Friendly Society returns
RUp	deposited plans
SR	sessions rolls

County Council Records

C/E	education department

Other Deposits

D/N/wsc	West Somerset Methodist Circuit records

Photostats and Microfilms

T/PH/ay	F. J. Ayres (TS. of the Revd. W. Holland's diary)
bscs	Bath Stamp and Coin Shop
no	Northamptonshire Record Office
pro	Public Record Office
rhs	D. R. Harris
win	Winchester College Records

NOTE ON ABBREVIATIONS

Among the abbreviations and short titles used the following, in addition to those listed in the Victoria History's *Handbook for Editors and Authors*, may require elucidation:

B.L.	British Library
Char. Don.	*Abstract of Returns of Charitable Donations made in 1787–8*, H.C. 511 (1816), xvi
Collinson, *Hist. Som.*	J. Collinson, *History and Antiquities of the County of Somerset* (3 vols., 1791)
Dioc. Dir.	*Bath and Wells Diocesan Directory (and Almanack)* (1908–) (Almanack discontinued 1948)
Dioc. Kal.	*(New) Bath and Wells Diocesan Kalendar* (1888–1907)
Downside Review	*Downside Review* (1880–)
E. Dwelly, *Par. Rec.*	E. Dwelly, *Parish Records* (priv. print. 1913–)
Educ. Enq. Abstract	*Abstract of Educational Returns*, H.C. 62 (1835), xli
Educ. of Poor Digest	*Digest of Returns to the Select Committee on the Education of the Poor*, H.C. 224 (1819), ix (2)
Forde Abbey Cart.	Cartulary of Forde Abbey, MS. at Forde Abbey, Dorset
H.M.C. Wells	Historical Manuscripts Commission, Series 12, *Calendar of the Manuscripts of the Dean and Chapter of Wells* (2 vols., 1907, 1914)
Livings Aug. Q.A.B.	*Livings Augmented by Queen Anne's Bounty, 1703–1815*, H.C. 115 (1814–15), xii; H.C. 114 (1837), xli; H.C. 122 (1867), liv
Maxwell Lyte, *Dunster*	H. C. Maxwell Lyte, *History of Dunster* (2 vols., 1902)
Nat. Soc. *Inquiry*	*Result of the Returns to the General Inquiry made by the National Society ... 1846–7* (1849)
P.R.O.	Public Record Office
Proc. Som. Arch. Soc.	*Proceedings of the Somersetshire Archaeological and Natural History Society* (from 1968 *Somerset Archaeology and Natural History*)
15th Rep. Com. Char.	*15th Report of the Charity Commissioners for England and Wales*, H.C. 383 (1826), xiii
Rep. Com. Eccl. Rev.	*Report of the Royal Commission on Ecclesiastical Revenues* [67], H.C. (1835), xxii
Rep. Com. Women and Children in Agric.	*Report of the Royal Commission on Children ... and Women in Agriculture* [4202-I], H.C. (1868–9), xiii
Rep. Som. Cong. Union (1896)	*Annual Report of the Somerset Congregational Union and of the Evangelist Society presented at the One-Hundredth Anniversary* (1896)
R.O.	Record Office
Sanders, *Eng. Baronies*	I. J. Sanders, *English Baronies* (1960)
Schs. Lists	Somerset County Council, Education Committee, *Lists of Schools* (1905–)
Sellick, *W. Som. Mineral Rly.*	R. Sellick, *West Somerset Mineral Railway* (1970)
S.R.O.	Somerset Record Office
S.R.S.	*Somerset Record Society* (for list of publications used in this volume see page xix)
S. & D. N. & Q.	*Somerset and Dorset Notes and Queries*
Som. Co. Gaz.	*Somerset County Gazette*
Som. Incumbents, ed. Weaver	*Somerset Incumbents*, ed. F. W. Weaver (1889)
Som. Protestation Returns, ed. Howard and Stoate	*Somerset Protestation Returns and Subsidy Rolls*, ed. A. J. Howard and T. L. Stoate (1975)
Som. Wills, ed. Brown	*Abstracts of Somersetshire Wills, etc., copied from the Manuscript Collections of the late Revd. F. Brown* (6 vols., priv. print. 1887–90)
Wedlake, *Watchet*	A. L. Wedlake, *History of Watchet* (2nd edn. 1973)
Wells Wills, ed. Weaver	*Wells Wills*, ed. F. W. Weaver (1890)
Youngs, *Local Admin. Units*	F. A. Youngs, *Guide to the Local Administrative Units of England*, i: *Southern England* (1979)

LIST OF
SOMERSET RECORD SOCIETY PUBLICATIONS
USED IN THIS VOLUME

i	*Bishop Drokensford's Register, 1309–27* (1887)
ii	*Somerset Chantries, 1548* (1888)
iii	*Kirby's Quest* (1889)
vi	*Pedes Finium, 1196–1307* (1892)
vii	*Cartularies of Bath Priory* (1893)
ix & x	*Register of Ralph of Shrewsbury, 1327–63* (1896)
xi	*Somersetshire Pleas, c. 1200–56* (1897)
xii	*Pedes Finium, 1307–46* (1898)
xiii	*Registers of Bishop Giffard, 1265–6, and Bishop Bowett, 1401–7* (1899)
xiv	*Cartularies of Muchelney and Athelney Abbeys* (1899)
xvi	*Somerset Wills, 1383–1500* (1901)
xvii	*Pedes Finium, 1347–99* (1902)
xviii	*Bellum Civile* (1902)
xix	*Somerset Wills, 1501–30* (1903)
xx	*Certificate of Musters, 1569* (1904)
xxi	*Somerset Wills, 1531–58* (1905)
xxii	*Pedes Finium, 1399–1485* (1906)
xxiii	*Quarter Sessions Records, 1607–25* (1907)
xxv	*Cartulary of Buckland Priory* (1909)
xxviii	*Quarter Sessions Records, 1646–60* (1912)
xxix & xxx	*Register of Bishop Bubwith, 1407–24* (1913–14)
xxxi & xxxii	*Register of Bishop Stafford, 1425–43* (1915–16)
xxxiii	*The Honour of Dunster* (1918)
xxxvi	*Somersetshire Pleas, 1255–72* (1921)
xl	*Medieval Wills from Wells, 1543–6, 1554–6* (1925)
xlix & l	*Register of Bishop Bekynton, 1443–65* (1934–5)
li	*Somerset Enrolled Deeds* (1936)
lii	*Registers of Bishop Stillington and Bishop Fox, 1466–94* (1937)
liv	*Registers of Bishop King and Bishop de Castello, 1496–1518* (1938)
lv	*Bishops' Registers, 1518–59* (1940)
lxi	*Stogursey Charters* (1946)
lxvii	*Sales of Wards, 1603–41* (1965)
lxxi	*Somerset Assize Orders, 1640–59* (1971)
lxxvi	*Somerset Maps* (1981)
lxxvii	*Calendar of Somerset Chantry Grants, 1548–1603* (1982)
extra ser.	*Some Somerset Manors* (1931)

WHITLEY HUNDRED

(*Part*)

WHITLEY hundred, belonging to the abbots of Glastonbury and located principally in the centre of the county, comprised the parishes of Ashcott, Blackford, Butleigh, Compton Dundon, Cossington, Greinton, High Ham, Holford, Holton, Middlezoy, West Monkton, Moorlinch, Othery, Podimore Milton, Shapwick, Street, Walton, Westonzoyland, Wheathill, and Woolavington.[1] The history of the hundred is deferred, but the history of Holford is given below because part of the parish, Newhall, lay in Williton hundred, because of its intimate relationship with the neighbouring parish of Dodington, itself in Williton hundred, and because of Holford's isolation from the main part of Whitley hundred. A plot of land at Leigh in Crowcombe was said to have been part of Whitley hundred in 1353.[2]

[1] *S.R.S.* iii. 115–24.

[2] S.R.O., DD/TB 12/1, ct. roll.

HOLFORD

HOLFORD, named after a crossing point on the stream in the deeply cut valley at the mouth of Holford Combe, lies on the north-eastern slopes of the Quantocks.[1] The ancient parish, to which the present article relates,[2] was shaped roughly like a **W**, its eastern arm detached from the remainder. The western arm, including Holford village, was a narrow band rarely more than 0.5 km. wide but some 3.5 km. from north to south along the course of Holford water. In the centre of the **W**, linked with the western arm by a narrow strip of woodland, a roughly triangular area included Newhall farm and part of the hamlet of Currill. The narrow eastern part of the parish, known as Batchwell, ran north-east from the Quantock scarp just south of Dowsborough for some 3.5 km., passing the southern edge of Dodington to the outskirts of Nether Stowey. The woodland and commons on the hills were bounded by watercourses and footpaths, with individual holdings in the 18th century divided by fences, heaps of stones, and landmarks named Lord's Bench, Nog Head, Wilmot's Pool, and Poor Oak well.[3] The whole parish was thought to measure 796 a. in 1881.[4] In 1884 Holford lost the central area called Newhall to Dodington, and in 1886 Batchwell was also added to Dodington.[5] Moorhouse and Woodlands, about 450 a. including 45 people in 9 houses, and Alfoxton, some 360 a. but only 1 house, were transferred to Holford from Kilton and Stringston respectively in 1886.[6] In 1901 the civil parish covered 1,083 a.[7] In 1933 the civil parish of Dodington was amalgamated with that of Holford to form the civil parish of Holford, measuring 1,316 ha. (3,253 a.) in 1971.[8]

The two main arms of the parish ran down over the Hangman Grits of the higher slopes of the Quantocks to the gravels and marls of the coastal shelf.[9] The western arm formed the eastern side of Holford Combe, and fell from c. 213 m. at its highest point to 122 m. at the broadening mouth of the combe. The eastern arm began near the 290 m. contour and ran, at first steeply across common and woodland, and then more gently, reaching 56 m. at Stogursey brook east of Perry Mill.

Holford village lies at the extreme western edge of the parish at the mouth of Holford Combe, at a point where the road west from Nether Stowey divided, one branch running as the Great Road or Old Stowey Lane westwards over the Quantocks to Staple in West Quantoxhead, the other skirting the northern end of the Quantock ridge. St. John's cross, probably marking the junction of the Great Road with the lane from Holford Combe, still stood in 1716.[10] The subsidiary settlement at Currill or Corewell, partly in Stringston parish, existed by the early 14th century.[11] Holford village expanded up Holford Combe from the early 19th century. In the 1930s there was residential development in the northern tip of the parish; in the 1950s Holford village expanded north-eastwards into the area that had been added from Kilton.

The eastern side of the triangular road pattern in Holford village was probably created when the lower route from Nether Stowey to Minehead was adopted by the Minehead turnpike trust in 1765,[12] in preference to the Great Road. Small alterations to the lanes in the east of the parish improved access to woodland at Five Lords' wood in 1788,[13] and involved the abandonment of part of an old road to Over Stowey.[14]

Small pieces of land at Currill c. 1300 may indicate the remains of open fields there,[15] but the shape of closes established in the east by the early 16th century do not suggest common arable.[16] In the latter area lay a medieval park, part of the Durborough estate and traceable by the field name Trivet's and Tripod's park.[17] One side of the park lay along the boundary with Dodington; another part of the boundary bank was 'taken down' in the mid 18th century.[18]

There was an alehouse by 1609 which was closed in 1613.[19] A cottage later called Burnell's or Holford inn was a public house by 1657, and survived as such until 1755 or later.[20] Another inn, the Fox and Goose, was established by 1716, and may have survived until after 1754.[21] In 1980 it was two private houses, of which one was known as Glenside. An inn in the village on the Minehead road was established by 1851.[22] By 1859 it was known as the Plough,[23] and remained in 1980.

The population in 1801 was 125.[24] By 1821 it had almost doubled, but thereafter it gradually decreased, falling to 145 by 1871. An increase to 169 by 1891 was in part due to boundary changes. By 1911 the total had fallen to 88, but within the next twenty years it had almost doubled to 171. Subsequent figures for the parish alone are not available.[25]

MANOR AND OTHER ESTATES. Two Domesday estates lay in the ancient parish of Holford. The larger, assessed at 1 hide, was held by Hugh of William de Mohun in succession to Alwold,[26] and

---

[1] Ekwall, *Eng. Place-Names* (1960), 245. This article was completed in 1980.
[2] S.R.O., tithe award.
[3] Huntington Libr., Stowe MSS., ST Maps 106–9 (maps 1764–5, c. 1784, 1791).
[4] *Census*, 1881.
[5] Ibid. 1891; *Local Govt. Bd. Order* 19,060.
[6] *Census*, 1891.
[7] Ibid. 1901.
[8] *Som. Review Order* 1933; *Census*, 1971.
[9] Geol. Surv. Map 1″, drift, sheet 295 (1956 edn.).
[10] S.R.O., DD/MDW 20, deed 1716; copy deed in possession of Mrs. Bunch, whose house, called Longstone, perhaps takes its name from the cross shaft.
[11] S.R.O., DD/AH 66/15.
[12] 5 Geo. III, c. 93.

[13] S.R.O., Q/SR, July 1788.
[14] Ibid. DD/AH 66/11.
[15] Ibid. 66/15.
[16] Ibid. 65/9.
[17] Ibid. 35/32, 66/11; ibid. D/P/hol 21/1/1; ibid. tithe award; Huntington Libr., Stowe MSS., ST Map 106.
[18] S.R.O., DD/AH 66/11.
[19] Ibid. Q/RL; *S.R.S.* xxiii. 82, 103.
[20] S.R.O., DD/MDW 20–21; ibid. Q/RL; Dyfed R.O., D/CAR 202.
[21] S.R.O., DD/MDW 20–21; ibid. Q/RL.
[22] P.R.O., HO 107/1920.
[23] Harrison, Harrod, and Co. *Dir. Som.* (1859).
[24] *V.C.H. Som.* ii. 350.
[25] Ibid.; *Census*, 1911–31.
[26] *V.C.H. Som.* i. 505.

can be traced as a fee held of the honor of Dunster until 1777.[27] By 1166 the fee was probably one of those held by William de Curci[28] (d. 1171), and descended as a mesne lordship with the barony of Stogursey, passing in 1224 to Joan, wife of Hugh de Neville of Essex (d. 1234). John de Neville (d. 1246)[29] was called to warrant the terre tenant against Reynold de Mohun in 1235,[30] and in 1358–9 another John de Neville claimed the mesne lordship,[31] which has not been traced later.

It is not known when the estate was subinfeudated, but since the church was surrounded by its lands, Robert son of Alfred, who gave the church to Stogursey Priory in 1175, is likely to have been the terre tenant.[32] By 1279 the estate was held by Matthew de Furneaux,[33] and it descended with the manor of Kilve[34] through the Furneaux family to Elizabeth Blount, whose daughter Alice succeeded in 1399 to the estate called *HOLFORD* manor.[35] Like Kilve it was held by the Rogers family from 1419 and passed to the Cunditts in 1664.[36] John Cunditt (d. 1771) seems to have sold his lands in Holford to John St. Albyn by 1746, and they were absorbed into the Alfoxton estate.[37]

In 1500 John St. Albyn of Chilton Trivet was holding land called the manors of *ALFOXTON AND LYMBER*, which included property in Holford.[38] Later in the 16th century the estate was known as Lymbards,[39] and by 1718 as the manor of Alfoxton with Lymberds and Holford.[40] The land in Holford thus seems to have descended in the St. Albyn family with the manor of Alfoxton in Stringston.

An estate called *NEWHALL*, held in 1066 by Merlesuain and in 1086 by Robert son of Roscelin of Ralph Pagnell, lay in the centre of the ancient parish.[41] The subsequent ownership is not certain, but it was probably attached to that estate in North Newton in North Petherton which descended from Robert de Odburville with the forestership of North Petherton. The occupant was charged with the service of attending at North Petherton park at fawning time, a service still discharged as a cash rent in the 1730s.[42] The tenant in 1642 was probably Thomas Clutsome.[43] By 1720 the estate belonged to the Dodington family and was a holding of 24 a.;[44] in 1840 Newhall farm was just over 90 a. in extent.[45] The buildings remaining in 1980 date from the 19th century, but stand on the site of an earlier house.

Part of the same section of the parish, known as *CURRILL*, was held by the Verneys in the 14th and earlier 15th centuries,[46] and George Dodington bought a house and land there in 1606.[47] From another George Dodington, owner in 1720, the estate descended with the manor of Dodington, passing to the Aclands in 1835.[48]

ECONOMIC HISTORY. Holford and Newhall between them included 4 ploughlands in 1086; Holford had 3 a. of meadow, 60 a. of pasture, and 4 a. of woodland, and Newhall included ½ league of woodland. Holford demesne was three times the size of the tenant holdings, but all but one of the 8 tenants on the two estates were bordars. The Holford estate had doubled in value since 1066.[49]

By 1327 Thomas Trivet held the largest estate in the parish, probably the land in the eastern area which was part of Durborough manor.[50] Simon Furneaux held lands worth only 40s. in 1359.[51] The Sydenham family had some land in the parish by 1500,[52] and the Lytes and the Verneys had small holdings at Currill and elsewhere.[53] By the late 16th century the Dodingtons had begun to acquire land in the parish,[54] and by the early 18th century owned Durborough manor and Newhall.[55]

Corn and peas were listed as tithable crops in the early 17th century. In the 1630s Durborough Hill was divided between sheep and tillage,[56] and in the 1640s land formerly under grass in the west part of the parish was ploughed and sown in rotation with oats, peas, barley, peas, and fallow, with a single application of lime.[57] Common rights on the higher ground seem to have been only gradually extinguished. By 1639 the Dodingtons held a fifth share in the former common, presumably the origin of the name Five Lords' wood.[58] Currill or Holford common remained for stocking cattle until after 1792,[59] but by 1840 it was occupied by Sir Peregrine Acland.[60] The marquess of Buckingham acquired some common turbary rights in intermixed holdings, but areas remaining uninclosed by 1819 had been reclaimed by Holford people.[61] There were still 64 a. of common in 1840,[62] and some survived in 1980 in the hands of the National Trust.[63]

Much of the former common was converted to woodland: Holford Edge, in Holford Combe, was coppiced by c. 1727, and in 1734 other parts of the same land were let for felling.[64] By 1764 Danesborough wood was planted, together with Custom or

[27] *S.R.S.* xxxiii, p. 351.   [28] Ibid. p. 5.
[29] Sanders, *Eng. Baronies*, 143.
[30] *S.R.S.* xxxiii, p. 28.
[31] Ibid. xvii. 185.
[32] Ibid. lxi, pp. 12–13.
[33] Ibid. extra ser. 316.
[34] Below, Kilve, manors.
[35] *S.R.S.* xxxiii, p. 106.
[36] Below, Kilve, manors.
[37] *S.R.S.* xxxiii, p. 345.
[38] Devon R.O., DD/4183.
[39] P.R.O., C 3/162/57.
[40] S.R.O., DD/MDW 21.
[41] *V.C.H. Som.* i. 510.
[42] S.R.O., DD/AH 21/2: notes by Thos. Palmer c. 1730 based on MSS. at Petherton Park.
[43] *Som. Protestation Returns*, ed. Howard and Stoate, 284.
[44] Ibid. DD/AH 37/26.
[45] Ibid. tithe award.
[46] Ibid. DD/AH 21/2.
[47] *S.R.S.* li, pp. 174–5.
[48] S.R.O., DD/AH 7/4, 37/26, 55/2.

[49] *V.C.H. Som.* i. 505, 510; cf. 104 a. of wood in Exon. Domesday, ibid. 505 n.
[50] *S.R.S.* iii. 122.
[51] *Cal. Inq. p.m.* x, p. 395.
[52] S.R.O., DD/WY 1/30.
[53] Ibid. DD/X/LY, p. 38; DD/AH 65/1, 9, 66/3; *Cal. Pat.* 1557–8, 263.
[54] *S.R.S.* lxvii, p. 148.
[55] Ibid. li, pp. 174–5; S.R.O., DD/AH 33/3, 37/13, 18, 21, 25–6, 28.
[56] S.R.O., D/D/Rg 272.
[57] Ibid. D/P/hol 2/1/1, memo. in par. reg.
[58] Ibid. DD/AH 37/3. The wood was also known as Five Lawn wood: ibid. DD/AH 66/11; ibid. tithe award; Huntington Libr., Stowe MSS., ST Map 106 (1764).
[59] S.R.O., DD/MY 35.
[60] Ibid. tithe award.
[61] Ibid. DD/AH 37/30; Huntington Libr., Stowe MSS., STG box 49, survey 1819.
[62] S.R.O., tithe award.
[63] Ibid. DD/NA; *Som. Co. Herald*, 13 July 1946.
[64] S.R.O., DD/MDW 19.

Newspring wood.[65] By 1840 the Aclands owned 146 a. of woodland out of a total of 178 a.[66]

By 1840 the three largest farms were known as Zesters, Newhall, and Winsors,[67] the first two created out of smaller units by the early 18th century and held from the 1760s onwards on short leases under the Dodingtons and the Grenvilles.[68] From 1835 the Aclands owned most of the parish, the farms equally divided between arable and grass.[69] By 1851 a farm of 210 a. had been created by uniting Newhall and Zesters.[70] By 1980 the land was largely under grass, and had been absorbed into holdings based outside the ancient parish.[71]

Cloth was made at Holford as elsewhere in the district. Weavers are found in 1584,[72] and 1684,[73] a tucker in 1606,[74] dyers c. 1590 and 1681,[75] and clothiers in 1680, 1688, 1698, and 1709.[76] Lewis Pollard (d. 1688), a clothier, left goods valued at over £328, including not only cloth and racking and finishing equipment but also raw materials and dye stuffs suggesting organized production.[77] There was a linen house in Holford by 1721,[78] a dye house by 1756,[79] and two fulling mills in 1664.[80]

The Dodington copper workings included an ore floor at Newhall and an adit there which was opened after 1787.[81] The manor court at Dodington in 1817 heard complaints about ore dressing at Newhall and about the unrailed state of shafts.[82] An extensive tannery was established in Holford Combe by 1840.[83] By 1856 it possessed a wide range of buildings including a bark mill, tan pits, saw pit, glue house, counting house, and carpenter's shop.[84] The tannery continued to operate until the beginning of the 20th century, and by 1906 the owner was also a road contractor.[85] By 1910 the dwelling house, across the stream in Kilve, had been converted into a private hotel, known in 1980 as the Combe House Hotel.[86] The site includes converted industrial buildings and a large iron water-wheel.

From the late 1890s apartments and boarding houses in the village,[87] and later the Combe House Hotel, catered for holiday makers, and a garage was established by 1931.[88]

MILLS. There was a mill at Holford in 1086.[89] Its site is not known, but the mill was part of the main holding and was thus presumably driven by Holford water. The continuous existence of the mill cannot be traced, but by 1718 a grist mill, known as Over Mill to distinguish it from Higher Mill in Kilve,[90] lay at the northern tip of the parish. It was still there in 1840 but had been demolished by 1886.[91]

By 1664 there were three fulling mills on the Rogers estate of Kilve and Holford, of which two were in Holford and one in Stringston.[92] One of the Holford mills had been built by c. 1590.[93] The other, described as lately built in 1664, was called Broadwood Mill, and a dye house stood near it.[94] It remained in use until 1832 or later.[95]

LOCAL GOVERNMENT. Most of the parish lay in Whitley hundred,[96] but Newhall was in Williton. Holford tithing extended beyond the parish boundary to include Perry Mill in Dodington.[97]

No record has been found of a separate manor court for any of the estates in the ancient parish. Tenants of Holford manor in the 17th century owed suit to Kilve manor court, sometimes called the court baron of Kilve and Holford.[98] The Dodingtons' tenants were required to do suit at Dodington manor court,[99] or in 1625 at Stogursey.[1]

One churchwarden administered parish affairs by the 1760s,[2] and there was a single overseer by the early 19th century. There is one reference to a meeting of inhabitants in 1824, and one to a vestry in 1828.[3] A parish house is recorded in 1699.[4] A poorhouse still existed in 1840 although the parish had been part of the Williton poor-law union since 1836.[5] The house was in 1980 part of the house known as Brackenside in Holford Combe. The parish became part of the Williton rural district in 1894, and of West Somerset district in 1974.[6]

CHURCH. In 1175 the church of Holford was given by Robert son of Alfred to Stogursey Priory.[7] Successive priors, or the Crown when the priory was in royal hands, held the patronage of the rectory[8] until the priory's estates passed to Eton College in 1440.[9] The living remained in the hands of the warden and fellows of Eton until 1913 when Dodington was united with Holford and the college shared the presentation with Lord St. Audries.[10] The college

[65] Huntington Libr., Stowe MSS., ST Maps 106–7; S.R.O., tithe award.
[66] S.R.O., tithe award; the schedule of the award is inaccurate.
[67] S.R.O., tithe award.
[68] Ibid. DD/AH 7/4, 37/26, 31, 33.
[69] Ibid. tithe award; ibid. DD/AH 55/2; above, manor.
[70] P.R.O., HO 107/1920.
[71] Local inf.
[72] S.R.O., DD/MDW 20.
[73] Ibid. DD/SP, inventory 1684.
[74] S.R.S. li, pp. 174–5.
[75] S.R.O., DD/GB 145; DD/MDW 15.
[76] Ibid. DD/MDW 19; DD/SP, inventory 1688; ibid. Q/SR 209/4.
[77] Ibid. DD/SP, inventory 1688.
[78] Ibid. DD/MDW 21.
[79] Ibid. DD/AH 13/1.
[80] Below.
[81] J. Hamilton and J. F. Lawrence, Men and Mining on the Quantocks (1970), 38.
[82] S.R.O., DD/AH 14/14.
[83] Ibid. tithe award.
[84] Ibid. DD/CCH 4/2.
[85] Kelly's Dir. Som. (1902, 1906).
[86] Ibid. (1910).

[87] Ibid. (1894, 1897, 1902, 1931).
[88] Ibid. (1931).
[89] V.C.H. Som. i. 505.
[90] Ibid. Q/REl; ibid. DD/MDW 21.
[91] Ibid. tithe award; O.S. Map 6″, Som. XXXVII. SW. (1886 edn.).
[92] S.R.O., DD/L 2/7/37.
[93] Ibid. DD/GB 145.
[94] S.R.S. xxxviii. 352; S.R.O., DD/MDW 15, 20–21.
[95] S.R.O., Q/REl.
[96] Ibid. DD/AH 21/2.
[97] Ibid. Q/REl.
[98] Ibid. DD/MDW 14, 21; DD/HC 6M; Devon R.O. 337B/28/13, 32/54.
[99] S.R.O., DD/AH 31/29; 37/31; 37/33.
[1] Ibid. 34/21, 37/10.
[2] 15th Rep. Com. Char. 491.
[3] S.R.O., D/P/hol 4/1/1.
[4] Ibid. DD/MDW 19.
[5] Ibid. tithe award.
[6] Youngs, Local Admin. Units, i. 428, 675–6.
[7] S.R.S. lxi, pp. 12–13; Cal. Papal Reg. i. 17.
[8] e.g. S.R.S. x, pp. 618, 627; xiii, p. 173; xxxi, pp. 40, 65; Cal. Pat. 1422–9, 352, 501; 1429–36, 182, 187.
[9] V.C.H. Som. ii. 170–1.
[10] Som. Incumbents, ed. Weaver, 378; Dioc. Dir. (1913).

ceded its patronage on the creation of the benefice of Quantoxhead in 1978.[11]

The net income of the living was £5 1s. 4d. in 1535.[12] Its reputed value was £50 c. 1668,[13] and no more than £70 in 1715.[14] The benefice was augmented in 1723 by a grant of £200 from Dr. Henry Godolphin, dean of St. Paul's and formerly provost of Eton, met by an equal grant from Queen Anne's Bounty.[15] It was said to be worth £200 in 1815[16] and £225 in 1851.[17] The living was subject to a small pension paid to Stogursey Priory by 1392 and later to Eton College.[18]

The tithes were worth £3 6s. 5d. in 1535.[19] By 1633 they were payable on crops and some stock, and included corn and wool tithes from Durborough Hill and 'hand tithes' (perhaps personal tithes) from 'servants and others' coming from parishes where such were due. Tithes of other stock, of mills, and of meadows had been commuted for moduses. The rector also claimed Easter offerings of 2d. from every communicant (1d. from natives at first communion) and 4d. for weddings, churchings, and certificates.[20] All remaining tithes were commuted in 1840 for a rent charge of £148.[21]

Glebe was worth 22s. in 1535.[22] By the early 17th century it amounted to c. 28 a.[23] In 1742 nearly 40 a. were bought in Stogursey with augmentation money. Just over 26 a. in Holford and nearly 33 a. in Stogursey were sold in 1893,[24] and in 1948 there were only 3 a. in Holford.[25] The rectory house in 1633 had a four-roomed plan with four chambers above.[26] It was almost entirely rebuilt c. 1815,[27] and was sold in 1978.

At least three medieval rectors were involved in abortive exchanges.[28] John Dickinson, rector 1530–44, acted for Thomas Cromwell during a visitation of Athelney Abbey in 1538.[29] Thomas Withers, the first known graduate rector of Holford when appointed in 1544, probably came from a Stogursey family.[30] Richard Bodley, rector by 1558 until his death in 1586, was reported in 1576 for not preaching the regular quarterly sermons and for not reading the services distinctly.[31] Henry Cox, rector from 1586, lived a little distance from the parish, but in 1593 was reported to have preached monthly.[32] His successor John Gibson (d. 1609) was suspected of being a drunkard.[33] John Slater, rector 1610–11, had been

at Eton and a fellow of King's College, Cambridge.[34] Michael Pollard, rector 1663–7, combined the living with Dodington.[35]

The rectors in the later 18th century were absentees who left the parish to curates.[36] William Chilcott, rector 1776–88, combined the living with Stogursey.[37] At the beginning of Chilcott's tenure of Holford there were 28 communicants.[38] George Buxton, rector 1788–1832, lived at Dorney (Bucks.). In 1815 the curate was John Audain of Nether Stowey, who also served Dodington.[39] From 1816 John Hole was resident curate until Buxton's death, and during his time one service was held every Sunday morning.[40] John Barnwell, rector 1832–66, was already vicar of Stogursey and by 1848 was rector also of Sutton Valence (Kent).[41] By 1840 Sunday services were held alternately morning and afternoon;[42] in 1851 the average attendance was 100 in the morning and 150 in the afternoon including at each service 30 Sunday-school pupils.[43] Henry Prentice, rector 1867–87 and a former curate of an Eton living, introduced two services with sermons each Sunday and monthly celebrations.[44]

The church of *ST. MARY THE VIRGIN*, dedicated to St. John by 1175[45] and to St. Mary by 1791,[46] is a small building comprising chancel with south vestry, nave, and west tower with north porch. The lower parts of the tower suggest a 12th-century origin, and there was refenestration in the early 16th century.[47] Before probable rebuilding at least of the chancel and north side of the nave between 1842 and 1844 the porch gave entrance to the western end of the nave, and the window on the north side of the chancel was further west. A west gallery was added during rebuilding, but was later demolished.[48] The vestry was added in 1888.[49] The nave contains some 17th-century pew ends. In the churchyard is a late medieval cross shaft with mutilated figures.

The registers date from 1558, but marriages were not entered between 1653 and 1660.[50] Of the six bells, two were cast in the early 16th century, one by Roger Semson of Ash Priors, the other by Thomas Jefferies of Bristol.[51] The plate was bought in 1844, partly from the proceeds of sale of the old silver.[52]

NONCONFORMITY. None known.

[11] S.R.O., D/P/hol 22/3/1.
[12] *Valor Eccl.* (Rec. Com.) i. 215.
[13] S.R.O., D/D/Vc 24.
[14] Ibid. DD/MDW 19.
[15] C. Hodgson, *Queen Anne's Bounty* (1846), pp. cxxxviii, ccxlii; *D.N.B.*
[16] S.R.O., D/D/B returns 1815.
[17] P.R.O., HO 129/313/4/8/8.
[18] *S.R.S.* lxi, p. 62; *Valor Eccl.* (Rec. Com.), i. 215.
[19] *Valor Eccl.* (Rec. Com.), i. 215.
[20] S.R.O., D/D/Rg 272.
[21] Ibid. tithe award.
[22] *Valor Eccl.* (Rec. Com.), i. 215.
[23] S.R.O., D/D/Rg 272.
[24] Inf. from Church Comm.
[25] *Crockford* (1948).
[26] S.R.O., D/D/Rg 272.
[27] Ibid. D/D/B returns 1815.
[28] *Cal. Pat.* 1374–7, 131; 1429–36, 182, 187.
[29] *L. & P. Hen. VIII*, xiii, pp. 287–8.
[30] *S.R.S.* lv, p. 105; Emden, *Oxford 1501–40*, p. 650.
[31] *S. & D. N. & Q.* xiii. 270; S.R.O., D/D/Ca 57.
[32] S.R.O., D/D/Ca 98.
[33] Ibid. D/D/Ca 151; D/P/hol 2/1/1.
[34] *Alum. Cantab. to 1751.*

[35] *Alum. Oxon. 1500–1714.*
[36] S.R.O., D/D/Vc 6, 9, 94; D/P/hol 2/1/1–4.
[37] R. E. Ballard, *Priory Church of St. Andrew, Stoke Courcy* (1977).
[38] S.R.O., D/D/Vc 81.
[39] Ibid. D/D/B returns 1815.
[40] Ibid. D/D/B returns 1815, 1827; ibid. D/P/hol 2/1/4; cf. ibid. T/PH/ay 1, Nov. 1815, Feb. 1817.
[41] Ballard, *Ch. of Stoke Courcy*; *Clergy List* (1848, 1859).
[42] S.R.O., D/D/V returns 1840.
[43] P.R.O., HO 129/313/4/8/8.
[44] *Crockford* (1874); S.R.O., D/D/V returns 1870.
[45] *S.R.S.* lxi, pp. 12–13; for St. John's cross, above, intro.
[46] Collinson, *Hist. Som.* iii. 457.
[47] Taunton Castle, Pigott Colln., water colour by J. Buckler, 1840.
[48] S.R.O., D/P/hol 4/1/1–2; Taunton Castle, Pigott Colln., water colour by J. Buckler, 1840.
[49] *Kelly's Dir. Som.* (1894).
[50] S.R.O., D/P/hol 2/1/1–5.
[51] Ibid. DD/SAS CH 16; local inf.
[52] S.R.O., D/P/hol 4/1/2; *Proc. Som. Arch. Soc.* xlvii. 165–6.

EDUCATION. An unlicensed schoolmaster was reported in 1603.[53] A schoolroom stood west of the church by 1840[54] and the school, supported by the rector and by voluntary contributions, continued until 1875 when it was replaced by one at Dyche in Stringston.[55] In 1847 it appears to have been a Sunday school only, with 38 children.[56]

CHARITIES FOR THE POOR. Three small charities were established in the 17th century: John Hembrow (d. 1631) gave £5, half the interest for the poor at Easter; Agnes Winsor (d. 1637) gave £5 for poor householders at Christmas; and Alexander Standfast of Kilve gave to the second poor of Holford a rent charge of 6s. 8d. to be given at Easter.[57] By the 1760s Winsor's and the whole capital of Hembrow's were held by the churchwarden and the whole income was paid to the poor in cash. No rent was received from Standfast's from 1802.[58] Bread costing £2 was given to the poor of Holford at Christmas 1813.[59] The Hembrow and Winsor charities produced 6s. between them by 1869, but details of Standfast's were not then known.[60] By 1955 the total income of the two former was c. 4s., and there were problems over the payment of Standfast's rent charge. The Standfast charity was probably lost soon afterwards.[61]

In 1891 Mrs. Jane St. Albyn gave £300, the interest to be given to the poor at Christmas at the discretion of the rector and churchwardens.[62] Unspecified benefactions were said to produce between £8 and £9, distributed in coal, in the early 1970s,[63] perhaps an accumulation of all the parish charities. No distributions were made after 1978.[64]

[53] S.R.O., D/D/Ca 134.
[54] Ibid. tithe award.
[55] P.R.O., HO 107/1920; *P.O. Dir. Som.* (1866); *Kelly's Dir. Som.* (1883).
[56] Nat. Soc. *Inquiry, 1846–7*, Som. 10–11.
[57] Holford ch., charity bd.
[58] *15th Rep. Com. Char.* 491.
[59] S.R.O., D/P/hol 2/1/4.
[60] *Digest Endowed Chars. 1869–71*, H.C. pp. 50–1 (1873), li.
[61] Char. Com., files, reg. of chars.
[62] Holford ch., charity bd.; Char. Com., reg. of chars.
[63] J. J. A. Hayman, *Brief Hist. of Holford* (1973), 7.
[64] Inf. from the rector, the Revd. W. H. Minshull.

WILLITON AND FREEMANORS HUNDRED

T HE HUNDRED lies near the western end of the county.[1] It occupies the southern slopes of Exmoor, the southern and eastern parts of the Brendon Hills, part of the broad valley between the Brendons and the Quantock Hills, and the north-western end of the Quantock ridge. Much of the hundred lies on high and often infertile ground where settlements are small and scattered, contrasting with the nucleated villages on the coastal shelf north of the Brendons and the Quantocks and those in the valley between them. Agriculture has long been the predominant activity, but extensive sheep farming made the production of woollen cloth a significant feature of many villages until the earlier 19th century. Iron ore mining on the Brendons made an impact on the area in the later 19th century. Exmoor and the Brendon Hill area became part of the Exmoor National Park created in 1954 and the Quantock Hills were designated an Area of Outstanding Natural Beauty in 1957.[2]

The Domesday hundreds of Williton and Winsford, including together just over 94½ hides,[3] were the origin of the later hundreds of Williton and Freemanors. Precise definition of Williton is not possible before the late 13th century, but Maud de Chandos's estate of Stowey and Maurice de Gaunt's holding of East Quantoxhead and Huish in Nettlecombe were in the hundred by 1212,[4] Huish then forming a single tithing uniting Lodhuish and Beggearn Huish, the latter soon afterwards to be joined with East Quantoxhead.[5] In 1225 Williton hundred seems to have included Crowcombe, Honibere in Lilstock, East and West Quantoxhead, Raddington, and Stogumber.[6] Kilve and Skilgate may have been included by 1242-3.[7] The borough of Watchet and Williton manor presented separately at the eyre in 1225.[8] Suit to the hundred from part of Crowcombe was withdrawn by Godfrey of Crowcombe before 1247 when he gave half his manor there to the prioress of Studley (Oxon.).[9]

In 1284-5 Williton hundred comprised Bicknoller, Chipstable, Crowcombe, Elworthy, Halsway in Stogumber, Honibere in Lilstock, Huish Champflower, Kilton, Kilve, Lodhuish in Nettlecombe, East and West Quantoxhead, Raddington, Sampford Brett, Skilgate, Stogumber, Stowey, Syndercombe in Clatworthy, Torweston, Westowe in Lydeard St. Lawrence, and Woodadvent in Nettlecombe.[10] In 1303 the same parishes and tithings were mentioned except Chipstable, Stogumber, and Raddington. Lilstock was substituted for Honibere. In addition were the tithings of Clatworthy and Nettlecombe and four small detached areas, Almsworthy in Exford, Briddicott in Carhampton, part of Brompton Regis, and Luxborough Piket in Luxborough.[11] All four detached areas had been part of Carhampton hundred in 1284-5.[12]

[1] The histories of the parishes of Brompton Regis, Brushford, Dulverton, Exton, Hawkridge, Upton, Skilgate, Winsford, and Withypool are reserved for treatment in a future volume.

[2] Som. C.C. *County Development Plan, First Review* (1964), 2-3.

[3] *V.C.H. Som.* i. 532.

[4] *Bk. of Fees*, i. 83.

[5] *Rot. Hund.* (Rec. Com.), ii. 125.

[6] *S.R.S.* xi, pp. 43-4, 106.

[7] Ibid. pp. 304-5.

[8] Ibid. p. 36.

[9] Below, Crowcombe, local govt.

[10] *Feud. Aids*, iv. 274-5.

[11] Ibid. 303.

[12] Ibid. 296.

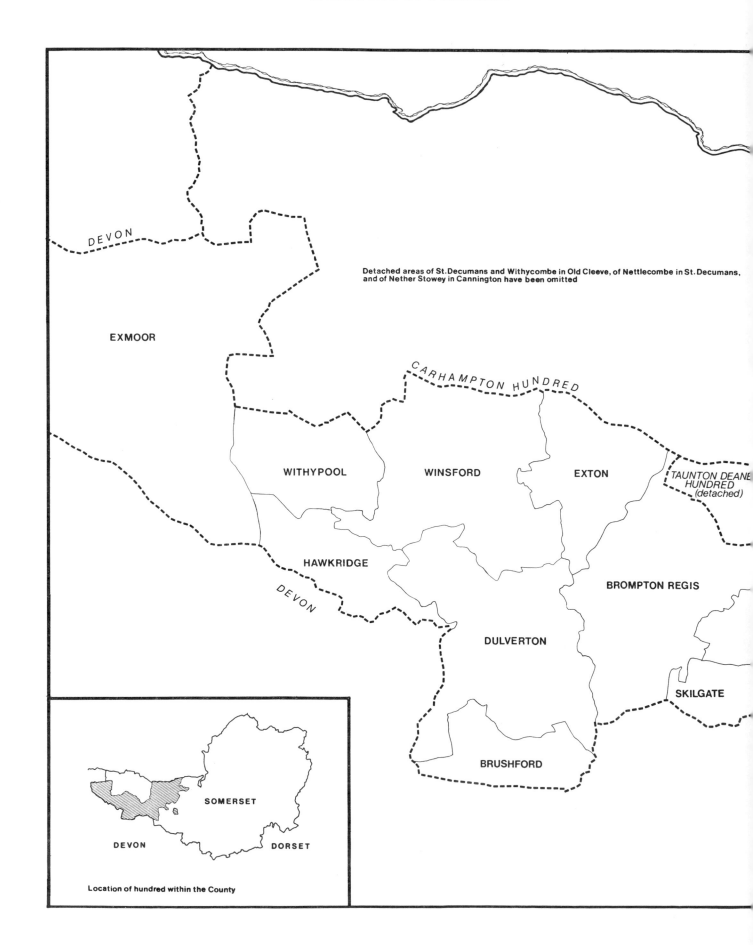

DEVON

Detached areas of St.Decumans and Withycombe in Old Cleeve, of Nettlecombe in St.Decumans, and of Nether Stowey in Cannington have been omitted

EXMOOR

CARHAMPTON HUNDRED

WITHYPOOL

WINSFORD

EXTON

TAUNTON DEANE HUNDRED (detached)

HAWKRIDGE

DEVON

BROMPTON REGIS

DULVERTON

SKILGATE

BRUSHFORD

SOMERSET

DEVON

DORSET

Location of hundred within the County

WILLITON AND FREEMANORS HUNDRED *c* 1840

LILSTOCK

KILTON

KILVE

EAST
QUANTOXHEAD

Watchet

WEST
QUANTOXHEAD

STRINGSTON

OLD
CLEEVE

ST. DECUMANS

ALFOXTON

HOLFORD

CODINGTON

Williton

New
hall

NETHER
STOWEY

SAMPFORD
Torweston
BRETT

Lower
Weacombe

Weacombe

Batchwell

HUNDRED

BICKNOLLER

NETTLECOMBE

Aller

CANNINGTON

Halsway

MONKSILVER

Leighland

CROWCOMBE

STOGUMBER

N

ELWORTHY

Willett

TAUNTON DEANE HUNDRED

Middleton

Clatworthy

BROMPTON
RALPH

East
Withy

CLATWORTHY

Syndercombe

KINGSBURY (WEST)
HUNDRED

HUISH
CHAMPFLOWER

UPTON

HALSE

RADDINGTON

CHIPSTABLE

HUNDRED

VON

MILVERTON

| 0 | 1 | 2 | 3 | 4 | 5 Kilometres |

| 0 | | 1 | | 2 | 3 Miles |

A list of vills purporting to form Williton hundred in 1316 included only Clatworthy, Crowcombe, Nettlecombe, and a part of Stogumber associated with Doniford in St. Decumans parish of those which had previously been within the hundred, but recorded Watchet and Williton, and others which both before and afterwards were described as free manors.[13] The hundred as constituted for fiscal purposes in 1327 was the same as 1284–5 with the addition of Clatworthy and Nettlecombe, established as part of the hundred since 1303, and Preston in Stogumber. That part of Crowcombe known as Crowcombe Studley was omitted, and Stowey was replaced by the tithing of Bincombe, locally in Over Stowey parish, probably that part of the estate of Stowey not included in the borough of Nether Stowey.[14] In 1346[15] Chipstable and Raddington were again not recorded, as in 1303, but Stogumber was named, together with the four detached areas. In 1428 the hundred was virtually unchanged, but Lodhuish was not named and Williton was included. Subsidy from Almsworthy and Briddicott was to be charged in Carhampton hundred.[16]

The hundred was combined for fiscal purposes with Freemanors hundred by 1569, when a joint tithing of Chipstable and Raddington was included,[17] but its constituent parts were separately recorded in 1652. The hundred then comprised all those places named in 1284–5 together with Clatworthy and Nettlecombe, and the tithing of Bincombe instead of Stowey. There were then four additions, Brompton Ralph, Brushford, Dulverton, and Winsford.[18] The Williton elements in the combined hundred lost Westowe by 1742[19] but gained Preston Bowyer in Milverton by c. 1730.[20] No legal union of the hundreds took place and the two were regarded as separate in 1856.[21]

Freemanors hundred was formed from a loose association of royal manors which in 1086 were either included in Williton hundred or were themselves described as the hundreds of Brompton Ralph, Brompton Regis, Dulverton, Cleeve, and Winsford.[22] Courts at Brompton Ralph,[23] Brompton Regis,[24] Dulverton,[25] Exton,[26] and Old Cleeve[27] were described as hundred courts during the Middle Ages, and these and other manors sent separate juries to eyres in the 13th century. The hundreds of 'Bruneland'[28] and Dulverton, and Winsford manor each sent jurors in 1225[29] and in 1242–3 the manors of Brompton Regis, 'Bruneland', Brushford, Clatworthy, Cleeve, Crowcombe, Dulverton, Huish Champflower, Nettlecombe, North Newton in North Petherton including Exton, Monksilver, Williton, and Winsford each appeared independently of any hundred.[30] Exton, North Newton, and detached areas later associated with them were connected until the mid 14th century with the forestership of North Petherton, whose occupants were bailiffs of Williton hundred.[31] Brompton Ralph, Brushford, Clatworthy, part of Crowcombe, Dulverton, Huish Champflower, Nettlecombe, and Winsford were described as free manors in 1274–6,[32] and the existence of a bailiff of the free manors in the late 13th century indicates some corporate identity.[33] Huish Champflower was established as part of Williton hundred by 1284–5,[34] and Clatworthy and Nettlecombe by 1303.[35] In 1316 the remaining free manors of the 1242–3 eyre, with the addition of Creech St. Michael, were arranged in two groups: Brompton Ralph,

[13] Ibid. 333.
[14] S.R.S. iii. 165–8.
[15] Feud. Aids, iv. 346–7.
[16] Ibid. 391–3.
[17] S.R.S. xx. 158–80.
[18] P.R.O., E 317/Som. 12.
[19] Below.
[20] S.R.O., DD/AH 21/2; S.R.S. iii. 302, 335 n.
[21] S.R.O., DD/TB 31.
[22] V.C.H. Som. i. 532.
[23] S.R.O., DD/L P32, deeds 1307–55.
[24] Ibid. DD/SAS PD 33.
[25] e.g. Cal. Pat. 1354–8, 214; Cal. Chart. R. 1327–41, 317.
[26] Cal. Pat. 1422–9, 135; 1476–85, 253.
[27] Below, Old Cleeve, local govt.
[28] The name was given both to Brown in Huish Champflower (S.R.S. xxv, p. 84), and to land in Brompton Regis (Proc. Som. Arch. Soc. liv. 92, 101).
[29] S.R.S. xi, pp. 60, 67, 322.
[30] Ibid. pp. 296, 303, 305–8, 322.
[31] Below.
[32] Rot. Hund. (Rec. Com.), ii. 119, 125, 138.
[33] S.R.O., DD/AH 60/11.
[34] Feud. Aids, iv. 275.
[35] Ibid. 303.

Creech, and the tithing of Preston Bowyer in Milverton which included Monksilver formed a small fiscal group entitled Free Manors; the remainder, with the addition of Clatworthy, the whole of Crowcombe, the joint tithing of Exton and Withypool replacing North Newton, Nettlecombe, a part of Stogumber linked with Doniford in St. Decumans, and Watchet, were said, probably in error, to constitute Williton hundred.[36] By 1327 those same places, together with Lyng but omitting half of Crowcombe and Watchet borough, were said to constitute Freemanors hundred for fiscal purposes.[37] In 1334, again for fiscal purposes, the Free Manors were listed together but not specifically described as a hundred. Two additions had then been made to the list of seven years earlier: Creech and Halse,[38] the latter part of Taunton hundred in 1086,[39] and in 1327 a free manor.[40] In 1346 only Exton and North Newton were said to be in the hundred,[41] and in 1402 the Free Manors were said to constitute Cathanger in Fivehead, Exton, and North Newton.[42]

Freemanors hundred had an independent existence in 1448 when it was granted away by the Crown with Williton hundred,[43] but the two were in practice combined by 1569. The Freemanors element then included both Cleeve and Old Cleeve, representing the two tithings in the parish, a tithing of Exton, Withypool, and Hawkridge replacing the former Exton and North Newton tithing, and a joint tithing of Halse and Dodington.[44] In 1642 the Freemanors element comprised Brompton Ralph, Brompton Regis, Brushford, Cathanger in Fivehead, Dulverton, Exton, Halse and Dodington, Hawkridge, Monksilver and Preston Bowyer, North Newton, Old Cleeve, Watchet, Williton, Winsford, and Withypool, and small areas at Low Ham in High Ham parish and Newhall in Holford.[45] Cathanger, Low Ham, Newhall, and North Newton were also considered to be part of Exton tithing.[46] Brompton Ralph, Brushford, Dulverton, and Winsford were said to be in Williton hundred in 1652.[47]

The two hundreds were effectively combined by 1742,[48] the only addition since 1642 being Upton tithing, probably formed out of Brompton Regis.[49] The only change made by 1841 was the inclusion of Exmoor forest.[50] The detached parts in the parishes of Fivehead, High Ham, and Over Stowey were still considered part of the hundred, the area at Low Ham being defined for the first time as part of the hamlet of Paradise, locally situated in Huish Episcopi parish. An undefined part of Exton was said to be in Carhampton hundred.[51]

The two hundreds, hitherto held by the Crown, were granted in 1448[52] to Sir John Stourton, Lord Stourton (d. 1462), and passed to successive holders of the title.[53] Edward, Lord Stourton (d. 1720), sold the hundreds to John Gore of Salisbury.[54] John's son, also John, conveyed them to his sisters in 1725[55] and they and their husbands conveyed them to John Glass of London in 1728.[56] Glass sold the hundreds to Thomas Carew of Crowcombe in 1733, and in 1754 Carew conveyed them to John Perceval, earl of Egmont.[57] Egmont (d. 1770) was succeeded by his son John (d. 1822) and by John's son, also John. The last died in 1835 and his son Henry, earl of Egmont, sold the hundreds to George Henry Carew of Crowcombe.[58] George died in 1842 and his heir

[36] Ibid. 333.
[37] S.R.S. iii. 177–82.
[38] Subsidy of 1334, ed. R. E. Glasscock, 265.
[39] Below, Halse, local govt.
[40] S.R.S. iii. 185.
[41] Feud. Aids, iv. 360.
[42] Ibid. 362–3.
[43] Cal. Pat. 1446–52, 160.   [44] S.R.S. xx. 158–80.
[45] Som. Protestation Returns, ed. Howard and Stoate, 282–96. Newhall occurs as Newkall: ibid. 284.
[46] S.R.S. xxiii. 315–16; Proc. Som. Arch. Soc. xxxv. 58–9.

[47] P.R.O., E 317/Som. 12.   [48] S.R.S. iii. 307–8.
[49] Som. Protestation Returns, ed. Howard and Stoate, 173, 285.
[50] S.R.S. iii. 335–6.
[51] Ibid. 334 n, 335 n.
[52] Cal. Pat. 1446–52, 160.
[53] Burke, Peerage (1949), 1146–7.
[54] S.R.O., DD/BR/fc 61.
[55] Ibid. DD/S/SH 1.
[56] Ibid. DD/X/HU (H/8).
[57] Ibid. DD/S/SH 1; Burke, Peerage (1949), 690.
[58] S.R.O., DD/TB 31.

Thomas G. W. Carew in 1855.[59] Thomas's brother and executor, John Francis Carew, conveyed them to his nephew G. H. W. Carew in 1856.[60] No reference to ownership has been found after 1868.[61]

The sheriff's tourn and hundred court for Williton hundred was held at Williton in 1391,[62] and a prison there had been mentioned in 1276.[63] The meeting place for both hundreds was at Stogumber by 1585,[64] and courts were held at the Red Lion inn there by 1652.[65] From 1741 until 1868 the hundred court met at Crowcombe.[66] In the mid 17th century the sheriff's tourn was held twice a year about Easter and Michaelmas, but the three-weekly courts were said to be 'much discontinued'. Each tithing was then represented by its tithingman and its jurors or posts; the tithingman of Torweston came with his rod only and the tithingman of Westowe came with one juror.[67] Between 1741 and 1743 a hundred court 'for trying actions' was held every three or four weeks. Each session was described as a court baron, and among the parties was the owner of the hundred.[68] Rolls of the 'court leet and view of frankpledge together with the court baron of the lord of the hundred' record annual meetings of the court for the periods 1761–1835 and 1837–68.[69]

In the 17th century all tithings except Williton and Watchet borough paid rents called tithing silver or 'certainties'.[70] The rents were said to be payable in the earlier 18th century[71] and were recorded in the court rolls until 1791.[72] The names of the tithingmen were no longer recorded in the rolls after 1842.

The office of bailiff of the hundred of Williton was held by successive foresters of North Petherton from Richard I's time until the 14th century.[73] A bailiff of the free manors was mentioned in the late 13th century.[74] A single high constable was in office in 1556[75] and 1576[76] but there were two by 1626.[77] At the Michaelmas tourn 1664 two high constables were chosen, one for the eastern and one for the western division,[78] and two continued to serve until 1868.[79] A steward of the hundred court at Stogumber was mentioned in 1649,[80] and a steward presided over the courts until 1868. There was a bailiff in the later 18th and the 19th century, and a keeper for the hundred pound, situated next to the manor pound at Williton.[81]

[59] Below, Crowcombe, manors.
[60] S.R.O., DD/TB 31.
[61] Ibid. DD/TB 12/9.
[62] *Cal. Inq. Misc.* v, p. 197.
[63] *Rot. Hund.* (Rec. Com.), ii. 125.
[64] S.R.O., DD/WY 6: acct. bk. of subsidy payments.
[65] P.R.O., E 317/Som. 12.
[66] S.R.O., DD/DP 59; DD/TB 12/9.
[67] P.R.O., E 317/Som. 12.
[68] S.R.O., DD/DP 59.
[69] Ibid. DD/TB 12/9.
[70] P.R.O., E 317/Som. 12.

[71] S.R.O., DD/S/SH 1.
[72] Ibid. DD/TB 12/9.
[73] Ibid. DD/AH 21/2: Thos. Palmer's notes *c.* 1730 based on Wroth MSS. then at Petherton Park.
[74] Ibid. DD/AH 60/11.
[75] Ibid. DD/WO 49/3.
[76] Ibid. D/P/bic 13/10/1.
[77] Ibid. D/B/bw 1960.
[78] Ibid. DD/WY 4/R2.
[79] Ibid. DD/TB 12/9.
[80] Ibid. DD/WY 6: acct. bk. of subsidy payments.
[81] Ibid. DD/TB 12/9.

BICKNOLLER

THE PARISH of Bicknoller, on the south-western slopes of the Quantocks 4 km. south-east of Williton, lay within the probable minster parish of Stogumber. The boundary with Stogumber and Sampford Brett is formed by the Doniford stream, that with Holford by the Quantock ridgeway, and that towards Crowcombe by two streams. The ancient parish was irregular in shape, stretching for 3 km. from east to west and 2.5 km. from north to south at its widest points.[1] In 1883 Halsway in Stogumber (*c.* 500 a.) was added to form the civil parish of Bicknoller, which by 1978 measured 774 ha. (1,912 a.).[2]

Bicknoller village and the former hamlet of Thorncombe lie beneath the Quantock scarp; the ground falls sharply from 320 m. on Thorncombe Hill to 76 m. on the settlement line, and then more gradually to 46 m. at Woolston, just above the Doniford stream. The Devonian Hangman Grits of the Quantocks give way to valley gravels and Keuper Marls, with outcrops of sandstone, conglomerates, and pebbles.[3] Stone was quarried at Woolston and Newton by 1457 (at Woolston possibly in 1438).[4] Woolston quarry, with a limekiln, was still open in 1904.[5] Gravel was dug on Quantock Moor, between Thorncombe and Bicknoller Hill, until *c.* 1905.[6]

Trendle Ring on the slope of Bicknoller Hill may represent permanent prehistoric settlement.[7] In the 11th century the recorded settlements were Newton and Woolston,[8] the former perhaps an alternative name for Bicknoller, whose regular street pattern shows characteristics of a planted village. Bicknoller is first mentioned by name in 1243,[9] and the present hamlet of Newton may derive its name from the presence there of the Domesday mill.[10]

The survival of a few 'furlong' field names suggests open-field farming around Bicknoller village, but Yard, Chapmanscombe, Chilcombe, Upcott, Thorncombe, Cottiford, Ford, and Culverhayes were established settlements by the early 14th century,[11] and by the 19th the first five had become centres of consolidated holdings.[12] The compact, regular street pattern of Bicknoller, on the slopes of the Quantocks, and its surviving thatched houses, dating mainly from the 16th to the 18th centuries, together with modern building of quality, contribute materially to the picturesque character of the village.

The road pattern seems to have been of two parallel routes between the Quantock scarp and the Doniford stream with lanes from Bicknoller village to the outlying hamlets. The route nearest the scarp, linking Halsway with West Quantoxhead through Thorncombe, was stopped at Thorncombe in 1830.[13] The lower road, which became the main route between Taunton and Minehead, was turnpiked in 1807.[14] Where it forms the parish boundary with lower Weacombe in Stogumber, north of Woolston Moor, it clearly follows an ancient course, though it was redirected across the moor, away from the earlier route through Woolston, as part of the turnpike improvement.[15] The West Somerset Railway, opened in 1862, was cut through the parish and involved road alterations and new buildings at Woolston and Yard.[16]

The Bicknoller inn, formerly the New Inn, is mentioned in 1841 but there were two licensed victuallers in 1736. One of these licences appears to have been revoked by 1755.[17] There were clothing clubs from the mid 19th century,[18] and a parochial lending library in 1877.[19] Tennis, fives, and bowls were played in the 16th and 17th centuries,[20] and wassailing on Old Twelfth Night continued at least until 1870.[21] Church and village meetings in the 19th century were held in the school, the vicarage house and grounds, and from the 1890s to 1910 in the parish room, built on the glebe by Mrs. Trefusis of Thorncombe House.[22] In 1948 Henry Bickersteth Mayor left a site and endowment for a village hall and playing field.[23]

There were 40 households in the parish in 1563,[24] at least 107 adult males were recorded in 1641,[25] and 237 persons were taxed in 1667.[26] In 1801 the population of Bicknoller was 246, falling to 204 in 1811. The population reached a peak of 372 in 1871, but fell to 270 in 1891 and to 211 in 1901, in spite of the addition of Halsway to the parish in 1883. The numbers rose again in the 20th century and in 1971 the population was 317.[27]

MANORS AND OTHER ESTATES. In 1066 the later parish of Bicknoller consisted of two estates: Woolston held by Britmar and Newton held by Alviet. By 1086 both were held by William de Mohun and they continued to be held of the honor of Dunster until 1620 or later.[28] The estate descended to William's great-granddaughter, Agnes, wife of

---

[1] S.R.O., tithe award. This article was completed in 1978.   [2] S.R.O., DD/CCH 62; *Census*, 1971.
[3] Geol. Surv. Map 1", drift, sheet 295 (1956 edn.).
[4] S.R.O., DD/CC 110079/18, 22.
[5] Ibid. D/P/bic 1/7/4.
[6] Ibid. 1/6/6; *W. Som. Free Press*, 2 Dec. 1905.
[7] L. V. Grinsell, *Prehist. Sites in Quantock Country*, 18; *Proc. Som. Arch. Soc.* cxiii, suppl. 27.
[8] *V.C.H. Som.* i. 504.
[9] *S.R.S.* xi, pp. 167–8.   [10] Below, econ. hist.
[11] *S.R.S.* iii. 166; *H.M.C. Wells*, i. 348–51.
[12] S.R.O., tithe award.
[13] Ibid. Q/SR Mich. 1830.
[14] 47 Geo. III, c. 27 (Local and Personal).
[15] S.R.O., DD/CC 10874; ibid. tithe award; ibid. Q/SR Epiph. 1812.

[16] Ibid. DD/CC 114484–5.
[17] Ibid., Q/RL; Dyfed R.O., D/CAR 202.
[18] S.R.O., D/P/bic 1/7/1–2, 1/7/6; Char. Com. files.
[19] S.R.O., D/P/bic 1/7/6.
[20] Ibid. DD/CC 131909/15; ibid. D/D/Ca 175, 235.
[21] Ibid. D/P/bic 1/7/1. Another parish custom was that of closing the road to a newly-married couple and charging them toll: ibid.
[22] Ibid. 1/7/6.
[23] Char. Com. files.
[24] B.L. Harl. MS. 594, f. 55.
[25] *Som. Protestation Returns*, ed. Howard and Stoate, 151.
[26] S.R.O., DD/WY 34.
[27] *Census*, 1801–1971.
[28] *V.C.H. Som.* i. 504; *S.R.S.* xxxiii, p. 325.

C

William de Windsor, who apparently held it in 1201 and 1202.[29] After his death Agnes divided the estate, giving half to her daughter Godehuda, wife of Nicholas Rolland, in frank marriage.[30] In 1230 and 1236 Agnes resisted Geoffrey de Kitenor's claim to ¼ fee at Woolston,[31] evidently the remaining part of the estate. Godehuda brought her land after Nicholas's death to her second husband Richard de Wayville,[32] no later than 1227, and he was holding an estate described as half the manor of *BICKNOLLER* in 1243.[33] Agnes probably retained the other half of the manor until her death. The late 13th century saw much litigation involving the descendants of Agnes. The main claimants were Godehuda's sons by her two marriages, William Rolland and Henry de Wayville, and the Windsor family, descendants of Agnes's son William. In 1280 Richard de Windsor was said to be holding two fees and Henry de Wayville one.[34] In 1283 Robert Rolland successfully claimed an estate in Bicknoller as heir to his grandmother Godehuda, and was awarded half the manor, which he then granted in fee to Richard de Windsor.[35] In 1286 Richard was returned as holder of the whole estate.[36] Disputes continued until the Wayvilles were awarded half the manor in 1291,[37] and in 1303 the property was shared between Richard de Windsor and James de Wayville, son of Henry de Wayville, claimant in 1286.[38]

In 1327 Richard de Windsor granted his half manor to Robert de Cormailles, and in 1330 Robert's brother Roger gave it to the chapter of Wells.[39] The other half was held by Thomas de Wayville in 1346, by John Wayville in 1376, and by him or another John in 1403.[40] Richard Wayville of Rodmell (Suss.), son of John, died in 1417 leaving his estate to be sold.[41] His widow Agnes quitclaimed her rights to trustees in 1423[42] and they in turn sold the estate to the executors of Nicholas Bubwith (d. 1424), bishop of Bath and Wells. It was acquired from the executors by the Wells chapter in 1430 and contributed to the maintenance of Bubwith's chantry in the cathedral until the 16th century.[43] The chapter held the united lordship from 1430 until 1857, when they were succeeded by the Ecclesiastical (later Church) Commissioners, the lords in 1977.

From 1622 if not earlier the manor house, called Wayfield, was let and from the 17th century until the 19th was occupied by successive manor bailiffs.[44] The house, in 1978 called Wayvile, is a late 16th-century house with late 17th-century additions. Further work was done in 1884 and 1904 when the rear was enlarged and the roof raised. In the 15th century the lessee of the manor held the manorial dovecot.[45]

In 1221 Agnes de Windsor granted in fee to Richard de Wechesford and his wife Maud an estate late of Richard of Thorncombe for the life of Maud.[46] It probably formed part of the lands Agnes gave to Godehuda her daughter, for in 1227 Godehuda and her husband Richard de Wayville held 1½ virgate in Thorncombe.[47] In 1281–2 Simon Brett, lord of Thorncombe, leased to his brother Adam Brett of Torweston an annual rent of £10 from his manor of *THORNCOMBE* and lands in Sampford Brett. In 1308, after obtaining a quitclaim from his mother Godehuda, John Brett, son of Simon, released to his uncle Adam Brett lands at Thorncombe and elsewhere. Simon Brett headed the subsidy assessment with Richard de Windsor in 1327.[48] John Brett held a virgate at Thorncombe of the Wells chapter's moiety of Bicknoller c. 1330.[49] By 1356 the Brett family had a substantial holding at Thorncombe[50] and early in the following century Thorncombe manor comprised lands and tenements in Bicknoller, Stogumber, and Crowcombe.[51] The estate continued in the hands of the Brett family throughout the 15th and 16th centuries. In 1609 Alexander Brett, then living in Lincolnshire, sold the manor with rents in Stogumber and all his pasture in Over Stowey to John Sweeting.[52] Members of the Sweeting family already held considerable estates in Bicknoller but their principal residence hitherto had been at Sampford Brett. At some time between the purchase of the Thorncombe estate and the drawing up of his will in 1619, John Sweeting (d. 1628) moved to Thorncombe where his descendants lived for over one and a half centuries.[53] The Sweetings appear to have been clothiers who, having invested in land at Bicknoller, Sampford Brett, Torweston, and Stogumber, were able to rise to the ranks of the gentry. The estate was divided between two brothers, John, of Thorncombe (d. 1646) and Robert, of Sampford Brett. John's son, John Sweeting (III), was elected coroner for Somerset in 1652 but was prevented from holding office owing to ill health. He died in 1688.[54] His son Joseph (d. 1707) was succeeded by Joseph's son Joseph (II) and his grandson Joseph (III) who died without issue in 1772. He was the last Sweeting to live at

[29] *S.R.S.* xxxiii, pp. 14, 16.
[30] Ibid. extra ser. 163–4.
[31] *Close R.* 1227–31, 395; *S.R.S.* vi. 85.
[32] *S.R.S.* extra ser. 163–4. A statement that Agnes gave Godehuda and Richard both parts of the manor cannot be borne out by any other evidence.
[33] *S.R.S.* vi. 67; xi. 167–8.
[34] *S.R.S.* xxxiii, p. 50. Wayville's fee was known as Combe [? Sydenham or Thorncombe] and Cottiford: ibid. pp. 49, 53, 72, 232.
[35] *S.R.S.* extra ser. 165–6.
[36] *Feud. Aids*, iv. 275.
[37] *S.R.S.* vi. 281; xxxiii, p. 50.
[38] *Feud. Aids*, iv. 302.
[39] *S.R.S.* xxxiii, p. 69; *H.M.C. Wells*, i. 324; ii. 594, 596–7, 623.
[40] *Feud. Aids*, iv. 347; *Cal. Inq. p.m.* xiii, p. 171; *S.R.S.* xxxiii, p. 116.
[41] *S.R.S.* xvi. 80–2.
[42] *Cal. Close*, 1422–9, 48–9.
[43] *Cal. Pat.* 1422–9, 396; *S.R.S.* ii. 160.
[44] S.R.O., DD/CC 110113, 110118, 1101121–3, 1101125–31.
[45] Ibid. DD/CC 110079/20.

[46] *S.R.S.* vi. 42. It is possible that the Domesday estate of Combe was Thorncombe; below, Combe Sydenham in Stogumber.
[47] Ibid. 67.
[48] S.R.O., DD/WO 1/MTD/II/2; *S.R.S.* iii. 166. Simon (fl. 1282) married Godehuda, da. of Hen. de Wayville: *S.R.S.* extra ser. 154.
[49] *H.M.C. Wells*, i. 348–9. The rent, 4½ 'slabbes' of iron, remained unpaid throughout the 15th century: S.R.O., DD/CC 110079/18–26. In 1512 an arbitration was sought by the chapter of Wells and the Bretts concerning this rent. The outcome is unknown but the rent was never paid: S.R.O., DD/WY 7/Z1f/6.
[50] Ibid. DD/WY 4/T.
[51] Ibid.; *Cal. Inq. p.m.* (Rec. Com.), iv. 389.
[52] Taunton Castle, Som. Arch. Soc. Libr., Hancock MS.; *V.C.H. Som.* iv. 233. The N. aisle of Bicknoller ch. was known as the Thorncombe aisle and until 1872 contained monuments to the Sweeting family. Part of the manor which lay outside the parish was sold to Sir John Wyndham: below, Stogumber, manor and local govt.
[53] *Som. Wills*, ed. Brown, iii. 87; M.I. Bicknoller ch.
[54] *S.R.S.* lxxi. 41; M.I. Bicknoller ch.

Thorncombe.[55] The estate was sold and subsequently divided.[56] For most of the 19th century Thorncombe house was owned by the Norris family.[57]

A house at Thorncombe was mentioned in 1334 when John Brett was licensed to have an oratory there for a year.[58] Thorncombe house was built in 1744.[59] The 5-bay front was rebuilt in the 19th century and additions made to the south and rear later in the century. The late 18th-century front door has been reused as the present side entrance.

ECONOMIC HISTORY. In 1086 the two Domesday estates, known as Woolston and Newton, together measured 5 hides.[60] By the 1330s[61] the estate of the chapter of Wells known as Bicknoller included 8 freeholdings in the parish, the largest of which was Thorncombe. There were 8 villeins each holding 24 a. for rent and services which included carting every other day, ploughing, mowing, harrowing, and making the water leat.[62] Seven 'lesser' villeins held 6 a. each, their services including mowing, driving the lord's cattle up to 240 miles, and taking turns at the office of oxherd. There were also seven cottars and 12 neifs. The neifs, two freemen, a cottar, and the tenant of Thorncombe owed 'slabbes' of iron. The chapter's demesne holding comprised a house and 75 a. of arable, with meadow, alder wood, and 'high' wood totalling a further 18¾ a., an area of waste on the hill for sheep pasture, and a further area there under cultivation. The whole estate was then worth £16 6s. 3½d.[63]

Actual receipts from the estate were usually much less than the valuation because the demesne was farmed in the 14th century. In the early 15th there were small receipts for wax and honey in addition to heriots and rents, including capons and cumin. After the acquisition of the entire manor by the chapter of Wells in 1430 the receipts rose to over £20.[64] In 1454–5 the chapter acquired a small estate in Bicknoller from Robert Bicknoller alias Jenkins whose family had held it since the 13th century.[65] In 1560 the communar of Wells received over £27 from the manor.[66]

The manor accounts do not provide particulars of the holdings. Until the mid 15th century the bailiff lived at Yard, a consolidated farm in the south-west corner of the parish, where the manorial bees were kept.[67] There were 25 holdings on the manor in 1571, excluding Idson in Stogursey, but including an estate of 300 a. which has not been identified. The capital messuage, Wayfield, was leased to a branch

of the Sweeting family with whom it remained until the death of Giles Sweeting in 1692.[68] Yard was held at the same time with Causey's or Kensey's, a 17½-a. holding adjoining, and Ford farm was held with Chilcombe. Most of the holdings, however, contained between 6 a. and 20 a., similar to the medieval units.[69] In 1650 there were 8 freeholds, 2 leaseholds, Wayfield and Jenkin's Bargain, and 34 copyholds excluding Idson.[70]

The largest freehold was Thorncombe, a consolidated holding in the south-east of the parish with a small estate at Cottiford near Woolston. Cottiford was occupied by fellmongers and a clothier in the 18th century but was divided into three cottages by 1888.[71] Upcott and Chapmanscombe were consolidated freeholds south-west of Thorncombe, measuring 65 a. and 35 a. respectively. A small freehold at Culverhayes to the south-west of Upcott was part of the manor of Avil in Dunster in the 18th century. In 1744 a reversionary lease was granted to a merchant of Bicknoller on conditions which included sending a man to clear the mill leat every Whitsun Thursday and keeping a beagle or spaniel.[72] Woolston Grange and Bottoms, together 44 a., were the property of the Slocombe family in the 16th and 17th centuries.[73] The 21-a. estate of Sir William Yea in Woolston was bought by Sir Alexander Acland-Hood in 1863.[74]

In 1838 the Thorncombe estate was 262 a. divided between two farms of over 100 a. and a smallholding. Wayfield, Upcott, and Yard each had about 60 a. of land; and there were 8 other holdings of between 35 a. and 50 a.[75] The number of houses in the parish increased from 40 in 1791 to 46 in 1831, and to 72 in 1877.[76]

In the late 16th century rye was being grown on Bicknoller Hill[77] and from the 17th century to the mid 19th there was a balance between arable and pasture farming. A joiner and farmer of Woolston in 1675 had a milkhouse and presshouse containing butter and 192 lb. of cheese, a ciderpress, corn, over 3 a. of hay, a clover rick, sheep, pigs, heifers, a cow, a horse, and seed for 5 a. of wheat.[78] Giles Sweeting of Wayfield (d. 1692) had a malthouse, salting house, milkhouse, horses, 12 cattle, 232 sheep, 12 pigs, ricks of wheat, barley, oats, hay, and peas, 10 a. of hay, 22 a. of wheat, and an assortment of implements. The total value of the inventory of his goods was £317.[79] The tithe award of 1838 listed 560 a. arable, 320 a. meadow and pasture, 75 a. houses, gardens, and orchards, and 340 a. of common.[80] In 1905 632 a. were under permanent grass, 356 a. were arable.[81] The main crops in 1883 were wheat, beans, barley,

---

55 Taunton Castle, Som. Arch. Soc. Libr., Hancock MS.; M.I. Bicknoller ch.
56 S.R.O., DD/BR/py 16; P.R.O., CP 43/67, rot. 151. The lands in Crowcombe passed to the Carew family and were enfranchised from Thorncombe in 1826: S.R.O., DD/TB 7/8.
57 Taunton Castle, Som. Arch. Soc. Libr., Hancock MS.
58 S.R.S. ix, p. 172.
59 Inf. from owner, Mr. J. Luttrell.
60 V.C.H. Som. i. 504.   61 H.M.C. Wells, i. 348–51.
62 They also served as 'wikmen'. It is not clear what this service entailed but it obviously did not include maintaining the sea walls which was the duty of the 'wikmen' on the Glastonbury estates: M. Williams, Draining of the Somerset Levels, 44.
63 H.M.C. Wells, i. 348–51.
64 S.R.O., DD/CC 110079/2–26.
65 H.M.C. Wells, ii. 570, 634, 672, 682. This is probably the estate known as Jenkins's Bargain which was leased to

the Sweeting family of Thorncombe from the mid 16th century: S.R.O., DD/CC 110002, 110114, 110117, 110119, 110124.
66 H.M.C. Wells, ii. 283.
67 S.R.O., DD/CC 110079/1–22.
68 Ibid. 110002, 110113, 110121.
69 Ibid. 110002.
70 Ibid. 110074.
71 S.R.O., DD/CCH 1/7; DD/BR/py 16.
72 Devon R.O. 1148MA 6/20.
73 S.R.S. li, pp. 1–2; S.R.O., DD/X/PLY.
74 S.R.O., DD/CCH 40/3.
75 Ibid. tithe award.
76 Collinson, Hist. Som. iii. 502; S.R.O., D/P/bic 1/7/1; 23/2.
77 S.R.O., DD/CC 131925A/10.
78 Ibid. DD/SP, inventory 1675.
79 Ibid. inventory 1692.
80 Ibid. tithe award.
81 Statistics supplied by the then Bd. of Agric. 1905.

oats, and turnips.[82] Clearly there was a shrinkage of arable. There were at least 13 holdings in 1976, only one of which was over 50 ha. (*c.* 90 a.). Two were specialist dairy farms and another was a fruit farm.[83]

Common land played a significant part in the farming of the parish. In 1572 there were complaints of unlicensed grazing of sheep on the commons and of farmers forcibly rescuing their impounded animals.[84] In 1593 after a dispute with tenants it was agreed to 'view, lay out and bound the Common Quantock'.[85] In 1838 there were 340 a. of common land at Woolston Moor, Bicknoller Hill, and Quantock Moor, the last settled by squatters.[86] In 1860 614 a. of enclosed land carried rights of common.[87]

There were 57 a. of wood recorded in 1086,[88] and timber from the rectory estate contributed to a barn and granary at Burnham in 1376.[89] Over 900 timber trees and several hundred saplings were growing on seven of the larger holdings in 1830,[90] and there were 25 a. of woodland in 1838.[91] By 1905 the area had been reduced to 16 a.[92]

Weavers, serge weavers, dyers, and clothiers occur in the parish from the early 17th century, and field names indicate racks in several places, besides a fulling mill or washing shed at Woolston.[93] A joiner who died in 1675 made shuttles.[94] George Taylor, a clothier, took an apprentice from Bathealton to learn the art of serge making in 1710 and Henry Pinn, a serge weaver, took two apprentices from North Petherton and Taunton.[95] Clothiers continued in business until the beginning of the 19th century, and included the Helliker family of Chilcombe.[96] Tanning and gloving were also carried out in the parish by the mid 16th at least until the late 17th century[97] and fellmongers continued at Cottiford until the 18th century.[98] In 1821 only 29 of the 50 families in the parish were employed in farming, and in 1831 9 were involved in trade and manufacture.[99]

There was a mill on the Newton estate in 1086 paying 3s. 4d.[1] It was divided with the manor in the early 14th century when half was worth 6s. 8d.[2] In 1367 the mill was farmed for 8s. In 1394–5 Thomas Mullward paid 6s. 8d. for the farm of the mill which was burnt down that year.[3] A new mill appears to have been built by 1420 when Richard Lawson was renting a piece of land on which it stood. The manorial mill was derelict.[4] There was a newly-erected water mill at Chapmanscombe in 1720, half of which belonged to Halsway manor in Stogumber.[5] It had disappeared by 1838 but Mill meadow and remains of a leat survived.[6] Robert Brett had a water mill on

his manor of Thorncombe in 1536 but it may have been outside the parish and is not referred to after 1593.[7] In 1796 a small water mill was in existence at Cottiford but nothing more is known of it.[8]

LOCAL GOVERNMENT. There are court rolls for the Wells chapter holdings in Bicknoller from 1367 to 1831 with gaps.[9] The manor included less than half the parish but lands outside the parish, including Combe Sydenham in Stogumber and Idson in Stogursey, were held of it.[10] Courts were held every summer at the church house in Bicknoller, and in some years an additional court was held. By the 19th century the court was held in the Audit Room at Wells and was concerned only with leases.[11] The manor court for Thorncombe appears to have been concerned only with admissions; no court rolls survive but the steward is mentioned in leases.[12] Apart from maintaining a pound and the highways the Bicknoller manor court dealt mainly with transfer of tenancies and nuisances. In 1368 John atte Yerd gave 6s. 8d. for the office of reeve; by the 17th century that office was held by the lessee of Wayfield, the manor house.[13] In the early 18th century various gentlemen were appointed gamekeepers for the manor.[14] No other manorial officers have been found.

From the 16th century the parish had two churchwardens, two overseers, and a tithingman.[15] The tithingman was responsible for collecting taxes, maintaining parish armour, weapons, the butts, a beacon, and stocks and issuing passes and warrants. During the Civil War he levied money to relieve Taunton and Langport and employed a trained soldier, either for defence or training purposes.[16] There were highway surveyors from 1768 and waywardens in 1846,[17] although in some years only one was elected or the office was combined with that of overseer. In 1854 a perpetual overseer and waywarden was elected but the following year two overseers and two waywardens were elected as usual. The vestry appears to have met only once a year at Easter. In 1854 a parish constable was chosen, from 1855 a poor law guardian,[18] and by 1873 a salaried assistant overseer.[19]

Paupers were given relief in cash or in kind[20] and parishioners in gaol were also relieved when necessary. In 1648 a prisoner was moved to Taunton house of correction which was more convenient than Ilchester for the parish officers to send him relief.[21] All parishioners with £50 a year had to take an apprentice, and the parish allowed 20s. each for

[82] *Kelly's Dir. Som.* (1883).
[83] Min. of Agric., Fisheries, and Food, agric. returns 1976.
[84] S.R.O., DD/CC 131907/21.
[85] Ibid. DD/CC 131925A/10.
[86] Ibid. tithe award.
[87] Ibid. DD/CCH 72.
[88] *V.C.H. Som.* i. 504.
[89] *H.M.C. Wells*, i. 276–7.
[90] S.R.O., DD/CC 110090.
[91] Ibid. tithe award.
[92] Min. of Agric., Fisheries, and Food, agric. returns 1976.
[93] S.R.O., DD/CC 10874, 110122, 110213–4; DD/AH 40/2; ibid. D/P/bic 13/3/74, 13/6/5.
[94] Ibid. DD/SP, inventory 1675.
[95] Ibid. D/P/bic 13/3/19, 23–4; 13/6/65.
[96] Ibid. DD/CC 110132.
[97] Ibid. DD/SAS PR 57; DD/CC 131925A/5; ibid. D/P/bic 13/3/74, 13/6/5.
[98] Ibid. DD/BR/py 16.

[99] *Census*, 1821; S.R.O., D/P/bic 23/2.
[1] *V.C.H. Som.* i. 504.
[2] *H.M.C. Wells*, i. 351.
[3] S.R.O., DD/CC 110079/9.
[4] Ibid. 110079/15.
[5] Ibid. DD/CCH 58.
[6] Ibid. tithe award.
[7] Ibid. DD/BR/py 16.
[8] Ibid. DD/WO, map of Stogumber 1796.
[9] Ibid. DD/CC, catalogue of chapter estate recs.
[10] Ibid. DD/CC 110002, 131907/18; *S.R.S.* lxvii, p. 65.
[11] S.R.O., DD/CC 110083–4.
[12] Ibid. DD/BR/py 16; DD/WY 7.
[13] Ibid. DD/CC 110074, 110079/1, 110089, 110113, 131921/2.
[14] *H.M.C. Wells*, ii. 489, 493.
[15] S.R.O., D/P/bic 4/1/1, 12/13/2, 13/2/13, 13/10/1.
[16] Ibid. 12/13/2; 13/2/1, 3, 5, 9–10.
[17] Ibid. 14/5/1–5.
[18] Ibid. 13/2/36.
[19] Ibid. 13/2/33.
[20] Ibid. 13/2/13.
[21] *S.R.S.* lxxi, p. 24.

clothing.[22] In 1836 the poor were supplied with furniture marked with the parish monogram.[23] The overseers in 1859 provided a man with a brass and leather armcap to enable him to work, presumably after an amputation.[24]

The parish took over the church house for paupers in 1580.[25] It was still occupied by poor people in the 1860s and continued to be repaired by the parish.[26] In 1888 it was occupied by the sexton, though a decade later it was used only to house pigeons and store wood.[27] The house stood by the pound on the north-western boundary of the churchyard and was of two storeys. The site was annexed to the benefice in 1900 and was planted with shrubs.[28] In 1836 the parish became part of the Williton poor-law union, and it remained in the Williton rural district until becoming part of the West Somerset district in 1974.[29]

CHURCH. Bicknoller church probably originated as a manorial chapel and the chapter of Wells as lord of Bicknoller paid towards the repair of the chancel in 1445.[30] Ingram of Bicknoller, chaplain, recorded in Edward I's reign,[31] probably served the church, which has not been found mentioned by name before 1368 when it was a chapel of Stogumber.[32] Since there was an endowment for the chaplain[33] the living was technically a perpetual curacy,[34] but it was called a vicarage in 1661[35] and in the 19th century.[36] In 1975 the living was linked with Crowcombe, and from the end of 1977 formed part of the united benefice of Bicknoller with Crowcombe and Sampford Brett, of which the incumbent is styled rector.[37] From 1368 or earlier the chaplain or curate was appointed and paid by the vicar of Stogumber;[38] the vicar continued to appoint to the living until 1977, when he became one of the patrons in turn of the united benefice.[39]

The chaplain of Bicknoller was paid £5 6s. 8d. in 1535[40] and £7 or £8 by 1574.[41] There was a small endowment by 1571[42] and in 1656 the income was increased to £50.[43] In 1661 it was worth only £20[44] and £15 in 1754.[45] In 1815 it had risen to £143, the result of an augmentation in 1770 by the trustees of Mrs. Pincombe and Mrs. Horner.[46] Further additions were made in 1864 and 1882, and a fund was set up in 1937 to ensure, by a voluntary rate, an income of £150. This fund, continued into the 1960s,

was designed to prevent the union of the parish with a neighbour.[47]

By 1812 the perpetual curate of Bicknoller received tithes worth £104.[48] These tithes must have been given by the vicar of Stogumber, perhaps the result of a petition for augmentation in 1686.[49] In 1838 the small tithes were commuted for a rent charge of £78.[50]

In 1571 the glebe consisted of 1 a. of orchard, ½ a. of meadow, and the herbage of the churchyard.[51] It was increased in 1774 when 21½ a. in the parish of St. John, Glastonbury, were purchased. Some of that land was sold in 1920,[52] and none remained in 1979.

There was a house for the curate by 1626[53] which was pulled down c. 1634. The vicar of Stogumber was accused in 1636 of not rebuilding it.[54] A replacement, said in 1815 to be 'a small cottage only', was then occupied neither by the incumbent nor his assistant curates.[55] In 1868 a wing was added to the 2-storeyed, thatched building which stood in the village street south-west of the church.[56] The wing alone survived a fire in 1883. A new house was built in 1883[57] and continued as the benefice house until 1956 when it was sold. A house was built in Trendle Lane to replace it in 1962.

The curate in 1554 was deprived for marriage, and the church was still without rood and tabernacle in 1557.[58] At least two curates in the early 17th century served without licence and no quarterly sermons were preached.[59] John Baynham, vicar of Stogumber, served the cure in person until 1642. Bartholomew Safford signed the parish register in 1643, but Thomas White signed as curate from then until 1645. Safford was minister in the parish from 1646 until 1662.[60] In 1686 the parish was said to be 'neglected and ill-supplied'.[61] During the 18th century there was a rapid succession of curates, and between 1784 and 1811 the living was vacant.[62] William Phelps, who held the benefice from 1811 until 1854, was also vicar of Meare, a botanist, and author of a *History of the Antiquities of Somerset*.[63] His curate lived at and also served Stogumber, holding services at Bicknoller in 1840 alternately morning and afternoon and every Sunday evening.[64] In 1851 morning and afternoon services were attended by 72 and 145 people respectively, including Sunday school children.[65] Under W. H. Hunnybun (1867–9) daily services and weekly celebrations were held at Bicknoller and weekly services at Woolston. J. E. Vernon (1869–77) found the Woolston services better

[22] S.R.O., D/P/bic 13/2/24.
[23] Ibid. 13/2/34.
[24] Ibid. 13/2/36.
[25] Ibid. 5/1/1.
[26] Ibid. 13/2/34, 36.
[27] Ibid. 1/7/2.
[28] Ibid. 1/7/6; 13/10/2.
[29] Youngs, *Local Admin. Units*, i. 673, 675–6.
[30] S.R.O., DD/CC 110079/13.
[31] *H.M.C. Wells*, ii. 571–2.
[32] S.R.O., DD/CC 110079/3.
[33] Below.
[34] S.R.O., D/D/B returns 1827.
[35] Ibid. DD/CC 110075.
[36] Ibid. D/D/V returns 1840.
[37] *Dioc. Dir.*
[38] S.R.O., DD/CC 110079/3.
[39] *Dioc. Dir.*
[40] *Valor Eccl.* (Rec. Com.), i. 226.
[41] *S. & D. N. & Q.* xiv. 63.
[42] S.R.O., D/D/Rg 360.
[43] *Cal. S.P. Dom.* 1655–6, 246. An augmentation in 1649 is mentioned by Crippen, *Nonconf. in Som.*

[44] S.R.O., DD/CC 110075.
[45] J. Ecton, *Thesaurus*, 36.
[46] C. Hodgson, *Queen Anne's Bounty* (1844), p. clxix.
[47] *Livings Augmented by Queen Anne's Bounty*, H.C. 122 (1867), liv; S.R.O., D/P/bic 10/2/1, 23/1.
[48] S.R.O., D/P/bic 23/1.
[49] Ibid. DD/CC 110089.
[50] Ibid. tithe award.
[51] Ibid. D/D/Rg 360.
[52] Ibid. D/P/bic 1/7/6; 23/1.
[53] Ibid. D/D/Rg 331.
[54] Ibid. D/D/Ca 310.
[55] Ibid. D/D/B returns 1815, 1827.
[56] Ibid. DD/CC E173.
[57] Ibid. D/P/bic 1/7/2.
[58] Ibid. D/D/Ca 22, 27.
[59] Ibid. D/D/Ca 134, 151, 180.
[60] Ibid. D/P/bic 2/1/1.
[61] Ibid. DD/CC 110089.
[62] Ibid. D/P/bic 23/1.
[63] Green, *Bibliotheca Somersetensis*, iii. 139.
[64] S.R.O., D/D/Bo; D/D/B returns 1815, 1827; D/D/V returns 1840.   [65] P.R.O., HO 129/313/5/2/2.

attended than those of the parish church, and introduced cottage lectures and vestments. W. B. Wood (1877–1910) abandoned vestments and daily services.[66]

There was a church house at Bicknoller. By 1580 it had been acquired by the parish as a poorhouse.[67]

In Edward I's reign land was given for three masses a year for Henry de Wayville and his family.[68] In 1504 the tenant of the land was required to find a taper before the figure of Our Lady at Bicknoller during daily mass, a torch at 'sacring time', and 3d. a year for the priest to pray for the souls of the Way-villes whose names were specified in the mass book.[69] The charge continued until 1547.[70] There were endowed lights in the church by 1530 including one called St. Saviour's light.[71]

The church of *ST. GEORGE*, of local stone with Ham stone dressings, has a chancel with north chapel, nave with north aisle and two-storeyed south porch, and a west tower. The small size of the nave and the thickness of its south wall, which is unbuttressed, suggest a 12th-century origin, which may be corroborated by a 12th-century pillar piscina in the chancel. The tower was added in the 15th century and at about the same time the chancel was refenestrated and may have been rebuilt. The porch, the nave window to the west, and the north aisle and chapel are of the early 16th century.

The heavily recut font is of the 15th century and there are fragments of medieval glass reset in the north window of the chancel.[72] The much-restored chancel screen, probably of *c.* 1500 and said to have come from Huish Champflower in 1726,[73] before 1842 included a rood loft.[74] A rood stair in the south wall is evidence of a screen in a similar position in the later Middle Ages. There are bench ends of the earlier 16th century and others of similar design were put in in 1932.[75] Two ancient stone altars have been lost;[76] the present altar is the top of a tomb chest which was brought in from the churchyard in the 1950s.[77] A gallery was built before 1781[78] and removed in 1871 during restoration by J. D. Sedding which included the removal of the plastered waggon roof and most monuments.[79] Further restoration and refurnishing took place in the 1920s and 1930s.[80]

There are four bells, the oldest of *c.* 1420–60 by Robert Norton of Exeter.[81] The plate includes an Elizabethan cup made in Exeter.[82] The registers date from 1557 and are complete except for burials 1640–76.[83]

NONCONFORMITY. One recusant is recorded in the early 17th century and two in 1642.[84] An Anabaptist was presented in 1664,[85] and in 1669 people were meeting at several houses in the parish. In 1670 Hannah Safford, widow of the former minister Bartholomew, was convicted of allowing a conventicle in her house with over 40 people, under her brother-in-law Thomas Safford. The tithingman was convicted for not giving assistance in suppressing the conventicle.[86] The vicar of Stogumber recorded the baptism of a child at a 'chimney church' at Upcott in Bicknoller in 1672.[87] In the same year Thomas Safford was licensed as a preacher anp ministered in Bicknoller and the neighbouring parishes until his death in 1704.[88] The first licensed places of worship were the houses of Hannah Safford and Richard Gillinge in 1672[89] followed by others in 1689, 1697, 1700, and 1726. The newly-erected house of William Cornish was licensed as a Presbyterian meeting-house in 1734.[90] In 1834 Wesleyan Methodists decided to introduce preaching into Bicknoller but abandoned the scheme in the following year. A preaching place was established at Woolston in 1869.[91] In 1894 the Wesleyans held an afternoon meeting at Cottiford,[92] and between 1895 and 1897 they held services at Woolston.[93] In 1883 the Salvation Army held meetings in Woolston and Bicknoller.[94]

EDUCATION. In 1609 the curate was accused of teaching without licence.[95] An infant school was started in 1828 and a day school in 1832; by 1835 they took 32 children together.[96] In 1846–7 there was a Sunday school, held in the church and united with the National Society, which was supported by subscriptions and took 42 children. A dame's school, whose 14 children attended the Sunday school, was supported by school pence. The educational wants of the parish were then said to be deplorable.[97] There was a day school in 1859.[98] The vestry in 1855 rejected the vicar's motion to start a school for the 'labouring class',[99] but in 1863 the Wells chapter gave a site for a school.[1] There were said to be 106 pupils enrolled in 1881[2] but by 1893 there were only 35 children on the books and the average attendances were much lower.[3] In 1905 average attendance had fallen to fourteen and in 1912 the school was closed.[4] A night school was held in the parish on Tuesdays and Thursdays in 1868.[5]

[66] S.R.O., D/P/bic 1/7/1–6.
[67] Above, local govt.
[68] *H.M.C. Wells*, ii. 571–2.
[69] *S.R.S.* liv, pp. 105–6.
[70] Ibid. ii. 45.   [71] Ibid.; *Wells Wills*, ed. Weaver, 9.
[72] Glass in the church was repaired in 1445–6: S.R.O., DD/CC 110079/19.
[73] Taunton Castle, Som. Arch. Soc. Libr., Hancock MS.
[74] F. B. Bond and B. Camm, *Rood Screens and Roodlofts*, i (1909), 148.
[75] S.R.O., D/P/bic 8/3/1.
[76] Taunton Castle, Som. Arch. Soc. Libr., Hancock MS.
[77] *Church Guide* (n.d.).
[78] S.R.O., D/P/bic 4/1/21.
[79] Ibid. 1/7/1, 7/4/1; D/D/Cf 71/4.
[80] Ibid. D/P/bic 8/3/1.
[81] Taunton Castle, Som. Arch. Soc. Libr., Hancock MS.
[82] *Proc. Som. Arch. Soc.* xlv. 163.
[83] S.R.O., D/P/bic 2/1/2–9.
[84] *S. & D. N. & Q.* v. 112; *Som. Protestation Returns*, ed. Howard and Stoate, 293.

[85] S.R.O., D/D/Ca 344.
[86] *Orig. Records of Early Nonconf.* ed. G. L. Turner, i. 8.
[87] S.R.O., D/P/stogm 2/1/2.
[88] *Calamy Revised*, ed. A. G. Matthews; S.R.O., D/P/bic 2/1/3.
[89] *Orig. Records of Early Nonconf.* ed. Turner, i. 613.
[90] S.R.O., Q/SR.
[91] Ibid. D/N/wsc 3/2/2.
[92] Ibid. D/P/bic 1/7/3.
[93] Ibid. D/N/wsc 3/2/4.
[94] Ibid. D/P/bic 1/7/2.
[95] S.R.O., D/D/Ca 160.
[96] *Educ. Enq. Abstract*, H.C. 62 (1835), xlii.
[97] Nat. Soc. *Inquiry, 1846–7*, Som. 4–5.
[98] *P.O. Dir. Som.* (1859).
[99] S.R.O., D/P/bic 13/2/36.
[1] Ibid.; ibid. C/E 26.
[2] Ibid. 1/7/4.
[3] Ibid. 1/7/2.
[4] Ibid. *Schs. Lists*; D/P/bic 18/7/1.
[5] Ibid. D/P/bic 1/7/1.

CHARITIES FOR THE POOR. In 1718 the parish held £32 in trust and in 1771 received a further £20 under the will of Giles Jenkins for the aged poor.[6] Distributions of cloth were made in 1783 and 1785.[7] By 1815 £15 capital had been lost and the two benefactions produced only £1 17s. a year.[8] By 1826 Jenkins' bequest had been lent out on private security and lost and £1 10s. was being paid out of the poor rate.[9] Eliza Warrington (d. 1901) gave the residue from £300, after the upkeep of a grave, to be divided between poor churchgoers.[10] By 1974 no distribution had been made for many years as there was 'little or no poverty' in Bicknoller. In the 1960s some of the

income had been used to augment the funds of the clothing club.[11]

The Bartholomew Thomas almshouses at Woolston were founded under a bequest by Lucy Thomas (d. 1902). She gave £3,000 for four almshouses for poor protestants of 55 or over of good character who were unable to work. Each inmate was to receive 5s. or 7s. 6d. a week. Six cottages were demolished to make way for the almshouses which were completed in 1905.[12] In 1908 there were couples in three of the almshouses and the fourth was divided between two single people.[13] Doles ceased by 1935, and in 1976 the occupants were contributing up to £4 a week.[14]

BROMPTON RALPH

BROMPTON RALPH lies on the eastern edge of the Brendons immediately north of Wiveliscombe. It occupies a steep slope divided into spurs by deep combes and rising from 76 m. in the extreme southeast to 183 m. in the village and then more sharply to 393 m. by the northern boundary. The parish is trapezoid in shape and measures approximately 3.5 km. north to south and between 3.5 km. and 4 km. east to west. Most of the western, northern, and eastern boundaries follow roads. In the south-east the boundary follows two streams which converge south of Moor Mill Farm.[15] The northern boundary near Holcombe Water was confirmed in 1505[16] and the southern was the subject of an agreement in 1437 or 1438.[17] The northern half of the parish is composed of Brendon Hill beds and the southern half of Morte Slates.[18] After the transfer to Tolland parish of a small detached part of Brompton Ralph called Brompton Cottage in 1883 the civil parish contained 1,107 ha. (2,736 a.).[19]

The earliest settlement in the parish was by the Brendon ridgeway where an unfinished Iron Age hillfort known as Elworthy Barrows survives.[20] Brompton or Bruneton, the farmstead by the Brendons,[21] was so called by the 8th century and presumably acquired the suffix Ralph from its lord, Ralph son of William, in late 12th century.[22] The village lies near the eastern boundary of the parish on the lower slopes of the Brendons. It consists of a scatter of cottages and farms, of various dates, around two greens. The larger, Brompton Green, lies beside the church and was allotted for recreation in 1845; the smaller was formerly the pound.[23] There are hamlets in the south at Pitsford Hill, which dates from at least the 12th century,[24] and Stone, mentioned in the

14th century, and in the north on the road to Elworthy Rooksnest and Colwell, the latter so called by 1327.[25] Scattered farms, mainly in the combes, include Westcott and Parswell, in existence by the 12th century,[26] Bowden, Hele, and Padcombe by 1327, and Burton by 1337.[27]

Most of the parish was inclosed by the 1380s,[28] but there was some common pasture on the Brendons until the 19th century.[29] A park and 'parkland' were mentioned in the late 14th century and the park formed part of the demesne of the Fulfords' manor in the 1440s and in 1568.[30] In 1614 both park and 'parkland' were let to tenants.[31] It is possible that there were two parks, a small one south of the village and a later addition occupied by the 19th-century farm called Parks.[32] There were 20 a. of woodland in 1086,[33] 28 a. in 1842,[34] and 48 a. in 1905.[35] Stone Wood in the south part of the parish is now part of a commercial woodland estate.

The parish was surrounded on three sides by turnpike roads but the village itself is served only by minor roads and lanes because of the precipitous nature of most of the ground. The turnpike from Wiveliscombe to Holcombe Water was opened in 1786 and followed the western boundary of the parish.[36] The old Bampton–Hartrow road, turnpiked by the Wiveliscombe trust in 1806, links the turnpike from Wiveliscombe to Holcombe Water with the Wiveliscombe–Elworthy road, also turnpiked in 1806, and forms the northern boundary of the parish.[37] There were tollhouses on the Elworthy road at Pitsford Hill and at the junction with the road to Tolland.[38] Several small lanes were laid out across Brendon Common when it was inclosed in 1845.[39]

In 1671 there was a 'drinkhouse' in the parish[40] and

[6] Ibid. 17/3/1–3.   [7] Ibid. 13/2/34.
[8] Char. Don. H.C. 511 (1816), xvi.
[9] 15th Rep. Com. Char. p. 438.
[10] S.R.O., D/P/bic 17/1/4.   [11] Char. Com. files.
[12] S.R.O., D/P/bic 17/5/1.   [13] Ibid. 1/7/2.
[14] Char. Com. files.
[15] O.S. Map 1/50,000, sheet 181 (1974 edn.). This article was completed in 1981.
[16] S.R.O., DD/WO 41/22.   [17] H.M.C. Wells, ii. 69.
[18] Geol. Surv. Map 1″, solid and drift, sheet 294 (1969 edn.); drift, sheet 295 (1956 edn.).
[19] Youngs, Local Admin. Units, i. 419; Census, 1971.
[20] V.C.H. Som. i. 190; L. V. Grinsell, Archaeology of Exmoor, 88.
[21] Ekwall, Eng. Place-Names (1960), 65; the identity of Ralph is incorrect: below.
[22] H. P. R. Finberg, Early Charters of Wessex, p. 115; below, manor.
[23] S.R.O., DD/WO 9/1; DD/WY 168; ibid. D/P/h.c 20/1/1.   [24] Proc. Som. Arch. Soc. xcviii. 120.

[25] S.R.S. iii. 182.
[26] Cart. Canonsleigh Abbey (Devon and Cornw. Rec. Soc. N.S. viii), 33.
[27] S.R.S. iii. 182; S.R.O., DD/SAS PR 57.
[28] S.R.O., DD/L P33/7.
[29] S.R.O., tithe award; ibid. DD/WO 9/1; D/P/h. c 20/1/1; DD/WY 168.
[30] Ibid. DD/L P33/4, 7; ct.roll, Brompton Fulford, in the possession of Mr. R. C. Hatchwell, Lt. Somerford, Wilts., 1978.
[31] S.R.O., DD/WY 47/3/43.
[32] Ibid. tithe award; ibid. DD/BR/gm 12.
[33] V.C.H. Som. i. 501.   [34] S.R.O., tithe award.
[35] Statistics supplied by the then Bd. of Agric. 1905.
[36] 26 Geo. III, c. 135.
[37] 46 Geo. III, c. 52 (Local and Personal); S.R.O., set of 1″ maps annotated by Sir Rob. Hall.
[38] S.R.O., tithe award.
[39] Ibid. D/P/h. c 20/1/1.
[40] Ibid. DD/SP, inventory 1671.

in 1721 two people were accused of selling beer without a licence.[41] The King's Head inn was established by 1823[42] and may be the same as the Carpenters Arms at Pitsford Hill first recorded by that name in 1842,[43] which remained open until 1920; in 1981 it was a general store.[44] In 1851 there was a beer house in the parish, possibly the Jackass tavern, which stood on the western boundary road in 1842.[45] It is now a cottage.

There were at least 106 adult males in the parish in 1641[46] and over 174 inhabitants in 1667,[47] a figure which rose to 406 in 1801. The population reached a peak of 530 in 1851, falling sharply to 436 in 1861 and then more gradually to 322 in 1901. Numbers continued to decline, reaching 179 in 1971.[48]

John Toms, glass stainer, was born in Brompton Ralph between 1813 and 1815.[49] His work can be seen in the churches at Clatworthy, Elworthy, Milverton, Monksilver, Nettlecombe, and Nynehead.[50]

MANORS AND OTHER ESTATES. Frithogyth, wife of King Aethelheard, gave 5 hides at Brompton to Glastonbury Abbey c. 729.[51] By 1066 the abbey had lost the estate to Brictric. William I granted it to William de Mohun, of whose honor of Dunster it was held until 1627 or later.[52] William's tenant in 1086 was Turgis.[53] In 1166 the estate was almost certainly one of the 5½ fees held by William son of Durand (d. before 1194) under William de Mohun.[54] Ralph, son of William and grandson of Durand, who gave his name to the estate to distinguish it from Brompton Regis, married Yolande, sister of his overlord William de Mohun, and secured a remittance of scutage from his estate at Brompton.[55] Ralph, who may have been dead by 1212, had three daughters: Lucy, wife of William Malet, Hilary, wife of John FitzUrse, and Isabel, wife successively of Hugh Peverel and of Nicholas FitzMartin.[56]

Lucy's inheritance was the senior estate held of Dunster and the other two shares were held of her.[57] Lucy (d. c. 1259) was succeeded by her daughter, also Lucy, who married Simon of Merriott (d. c. 1276) and Thomas of Timworth (d. c. 1296).[58] Lucy the younger was dead by 1316 and her manor of *BROMPTON RALPH* descended to her second son Walter of Merriott, clerk (d. 1345), incumbent of Withycombe, and then to Walter's nephew Simon of Merriott.[59] Simon died before 1372 when his

widow Margery was the wife of Thomas Willington. Thomas purchased the reversion from Sir John of Merriott, Simon's heir, through trustees c. 1373. When Margery died c. 1390 Brompton Ralph passed in turn to Thomas Willington's nephews, Ralph Willington, who died a minor, and his brother John, who also died a minor and insane in 1396.[60]

John's heirs were his sister Isabel, wife of William Beaumont, and John Wroth, son of his other sister Margaret. Brompton Ralph passed to John, then a minor. John died still under age in 1412 and his widow Joyce conveyed the manor to John's sister Elizabeth (or Joan), wife of Sir William Palton.[61] Elizabeth (d. 1440) and Sir William (d. 1450) had no issue and their estate passed to Elizabeth's cousin Thomas Beaumont (d. 1451) and to his son William (d. 1453).[62]

William died without legitimate issue and his brother Philip (d. 1473) settled Brompton Ralph on William's widow Joan. In 1470 Philip transferred his estate to trustees and, under a settlement of 1485, Brompton Ralph was conveyed to Philip's half brother Thomas Beaumont (d. 1488) with remainder to Hugh and John, Thomas's brothers.[63] In 1500 John Basset, son of Philip Beaumont's sister Joan, was acknowledged as Hugh's heir at the request of Giles, Lord Daubeney (d. 1508), who intended to marry his son Henry to one of John's daughters. In 1504 Brompton Ralph was settled on Daubeney and his heirs with remainder to Sir John Basset and his heirs if the marriage did not take place. Henry Daubeney (cr. earl of Bridgwater 1538) did not marry a Basset and died without issue in 1548. The manor reverted to the Bassets. Sir John Basset's son John had died leaving an infant heir, Arthur, and in 1548 the estate was settled on John's widow Frances and her second husband Thomas Moncke.[64]

Although Frances had male issue by both her husbands the Brompton Ralph estate appears to have been sold. During the later 16th century it came into the hands of the Hobbes family of Stogursey and they held the chief manor in 1614.[65] In 1620 the property, described as half the manor of Brompton Ralph, was settled on Edward Hobbes and his wife Eleanor.[66] Edward (d. before 1642) was succeeded by his son Thomas (d. 1657), his grandson Edward (d. 1693), and his great-grandson John, who last sold the estate to Nathaniel Brewer in 1711.[67] The purchaser was probably Nathaniel Brewer the younger (d. 1729). About 1721 Nathaniel's daughter and

[41] Ibid. DD/HC 6L.
[42] Ibid. Q/RL.
[43] Ibid. tithe award.
[44] *P.O. Dir. Som.* (1861, 1875); *Kelly's Dir. Som.* (1910); inf. from Mrs. Hutchings, Lydeard St. Lawrence.
[45] P.R.O., HO 107/1920; S.R.O., tithe award.
[46] *Som. Protestation Returns*, ed. Howard and Stoate, 152.
[47] S.R.O., DD/WY 34: part of the list is illegible.
[48] *Census*, 1801–1971.
[49] P.R.O., HO 107/1920.
[50] *S. & D. N. & Q.* xxv. 179–82.
[51] H. P. R. Finberg, *Early Charters of Wessex*, 115.
[52] *V.C.H. Som.* i. 408, 501; *S.R.S.* xxxiii, p. 333.
[53] *V.C.H. Som.* i. 501.
[54] *Red Bk. Exch.* (Rolls Ser.), i. 226.
[55] *S.R.S.* xxxiii, pp. 6, 52.
[56] Ibid. pp. 33, 37, 55.
[57] *S.R.S.* vi. 111, 117, 195, 207.
[58] *Rot. Hund.* (Rec. Com.), ii. 119; *S.R.S.* xxxiii, pp. 49, 53, 59; xli, 95; *Cal. Inq. p.m.* ii, pp. 178, 351.

[59] *S.R.S.* xxxiii, pp. 70–1; *Cal. Inq. p.m.* viii, p. 159; ix, p. 390.
[60] *S.R.S.* xvii, 84; xxxiii, pp. 113, 115, 118; *Cal. Inq. p.m.* xvi, p. 260; *Cal. Inq. Misc.* v, p. 142; *Cal. Pat.* 1396–9, 434; P.R.O., C 136/96, no. 55.
[61] *Cal. Pat.* 1396–9, 434; *Cal. Fine R.* 1399–1405, p. 31; *Cal. Close*, 1409–13, 382, 430, 434; P.R.O., C 137/86, no. 25; *S.R.S.* xxxiii, pp. 114, 115, 196, 209, 220.
[62] *Cal. Close*, 1447–54, 152, 216; P.R.O., C 149/638, no. 28.
[63] P.R.O., C 140/67, no. 64; Devon R.O. 48/25/9/3; *Cal. Inq. p.m. Hen. VII*, i, pp. 58, 119–20.
[64] P.R.O., CP 40/958, rott. 537–40; CP 40/974, rot. 541; C 54/399, no. 9; C 142/25, no. 22; CP 25(2)/62/498/2 Edw. VI Mich.
[65] P.R.O., C 3/85/11; CP 25(2)/206/29 and 30 Eliz. I Mich.; C 142/519, no. 86.
[66] P.R.O., CP 25(2)/347/18 Jas. I Mich.
[67] S.R.O., DD/WY 20/52; P.R.O., CP 25(2)/869/5 Wm. & M. Trin.; CP 25(2)/962/11 Anne East.; Wilts. R.O. 754/71.

eventual heir Joan married David Yea the younger, whose family already owned land in Brompton Ralph through two earlier marriages into the Hobbes family. Joan (d. 1781) was succeeded by her eldest surviving son, Sir William, who settled the manor on his son William Walter (d. 1804).[68]

Jane Yea, widow of William Walter, died in 1829 and the estate was sold to Mary Stephens and her daughter, also Mary. On the death of Mary Stephens the younger in 1854 the property was sold to Samuel Mogg and four others. Mogg acquired the whole estate which he sold in 1861 to Edward Portman, Baron Portman,[69] who was said in 1872 to hold an equal third share in the manor. Lord Portman (cr. Viscount 1873) died in 1888 and was succeeded by his son William Henry, Viscount Portman (d. 1919).[70] The property appears to have been sold to George Elliot by 1923 and in 1931 it was in the possession of Ernest Henry Elliot.[71] No further reference to lordship has been found.

Hilary FitzUrse's share of the manor passed to her son Ralph (d. by 1269). Ralph's widow Isabel, later wife of William de Raleigh, held the share and survived her son John FitzUrse (d. c. 1280). On her death it passed to John's son Ralph (d. c. 1321), and descended like the manor of Williton Fulford, being divided into two shares after 1388.[72] James Durburgh (d. 1416) was succeeded in his share by his son John, and later by his brother Ralph, who seems to have conveyed his estate c. 1428 to trustees including John, parson of Bradford; John held the fee in 1429.[73] By 1433 the estate was sold to John Spencer (d. before 1472) who granted it in trust to John Monk or Mounhun, named lord in 1475.[74] By 1490 it had been sold, to raise portions for Spencer's daughters, to Sir Thomas Fulford and was thus united with the other share.[75]

The manor of *BROMPTON FULFORD* was settled on Thomas Fulford's son Sir Humphrey (d. 1508) and his wife Florence (d. 1524) Sir Humphrey died without issue and was succeeded by his nephew John Fulford (d. 1544).[76] John's wife Dorothy (d. after 1551) held the manor for life and was followed by her son Sir John (d. 1580), Sir John's son Sir Thomas (d. 1610), and Sir Thomas's son Francis.[77] In 1620 Francis Fulford and his wife Elizabeth sold Brompton Fulford to William Lacey of Hartrow, in Stogumber, in whose family it descended with

Elworthy manor until 1811.[78] The manor was held jointly by two sisters, Elizabeth and Mary Escott, their respective husbands Daniel Blommart and Thomas Sweet Escott, and their heirs from 1811 until 1872 or later.[79] No further reference to the lordship has been found.

The capital messuage of Brompton Fulford was divided with the estate after 1388 and one share contained a hall with chamber adjoining, and a cellar (*salarium*) or undercroft beneath the two.[80] In the 16th century it was let to tenants[81] and in 1614 the barton was divided.[82] No further reference to the house has been found.

The third of the original manor that was inherited by Isabel, wife successively of Hugh Peverel (d. c. 1259) of Ermington (Devon) and of Nicholas Fitz-Martin, was sold before 1277 to John of Heghton or Hetherton and his wife Christine of Washford.[83] Christine's conveyance of her estate in Brompton Ralph to Adam of Bawdrip was challenged by Thomas of Timworth and his wife Lucy, holders of the chief part of the manor, and by the heirs of John de Hetherton.[84] Adam's right was upheld and he was holding part of a fee in Brompton Ralph between 1280 and 1285.[85] Adam, who was coroner for Somerset, died c. 1296 leaving his heir John a minor.[86] In 1351 John of Bawdrip, probably grandson of John, granted his estate in Brompton Ralph to his mother Orange, widow of Hugh of Bawdrip, to hold in dower. She was holding it in 1359 when he sold the reversion in order to pay his debts.[87] By 1389 the Bawdrips' part of the manor was owned by Joan Sydenham, wife of Richard Cave, and Julian, wife of William Barwe. In 1429 an estate in Brompton Ralph was settled on Joan and her second husband Ralph Bosom for life and then on their daughter Joan, but John Hamelyn, possibly a trustee, was recorded as holding part of a fee in 1429 and 1442.[88] The younger Joan Bosom was probably Joan, wife of Martin Jacob, who died in possession of a share in the manor of Brompton Ralph in 1485. Her heir was her grandson John Jacob but her daughter-in-law Elizabeth (d. 1510), mother of John, held the estate for life.[89] John Jacob or his heirs sold the estate, known in 1510 as the manor of *BROMPTON JACOB*,[90] before 1541 to Michael Malet who in 1542 settled it on his wife Joan. Michael died in 1547 and Joan married John Fry.[91] By 1575 Joan had been succeeded by her

[68] S.R.O., DD/HC 6G, 6L; Wilts. R.O. 754/83, 85; P.R.O., CP 25(2)/1399/22 Geo. III Hil.; A. J. Monday, *Hist. Family of Yea* (Taunton, 1885), p. lviii; *Proc. Som. Arch. Soc.* xxix. 64; S.R.O., DD/RR 3, 6, 48.
[69] S.R.O., DD/BR/vi 9; DD/SAS SE 25; DD/WY 168; DD/CCH 6/4; ibid. tithe award; Monday, *Family of Yea*, p. lxvi.
[70] S.R.O., DD/CCH 77; *P.O. Dir. Som.* (1875); *Kelly's Dir. Som.* (1883, 1889); Burke, *Peerage* (1949), 1618–19.
[71] *Kelly's Dir. Som.* (1911, 1923, 1931); Burke, *Peerage* (1949), 1618–19.
[72] *Proc. Som. Arch. Soc.* lxviii. 97–102; below.
[73] *S.R.S.* xxii. 71–2; xxxiii, pp. 128, 197; extra ser. 198, 260; *Feud. Aids*, iv. 438; S.R.O., DD/SAS PR 57.
[74] *S.R.S.* xxxiii, pp. 208, 213, 220, 232; S.R.O., DD/DR/d 5; P.R.O., C 1/40, no. 112.
[75] *S.R.S.* extra ser. 199.
[76] *Cal. Inq. p.m. Hen. VII*, i, pp. 266, 270; P.R.O., CP 40/977, rot. 149; C 142/25, no. 43; *S.R.S.* xxxiii, pp. 261, 271, 275, 281, 282.
[77] S.R.O., DD/DR/d 9; DD/DR 3, 68; DD/WY 10; P.R.O., C 142/330, no. 93; C 3/65/2; C 3/170/8; CP 25(2)/260/24 Eliz. I East.; *Cal. Proc. Chanc. Eliz.* (Rec. Com.), i. 313; *S.R.S.* xxxiii, pp. 296, 310.

[78] Below; S.R.O., DD/DR 3, 32; DD/CCH 77; DD/BR/gm 12; Wilts. R.O. 754/74; Devon R.O. 74B/MT 1812–13; P.R.O., CP 25(2)/347/18 Jas. I Trin. and Mich.; CP 25(2)/961/2 Anne Hil.; CP 25(2)/1057/11 Geo. I Mich.; C 142/462, no. 100; *S.R.S.* xxxiii, p. 333; lxvii, p. 33.
[79] S.R.O., DD/CCH 77, 79, 80, 81; DD/WY 168.
[80] Ibid. DD/L P33/7.
[81] Ibid. DD/DR/d 9; Devon R.O. 2229M/M1.
[82] S.R.O., DD/WY 47/3.
[83] *S.R.S.* vi. 87; xxxiii, p. 33; *Cal. Inq. p.m.* i, p. 134.
[84] *S.R.S.* vi. 244; xli. 95, 193; xliv. 291, 314.
[85] *S.R.S.* xxxiii, pp. 49, 53, 59; *Cal. Inq. p.m.* ii, p. 178.
[86] *Cal. Inq. p.m.* iii, p. 434.
[87] *Cal. Pat. 1292–1301*, 187; *Cal. Inq. p.m.* xiii, p. 75; deed in the possession of Mr. J. S. Cox, St. Peter Port, Guernsey, 1969.
[88] *Cal. Inq. p.m.* iii, p. 119; *Cal. Inq. Misc.* v, pp. 142, 147; *Cal. Close, 1389–92*, 220; *S.R.S.* xxii. 77; xxxiii, pp. 197, 209.
[89] *Cal. Inq. p.m. Hen. VII*, i, p. 58; *S.R.S.* xix. 140–1; P.R.O., C 142/25, no. 41.
[90] S.R.O., DD/AH 11/9.
[91] P.R.O., STAC 1/30/120; C 3/197/25; C 142/87, no. 85; S.R.O., DD/AS 23.

son Richard Malet.[92] Richard was succeeded in 1614 by his son Arthur (d. 1644) who was in turn succeeded by his kinsman Thomas Malet of Poyntington (Dors.).[93]

Sir Thomas Malet (d. 1665) was succeeded by his son Sir John (d. 1686), by Sir John's son Baldwin (d. before 1704), and by Baldwin's son William (d. before 1736).[94] William's daughter Anne was also dead by 1736, leaving as her heir her uncle, Baldwin Malet, rector of Street, who probably sold the manor to Edward Dyke of Tetton, Kingston St. Mary. Most of the land had already been sold in the 17th century to William Lacey and John Hobbes, holders of the other two parts of the manor. Dyke's descendant, Thomas Dyke Acland, was in possession of a rent charge in Brompton Ralph in 1800. No further reference to the estate has been found and no rights for this share of the manor were claimed in 1842.[95]

An estate in the north part of the parish including part of Colwell (now Colwell farm) and Shorney (now Combe Shorney farm) was described as the manor of *BROMPTON RALPH* in 1602 when it was in the possession of Joan Saffin, widow (d. 1603), and her son Edward Saffin. After Edward's death without issue in 1621 the manor appears to have been held jointly by his widow Joan (d. *c.* 1657) with her second husband John Boys (d. before 1646) and Edward, son of John Saffin of Halberton (Devon), probably her first husband's nephew. Edward Saffin gave to his two brothers, John and Hugh, his half of the manor in 1656 probably in trust for his marriage. In 1674 Edward's brother or son, John Saffin of Halberton, sold the estates to the tenants free of any manorial services.[96]

A large freehold estate at Westcott, part of the manor of Brompton Fulford, came to be regarded as a separate manor and had its own courts by 1628.[97] From the late 16th century it was held partly by the Wyndham family and partly by the Dykes of Brompton Regis until 1648 when John Wyndham acquired the entire estate by exchange.[98] The property descended with Orchard Wyndham.[99] In 1763 Charles, earl of Egremont, referred to his manor of *BROMPTON RALPH* and demanded suit of court and heriots from his tenants.[1] By the 19th century claim to a manor was no longer made but in 1842 Egremont successfully asserted rights in the commons then being inclosed.[2]

Parswell was given between 1196 and 1204 by Ralph son of William to Canonsleigh Abbey (Devon).[3] Land called Hyndon, formerly belonging to Canonsleigh and possibly part of the same estate, was sold to

Roger Bluet of Holcombe Rogus (Devon) in 1548.[4]

Property in the south part of the parish, including Moor mill, was among the possessions of the order of St. John of Jerusalem, probably as a result of a grant by Ralph son of William.[5] It later formed part of the senior third of the manor.[6]

ECONOMIC HISTORY. In 1086 the estate included $3\frac{1}{2}$ hides of arable, of which only 1 virgate was in demesne, worked by 7 serfs, and 6 a. of meadow, 20 a. of wood, and a league of pasture. Livestock included 12 she-goats and 107 sheep.[7] There were 16 villeins and two bordars in 1086 and the total of 20 taxpayers in 1327 suggests that the number of occupiers was then about the same.[8]

The largest individual farms on Maud FitzUrse's estate in 1383 were at Westcott, Hele, and Pitsford.[9] John Hale, a freeholder in 1389, had a messuage and carucate of land worth 10s. a year, and his goods included 9 qr. of rye and 60 qr. of oats.[10] The rental of Brompton Fulford manor in 1491–2[11] included substantial rents from the demesne, let by 1440 and probably much earlier.[12] Evidence for farming practice is scarce, but the fields named in the division of the manor in 1383 were almost all inclosed.[13] Rye was grown in the Middle Ages and later.[14] Sheep were a common concern for the manorial court in the 16th century[15] and were grazed both on Brendon common[16] and also in the south part of the parish. In the early 17th century Middle Westcott Down was said to measure 60 a. and Higher Westcott Down 40 a. Names such as Sheep Washing meadow suggest the importance of sheep in the parish.[17] Farming inventories included a flock of 10 sheep in 1687[18] and one of 36 sheep in 1730.[19]

By the early 19th century many of the downs had been divided into smaller fields and in some cases ploughed. In 1801 James Bernard, lord of Clatworthy manor, was awarded a silver goblet by the Wiveliscombe Agricultural Society for planting potatoes and turnips on 20 a. of Brendon common in Brompton Ralph. Bernard had offered it to the tenants 30 years before if they would till it but they preferred to use it for common pasture because they could graze the whole of the common.[20]

Very little consolidation of holdings had taken place and some holdings had been divided by 1842 when the largest farm was 143 a. and only four other farms measured over 100 a. Fourteen farms had between 50 a. and 100 a., 17 had between 20 a. and 50 a.,

---

[92] P.R.O., CP 25(2)/260/17 Eliz. I Hil.; C 3/85/11.
[93] P.R.O., C 142/519, no. 86; *S.R.S.* xxiii. 352; *Cal. Cttee. for Compounding*, ii. 1512.
[94] P.R.O., C 66/2959, no. 24; CP 25(2)/717/29 and 30 Chas. II Hil.; S.R.O., DD/DR 3; DD/AH 38/2; DD/WO 34/3; Wilts. R.O. 754/71.
[95] *Cal. Treas. Papers*, 1702–7, 300, 346; Wilts. R.O. 754/71; ibid. 490/1141; S.R.O., DD/WY 168; DD/AH 38/1, 39/1.
[96] S.R.O., DD/DR 3, 68; DD/CCH 58; D/P/b. ra 2/1/1; Wilts. R.O. 754/71; *Som. Wills*, ed. Brown, ii. 25; ibid. v. 69.
[97] S.R.O., DD/WY 38/13; 47/3; 60.
[98] Ibid. 1/c; 11/E2; 20/3M; 47/2; 52; 60.
[99] Below, St. Decumans, Orchard manor.
[1] S.R.O., DD/WY 56.
[2] Ibid. 168; ibid. survey 1801; ibid. D/P/h. c 20/1/1.
[3] *Cart. Canonsleigh Abbey* (Devon and Cornw. Rec. Soc. N.S. viii), 33.
[4] *Cal. Pat.* 1547–8, 264; *L. & P. Hen. VIII*, xxi, p. 93.

[5] T. Hugo, *Hist. Mynchin Buckland Priory and Preceptory* (London, 1861), 95, 134, 175–6.
[6] Below, econ. hist.
[7] *V.C.H. Som.* i. 501.
[8] *S.R.S.* iii. 182.
[9] S.R.O., DD/L P32/20.
[10] *Cal. Inq. Misc.* v, p. 142.
[11] Ct. roll, Brompton Fulford, in the possession of Mr. Hatchwell, 1978.
[12] S.R.O., DD/L P33/4.
[13] Ibid. P33/7.
[14] P.R.O., STAC 1/30/120; S.R.O., DD/SP, inventory 1684; DD/L P33/4.
[15] Ct. roll, Brompton Fulford, in the possession of Mr. Hatchwell.
[16] S.R.O., D/D/Rg 332; DD/DR 32; Wilts. R.O. 754/83; Devon R.O. 2229M/M1.
[17] S.R.O., DD/WY 11/E2.
[18] Ibid. DD/SP, inventory 1687.
[19] Ibid. inventory 1730.　　[20] Ibid. DD/TB 26; 57/55.

and there were 13 farms with less than 20 a., in addition to several cottage holdings. Most of the farmhouses appear to have been rebuilt during the 19th century.[21] The pattern of holding remained little changed into the 20th century with many of the units let as hill farms and almost entirely given over to pasture.[22] In 1905 there were 1,117 a. of arable and 1,203 a. of grass,[23] but by 1976 a return relating to three quarters of the parish included only 250 a. of arable. Most of the farms in 1976 were small; only three were over 120 a. and they were devoted to dairying and sheep rearing.[24]

Agriculture was always the main occupation in the parish. In 1821 53 houses were occupied by 69 families of whom 57 were engaged in agriculture.[25] There was some cloth making in the late 17th century. In the 1680s there were weavers, a woolcomber, and a clothier at work.[26] The Brewers were clothiers in the parish in the 17th century.[27] Other craftsmen at this period were a carpenter, a cooper, a tailor, and tanners.[28] One tanner was also a shopkeeper, with stock in 1685 including sugar, raisins, tobacco and 'strong water'.[29] In 1851, in addition to masons, carpenters, a thatcher, and smiths, there were shoe-makers, tailors, dressmakers, an ironmonger, drapers, a grocer, a baker, and a shopkeeper. In 1871 the parish was the home of a sculptor.[30]

Stone was quarried in several parts of the parish by the 1840s, partly for roads.[31] A limekiln, described as new in the 1840s, was probably producing lime for agriculture.[32] In 1845 a part of the common was inclosed as a parish quarry.[33] In 1872 and 1876 the Ebbw Vale Steel, Iron, and Coal Co. was licensed to search for iron ore.[34] A mine was opened at Yeanon, in the north-west corner of the parish, in 1872 and an engine installed. A shaft was eventually sunk to 375 ft. with seven levels but work had ceased by 1877.[35]

There was a mill in Brompton Ralph in 1086 paying 30d., possibly that later known as Moor mill.[36] Moor mill was referred to in 1491–2.[37] In 1544 the mill, also known as Elsam mill, which had belonged to the Hospitallers, was granted to Roger and Robert Taverner and was probably the mill which was in the possession of the Hobbes family from 1587 or earlier.[38] The mill was referred to as Moor mill in 1636 and 1680 and as Elsam mill from 1776.[39] Pool mill is recorded in 1799.[40] Both Pool and Moor mills descended with the senior third of the manor and

were still in use in the 1880s.[41] Milling had ceased at Pool mill by 1894 but Moor mill was still in use in 1902 and in 1906 was occupied by a wood turner.[42] The remains of the leats at Moor mill are still visible on both sides of the lane. The house at Pool mill in Stone wood was in a ruinous condition in 1981 when some walling, probably from the mill building, remained.

LOCAL GOVERNMENT. With the exception of the 'Temporal lands' in the north-east of the parish, which were possibly connected with the Templar estate in Williton and were held to be in the tithing and manor of Williton,[43] the parish was a single tithing.

In 1274 Simon of Merriott took all strays on his share of Brompton Ralph manor by ancient custom, and in 1280 Isabel FitzUrse claimed rights of warren, gallows, and assize of bread and of ale on her part of the manor.[44] Courts for Brompton Fulford were held by 1396, and records survive for 1568 and 1569 when courts appear to have been held twice a year; in the 17th century they were held in the upper room of the parish house.[45] Court records survive for Brompton Jacob in 1510 and for the Saffins' manor in 1602.[46] In the 18th century the only court was that for the chief manor and records survive for the years 1719 to 1788. A steward, bailiff, two constables, and a tithingman were appointed.[47] There was a pound in the 18th and 19th centuries and a new one was built in 1814.[48]

Accounts of the two churchwardens survive from 1767.[49] In 1608 the parish possessed a 'book to direct the overseers of the poor'.[50] The two overseers, whose accounts survive from 1795, distributed cloth, clothing, and pairs of cards for carding wool. In 1800 they employed a physician for the poor, and in 1828 paid a man to collect furze for the poor.[51] There were by 1838 two surveyors and an assistant responsible for 12 miles of parish roads. In 1840 the vestry decided to use part of the highway rate to clothe poor children. By 1865 the one surveyor or waywarden combined the office with that of parish guardian.[52]

A public parish meeting was held from at least 1768[53] and a select vestry was set up in 1823, meeting monthly. It appointed parish officers, according to a rota of property.[54]

[21] Ibid. tithe award.
[22] Ibid. DD/WY 145; DD/SAS SE 25; Devon R.O. 547B/3477.
[23] Statistics supplied by the then Bd. of Agric. 1905.
[24] Min. of Agric., Fisheries, and Food, agric. returns 1976.
[25] Census, 1821.
[26] S.R.O., DD/SP, inventories 1684; DD/DR 3; ibid. Q/SR 157/45.
[27] Ibid. DD/DR 3.
[28] Ibid. DD/SP, inventories; DD/SAS C/59/12; ibid. Q/SR 163/10–13.
[29] Ibid. Q/SR 163/10–13.   [30] P.R.O., HO 107/1920.
[31] S.R.O., tithe award.   [32] Ibid. DD/SAS C/2492.
[33] Ibid. D/P/h. c 20/1/1.
[34] Ibid. DD/CCH 4/6; 77.
[35] Sellick, W. Som. Mineral Railway, 41.
[36] V.C.H. Som. i. 501.
[37] S.R.O., DD/L P32/27.
[38] P.R.O., CP 25(2)/206/29 & 30 Eliz. I Mich.; CP 25(2)/347/18 Jas. I. Mich.; CP 25(2)/962/11 Anne East.; L. & P. Hen. VIII, xix, p. 636; Hugo, Hist. Mynchin Buckland, 95, 134, 175–6.

[39] S.R.O., D/P/b. ra 4/1/1; DD/DR 68.
[40] Ibid. Q/REl, Williton.
[41] P.R.O., HO 107/1920; Kelly's Dir. Som. (1889); Monday, Hist. Family of Yea, p. lxvi; S.R.O., DD/SAS SE 25; DD/CCH 6/4; ibid. Q/REl, Williton; Wilts. R.O. 754/83.
[42] Kelly's Dir. Som. (1894, 1902, 1906).
[43] Cal. Pat. 1550–3, 80; 1563–6, 371.
[44] Rot. Hund. (Rec. Com.), ii. 119; Proc. Som. Arch. Soc. lxviii. 98.
[45] S.R.O., DD/DR 3; DD/SAS PR 57; DD/WY 47/3/43; P.R.O., C 3/170/8; ct. roll, Brompton Fulford, in possession of Mr. Hatchwell; below, church.
[46] S.R.O., DD/DR 3; DD/AH 11/9.
[47] Ibid. DD/HC 6L; Som. Protestation Returns, ed. Howard and Stoate, 152.
[48] S.R.O., DD/SAS SE 25; DD/CCH 6/4.
[49] Ibid. D/P/b. ra 4/1/1.
[50] Ibid. 2/1/1.
[51] Ibid. 13/2/1–2.
[52] Ibid. 9/1/1; DD/SAS (C/2492), surveyor's acct. bk.
[53] Ibid. D/P/b. ra 4/1/1.
[54] Ibid. 9/1/1.

A poorhouse was rented in 1803–4.[55] It was large and stood south of the village opposite the Congregational chapel. It was still called the poorhouse in 1842 when it was let by the owner to several people.[56] Brompton Ralph joined the Williton poor-law union in 1836; it was part of the Williton rural district from 1894 until 1974 when it became part of the West Somerset district.[57]

CHURCH. The church at Brompton Ralph, a rectory, was established by 1291.[58] The advowson descended with the FitzUrse manor, and after the division of that estate in 1388 the two owners presented in turn.[59] The advowson continued to descend with Brompton Fulford manor, although presentations were occasionally made by lessees, until 1811 from which time the Sweet Escotts and Blommarts presented alternately until 1895.[60] From 1896 until c. 1899 William Hancock was patron and in 1901 the advowson was held by the rector, A. E. Wansborough. Mrs. Ethel Wansborough was the patron until her death c. 1938, after which the advowson passed to the bishop.[61] In 1961 the Lord Chancellor acquired the advowson by exchange, and he was patron in 1980.[62] From 1926 the benefice was held with Tolland, but since 1969 it has formed part of a united benefice with Monksilver and Nettlecombe, which since 1977 has been held in addition with Stogumber.[63]

In 1291 the church was worth £6 13s. 4d.[64] but it had increased in value to £17 10s. 3d. by 1535,[65] and to £100 c. 1668.[66] The net income was £347 in 1831.[67] In 1535 the tithes were worth c. £14 10s.[68] In 1626 the rector and parishioners declared that no tithe went out of the parish, but in the same year the rector of Clatworthy claimed tithe wool from a close called Farthings in Brompton Ralph.[69] In 1842 the tithes were commuted for a rent charge of £410.[70]

The glebe was valued at 40s. in 1535[71] and in 1626 it comprised closes, orchard, and garden totalling 108 a., the area in 1842.[72] The glebe remained intact until the 20th century and was increased to 113 a. with one allotment of inclosed land in 1845.[73] Some land had been sold by 1923 when only 88 a. remained.[74] It probably formed the nucleus of Glebe

Farm which lies north-west of the rectory house.

The parsonage house was said to be ruinous in 1547.[75] In 1626 there were three houses on the glebe; the rector lived in a house beside a green, and one of the other houses, perhaps an earlier residence, adjoined the churchyard.[76] A large house, nearly 1 km. north-west of the church, may be identified with the early 17th-century residence.[77] It was described as fit in 1831[78] but was not suitable for the 'numerous family' of Thomas Sweet Escott, who lived at his family home at Hartrow.[79] In 1862 a new house was begun in the Gothic style immediately south of the old one. It was completed and occupied in 1864 by a curate. In 1884 the house was let out with the glebe lands.[80] It was sold c. 1969.

The first known rector of Brompton Ralph was John FitzUrse (1316–1329), son of the patron, who was licensed to be absent for study 1316–22.[81] Dr. Thomas Hope, rector 1454–72, a native of Worms, was a pluralist who appears to have spent most of his time at the papal curia.[82] Thomas Trebyll, instituted in 1524, was deprived in 1554,[83] and his successor, Richard Lambert, remained rector until his death in 1587.[84] John Hite, rector from 1643, was ejected in 1647 but restored in 1660.[85] Three generations of the Camplin family were rectors from 1689 until 1781; Thomas, rector 1752–81, was also vicar of Chard, and archdeacon of Taunton from 1767 until 1782.[86] During his time communion was celebrated quarterly.[87] Between 1781 and 1895 the benefice was, with one exception, held by members of the Sweet Escott family.[88] In 1815 two services were held each Sunday, a pattern which still continued until 1870, when the number of celebrations a year had increased to six.[89] In 1851 morning and afternoon services were attended by 140 and 158 people respectively, including 50 Sunday-school children.[90] Average attendance in 1862 was 81 in the morning and 83 in the evening.[91]

In the 1530s there were lights of the High Cross and All Souls and in 1548 an endowed lamp.[92]

There was a church house by 1598 part of which was leased by the parishioners from the lord of Brompton Fulford.[93] In 1641 it was described as the parish house on the south side of the churchyard, and the upper chamber was reserved as a courtroom.[94] It was said to be in a dangerous state in 1772 and in the

55 Ibid. 13/2/1.
56 Ibid. tithe award.
57 Youngs, *Local Admin. Units*, i. 673, 675–6.
58 *Tax. Eccl.* (Rec. Com.), 198.
59 *S.R.S.* i. 17, 117; ix, p. 743; xii. 110; xxii. 20, 71–2, 174; xlix, p. 251; lii, p. 14; S.R.O., DD/L P33/7; DD/DR 68, d 5.
60 *S.R.S.* lii, p. 168; liv, pp. 12, 16, 50, 68, 108, 174, 184; *Som. Incumbents*, ed. Weaver, 320; *Kelly's Dir. Som.* (1889, 1895); P.R.O., C 142/330, no. 93.
61 *Dioc. Kal.*; *Dioc. Dir.*; *Char. Com.* files.
62 Inf. from Dioc. Regy.; *Dioc. Dir.*
63 *Dioc. Dir.*
64 *Tax. Eccl.* (Rec. Com.), 198.
65 *Valor Eccl.* (Rec. Com.), i. 222.
66 S.R.O., D/D/Vc 24.
67 *Rep. Com. Eccl. Revenues*, pp. 128–9.
68 *Valor Eccl.* (Rec. Com.), i. 222.
69 S.R.O., D/D/Rg 332, 337.
70 Ibid. tithe award.
71 *Valor Eccl.* (Rec. Com.), i. 222.
72 S.R.O., D/D/Rg 332; ibid. tithe award.
73 Ibid. DD/CCH 80; D/P/b. ra 4/3/1; *Kelly's Dir. Som.* (1910).
74 *Kelly's Dir. Som.* (1923).
75 S.R.O., D/D/Ca 17

76 Ibid. D/D/Rg 332; inf. from Mr. Graham Durling.
77 S.R.O., D/D/Rg 332.
78 *Rep. Com. Eccl. Revenues*, pp. 128–9.
79 S.R.O., D/D/B returns 1827; D/D/V returns 1840; D/P/b. ra 1/6/1.
80 Ibid. D/P/b. ra 2/1/6, 2/1/9; DD/CCH 80; ibid. tithe award; *P.O. Dir. Som.* (1866).
81 *S.R.S.* i. 17, 117, 139, 305.
82 *Cal. Papal Reg.* xi. 86, 118, 324–5, 329, xiii (1), 316–7; *S.R.S.* xlix, pp. xxviii, 33, 210–11, 251, 350–71, 388; Emden, *Biog. Reg. Univ. Oxon.* ii. 959–60.
83 *S.R.S.* lv, p. 124.
84 S.R.O., D/P/b. ra 2/1/1.
85 *Walker Revised*, ed. A. G. Matthews; S.R.O., D/P/b. ra 2/1/1.
86 Le Neve, *Fasti, 1541–1857, Bath and Wells*, 17; S.R.O., D/D/Bo; M.I. in ch.
87 S.R.O., D/P/b. ra 4/1/1.
88 Ibid. D/D/Bi; D/P/b. ra 2/1/4–9.
89 Ibid. D/D/B returns 1815, 1827; D/D/V returns 1840, 1843, 1870; D/P/b. ra 2/1/6.
90 P.R.O., HO 129/313/5/8/10.
91 S.R.O., D/P/b. ra 2/1/6.
92 *Wells Wills*, ed. Weaver, 30; *S.R.S.* ii. 46.
93 S.R.O., DD/WY 47/3/43; Devon R.O. 2229M/M1.
94 S.R.O., DD/DR 3.

following year had fallen down.[95] In 1780 the church-wardens employed a man to dispose of its materials.[96]

The church of the *ASSUMPTION OF OUR BLESSED LADY*, so dedicated by 1532[97] but later known simply as the church of the *BLESSED VIRGIN MARY*, comprises a chancel with north organ chamber and vestry, nave with north aisle and south porch, and west tower. The south doorway and tower arch are of the 15th century and the large window in the south aisle dates from the 16th century. The church was said to have been largely rebuilt in 1738,[98] and much work was done on the church and tower in 1797 and 1804.[99] A gallery existed in 1814 and 1826 and the north aisle was built in 1847 by William Sweet Escott, rector 1842–54 and 1879–84.[1] A singing gallery was erected in 1854.[2] The church was restored in 1880–1 by Samuel Shewbrooks. The chancel was completely rebuilt to a new plan.[3]

Some of the original fittings remain, including a 16th-century font with a carving of the green man and a 17th-century cover, 16th-century benches, and an early 19th-century pulpit. The 15th-century Welsh-style screen was taken to Hartrow by the rector during the restoration of the church in the 1880s. Some pieces were recovered early in the 20th century and incorporated into a reconstructed screen designed by F. Bligh Bond in 1913.[4] The communion rail is dated 1677.

There are two pre-Reformation bells, one of which, named Gabriel, was probably made in Exeter in the 14th century and bears an inscription in English.[5] The church possesses a chalice and cover of 1573.[6] The registers date from 1558 and are complete.[7]

NONCONFORMITY. A conventicle was held in 1637[8] and a recusant was mentioned in 1641.[9] In 1669 a nonconformist, John Galpin, taught in the parish.[10]

The Congregational chapel was opened in 1840 with the assistance of the ladies of the chief manor of Brompton Ralph, following open air and cottage meetings.[11] In 1851 the chapel was described as an 'out station' of Wiveliscombe Independent chapel and the average attendance at evening service was 60 people.[12] The chapel, at the crossroads south of the village, is a plain whitewashed building with narrow lancet windows. In 1974 it was registered as an independent chapel[13] and was still open in 1981 with *c.* 8 members and a small Sunday school.[14]

EDUCATION. In 1606 children were taught by the parish clerk.[15] From 1792 the churchwardens paid a man 2*d.* a week to teach six poor children.[16] By 1819 a Sunday school had been established but only 20–30 children attended.[17] In 1826 there was a day school with 28 boys and a Sunday school for 40 girls,[18] but in 1835 only 22 children went to the day and Sunday schools, which were supported by the rector and small weekly payments from parents.[19] By 1847 there were 88 children at the day and Sunday schools.[20] Both schools were still in existence in 1851, endowed from 1844 with £11 a year.[21] In 1859 there was said to be a small day school for girls.[22]

A school board for Brompton Ralph and Tolland was formed compulsorily under an order of 1875, and a school built in 1877 on the Elworthy–Wiveliscombe road was conveyed to the board in 1878.[23] There were 67 children on the books in 1903 but numbers fell rapidly and by 1960 there were only 18. The school closed in 1966 and in 1981 was a private house.[24]

The Sunday school room, north of the church, was purchased in 1927 for use as a parish institute.[25]

CHARITIES FOR THE POOR. A sum of £36 given by several people was held by the Yea family in the 18th century, and payments were made to the poor during the 1730s, but not after 1757.[26] Mary Stephens (d. 1854), lady of the chief manor of Brompton Ralph, left £150 to provide blankets for people not in receipt of public relief. Payments in money or groceries were made during the 1960s and 1970s. By 1981 the charity income of *c.* £4 a year provided Christmas puddings for the elderly. In 1947 the Medlands charity existed as a clothing club and probably accounted for a sum of £105 invested in war stock.[27] It had been lost by 1981.

[95] Ibid. DD/HC 6L.
[96] Ibid. D/P/b. ra 4/1/1.
[97] *Wells Wills*, ed. Weaver, 30.
[98] Collinson, *Hist. Som.* iii. 506.
[99] S.R.O., D/P/b. ra 4/1/1.
[1] Ibid. 4/1/1, 9/1/1; *Som. Co. Gaz.* 2 July 1881.
[2] S.R.O., D/P/b. ra 2/1/6.
[3] Ibid. 4/1/1; *Som. Co. Gaz.* 2 July 1881; *Proc. Som. Arch. Soc.* lii. 60; lxix, p. xxx. No evidence has been found for work by H. Parsons as mentioned in Pevsner, *South and West Som.* 101.
[4] *Proc. Som. Arch. Soc.* lii. 60; lxix, p. xxx; elevation in ch.
[5] S.R.O., DD/SAS CH 16.
[6] *Proc. Som. Arch. Soc.* xlix. 30.
[7] S.R.O., D/P/b. ra 2/1/1–9.
[8] T. H. Peake, 'Clergy and Church Courts in diocese of Bath and Wells 1625–42' (Bristol Univ. M. Litt. thesis 1978), 437.
[9] *Som. Protestation Returns*, ed. Howard and Stoate, 287.
[10] *Orig. Records of Early Nonconf.* ed. G. L. Turner, i. 8.

[11] *Rep. Som. Cong. Union* (1896); S.R.O., tithe award.
[12] P.R.O., H.O. 129/313/5/8/11.
[13] G.R.O. Worship Reg.
[14] Inf. from the minister.
[15] S.R.O., D/D/Ca 151.
[16] Ibid. D/P/b. ra 4/1/1.
[17] *Educ. of Poor Digest*, H.C. 224 (1819), ix (2).
[18] *Ann. Rep. B. & W. Dioc. Assoc. S.P.C.K.* (1825–6).
[19] *Educ. Enq. Abstract*, H.C. 62 (1835), xlii.
[20] Nat. Soc. *Inquiry, 1846–7*, Som. 4–5.
[21] *P.O. Dir. Som.* (1851); *Lond. Gaz.* 3 May 1844, p. 1505.
[22] *P.O. Dir. Som.* (1859).
[23] S.R.O., C/E 26; DD/CCH 5/5; D/P/b. ra 9/1/1; *Lond. Gaz.* 19 Feb. 1875, p. 708.
[24] S.R.O., *Schs. Lists*; ibid. C/E 26.
[25] Char. Com. files; S.R.O., tithe award.
[26] S.R.O., D/P/b. ra 13/1/1; *15th Rep. Com. Char.* p. 438.
[27] Char. Com. files; S.R.O., D/P/b. ra 9/1/1; inf. from he Revd. R. N. Swinburn.

CHIPSTABLE

THE ANCIENT parish of Chipstable lay on the southern slopes of the Brendons 4 km. west of Wiveliscombe.[28] It was in two parts, both treated below. The main part of the parish, roughly rectangular in shape, measured 2 km. from east to west and 3.5 km. from north to south. A detached area some 2.5 km. north of the northern boundary, beyond Huish Champflower and reaching to the Brendon ridgeway, included East Withy and Chitcombe farms.[29] In 1881 the total area was 2,252 a.[30] In 1884 the detached area was added to Huish Champflower, reducing the parish to 1,936 a.[31] In 1933 Raddington was joined with Chipstable to form the civil parish of Chipstable, giving a total area of 1,398 ha. (3,454 a.).[32]

The parish occupies land which falls from 338 m. on Heydon Hill in the north-west to c. 120 m. in the extreme south-east, on slates, siltstones, and sandstones of the Pilton and Pickwell Down beds.[33] Its western boundary with Raddington is marked largely by the wide Old Way.[34] The River Tone marks the eastern boundary, its narrow, steep-sided valley heavily wooded in the north, but widening sufficiently further south for the establishment of two farmsteads and the straggling hamlet of Waterrow at two crossing places. From Waterrow another valley runs north-west across the parish to Chipstable village, at the 250 m. contour. The south end of the parish includes a shallow valley beyond the abrupt southern slope of Biballs Hill.

Chipstable village comprises the church, former and present rectory houses, former school, two farms, and a few cottages. Waterrow is the name given from the mid 19th century to scattered settlements in the Tone valley formerly called East and West Skirdall or Skirdle, which became the largest settlement.[35] Cottages at Elms Green, south of Chipstable village, and at Bulland were mentioned in the mid 19th century.[36] Farms are spread widely through the rest of the parish: Chitcombe and East Withy were established by 1306,[37] Withycombe, Trowell, Severidges, and Above Church by 1327,[38] and Pinkhouse by 1451.[39] Trowell Farm is a 15th-century long house with linenfold panelling similar to work at Muchelney Abbey.[40] Furze and heath were found, probably near the Chipstable–Raddington boundary, in the 1440s.[41] There were areas of common pasture on Heydon (264 a.), Lydon (32 a.), and Biballs (14 a.) hills until they were inclosed in

1837,[42] but no common arable fields have been traced. Field names and shapes indicate a park on the demesne in a watered valley in the centre of the parish.[43] Woodland on Heydon Hill and elsewhere was established in the 1830s by John Stone, lord of the manor, and was then 'abounding with black and other game'.[44]

From 1786 the turnpike road from Wiveliscombe to Bampton (Devon) entered the parish over Yeo Bridge[45] and from Waterrow climbed Biballs and Shute hills before descending into Raddington.[46] The route was improved c. 1824, entering Waterrow further south over Biballs Bridge and curving southwards into the valley below Shute Hill.[47] The same valley was the route of the Devon and Somerset railway, opened in 1873, which entered the parish over Waterrow viaduct.[48] Venn Cross station, partly in Chipstable and partly in Clayhanger (Devon), was closed with the line in 1966.[49]

The Travellers' Rest inn, immediately north of Biballs Bridge, was established in 1819, and continued until 1851 or later.[50] The Rock House inn, later the Rock inn, also at Waterrow and in 1840 a private house and smithy,[51] had become an inn by 1851.[52] It was still open in 1982.

A total of 56 people signed the Protestation in 1642.[53] There were 301 people in the parish in 1801. After a fall to 288 in 1811, the total rose each decade, reaching 395 in 1851. Then began a steady decline, the figure of 420 in 1871 including the families of workmen building the railway. By 1901 the population was 265, and in twenty years it reached 277. In 1931 the total of 335 included the inhabitants of Raddington ecclesiastical parish. In 1971 the population of the civil parish, which included Raddington, had fallen to 273.[54]

MANOR AND OTHER ESTATES. Celric held *CHIPSTABLE* in 1066, but by 1086 he had been succeeded by the monks of Muchelney.[55] The monks remained in possession until their house was surrendered to the Crown in 1538,[56] the manor having in the mid 15th century been assigned to the monastic cook.[57] The Crown almost immediately sold the manor to Edward Seymour, earl of Hertford,[58] who sold it later in the same year to Roger (later Sir Roger) Bluet of Greenham in Stawley.[59] The Bluets were said to hold of the Crown in chief in 1615.[60]

[28] This article was completed in 1982.
[29] S.R.O., tithe award; the detached area is treated here.
[30] *Census*, 1881.
[31] Ibid. 1891.
[32] *Som. Review Order* (1933); *Census*, 1971.
[33] Geol. Surv. Map 1", solid and drift, sheet 294 (1969 edn.).
[34] Below, Raddington, introduction.
[35] Devon R.O. 74B/MT 1822.
[36] P.R.O., HO 107/1921.
[37] S.R.O., DD/WY 5/F1/1.
[38] *S.R.S.* iii. 168–9.
[39] N. Yorks. R.O., Swinton MSS., ZJx.
[40] S.R.O., DD/V Wlr.
[41] *S.R.S.* xxii. 198.
[42] S.R.O., DD/CPL 8; ibid. Q/RDe 90.
[43] Ibid. tithe award.
[44] Ibid. DD/CPL 8.

[45] Known as Yeah Bridge in 1840, possibly after the Yea family: ibid. tithe award.
[46] 26 Geo. III, c. 135 (Local and Personal).
[47] S.R.O., Q/RUp 74.
[48] R. Madge, *Railways Round Exmoor* (Dulverton, 1971), 7–8.
[49] S.R.O., DD/WI 2; Madge, *Railways Round Exmoor*, 9.
[50] Ibid. Q/RL; ibid. tithe award; P.R.O., HO 107/1921.
[51] S.R.O., tithe award.
[52] P.R.O., HO 107/1921.
[53] *Som. Protestation Returns*, ed. Howard and Stoate, 154–5.   [54] *V.C.H. Som.* ii. 351; *Census*, 1911–71.
[55] *V.C.H. Som.* i. 468.
[56] *L. & P. Hen. VIII*, xiii (1), p. 64.
[57] N. Yorks. R.O., Swinton MSS., ZJx.
[58] *L. & P. Hen. VIII*, xiii (1), p. 64; S.R.O., DD/AB 19.
[59] P.R.O., CP 25(2)/36/239/30 Hen. VIII Trin.
[60] Ibid. C 142/351, no. 104.

Sir Roger Bluet, alive in 1548,[61] was followed by his son John (d. 1584)[62] and by John's son Richard (d. 1615). Richard was succeeded by his grandson John Bluet, a minor.[63] John died in 1634, when his four surviving daughters, the oldest aged nine, shared the estate.[64] Much of the land was sold from the 1680s onwards, but quarter shares in the chief rents of the ancient freeholds of the manor and the church house were retained by the descendants of some of the Bluet daughters until the mid 18th century.[65]

Anne, the eldest daughter of John Bluet, married Cadwallader Jones of Greenham before 1652.[66] Her son, also Cadwallader, had succeeded to his mother's estate by 1687,[67] and John Jones of Burlescombe (Devon) retained a share of the chief rents until 1715, when he sold them to the rector of Chipstable, Simon Richards.[68] John Bluet's second daughter, Mary, married first Sir James Stonehouse and in 1659 John (later Sir John) Lenthall of Besselsleigh (Berks., now Oxon.).[69] William Lenthall (d. 1686),[70] son of Mary, was followed by his son John. John sold most of his property in Chipstable in 1706 and 1707, his share of the manor passing in 1706 to Miles Corbett of Lyons Inn, London.[71] Before 1743 the share had been acquired by David Yea of Oakhampton in Wiveliscombe, who in that year sold it to Simon Richards.[72]

John Bluet's third daughter, Dorothy, married Henry Wallop of Farleigh Wallop (Hants). Their son John (d. 1694) was succeeded first by his elder son Bluet (d. 1707) and then by his younger son John (cr. Baron Wallop and Vct. Lymington 1720, and earl of Portsmouth 1743).[73] Lord Lymington sold his share of the demesne, Chipstable farm, to David Yea in 1726,[74] but retained his share of the chief rents, the church house, and other land until 1742, when he sold his estate to Gregory Jeane of Bradford on Tone. In the following year Jeane sold his share of the chief rents and the church house to Simon Richards.[75]

John Bluet's fourth daughter, Susan, married John Basset of Heanton Punchardon (Devon). Their son John (d. 1686) was succeeded by his son, also John (d. 1721). John Basset was followed by his son Francis John, who in 1739 conveyed his share of the chief rents and the church house to Simon Richards.[76]

By 1743, therefore, Simon Richards was in possession of the chief rents of the former manor, and of other former manorial demesne holdings including the church house. His estate, known as the manor or reputed manor, passed on his death in 1751 to his brother Richard, and then to Richard's nephew Simon Richards (d. 1804), rector from 1784. The manor was settled on Simon and his wife Anne in 1782 and was conveyed by Anne to her son, Simon Slocombe Richards, when he became rector in 1809.

Richards sold the manor to John Carige of Wiveliscombe in 1815, and in 1818 it passed to Charles Templer of Honiton (Devon), curate 1818–28 and lessee of the glebe and tithes.[77] Templer sold the manor in 1827 to John Stone; and Stone, then living in Bath, sold it in 1839 to Arthur Capel of Stroud (Glos.).[78]

Arthur Capel died in 1889 and was succeeded by his son Arthur (d. 1931) and then by his grandson, Air Vice Marshal Arthur John Capel. On the latter's death in 1979 the estate passed to his daughter, Mrs. Anne Deshon.[79]

Chipstable farm, based on the capital messuage of the manor, was divided like the manor into four parts. By 1687 at least one quarter was let to the Langdon family, and passed to George Musgrave (d. 1721) of Nettlecombe under a lease of 1698.[80] George's second son, Dr. Richard Musgrave of Dulverton,[81] held three shares of the farm by 1726, but in the same year a reversionary lease to David Yea of Oakhampton began his family's connexion with the farm which continued until 1802.[82] In 1726 Richard Musgrave reserved the hall, parlour, and buttery, and the rooms over them, together with a garden and stable.[83] The house was described as newly built in 1802.[84]

Between 1827 and 1838 John Stone, as lord of the manor, built a house called Bulland Lodge in the north-east corner of the parish on part of his farm of Withycombe.[85] Surrounded by gardens and woodland, with lodges, coach houses, and stables, the house was described as 'very eligible and peculiarly beautiful'. It was extended to designs by Richard Carver c. 1840.[86] The house was occupied by the Capel family until 1980.

There were five medieval freeholds on the manor. One, later identified as Halsdown farm, was held in 1461 by Henry Perys, probably in succession to the Brooke family, Lords Cobham, who held in 1448.[87] George Stewkeley (d. 1494), of Marsh in Dunster, was holding it by 1490, and was succeeded by his son Peter, then a minor.[88] Peter's son Hugh (d. 1585) was followed by Hugh's son Sir Thomas (d. 1639). Sir Thomas's son Hugh (cr. Bt. 1627) died in 1642, and was followed by his son, also Hugh, who died without male heirs in 1719.[89] The rent for Halsdown was still recorded in Sir Hugh's name in 1741,[90] but it was not claimed later.

Chitcombe and East Withy were freeholds by 1324.[91] The Dyke family held a freehold by 1461, probably in succession to Thomas Bratton,[92] which was identified as East Withy farm by 1637.[93] The freehold descended in the Dyke family to Elizabeth (d. 1752) daughter of Thomas Dyke, who married

[61] Ibid. CP 40/1138, rot. 303.
[62] Ibid. C 142/206, no. 1.
[63] Ibid. C 142/351, no. 104; *S.R.S.* lxvii, pp. 88–9.
[64] Ibid. C 142/475, no. 105; *S.R.S.* lxvii, pp. 8–10.
[65] Below.
[66] P.R.O., CP 25(2)/593/1659 Mich.; S.R.O., DD/X/CG.
[67] S.R.O., DD/DP 12/8; DD/X/CG; Devon R.O. 74B/MT 1824(b).   [68] S.R.O., DD/HB 7.
[69] Ibid. DD/DP 11/3; DD/SF 408.
[70] *Le Neve's Pedigrees of Knights* (Harl. Soc. viii), 324.
[71] S.R.O., DD/HB 7; DD/DP 11/3, 12/13; DD/SF 1036; DD/X/CG.   [72] Ibid. DD/HB 7.
[73] *Complete Peerage*, x. 610–12.   [74] S.R.O., DD/DR 6.
[75] Ibid. DD/HB 7; DD/X/CG; DD/CPL 88.
[76] Ibid. DD/HB 7; DD/X/CG; DD/CPL 70.
[77] Ibid. DD/CPL 69; ibid. Q/REl; ibid. D/P/chip 2/1/4; cf. *Taunton Courier*, 17 June 1813 for sale notice.

[78] S.R.O., DD/CPL 8, 69–70.
[79] Burke, *Land Gent.* (1914), 320; *Who Was Who, 1971–80*; local inf.
[80] S.R.O., DD/DR 6.
[81] *Som. Wills*, ed. Brown, iii. 40–1.
[82] S.R.O., DD/DR 6; DD/WO 11/3; DD/HC 6L; DD/MY 35.
[83] Ibid. DD/DR 6.
[84] Ibid. DD/MY 35.   [85] Ibid. DD/CPL 70.
[86] Ibid. 8.
[87] N. Yorks. R.O., Swinton MSS., ZJx.
[88] *Cal. Inq. p.m. Hen. VII*, i, p. 402.
[89] Maxwell Lyte, *Dunster*, 417; G.E.C. *Baronetage*, ii. 27.
[90] S.R.O., DD/CPL 88.
[91] *S.R.S.* xlii. 87.
[92] N. Yorks. R.O., Swinton MSS., ZJx.
[93] S.R.O., DD/SL 7.

Sir Thomas Acland, Bt. Their son John Dyke Acland (d. 1778) was succeeded by his son, also John, who was named as a freeholder in 1782.[94] The freehold continued in the family, passing through the marriage of Elizabeth Dyke Acland with Henry George Herbert, Lord Porchester, later earl of Carnarvon, to the Herbert family. It was sold by the 4th earl of Carnarvon c. 1886.[95]

John Sydenham held a freehold by 1448 which may be identified as half of Bovey farm in 1741.[96] The chief rent was said in 1782 to be payable by the Revd. Alexander Webber.[97] The fifth medieval freehold, described in 1741 as at Sedgebarrow,[98] was held by Robert Tanfield from 1460 and by 1637 was occupied by John Talbot.[99] Men of that name were owners until 1741,[1] but by 1782 the rent was owed by Thomas Wright.[2] The estate has not been located. Sir John Davie of Bittescombe in Upton was charged with a chief rent in 1782 for land called Monkton meadow in succession to James Welsh, who had held it in 1715.[3] It may be the land held with Bittescombe manor in 1554.[4]

ECONOMIC HISTORY. Chipstable gelded for 2½ hides in 1086 but there were 6 ploughteams, of which 1 was in demesne with 2 serfs, and 5 were worked by 16 villeins and 2 bordars. There was only ½ a. of meadow, but 100 a. of pasture; and woodland measured ½ league long by 2 furlongs broad.[5] The release in 1461 of a freeholder occupying customary land from the obligation to plough for 1 day, make hay for 2 days, and thatch the lord's barn[6] may indicate the dispersal of the former demesne farm. Certainly by 1535 the monks of Muchelney had let their land in Chipstable, and rents produced £11 16s. 4½d.[7] At Severidges Farm, the centre of a holding of c. 60 a. of land in 1399,[8] the presence in the 16th century of a corn-drying kiln and a curing chamber suggests mixed farming.[9] By 1543 part of the common pasture on Heydon Hill was being cultivated.[10] Nevertheless pasturage and particularly sheep farming appear to have been more important than arable farming. Pasture held in severalty and straying sheep were recorded in the 15th century.[11] In 1535 the rector's tithes of wool and lambs were valued at £4 18s., compared with the £5 11s. from all other tithes.[12] In 1643 a tenant farmer at Hilland had sheep valued at £17 10s., wool valued at £1 6s., and only 5 cattle; Thomas Sedgeborrow (d. 1642) had sheep valued at £79, wool at £22, and cattle at £39, compared with corn at £75; Gregory Robbins (d. 1683),

a carpenter, had 70 sheep and lambs representing a quarter of the value of his entire possessions.[13]

From the later 17th century the established tenant farms were converted to freeholds, although the process was prolonged because of the division of the manor. The Surrage family, for instance, bought the freehold of one quarter of Trowell farm in 1687, but did not acquire the last quarter until 1739.[14] The freehold of Bulham, later Bulland, was similarly acquired by the Hellings family in four stages between 1701 and 1739.[15] By 1741 all but three small farms and a few cottages had been converted to freeholds.[16]

Sub-leases for terms of years were already established practice before the conversion to freeholds had been completed. Three parts of Chipstable farm were let from 1727 for 21 years, with covenants to prevent more than two successive arable crops, ploughing pasture less than six years old, and cutting clover and trefoil before it was three years old. Part of the former park was then under flax.[17] A rent of 6d. an acre was payable for ploughing the commons.[18] By 1806 oats was the largest corn crop, a dairy was established at East Shutt, and bullocks were raised at East Withy.[19] In 1810 the farmer at East Withy had a flock of 100 sheep.[20]

By 1796 there were 20 farms in the parish, ranging from Chipstable farm (207 a.) and East Withy (154 a.) to a holding of 20 a., more than half measuring over 50 a. Sir William Yea held both Chipstable farm and Halsdown.[21] By 1803 the former was divided into six units.[22] There were 14 farms of over 50 a. in 1840, including the 257 a. of new inclosures on Heydon Hill, then owned by Arthur Capel, part of which was later to become North Combe farm.[23] By 1851 consolidation of farms in the south part of the parish had resulted in a holding of 340 a. at West Bovey and other increases at Wadhams and Trowell.[24] The Capels acquired Wadhams, Marshes, and Millbeer farms in the 1890s[25] to build up a substantial estate in the north-east quarter of the parish, based in the 1980s at Withycombe farm.

In 1840 there were an estimated 1,030 a. of pasture, 800 a. of arable, and 112 a. of wood.[26] In 1905, excluding East Withy and Chitcombe, there were 1,130 a. of grassland, 537 a. of arable, and 203 a. of wood.[27] In 1976 four fifths of the civil parish of Chipstable, including Raddington, were under grass; there were ten dairy farms and five farms specializing in cattle and sheep.[28]

Two clothiers in the parish were accused of illegal trade practices in 1631.[29] A fuller was living in

[94] Burke, *Peerage* (1949), 14, S.R.O., DD/CPL 69.
[95] Burke, *Peerage* (1949), 359; *Kelly's Dir. Som.* (1883, 1889).
[96] N. Yorks. R.O., Swinton MSS., ZJx; S.R.O., DD/CPL 88.
[97] S.R.O., DD/CPL 69.
[98] Ibid. 88.
[99] N. Yorks. R.O., Swinton MSS., ZJx; S.R.O., DD/SL 7.
[1] S.R.O., DD/CPL 88.
[2] Ibid. 69.
[3] Ibid. 69; DD/HB 7.
[4] P.R.O., C 142/101, no. 106.
[5] *V.C.H. Som.* i. 468.
[6] N. Yorks. R.O., Swinton MSS., ZJx.
[7] *Valor Eccl.* (Rec. Com.), i. 193. For later rents see Devon R.O. 1936M/M5; S.R.O., DD/SL 7; ibid DD/X/FRC.
[8] *S.R.S.* xvii. 211–12.
[9] *Proc. Som. Arch. Soc.* cxv. 46; cxvi. 101–3.

[10] Devon R.O. 1936M/M5.
[11] N. Yorks. R.O., Swinton MSS., ZJx.
[12] *Valor Eccl.* (Rec. Com.), i. 223–4.
[13] S.R.O., DD/SP inventories.
[14] Devon R.O. 74B/MT 1824(b).
[15] S.R.O., DD/CPL 70.
[16] Ibid. 88.
[17] Ibid. DD/DR 6.
[18] Ibid. DD/CPL 88.
[19] Ibid. DD/HC 6F.
[20] Ibid. DD/CPL 93.
[21] Ibid. DD/HC 6L.
[22] Ibid. Q/REl.
[23] Ibid. tithe award; O.S. Map 6″, Som. LXVIII. NE. (1888 edn.).
[24] P.R.O., HO 107/1921.
[25] S.R.O., DD/CPL 13.
[26] Ibid. tithe award.
[27] Statistics supplied by the then Bd. of Agric. 1905.
[28] Min. of Agric., Fisheries, and Food, agric. returns 1976.
[29] *S.R.S.* xxiv. 165.

Chipstable between 1824 and 1827.[30] Two smithies and several workshops were established near the turnpike road at Waterrow by 1840,[31] and a tradition of agricultural machinery manufacture, begun by 1823 in the person of a share maker,[32] was continued with a machine maker in 1851.[33] The firm of W. H. Pool and Sons at Waterrow, founded by Henry Pool, carpenter, in 1847, were patentees of a calf feeder in the 1870s, and sold a wide range of farming machinery. A. J. Pool (d. 1957), who continued the business and made oil engines, was also a professional photographer.[34] In the later 19th century there were several shops at Waterrow, by that time the largest settlement in the parish.[35]

MILLS. There was a mill at East Withy, on the border with Huish Champflower, before 1187,[36] but no further trace of it has been found. A tenant was released from his obligation to procure a millstone for the lord in 1461.[37] There were said to be two mills on the manor by 1538,[38] and there were two in 1637 and 1647, one a corn mill, the other a fulling mill.[39] The former, known as Bullworthy's after the tenant in 1652,[40] was occupied by Roger Bishop in 1721 and by John Rossiter in 1766,[41] and was owned and occupied by Bishop Stone in 1840.[42] The mill, known as Manor mill, stood north of Waterrow, and remained in use until c. 1908.[43] It was driven by a long leat which was diverted from the River Tone at Yeo Bridge.[44] A second mill stood in 1840 in the centre of Waterrow.[45] It has not been traced later.

LOCAL GOVERNMENT. Court rolls for the manor have survived for nine sessions during the period 1448–51 and for ten sessions between 1459 and 1465.[46] Courts seem to have been held until the last tenant farms were sold in the mid 18th century. The tenant of the manor house from 1718 had to provide lodging for the steward, his servants, and two horses for two days and two nights twice a year.[47] In the 15th century the court nominated three or four men for appointment as reeve, and the reeve received the income from some woodland to support himself in office.[48]

Chipstable tithing was joined with Raddington by 1569.[49] The parish had two churchwardens and two overseers by 1642.[50] No records of parochial government have been traced. The overseers repaired the church house in the 18th century and may have used it as a poorhouse.[51] The parish became part of the Wellington poor-law union in 1836, and was in the Wellington rural district from 1894 and Taunton Deane district, later Borough, from 1974.[52]

CHURCH. Ownership of the church of Chipstable was confirmed to the monks of Muchelney in 1239.[53] The benefice remained a sole rectory until 1929, when it was united with Raddington.[54] From 1967 until 1971 the living was held as a curacy-in-charge with Huish Champflower and Clatworthy, to which it was united in 1971.[55]

The advowson descended with the manor in the possession of the monks of Muchelney until 1538, but the Crown presented to the living in 1305 and 1463 when the abbacy was vacant.[56] After the Dissolution the descent of the patronage has not been traced until 1597 when a rector was presented by grant of John Bluet of Greenham.[57] Both the Crown and another John Bluet presented in 1629 at a single vacancy.[58] At the next presentation in 1670, after the division of the manor, Cadwallader Jones and his wife Anne appointed a rector.[59] In 1695 Joseph Wyatt was said to be patron as son and heir of the previous rector,[60] but in 1707 the presentation was made by Gregory Jeane, appointed for that turn in respect of the Wallop share of the manor.[61] The advowson was subsequently acquired by Simon Richards, rector 1707–51, and it descended to his son Simon, who was appointed rector by the bishop at his own request in 1751.[62] The Richards family retained the advowson: Richard Richards, the last rector's uncle, presented in 1781,[63] John Harvey, as a trustee of Simon Richards of Chipstable, in 1784,[64] and Anne Richards, Simon's widow, in 1806.[65] Simon Slocombe Richards was instituted at his own request in 1809.[66] The advowson passed, probably on the death of S. S. Richards in 1853,[67] to Charles Dare of North Curry and Samuel Knight Pollard of Taunton, and they presented Dare's son Walter in 1855.[68] In 1857 the patrons were Charles Dare and John Rendell of Taunton.[69] By 1875 the advowson had been acquired by the rector, William Nicholetts, and it remained in his family until transferred to the bishop of Bath and Wells in 1937.[70]

The living was assessed at £11 1s. 6d. net in 1535,[71] and was said to be worth £80 c. 1668.[72] The net income was £340 in 1831.[73] Tithes were assessed at £10 9s. in 1535,[74] and a tithe rent charge of £263 16s.

[30] S.R.O., D/P/chip 2/1/4.   [31] Ibid. tithe award.
[32] Ibid. D/P/chip 2/1/4.   [33] P.R.O., HO 107/1921.
[34] Morris and Co., *Dir. Som.* (1872); *Kelly's Dir. Som.* (1889); P.R.O., HO 107/1921; *Exmoor Rev.* (1977), 41–3, 46; (1980), 81–3.
[35] *P.O. Dir. Som.* (1866, 1875).
[36] *S.R.S.* xxv, pp. 188–9.
[37] N. Yorks. R.O., Swinton MSS., ZJx.
[38] P.R.O., CP 25(2)/37/239/30 Hen. VIII Trin.
[39] S.R.O., DD/SL 7; DD/X/FRC.
[40] Ibid. DD/X/CG.
[41] Ibid. DD/CPL 91; ibid. Q/REl.
[42] Ibid. tithe award.
[43] *Kelly's Dir. Som.* (1906, 1910).
[44] O.S. Map 6", Som. LXIX. NW. (1888 edn.).
[45] S.R.O., tithe award.
[46] N. Yorks. R.O., Swinton MSS., ZJx.
[47] S.R.O., DD/DR 6.
[48] N. Yorks. R.O., Swinton MSS., ZJx, 1449, 1451.
[49] *S.R.S.* xx. 165–6.
[50] *Som. Protestation Returns*, ed. Howard and Stoate, 155.
[51] S.R.O., DD/CPL 91.

[52] Youngs, *Local Admin. Units*, i. 421, 673, 676.
[53] *S.R.S.* xiv, pp. 51–2.   [54] S.R.O., D/P/chip 1/7/1.
[55] *Dioc. Dir.*; inf. from Dioc. Regy., Wells.
[56] *Cal. Pat.* 1301–7, 315; 1461–7, 283.
[57] *Som. Incumbents*, ed. Weaver, 334.
[58] Ibid.; P.R.O., E 331/Bath and Wells/3.
[59] *Som. Incumbents*, ed. Weaver, 334.
[60] S.R.O., D/D/B reg. 24, f. 10v.
[61] E. Dwelly, *Par. Rec.* viii. 7; S.R.O., D/D/B reg. 25, f. 8; ibid. D/P/chip 2/1/1.
[62] S.R.O., D/D/B reg. 27, f. 318.
[63] Ibid. 32, f. 46v.; ibid. DD/CPL 69.
[64] Ibid. D/D/B reg. 32, f. 70v.
[65] Ibid. 33, f. 25; Devon R.O. 74B/MT 1823.
[66] S.R.O., D/D/B reg. 33, f. 52.
[67] Ibid. D/P/crch 2/1/7.
[68] Ibid. D/D/B reg. 37, f. 75v.   [69] Ibid. f. 193.
[70] *P.O. Dir. Som.* (1875); S.R.O., D/P/chip 1/7/2.
[71] *Valor Eccl.* (Rec. Com.), i. 223–4.
[72] S.R.O., D/D/Vc 24.
[73] *Rep. Com. Eccl. Revenues*, pp. 132–3.
[74] *Valor Eccl.* (Rec. Com.), i. 223–4.

was agreed in 1842, including £11 4s. from the newly inclosed commons, £6 from glebe when let, and 8s. from the mills.[75] The glebe was worth 21s. in 1535.[76] There were 37 a. in 1571[77] and the same amount in 1840,[78] of which c. 26 a. were sold in 1924.[79]

In the early 17th century the rectory house was a building of two storeys, having a parlour, hall, kitchen, buttery, and malt house on the ground floor, and chambers including a study above. The house was newly repaired c. 1629. The adjoining farm buildings included a two-storeyed barn.[80] The house was said to be 'in decent repair for an old house' when occupied by the curate in 1840.[81] It was rebuilt on a large scale c. 1870, and c. 1967 was sold, to be replaced c. 1975 by a new house to the south. The former rectory house was known in 1982 as the Grange.[82]

John de Wamberg, appointed rector in 1326, was at the same time licensed to receive holy orders and to be absent for study.[83] Master John Petherton, rector 1409–19 and a licensed preacher in the diocese,[84] was succeeded for a short time by Master John Storthwayt, later a prominent diocesan official.[85] Nicholas Browne, rector by 1584 and until 1597, let the parsonage to a local farmer with the obligation to find a curate.[86] There was some neglect in the 1620s, when the rector of Stoke Pero acted as curate.[87] Rectors seem to have been resident during the 18th century, including three members of the Richards family, who were also lords of the manor and patrons. A fourth member, S. S. Richards, rector from 1809, was absent in 1815 because of illness,[88] and seems never to have lived in the parish thereafter. He died in 1853.[89] In 1815 a schoolmaster from Wellington served both Chipstable and Raddington, and held one service in Chipstable each Sunday.[90]

In 1840 the curate occupied the rectory house and held both morning and afternoon services.[91] On Census Sunday 1851 the morning congregation totalled 162, including 52 children from the Sunday school; the afternoon congregation was 172 with the same number of children.[92] William Nicholetts, rector 1857–1901, lived in the parish, rebuilt the church and rectory house, and, according to a churchwarden, visited the sick 'with great delight'. By 1870 he was preaching two sermons each Sunday, and celebrations of communion increased from four to six each year.[93] Cottage meetings held at Waterrow in the earlier 19th century were resumed in 1854.[94]

A church house was being leased by the lord of the manor to the churchwardens by 1647.[95] Quarter shares in the house were bought by the rector from the Bluet heirs in 1715, 1739, and 1743.[96] The church hall at Waterrow, used for both services and social activities, was designed by A. B. Cottam and built in 1908.[97]

The church of *ALL SAINTS* was so dedicated by 1531.[98] The medieval building, comprising chancel, nave with south aisle and south porch, and west tower, with windows of the 15th and early 16th centuries,[99] was demolished except for the tower in 1869, and was replaced by a building in the Geometrical style by Benjamin Ferrey.[1] The old arcade, with angel capitals, and bench ends carved with the Bluet arms, Renaissance heads, and a huntsman, were retained.

Five bells were recast in 1861 and a sixth was added in 1901.[2] The plate includes a cup of 1792.[3] The registers date from 1694, but volumes from 1559 were in existence in 1812.[4]

NONCONFORMITY. Cottage meetings organized by Congregationalists from Wiveliscombe were held at Waterrow from 1854 and a Sunday school was established there in 1885. Bethel chapel was built in 1890, and was considered unsectarian in its allegiance. It was in use in 1982.[5]

EDUCATION. There was a schoolmaster in the parish in 1675.[6] By 1819 there was a school where a few children were taught to read,[7] and by 1825 there were three day schools and two Sunday schools, with a total of 34 pupils.[8] No school survived into the next decade, but day schools were re-started in 1830 and 1831, having 22 pupils between them by 1835. A new Sunday school was started in 1833.[9] A building, comprising a dwelling on the ground floor and a schoolroom above, was conveyed for a school in 1836.[10] The school was linked with the National Society by 1847 and was supported by subscriptions. In 1847 it had 26 children.[11] The building continued in use until 1876, and later became a church hall. It was largely rebuilt after a fire c. 1961,[12] and in 1980 had been converted to a dwelling called the Old School House. The National school was replaced in 1876 by a board school 1 km. south-east of the village opposite Chipstable Farm.[13] The school, which until the 1930s had over 50 pupils, took juniors only from 1937, and was closed after fire damage in 1956. The children were transferred to Wiveliscombe.[14]

[75] S.R.O., tithe award.
[76] *Valor Eccl.* (Rec. Com.), i. 223–4.
[77] S.R.O., D/D/Rg 336.
[78] Ibid. tithe award.   [79] Ibid. DD/CPL 13.
[80] Ibid. D/D/Rg 336.   [81] Ibid. D/D/V returns 1840.
[82] Inf. from the rector, the Revd. M. Balchin.
[83] *S.R.S.* i. 258.
[84] Ibid. xxx, p. 351.
[85] Emden, *Biog. Reg. Univ. Oxon.* iii. 1792–3.
[86] S.R.O., D/D/Ca 98; P.R.O., C2/Eliz. I/T 6/39.
[87] Dwelly, *Par. Rec.* ix. 137–9; S.R.O., D/D/Ca 235.
[88] S.R.O., D/D/B returns 1815; Dwelly, *Par. Rec.* viii. 67.
[89] S.R.O., D/P/crch 2/1/7.
[90] Ibid. D/D/B returns 1815.
[91] Ibid. D/D/V returns 1840; ibid. tithe award.
[92] P.R.O., HO 129/314/1/3/5.
[93] S.R.O., D/D/V returns 1870.
[94] A. T. Cameron, *Chipstable, Brief Sketch of Parish and Church* (Beverley, 1919), 36; *Rep. Som. Cong. Union* (1896).
[95] S.R.O., DD/X/FRC.   [96] Ibid. DD/HB 3.
[97] Cameron, *Chipstable*, 31–4.
[98] *Wells Wills*, ed. Weaver, 57.
[99] Taunton Castle, Braikenridge Colln., watercolour (1849) by W. W. Wheatley.
[1] Wells Dioc. Regy., Muniment Bk. vi. 59.
[2] S.R.O., DD/SAS CH 16; Dwelly, *Par. Rec.* viii. 165.
[3] *Proc. Som. Arch. Soc.* xlv. 165.
[4] S.R.O., D/P/chip 2/1/1–5; Dwelly, *Par. Rec.* ix. 166.
[5] *Rep. Som. Cong. Union* (1896); Cameron, *Chipstable*, 36.
[6] *S.R.S.* xxxiv. 183, 189.
[7] *Educ. of Poor Digest*, H.C. 224 (1819), ix (2).
[8] *Ann. Rep. B. & W. Dioc. Assoc. S.P.C.K.* (1825–6).
[9] *Educ. Enq. Abstract*, H.C. 62 (1835), xlii.
[10] S.R.O., DD/CPL 83; ibid. D/P/chip 18/1/1. For accts. 1838–43, see D/P/chip 18/3/1.
[11] Nat. Soc. *Inquiry*, 1846–7, Som. 6–7.
[12] Char. Com. files.
[13] *Lond. Gaz.* 23 Jan. 1874, 285; S.R.O., C/E 26.
[14] S.R.O., *Schs. Lists*; ibid. C/E 85.

CHARITIES FOR THE POOR. Five sums of £5 had been given to the parish by the 1780s for the benefit of the second poor. Two of those sums were given by John Talbot and George Huish at unknown dates; the remainder were bequeathed by John Parrat in 1712, James Surrage in 1716, and John Hellings in 1762. In 1826 the interest of 25s. was being paid at Easter to about twenty people not otherwise relieved.[15] In 1843 the charities, said to have been distributed in bread, were declared to have been 'lost for many years'.[16]

CLATWORTHY

THE PARISH of Clatworthy lies on the southern side of the Brendon ridge, its village 4.5 km. northwest of Wiveliscombe. It measures 4 km. from north to south, and between 2 km. and 3 km. from east to west, and its area is 1,199 ha. (2,964 a.).[17] The northern and eastern boundaries are largely followed by roads, the limit to the west is partly the river Tone, and the boundary in the south-east is a stream known by 1720 as Sharcombe Water.[18]

The parish lies around the junction of six narrow and steep-sided combes, their waters together forming the headwaters of the river Tone. The valley so formed has since 1960 been flooded to form Clatworthy reservoir, with a surface area of 52.6 ha. and a capacity of 1,180 million gallons.[19] The surrounding land, light loam over slates,[20] rises to 373 m. near Tripp Barrow in the north, and reaches just over 300 km. around the reservoir, falling only in the south-east, where the Tone flows beneath the modern dam and through the small valley below Clatworthy village. The two main sources of water form two significant valleys in the northern half of the parish. One rises at Beverton Pond in Huish Champflower and is generally regarded as the Tone.[21] Its course formed the boundary between two estates in the 13th century,[22] A second stream, rising in Elworthy parish, was also an estate boundary, and in the early 13th century was known as the Tan, indicating a different origin for the Tone.[23] A ford, known in the 16th century as Oakhamford,[24] and later as Holcombe Water, was in the late 13th century known as Tanford, and the valley itself, later called Tripp Bottom, was called Tonecumbe c. 1300.[25]

There are two round barrows in the north end of the parish,[26] and an Iron-Age enclosure east of Clatworthy wood and the reservoir. The enclosure is roughly triangular in shape, with a rounded apex to the east.[27] 'Land at le Catell' was mentioned in 1385, and the 'Castellwall' in 1435.[28] The name Syndercombe, and iron slag found there and along the banks of the reservoir, are evidence of early ironworking, although no datable site has been found. Similar claims have been made for early origins of the 19th-century Carew and Roman iron mines.[29]

The village of Clatworthy, called Clatworthy Town in the 17th century,[30] lies in the south-east corner of the parish, on a hillside above the Tone. It consists of a few houses and cottages once grouped around a green at the junction of four lanes, on the south side of the parish church. The green was partly built over in the 18th century, and included a sawpit in 1839.[31] The possible manor house, the church house, and the rectory house all stood in the village. Syndercombe was at the centre of a separate estate by 1066,[32] and Week in the north, named by 1327, was regarded as a 'village' c. 1610.[33] Scattered farmsteads elsewhere were medieval if not earlier. Sedgeborough (Segbroc in 1226) and Tripp were established by the early 13th century, the former a grange of Forde Abbey (Devon, now Dors.) c. 1300.[34] Dudderidge, Westcott, and Hudford appeared by the end of the 15th century,[35] Fryan by the 16th,[36] and Mill Town by the 18th.[37] Dukesham, between Syndercombe and 'Bruneland', possibly Brown in Huish Champflower, was an estate name in the late 12th century.[38] Dudderidge and Syndercombe were both submerged in the creation of the reservoir.

Furlongs on Forde Abbey's grange at Sedgeborough c. 1300[39] and the 14th-century field name Fischforlong, later Fisherlands,[40] north east of Clatworthy village, suggest areas of open-field arable, though most of the parish was probably inclosed, except the high ground north of Tripp Farm and the eastern slope of Tripp Bottom, still known as Sedgeborough common in the 19th century.[41] Common pasture in Brendon is clearly indicated in Domesday and a manorial lease of 1435 included the right to pasture there,[42] although such common grazing was not expressly granted in most leases. In 1644 10s. 10d. was paid to the lord for 'doune rents' and these may possibly be identified with rents paid in the 18th century by between four and six 'rangers of common',

[15] 15th Rep. Com. Char. 440; Char. Don. H.C. 511 (1816), xvi.
[16] S.R.O., D/D/V returns, 1843; Cameron, Chipstable, 16.
[17] Census, 1971. This article was completed in 1978.
[18] S.R.O., DD/TB 12/12.
[19] Rep. Chief Engineer, W. Som. Water Bd. (1964); below plate facing p. 124.
[20] Geol. Surv. Map 1″, solid and drift, sheet 294 (1969 edn.).
[21] O.S. Nat. Grid 018340.
[22] Cal. Close, 1227–31, 587.
[23] Forde Abbey, cart., pp. 368–72.
[24] S.R.O., DD/WO 41/22 (1505).
[25] Forde Abbey, cart., pp. 370, 372.
[26] Proc. Som. Arch. Soc. cxiii, suppl. 28.
[27] V.C.H. Som. ii. 489–90.
[28] S.R.O., DD/TB 6/1, 54/13.

[29] Sellick, W. Som. Mineral Rly. 11–12; inf. from Mr. M. A. Aston.
[30] S.R.O., DD/TB 14/1.
[31] Ibid. 9/2–3.
[32] V.C.H. Som. i. 514; below, manors.
[33] S.R.S. iii. 7; S.R.O., DD/TB 12/3, 12.
[34] Forde Abbey, cart., pp. 366–7, 371; Cal. Close, 1227–31, 587.
[35] S.R.O., DD/TB 9/2, 12/3, 54/13; P.R.O., SC 2/200/42.
[36] Cat. Anct. D. v, A 13547; S.R.O., DD/WO 41/22.
[37] S.R.O., DD/TB 9/2.
[38] S.R.S. xxv, pp. 82–5.
[39] Forde Abbey, cart., p. 371.
[40] S.R.O., DD/TB 54/13; Devon R.O., B.R.A. 456.
[41] O.S. Map 6″, Som. LVIII. NE. (1887 edn.).
[42] V.C.H. Som. i, 501, 514; S.R.O., DD/TB 54/13.

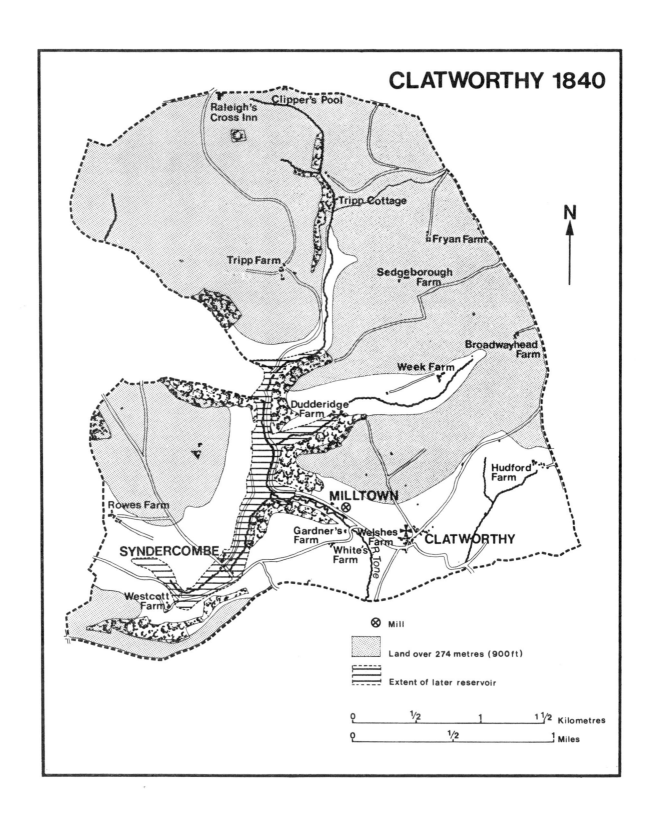

CLATWORTHY 1840

Clipper's Pool

Raleigh's Cross Inn

Tripp Cottage

Fryan Farm

Tripp Farm

Sedgeborough Farm

N

Broadwayhead Farm

Week Farm

Dudderidge Farm

Hudford Farm

MILLTOWN

Rowes Farm

Gardner's Farm

Welshes Farm

CLATWORTHY

White's Farm

R. Tone

SYNDERCOMBE

Westcott Farm

⊗ Mill

Land over 274 metres (900ft)

Extent of later reservoir

| 0 | ½ | 1 | 1½ | Kilometres |

| 0 | ½ | 1 | Miles |

rents which totalled £5 10s. in 1720.[43] Syndercombe manor farm had pasture for 200 sheep in 1690.[44] The tenant in 1724 was granted liberty to inclose any part of the common which belonged to the farm and had evidently exercised that right by 1780.[45] The unlawful cutting of furze, heath, and turf on the commons, regarded as the property of the lord, was presented in 1733 and leases of 1779 and 1780 reserved the lord's right to inclose any of the common land.[46] The rights of the tenants were limited to the 'western common' in 1793 and some were presented for cutting turf elsewhere than on 'the usual bogs' as late as 1821. Eighteen tenants were fined for taking turf on the lord's waste in 1825 and fixed rents had been imposed by 1831 for turbary licences.[47] The Brendon commons were inclosed by Act of Parliament in 1845 when 141 a. were allotted to Clatworthy. The Carews received 51 a.[48] Woodland on the north-eastern slopes of the reservoir was matched on the opposite hillside in the mid 14th century by similar growth on the Syndercombe estate.[49] In 1287 the lord of Clatworthy reserved to himself the chase between Tripp and Sedgeborough up to Brendon, in country that was presumably well wooded.[50] A Wiveliscombe man was accused of hunting over the lord's demesne in 1504.[51] Hunting was organized for the tenants in 1733, though in 1738 one tenant was presented for hunting on 'Peasewell common' on Brendon.[52] The Clatworthy estate was described as providing 'capital partridge and rough shooting' in 1911, when it included 150 a. of pheasant coverts, and a keeper's lodge with kennels and game house.[53] Field names suggest a park or parks. Land called Westpark was mentioned in 1400, the Park and Burchen Park in 1566 (probably west of Week Farm), Higher and Lower Park in 1592, and Middle and Easter Park c. 1610.[54] The name Park was recorded north of Clatworthy village in 1780.[55]

A victualler built a cottage on the village green soon after 1729 and was licensed in 1736. Manor court dinners were held there until 1772 or later.[56] Raleigh's Cross inn on the northern boundary was mentioned in 1837 and was then also a farmhouse.[57] The reservoir attracts fishermen, sailors, and picnickers.

There were 53 adult males in the parish in 1641[58] and 99 taxpayers in 1667.[59] The population rose from 197 in 1801 to 280 by 1821 and then, after a slight fall, reached 323 in 1851. Within the next fifty years it was halved, and had fallen to 118 in 1921. Thereafter there was little change until the 1950s, but by 1961, with a total of 54 inhabitants, Clatworthy had the second lowest population in the county. There were 82 inhabitants in 1971.[60]

MANORS AND OTHER ESTATE. The manor of *CLATWORTHY* was owned in 1066 by Alviet, a woman. By 1086 the overlordship was held by William de Mohun (d. after 1090) and descended with the barony of Dunster.[61] The overlordship was still recognized in 1777.[62]

The terre tenant in 1086 was Ogis, predecessor of the Arundels in two other estates.[63] Clatworthy was probably one of three fees which Roger (I) Arundel held in 1166 and which he may have held by 1135.[64] He granted lands in the manor to Forde Abbey by 1189,[65] and both he and his son Roger (II) were dead by 1204. They were followed in successive generations by Thomas (fl. 1220–7) and Roger (III) Arundel (fl.1268, d. by 1296).[66] Roger (IV) Arundel, probably son of the last, was lord in 1303 and was succeeded by his son John (I) (fl. 1316–28).[67] Thomas Arundel (d. 1335), probably John's brother, held the manor by 1331 and was followed by two daughters, Margaret and Isabel, between whom the estate was partitioned.[68]

Margaret married Philip de Hul, known generally as Philip of Clatworthy, and in 1343 they settled their share on John son of Peter de Bradeston for life with successive remainders to their own children.[69] John de Bradeston held the estate in 1346 but by 1370 it had passed to Philip and Margaret's eldest son John, who adopted the surname Arundel.[70] John (II) Arundel was probably succeeded by John (III) (d. c. 1419), and then by the latter's son John (IV), who was dead by 1442.[71] John (V), son of the last, held the share in 1475, and presented to the rectory in 1486. John (VI), described as of Bagborough, did fealty in 1493.[72] The estate had passed to George, son of John (VI), by 1501, and he still held it in 1509. Before 1521 he was succeeded by his son Thomas Arundel of West Bagborough (d. 1554).[73] In 1563 Thomas's son William Arundel sold his half of the manor to Richard Malet of West Quantoxhead, owner of the other half.[74]

The second share was inherited on the death of Thomas Arundel in 1335 by Isabel, wife successively of Simon Chapman of Taunton and William Lambrook. William was lord in 1344 and 1346.[75] From him the share passed by 1380 to Henry Lambrook. Henry's wife Joan held it in 1387 and had taken it to her second husband, Nicholas Wynnegod, by 1392.[76] John Lambrook (d. c. 1420), probably Henry's son,

43 S.R.O., DD/TB 9/2, 12/12, 14/1.
44 P.R.O., E 134/4 Wm. and Mary Trin./2.
45 S.R.O., DD/TB 8/2; ibid. outsize 5.
46 Ibid. DD/TB 8/5, 9/2, 9/26 (lease 11 Aug. 1779).
47 Ibid. DD/TB 9/3.   48 Ibid. Q/RDe 112.
49 Cat. Anct. D. v, A 11079.
50 Forde Abbey, cart., pp. 367–8.
51 S.R.O., DD/TB 54/13.   52 Ibid. 9/2, 14/5.
53 Ibid. DD/CH 86/2.
54 Ibid. DD/TB 12/3, 12/8, 12/12.
55 Ibid. DD/TB outsize 5.
56 Ibid. Q/RL; ibid. DD/TB 8/3, 9/2, 10/11/1.
57 S.R.O., tithe award; Sellick, W. Som. Mineral Rly. 60–1.
58 Som. Protestation Returns, ed. Howard and Stoate, 155.
59 S.R.O., DD/WY 34.   60 Census, 1801–1971.
61 V.C.H. Som. i. 501; Sanders, Eng. Baronies, 114; S.R.S. extra ser. 205–18.
62 S.R.S. xxxiii, p. 351.
63 V.C.H. Som. i. 490–1.
64 Red Bk. Exch. (Rolls Ser.), i. 226.

65 G. Oliver, Monasticon Dioc. Exon. 346; Forde Abbey, cart., pp. 365–6.
66 S.R.S. vi. 41, 69; xxxvi. 55; Rot. Hund. (Rec. Com.), ii. 119, 125, 138; Cal. Inq. p.m. ii, pp. 177, 352; Hist. MSS. Com. 5, 6th Rep., p. 345.
67 Feud. Aids, iv. 304, 334; S.R.S. i. 201, 278, 285; Forde Abbey, cart., pp. 371–2.
68 Cal. Inq. p.m. vii, pp. 220, 505.
69 S.R.S. xii. 220; Forde Abbey, cart., p. 376.
70 Feud. Aids, iv. 347; S.R.O., DD/TB 54/13.
71 S.R.S. xxxiii, pp. 166–7; ibid. extra ser. 209.
72 S.R.O., DD/TB 54/13; S.R.S. lii, p. 140.
73 S.R.O., DD/TB 54/13; S.R.S. xxxiii, pp. 248, 262; P.R.O., C 142/37, no. 118; C 142/104, no. 105. A reference to John Arundel as lord in 1520 (S.R.S. xxxiii, pp. 268) probably relates to an earlier owner as a deed of 1522 (S.R.O., DD/TB 54/13) describes Thomas as son and heir of George, who was son and heir of John Arundel.
74 S.R.O., DD/TB 54/13.
75 S.R.S. extra ser. 211; Feud. Aids, iv. 347.
76 S.R.S. xxxiii, pp. 93, 97; Cal. Close, 1392–6, 12.

held it by 1400 and was succeeded by his widow Eleanor, who was still in possession in 1432.[77] By 1442 the estate had passed to Margaret (d. 1491), daughter and heir of John and Eleanor, and wife of William Cloutsham.[78] The elder of Margaret's two daughters and coheirs, also Margaret, died unmarried and the estate descended to the younger, Elizabeth (d. 1510), married in turn to William Jacob and John FitzJames.[79] Elizabeth's son John Jacob held the property in 1530, and it was soon afterwards called the manor of *CLATWORTHY JACOB*. John's half brother, Aldred FitzJames, sold it in 1540 to John's widow's nephew Michael Malet (d. 1547) of West Quantoxhead.[80] Michael's widow Joan, who succeeded under a settlement, married John Fry, patron of the living in 1555, but the estate passed in 1563 to her son Richard Malet, who reunited the two shares in the same year.[81]

Malet sold the manor to Thomas Carew of Crowcombe in 1582 and thereafter it descended through the Carew family with the manor of Crowcombe Carew.[82] The Clatworthy estate was put up for sale by Mrs. E. M. Trollope in 1911 but only Broadway Head farm was then sold. Most of the estate was later disposed of although in 1978 the lordship was still retained by Mrs. Trollope's grandson, Major T. F. Trollope-Bellew.[83]

A manor house stood probably near the church, but the partition of the manor in the 14th century may have reduced it to the status of a copyhold tenement. It may possibly be identified with the farm called Welches which stood immediately east of the church and was leased to John Welsh in 1649. The lessee was then required to provide entertainment, food, and lodging for the lord, his steward, bailiff, and two servants whenever the manor court was held or pay an additional 20s. a year in rent.[84] The farmhouse has been demolished in recent years and the site was occupied by farm outbuildings in 1978. A chapel, probably attached to the manor house, was described as new in 1272.[85]

The manor of *SYNDERCOMBE* was held by Cerric in 1066. By the time of Domesday the overlordship had passed to Turstin son of Ralph[86] from whom it apparently descended with the barony of North Cadbury. Turstin was succeeded by Wynebald de Ballon (fl. 1092–1121), whose daughter married Henry de Newmarket (d. 1198). Henry was followed in turn by his sons William (d. 1204) and James (d. 1216). The overlordship evidently passed to James's daughter and coheir Isabel, wife of Ralph (I) Russel (d. c. 1250), and their son Ralph (II) (d. 1278) whose heirs were described as overlords in 1286.[87] The

property then passed successively to Ralph's son James (d. 1280) and his grandson, Ralph (III) Russel (d. 1295), and the latter's widow Eleanor received the overlordship as part of her dower in 1297.[88] Robert Russel (d. 1297), uncle and heir of Ralph (III) and mentioned as overlord in 1303, was followed by his brother Sir William (d. 1311) and Sir William's son Theobald (d. 1340).[89] Thereafter the overlordship descended as a freehold of Horsington manor, and continued in the Russel family to Theobald's son, Sir Ralph (d. 1375), and grandson, Sir Maurice (d. c. 1416).[90] Sir Maurice's son Thomas Russel (d. 1431) was succeeded by his second cousin Sir Theobald Gorges (d. 1470), and then by the latter's younger son Richard (d. 1480). Richard's son Marmaduke (d. 1510) left two daughters, Elizabeth and Maud, who held the overlordship jointly in 1514–15.[91] In 1623 the manor was held of the king as of his manor of Stalbridge (Dors.), but by 1656 the lords of Syndercombe were regarded as freeholders of Clatworthy manor and so continued until at least 1788.[92]

The terre tenancy was held at Domesday by Hugh although its subsequent descent is not recorded until Henry II's reign when Matthew de Gatemore, also called Matthew de Skilgate, was lord.[93] By 1225 the manor had passed into the hands of Richard de Mucegros (I) (fl. 1221–49) of Woollas Hall, Eckington (Worcs.).[94] Richard was probably succeeded by Robert, described as of Woollas Hall in 1256, and then by Richard de Mucegros (II) (fl. 1274–1304), who held the manor in 1286.[95] John de Mucegros held it by 1297 and William de Mucegros by 1303.[96] Sarah de Mucegros had lands in Syndercombe in 1327, possibly as William's widow, and in 1340 Robert Mucegros settled the manor on his son Richard and another, although Robert was still lord in 1346.[97] From Richard descended Henry Mucegros who held the manor in 1428.[98] Henry was succeeded by William Wollashull (d. 1453), probably his cousin, who also held Woollas Hall and who in 1436 settled the estate on his daughter Joan, wife of John (later Sir John) Vampage (I) (d. c. 1471).[99] The estate then descended through successive generations to John (II) (d. 1490), Robert (d. 1516), and John (III) Vampage (d. 1548), the last of whom sold it in 1540 to John Sydenham of Leigh (d. 1547).[1]

From that time the estate was often described as the manor or manors of *SYNDERCOMBE AND TRIPP*. John Sydenham was succeeded by his son also John,[2] and then by the latter's sister, Margaret, wife of Robert Hensleigh. The property formed part of the marriage settlement of Robert's son, John

[77] S.R.O., DD/TB 9/3; S.R.S. xvi. 103; xxxiii, pp. 108, 172, 197, 200, 202; *Feud. Aids*, iv. 439.
[78] *S.R.S.* extra ser. 142, 212; *Cal. Inq. p.m. Hen. VII*, i. p. 291.
[79] P.R.O., C 142/25, no. 41; *S.R.S.* xix. 140–1.
[80] S.R.O., DD/TB 9/2, 54/13; *S.R.S.* extra ser. 212–13; C 142/87, no. 85; CP 40/1106, Carte, m. 17.
[81] *S.R.S.* extra ser. 213; S.R.O., DD/TB 54/13.
[82] S.R.O., DD/TB 54/13.
[83] Ibid. DD/CH 86/2; *Som. Co. Gaz.* 12 Aug. 1911; inf. from Major T. F. Trollope-Bellew.
[84] S.R.O., DD/TB 8/1.   [85] Ibid. DD/AH 21/2.
[86] *V.C.H. Som.* i. 514.
[87] Sanders, *Eng. Baronies*, 68; *Feud. Aids*, iv. 275.
[88] Sanders, *Eng. Baronies*, 68; *Cal. Close, 1296–1302*, 84.
[89] Sanders, *Eng. Baronies*, 68; *Feud. Aids*, iv. 303.
[90] *Cal. Inq. p.m.* xiv, p. 206; *S.R.S.* extra ser. 393.
[91] P.R.O., C 139/55, no. 39; C 140/35, no. 59; C 140/78, no. 93; C 142/25, no. 56; S.R.O., transcripts file 2/51.

[92] P.R.O., WARD 7/69, no. 222; Devon R.O., B.R.A. 456; S.R.O., DD/TB 9/3.   [93] *S.R.S.* xxv, pp. 82–5.
[94] *V.C.H. Som.* i. 514; *S.R.S.* vi. 370; xi. 91. Richard de Mucegros was probably son of Robert (fl. 1207) and grandson of Richard de Mucegros (d. c. 1200), both possibly former lords of Syndercombe: *Trans. and Proc. Birmingham Arch. Soc.* xlvii, pedigree facing p. 15.
[95] *Trans. Birmingham Arch. Soc.* xlvii. 29–30; *Feud. Aids*, iv. 275.
[96] *H.M.C. Wells*, ii. 573–4; *Cal. Close, 1296–1302*, 84; *Feud. Aids*, iv. 303.
[97] *S.R.S.* iii. 168; *Cat. Anct. D.* v, A 11079; *Feud. Aids*, iv. 346.
[98] *Feud. Aids*, iv. 392.
[99] *Cat. Anct. D.* i, C 1747; *Trans. Birmingham Arch. Soc.* xliii. 75–6; xlvii. 30–1.
[1] *Trans. Birmingham Arch. Soc.* xlvii. 75–6; *Cat. Anct. D.* iv, A 6162–4; v, A 13057; *Visit. Worcs.* 1569 (Harl. Soc. xxvii), 69.   [2] *Cat. Anct. D.* v, A 12753.

Hensleigh, and his wife Cecily. Cecily's life interest was carried to her second husband Gawain Malet, and the estate later passed to John's brother, Henry Hensleigh (d. 1623) of Spaxton.[3] Henry was followed by his son John, probably the John Hensleigh who sold half the manor to John Carew in 1665.[4]

The half retained by John Hensleigh was called the manor of *SYNDERCOMBE* in 1679 but thereafter was usually described as the farm and mill of Syndercombe.[5] In 1702 John Hensleigh's son, also John, sold the estate to John Periam (d. 1711) of Milverton, who left it to his son John (d. 1775), of Hill in Bishop's Lydeard.[6] The last was succeeded by his great-nephew John Lethbridge (cr. Bt. 1804, d. 1815), then by Sir Thomas Buckler Lethbridge, Bt. (d. 1849) son of John, who added Tripp farm to the estate *c.* 1817.[7] The lands passed successively to Sir Thomas's son, Sir John Hesketh Lethbridge, Bt. (d. 1873), and to his grandson, Sir Wroth Acland Lethbridge, Bt. They were sold in 1875–6 to the Carews.[8]

The estate sold to the Carews in 1665 carried the title of manor of *SYNDERCOMBE AND TRIPP* and the manor courts, and descended with the Clatworthy manor through the Carew and Trollope families. The lands were sold during the present century but the lordship has continued in the Trollope-Bellew family.[9]

Syndercombe manor house was mentioned in 1432 and described as a mansion house in Elizabeth I's reign.[10] It passed with the half of the manor retained by John Hensleigh in 1665, was held by the Periam and Lethbridge families, and in 1874 was described as built of cob and thatched, and comprising a kitchen, two parlours, dairy, cheese room, and six bedrooms.[11] By 1911 it had been rebuilt in stone with a slate roof, but since 1960 the site has been submerged in Clatworthy reservoir.[12]

Before 1189 Roger (I) Arundel granted to Forde Abbey (Devon, now Dors.) ½ hide of demesne at 'Bromdun' or 'Brundon', and a virgate at 'Sedgebrook'.[13] The grant probably excluded the present Sedgeborough farm, as the bounds between Sedgebrook Arundel and Sedgebrook Abbatis were established in 1287.[14] The estate was held as 'Bromdun' and 'Sedgebrook', or later as 'Fryron' until the abbey was dissolved in 1539.[15] In 1545 William Affryren's holding there passed to Crown agents, and their successor sold the property in 1548 to John Sydenham, lord of Syndercombe, subject to a lease to John Fryern.[16] It seems likely that the estate was the origin of the present Fryan farm, north of Sedgeborough. The farm passed with half of Syndercombe

to the Carew family in 1665, and thereafter descended with the main estate.[17]

ECONOMIC HISTORY. Before the Conquest the parish was divided into two estates to form the manors of Clatworthy and Syndercombe, and it is probable that Tripp was included with Syndercombe. In 1086 Clatworthy manor gelded for 1½ hide and had land for 7 ploughs. Half the estate was demesne with 2 ploughs and 2 serfs, and the remaining 3 virgates were worked by 16 villeins and 5 bordars with 5 ploughs. There were then 5 a. of meadow, 25 a. of woodland, and pasture ½ a league by 4 furlongs, probably on the Brendons. Stock comprised a riding-horse, 8 cattle, 20 swine, 100 sheep, and 30 she-goats. The value had doubled since the Conquest to 40s. Syndercombe manor gelded for a single hide and had 5 ploughlands. One quarter was then held in demesne with one plough, and 7 villeins and 7 bordars held 3 ploughs on their 3 virgates. There were 17 a. of meadow, a square league of pasture, and 50 a. of woodland, and its pre-Conquest value of 20s. remained unchanged in 1086.[18]

With only the slightest indication of any open-field system and medieval references to most of the present farms, it seems likely that most of the land was farmed in closes from an early date with progressive encroachment on uninclosed wastes and commons, giving rise to disputes such as that in 1221 between Thomas Arundel and the abbot of Forde over Arundel's common pasture. Arundel claimed common for himself and his men and the right to take strays over the abbot's land at Sedgeborough after the hay had been carried, but in 1227 granted to the abbot similar rights over a ¼ hide of his own land.[19] Apart from the subdivision of the main manor in 1335 there is no hint of abrupt changes on either estate and the farming pattern is one of amalgamation of small holdings to create larger farms. The figures of 11 taxpayers in Clatworthy tithing and 4 at Syndercombe in 1327 indicate that Clatworthy was still the larger settlement.[20]

Labour services on Clatworthy manor included a harvest day and an afternoon from a tenant of 10 a. in 1370, and comparable services or their monetary equivalents continued to be demanded from two tenants as late as 1775.[21] A plot of demesne was leased by 1429[22] and most of the enclosed demesne had probably passed into the hands of the tenants by the 15th century. Between 1399 and 1402 the Clatworthy lords concentrated their efforts on conserving woodland and fishing from the depredations of

[3] G. F. Sydenham, *Hist. Sydenham Fam.* 200 ff.; *Cal. Proc. Chanc. Eliz.* (Rec. Com.), ii. 209; P.R.O., WARD 7/69, no. 222.

[4] P.R.O., WARD 7/69, no. 222; CP 25(2)/715/17 Chas. II Mich.

[5] Ibid. CP 25(2)/718/31 Chas. II Mich.; CP 25(2)/869/ 3 Wm. and Mary Trin.

[6] Ibid. CP 25(2)/961 1 Anne Mich.; S.R.O., DD/GC 64; DD/SAS HV 68/5.

[7] S.R.O., DD/X/LGV, correspondence; Burke, *Peerage* (1949), 1211.

[8] Burke, *Peerage* (1949), 1211–12; S.R.O., DD/SAS C/2273, 1.C.8.1; DD/CH 86/2.

[9] S.R.O., DD/TB 19 (hist. of Clatworthy); DD/CH 86/2; inf. from Maj. T. F. Trollope-Bellew.

[10] P.R.O. SC 2/200/42; *Cal. Proc. Chanc. Eliz.* (Rec. Com.), ii. 209.

[11] S.R.O., DD/SAS C/2273, 1.C.8.1.

[12] Ibid. DD/CH 86/2.

[13] Forde Abbey, cart., pp. 365–8; *Cal. Chart. R.* 1300–26, 208.

[14] Forde Abbey, cart., pp. 366–7. A copyhold grant of a tenement called Sedgebrook was made by John Arundel in 1400: S.R.O., DD/TB 12/3.

[15] Forde Abbey, cart., pp. 374, 377–8; Dugdale, *Mon.* v. 383–4; S.R.O., DD/WO 41/22.

[16] *L. & P. Hen. VIII*, xx (1), p. 661; *Cat. Anct. D.* v, A 13547.

[17] 'Fryeron House' was considered as part of the manor of Syndercombe and Tripp in 1683: Devon R.O., B.R.A. 456.

[18] *V.C.H. Som.* i. 501, 514.

[19] *Cur. Reg. R.* ix. 101; *S.R.S.* vi. 69.

[20] *S.R.S.* iii. 168.

[21] S.R.O., DD/TB 9/3, 54/13.

[22] Ibid. 54/13.

tenants, and presentments at Syndercombe manor court in 1432 and 1435 reflect similar action.[23] The conservation of woodland and fishing was still the principal concern on Clatworthy manor during the 16th century and in 1502 efforts to define tenement boundaries resulted in orders to tenants to raise a 'lanchard' or baulk and to erect boundary stones.[24]

Clatworthy manor was worth £6 a year in 1491,[25] but annuities granted from manorial income in 1522 suggest increasing value.[26] Until the mid 16th century tenants held almost wholly on lives, but a reversionary grant of Hudford farm in 1568 was a lease for 21 years.[27] By 1606 there were at least five leaseholders among 27 holdings amounting in total to 1,336 a.[28] Income from rents was £18 19s. 6d. in 1641–2 and fluctuated around £15 from 29 holdings up to 1646.[29] By the early 18th century the landlords, following their policy in Crowcombe, had converted to rack rents on short leases. In 1720–1 there were twelve such holdings, together with eight customary holdings. The gross income in consequence rose from £347 0s. 7d. in 1720–1 to £427 9s. 3d. in 1740–1. Arrears mounted towards the end of the century, rising from £290 10s. on a basic rental of £535 in 1771 to over £574 in 1780.[30] The same period saw the consolidation of holdings; four tenements at Tripp became a single unit, East and West Hudford another. Sedgeborough joined with Broadway Head and, from 1745, Welches with Week.[31]

Tenants in the 17th and 18th centuries accepted a wide variety of obligations. Farlieus or heriots still survived[32] and capon rents remained until at least 1737.[33] Tree-planting and the maintenance of coppice were regular requirements, the occupier of Duddridge farm in 1763 agreeing to take 500 young trees from Crowcombe to plant on his holding.[34] One tenant was to provide carriage on one day a year for tile stones from the Carew quarries to Stoodleigh (Devon) and Crowcombe.[35] Manuring and planting clauses occur on a lease of Sedgeborough in 1742 and new buildings were required of the tenant at Week in 1804.[36]

By the 18th century two freeholds had been created within the tithing of Syndercombe. Westcott farm of c. 90 a. passed through the families of Escott and Leigh, and c. 1828 to the Revd. Thomas Tudball (d. 1864).[37] The second freehold, totalling over 350 a., included Rowes, Whites and Ways Down Glasses, and Gardeners, and descended from the Darch family to Alexander Webber c. 1832.[38] By 1837 the Carews held 1,365 a., the largest farms being Fryan (355 a.), Hudford (206 a.), Week (160 a.), Welches (151 a.), and Broadway Head (124 a.). Sir Thomas Buckler Lethbridge held 765 a., including Tripp (450 a.) and

Syndercombe (250 a.). Alexander Webber had 356 a. of which Rowes accounted for 150 a. and Whites and Gardeners for 103 a. There were a further four farms of over 50 a.: Westcott, Mill Town, Duddridge, and the glebe.[39] By 1851 Syndercombe had grown to 300 a. and Sedgeborough to 212 a., and by 1871 Westcott had doubled in size to 180 a. and Whites increased to the same figure. Raleigh's Cross inn was a farm of 160 a. by 1871, much of its land outside the parish.[40] Tripp (515 a.) and Syndercombe (287 a.) were tenanted together in 1876 and by 1911 the Trollope family held 2,161 a. between ten farms.[41] The estate was gradually sold off during the 20th century, largely to the tenants.[42]

Thomas Carew, writing in the mid 18th century, commented that 'the lower part of the soil, being watered by the springs from the adjacent hills, is very fertile and the other parts lying near the commons is good arable land upon which are fed large flocks of sheep, which yield no small profit to their owners'.[43] Small areas of common had been ploughed in the early 17th century,[44] but the extent of the arable is not clearly known, though Syndercombe manor farm in 1690 comprised 300 a. of which 30 a. were sown with barley and 4 a. with wheat and rye.[45] In 1837 arable totalled 1,372 a. compared with 1,067½ a. of grassland and 190 a. of woodland.[46] The inclosure of 1842 led to a further slight increase in arable.[47] By 1905 of 2,664 a. in the parish there were 1,408 a. of arable, 1,022 a. of grassland, and 234 a. of wood and plantation. In 1911 the Trollope estate included 'some of the best stock-raising farms in this noted cattle and sheep district'.[48] In 1976 of 2,453 a. returned there were 1,564 a. of grass and 9 a. of woodland. There were then 8,213 sheep, 1,244 cattle, and 393 poultry. Of the 11 holdings returned most were devoted to stock raising.[49]

A 60-year lease of mining rights on the Lethbridge lands at Tripp was made to the Ebbw Vale Company in 1855,[50] and it was probably under that lease that the Roman and Carew mines were opened in 1865. A steam engine was installed at the Carew mine by 1868 for pumping, sinking, and winding the ore.[51] A branch line to link the mines with the West Somerset Mineral Railway was started but never completed, and both mines were closed by 1873.[52]

There was a mill in 1086 paying 6d. a year,[53] probably the later manor mill. After the subdivision of the manor, Henry Lambrook granted his share of the mill and watercourse to John Arundel in 1370,[54] and thereafter the mill descended with the Arundel estate.[55] In 1504 each tenant was required to spend one day a year scouring the mill leat.[56] The mill was worked by a succession of tenants including a tailor

---

[23] Ibid. 12/3; P.R.O., SC 2/200/42.
[24] S.R.O., DD/TB 54/13.
[25] P.R.O., C 142/37, no. 118.
[26] S.R.O., DD/TB 54/13.   [27] Ibid. 8/5.
[28] Ibid. 12/8, 12/12.   [29] Ibid. 14/1.
[30] Ibid. 10/11/1–2, 12/4, 14/5, 14/13.
[31] Ibid. 8/2, 8/5.   [32] Ibid. 14/1, 54/14.
[33] Ibid. 23 (lease 1737).   [34] Ibid. 8/1, 8/2.
[35] Ibid. 8/1.   [36] Ibid. 8/5.
[37] Ibid. 9/2, 9/3; ibid. Q/RE; Q/REr; ibid. DD/SAS, deeds 7(4), probate 1773; *Alum. Oxon. 1715–1886*, s.v. Tudball.
[38] S.R.O., Q/RE; Q/REr; ibid. DD/BR/py 166; DD/TB 9/2, 9/3.
[39] Ibid. tithe award.
[40] P.R.O., HO 107/1920; RG 10/2356.
[41] S.R.O., DD/SAS C/2273, 1.C.8.1; DD/CH 86/2.

[42] Inf. from Maj. T. F. Trollope-Bellew.
[43] S.R.O., DD/TB 19 (hist. of Clatworthy).
[44] Ibid. DD/TB 9/2.
[45] P.R.O., E 134/4 Wm. and Mary Trin./2.
[46] S.R.O., tithe award.
[47] S.R.O., DD/CH 86/2.
[48] Statistics supplied by the then Bd. of Agric. 1905.
[49] Min. of Agric., Fisheries, and Food, agric. returns 1976.
[50] S.R.O., DD/CCH 72 (lease 1855).
[51] Sellick, *W. Som. Mineral Rly. 33*; *Proc. S. Wales Inst. of Engineers*, vi. 83.
[52] Sellick, *W. Som. Mineral Rly.* 33, 41, 54.
[53] *V.C.H. Som.* i. 501.
[54] S.R.O., DD/TB 6/1.
[55] Ibid. 12/3.
[56] Ibid. 54/13.

from Brompton Ralph,[57] and a miller who was required to produce his peck (and later half peck) measure and toll dish for inspection at the manor court. Tenants were fined for grinding malt in a handmill and not at the manor mill in 1676 and 1680.[58] From the 1730s the mill was in bad repair and in 1742 a Huish Champflower miller was given a lease on condition that he built a mill house, grist mill, and malt mill there.[59]

Part of the buildings were then converted to a fulling mill. The water course was regularly diverted to drive a threshing machine between 1815 and 1826, and the tenant of Tripp farm claimed in 1828 similarly to have taken water for at least 40 years.[60] The mill continued to grind flour, probably until the 1930s.[61] The site was obliterated in the construction of Clatworthy reservoir. The mill stood near the farm and hamlet of Mill Town on the north-east bank of the Tone and was driven by a leat running along the hillside. In 1911 it had an overshot wheel, two pairs of mill stones, and a pit wheel with crown and pinion wheels.[62]

A mill by a ford, mentioned in the 12th and 13th centuries, stood near the boundary of Ford Abbey's estate at Fryan and Sedgeborough.[63]

A watermill and watercourses formed part of Syndercombe manor by 1340.[64] The mill was leased with the manor farm in 1502.[65] It was occupied in 1690 with 4 a. of land, and was recorded as belonging to the farm in 1704.[66] In 1842 the leat could be seen running north-east beside Syndercombe farm, and the field names Higher and Lower Mill mead survived in the vicinity.[67]

A blade mill and leat formed part of the Arundel demesne in 1514.[68]

A market or fair for sheep and cattle was held near Raleigh's Cross inn in August and September each year from the beginning of the 20th century.[69] In 1960 the site was moved to the field west of the inn.[70]

LOCAL GOVERNMENT. The parish was divided into two tithings until the 18th century, representing the manors of Clatworthy and Syndercombe.[71] Clatworthy was described as a free manor in 1274 when Roger Arundel by 'ancient custom' took all strays, and in 1275–6 he claimed the right to gallows and the assize of bread and ale.[72] There are court rolls and books for the manor for 1399–1402,[73] 1501–5,[74] 1537,[75] 1596, 1606,[76] 1607,[77] 1656–84,[78] 1674–81,[79] and 1720–1,[80] and court papers for 1720–56, 1759, and 1788–1840.[81] The earliest rolls describe sessions as hundreds and halmotes but by 1501 they were called courts leet, with views of frankpledge and courts

baron added by the 17th century. Courts were generally held twice a year, at first at Hockday or Easter and Michaelmas. In 1747 the meeting place was apparently an alehouse in the village, where court dinners were held from 1744.[82] The only officer regularly appointed in court was the tithingman, who occurs from 1402, although the bailiff was occasionally mentioned with a steward. A crier was paid fees in 1755, and a pound keeper was elected between 1829 and 1840. Court business included breaches of the assize of ale, damage caused by strays, rights of way, illicit felling of timber, and repair of dilapidated buildings. After the Restoration the oath of allegiance was taken in court by residents as they came of age. The butts were presented as unrepaired in 1607, the stocks and pillory in 1660–1 and 1731–2, and the cucking stool in 1677 and 1731.

Court rolls survive for the manor of Syndercombe for the years 1432 and 1435,[83] and a court book for Syndercombe and Tripp for 1683.[84] In the 15th century the court's business included presentments of ruinous buildings, felling timber, illegal fishing, and the presentment of *nativi* who were living at Wiveliscombe. A court was held for Clatworthy, Syndercombe, and Tripp in 1755 and Syndercombe was included in a court held for Clatworthy manor in 1759.[85] It is doubtful, however, whether any individual court for Syndercombe was regularly held after the Carews bought half the estate in 1665. A reeve was mentioned in 1435.

There were 2 churchwardens by 1626, and 2 overseers of the poor[86] and 2 surveyors of the highways by 1678.[87]

The former church house, standing south of the church, was converted to shelter the poor, probably by 1721.[88] By 1826 it was described as a house of four dwellings and garden, and it was in disrepair in 1830.[89] It was later demolished and the site was occupied by modern housing in 1978. The parish became part of the Williton poor-law union in 1836. It was included in Williton rural district in 1894 and since 1974 it has formed part of the West Somerset district.[90]

CHURCH. There was probably a priest at Clatworthy by 1189, and a parson is mentioned in 1287.[91] By 1321 the living was described as a rectory, and was in the gift of the lords of Clatworthy manor.[92] After the manor was divided in 1335 alternate presentations were normally made by the owners of the two halves.[93] The bishop presented in 1346, John Fry as second husband of Michael Malet's widow in 1555, and John Wood as husband of Dorothy, sister of Richard

57 Ibid. 8/1, 12/5, 54/13; Devon R.O., B.R.A. 456.
58 S.R.O., DD/TB 8/2, 9/2.
59 Ibid. DD/TB 8/2–3, 9/3, 14/5; ibid. D/P/clat 4/1/1.
60 Ibid. DD/TB 9/3.
61 Ibid. 8/4, 9/3; ibid. D/P/clat 2/1/4; ibid. tithe award; *Kelly's Dir. Som.* (1889–1939).
62 S.R.O., DD/CH 86/2.
63 Forde Abbey, cart., pp. 365–8.
64 *Cat. Anct. D.* v, A 11079; P.R.O., SC 2/200/42.
65 P.R.O., REQ 2/15, no. 122.
66 S.R.O., DD/MGR 1, abst. of will of John Periam.
67 Ibid. tithe ward.   68 Ibid. DD/TB 54/13.
69 Ibid. DD/CH 86/2; inf. from Mr. R. C. Notley, Monksilver. Folk tales relating to the market are frequent.
70 Inf. from Mr. Notley; plate facing p. 76.
71 *S.R.S.* iii. 168; S.R.O., DD/TB 19 (hist. of Clatworthy); *Som. Protestation Returns*, ed. Howard and Stoate, 155.

72 *Rot. Hund.* (Rec. Com.), ii. 119, 125.
73 S.R.O., DD/TB 12/3.   74 Ibid. 54/13.
75 Ibid. 9/2.   76 Ibid. 12/8.
77 Ibid. 9/2, 12/8.   78 Devon R.O., B.R.A. 456.
79 S.R.O., DD/TB 12/5.   80 Ibid. 12/12.
81 Ibid. 9/2–3.
82 Ibid. 13/3; ibid. Q/RL.
83 P.R.O., SC 2/200/42.
84 Devon R.O., B.R.A. 456.
85 S.R.O., DD/TB 9/2.
86 Ibid. D/D/Rg 337.
87 Ibid. DD/TB 12/5.
88 Ibid. 12/12; DD/TB outsize 5.
89 Ibid. DD/TB 8/3, 8/5, 9/3.
90 Youngs, *Local Admin. Units*, i. 675–6.
91 Forde Abbey, cart., pp. 365–8, 374.
92 *S.R.S.* i. 201.
93 *S.R.S.* ix, p. 413; ibid. extra ser. 208.

Malet, in 1570.[94] Henry Byam, rector of Luccombe, presented his brother John in 1616,[95] and John succeeded to the advowson by grant of John Carew.[96] The Lords Commissioners appointed in 1653,[97] but Francis Byam was patron in 1660 in succession to Sarah, John Byam's daughter.[98] Thereafter the advowson descended with the manor of Crowcombe Carew through the Carew and Trollope families to the Trollope-Bellews.[99] From 1951 the living was held with Huish Champflower and from 1967 also with Chipstable. A united benefice was created in 1971, when Major T. F. Trollope-Bellew became patron with one turn in three.[1]

The church was valued at £5 in 1291, £13 10s. 3½d. net in 1535, and £80 c. 1668.[2] In the early 18th century it was worth £120, £160 c. 1760, and by 1831 £310 net.[3] In 1535 the tithes of wool and lambs totalled £4 and personal tithes £4 6s.[4] In 1626 the tithes on lambs were to be taken on St. Mark's day (25 April) when of thirteen lambs the owner might choose the first two, the parson a third, the owner the next nine, then the parson another. For every lamb under the number of seven the owner paid the parson 1d. each; if there were between seven and nine the parson took one lamb and paid the owner 1d. for each animal. Tithe butter and cheese were taken at Midsummer and Michaelmas. Every householder and his wife paid 2d. each at Easter, their children while at home 1d., but menservants paid 4d. and maidservants 3d. The rector also received tithe wool from a close called Farthings in Brompton Ralph parish.[5] Compositions in lieu of tithes produced £68 until 1744 when tithes were again taken in kind.[6] The tithes were commuted for a tithe rent charge of £283 in 1837.[7] 'Churcheset' or tithes of grain from Syndercombe manor were payable to the rector to Stogumber in 1308–9.[8]

The glebe was valued at £4 0s. 8d. in 1535,[9] and in 1626 amounted to 85¼ a., including 30 a. at 'Tichicoombe', and 14a. in Clatworthy wood,[10] allotted to the parson in lieu of tithe wood.[11] The glebe was leased for £52 in 1744.[12] There were 93 a. of glebe in 1837, and the same area in 1939.[13] Under the inclosure award of 1842 just over 4 a. were allotted to the rector but were apparently sold soon after.[14]

The parsonage house in 1626 had six ground-floor rooms and five upper rooms, under a thatched roof, with a stall, stable, and hayloft, and stood between two walled courts, a further court having a barn, all on the south side of the road east of the church.[15]

Shortly before 1761 part of the house was taken down and the remainder was 'in a very indifferent state'.[16] The house was remodelled, extended, and repaired in 1814 by John Carter.[17] Extensive alterations were made in the late 19th century; it was sold c. 1951.

Richard Atte Ash, rector 1321–6, was instituted when only a subdeacon and was licensed to be absent for study.[18] John de Sydenhale, rector before 1347, was the only known medieval graduate, although Alexander Arundel, rector 1486–1525 and presumably related to the patron, was licensed for absence to study for three years from 1503.[19] John Skelton, B.Can.L., rector from 1525 until 1535 or later, held the living with West Quantoxhead, and Hugh Wood, LL.B., rector 1570–8, was a former fellow of New College, Oxford, and not resident.[20] William Mascall, rector 1578–1616, was 'old and sick' in 1612, and did not catechize. He was succeeded by his son-in-law John Byam, rector 1616–53,[21] who also held Dulverton from 1625. Byam was accused in 1636 of preaching irregularly, and was imprisoned c. 1646 for urging the royalist governor of Dunster Castle to hold out against Parliament. He was ordered to be removed from the parsonage house in 1648 but was involved in litigation over his livings until 1652.[22] His successor, John Gibbes, was appointed in 1653 and survived the Restoration. Stephen Pierce, rector 1677–1707, held the rectory with Chipstable; Ayshford Sanford, rector 1721–5, with West Monkton; and Henry Lockett, rector 1744–79, with Crowcombe.[23] Lockett was accused by the patron of consistently failing to provide resident assistant curates and of leasing the parsonage house and refusing it to a curate.[24] Communion was administered three or four times a year in the later 18th century and there were between 20 and 40 communicants in 1776.[25] There were resident rectors from 1810.[26] William Bernard also served Huish Champflower in 1815; by 1840 there were two Sunday services.[27] In 1851 there were morning and afternoon services attended by 109 and 160 people respectively on Census Sunday.[28] By 1870 there were monthly celebrations.[29]

There was a high cross, a light for the dead, and a fraternity in the 1530s,[30] and a church house by 1644.[31]

The church of *ST. MARY MAGDALENE*, on sloping ground above the village, comprises a chancel with north organ chamber and vestry, a nave with large south porch, and a western tower, the whole in

[94] *S.R.S.* x, p. 528; lv, p. 137; *Som. Incumbents*, ed. Weaver, 335.
[95] P.R.O., E 331/Bath and Wells/1; C. E. H. Chadwyck Healey, *Hist. W. Som.* pedigree facing p. 170.
[96] *Som. Incumbents*, ed. Weaver, 335.
[97] P.R.O. Institution Bks. index A2.
[98] *Som. Incumbents*, ed. Weaver, 335.
[99] Below, Crowcombe, manors.
[1] *Dioc. Dir.*
[2] *Tax. Eccl.* (Rec. Com.), 198; *Valor Eccl.* (Rec. Com.), i. 222; S.R.O., D/D/Vc 24.
[3] S.R.O., DD/TB 15/1; 27 (letter 1744); *Rep. Com. Eccl. Revenues*, pp. 132–3.
[4] *Valor Eccl.* (Rec. Com.), i. 222.
[5] S.R.O., D/D/Rg 337.
[6] Ibid. DD/TB 27 (letter 1744).
[7] S.R.O., tithe award.
[8] *H.M.C. Wells*, ii. 573–4.
[9] *Valor Eccl.* (Rec. Com.), i. 222.
[10] S.R.O., D/D/Rg 337.   [11] Ibid. DD/TB 12/12.
[12] Ibid. DD/TB 27 (letter 1744).
[13] Ibid. tithe award; *Kelly's Dir. Som.* (1939).
[14] S.R.O., Q/RDe 112.

[15] Ibid. D/D/Rg 337.   [16] Ibid. DD/TB 15/1.
[17] Ibid. DD/TB outsize 5, inserted drawings; H. M. Colvin, *Biog. Dict. Eng. Architects, 1660–1840*, 125–7.
[18] *S.R.S.* i. 201, 230.
[19] *S.R.S.* x, p. 548; lii, p. 140; liv. p. 80; lv, p. 40; Le Neve, *Fasti, 1300–1541, Bath and Wells*, 46, 68.
[20] *S.R.S.* lv, p. 40; *Valor Eccl.* (Rec. Com.), i. 222, 224; *Alum. Oxon. 1500–1714*; S.R.O., D/D/Ca 57.
[21] *Som. Incumbents*, ed. Weaver, 335; S.R.O., D/D/Ca 175; ibid. D/P/clat 2/1/1; *Alum. Oxon. 1500–1714*.
[22] *Walker Revised*, ed. A. G. Matthews, 310; S.R.O., D/D/Ca 310; *Alum. Oxon. 1500–1714*.
[23] *Som. Incumbents*, ed. Weaver, 335; *Alum. Oxon. 1500–1714, 1715–1886*; *Alum. Cantab. to 1751*.
[24] S.R.O., DD/TB 15/1–3.
[25] Ibid. D/P/clat 4/1/1; ibid. D/D/Vc 88.
[26] Ibid. D/P/clat 2/1/1–3; ibid. D/D/B returns 1815; *Rep. Com. Eccl. Revenues*, pp. 132–3.
[27] S.R.O., D/D/V returns 1840, 1843.
[28] P.R.O., HO 129/313/5/7/9.
[29] S.R.O., D/D/V returns 1870.
[30] *Wells Wills*, ed. Weaver, 59–60.
[31] S.R.O., DD/TB 14/1; above, local govt.

rendered local stone. The building probably dates from the 12th century, but in the late Middle Ages the nave seems to have been lengthened and the porch and tower added. Other new work included windows in the nave, one containing contemporary glass, and the rood stair. There is a plain, probably 12th-century, font. The pulpit and pews were installed in 1819,[32] and the vestry, partly later the organ chamber, was added by 1848.[33]

The parish registers survive from 1561 but lack entries for the years 1644 and 1651–4.[34] The four bells include one, the oldest, cast by George Purdue in 1599.[35] The plate includes a cup given in 1757 and an almsdish given by the rector in 1797.[36]

NONCONFORMITY. There were three 'popish recusants' in the parish in 1664–5.[37]

EDUCATION. There was a school in the parish serving both Clatworthy and Huish Champflower in 1818. It was partly supported by subscription, and 25 children were taught.[38] Before 1825 there were both day and Sunday schools, the former with 21 pupils and the latter with 14,[39] but by 1835 children

were attending a school in an adjoining parish,[40] known by 1847 as the Huish Champflower and Clatworthy village school.[41]

A National school was built in Clatworthy in 1840.[42] In 1846–7 there were 33 pupils attending on weekdays and 41 in the Sunday school.[43] William Edbrooke, the former village blacksmith, was master by 1851[44] and was succeeded in 1863 by his brother-in-law J. P. Nation,[45] schoolmaster and village shop-keeper for 35 years until his death in 1908.[46] There were 60 children attending in 1877 although numbers later declined with the parish's population to 42 in 1883 and 36 in 1889,[47] and to 26 by 1903. Numbers rose to 37 by 1930 but fell to 27 by 1940. The school was closed in 1948. Junior pupils were then sent to Huish Champflower and seniors to Wiveliscombe.[48] The former schoolroom lies at the north-eastern end of the village.

CHARITIES FOR THE POOR. The parish acquired an allotment of 1 a. at Raleigh's Cross for exercise and recreation in 1845. It was sold for £300 in 1968, and the investment income of £21 15s. has been used to provide a party and Christmas presents for the children of the parish.[49]

OLD CLEEVE

THE PARISH of Old Cleeve,[50] so called[51] to distinguish its main settlement from the Cistercian abbey founded in the valley to the south at the end of the 12th century,[52] occupies a coastal ridge between the Washford and Pill rivers, some 3 km. wide along the shore, and stretches for 9.5 km. south, largely along the western side of the Washford river valley, to the Brendon ridgeway. The parish is irregular in shape, narrowing to 1 km. at Roadwater but widening at its southern end around the hamlet of Leighland, or Leighland Chapel, on an outlier of the Brendons, and spreading some 2 km. along the ridge at its southern boundary, where the land reaches 400 m. The eastern boundary of the ancient parish followed the Washford river for much of its course, with three important exceptions. One was north of the village of Washford, which lies between Old Cleeve village and the abbey, where part of the boundary of Old Cleeve parish projects across the river, apparently following the boundary of an

estate described in the 10th century.[53] The second was the site of the abbey, 1 km. to the south, where a level precinct could be formed only east of the river.[54] The third exception was a steep-sided combe in the south-east corner of the parish, known in the 16th century as View's End,[55] which included the hamlet of Chidgley. The area was given to the monks of Cleeve before 1202 and may then have been added to the parish. Part of its boundary was already marked by a ditch dug by the monks.[56]

The western boundary follows streams and lanes for short distances, but is more often marked by hedges. In the extreme south a band of common land was incorporated into the parish before 1801.[57] The south-western angle of the boundary is marked by a stone variously known as Fournaked Boys[58] or as Naked Boys stone,[59] a name probably deriving from woodland there which had once been attached to the medieval estate of Fernacre.[60]

The ancient parish was increased in size by the

[32] S.R.O., DD/TB outsize 5.
[33] Ibid. DD/SAS (C/2402), 49.
[34] Ibid. D/P/clat 2/1/1–6.
[35] Ibid. DD/SAS CH 16.
[36] Proc. Som. Arch. Soc. xlv. 165.
[37] S.R.O., D/D/Ca 344.
[38] Educ. of Poor Digest, H.C. 224 (1819), ix(2).
[39] Ann. Rep. B. & W. Dioc. Assoc. S.P.C.K. (1825–6).
[40] Educ. Enq. Abstract, H.C. 62 (1835), xlii.
[41] Nat. Soc. Inquiry, 1846–7, Som. 10–11.
[42] S.R.O., C/E 26; cf. c. 1848: Kelly's Dir. Som. (1906). 'The school' was mentioned in 1840 and 1843: S.R.O., D/D/V returns 1840, 1843.
[43] Nat. Soc. Inquiry, 1846–7, Som. 6–7.
[44] P.R.O., HO 107/1920; S.R.O., D/P/clat 2/1/4, 2/1/6.
[45] S.R.O., C/E, box 6.

[46] M.I. in chyd.
[47] S.R.O., C/E, box 6, log bks.; Kelly's Dir. Som. (1883, 1889).
[48] S.R.O., C/E, box 6, log bks.; ibid. Schs. Lists.
[49] Char. Com. files.
[50] This article was completed in 1982.
[51] Cal. Pat. 1385–9, 370.
[52] V.C.H. Som. ii. 115–18.
[53] Proc. Som. Arch. Soc. xcviii. 122, 125.
[54] Below.
[55] S.R.O. transcripts file 3/2.
[56] B.L. Add. Ch. 11162.
[57] S.R.O., Q/RDe 2.
[58] S.R.S. lxxvi, Greenwood's map.
[59] O.S. Map 6", Som. LVIII.SE. (1887 edn.).
[60] B.L. Add. Ch. 11161.

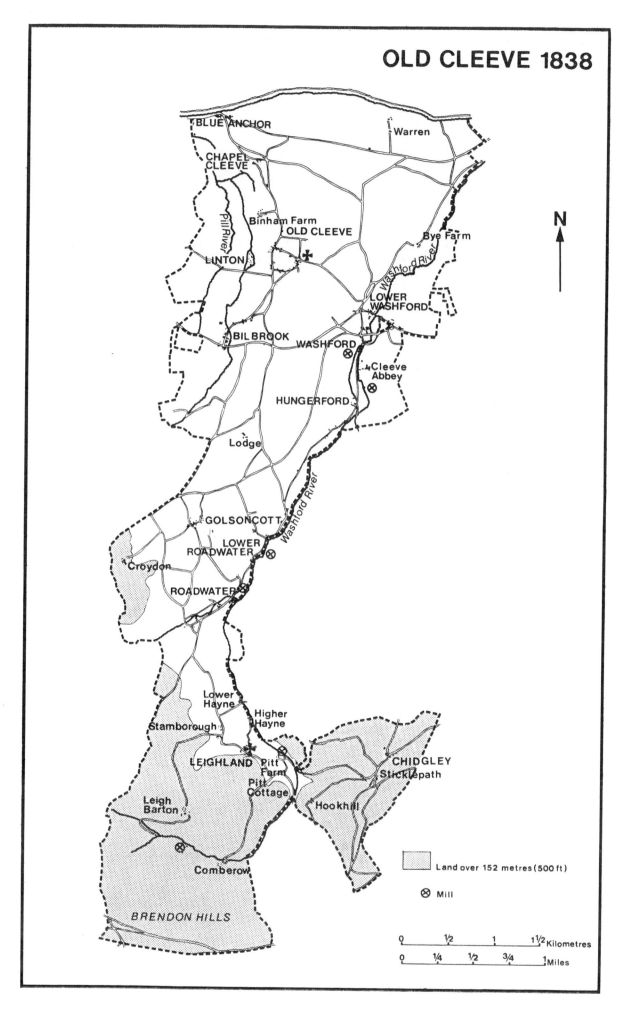

OLD CLEEVE 1838

N

BLUE ANCHOR
Warren
CHAPEL CLEEVE
Pill River
Binham Farm
OLD CLEEVE
Bye Farm
LINTON
Washford River
LOWER WASHFORD
BILBROOK
WASHFORD
Cleeve Abbey
HUNGERFORD
Lodge
Washford River
GOLSONCOTT
LOWER ROADWATER
Croydon
ROADWATER
Lower Hayne
Higher Hayne
Stamborough
LEIGHLAND
Pitt Farm
Pitt Cottage
CHIDGLEY
Sticklepath
Leigh Barton
Hookhill
Comberow
BRENDON HILLS

Land over 152 metres (500 ft)

⊗ Mill

| 0 | ½ | 1 | 1½ Kilometres |
| 0 | ¼ | ½ | ¾ | 1 Miles |

transfer of small parcels from Withycombe in 1882 and 1886 and of parts of Washford (7 houses, 34 people) from St. Decumans in 1882, Doniford or Dorniford (1 house, 3 people) from Monksilver in 1884, and Timwood (1 house, 10 people) from St. Decumans in 1886.[61] In 1971 the parish measured 2,105 ha. (5,203 a.).[62]

Between the narrow bands of alluvium and river gravel of the Pill and Washford rivers lies a ridge of marl, rising around Cleeve Hill (85 m.) in the north where it forms along the coast part of a faulted and unstable area of shale, limestone, and clay, the site of extensive Mesolithic activity.[63] Lime, gypsum, and alabaster have been extracted along the cliffs and bricks and tiles were made at Blue Anchor, in the extreme west.[64] The alluvium of the Washford river stretches southwards through Lower Roadwater and Roadwater, one branch thereafter reaching the 122 m. contour in the valley below Leighland. From the site of Cleeve Abbey on the alluvium, the underlying rocks change from Upper Sandstone and Pebble Beds with a narrow band of limestone to the slates and siltstones of the Cutcombe Slate Beds and finally, on the Brendon ridge, to the slates and silts of the Sticklepath Slates and the Brendon Hill Beds.[65] Lime was burned at Roadwater in the 18th and 19th century[66] and at Golsoncott, over the hill to the north-west, in the 19th, and there was a slate quarry at Glasses, south-west of Roadwater, by 1851.[67] There was a quarry for tile stones near Leighland in the early 19th century.[68] Attempts to extract iron ore at Timwood between 1907 and 1909 were abandoned.[69]

The parish contains 9 villages or hamlets and 14 farmsteads. In the centre of the northern end is Old Cleeve village, an irregular cluster of cottages, many of them thatched and mostly dating from the 18th and 19th centuries, which lie west and south-west from the parish church. Its name perhaps derives from its prominent position on the hillside. One km. north of Old Cleeve village lies Chapel Cleeve, founded in the mid 15th century when the chapel of St. Mary was built there to replace one destroyed in 1452 by a landslip.[70] On the south side of the chapel was a stone building which served as an inn for pilgrims to the chapel until the dissolution of Cleeve Abbey.[71] Part of the inn was incorporated into a dwelling which later became Chapel Cleeve Manor. Its ground floor was occupied in 1981 as the Hospice Bar of the Chapel Cleeve Manor Hotel. From the 1930s houses were built west and north of Chapel Cleeve Manor and from the 1950s within its grounds. North-west of Chapel Cleeve a sea-bathing resort was established in the late 18th century known as Cleeve Bay and later as Blue Anchor.[72]

Washford, 1 km. south-east of Old Cleeve village, appears to have originated as a settlement by a ford mentioned in the 10th century.[73] It comprises three distinct elements: Lower Washford at the site of the ford, the Hill to the south-east, mentioned before 1221,[74] which by the 19th century was the largest settlement, and a regular group of houses north of Washford mill which may be the New Street mentioned in 1508,[75] perhaps established in connexion with the adjoining fulling mills.[76] The road pattern in the hamlet probably developed from a route across the ford leading north-west along the course of Monks' Path[77] to Old Cleeve village or south-west to Bilbrook. A branch from the Hill led south-west past the abbey to Roadwater, a course modified at its northern end when the railway was built c. 1856.[78] The houses in Washford date largely from the 19th century, but Croft Cottage in Lower Washford is medieval in origin.[79] There was extensive building at Washford in the 1960s and 1970s. Bilbrook, 1.5 km. south-west of Old Cleeve village, is a small hamlet by the Pill river which was established by 1221.[80]

The Cistercian abbey of Cleeve occupied a site in the 'flowery vale' south of Washford from c. 1198.[81] Its precinct was bounded on the west by the Washford river and on the north and east by a moat known as the Black Ditch.[82] It is possible that the moat was the original course of the river.[83] The surviving buildings comprise ranges on the east and south of a cloister, the west cloister alley, a later farmhouse adjoining the south-west corner of the cloister, and a gatehouse to the north-west between two courts. Only the foundations of the monastic church have survived north of the cloister, and the reredorter to the south-east of the eastern range was being excavated in 1982. The site was taken into the guardianship of the Ministry of Works in 1951.[84]

South of the abbey is the hamlet of Hungerford, mentioned in 1536,[85] and the site of the abbey grange called Stout.[86] Small fields called Stout each side of the road running south-west up the valley represent the medieval Stout Green, towards the southern end of which stood the chapel of St. Pancras.[87] Substantial remains of the 14th-century building survive in a cottage of the same name, formerly corrupted to Prancard's chapel[88] or Pranketts.[89] By the early 16th century the abbey had established two other substantial granges where Bye Farm, north of Washford, and Binham Farm, south of Chapel Cleeve, stand; the main range of Binham Farm was built probably in the late 16th century and the central porch added, with interior decorative plasterwork, in 1624.[90] Linton, formerly London, west of Old Cleeve village, was mentioned in the 16th century.[91]

[61] Census, 1891.   [62] Ibid. 1971.
[63] Geol. Surv. Map 1″, solid and drift, sheet 294 (1969 edn.); O.S. archaeological surv.
[64] Below, econ. hist.
[65] Geol. Surv. Map 1″, solid and drift, sheet 294 (1969 edn.).
[66] S.R.O., DD/WO 35/5; ibid. D/P/lei 2/1/3.
[67] P.R.O., HO 107/1920.
[68] S.R.O., DD/WO 35/4.
[69] Sellick, W. Som. Mineral Rly. 73–5.
[70] Below, churches.
[71] Leland, Itin. ed. Toulmin Smith, i. 165; below, plate facing p. 44.
[72] R. Warner, Walk Thro' Western Counties (1800), 79; below, econ. hist.
[73] Proc. Som. Arch. Soc. xcviii. 122.

[74] Cat. Anct. D. v, A 10384.
[75] S.R.O., DD/AH 11/9.   [76] Below, mills.
[77] Below.   [78] Below.
[79] S.R.O., DD/V Wlr.
[80] Cur. Reg. R. x, p. 235.
[81] Dugdale, Mon. v. 732; below, plate facing p. 61.
[82] S.R.O., DD/AH 11/9 (1510).
[83] The suggestion of Dr. A. W. G. Court, Washford.
[84] Cleeve Abbey (H.M.S.O. 1959).
[85] P.R.O., SC 6/Hen. VIII/3127.
[86] S.R.O., DD/AH 11/9.   [87] Ibid.; ibid. tithe award.
[88] Ibid. DD/SAS C77/27–8; C432/5.
[89] Ibid. tithe award.
[90] Below, econ. hist.; plate facing p. 44; date on porch.
[91] P.R.O., SC 6/Hen. VIII/3127; S.R.O., D/P/cle.o 2/1/11, burial 1838.

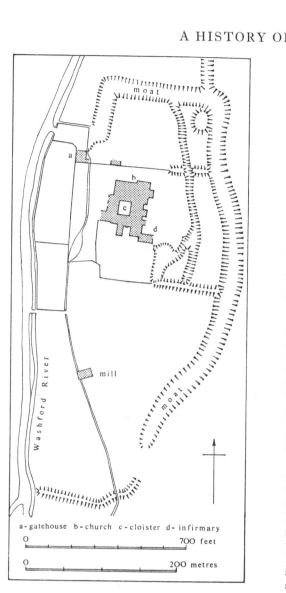

a - gatehouse b - church c - cloister d - infirmary

0 ————————————— 700 feet

0 ————————————— 200 metres

CLEEVE ABBEY PRECINCT

In the narrow central part of the parish Road-water, formerly Rode,[92] in the river valley, was the site of a mill by 1243,[93] and later of a bridge over the Washford river around which a settlement had grown up by the end of the Middle Ages.[94] The settlement continued to grow northwards, where the valley widens, to form Lower Roadwater. Buildings there are mostly of the 18th, 19th, and 20th centuries, but Oatways at Roadwater survives from the Middle Ages. To the west of Roadwater, occupying high but sheltered positions on the northern edge of the Brendons, the later abbey grange of Croydon and the hamlet of Golsoncott were recorded by 1221,[95] the first apparently as a habitation, the second suggesting in the last part of its name that it was a pre-Conquest farmstead.[96]

In the southern end of the parish the hamlet of

Leighland had a chapel by 1320.[97] Stamborough was named in 1298,[98] and Leigh Barton was a grange of Cleeve Abbey by the 16th century.[99] Isolated farms lie further south on the slopes of the Brendons. The short-lived industrial village of Brendon Hill, on the Brendon ridge, is mentioned below.[1]

The Saxon 'herpath' at Washford[2] presumably continued westwards perhaps to the royal estate of Carhampton or beyond. The known medieval routes in the parish indicate north-south travel. A road called Portway[3] was probably a route from Watchet to Old Cleeve village, and Clydens Cross, possibly of the 12th century, marks the northern end of a road from there to Lower Washford along Monks' Path.[4] There was a more direct route from Watchet to Washford and Cleeve Abbey along the Washford river valley beside Kentsford.[5] Other routes led south up the Brendons: one from Bilbrook up Forches Lane to Croydon, another from Old Cleeve village up Old Cross Hill, climbing to Golsoncott or dropping down into Lower Roadwater. A third route, from Washford, also led to Golsoncott and Croydon. The principal road from Washford southwards, passing Cleeve Abbey, was causewayed between the river crossing at Abbey Bridge, by Washford mill, and Road Bridge at Roadwater.[6] The road may have continued southwards over the Brendons to Bampton (Devon), for the name Market-path wood survived in the later 19th century south-west of Comberow Farm.[7]

By the 18th century the principal routes through the parish included the road between Hungerford, Washford, and Bilbrook which formed part of the road from Taunton and Hartrow Gate to Minehead. It was turnpiked by the Minehead trust in 1765. A second route adopted by the same trust at the same time ran north from Carhampton and over Mouth Bridge or Pill Bridge (built 1676) to Blue Anchor and then east over Cleeve Hill to Watchet.[8] The same trust extended its control over the road east from Washford to Williton in 1807.[9] The road from Williton to Bampton, following the parish boundary for a short distance west from Raleigh's Cross, was turnpiked by the Minehead trust in 1765.[10]

Field names and boundaries indicate former open arable fields north-east and south of Old Cleeve village and north-west of Leighland. There was common grazing on Brendon Hill and between the Pill river and Chapel Cleeve at Cleeve Alders.[11] A new park was established at Stout by 1507[12] and field names indicate others south of Golsoncott and west of Leighland. Woodland, by the mid 19th century amounting to some 300 a., was concentrated in the combes south of Leigh Barton, with copses and smaller woods in the valleys south and south-west of Roadwater.[13] Trowden wood and the wood called the Castle were established near Washford by 1633.[14] Further north, woods were planted around the rebuilt Chapel Cleeve Manor in the early 19th century.[15]

[92] S.R.S. xi, p. 306.   [93] Below, mills.
[94] P.R.O., SC 6/Hen. VIII/3127.
[95] Cat. Anct. D. iv, A 10384.
[96] Cal. Pat. 1225–32, 164 gives Croydon as Crandon, probably for Craudon.
[97] Below, churches.
[98] Cal. Pat. 1292–1301, 422.   [99] Below, econ. hist.
[1] Below.
[2] Proc. Som. Arch. Soc. xcviii. 122.
[3] S.R.O., DD/AH 11/9.

[4] O.S. archaeological surv.   [5] S.R.O., DD/L P32/7.
[6] Ibid. DD/AH 11/9; ibid. D/P/cle.o 14/5/2.
[7] O.S. Map 6", Som. LVIII. NE. (1887 edn.).
[8] 5 Geo. III, c. 93; S.R.O., D/P/cle.o 14/5/1.
[9] 47 Geo. III, c. 27 (Local and Personal).
[10] 5 Geo. III, c. 93.   [11] S.R.O., tithe award.
[12] Ibid. DD/AH 11/9.
[13] Ibid. tithe award; O.S. Map 6", Som. XLVII. SE., LVIII. NE. (1887 edn.).   [14] S.R.O., DD/WY 47/1/12.
[15] Ibid. tithe award; below, manors.

The opening of the Brendon iron mines from 1851 involved the creation of the mining village of Brendon Hill c. 1854. Within a decade there were 60 dwellings, together with shops, a church, and a chapel.[16] When the mines were closed in 1883 the village quickly contracted, leaving only one terrace, a few cottages, a chapel, and one substantial house by 1887.[17] The chapel and a few houses survived in 1982. The first part of the railway linking the mines with the coast at Watchet was opened in 1856, and in the following year, when the line reached Comberow, there were stations at Washford and Roadwater and sidings near Torre. The next stage was an incline from Comberow to the summit of the Brendon ridge, on which trucks were pulled by wire ropes. The incline was finished in 1861. The line took passengers as well as iron ore, and it survived the closure of the mines until 1898, and was revived with the mines between 1907 and 1910.[18]

A second line, following the mineral railway up the Washford river valley to Washford, was built in 1874 to serve Minehead, and a station was built on the west side of Washford. Known as the West Somerset Railway, it operated until 1971. In 1976 it was reopened under private enterprise[19] and continued in 1982.

A house called the Blue Anchor, probably an inn, stood 'on the strand' beside the coast road from Watchet to Minehead by 1678.[20] It continued in use until c. 1860.[21] There were at least five other inns in the parish by 1736, one of which was in Roadwater.[22] They included the White Horse at Hungerford, established by 1730,[23] and the Four Bells, later the Red Lion (1741–8), and finally the Bell (from 1749), in Old Cleeve village opposite the old school, which survived until the early 19th century and later was rebuilt as a smithy.[24] The Valiant Soldier in Roadwater was so named by 1770,[25] and like the White Horse was in business in 1981. The New Inn, also at Roadwater, was open by 1809 and continued until the late 1920s.[26] In the 1840s there was an inn at Leighland which survived for at least a decade[27] and by 1851 another was open at Washford, perhaps that known in 1852 as the Royal Oak and in the 1860s as the Wheatsheaf.[28] The Roadwater inn, using that name in 1939 but in business by 1923, was closed in the early 1970s.[29]

The appearance of the railway and the development of the holiday industry brought hotels and guests houses to the parish. The Railway Hotel was built by Washford station by 1875. By 1861 the Blue Anchor Family Hotel was built near the Blue

Anchor inn and presumably took over its business. Soon afterwards the Cleeve Bay inn was established, providing 'excellent accommodation'.[30] Another lodging house, known as Whitehall, near Old Cleeve village, was in business by 1883, and in the 1920s Vale House above Roadwater offered accommodation to holiday makers. By the 1930s more boarding and guest houses had opened,[31] and by 1981 there were two hotels[32] and a guest house at Bilbrook, beside the Minehead road, and Chapel Cleeve Manor had become an hotel. A camping ground established in Blue Anchor in the 1930s[33] was the beginning of a large-scale holiday development for caravans and tents which occupies, with ancillary shops and restaurants, much of the land running for more than a kilometre along the promenade into Carhampton parish. There was a caravan park at Warren Bay, east of Blue Anchor, in 1982.

There was a friendly society at Roadwater by 1802,[34] and a strong temperance society was founded there in 1868. An annual revel was held in September.[35]

In 1563 there were 74 households in Old Cleeve tithing and 21 in Leighland.[36] There were 323 adults paying the subsidy in 1667.[37] In 1801 the population was 1,040. It rose to 1,550 by 1851 and, notwithstanding the creation of the mining settlement at Brendon Hill, decreased slightly to 1,529 in 1861 and rose only to 1,689 by 1871. After 1881 the closure of the iron workings brought a rapid fall, to 1,307 by 1901.[38] Thereafter growth in the next decade was followed by contraction, but there was some significant expansion in the 1920s and after two decades of stability the population was 1,677 in 1971.[39]

J. W. North (1842–1924), painter, lived for short periods at Bilbrook and Stamborough in the 1870s.[40] R. W. Macbeth (1848–1910), artist and etcher, lived at Bilbrook in the 1880s and 1890s,[41] and Hubert (later Sir Hubert von) Herkomer (1849–1914), painter and teacher, lived at Lodge House from 1892 until after 1897.[42] James Vickery (1833–1910), a lesser known artist, was born in the parish.[43]

MANORS AND OTHER ESTATES. Cleeve formed part of the estate of Earl Godwin and T.R.E. was held by Earl Harold. It was held by the Crown in demesne in 1086.[44] Before 1102 it had probably been granted to Robert FitzGerold, when it included an estate known as Lege, identified as Leighland.[45] Robert's land descended to his nephew

[16] Sellick, W. Som. Mineral Rly. 55–8.
[17] O.S. Map 6″, Som. LVIII. NE. (1887 edn.).
[18] Sellick, W. Som. Mineral Rly. 19–26, 46, 68, 71–5; below, plate facing p. 45.
[19] E. T. Macdermot, Hist. G.W.R. rev. C. R. Clinker, ii. 87, 92; J. A. Stanistreet, W. Som. Rly. Official Guide.
[20] S.R.O., DD/SAS C 77/27.
[21] Ibid. DD/L 2/11/63, 2/12/65–6; P.O. Dir. Som. (1861, 1866).
[22] S.R.O., Q/RL.   [23] Ibid. D/P/cle.o 13/2/1.
[24] Ibid. DD/L 2/11/65; D/P/cle.o 4/1/1, 13/2/1–2, 14/2/1.   [25] Ibid. DD/WO 8A/4.
[26] Ibid. Q/RL; Kelly's Dir. Som. (1923). It may have been known as the Knapp inn in the 1860s: P.O. Dir. Som. (1861, 1866).
[27] S.R.O., D/P/lei 2/1/3; ibid. DD/DP 99–100.
[28] P.R.O., HO 107/1920; P.O. Dir. Som. (1861, 1866).
[29] Kelly's Dir. Som. (1923, 1939); S.R.O., Q/REr.
[30] P.O. Dir. Som. (1861, 1866, 1875).
[31] Kelly's Dir. Som. (1883, 1923, 1931, 1935, 1939).
[32] The Dragon House Hotel occupies a former farmhouse known as the Dragon or Dragon House since 1768: S.R.O., D/P/cle.o 14/5/3.
[33] Kelly's Dir. Som. (1935).
[34] S.R.O., DD/HC 6E/7–9.
[35] Inf. from Dr. A. W. G. Court.
[36] B.L. Harl. MS. 594, f. 55.   [37] S.R.O., DD/WY 34.
[38] V.C.H. Som. ii. 351.   [39] Census, 1911, 1971.
[40] Inf. from Dr. Court based on conversations with Miss B. V. North; C. Wood, Dict. Victorian Painters (1971).
[41] D.N.B.; Kelly's Dir. Som. (1889–1897).
[42] H. Herkomer, The Herkomers (1910), ii. 66–71; Kelly's Dir. Som. (1894, 1897).
[43] H. G. Harris, Zummerzet Volk and Devonshire Diversions (c. 1911), 29–30.
[44] V.C.H. Som. i. 437.
[45] Cal. Doc. France, ed. Round, p. 127; Sanders, Eng. Baronies, 17. The separate Domesday holding of Lege has been identified as part of Nether Stowey: below, Nether Stowey, manors.

William de Roumare (cr. earl of Lincoln *c.* 1141), who had died by 1161. William was followed by his grandson, William de Roumare (d. *c.* 1198).[46] Between 1186 and 1191 William gave all his land of Cleeve for the establishment of a Cistercian monastery which was colonized from Revesby (Lincs.) in 1198.[47] At or soon after its foundation Cleeve Abbey received the holdings of Hubert de Burgh, grantee of much Roumare land,[48] and estates at Croydon, Golsoncott, Bilbrook, and the Hill at Washford, which had formerly been held by the Benniworth family, retainers of the Roumares from Benniworth (Lincs.), all presumably once part of Robert Fitz-Gerold's estate.[49] The complete holding, later known as the manor of *OLD CLEEVE*,[50] continued in the possession of the monks until the surrender of the abbey in 1536.[51]

The manor was granted by the Crown in 1538 to Robert Radcliffe, earl of Sussex (d. 1542), in tail male, and in 1542 to him and his wife Mary, later wife of Henry FitzAlan, earl of Arundel, subject to the leases granted in 1537 to Anthony Busterd of the abbey site and lands, and the chapel of St. Mary.[52] The countess of Arundel was succeeded in 1557 by her son Sir John Radcliffe.[53] Sir John was still in possession in 1567 and probably in 1572, when the reversion was granted to Thomas Radcliffe, earl of Sussex (d. 1583), Sir John's nephew.[54] Thomas was succeeded by his brother Henry, earl of Sussex, who held the manor by 1592.[55] Henry died in the following year and his heir, Robert Radcliffe, in 1602 sold it to Thomas (later Sir Thomas) Stewkeley of Marsh (Som.) and Hinton Ampner (Hants).[56]

Sir Thomas Stewkeley died in 1639 and his son Sir Hugh (cr. Bt. 1627) in 1642. Sir Hugh's son, also Sir Hugh, died in 1719 without male issue,[57] and after a suit in Chancery his widow Mary, later wife of Thomas Foley, Lord Foley of Kidderminster, sold the estate to Thomas Musgrave of Nettlecombe in 1723.[58] Musgrave died shortly afterwards, leaving the manor to his great-nephew George Musgrave (d. 1724) and others in trust for George's son, also George. George Musgrave the younger succeeded to the estate between 1735 and 1739, but died in 1742, and was followed in succession by his son Thomas (d. 1766) and his daughter Juliana, married in 1767 to Sir James Langham, Bt.[59] Lady Langham offered the estate for sale to James Fownes Luttrell in 1799, but it was sold in the following year to Edmund Trowbridge Halliday of Bishop's Lydeard.[60]

Edmund Halliday died *c.* 1813 and was followed by his son John (d. 1826) and by his grandson, also

John Halliday (1816–97).[61] In 1870 George Fownes Luttrell bought part of the land[62] which seems to have descended with the Dunster estates until 1949, but G. S. Lysaght is said, probably in view of his ownership of Chapel Cleeve Manor from 1912, to have been lord of the manor.[63]

The dwelling house which was adapted from buildings on the abbey site after the surrender, presumably including the abbot's lodgings, came to be known as the mansion or capital messuage of the manor.[64] It was occupied by a succession of tenant farmers. The farmhouse was handed over with the abbey ruins to the Ministry of Works in 1951, but the house itself is not open to the public.[65]

A new house, incorporating at its north-east corner the remains of the medieval inn formerly serving St. Mary's chapel at Chapel Cleeve, was designed by Richard Carver and built between 1818 and 1823. It is in the Tudor style and had a symmetrical front of five bays with a central octagonal entrance hall flanked by reception rooms leading to a top-lit staircase. There was an octagonal tower to the west.[66] In 1913–14 the house was extended westwards in a similar style. The new interiors were fitted with oak panelling, richly decorated ceilings by Bankart, and an old overmantel from a house in Taunton. The grounds were planted with yew hedges and walks.[67] After the death of G. S. Lysaght in 1951[68] parts of the grounds were sold for building sites and the mansion itself later became an hotel.

The lords of *WASHFORD* were owed services in the late 13th century,[69] but their identity has not been discovered. A house, land, and rent in Washford were held of Cleeve Abbey as ⅛ knight's fee before 1359 evidently by Hugh of Bawdrip, lord of Bawdrip manor, for his widow Orange had dower there until 1366 or later.[70] John of Bawdrip had succeeded Hugh by 1359,[71] but before 1362 granted his estate there in fee to Sir John Combe (d. 1362), receiving it back for life. Early in 1365 Sir John's son, John, a minor, attempted to take possession of the estate, but Bawdrip continued to hold his life interest until later in the same year when he granted it to William Style. Style remained in possession until 1368 when Sir John's widow and executrix, Margaret, gained entry.[72] Later record of the son John has not been found, but Margaret apparently married Thomas Beaupyne (d. by 1404) and as his widow granted the estate to William Wroughton and his wife Margaret.[73] Wroughton died in 1408[74] and his widow later married John Blaket and received a quitclaim from the abbot and convent of Cleeve,

[46] Sanders, *Eng. Baronies*, 17–18.
[47] Dugdale, *Mon.* v. 732; B.L. Cott. MS. Tib. E. viii, f. 208; *Proc. Som. Arch. Soc.* vi. 22–3.
[48] *Red Bk. Exch.* (Rolls Ser.), i. 125, 235 n.; *Complete Peerage*, vii. 133–42.
[49] Dugdale, *Mon.* v. 732, 734; *Cur. Reg. R.* x. 137, 235; xi. 235–6, 333, 420; *Cal. Chart. R.* i. 59; *Pat. R. 1225–32*, 164.   [50] P.R.O., C 1/125, no. 1.
[51] Ibid. SC 6/Hen. VIII/7298. The date 1537 usually given is based on an undated letter in *L. & P. Hen. VIII*, xii (1), p. 2.
[52] *L. & P. Hen. VIII*, xiii (1), p. 64; xvii, p. 105.
[53] P.R.O., C 142/112, no. 151; C 3/151/18.
[54] *Cat. Anct. D.* v, A 12601; *Cal. Pat. 1569–72*, pp. 368–9.
[55] S.R.O., DD/SAS C 432/5.
[56] P.R.O., C 142/241, no. 109; ibid. CP 25(2)/207/44 & 45 Eliz. I Mich.
[57] Ibid. C 142/498, no. 45; G.E.C. *Baronetage*, ii. 26.
[58] S.R.O., DD/MY 10.

[59] Ibid. DD/SAS FA 179; DD/L 2/11/63; *Som. Wills*, ed. Brown, iii. 40–41.
[60] S.R.O., DD/MY 10, 32.
[61] Ibid. DD/MY 32; Burke, *Land. Gent.* (1894), 864–5, where the death of Edm. Halliday is given as 1790.
[62] Maxwell Lyte, *Dunster*, i. 274.
[63] e.g. *Kelly's Dir. Som.* (1923).
[64] S.R.O., DD/MY 9 (1685); DD/L 2/11/64; ibid. D/P/cle.o 23/3.
[65] *Cleeve Abbey* (H.M.S.O. 1959), 4.
[66] S.R.O., T/PH/bscs: photocopies of letters of Carver to John Halliday.
[67] *Som. Country Houses and Villages* (Truman Press 1931–2), 75–6; plate opposite.
[68] Inscr. in ch.   [69] S.R.O., DD/WO 10/1.
[70] *Cal. Close, 1354–60*, 617; *Cal. Pat. 1364–7*, 262.
[71] *Cal. Close, 1354–60*, 617.
[72] *Cal. Inq. p.m.* xiii, pp. 75–6.
[73] *Cal. Close, 1402–5*, 346–7; *1405–9*, 425–6.
[74] P.R.O., C 137/74, no. 50A.

CHAPEL CLEEVE MANOR, OLD CLEEVE, FROM THE SOUTH-EAST

BINHAM FARM, OLD CLEEVE: OVERMANTEL

LILSTOCK HARBOUR, *c.* 1907

WEST SOMERSET MINERAL RAILWAY, BRENDON HILL INCLINE, *c.* 1865

apparently to cancel a grant to them made in 1366.[75] From 1421 Blaket held Margaret's estate by the curtesy of England,[76] and was later knighted. By 1440 the estate had passed to John Wroughton of Broad Hinton (Wilts.),[77] grandson of William Wroughton.[78] John died in 1496 holding what was described as Washford manor.[79]

Sir Christopher Wroughton (d. 1515), son of John, was followed by his grandson William Wroughton, a minor.[80] In 1542 William sold the manor, with lands in St. Decumans parish, to John Wyndham, together with the reversion of his mother's dower.[81] The manor then descended in the Wyndham family like Williton manor,[82] and was held by G. C. Wyndham of Orchard Wyndham at his death in 1982. The Wyndham estate at Washford included land formerly belonging to Taunton Priory, bought from Crown agents in 1545,[83] together with other former monastic land acquired in 1611.[84]

The capital messuage was known as the Farm or Washford Farm from the 16th century.[85] In 1573 it was let by John Wyndham to his youngest son Charles, who was in the service of the earl of Sussex.[86]

The grange of *LEIGH*, later known as Leigh Barton, was part of the original grant by William de Roumare to Cleeve Abbey,[87] and was let by the abbot from 1527 to John Sydenham for 99 years.[88] John died in 1547,[89] and was succeeded by his son, also John. The latter's widow Ursula (d. 1608), who in 1596 assigned a third of her estate to John Trevelyan of Nettlecombe,[90] gave a similar share to her kinsman Robert Poyntz before 1606.[91] Poyntz was in possession of Leigh, apparently in fee, by the time of his death in 1611, and it then passed to his son Giles, a minor.[92] The estate was confiscated in 1649 but Giles had recovered possession by his death in 1666.[93] Clement Poyntz, son of Giles, died unmarried in 1685 leaving Leigh to his mother Prudence.[94] She died in 1691 and was succeeded by her kinsman Robert Rowe of Kingston in Staverton (Devon).[95] The Rowe family held the land for nearly a century, Robert being succeeded on his death c. 1745 by his son John (d. 1787). Israel Noke, owner by 1787, was followed by members of the James family.[96] In 1982 Leigh Barton farm was owned by Mr. P. E. White.

The farmhouse is of the 19th century, but at the rear are the remains of a chapel, and an annexe, dated 1627, which provided accommodation for the chaplain of the Catholic Poyntz family.[97]

The *RECTORY* of Old Cleeve, comprising the patronage and the great tithes of the parish, was acquired by the Crown at the Dissolution. From 1563 the rectory and tithes, but not the patronage, were leased to George Sydenham.[98] Nicholas Hilliard, probably the miniature painter, was given a reversionary interest to date from 1586,[99] but before he took possession the estate passed to Vincent Goddard and then to Conan Prowse, presumably as undertenants.[1] Hilliard surrendered his lease to the Crown, and Conan Prowse became owner c. 1607.[2] In 1608 Prowse sold the estate to Dr. John Layfield (d. 1617), rector of St. Clement Dane's and one of the revisers of the Bible.[3]

Dr. Layfield's widow Bridget succeeded her husband, and the family held the estate for more than a century.[4] In 1656 it passed from Dr. Edward Layfield (d. 1680), archdeacon of Essex, to John Layfield, perhaps to avoid confiscation.[5] It was later owned by Edward's son Dr. Charles Layfield (1649–1715), residentiary canon of Winchester, who by will left the impropriation to the Revd. Benjamin Culme, his nephew by marriage, for life, with the intention that it should pass to the church, presumably to the benefice, or, if his debts were larger than his assets, be sold below its full value to a clergyman.[6] In 1733 the great tithes, together with an endowment for Leighland, were settled on successive incumbents, subject to Culme's life interest.[7]

ECONOMIC HISTORY. AGRICULTURE. The Domesday estate of Cleeve paid geld for $4\frac{1}{4}$ hides, but there was land for 33 ploughs, 24 a. of meadow, woodland measuring 1 league by $\frac{1}{2}$ league, and grazing for at least 300 sheep and 50 she-goats. Only 21 ploughs were recorded.[8] Most of this estate came into the hands of Cleeve Abbey in the late 12th century, partly by grants of William de Roumare and his retainers,[9] partly in the form of gifts of small parcels situated on the edges of the estate. The grant by Robert, son of Hugh of Woodadvent, added land near Hayne beyond the ditch which the monks had dug, and included pasture in Woodadvent for 300 sheep, 60 cattle, and 60 pigs.[10] Another grant comprised a fishery on the border with Withycombe.[11] Small additions were made to the estate in the parish

[75] *Cal. Close*, 1409–13, 318; *Cal. Pat.* 1364–7, 262.
[76] *Cal. Fine R.* 1413–22, 386–7.
[77] *S.R.S.* xxxii, pp. 252–3.
[78] *Wilts. Pedigrees* (Harl. Soc. cv–cvi), 219.
[79] *Cal. Inq. p.m. Hen. VII*, i, p. 541.
[80] J. C. Wedgwood, *Hist. Parl., Biogs.* 975.
[81] S.R.O., DD/WY 8/G2.
[82] Below, St. Decumans, manors.
[83] S.R.O., DD/WY 8/I2.
[84] Ibid. 8/S2.
[85] Ibid. 8/G2; 46/2; 47/2/20; 65.
[86] Ibid. 8/G2.
[87] *Cal. Doc. France*, ed. Round, p. 127.
[88] P.R.O., SC 6/Hen. VIII/3127.
[89] *S.R.S.* xxi. 96.
[90] S.R.O., DD/WO 11/3.
[91] *Som. Wills*, ed. Brown, i. 71; J. Maclean, *Family of Poyntz* (Exeter, 1886), 268.
[92] *S.R.S.* lxvii, pp. 143–4.
[93] *Cal. Cttee. for Compounding*, iv. 310; Maclean, *Family of Poyntz*, 271, 280.
[94] Maclean, *Family of Poyntz*, 272–3; S.R.O., D/P/lei 4/1/2, 4/3/1.
[95] Maclean, *Family of Poyntz*, 274.
[96] S.R.O., D/P/cle.o 13/2/1, 3–4; ibid. DD/WO 35/4.
[97] Ibid. DD/V Wlr 18.2; below, Roman Catholicism.
[98] *Cal. Pat.* 1560–3, 507; 1563–6, p. 238.
[99] Ibid. 1572–5, p. 29.
[1] S.R.O., DD/L 2/11/61; P.R.O., E 134/31 Eliz. I East./24.
[2] P.R.O., C 66/1400, m. 33; C 66/1721, m. 9.
[3] Ibid. CP 25(2)/345/6 Jas. I East.; *Alum. Cantab. to 1751*; *D.N.B.*
[4] P.R.O., E 134/16 Jas. I Mich./16.
[5] Ibid. CP 25(2)/593/1656 East.; *Alum. Cantab. to 1751*.
[6] S.R.O., transcripts file 3/2, no. 6.
[7] Ibid. no. 8.
[8] *V.C.H. Som.* i. 437.
[9] Above, manors.
[10] B.L. Add. Ch. 11162; below, Nettlecombe, intro.
[11] B.L. Add. Ch. 11161.

until the end of the 13th century.[12] By the earlier 16th century most of the abbey's lands were divided between five granges, Stout, Croydon, Leigh Barton, Bye, and Binham,[13] with small holdings in each of the scattered hamlets of the parish.[14]

Cash rents had been introduced on the estate by 1367,[15] and a manumission was made in 1383,[16] but services were still demanded in 1510 when a cottager requesting the addition of his son's life in a lease offered as a fine seven days' ploughing, and the son promised a cash fine and $\frac{1}{2}d.$ for hundred wite. A much larger holding, at Linton, was at the same date subject to hundred wite, heriots, the supply of reed, and hoeing for one day and reaping for two.[17] The abbey's financial difficulties[18] may have prompted the leasing of granges, hitherto kept in hand. The park at Stout grange was let by 1507,[19] and before 1517 Croydon grange was let to the Prowse family. In the latter year the tenants took a lease of the 172-a. farm with 24 a. of wood and the tithes for the low rent of £4 17s. and the obligation to provide dinner and supper once each autumn for the abbot and his retinue.[20] The grange of Bye was divided, and in 1526 new tenants took a lease for two lives of some of its land in succession to a tenant at will, subject to twice-yearly suit of court and mill suit at Washford.[21] In 1532 John Underhay, a Taunton clothier,[22] took an 80-year lease of land at Kentsford and pasture for 60 sheep at Bye and of 60 a. and tithes at Shortmarsh, for the first 20 years at a rent of a grain of wheat and thereafter for 26s. 8d. a year.[23]

Leigh Barton remained a single holding, let on a 99-year lease from 1527, rent free for the first 14 years.[24] Binham grange was divided into at least five parts in the period 1533–5, each let for 61 years.[25] Land and the mills at Washford were let on favourable terms to members of the family of the last abbot.[26] The abbey's evident need for cash led it to mortgage its flock of 1,200 sheep.[27]

In 1536 the gross income of the abbey from lands in the parish amounted to £190 18s. 6½d., comprising £102 12s. 6½d. from the former granges, mills, and other land let to farm, together with manorial profits, the whole described as the manor of Old Cleeve, £16 13s. 4d. from the rectory, and £72 2s. 8d. from 632 a. of demesne in hand and other profits including £20 from offerings at St. Mary's chapel. The net value was £166 1s. 2½d.[28] The abbey estate was taken over by the Crown in September 1536.[29] The fragmentation of the estate under long leases,

involving the tithes as well as the land,[30] was partially reversed under Henry, earl of Sussex, who in effect reconstituted the grange at Binham for Robert Boteler, one of his retainers, in 1592, making a farm of 152 a., to which was added a renewed lease of the site of the abbey and Stout grange comprising c. 104 a.[31] The remaining lands in the parish were by 1642 in divided occupation. The lord of Old Cleeve manor, Sir Hugh Stewkeley, then held the former Boteler farms, but the largest owner-occupier was Giles Poyntz of Leigh, with the former grange of Leigh and all tithes south of Road Bridge.[32] By the 1680s Stewkeley's holding comprised the abbey site and Stout farm, and much of the land lying north of Old Cleeve village, between the former granges of Binham and Bye, the whole amounting in 1685–6 to 732 a.[33] Other substantial holdings included the Wyndham estate of Washford, with small holdings in Roadwater, based on the 80-a. Washford farm[34] and later to be augmented by the farm attached to Stamborough House;[35] the Speed family holding at Bye farm;[36] the Churchey farm at Stamborough;[37] and the Prowse farm at Croydon, converted from leasehold to freehold by the sale to George Prowse in 1600.[38]

In the northern part of the parish, fields such as Watchet Hill close (123 a.)[39] near the coast and Highbecks (100 a.)[40] north-west of Washford may have taken the place of medieval open fields when grange farming was established, and by the late 16th century there were traces of only two 'furlong' names.[41] Considerable areas of arable survived, 160 a. being leased with Croydon grange in 1517.[42] In Golsoncott, Roadwater, Bilbrook, Stout, and Washford together 385 a. were under crops in 1588, of which 50 a. were under oats and the rest under wheat, rye, barley, beans, and peas.[43] In the northern part of the parish in 1608 there was about twice as much land under wheat as under either oats or barley.[44]

Traces of common grazing were still apparent in the 17th century. Land called Cleeve Alders, beside the Pill river west of Chapel Cleeve, was subject to common rights, and lessees could take as many alders and willows each year as a man could cut in a day.[45] Rights to take fuel from there continued until 1730[46] or later and rights to pasture until 1794.[47] There was also shared woodland, and areas of furze attached to Binham in the 16th century may have been common in origin.[48] Townings mead at Washford may also have been common.[49] The lease of the

[12] S.R.O., DD/L P32/1; *Cat. Anct. D.* iv, A 6151; *Cal. Pat.* 1281–92, 466; 1292–1301, 422.
[13] Below.   [14] P.R.O., SC 6/Hen. VIII/3127.
[15] B.L. Add. Ch. 11164.
[16] *Cal. Pat.* 1396–9, 484.   [17] S.R.O., DD/AH 11/9.
[18] Windsor, St. George's Chapel, MS. IV.B.2, ff. 40–1.
[19] S.R.O., DD/AH 11/9.
[20] *Cat. Anct. D.* v, A 13069.
[21] Ibid. iii, A 5963.
[22] *S.R.S.* xxi. 202.
[23] P.R.O., SC 6/Hen. VIII/3127; S.R.O., DD/SAS PR 57.
[24] P.R.O., SC 6/Hen. VIII/3127; *Proc. Som. Arch. Soc.* vi. 55–6.
[25] S.R.O., DD/SAS PR 57; P.R.O., SC 6/Hen. VIII/ 3127.   [26] *Cat. Anct. D.* v, A 12456.
[27] P.R.O., E 315/91, ff. 26, 32v., 33.
[28] Ibid. SC 11/567. The rental for Old Cleeve manor is repeated in ibid. SC 12/14, no. 34; cf. the incomplete valuation in *Valor Eccl.* (Rec. Com.), i. 217–18.
[29] P.R.O., SC 6/Hen. VIII/3127, 7298.

[30] Ibid. E 134/31 Eliz. I East./24.
[31] S.R.O., DD/SAS C432/5.
[32] *Som. Protestation Returns*, ed. Howard and Stoate, 294–5; P.R.O., E 134/16 Jas. I Mich./16.
[33] S.R.O., DD/MY 9.   [34] Ibid. DD/WY 7/Z1.
[35] Ibid. 46/2/25B, 26(1); 47/1/2A, 3, 5, 12.
[36] *S.R.S.* lxvii, p. 148.
[37] P.R.O., C 142/535, no. 24; S.R.O., DD/SAS C77/ 28 (1675); DD/WY 7/Z1.
[38] S.R.O., DD/SAS C77/28 (1605); *S.R.S.* xxi. 143.
[39] S.R.O., DD/MY 9.
[40] P.R.O., STAC 4/1/41.
[41] Ibid. C145/535, no. 24; S.R.O., DD/SAS PR 57.
[42] *Cat. Anct. D.* v, A 13069.
[43] P.R.O., E 134/31 Eliz. I East./24.
[44] S.R.O., DD/SAS PR 57.
[45] *Cat. Anct. D.* iii, A 5963.
[46] S.R.O., DD/L 2/11/63.
[47] *S. & D. N. & Q.* xii. 241.
[48] *Cat. Anct. D.* v, A 12601.
[49] S.R.O., DD/WY 47/1/12.

main farm at Washford in 1631 included a small meadow and the use of water to improve it when not needed for an adjoining meadow.[50]

The payment of heriots survived in 1721, and suit to Washford mill remained a feature of Old Cleeve manor, but short leases and husbandry clauses were introduced for Abbey farm by 1700. That farm was then let for 7 years for £23, but no more than 140 a. was to be ploughed in any year, and no more than four grain crops, one being peas, was permitted.[51] The rent remained constant during the earlier 18th century.[52]

The purchase of the manor in 1721 was keenly contested between Edward Stawell and Thomas Musgrave. It then comprised 23 copyhold and 45 leasehold tenancies. Quit rents were worth £37 18s. 10d. and the main holding, the Abbey farm and the former Stout grange, was let for £230 a year. The whole estate comprised 625 a. of tithe-free former abbey demesne[53] and a farm at Chapel Cleeve which had been bought from the Layfield family by 1684.[54] The Musgraves continued the policy of purchase, adding land at Bilbrook in 1724[55] and both parts of Binham in 1763.[56] By 1794 eight farms had been established covering a total of 1,276 a.,[57] including Abbey farm which comprised 569 a. based on the former abbey buildings with 'every conveniency suitable to a large farm'.[58] There were four more farms of over 100 a. in the north. In the south the largest farm was still Leigh Barton, with extensive tracts of woodland, the Trevelyans' farm at Golsoncott, and smaller units at Croydon, Lodge, Stamborough, and Comberow.[59] Husbandry clauses in leases of farms on Old Cleeve manor required the strict application of dung or lime, Welsh lime being needed in half the quantities of the inferior English. Turnips, tares, or peas were to be grown before dressing, and no more than two successive crops of grain or beans were permitted.[60]

Amalgamation of scattered holdings by the Hallidays[61] and the purchase of small pieces of hill land by the Trevelyans[62] was part of a pattern of consolidation, particularly in the south, which by 1838 had made Leigh Barton the largest holding in the parish with 784 a., and had created a new farming unit at Hungerford out of the divided Abbey farm. By that date Old Cleeve farm measured 220 a., and twelve other units measured 100 a. or more.[63] By 1851 the farmer at Leigh Barton employed 24 men, women, and boys. At Bye farm (160 a.) there were 13 labourers, at Chidgley (200 a.) and Binham (246 a.) 10 each, and at Old Cleeve farm (216 a.) 9 men.[64]

The parish was almost equally divided between grassland and arable in the 1830s,[65] a balance which was virtually unchanged in 1980. Sheep were kept on the farms on the Brendons in the early 19th century, and a lambing shed was built at Chidgley.[66] A man living at Washford drove sheep from there to Bristol in the 1820s and 1830s.[67] Oxbow makers active in Old Cleeve until the 1850s or later indicates the continued use of oxen in the district.[68] The presence of a corn factor at Washford by 1838 and the establishment of the cattle market there by the 1890s[69] were in part because of good communications, and in part because of the produce of the parish. Corn growing and dairying were the main farming activities of the 1970s when there were still twelve farms of over 50 ha.[70]

TRADE AND INDUSTRY. Weaving and fulling were established in the parish by 1243[71] and there was a fulling mill, probably at Washford. A merchant mentioned in 1296[72] may have been concerned in the cloth trade. Cloth manufacture was probably most significant in the 17th century, involving three generations of the prosperous Bickham family[73] and at least seven other clothiers, a dyer, and weavers in the second half of the century.[74] At least two clothiers had business connexions in Taunton and Cullompton (Devon).[75] There is some evidence of contraction in the 18th century, but the Winter family of Roadwater continued to produce cloth, probably at Leighland, in 1815.[76] The fulling mill at Washford, whose tenant in the early 18th century had links with a Gloucestershire clothier,[77] continued in use until the 1840s.[78]

Seaweed, collected from the foreshore by the mid 16th century,[79] was still burnt and exported to Bristol for making bottles in the mid 19th century.[80] Laver was also collected and boiled in commercial quantities in the 1820s and 1830s.[81] By the 1830s bricks were being made at Blue Anchor,[82] a tannery was established at Linton,[83] and lime kilns were in operation in several places.[84] Increasing economic activity before the appearance of the railway is evident from the coal merchant established at Blue Anchor, where boats had occasionally discharged since the early 18th century,[85] the shops at Bilbrook, Old Cleeve, Leighland, and Roadwater, and the cabinet maker at Washford.[86] The iron-mining settlement at Brendon Hill, with a warehouse and two shops,[87] and the railways which linked the mines to Watchet stimulated business in the parish and provided considerable employment. Cleeve Bay,

[50] Ibid. DD/WY 65.
[51] Ibid. DD/SAS C77/27.
[52] Ibid. C77/28.
[53] Ibid.; ibid. tithe award.
[54] Ibid. DD/SAS C432/5.
[55] Ibid. DD/MY 14.
[56] Ibid. 12/9.
[57] S. & D. N. & Q. xii. 241; S.R.O., D/P/cle.o 23/3.
[58] S. & D. N. & Q. xii. 241.
[59] S.R.O., DD/WO 35/8, 44/11-12, 50/7-12, 52/4.
[60] Ibid. DD/L 2/11/64.
[61] Ibid. 2/12/65.
[62] Ibid. DD/WO 8/4.
[63] Ibid. tithe award.
[64] P.R.O., HO 107/1920.
[65] S.R.O., tithe award.
[66] Ibid. DD/WO 14/9.
[67] Ibid. D/P/cle.o 2/1/4.
[68] Ibid. 2/1/4-5; P.R.O., HO 107/1920.
[69] Below, markets and fairs.
[70] Min. of Agric., Fisheries, and Food, agric. returns 1976.

[71] S.R.S. xi, pp. 305-6.   [72] S.R.O., DD/L P32.
[73] Som. Wills, ed. Brown, ii. 67; iii. 87-8.
[74] S.R.O., DD/SAS C77/27, 28; C432/5; DD/WY 65; ibid. Q/SR 103/28.   [75] Ibid. DD/WY 65.
[76] Ibid. DD/WO 35/5; DD/L 2/11/63; DD/SAS PR 485; ibid. D/P/cle.o 13/6/1; ibid. transcripts file 3/2, no. 12.
[77] Ibid. DD/L 2/11/63.
[78] Ibid. tithe award; DD/L 2/11/64; P.R.O., HO 107/1920.
[79] Cat. Anct. D. iii, A 5504; S.R.O., DD/SAS PR 485; DD/SAS SX 66 (1626); ibid. D/P/cle.o 23/3.
[80] V.C.H. Som. ii. 361.
[81] S.R.O., D/P/cle.o 2/1/4.
[82] Ibid. tithe award.
[83] Ibid. D/P/cle.o 2/1/4, 13/6/1.
[84] S.R.O., tithe award.   [85] Wedlake, Watchet, 84.
[86] P.R.O., HO 107/1920.
[87] Sellick, W. Som. Mineral Rly. 58; above, intro.

later known as Blue Anchor, was an established holiday resort by the 1860s,[88] but much of the increased activity was connected with agriculture and was made possible by improved transport. By 1883, for example, John Gooding of Warren farm had established himself as a cement and manure manufacturer. By 1889 John Wood and Sons at Linton were making gloves and gaiters, and dressing skins, and an engineer and wagon builder was in business at Roadwater. Shops were established in the larger hamlets, most at Washford, including one for stationery and fancy goods, and another for patent medicines. By 1910 there was one shop in Old Cleeve village, thirteen shops and small businesses at Roadwater and Leighland, and six at Washford. Two banks had branches at Washford.[89] The number of shops fell sharply before the Second World War, and among the small businesses only the sheepskin factory at Linton survived in 1981. In the 1970s ornamental ironwork was made at Roadwater by Harry Horrobin in premises which, from 1978, were occupied by the Singer Instruments Co. Ltd., manufacturers of micromanipulators for making precise measurements in scientific research.[90] By the late 1930s a camping ground had been established at Blue Anchor, there were guest houses at Bilbrook and Roadwater, and a garage and a filling station had been opened on the increasingly popular holiday route through Washford and Bilbrook to Minehead.[91]

MARKET AND FAIRS. A market on Wednesdays and fairs on St. James' day (25 July) and the feast of the Exaltation of the Holy Cross (14 September) and the three days following each were granted to the monks of Cleeve in 1466.[92] A field called Fairclose was mentioned in 1510,[93] but no further reference to the fairs has been found. A site by Washford mill was occupied by shambles in 1522,[94] and shambles, probably at Chapel Cleeve, were in use in 1536.[95]

Cattle auctions were held on the first Monday each month by 1894 in a field beside Washford station.[96] Markets were still held there in the late 1960s,[97] but the site was occupied by houses in the late 1970s.

MILLS. There were two mills on the Domesday estate at Cleeve.[98] By 1243 there were three corn mills, one probably at Washford, and another at Roadwater.[99] By 1507 there was a mill in Leighland tithing, perhaps the customary mill for tenants of land above Road Bridge.[1] There were at least three millers on the manor in 1507–9,[2] and by 1536 there were four corn mills.[3]

One of the mills, at Washford, later known as Lower mills or Washford mill, was the customary mill for tenants of the northern part of the manor until 1606 or later.[4] The mill was let to members of the Dovell family by 1510,[5] until 1557 when it passed to the Sydenhams.[6] The Sydenhams still held it in 1669.[7] It was held by William Rawle from 1745 until 1772.[8] Grinding continued there until c. 1935.[9] A water-powered turbine roller was introduced by 1906[10] and was still in use in 1981 when the business was part of a milling consortium.[11]

A mill on the south side of the abbey precinct became the customary mill of the manor in the 17th century[12] and was held by the tenants of Abbey and Stout farms, who sometimes sublet to millers.[13] Suit of mill was included in manor leases until 1838,[14] and milling ceased probably during the First World War.[15]

Manor mill at Lower Roadwater, perhaps successor to the 13th-century mill,[16] was the customary mill for the tenants of Leighland until the earlier 17th century, when tenements with mill suit were taken in hand and the mill stream and mill head diverted.[17] A second mill seems to have been built c. 1620.[18] One mill, known as Road mill in the 18th century,[19] continued in use until the First World War.[20]

There was a corn mill at Leighland in 1672.[21] It may have been the later Pitt mills, known for a time as Webb's mill,[22] which continued in use until the later 19th century.[23] There were also several mills in the immediate vicinity: at Leigh, south of Leigh Barton, by 1814; at Chidgley by 1828;[24] and below Vale House and at Roadwater by 1838. Chidgley mill had closed by 1838 when Vale House mill was described as a factory.[25] By 1906 Vale mill and Roadwater mill were in operation together to process manure and seed as well as flour. All four mills probably ceased working during the First World War.[26]

There was a fulling mill, probably at Washford, by 1243.[27] Possibly the same mill was mentioned in 1507,[28] and by 1536 two fulling mills, possibly under

[88] *P.O. Dir. Som.* (1861, 1866).
[89] *Kelly's Dir. Som.* (1883, 1889, 1910).
[90] Inf. from Mr. A. E. Saunders-Singer.
[91] *Kelly's Dir. Som.* (1939).
[92] *Cal. Pat.* 1461–7, 527; below, churches.
[93] S.R.O., DD/AH 11/9.
[94] *Cat. Anct. D.* v, A 12456.
[95] P.R.O., SC 6/Hen. VIII/3128.
[96] *Kelly's Dir. Som.* (1894).
[97] Inf. from Dr. A. W. G. Court.
[98] *V.C.H. Som.* i. 437.
[99] *S.R.S.* xi, pp. 305–6.
[1] S.R.O., DD/AH 11/9; DD/SAS SX 66.
[2] Ibid. DD/AH 11/9.
[3] P.R.O., SC 12/14, no. 34.
[4] *Cat. Anct. D.* v, A 13069; S.R.O., N/71, deed 1606, Sussex to Prowse.
[5] *Cat. Anct. D.* v, A 12456.
[6] P.R.O., STAC 4/1/41.
[7] *S.R.S.* lxvii, p. 65; S.R.O., DD/SAS BK 87; DD/SAS HV 7.

[8] S.R.O., D/P/cle.o 4/1/1, 13/2/1.
[9] Local inf.
[10] *Kelly's Dir. Som.* (1906).
[11] Local inf.
[12] S.R.O., DD/SAS C77/27.
[13] Ibid. D/P/cle.o 4/1/1, 13/2/1.
[14] Ibid. DD/L 2/12/65: Halliday to Court.
[15] *Kelly's Dir. Som.* (1910, 1923).
[16] *S.R.S.* xi, pp. 305–6.
[17] S.R.O., DD/SAS SX 66.
[18] Ibid. DD/SAS C432/6.
[19] Ibid. D/P/cle.o 14/5/3.
[20] *Kelly's Dir. Som.* (1914, 1919).
[21] S.R.O., DD/L 2/11/63: deed 1694/5.
[22] Ibid. DD/WO 17/9, 17/10, 17/14.
[23] Ibid. D/P/cle.o 4/1/1; 14/2/1; D/P/lei 2/1/3.
[24] Ibid. D/P/lei 2/1/3; ibid. DD/WO 35/4.
[25] Ibid. tithe award.
[26] *Kelly's Dir. Som.* (1906, 1914, 1919).
[27] *S.R.S.* xi, pp. 305–6.
[28] S.R.O., DD/AH 11/9.

one roof, were let by the abbey.[29] John Sydenham (d. 1627) acquired the mill,[30] but before 1673 it had passed to Sir Hugh Stewkeley.[31] It was operated in the earlier 18th century by Richard Woollcott and from 1801 was held by the Gooding family.[32] By 1861 cloth production had ceased, and the buildings were used for the Goodings' manure and cement business.[33] Only a fragment of the mill buildings in Willow Grove survived in 1982.

By 1672 Sir Hugh Stewkeley owned a fulling mill at Leighland,[34] and a fulling mill at Bye was mentioned in 1688.[35]

LOCAL GOVERNMENT. In 1086 Old Cleeve was a separate hundred,[36] one of eleven which by 1327 constituted the hundred of Free Manors.[37] Courts of the manor were called hundred courts in the early 16th century, when the parish was divided between the tithings of Old Cleeve and Leighland. Sessions were held every three or four weeks, and courts leet at Michaelmas and Easter dealt with business from each tithing separately. A halmote court was also held at Michaelmas 1508. Draft court books covering the period 1507–13 include a session before the chief steward of the abbey, John Bourchier, Lord Fitzwarren, at Easter 1508. Court officers were two tithingmen, chosen at Michaelmas, a reeve for Leighland, a woodward, aletasters, and two constables.[38]

By the early 17th century an annual court, held at Michaelmas for Old Cleeve, appointed two constables, a tithingman, and two bread weighers and aletasters. Courts baron were held as necessary for admitting tenants. Court rolls for the periods 1611–24[39] and 1625–38[40] include orders for the repair of the butts, the tumbrel or cuckingstool, the crow net, and the pound. The last direct evidence of a court relates to 1654,[41] but a lease granted in 1838 included the obligation to do suit to both court and mill.[42]

From the 16th century the tenants of Washford manor owed suit to a manor court there, and records survive from 1562,[43] 1572–4,[44] 1598–1600,[45] 1614,[46] 1634,[47] 1639,[48] 1652, and 1684.[49] No record of officers has been found, but a pound stood in the yard of the capital messuage.[50] Chidgley lay within the tithing of Woodadvent in Nettlecombe and Rowdon manor in the 16th century.[51] Presentments relating to tenants in Golsoncott and Roadwater survive for the period 1709–46 and for 1755.[52]

By the 1620s the parish had been divided between

higher and lower sides. The higher side, administered by the sideman at Leighland, bore a quarter of certain parish charges, such as rent of the church house at Old Cleeve. The sideman was also known as the 'fourthman'. Accounts of sidemen survive for several years between 1621 and 1637 and of their successors, known as chapel wardens, for the period 1660–1706.[53] By the early 18th century two wardens and four overseers administered the whole parish, but the Leighland accounts were still compiled separately.[54] The vestry, amounting to a dozen or more members, nominated one of the wardens by 1783.[55] By the 1730s there were two constables and three highway surveyors.[56]

Treatment of the poor in the 18th century included not only regular weekly payments and gifts of clothing but also cash to redeem tools, to send children to school, or to board a patient at Wellington for special medical care.[57] By the 1720s, and probably much earlier, the overseers were renting the church house at Old Cleeve, and it continued to be rented for much of the 18th century.[58] About 1730 a workhouse was fitted out at Washford, and from 1741 the officer in charge was paid to dispose of the products made there, to serve vestry orders, and to place pauper apprentices. In 1748 a local soap boiler, then in charge of the workhouse, agreed for £200 a year to house, clothe, and feed the paupers, to pay for parish indentures, and to find funeral charges.[59] Terms were agreed in 1747 by the vestry with a doctor for care of the sick and with a carpenter for pauper coffins. In 1750 cash payments were revived for individual paupers, and in the following year food was also given, but in 1758–9 a workhouse governor was again given a lump sum to house and feed paupers while in 1759 payment of out-relief by the overseers was deliberately limited.[60] Grants of food and cash were resumed in the 1780s, and the workhouse continued to be occupied.[61] When its lease was renewed in 1806 it probably provided only shelter for the poor, but its old name persisted.[62] The building was still standing in 1839 near the river in Lower Washford, west of the site of the present school.[63] The parish became part of the Williton poor-law union in 1836, the Williton rural district in 1894, and the West Somerset district in 1974.[64]

CHURCHES. The church of Cleeve was given by Robert FitzGerold to the abbey of Bec-Helloin (Eure) early in the 12th century.[65] One of Robert's successors, William de Roumare (II), seems to have

[29] P.R.O., SC 12/14, no. 34.
[30] S.R.S. lxvii, p. 65.
[31] S.R.O., DD/SAS HV 7; DD/SAS C77/27.
[32] Ibid. DD/L 2/11/63–4, 2/12/65; DD/MY 23.
[33] P.O. Dir. Som. (1861).
[34] S.R.O., DD/L 2/11/63.
[35] P.R.O., CP 43/423, rot. 18.
[36] Domesday Bk. Som. ed. C. and F. Thorn, p. 370; above, Williton and Freemanors, hund. article.
[37] S.R.S. iii. 181.
[38] S.R.O., DD/AH 11/9.
[39] Ibid. DD/SAS C432/6.
[40] Ibid. DD/SAS SX 66.
[41] S.R.S. xxviii. 255.
[42] S.R.O., DD/L 2/12/65: Halliday to Court.
[43] Ibid. DD/WY 65.
[44] Ibid. 46/2/25A.
[45] Ibid. 46/2/27.
[46] Ibid. 46/3/52.
[47] Ibid. 47/1/12.

[48] Ibid. 46/2/26/1.
[49] Ibid. 46/2/25B.
[50] Ibid. 46/2/25A.
[51] Ibid. DD/WO 2/1, 35/1, 62/4.
[52] Ibid. 35/5.
[53] Ibid. D/P/lei 4/1/1–3; ibid. transcripts file 3/2, no. 22.
[54] Ibid. D/P/lei 4/1/2; D/P/cle.o 13/2/1.
[55] Ibid. D/P/cle.o 4/1/1; 13/2/1–3.
[56] Ibid. 14/5/2.
[57] Ibid. 13/2/1, sub anno 1745.
[58] Ibid. 13/2/1; ibid. DD/X/BOU 6.
[59] Ibid. D/P/cle.o 13/2/1.
[60] Ibid. 13/2/2.
[61] Ibid. 13/2/3.
[62] Ibid. DD/L 2/12/65.
[63] Ibid. tithe award.
[64] Youngs, Local Admin. Units, i. 675–6.
[65] Cal. Doc. France, ed. Round, p. 127; Eng. Lands of Abbey of Bec (Camd. 3rd ser. lxxiii), 142.

ignored the grant, and gave the church to Wells Cathedral between 1189 and 1192.[66] He himself also presented clerks to the living, but between 1192 and 1197 Bec's claims were recognized, and the abbey was licensed to appropriate the rectory. In 1199 the counter-claim of Wells was met by making the rectory a prebend in the cathedral, to be held by successive abbots of Bec.[67] Almost immediately Bec leased the prebend to the abbey of Cleeve, which continued to hold it until the Dissolution.[68] The later descent of the estate is given above.[69]

A vicarage was ordained c. 1197, and its endowment was increased in 1320.[70] The benefice, because it had been endowed in 1733 with great tithes, was called a rectory from 1866.[71] Leighland, which had had a chapel since 1320, became a district chapelry in 1865.[72] The vicarage of Leighland was united with the rectory of Treborough in 1950, and the livings of Old Cleeve, Leighland, and Treborough were united in 1955.[73]

The advowson was leased to the convent of Cleeve by Bec, though the Crown presented in 1387 on the grounds that the owner was an alien.[74] Hugh Stevyne of Stogumber, 'clothman', presented in 1557,[75] and the Crown on vacancies in 1563, 1572, and 1598. Peter Smithweeke presented in 1608,[76] but by 1624 the vicar, Edmund Brickenden, had acquired the advowson, and in turn sold it to his curate, John Tratt.[77] Richard Stockman of Durleigh presented in 1633 and Hugh Jenkins, who succeeded his father as vicar in 1664, was probably presented by his own mother.[78] The Crown was patron again in 1677, but at the next vacancy in 1698 Elston Whitlock was presented by Charles Sims, clerk.[79] John Whitlock of Old Cleeve presented Escott Richards in 1705, and in 1713 Charles Mitchell was presented by Thomas Luttrell, M.B., by grant of Elston Whitlock, John Whitlock, and John Jenkins.[80] At the next vacancy in 1735 the right was disputed between John Jenkins of Hartland (Devon) and Martha Layfield of Studland (Dors.), the latter heir to the patronage as devised by Dr. Charles Layfield (d. 1715).[81] The Revd. Benjamin Culme, husband of Judith Layfield, was patron in 1740,[82] but thereafter the patronage was held by or for successive incumbents. James Newton presented himself in 1782, and his trustees acted in 1803 and 1807, in the second year appointing his son William, vicar 1807-48.[83] William Newton's widow sold the next presentation in 1848 to the Revd. A. F. Luttrell,[84]

and Luttrell presented in 1851.[85] Thomas Bedford presented himself in 1858,[86] the bishop collated by lapse in 1863,[87] and John Blurton Webb presented both himself in 1865 and his successor in 1873.[88] William Walter Herringham, rector 1873-1904, purchased the living for his son, but the latter chose an army career and the advowson passed to Selwyn College, Cambridge, in 1925.[89] The college has the right to present to the united benefice for two turns out of three.[90]

The vicarage was worth £7 net in 1535,[91] and its reputed value was £6 c. 1668.[92] The endowment was increased by £200 capital in 1724, half provided by the patron, Benjamin Culme, half by Dr. Godolphin, dean of St. Paul's.[93] The income was much increased by a settlement of 1733.[94] By 1831 the average income was £466 net.[95] The tithes and other offerings constituted the whole gross value of the vicarage in 1535,[96] and comprised all but the corn tithes of the parish, but in 1636 it was said that the lay rector took tithe hay from certain fields.[97] In 1839 the vicar was awarded a rent charge of £600 15s. in place of both great tithes, which he held under the settlement of 1733, and small tithes.[98] In 1606 the glebe was limited to a small orchard and a garden.[99] It amounted to only just over 3 a. in 1839, the area of the vicarage house and garden.[1]

The vicar in 1320 lived in the house anciently assigned to the incumbent.[2] John Sym or Symmes, on resigning the living in 1448, was given a chamber he himself had built west of the hall of the vicarage house, with a small garden.[3] In the 17th century the vicarage buildings included a bakehouse, barn, stable, and dairy.[4] The house was rebuilt on a large scale on its commanding site probably by James Newton, vicar 1782-1802. It was replaced by a dwelling on an adjacent site in 1939,[5] and was known in 1982 as Old Cleeve House.

Ralph Free was appointed vicar in 1460 on condition that he studied for several months and resigned if he failed an examination.[6] John Dovell, vicar 1520-5, was a member of a prominent local family which included the last abbot of Cleeve.[7] A succession of curates and 'sundry serving priests that departed within the quarter' cared for the parish early in Elizabeth I's reign after resident vicars under Mary.[8] Robert Evans, vicar 1598-1608, was accused in 1603 of administering communion to people kneeling in their seats.[9] Edmund Brickenden, vicar from 1608,[10]

[66] H.M.C. Wells, i. 489; S.R.S. lvi. 98.
[67] Cal. Doc. France, pp. 129-30.
[68] H.M.C. Wells, ii. 549; Eng. Lands of Bec, 142.
[69] Above, manors.
[70] S.R.S. i. 185-6; H.M.C. Wells, i. 386-7.
[71] S.R.O., D/D/B reg. 39, ff. 57v.-58; above, manors.
[72] Lond. Gaz. 4 Apr. 1865, p. 1877.
[73] Dioc. Dir.   [74] Cal. Pat. 1385-9, 370.
[75] S.R.S. lv, p. 149.
[76] Cal. Pat. 1560-3, 480; 1569-72, p. 416; Som. Incumbents, ed. Weaver, 336.
[77] A. L. Humphreys, Fragments Illustrating Local History Gathered Round my Room (1892 priv. print.); Som. Co. Herald, 16 Feb. 1924.
[78] Som. Incumbents, ed. Weaver, 336.
[79] S.R.O., D/D/B reg. 24, f. 15v.
[80] Ibid. D/D/B reg. 26, ff. 21-2.
[81] Ibid. transcripts file 3/2, no. 6; ibid. D/D/B reg. 26, ff. 21-2. Martha Layfield proved her case on the strength of 'deeds mislaid'.
[82] S.R.O., D/D/B reg. 26, ff. 21-2; Hutchins, Hist. Dorset, i. 654.
[83] S.R.O., D/D/B reg. 33, ff. 4, 38.
[84] Ibid. DD/L 2/12/66.

[85] Ibid. D/D/B reg. 36, f. 252.
[86] Ibid. D/D/B reg. 38, f. 247.
[87] Ibid. ff. 249-50.
[88] Ibid. D/D/B reg. 39, ff. 29, 204v.
[89] Inf. from the Bursar, Selwyn Coll., Cambridge, who holds related papers dating from the mid 18th cent.
[90] Dioc. Dir.
[91] Valor Eccl. (Rec. Com.), i. 221.
[92] S.R.O., D/D/Vc 24.
[93] C. Hodgson, Queen Anne's Bounty (1864), p. ccxliii.
[94] Above, manors.
[95] Rep. Com. Eccl. Revenues, pp. 132-3.
[96] Valor Eccl. (Rec. Com.), i. 221.
[97] S.R.O., D/D/Rg 353.
[98] Ibid. transcripts file 3/2, no. 8; ibid. tithe award.
[99] Ibid. D/D/Rg 353.   [1] Ibid. tithe award.
[2] H.M.C. Wells, i. 386-7.   [3] S.R.S. xlix, pp. 85-6.
[4] S.R.O., D/D/Rg 353.
[5] Ibid. DD/X/BOU 6; inf. from the rector, the Revd. C. H. Townsend.   [6] S.R.S. xlix, p. 339.
[7] Som. Incumbents, ed. Weaver, 336; above, econ. hist.
[8] S. & D. N. & Q. xiv, p. 64; xv, p. 203.
[9] S.R.O., D/D/Ca 134.
[10] Som. Incumbents, ed. Weaver, 336.

was resident rector of East Quantoxhead;[11] John Tratt, his curate, was murdered by four parishioners in 1624.[12] John Jenkins, vicar from 1633, seems to have been undisturbed during the Interregnum, and was succeeded in 1664 by his son, then still an undergraduate.[13] There were resident curates in the 1670s and again between 1735 and 1782,[14] perhaps indicating that the vicars were non-resident.

In 1776 there were 17 communicants.[15] By 1815 William Newton, resident at Old Cleeve, was also serving as curate of Withycombe, and held one service in his own parish each Sunday, alternately morning and afternoon.[16] By 1840 two services were held each Sunday, but by 1843 one service was dropped on alternate Sundays.[17] A wet and stormy day reduced the congregation on Census Sunday 1851 to 283 in the morning and to 406 in the afternoon, including just over 50 Sunday-school children at each service.[18] A resident rector and a curate served the parish by 1870, and communion was celebrated monthly and on holy days.[19]

By 1886 a mission church and schoolroom had been built at Lower Roadwater; the church was later known as St. Luke's.[20] In 1909 another mission church, later dedicated to St. Mary, was built at Washford.[21] Both were in regular use in 1982.

There were seven lights in the parish church in 1346,[22] and an endowed light in 1548.[23] A church house belonging to the manor was rented by the parish in the early 17th century.[24] It stood at the entrance to the churchyard, and was later used as a poorhouse.[25] It was rebuilt in 1811 and was used as a school from then until 1855, and subsequently as a parish room.[26]

The church of ST. ANDREW, so dedicated by 1346,[27] overlooks the village of Old Cleeve. It comprises a chancel with north organ chamber and vestry, a nave with south transeptal chapel, south aisle, and south porch, and a west tower. Herringbone masonry and a break in the north wall suggest a smaller nave in the 12th century or earlier. The chancel was rebuilt in the 13th century when the south chapel was either added or altered.[28] The aisle and porch were built in the mid 15th century, and nave and aisle may have been extended westwards early in the 16th century. The tower was probably being built in 1533.[29] The chancel needed extensive repair in 1563.[30] Part of the roof remained thatched until 1765 or later. A singing loft was built by 1764.[31] The chancel was restored c.

1844[32] and the organ chamber added in 1885.[33]

There is a monument of c. 1425 in Beer stone to a civilian, his feet resting on a cat with a rat.[34] Medieval tiles surround the base of the 15th-century font, and two medieval bench ends are in the panelling behind the altar. The poor box is dated 1634, and the pebbled porch floor 1674. The brass candelabrum by Thomas Bayley of Bridgwater, given in 1770, was regarded in 1870 as 'unsightly' and was removed to the schoolroom.[35] New communion rails were put up in 1791.[36] There is glass by Morris and Co., Kempe, Sir Henry Holiday, and Comper,[37] a brass lectern of 1911 by Omar Ramsden and Alwyn Carr in the Arts and Crafts style, and a tower screen by local artists Rachel Reckitt and James Horrobin c. 1975.[38] The plate includes a chalice of 1573 by 'I.P.' and a paten of 1639.[39] There are six bells.[40] The registers date from 1661.[41]

The chapel at Leighland existed in 1320, when the vicar of Old Cleeve was charged to read the gospel and to administer holy water and bread there, and to celebrate mass there three times a year.[42] The vicar paid a chaplain to serve it in 1535.[43] A curate of Leighland was in the 1570s receiving £3 a year and his board,[44] presumably from the vicar of Old Cleeve against whom the inhabitants petitioned the bishop in 1668 because he was not paying the curate's stipend.[45] In 1733 the curacy was endowed by the patron and Queen Anne's Bounty to give a stipend of £30 a year.[46] By 1831 the benefice was worth £40 net,[47] and it was augmented in 1847 and 1867.[48] In 1865 the area of Leighland and Roadwater was created a district chapelry,[49] and the living came to be known as a vicarage. It was in the patronage of the rector of Old Cleeve.[50] In 1870 services were said to be maintained largely by voluntary subscriptions,[51] and in 1905 the living was worth only £94.[52] It was increased in 1905–6 partly by a bequest of £500 by Camilla, Lady Somers (d. 1904), daughter of William Newton, formerly vicar of Old Cleeve.[53] There were further augmentations in 1926–8, producing a net income of £290 by 1931.[54] In 1955 the united benefice of Leighland and Treborough, formed in 1950, became part of a united benefice with Old Cleeve.[55]

The chapel was regarded in 1548 as a chantry, and a small house and some land belonging to it were sold,[56] but by 1554 a group of inhabitants of Leighland had acquired what was then called the church house, to be used for the profit of the chapel or of the

---

[11] S.R.O., D/D/Cd 81, case of E. Quantoxhead rectory ho. 1635.
[12] A. L. Humphreys, *Fragments Illustrating Local History*; *Som. Co. Herald*, 16 Feb. 1924.
[13] S.R.O., D/D/Rr 317; *Som. Protestation Returns*, ed. Howard and Stoate, 166; *Alum. Oxon. 1500–1714*.
[14] S.R.O., D/P/cle.o 2/1/1–2.
[15] Ibid. D/D/Vc 88.
[16] Ibid. D/D/B returns, 1815.
[17] Ibid. D/D/V returns, 1840, 1843.
[18] P.R.O., HO 129/303/3/4/4.
[19] S.R.O., D/D/V returns, 1870.
[20] O.S. Map 6″, Som. XLVII. NE. (1886 edn.); local inf.
[21] Photographs in ch.; local inf.
[22] *S.R.S.* xlviii, pp. 103–4.
[23] *S.R.S.* ii. 47; *Cal. Pat.* 1548–9, 287.
[24] S.R.O., D/P/lei 4/1/1; D/P/cle.o 5/1/2.
[25] Ibid. DD/X/BOU 1–6, 8; above, local govt.
[26] Inscr. on building; below, education.
[27] *S.R.S.* xlviii, pp. 103–4.
[28] Taunton Castle, Braikenridge Colln., water colour 1845.
[29] *Wells Wills*, ed. Weaver, 77.
[30] *Cal. Pat.* 1560–3, 507; 1563–6, p. 238.
[31] S.R.O., D/P/cle.o 4/1/1.
[32] Ibid. DD/X/VZ, sale cat., 1848.   [33] Inscr. in ch.
[34] *Proc. Som. Arch. Soc.* lxviii. 56.
[35] S.R.O., D/D/V returns, 1870.
[36] Ibid. D/P/cle.o 4/1/1.
[37] Pevsner, *South and West Som.* 267.
[38] Local inf.
[39] *Proc. Som. Arch. Soc.* xlv. 170–1.
[40] S.R.O., DD/SAS CH 16.
[41] Ibid. D/P/cle.o 2/1/1–12.   [42] *S.R.S.* i. 185–6.
[43] *Valor Eccl.* (Rec. Com.), i. 221.
[44] *S. & D. N. & Q.* xiv. 64.
[45] S.R.O., D/P/lei 4/1/2.
[46] Ibid. transcripts file 3/2, no. 8.
[47] *Rep. Com. Eccl. Revenues*, pp. 142–3.
[48] *Livings Augmented by Queen Anne's Bounty*, H.C.122 (1867), liv.
[49] *Lond. Gaz.* 4 Apr. 1865, p. 1877.
[50] *Clergy List* (1869).
[51] S.R.O., D/D/V returns, 1870.
[52] Ibid. D/P/lei 3/3/1.
[53] Ibid.; *Complete Peerage*, xii (1), 35.
[54] S.R.O., D/P/lei 3/3/1.
[55] *Dioc. Dir.*   [56] *S.R.S.* ii. 47.

inhabitants. The house was let subject to its use as a church house for a month each year,[57] and in 1637 it was provided that the tenant be given good notice of the public use of the lower hall, buttery, and chamber above.[58] The 'chapel chamber' continued to provide an income for the chapel wardens, and was rebuilt in 1683–4.[59] In 1847 it was 'dilapidated and decayed'; it was rebuilt and extended in 1877 by C. E. Giles and Robinson of London as a vicarage house.[60] About 1955 it became a private house.[61]

Curates from the mid 16th century were not resident,[62] and one was excommunicated for serving without a licence.[63] Robert Evans, vicar of Old Cleeve, in 1601 accused of failing to serve the cure, denounced the inhabitants from the pulpit, referring to Leighland as a place 'where an idol hath been'.[64] In 1776 there were said to be c. 20 communicants.[65] In 1827 there was a service each Sunday, alternately morning and afternoon.[66] From 1847 until 1856 the living was held by the rector of Treborough, and in 1851 services were held in each place on alternate Sundays. On Census Sunday there were 153 people at the afternoon service at Leighland, but 80 was the average number attending.[67] From the late 1850s the incumbent also had care of Roadwater, where he lived.[68] In 1870 two services were held at Leighland each Sunday.[69]

The church of *ST. GILES*, succeeding to the dedication of the medieval chapel,[70] was built in 1861–2 by C. E. Giles.[71] It replaced a late-medieval single-cell building with a western bellcot and a large southern porch which had probably been a tower, its upper part converted to a gabled room perhaps in the 18th century.[72] The church of 1861–2 comprises a chancel with north vestry, and a nave with south porch and western bellcot in a plain geometrical style. Medieval tiles, probably from Cleeve Abbey, have been laid around the font. The chalice of 1670 replaced an older one, lost by 1664.[73] The bell, dated 1758, by Thomas Bayley was replaced by one from the redundant church of Bickenhall in 1981.[74] Entries relating to Leighland marriages and burials are found in the Old Cleeve parish registers until 1755, when separate registers begin. Baptism registers date from 1784.[75]

There was a chapel of *ST. MARY* 'by the sea' in 1320.[76] The building was damaged in 1398[77] and destroyed by a landslip in 1452. It was replaced by a chapel on a new site inland, consecrated, with a small burial ground, in 1455 and apparently rebuilt or extended c. 1466.[78] At the Dissolution the chapel was let to Anthony Busterd,[79] and was probably demolished by 1565.[80] The chapel, a focus of pilgrimage, public ceremony, probate business, and oath taking,[81] presumably contained the statue of the Virgin brought from the earlier site.[82] It had four bells.[83]

An iron church had been built for the workers at the Brendon Hill iron mines by 1861.[84] For a while it was served by a full-time minister.[85] On the closure of the mines in the 1880s it was re-erected in Watchet.[86]

The Community of the Glorious Ascension occupied a converted barn north-east of Old Cleeve village between 1969 and 1979.[87]

ROMAN CATHOLICISM. About 1624 Philip Powell or Morgan, later martyred at Tyburn, became chaplain to the Poyntz family at Leigh Barton. Powell left Leigh c. 1642, and was followed by a succession of priests, usually Benedictines, who regarded Leighland as the centre of a mission in West Somerset.[88] In 1627 Giles Poyntz built a chapel and an annexe for the priest behind his house.[89] Giles was one of a group of 8 recusants reported in 1642,[90] and 12 were presented in 1664.[91] Prudence Poyntz (d. 1691), Giles's second wife, leaving Leigh to her kinsman Robert Rowe, apparently required that Rowe should either maintain a chaplain in the house or pay him for an agreed number of masses. Should the family fail to keep a chaplain they were to pay £300 to the Benedictine province.[92] There were resident chaplains at Leigh until 1767,[93] but thereafter the chapel was used only occasionally. A priest celebrated monthly for five 'reputed papists' in 1776,[94] and a priest from Dunster was evidently visiting Leigh later in the century. A French émigré priest may have used the chapel c. 1808.[95]

PROTESTANT NONCONFORMITY. A room in the house of George Giles, probably at Linton,[96] was licensed in 1792 for use by a group of Methodists.[97] Meetings were transferred to the Green Dragon at Bilbrook in 1794,[98] and that house was licensed for worship in 1795.[99] Services were still held there in 1810. Preaching began at Washford in 1800,[1] and houses there were licensed in 1803, 1805, and 1806.[2]

[57] *Cat. Anct. D.* v, A 12519.
[58] S.R.O., transcripts file 3/2.   [59] Ibid. D/P/lei 4/1/2.
[60] S.R.O., transcripts file 3/2, no. 14; D/P/lei 3/4/2–5.
[61] Local inf.
[62] *S.R.S.* xxi. 105; S.R.O., D/P/lei 4/1/2; ibid. D/D/ subscription bk. 2, 3.
[63] S.R.O., D/D/Ca 57.   [64] Ibid. D/D/Cd 32.
[65] Ibid. D/D/Vc 88.   [66] Ibid. D/D/B returns, 1827.
[67] Ibid. D/P/lei 2/1/3; P.R.O., HO 129/313/3/4/5; cf. S.R.O., DD/X/BOU 11–14.
[68] *P.O. Dir. Som.* (1861).
[69] S.R.O., D/D/V returns, 1870.   [70] *S.R.S.* i. 185–6.
[71] S.R.O., D/P/lei 8/3/1.
[72] Plate facing p. 141; there was a tower in 1674: S.R.O., D/P/lei 4/1/2.
[73] S.R.O., D/P/lei 4/1/2; D/D/Ca 341/2: *Proc. Som. Som. Arch. Soc.* xlv. 167.   [74] Local inf.
[75] S.R.O., D/P/lei 2/1/1–3; D/P/cle.o 2/1/1–2.
[76] *S.R.S.* i. 186. The site is at O.S. Nat. Grid 041437.
[77] *Reg. Edmund Stafford*, ed. F. C. Hingeston-Randolph, 62; *Cal. Papal Reg.* v. 400.
[78] *S.R.S.* xlix, pp. 178–9, 251–2. The grant of a fair in 1466 was said to be for its rebuilding: *Cal. Pat.* 1461–7, 527.   [79] *L. & P. Hen. VIII*, xiii (1), p. 579.
[80] *Cal. Pat.* 1563–6, p. 238.
[81] S.R.O., DD/WO 62/2: *S.R.S.* xvi. 175; xxi. 14;

xxxiii, p. 103; liv, p. 189; *Cal. Pat.* 1461–7, 527; *Wells Wills*, ed. Weaver, 98; *Cal. Inq. p.m. Hen. VII*, i, p. 253.
[82] *S.R.S.* xliv, p. 178; *Cal. Pat.* 1461–7, 527.
[83] *V.C.H. Som.* ii. 116.
[84] Sellick, *W. Som. Mineral Rly.*, 58.
[85] S.R.O., D/P/lei 2/1/3.
[86] Below, St. Decumans, churches.
[87] Inf. from Brother Kenneth, C.G.A.
[88] *Downside Rev.* xii. 240–7.
[89] S.R.O., DD/V Wlr. 18.2: the date and the initials of Giles, his first wife Agnes, and perhaps his aunt Temperance.
[90] Maclean, *Family of Poyntz*, 274 and n.
[91] *Som. Protestation Returns*, ed. Howard and Stoate, 166, 294–5.   [92] S.R.O., D/D/Ca 341/2.
[93] *Downside Rev.* xii. 241–7; *Catholic Religion in Som.* (1826), 54 sqq.
[94] S.R.O., D/D/Vc 88.   [95] *Downside Rev.* xii. 248.
[96] Mr. Giles of Linton was a leading Methodist in 1800: W. Symons, *Early Methodism in W. Som.* [c. 1894], 6.
[97] S.R.O., D/D/Rm II, p. 126; cf. A. G. Pointon, *Methodists in W. Som.* (Minehead, 1982).
[98] Symons, *Early Methodism*, 6.
[99] S.R.O., D/D/Rm II, p. 158.
[1] Symons, *Early Methodism*, 8, 14.
[2] S.R.O., D/D/Rm, box 2.

A chapel was built in Lower Washford in 1811, and by 1814 the society had 21 members. A new chapel, in the part of St. Decumans parish that was transferred to Old Cleeve in 1882, was opened in 1826,[3] and was in use in 1982. On Census Sunday 1851 there were afternoon and evening services, with 184 attenders in the afternoon including 44 from the Sunday school and 117 in the evening. Average attendances were 195 in the morning, 250 in the afternoon, and 140 in the evening.[4] In 1903 there were two services on Sundays and evening meetings on Wednesdays and Fridays. Membership was 58 in 1923, 72 in 1943, and 42 in 1959.[5]

A house at Roadwater was used by a group of Methodists in 1812,[6] and in 1814 there were 16 members. A chapel was planned by Wesleyans in 1827,[7] but in the following year the idea was abandoned because of the presence of Bible Christians there.[8] Wesleyan services were discontinued in 1842.[9] The Bible Christians built a chapel near the Valiant Soldier inn in 1841.[10] Twice enlarged, it was replaced in 1907 but continued to be used as a schoolroom until the early 1930s.[11] There was a Sunday school of 32 on the morning of Census Sunday 1851, and 31 children joined the congregation of 122 in the afternoon. There were 100 people at the evening service. Average numbers were 140 for a morning service, 170 in the afternoon, and 100 in the evening.[12] Ebenezer chapel, Roadwater, built in 1907,[13] was in use in 1982.

Beulah chapel on Brendon Hill was opened by the Bible Christians to serve the Brendon iron workers in 1861 in succession to a preaching room nearby at Beverton in Huish Champflower parish. It fell into disrepair after the closure of the mines but was restored and reopened in 1910,[14] and regular services were held there in 1982. The Wesleyans used a loft over a stable at Sea View House on Brendon Hill while the mines were working.[15]

Afternoon open-air services were held by Wesleyans at Bilbrook from 1871 and a room was obtained in 1873. Weekday meetings were held in 1885 but services were discontinued in 1889. Cottage services were resumed two years later, but ceased to be held in 1914.[16]

EDUCATION. By 1730 there was a dame school in the parish, and by 1739 children were also being taught in the workhouse. Payments by the overseers for schooling continued until the 1750s or later and were resumed in the early 19th century.[17] From 1811 a school was held at the former church house, for a time conducted on Dr. Bell's system. The master also held a free Sunday school, but by 1818 the school,

'not answering as well as it used to do', was forsaken by children from the southern part of the parish in favour of the school at Nettlecombe.[18]

In 1835 it was one of four schools, one taking 14 infants only, the others a total of 85 children, all supported by parents' payments.[19] By 1847 66 children attended the church day school, and 112 children on Sundays. The school was then united with the National Society, and was principally supported by the vicar.[20] In 1855 a new school building was opened at Lower Washford to replace the small room at Old Cleeve. It continued in connexion with the National Society, and in 1903 there were 178 children on the books. The building was also used for evening continuation classes and for Sunday evening services during the winter.[21] The school, of voluntary controlled status, had 110 pupils in 1950, and pupils were then taken until the age of 13 years. From 1957 infants and juniors only were taken, and from 1971 it was a First School. In 1980 there were 56 pupils on the books.[22]

There was probably a school at Leighland by 1841.[23] By 1847 the day and Sunday schools had 44 children on the books, and were supported by subscriptions and school pence.[24] A free school at Leighland, established by 1861,[25] was probably new, but it seems not to have survived for long. A new school was built there in 1873 after the curate of Leighland had failed to establish one at Roadwater.[26] In 1903 it had 87 pupils, and was then partly supported by a voluntary rate.[27] Average attendance was 63 in 1930, but numbers thereafter fell rapidly. No children over 11 years were taken after 1950, and the school was closed in 1957, when there were only 11 children on the register.[28]

By 1861 a school was established in the iron church at Brendon Hill for the miners' children. It was supported at first by the mining company, but presumably ceased with the closure of the mines in 1883.[29]

In 1875 there were, in addition to the schools at Washford, Leighland, and Brendon Hill, an infants' school at Old Cleeve, perhaps housed in the old school buildings, and a Wesleyan school at Washford.[30] In 1877 a site at Roadwater was given for a National school. That site may have been the origin of the mission church there, for the school building was also to be used for services.[31] An infants' school was still held in the mission church in 1889, with average attendance of 35 children, but no later record of it has been found.[32] Evening continuation classes were held at Roadwater between 1909 and 1919.[33]

CHARITIES FOR THE POOR. Twenty-eight people, including Lady Radcliffe and John Syden-

[3] Symons, *Early Methodism*, 16, 47.
[4] P.R.O., HO 129/313/3/5/10.
[5] S.R.O., D/N/wsc 3/2/4.
[6] Ibid. D/D/Rm, box 2; cf. Symons, *Early Methodism*, 51.
[7] Symons, *Early Methodism*, 16, 51.
[8] S.R.O., D/N/wsc 3/2/2.
[9] Ibid.; Symons, *Early Methodism*, 52.
[10] P.R.O., HO 129/313/3/4/6.
[11] Pointon, *Methodists in W. Som.* 52; inf. from Dr. A. W. G. Court, Washford. For a drawing, L. H. Court, *Romance of a Country Circuit* (1921), facing 100.
[12] P.R.O., HO 129/313/3/4/6.
[13] Court, *Country Circuit*, 98.
[14] Sellick, *W. Som. Mineral Rly.* 58; Pointon, *Methodists in W. Som.* 46.

[15] Sellick, *W. Som. Mineral Rly.* 58.
[16] S.R.O., D/N/wsc 3/2/4-5, 3/2/9.
[17] Ibid. D/P/cle.o 13/2/1, 5.
[18] *Educ. of Poor Digest*, H.C. 224 (1819), ix (2); inscr. on building; S.R.O., DD/X/BOU 1-8.
[19] *Educ. Enq. Abstract*, H.C. 62 (1835), xlii.
[20] Nat. Soc. *Inquiry, 1846-7*, Som. 6-7.
[21] S.R.O., C/E 27; ibid. DD/EDS plans.
[22] Ibid. *Schs. Lists.*   [23] Ibid. D/P/lei 2/1/3.
[24] Nat. Soc. *Inquiry, 1846-7*, Som. 6-7.
[25] *P.O. Dir. Som.* (1861).
[26] S.R.O., DD/WO 37/15; ibid. C/E 17.
[27] Ibid. C/E 27.   [28] Ibid. *Schs. Lists.*
[29] Sellick, *W. Som. Mineral Rly.* 58.
[30] *P.O. Dir. Som.* (1875).   [31] S.R.O., DD/CCH 5/5.
[32] *Kelly's Dir. Som.* (1889).   [33] S.R.O., C/E 17.

ham, with gifts ranging between £1 and £40, were regarded as parish benefactors, having during the 16th and 17th centuries given sums which the parish retained as stock.[34] The only precisely known bequests were the interest on £8 given by Ellen Bickham (d. 1646) and her son Aldred (d. 1671), to buy two shifts for two poor women at Easter.[35] In addition Mary Whitlock (d. 1715) gave the interest on £10 to the second poor at Michaelmas.[36] Some of the capital of all the gifts was invested in land later known as the parish meadow, and the remainder was lent at interest, the income paid out as 'gift money' at Christmas and Easter. In 1730 nearly 40 people in the lower side of the parish shared £5 12s. 6d., and £1 16s. was paid to 13 at Leighland.[37] By 1760 holders

of capital were not paying interest regularly, but regular payments continued to be made by the overseers until 1796.[38] Increased rent from the land improved the charity's revenue, and in 1826 it was recommended that doles should be shared according to need, either in clothing or in cash.[39]

The charity was regulated in 1843 under the name of 'Sydenham *alias* various charities'. Trustees were then appointed to distribute cash in April or May each year. The total regular income was £16 16s. 6d. In 1896 £18 10s. was shared between parents whose children had attended regularly at school, 28 people over 60, 26 widows, and 19 couples over 60. In 1963 just over £26 was shared between 22 widows, 12 married couples, and 13 single people.[40]

CROWCOMBE

THE PARISH of Crowcombe lies on the south-west slope of the Quantocks. Shaped like a lozenge, it covers 1,324 ha. (3,271 a.)[41] and stretches from the Quantock ridgeway in the north-east to the upper reaches of the Doniford stream. The stream divides the parish from Stogumber and was variously described as the water of Trowbridge in 1243, Leigh water in 1498, and later simply as Water.[42] A stream similarly divides Crowcombe from Bicknoller in the north-west. On the south and south-east the boundary crosses the former common of Crowcombe Heathfield and follows a lane and a bank through Triscombe, the probable course of the Saxon 'herpath' to the Brendons.[43]

Crowcombe village, which once included a borough and a market, lies in the centre of the parish at the foot of a combe from which it takes its name. Above it the scarp of the Quantocks rises over Keuper marl on the lower slopes, giving way to the Hangman Grits of the higher ground, reaching 337 m. on Great Hill and 335 m. at Hurley and Fire beacons.[44] Below the village there are large areas of sandstone with outcrops of valley gravel. Heddon common, in the extreme north-west, lay on an area of pebble beds and lower marls.[45] Sandstone was quarried by 1513[46] and marl was used in the earlier 18th century for brickmaking.[47] Copper extraction was at least suggested in the 18th century.[48]

Three and possibly four Bronze Age barrows mark the course of the Quantock ridgeway,[49] but no direct evidence of prehistoric settlement has been found in the parish. Crowcombe village is a linear settlement

along a road known in the 18th century as Taunton street.[50] At a bend in the centre of the street stands the church, church house, market cross, and former manor house, and the southern section, known as Church Town, probably represents the earliest phase of settlement. The area north-west of the bend was known as the borough, and was probably laid out by the early 13th century.[51]

The settlement pattern of scattered farmsteads, known c. 1600 as villages,[52] may be traced from the later 13th century, but its origin may be much earlier. Water and Leigh (Layaa) are mentioned in 1267, Triscombe in 1278,[53] Hurley (Hyerlegh), Cooksley, Roebuck (Ralbock, Rabbock) by 1327,[54] Lawford in 1352, Slough in 1353, Flaxpool in 1355, Wharncliffe (Wormeclyve) in 1360, Combe in 1363, Poundisford (Pouresford) in 1365, Little Quantock in 1391, and Roebuck Gate (Mounselysrabbok) in 1415.[55] Quarkhill was established by the 15th century.[56] Only Cooksley and Combe have not survived. The farmsteads vary in size according to the amount of land allotted to each farm during the later 18th century, when most of the principal farmhouses were rebuilt.[57]

There were probably several sets of open arable fields, some of which survived into the 15th century.[58] Common pasture at Heddon, Crowcombe Heathfield, and on the Quantocks, occupying together about a third of the parish, survived until inclosure in 1780.[59] On the Quantocks parts remain open for the grazing of cattle and horses. Some of the scattered woodland was felled in the 18th century to build Crowcombe Court.[60] Plantations were made on the

[34] Ibid. D/P/lei 4/1/2 (1667). Lady Radcliffe was presumably the widow of Sir John Radcliffe, lord of the manor 1557–c. 1572.
[35] *15th Rep. Com. Char.* 440; *Som. Wills*, ed. Brown, iii. 88.
[36] M.I. in ch.
[37] S.R.O., D/P/cle.o 13/2/1; *15th Rep. Com. Char.* 440.
[38] S.R.O., D/P/cle.o 13/2/2, 4.
[39] *15th Rep. Com. Char.* 440.
[40] Char. Com. files.
[41] *Census*, 1971. This article was completed in 1977.
[42] *S.R.S.* xi, p. 307; S.R.O., DD/TB 12/1.
[43] O.S. Map 1/25,000, ST 13 (1962 edn.); S.R.O., Q/RDe 138.
[44] O.S. Map 1/50,000, sheet 181 (1974 edn.).
[45] Geol. Surv. Map 1", drift, sheet 295 (1956 edn.).
[46] S.R.O., DD/TB 12/1, containing a reference in 1513 to Quarry close.

[47] Ibid. DD/TB 13/1/1–3.
[48] Hants R.O., microfilm 86, no. 1430. A royalty of the 'seventh dish' to the lord was suggested: Dyfed R.O., D/CAR 86.
[49] *Proc. Som. Arch. Soc.* cxiii, suppl. 29; L. V. Grinsell, *Prehist. Sites in Quantock Country*, 12.
[50] S.R.O., DD/SAS PR 85, ct. roll 1767.
[51] Ibid. DD/TB 5/1; 6/8; 19 (hist. of Crowcombe); 55/24; Dugdale, *Mon.* iv. 225.
[52] S.R.O., DD/TB 12, survey c. 1600.
[53] *S.R.S.* xli. 131; S.R.O., DD/TB 19, abstr. of deeds.
[54] *S.R.S.* iii. 166.
[55] S.R.O., DD/TB 5/1, 12/1–2.
[56] Ibid. DD/TB 12/5; ibid. DD/V Wlr. 6.1.
[57] Ibid. DD/TB (C/1094), survey bk. 1796.
[58] Ibid. DD/TB 12/1.
[59] Ibid. DD/TB 19 (hist. of Crowcombe); ibid. Q/RDe 138.
[60] Ibid. DD/TB 13/1/1–3.

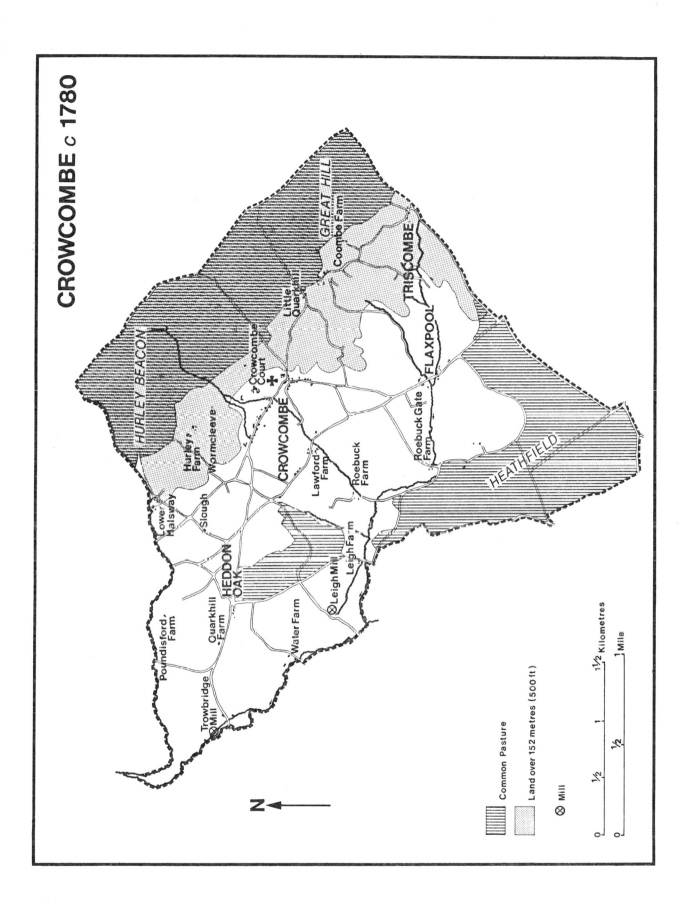

CROWCOMBE c 1780

HURLEY BEACON

GREAT HILL

Coombe Farm

Little Quarkhill

TRISCOMBE

Crowcombe Court

FLAXPOOL

Hurley Farm

Wormcleeve

CROWCOMBE

Roebuck Gate Farm

Lower Halsway

Slough

Lawford Farm

Roebuck Farm

HEATHFIELD

HEDDON OAK

Poundisford Farm

Quarkhill Farm

Water Farm

Leigh Mill

Leigh Farm

Trowbridge Mill

N

Common Pasture

Land over 152 metres (500 ft)

⊗ Mill

½   1   1½ Kilometres

0

0   ½   1 Mile

55

lower slopes of the Quantocks, particularly during the 19th century,[61] and there were 484 a. of woodland in 1802 and 403 a. in 1905.[62]

A chase between the lord's court and 'Cricktenes Hull' was mentioned in 1295.[63] A park called Carew Park, evidently by c. 1600 used merely as pasture, lay south-east of the village towards Flaxpool, near the manor fishponds.[64] Sir John Carew was licensed to create a park and warren in 1616.[65] The park created west of the new house in the 18th century was stocked with fallow deer until 1820.[66]

The ancient Quantock ridgeway and a parallel road running beneath the scarp linking several hillside settlements were the two principal routes in the parish. As late as the 19th century the ridgeway continued in use for carriages when parts of the lower route were waterlogged.[67] The main route through the village, turnpiked by the Minehead trust in 1807,[68] then formed the principal road between Taunton and Watchet. There was a secondary route in the valley further west through Lawford, part of which was adopted when the village was bypassed in 1929.[69] An elaborate network of lanes gave access to the mills on the western boundary, to the scattered farms, and to the commons. The railway from Taunton to Watchet, running through the valley in the west part of the parish, was opened in 1862. Two stations, Stogumber and Crowcombe or Crowcombe Heathfield, stand within the parish boundaries. The line was closed in 1971,[70] but was reopened by the private West Somerset Railway Co. in 1977.[71]

There was an innkeeper in the parish by 1620 and a victualler in 1681, and by 1736 two inns had been established.[72] The Lions or Three Lions, recorded in 1747, has been known as the Carew Arms since 1814.[73] The Railway inn at Stogumber station was open by 1894 and closed c. 1970.[74]

There was a bowling green in the parish in 1733.[75] The Stogumber and Crowcombe Benefit Society was mentioned from 1812 and the Crowcombe Friendly Society, probably founded in 1858, was disbanded c. 1911. The latter held its feast day on Whit Monday.[76] An 'old-established' men's institute and reading room occupied the church house in 1908.[77] The Kesteven recreation ground was given to the parish in 1919 by Mrs. E. M. Trollope in memory of her son Thomas Carew Trollope, Lord Kesteven (d. 1915).[78]

The population appears to have fallen sharply as a result of the Black Death in 1349.[79] The parish contained c. 70 houses in 1791 but had formerly been 'much more populous'.[80] The population rose from 575 in 1801 to 691 in 1831, declined to 573 in 1861, and rose to 594 in 1871. There followed the normal abrupt fall to 440 in 1881 and 374 in 1901. The recovery thereafter was only marginal: 433 in 1921 and 1931, 405 in 1951, and 434 in 1971.[81]

Thomas Griffith, formerly cook to George II and probably later employed at Crowcombe Court, died in the parish in 1776.[82]

MANORS. An estate at 'Cerawicombe', probably at Crowcombe, and described as of 6 hides, was held by Glastonbury Abbey in 854, when it was exempted by King Ethelwulf of the West Saxons from all secular dues as part of his second 'decimation'. In 904 ten *manentes* at 'Crawancombe' or Crowcombe held by the bishop of Winchester were granted to Edward the Elder in part exchange for the manor of Taunton, a transaction confirmed by King Edgar.[83] Thereafter the estate seems to have continued in the possession of the West Saxon kings, passing probably to Earl Godwin and, on his death in 1053, to his widow Gytha. In the same year she granted it to the church of Winchester, but the church lost it before 1086 when the manor had passed to Robert, count of Mortain (d. 1090).[84] His son William forfeited his lands in 1106 but the Crown did not regrant the overlordship of Crowcombe, and the manor was still described as of the fee of Mortain in 1428.[85]

In 1086 Crowcombe was held under the count of Mortain by Robert son of Ives, known as Robert the constable, the ancestor of the Beauchamp family. On the extinction of the Mortain holding the Beauchamps became tenants in chief, and the overlordship descended in the Beauchamp family like the manor of Stoke sub Hamdon.[86] After the death of Sir John de Beauchamp in 1361 the Biccombe half of the manor was assigned to his widow Alice (d. 1383) and the Studley half to his sister Cecily, widow of Roger Seymour.[87] Thereafter the overlordship passed to successive members of the Seymour family[88] and was last recorded in 1605, when Crowcombe was held of Sir Edward Seymour, earl of Hertford, as of his manor of Hatch Beauchamp.[89]

The terre tenant was possibly Wimond (I) of Crowcombe, who had died by 1130 leaving two daughters, the wives of Simon son of Robert and of Reynold Heirun. Simon and Reynold occur in 1158, and in 1166 Wimond (II) of Crowcombe and Reynold Heirun jointly held 1 fee in Somerset under Henry Lovell while Simon son of Robert held 1 fee under Robert de Beauchamp.[90] Wimond was still living in

[61] Ibid. tithe award; O.S. Map 6″, Som. XLVIII. SE. (1886 edn.).
[62] S.R.O., tithe award; statistics supplied by the then Bd. of Agric. 1905.
[63] S.R.O., DD/TB 5/1.
[64] Ibid. DD/TB 12, survey c. 1600; ibid. tithe award.
[65] *S. & D. N. & Q.* vi. 55.
[66] Inf. from Maj. T. F. Trollope-Bellew, Crowcombe.
[67] Local inf.   [68] 47 Geo. III, c. 27 (Local and Personal).
[69] Local inf.
[70] D. St. J. Thomas, *Regional Hist. of Railways of G.B.* i. 26.   [71] Local inf.
[72] S.R.O., DD/TB 6/11, bond 1620; DD/SAS PR 85; ibid. Q/RL; *S.R.S.* xxviii. 352.
[73] S.R.O., DD/TB 13/3, 53/9, 55/23.
[74] *Kelly's Dir. Som.* (1894); inf. from Maj. Trollope-Bellew.   [75] S.R.O., DD/TB 28, acct. 1733.
[76] Ibid. DD/TB 29, bond 1812; ibid. D/P/crow 23/3; ibid. C/E 23/3; M. Fuller, *West Country Friendly Socs.* 135.
[77] S.R.O., D/P/crow 8/3/1-3; Char. Com. files.
[78] Char. Com. files.
[79] *Cal. Inq. p.m.* ix, p. 142.
[80] Collinson, *Hist. Som.* iii. 513; *Som. Protestation Returns*, ed. Howard and Stoate, 155–6, 292.
[81] *V.C.H. Som.* ii. 351; *Census*, 1911–71.
[82] S.R.O., D/P/crow 2/1/2.
[83] H. P. R. Finberg, *Early Charters of Wessex*, pp. 122, 128, 144, 211.
[84] Ibid. p. 150; *Ann. Mon.* (Rolls Ser.), ii. 26; *V.C.H. Som.* i. 407, 474.
[85] Sanders, *Eng. Baronies*, 14; *Feud. Aids*, iv. 392.
[86] *V.C.H. Som.* iii. 238. Rob. (I) de Beauchamp fl. 1092–1113, Rob. (II) fl. 1150–81: Sanders, *Eng. Baronies*, 51.
[87] *V.C.H. Som.* iii. 238; *Cal. Inq. p.m.* xi, p. 25; *Cal. Close*, 1360–4, 449.   [88] *V.C.H. Som.* iv. 212.
[89] S.R.O., DD/TB 27, inquisition 1605.
[90] *Red Bk. Exch.* (Rolls Ser.), i. 234; Collinson, *Hist. Som.* iii. 515.

1184.[91] His estate possibly passed to Richard of Crowcombe[92] and thence to Godfrey of Crowcombe, recorded from 1208, who was lord of a manor of Crowcombe by 1227[93] and a prominent Crown servant.[94] Before his death by 1247, Godfrey granted what was later described as half the manor with the advowson to Studley Priory (Oxon.).[95]

The priory held the estate, known usually as the manor of *CROWCOMBE STUDLEY*, until its dissolution in 1539. In 1540 the Crown sold the manor to John Croke (d. 1554), controller of the hanaper.[96] Croke was succeeded by his son Sir John Croke, who conveyed it in 1598 to his sons, John and George.[97] A year later the sons jointly sold it to George, later Sir George, Kingsmill (d. 1606), justice of Common Pleas. From Sir George the manor seems to have passed in turn to his nephew Sir William Kingsmill (d. 1619) and the latter's son Sir Henry (d. 1624). Under Sir Henry's will the estate passed to his brother Sir Richard (d. 1663) subject to a lease of two thirds to his widow Bridget, the lease later causing financial difficulties.[98] Sir Richard Kingsmill was succeeded by Anne Kingsmill (d. 1682), widow of Sir Henry's son and heir Sir William, and then by her son Sir William (d. 1698).[99] William Kingsmill, son of the last and a lunatic, survived until 1766 when he was succeeded by his niece Elizabeth, wife of Capt. Robert Brice, R.N., who himself took the name of Kingsmill in 1766.[1] In 1789 Robert Kingsmill sold the manor to Sir Robert Bateson Harvey, Bt. (d. 1825), of Langley Park (Bucks.),[2] from whom it passed to his illegitimate son Robert Harvey (d. 1863), and then to Robert's son Sir Robert Bateson Harvey (d. 1887) and his grandson Sir Robert Greville Harvey. The last named sold the manor in 1894 to Ethel Mary Trollope of Crowcombe, owner of the other manor in the parish.[3]

That half of Crowcombe later known as the manor of *CROWCOMBE BICCOMBE* or *CROWCOMBE CAREW* was owned by Simon of Crowcombe in 1236. Simon of Crowcombe, probably Simon's son, may have died by 1280 and was succeeded by his son, also Simon (d. c. 1322).[4] The latter's eldest son Simon of Crowcombe died childless in 1349, when he was succeeded by his

niece Iseult.[5] By 1353 she had married John Biccombe (fl. 1363),[6] who was succeeded before 1390 by Robert Biccombe (d. c. 1401).[7] Robert's widow Emme seems to have married Thomas Wooth (d. 1407), and he held his first court at Crowcombe in 1401 and had the marriage of Robert's heir Richard Biccombe.[8] Hugh Biccombe, son of Richard, succeeded in 1457 and was himself followed in 1459 by his son Robert (d. 1523).[9] Robert's son Richard died in the same year as his father, leaving the estate subject to the life interests of two widows.[10] Hugh (d. 1568), son of Richard, left two daughters, and Crowcombe was allotted to Elizabeth, wife of Thomas Carew of Camerton, subject to the life tenancy of Hugh's widow, also Elizabeth.[11]

Thomas Carew, once suspected of complicity in the Babington plot,[12] died in 1604 and was followed in turn by his son Sir John (d. 1637), of Rifton in Stoodleigh (Devon), and Sir John's son Thomas (d. 1662).[13] John Carew, son of the last, died in 1684 and was succeeded first by his son Thomas and then by his brother, also Thomas, both of whom died in 1691. Thomas the elder was succeeded by his son Thomas (d. 1719) and by the son's son, also Thomas (d. 1766).[14] Thomas Carew was survived by two daughters, Mary (d. 1774) and Elizabeth (d. 1805), wife of James Bernard.[15] Bernard held the manor until his death in 1811, and was succeeded by Mary, daughter of his wife's first cousin, John Carew of Camerton.[16] Mary (d. 1852) married George Henry Warrington (d. 1842) of Pentrepant in Selattyn (Salop.), and Warrington took the additional name of Carew. He was followed by his son Thomas G. W. Carew (d. 1855) and his grandson G. H. W. Carew (d. 1874). The latter's son, E. G. Carew, died childless in 1886, and the estate passed to his sister Ethel Mary, wife of Robert Cranmer Trollope. On her death in 1934 Mrs. Trollope was succeeded in turn by her grandsons A. J. Trollope-Bellew (d. 1942) and Major T. F. Trollope-Bellew, lord of the manor in 1977.[17]

A manor house was mentioned in 1295.[18] By the mid 14th century the site, evidently immediately north or west of the church, included dovecots and a fishpond.[19] John Carew laid out a court and garden in 1676.[20] The house was pulled down in 1724 and

[91] *Pipe R.* 1177 (P.R.S. xxvi), 21; *Cal. Doc. France*, ed. Round, p. 180.   [92] *S.R.S.* viii. 149–50; extra ser. 86.
[93] *Rot. Chart.* (Rec. Com.), 176; *Cal. Chart R.* 1226–57, 54.
[94] *Rot. Litt. Claus.* (Rec. Com.), i. 627; *Cal. Pat.* 1225–32, 9; 1232–47, 2, 110; Dugdale, *Baronage*, i. 697.
[95] *S.R.S.* xxxv. 2; *Rot. Hund.* (Rec. Com.), ii. 125; Dugdale, *Mon.* iv. 255.
[96] *Valor Eccl.* (Rec. Com.), ii. 186; *L. & P. Hen. VIII*, xv, p. 115.
[97] Hants R.O., microfilm 86, no. 805; Burke, *Commoners*, i. 356–7.
[98] Bridget (d. c. 1672) was followed by her second son Daniel (d. 1679) and then by his sons Daniel and John. The remainder was assigned by Daniel and by John's daughter, Elizabeth Tazwell, to Sir Wm. Kingsmill in 1698: Hants R.O., microfilm 86, nos. 806, 808, 811–12, 814–20, 827–33, 1314; ibid. 90 M 72/PZ 20, pedigrees of Kingsmill; S.R.O., DD/SAS PR 85; *S.R.S.* lxvii, pp. 180–2; *London Visit. Pedigrees, 1664* (Harl. Soc. xcii), 134.
[99] S.R.O., DD/SAS PR 85; Hants R.O., microfilm 86, no. 815; ibid. 90 M 72/PZ 20.
[1] Hants R.O., microfilm 86, nos. 839, 846, 853, 856, 860, 876, 878, 884; ibid. 90 M 72/PZ 20; G.E.C. *Baronetage*, v. 331–2.
[2] Hants R.O., microfilm 86, no. 887; G.E.C. *Baronetage*, v. 426.
[3] S.R.O., DD/CH 9, abstr. of title; ibid. draft conveyance, 1894.

[4] *S.R.S.* xxxv. 2; xliv. 241; *S. & D. N. & Q.* vi. 159–61.
[5] *Cal. Close* 1279–88, 403; *Cal. Inq. p.m.* ix, p. 142; *S.R.S.* xxxv. 88, 93; *S. & D. N. & Q.* vi. 161–2; S.R.O., DD/TB 5/1.
[6] *Cal. Close*, 1360–4, 449; *S.R.S.* x, pp. 744–5; extra ser. 288; S.R.O., DD/TB 12/1, ct. rolls, 1353, 1363.
[7] S.R.O. DD/TB 5/1; *S.R.S.* extra ser. 289–90.
[8] *S.R.S.* extra ser. 290; xvi. 27–9.
[9] S.R.O., DD/TB 12/1, ct. roll, 1457; P.R.O., C 139/177, no. 44; C 1/29, no. 491.
[10] P.R.O., C 142/40, no. 49; C 142/81, no. 188.
[11] Ibid. C 142/150, no. 196; a son John was disinherited by a settlement made before his birth c. 1566.
[12] *Acts of P.C.* 1586–7, 275, 293, 337.
[13] S.R.O., DD/TB 57/42; P.R.O., CP 25(2)/345/5 Jas. I Trin. The date of Thomas's death, the succession after 1683, and two later dates (below) given in Burke, *Land. Gent.* (1952), 153 are incorrect.
[14] S.R.O., DD/TB 29, 57/52; M.I. of Thomas Carew (d. 1766) in Crowcombe ch.   [15] S.R.O., DD/TB 55/24.
[16] Ibid. DD/TB 57/52; Burke, *Land. Gent.* (1952), 153.
[17] Burke, *Land. Gent.* (1952), 153, where, however, the dates of death of T. G. W. and G. H. W. Carew are incorrect; inf. from Maj. Trollope-Bellew.
[18] S.R.O., DD/TB 5/1.
[19] Ibid. DD/TB 5/1, 19/2, 57/52; inf. from Maj. Trollope-Bellew.
[20] Dyfed R.O. D/CAR 157.

was replaced by the present Crowcombe Court.[21] During demolition bags of silver were discovered behind panelling in the hall.[22]

Crowcombe Court, so named by 1741,[23] was built on a new site c. 250 m. from the old house. It is of brick and has been described as the finest house of its date in the county south of Bath.[24] Thomas Parker of Gittisham (Devon) began the design and building, taking advantage of the sloping site by placing the house at the east end of a courtyard flanked by long two-storeyed service and stable ranges. Some apartments were habitable by 1725, and by 1727 the roof was on and 'most of the rooms within doors finished'.[25] Nathaniel Ireson of Wincanton was engaged as architect and builder in 1734 and, apart from some internal panelling and other furnishings, had completed the house by 1739.[26] Because of the slope the elevation is of four storeys on the west and three on the other sides. The extent to which Ireson rebuilt or enlarged Parker's house is not clear. The five bays of the front towards the courtyard probably represent the width of the earlier house, but the line of the front may have been moved westward by one bay to incorporate an open arcade which is linked to the service ranges by quadrants. The extra bay extends the otherwise symmetrical south front of seven bays, which has a projecting centre of three bays with an entrance approached by steps. At the west end of the elevation a short two-storeyed wing was built against the back of the south quadrant and partly disguises the end of the stable range.

The main rooms and the staircase were richly fitted out with plasterwork and chimneypieces, but the two drawing rooms on the east front were replanned and redecorated by Edward Barry c. 1870. Barry also provided new entrance steps and may have made other alterations to the south front, lowering the sills of some of the windows and possibly altering the heads of those flanking the entrance. The staircase and centre of the house were damaged by fire in 1963, but after occupation as a school in the 1970s[27] the house was being restored in 1981.

Thomas Carew, who sold six manors to pay for the house, and spent £4,122 on the work up to 1734,[28] also laid out ornamental and kitchen gardens south of the house[29] and extended the park, planting the woods on the hillside to the east. After 1766 James Bernard built a hot-house and removed the ornamental gardens to achieve a naturalistic 'modern style'. He also laid out walks in the woods and the combe north-east of the house, where he set up a succession of weirs across a stream, a rustic bridge (dated 1776), and a cruciform 'ruin', using medieval tracery and doors, traditionally said to have come from Halsway Manor in Stogumber but perhaps from the former Crowcombe manor house.[30]

BOROUGH. Part of the village, between the market cross and Townsend, north-west from the church, was described as a borough in the early 13th century.[31] No borough charter survives, but burgage holders owed rent rather than customary services.[32] The borough was attached to Crowcombe Studley manor by 1247.[33] A court called Crowcombe Burgus court met between 1633 and 1635[34] but there is no other evidence of a borough court. A portreeve was elected in the Crowcombe Biccombe manor court between 1363 and 1495 and in the Crowcombe Studley manor court in the 18th century. Burgage tenants were liable for repair of the market cross in 1724 and for providing a pillory and stocks up to 1730.[35] The borough was conveyed by name with Crowcombe Studley manor in 1894, and 'borough' and 'burgage' survive in field and tenement names.[36]

ECONOMIC HISTORY. The Domesday estate comprised 1 hide in demesne, with 3 ploughteams and 6 serfs, while the remaining 9 hides were farmed with 10 teams by 31 villeins and 10 bordars. Demesne stock included 26 beasts, 26 swine, 70 sheep, and 28 she-goats. There were 11 a. of meadow, 20 a. of woodland, and pasture 1 league long and ½ league broad.[37] Open-field arable survived until the early 15th century in parts of the parish, though the existence of the 'great field of Leigh' in 1352 may suggest separate sets of fields for some of the outlying farmstead hamlets.[38] An enclosure at Triscombe was still called after an earlier furlong in 1828.[39] By 1405 small plots of common on Quantock were ploughed, and by the 1430s parts of the commons at Heddon and Heathfield were similarly under cultivation, at Heathfield for growing rye. Land so ploughed was known as 'betelond'. Allotments of common were cultivated by 20 tenants in 1453, and 21 a. by 28 tenants in 1508.[40] It is not certain how long the practice continued, but early in the 18th century parts of the commons could be tilled on payment of a small rent.[41]

Common pasture on Quantock was subject in 1301 to annual renders of 12 slabs of iron to Stogursey Castle from as many tenants.[42] Parts of Heddon common were evidently inclosed for pasture by the early 16th century,[43] though the importance of the remainder for sheep grazing is clear from continuing disputes.[44] In the 14th and 15th centuries there were at least six areas of woodland.[45]

[21] S.R.O., DD/TB 24, letter from H. Sanford to Mrs. Carew, 6 Nov. 1725; DD/TB 29. A weather vane on the southern stable block bearing the initials of Thos. and Mary Carew is dated 1725.
[22] S.R.O., DD/TB 13/1; 29. One of the coins was dated 1662 and the money was supposed to have been hidden during Monmouth's rebellion: ibid. DD/TB 29.
[23] Ibid. DD/TB 14/5; below, plate facing p. 60.
[24] Pevsner, South and West Som. 142–3.
[25] S.R.O., DD/TB 29.
[26] Ibid. DD/TB 13/2; 18/11; 25; Proc. Som. Arch. Soc. lxxxiii. 43–4.
[27] Pevsner, South and West Som. 143.
[28] S.R.O., DD/TB 13/1.
[29] Painting of Crowcombe Court, c. 1740: Country Life, 22 Apr. 1933, 418; photograph in S.R.O., T/PH/so 2.
[30] S.R.O., DD/TB (C/1094), survey 1796; view in Collinson, Hist. Som. iii. opp. 516.

[31] S.R.O., DD/TB 19 (hist. of Crowcombe).
[32] Ibid. 26, leases 1596, 1637.
[33] Dugdale, Mon. iv. 255.
[34] Dyfed R.O., D/CAR 154.
[35] S.R.O., DD/SAS PR 85; ibid. DD/TB 12/1.
[36] Ibid. DD/CH 9, draft conveyance 1894.
[37] V.C.H. Som. i. 474.
[38] S.R.O., DD/TB 12/1–2, 19/2.
[39] Ibid. 10/6.
[40] Ibid. 12/1, ct. rolls.
[41] Ibid. DD/SAS PR 85.
[42] Ibid. DD/TB 5/1, deed 1522; Cal. Inq. p. m. iv, p. 341.
[43] Ibid. DD/TB 12/1.
[44] S.R.S. xxvii. 246–51.
[45] Leigh wood and Westwood, Haygrove and Hill wood, Watermans wood, Cookley wood, Stones wood, and Heddon wood: S.R.O., DD/TB 12/1, ct. rolls; ibid. tithe award; O.S. Map 6", Som. XLVIII. SE. (1886 edn.).

The existence of a borough, market, and fair by the 13th century indicates an attempt to expand the potential value of the estate.[46] Crowcombe Biccombe manor after 1247 was entirely rural.[47] By 1342 rents amounted to £8 15s. 3d., there were four free tenants, and the demesne farm comprised 2 carucates of arable, 20 a. of meadow, 20 a. of woodland, and 3 a. of moor.[48] The annual value had fallen to £3 2s. by 1349 and rents were only 5s. because 'the tenants were dead of the plague',[49] though there was partial recovery by 1352 when the income included cash from the sale of summer pasture at Leigh and elsewhere and from the sale of grain.[50] The four free tenants occupied farms on the parish boundary: Roebuck, Cooksley, Water, and 'Haynelond'. Roebuck was held by the Mansels possibly by 1342 and descended through the Orchards and Sydenhams to the Laceys of Hartrow.[51] Water was occupied by the Stradlings between 1462 and 1606, and 'Haynelond', north of Triscombe farm, was held by the Bretts from the 15th century.[52] Grimes farm, formerly Grimes Hays or Grimesland, was held by the Steyning family as a freehold of Crowcombe Studley manor from 1462 until the 17th century.[53] Customary tenants on Biccombe manor numbered at least 38 in 1414. Some tenants there were still described as neifs until 1360 or later. The demesne of Biccombe was being leased by 1479.[54]

By c. 1600 the demesne on Biccombe manor totalled 356 a. which were held in hand with the manor house. There were in addition 45 tenant holdings amounting to over 560 a., the largest being two at Roebuck.[55] Income from the estate rose from £20 in 1605 to £241 9s. 10d. in 1655, largely because the demesne was let.[56] Customary services and renders were still required of tenants: in 1614 one agreed to supply a man for a day's work on the demesne farm at three days' warning, to provide a fat capon at Christmas and a fat hen at the Purification, to replant three trees for every one felled for building and two for each cut for firewood, and not to take pheasant or partridge.[57] Similar covenants were required of another tenant in 1646.[58] In 1644 the lord was still receiving capons, hens, and geese from 26 tenants.[59]

Rack renting was evidently introduced on both manors in the later 17th century. By 1720 Biccombe manor had 35 tenants, and of the total rent of £536 William Shurt paid £169 for Leigh mills and the Barton.[60] By 1724 Crowcombe Studley comprised 832 a. shared among 69 tenements, the largest amounting to 47 a.[61] Holdings were gradually

combined thereafter, and by 1761 there were only 19 tenants.[62] The Biccombe estate had been allowed to run down,[63] and Thomas Carew had been gradually inclosing common pasture on the hillside above the village to form the park attached to his new house.[64] James Bernard's improvements to the estate involved the creation of new and larger leasehold farms and the inclosure of most of the commons in the west of the parish. At Roebuck seven tenements were combined and a new farmhouse was built, to create a holding of 120 a. in 1767. A new farmhouse was built at Hurley in 1777 around which a farm of 119 a. was formed in 1791. At Flaxpool several tenements were united with part of the manor farm and let; in 1793 a further farm was added to create a holding of 425 a., the largest in the parish. The farmhouse, newly built in 1789, was expensively altered in 1793 'by way of inducement for a good farmer from Norfolk to come down and settle here, in order to introduce the Norfolk and other good husbandry'. The farm was for a time called Norfolk farm. In contrast several small leaseholds still survived.[65]

The common at Heddon and Crowcombe Heathfield and part of that on Quantock, 600 a. in all, was inclosed in 1780 under an Act of 1776.[66] The soil there had been described some years earlier as 'very indifferent' for want of manure, but areas already then inclosed were 'good fertile land'.[67] Nearly half the inclosed land was in tillage in 1791 although the ground in general was 'capable of very considerable agricultural improvement'.[68] Part of Heddon common was planted with wood.[69]

By 1828 both main estates had been reorganized to give four large farms and a number of small holdings: Flaxpool, Water, Hurley, and Roebuck belonged to Crowcombe Biccombe, Little Quantock, Lawford, Quarkhill, and another farm at Flaxpool to Crowcombe Studley.[70] In 1842 the Biccombe estate was 1,418 a. and the Studley estate 1,382 a., the largest farms being Hurley (253 a.) and Little Quantock (335 a.). The only large freeholds were Heathfield (81 a.), created from former common, the glebe (63 a.), Slades (57 a.), and Brewers Water with Grimes (49 a.).[71]

In 1851 there were 12 farms of over 100 a., the two largest being Roebuck (340 a.) and Quantock (270 a.).[72] During the later 19th century there were minor changes in the size of some holdings[73] and a major change when the two manors were united in 1894 to create the Crowcombe Court estate.[74] In the same period the acreage under arable declined, from 1,190 a. in 1842 to 763 a. by 1905.[75] By 1976 over

---

[46] Above, borough; below, market and fair.
[47] *Cal. Close*, 1279–88, 403; S.R.O., DD/TB 19 (hist. of Crowcombe).
[48] *S.R.S.* xii. 212.
[49] S.R.O., DD/TB 19/2.
[50] Ibid. 12/2.
[51] Ibid. 12/1; DD/DR 8; *S.R.S.* xii. 212; lxvii, p. 33. It descended with Hartrow until the 19th century or later.
[52] S.R.O., DD/TB 5/2, 7/8, 12/1, 12/5.
[53] Ibid. 5/1, deed 1462; P.R.O., C 142/7, no. 18; *S.R.S.* lxvii, p. 149.
[54] S.R.O., DD/TB 12/1.   [55] Ibid. 12, survey.
[56] Ibid. 14/1.
[57] Ibid. 7/1.
[58] Ibid. 23, lease 1646.
[59] Ibid. 14/1.
[60] Ibid. 12/12.
[61] Ibid. bk. of maps, 1724; Hants R.O., microfilm 86, no. 930.

[62] Hants R.O., microfilm 86, no. 931.
[63] S.R.O., DD/TB 19, accts.
[64] *S.R.S.* xxvii. 246–51; S.R.O., DD/TB (C/1094), survey 1796.
[65] S.R.O., DD/TB (C/1094), survey 1796. The tenant of Norfolk fm. was George Legge of Wymondham, Norf.
[66] S.R.O., Q/RDe 138; 16 Geo. III, c. 73 (Priv. Act).
[67] Ibid. DD/TB 19 (hist. of Crowcombe).
[68] Collinson, *Hist. Som.* iii. 514; R. Locke, *Survey of Som.* 72.
[69] O.S. Map 6", Som. XLVIII. SE. (1886 edn.).
[70] S.R.O., DD/TB 10/6.
[71] Ibid. tithe award.
[72] P.R.O., HO 107/1920.
[73] *Kelly's Dir. Som.* (1883–1939).
[74] Inf. from Maj. Trollope-Bellew.
[75] S.R.O., tithe award; statistics supplied by the then Bd. of Agric. 1905.

84 per cent of the farmland was under grass.[76] Dairying increased sharply, with only 60 cows in 1828[77] and well over 1,000 in 1976. Among specialist holdings was a fruit farm at Quarkhill.[78]

The mid 14th-century fulling mill suggests early cloth manufacture, and tailors are found in the parish from 1615.[79] In 1617 a weaver founded a charity with money to be lent to clothiers and weavers of the parish, and Robert Pyke, clothier, was prosecuted in 1631 for not pressing his cloth.[80] Weavers, a dyer, and a woolcomber were working in the 17th century,[81] and a clothier was still renting the fulling mill in 1673.[82] The trade seems to have declined thereafter.

Bark from the woodlands supplied tanners in the 17th century, one of whom in 1676 leased the 40-a. Watermans wood.[83] In 1725 the bark of 500 oaks felled in the same wood for the building of Crowcombe Court was offered for sale.[84] A tanhouse at Leigh was mentioned in 1741 and a tanyard in 1809.[85] Tan House meadow survived as a field name south of Lawford in 1828, and in 1842 there was an extensive tanyard west of the village street behind the house called Timewell in 1977.[86]

A quarry had been opened by 1513.[87] A tenant of Biccombe manor in 1646 was required to do one day's work each year with a man and horse carrying tile-stones from the quarry[88] and limestone quarries at Lawford and Townsend Lane provided stone and lime for building Crowcombe Court in 1725. The bricks used for the Court were made in the parish, probably in the Brickfield, near the southern end of the village, by John and Richard Newick, brick-makers, and fired by furze cut in Crowcombe Heath-field.[89] In 1727 bricks were being fired in kilns thatched with reed and those surplus to Thomas Carew's needs were sold.[90] Carew allowed the rector clay to make bricks and gave him a kiln to rebuild part of the parsonage house in 1733.[91] A lease of the Roebuck lands in 1756 licensed the tenant to quarry stone for limeburning on the premises.[92] There were further quarries at Halsway, Little Quantock, and Triscombe, and the sites of limekilns are suggested by field names south-east of Trowbridge mill and at Lawford.[93]

Reference to other occupations include a glover in 1710, a staymaker in 1794, and a land surveyor, Charles Chilcott, practising from the parish between 1797 and 1837.[94] A horse breaker was recorded in 1836, a grocer and ironmonger had opened a shop by

1839, and there was a surgeon in 1843.[95] A veterinary surgeon was there in 1859, three resident hawkers in 1871, two road contractors and a coal dealer in 1897, and a cattle-food agent in 1914.[96]

MARKET AND FAIRS. In 1227 Godfrey of Crow-combe was granted the right to hold a weekly market on Fridays and an annual fair on the eve, day, and morrow of All Saints (31 October to 2 November). The day of the market was altered to Monday in 1230,[97] and the market and fair tolls were included in the grant of half the manor to Studley Priory before 1247.[98] They were nominally con-veyed with Crowcombe Studley manor in 1599, but both market and fair had then probably long been discontinued.[99]

Thomas Carew revived the market, probably in 1764, and provided stalls for butchers and bakers and tubs for corn and fruit free of charge. The con-cession was to continue for one year from 31 Octo-ber, the first day of the medieval fair. By 1767 the fair had been revived and another established on the first Friday in May, principally for the sale of cattle and drapery.[1] By 1791 the market had been 'dropped for many years' although the October fair then con-tinued.[2] A market house adjoining the Carew Arms was converted to a stable for the inn in 1799,[3] and no later reference to either fair or market has been traced.

The 14th-century cross at the south-eastern end of the borough may mark the site of the medieval market.

MILLS. Two mills were mentioned in 1342, and a water grist mill formed part of the Crowcombe Biccombe manor in 1349.[4] The latter was probably Leigh mill, leased from 1353 for the rent of one bushel of corn a week and to which the tenants owed suit of multure. The mill was ruinous in 1438–9 and the tenants had failed to scour the leat.[5] In 1641 the mill was held with a hopyard and a wood above the mill pond.[6] Manor leases by 1646 required tenants not only to grind corn and malt and make their 'pillcorn' at Leigh mill, but also to provide a man for between one and three days each year to repair the weirs and scour the leat, pond, and mill tail.[7] The miller complained in 1676 of the diversion of the mill stream as far away as Triscombe.[8] By 1745 the mill had three wheels.[9] In 1778 mill and mill house were burnt.[10] The property was rebuilt by a

[76] Min. of Agric., Fisheries, and Food, agric. returns 1976.
[77] S.R.O., DD/TB 10/6.
[78] Min. of Agric., Fisheries, and Food, agric. returns 1976.
[79] Below, mills; S.R.O., DD/TB 7/1; DD/TB 23, lease 1609.
[80] S.R.O., D/P/crow 17/1/1; S.R.S. xxiv. 165.
[81] S.R.O., DD/PLE 59, deed 1653; DD/TB 19, lease 1656; DD/SF 922, 3120; DD/SP, inventory 1664.
[82] Ibid. DD/TB 24, lease 1673.
[83] Ibid. 7/1, 7; DD/TB 23, lease 1606; DD/SF 1676.
[84] Ibid. DD/TB 13/1/1.
[85] Ibid. 32 (agreemt. 1809); 55/28.
[86] Ibid. 7/4, 10/6; ibid. tithe award.
[87] Ibid. DD/TB 12/1.
[88] Ibid. 26, lease 1646.
[89] Ibid. 13/1/1–3.
[90] Ibid. 29, receipts 1727–8.
[91] Ibid. 15/2.
[92] Ibid. 24, lease 1756.
[93] O.S. Map 6″, Som. XLVIII. SE. (1886 edn.); S.R.O., tithe award.
[94] S.R.O., D/P/crow 13/2/1; DD/TB 7/3–4.
[95] Ibid. D/P/crow 2/1/3; DD/CCH 8/2.
[96] Harrison, Harrod, & Co. Dir. Som. (1859); Kelly's Dir. Som. (1897–1914).
[97] Cal. Chart. R. 1226–57, 54, 117; Close R. 1227–31, 319.
[98] Dugdale, Mon. iv. 255.
[99] Hants R.O., microfilm 86, no. 806. Crowcombe is not in the list of Somerset market towns of 1742: Compleat Hist. of Som. (1742).
[1] S.R.O., DD/TB 11/9; Sherborne Mercury, 19 Nov. 1764; Bk. of Fairs (1767).
[2] Collinson, Hist. Som. iii. 514.
[3] S.R.O., DD/TB 54/16, endorsement on lease 1798.
[4] Ibid. 5/1; P.R.O., C 135/94, no. 1.
[5] S.R.O., DD/TB 12/1, ct. rolls.
[6] Ibid. 14/1, accts.
[7] Ibid. 7/1; 23, lease 1645/6.
[8] Ibid. 12/5.
[9] Dyfed R.O., D/CAR 90.
[10] S.R.O., DD/TB 55/23.

CROWCOMBE COURT FROM THE SOUTH-EAST

WEACOMBE HOUSE, WEST QUANTOXHEAD, FROM THE WEST

CLEEVE ABBEY, OLD CLEEVE: THE CLOISTER FROM THE NORTH-WEST

CROWCOMBE CHURCH HOUSE FROM THE SOUTH

Stogumber miller by 1780, and was renamed New mill.[11]

In 1803, as a precaution against invasion, the miller undertook to supply two sacks of flour a day in summer and four in winter, and to bake 120 quartern loaves daily.[12] A new miller in 1840 agreed to allow water to be taken to drive a threshing machine at Roebuck Farm.[13] The mill had apparently ceased to grind by 1875.[14] The mill house, leat, and pond survived in 1977, when the house was known as Leigh Mills Farm. The mill itself, an extension of the house to the north, had long been demolished.[15]

A fulling mill on Crowcombe Biccombe manor was leased in 1353. By c. 1423 it was ruinous. It apparently continued in use until c. 1720[16] but was not mentioned thereafter. It was described c. 1600 as at Leigh under Heddon, and field names indicate that it lay near the present Leigh Farm.[17]

There was a mill at Trowbridge near the northwest corner of the parish, in 1498–9.[18] A grist mill and malt mill called Trowbridge mills with a former dye house, converted to a kitchen, and 'fire house' were let in 1691. The mills formed part of Crowcombe Studley manor and the tenants of that estate owed suit of multure to them. The building of head weirs and sluices and failure to scour the leat were presented in the earlier 18th century, and a sluice at Water Farm prevented the mill from grinding between 1741 and 1742.[19] The mill was held with Quarkhill farm in 1897 and later with Kingswood mill in Stogumber.[20] After a fire c. 1914 had gutted the mill the upper part of the building was demolished[21] and in 1977 the remainder was used as a barn. The course of the leat can be traced, and apparently drove an overshot wheel.

Thomas Colford held a 'little' mill on Crowcombe Biccombe manor in 1414,[22] not afterwards recorded.

LOCAL GOVERNMENT. Apart from a plot of arable at Leigh, regarded as part of Whitley hundred in 1353,[23] the parish was evidently divided in the Middle Ages into two tithings corresponding to the two manors.[24] Crowcombe later constituted a single tithing within Williton hundred, the tithingman being chosen at both manor courts.[25] Godfrey of Crowcombe was said to have withdrawn suit from the hundred court and the gift of his manor to the prioress of Studley before 1247 was quit from suit of court to the county, sheriff's tourn, and hundred.[26] The Studley estate in 1276 was thus described as a 'free manor', with right to gallows and assize of

bread and of ale[27] and in 1327 was considered among the free manors. In 1370 Studley claimed the assize, the chattels of felons and fugitives, waifs and strays, and infangthief and outfangthief, although the Crown challenged those liberties.[28] In the 16th century the same estate claimed strays from all commons in the parish.[29]

A court book for Crowcombe Studley manor covers the period 1717–42. The court, described as court baron, sometimes with view of frankpledge, met usually once a year in October, and a constable, portreeve, and tithingman were elected annually.[30] The constable, mentioned from 1642, had responsibility for the repair of the pound, the stocks, and the armour of the parish.[31]

Court rolls and books for the manor of Crowcombe Biccombe survive in fairly complete series for the years 1350–66, 1400–26, 1451–85, 1494–1508, 1513–14, 1527,[32] 1606, 1648–55, and 1674–81,[33] and court papers for 1788–1839.[34] In the 14th century three courts were held each year, decreasing to two lawday courts usually held at Hockday and Michaelmas by the 15th century. Court business was largely concerned with dilapidated buildings and breaches of common rights and customs, particularly taking furze and felling trees, and scouring and maintaining watercourses. The courts appointed a hayward until the mid 17th century, a tithingman until 1832, and one portreeve, and occasionally two, between 1363 and 1495. The court was apparently still being held in the church house in 1876.[35]

There were generally two churchwardens and four, but by 1642 two, overseers of the poor. The overseers were again increased to four in number by 1742, after which the churchwardens sometimes served as additional overseers.[36] Waywardens were mentioned in 1689 and two were nominated during the period 1839–45.[37] An assistant overseer was appointed between 1820 and 1830.[38] The vestry issued badges to the poor in 1707, agreed in 1767 to prosecute the overseers if they relieved any pauper not wearing a badge,[39] and subsidized the emigration of poor families to Australia in 1849 and 1854.[40]

The former church house was used as a poorhouse by 1696 and two cottages at its southern end were later devoted to the same purpose; during the 18th and 19th centuries the ground floor housed paupers.[41] The parish joined Williton poor-law union in 1836, was part of Williton rural district from 1894, and since 1974 has been in West Somerset district.[42]

CHURCH. A rector of Crowcombe was mentioned

[11] Ibid. 7/3, 55/24.
[12] MS. in possession of Maj. Trollope-Bellew.
[13] S.R.O., DD/TB 7/4.
[14] P.O. Dir. Som. (1875).
[15] Local inf.
[16] S.R.O., DD/TB 7/1, 12/1, ct. rolls; DD/TB 12, survey c. 1600; 12/8 survey; DD/TB 24, lease 1673.
[17] Ibid. DD/TB 7/1; 12, survey c. 1600, bk. of maps, 1768.
[18] B.L. Royal MS. 14.B.VII.
[19] S.R.O., DD/SAS PR 85.
[20] Kelly's Dir. Som. (1897–1906).
[21] Local inf.
[22] S.R.O., DD/TB 12/1, rental 1414.
[23] Ibid. 12/1, ct. roll.
[24] S.R.S. iii. 166, 178; Subsidy of 1334, ed. R. E. Glasscock, 265.
[25] S.R.O., DD/TB 12/9, 23/3; DD/SAS PR 85.

[26] Dugdale, Mon. iv. 255.
[27] Rot. Hund. (Rec. Com.), ii. 120–1, 125; S.R.S. iii. 179.   [28] Cal. Close, 1369–74, 164.
[29] S.R.S. xxvii. 246–61.
[30] S.R.O., DD/SAS PR 85; Dyfed R.O., D/CAR 155.
[31] S.R.O., DD/TB 21/7; Som. Historical Studies (Bristol Univ. 1969), 36–50.
[32] S.R.O., DD/TB 12/1; 30, ct. rolls.
[33] Ibid. 12/5, 12/8; Dyfed R.O., D/CAR 156.
[34] S.R.O., DD/TB 9/1.
[35] Ibid. 23/3; Dyfed R.O., D/CAR 156.
[36] S.R.O., D/P/crow 13/2/1–4.
[37] Ibid. 9/1/2, 13/2/1.
[38] Ibid. 9/1/1–2.
[39] Ibid. 13/2/1, 3.
[40] Ibid. 2/9/1.
[41] Ibid. 13/2/1–4.
[42] Youngs, Local Admin. Units, i. 673, 675–6.

in 1226.[43] Godfrey of Crowcombe granted the advowson of the rectory in or before 1247 with his half of the manor to Studley Priory.[44] After the Dissolution the patronage descended with the manor of Crowcombe Studley, though the presentation was rarely made by its owners.[45] Parliamentary commissioners appointed a rector in 1645.[46] At least one turn was granted to John Farthing, rector 1672–97, and in 1707 two turns were given to John's son Samuel, rector 1700–32. Samuel's son-in-law Henry Lockett, rector 1732–91, surrendered the second turn in 1773.[47] The lord of the manor presented twice in 1779 and in 1806 Thomas Galley presented his own son.[48] The advowson was not sold to the Carews with Crowcombe Studley manor in 1894, and by 1901 had been conveyed to Mrs. E. M. Young of Crowcombe House, who presented her son H. C. Young in that year. Young succeeded his mother and on his death in 1943 he was followed by his brother and sister, Dr. B. Michell Young and Miss L. Young, as joint patrons. They held the advowson until c. 1949 when it was transferred to the bishop of Bath and Wells.[49] The living was held with Bicknoller from 1975, and both livings were united with Sampford Brett in 1978. The patronage of the united benefice is exercised jointly by the bishop and the vicar of Stogumber.[50]

The church was valued at £10 13s. 4d. in 1291.[51] In 1535 it was assessed at £33 5s. 8½d., but in 1576 it was said to be worth £60 though the patron was apparently holding the benefice at farm and paying the rector £22 a year.[52] The living was valued at £100 c. 1668 and in the mid 18th century at over £150.[53] In 1815 the income was given as 'over £150' and between 1861 and 1883 as £450.[54]

The tithes of corn with oblations and obventions were worth 53s. 4d. in 1341.[55] By 1535 predial tithes produced £16 12s. 10d., tithes of wool and lambs £8 0s. 4d., and personal tithes and oblations £6 12s. 6½d.[56] In the mid 17th century claims were made to mortuaries and to moduses of 4d. an acre on ancient meadow and 1d. in the shilling on rents paid by 'foreigners'.[57] Tithes were farmed by the early 18th century, but disputes c. 1760 followed the rector's attempt to collect them for his own use.[58] In 1826 the tithes were worth £275 net and included customary payments on stock. They were commuted in 1842 to a rent charge of £358 10s.[59]

The glebe was valued at 40s. in 1341 and 1535,[60] and there were 30½ a. by 1606.[61] Allotments of

nearly 36 a. at Crowcombe Heathfield in lieu of common pasture made a total of 63 a. in 1842.[62] Sales in the 1930s had reduced the total to 45 a. by 1940.[63]

A parsonage house was mentioned in 1385.[64] In the early 17th century it comprised entry, hall, parlour, kitchen, buttery, and cellar or inner buttery, with six rooms above, together with farm buildings, some of which were described as lying 'at both ends' of the house.[65] The south front was rebuilt in brick in 1733, evidently after a fire. The house was extended, refitted, and reroofed in the 18th and 19th centuries[66] but retains a medieval hall of three bays and the remains of an arch-braced roof. It was sold in 1976[67] and has since been known as the Old Rectory.

Geoffrey Lavington, rector, was licensed to be absent to study in 1320 and his successor John de Shiplake, rector from 1326 until 1331 or later, was licensed to be absent in Hugh Audley's service.[68] John Caam had licence to let his church to farm in order to study at Oxford in 1335 and James de Molton was granted a papal licence to hold the prebend of Howden (Yorks. E. R.) with the rectory in 1343.[69] William Tybard, rector 1459–70, held the living while president of Magdalen College, Oxford, and occupying two other benefices.[70] John Baker, rector 1513–20, was also canon of Salisbury and held at least three other livings while rector.[71] In 1523 Crowcombe was the first living to be given to Richard Pates, later bishop of Worcester.[72] In 1577 it was claimed that the rectors had not resided for 30 years.[73] Robert Kingman, rector 1641–5, and also rector of High Ham, was deprived of Crowcombe by the parliamentary commissioners in favour of Henry James, rector 1645–73, who had suffered financially as vicar of Kingston St. Mary because of the sieges of Taunton.[74] Henry Lockett, rector 1732–91, was also rector of Clatworthy and prebendary of Wells. He acted as unpaid bailiff for his friend, Thomas Carew of Crowcombe Court, until 1755 when they quarrelled over the conduct of Carew's steward. Their petty disagreements, continuing until Carew's death in 1766, involved most facets of parochial life, including tithes, charities, and school.[75] Charles Galley, rector 1806–21, was non-resident because of his wife's illness.[76] Under Daniel Campbell, rector 1827–53, the living was sequestered for debt, and in 1828 the patron, Robert Harvey, apologized to G. H. W. Carew for 'having introduced such an

[43] Forde Abbey, cart., p. 367.
[44] Dugdale, *Mon.* iv. 255.
[45] *Som. Incumbents*, ed. Weaver, 348.
[46] S.R.O., D/P/crow 2/1/1.
[47] Ibid. D/D/B reg. 24, ff. 12, 19; reg. 26, f. 12; Hants R.O., microfilm 86, nos. 809–10.
[48] S.R.O., D/D/B reg. 32, ff. 26, 29; reg. 33, f. 26.
[49] *Kelly's Dir. Som.* (1902–39); *Dioc. Dir.*
[50] *Dioc. Dir.*
[51] *Tax. Eccl.* (Rec. Com.), 198.
[52] *Valor Eccl.* (Rec. Com.), i. 216; S.R.O., D/D/Ca 57.
[53] S.R.O., D/D/Vc 24; DD/TB 19 (hist. of Crowcombe).
[54] Ibid. D/D/B returns 1815; *P.O. Dir. Som.* (1861–75); *Kelly's Dir. Som.* (1883).
[55] P.R.O., E 179/169/14.
[56] *Valor Eccl.* (Rec. Com.), i. 216.
[57] P.R.O., E 134/1657 Mich./13; E 134/18 Chas. II Mich./12; S.R.O., DD/TB 26, draft petn. 1668.
[58] S.R.O., DD/TB 15/2–4.
[59] Ibid. DD/TB 11/3; ibid. tithe award.

[60] P.R.O., E 179/169/14; *Valor Eccl.* (Rec. Com.), i. 216.
[61] S.R.O., D/D/Rg 266.
[62] Ibid. DD/TB 11/3; ibid. tithe award.
[63] *P.O. Dir. Som.* (1861–75); *Kelly's Dir. Som.* (1883–1931); S.R.O., D/P/crow 3/4/1.
[64] S.R.O., DD/TB 5/1, grant 1385.
[65] Ibid. D/D/Rg 266.
[66] Ibid. DD/TB 15/2; ibid. DD/V Wlr. 6.2.
[67] Inf. from Maj. Trollope-Bellew; S.R.O., D/P/crow 23/5/6.
[68] *S.R.S.* i. 251, 305; ix, pp. 62, 91.
[69] *S.R.S.* ix, pp. 250, 297, 416; *Cal. Papal Reg.* iii. 96; *Cal. Papal Pets.* i. 21, 30.
[70] Emden, *Biog. Reg. Univ. Oxon.* iii. 1874–5.
[71] Ibid. i. 94.
[72] Ibid. 1501–40, 435–6.
[73] S.R.O., D/D/Ca 57.
[74] Ibid. D/P/crow 2/1/1; DD/TB 26, draft petn. 1668.
[75] Ibid. DD/TB 15/2–4.
[76] Ibid. D/P/crow 1/6/1–2; D/D/B returns 1815; *Alum. Oxon. 1715–1886.*

unpleasant rector among you'.[77] Edwin Hotham, rector 1853–75 and related to Harvey, was non-resident because of sickness from 1864 until 1869.[78]

Chaplains were serving the parish in 1450 and 1468, and there was a curate and a stipendiary in 1532.[79] There were two guild lights in 1530 and in 1534 there was a brotherhood attached to the church.[80] In 1577 the church lacked a bible of the 'largest volume' and quarterly sermons.[81] During the 18th century communion was celebrated three or four times a year.[82] By the early 19th century services were held twice on Sundays, and there were sermons at each by 1840.[83] The dilapidated state of the chancel had been twice presented by 1843 but no repairs could be undertaken while the rectory was under sequestration.[84] The living was still under sequestration in 1851. In that year 164 people attended morning service and 227 were present in the afternoon.[85] By 1870 there were monthly celebrations of communion.[86]

Hugh Biccombe and the prioress of Studley were supposedly the founders of a charity which included the later church house, and which may therefore have existed by 1459 when Hugh died.[87] A house and garden opposite the churchyard, jointly held by the lords of the two manors, were granted to a group of parishioners in 1514, and a condition was made in 1515 that the house should be rebuilt within four years.[88] The new building, known as the parish or church house, was sublet between 1657 and 1669 and was later used as a poorhouse and a school.[89] In 1908 the first floor became a parish room and the ground floor a men's institute and reading room. The property was requisitioned for an army canteen between 1940 and 1944, but by 1977 the whole building was used as a parish hall.[90] The building, of local red sandstone, retains evidence of its original use in the separate entrances on the ground floor for the brewery and bakery and the external stair giving access to the first floor hall.

Simon of Crowcombe, perhaps a relation of the lord of the manor, was licensed in 1344 to have divine service celebrated in his oratory at Leigh.[91]

The church of the *HOLY GHOST*, in local red sandstone with grey stone dressings, stands in the centre of the village, beside a former entrance to Crowcombe Court. The dedication, recorded in the 18th century, was alternatively given as the Holy Trinity in 1861 and the Holy Cross in 1869.[92] The building comprises chancel with south chapel, nave with north chapel, south aisle, and south porch, and a west tower. The tower with its former spire was built in the 14th century, but the remainder, with the exception of the north chapel and the 14th-

century north wall, probably belongs to the early 16th century and includes a sumptuous south aisle and fan-vaulted porch. Bench ends with folk carvings, Renaissance details, and the arms of Crowcombe, Biccombe, and Carew, include the date 1534, but were evidently added throughout the 16th century. The north chapel was built by Thomas Carew in 1655 as the manor pew above a family vault.[93] Lightning struck the church in 1725, severely damaging the 80-ft. spire, tower, and bells, the debris destroying the screen, rails, altar, and much of the glass. The present screen, rails, altar, and pulpit were made in 1729 by Thomas Parker, architect of Crowcombe Court.[94] The upper section of the former spire, placed on top of the tower until the 1950s, stands in the churchyard east of the church. A singing gallery was built by subscription in the tower arch in 1785 and removed in 1856.[95] The building was restored in 1869–70, when all the roofs were renewed following the designs of those restored after the storm of 1725.[96] The font is of early 16th-century date and carries carvings including figures probably of a prioress of Studley and a lord of Crowcombe Biccombe. A wrought iron chandelier by James Horrobin of Roadwater was given in 1974. Monuments to seven servants of the lords of Crowcombe Carew manor, 1730–1815, are set on the outside walls of the north chapel.

In the churchyard south of the church stands a 14th-century cross with a restored head and three figures identified as a bishop, St. John the Baptist, and a woman, possibly a prioress of Studley.[97]

The plate includes a paten of 1719, a large flagon of 1729, and a chalice and dish of 1734.[98] There are six bells including one of the second quarter of the 15th century perhaps by John Gosselin of Bristol and another of the period 1410–40 by Robert Norton of Exeter.[99] The parish registers date from 1641 but lack entries for the period 1642–53.[1]

NONCONFORMITY. Two ministers were teaching in the parish in 1669.[2] There were eight Anabaptists in 1776, and a Roman Catholic and his widow died in 1784 and 1785 respectively.[3] Private houses were registered for nonconformist worship in 1842, 1844, and 1845, the last two by the Baptist minister from Stogumber.[4] A small Baptist chapel or mission room was built in 1890 and stands in the village street at right angles to the road. It was closed in 1916, 'there being no nonconformists resident in Crowcombe'. In 1921 the Somerset Congregational Union bought a site for a chapel, but it was never built on and the land was sold in 1961.[5]

---

[77] S.R.O., D/P/crow 11/1/1; ibid. DD/TB 15/20.
[78] Ibid. D/P/crow 1/6/3–6.
[79] *S.R.S.* xlix, pp. 140, 399; lii, p. 28; S.R.O., D/D/Vc 20.
[80] *Wells Wills*, ed. Weaver, 66–7.
[81] S.R.O., D/D/Ca 57, 235.
[82] Ibid. D/P/crow 4/1/1–2.
[83] Ibid. D/D/B returns 1815, 1827; D/D/V returns 1840.
[84] Ibid. D/D/V returns 1843.
[85] P.R.O., HO 129/313/5/3/3.
[86] S.R.O., D/D/V returns 1870.
[87] *Char. Don.* H.C. 511 (1816), xvi.
[88] S.R.O., DD/TB 5/1; Dyfed R.O., D/CAR 13; above, plate facing p. 61.
[89] Above, local govt.; below, education.
[90] S.R.O., D/P/crow 8/3/1–3.

[91] *S.R.S.* x, p. 495.
[92] S.R.O., DD/TB 19 (hist. of Crowcombe); *P.O. Dir. Som.* (1861); *Proc. Som. Arch. Soc.* xv. 6.
[93] Inscription in ch.; S.R.O., DD/TB 19 (hist. of Crowcombe) states that it was built in 1652.
[94] *S. & D. N. & Q.* iii. 275; S.R.O., D/P/crow 4/1/1.
[95] S.R.O., D/P/crow 4/1/1; *Proc. Som. Arch. Soc.* liv. 59.
[96] *Proc. Som. Arch. Soc.* liv. 61; *P.O. Dir. Som.* (1875).
[97] *Proc. Som. Arch. Soc.* liv. 61.
[98] Ibid. xlvii. 163–5.
[99] S.R.O., DD/SAS CH 16/1.
[1] Ibid. D/P/crow 2/1/1.
[2] *Orig. Rec. Early Nonconf.* ed. G. L. Turner, i. 9.
[3] S.R.O., D/D/Vc 88; ibid. D/P/crow 2/1/1.
[4] Ibid. D/D/Rm, box 2; ibid. DD/X/HYA C/799.
[5] *Kelly's Dir. Som.* (1906); Char. Com. files.

EDUCATION. There was a schoolmaster in the parish before 1687.[6] From 1704 until 1758 the overseers paid the interest on £10 given by John Liddon to teach one or two poor children.[7] They were presumably sent to an existing school until the parish charity school was founded under the will of the Revd. Dr. Henry James (d. 1717), son of a former rector, who gave £100 to buy land.[8] The school was open in 1718 when it took 4 boys and 1 girl, the master receiving rent from land in Bishop's Lydeard.[9] A second endowment, originally made by Elizabeth Carew of Stoodleigh (Devon) by will proved in 1669 for the general benefit of the poor, was appropriated by Thomas Carew to support the school. Carew himself, who had been paying the schoolmaster since 1732[11] or earlier, in 1733 added a further endowment, and is said also to have appropriated the bread charity of William Gill.[12] In 1759 the school had 36 boys and 6 girls,[13] and Carew's endowment taught and clothed 15 boys and taught 4 other boys.[14]

By 1776 the school had 48 boys and girls of whom 15 boys were still clothed by Carew's charity.[15] The master, James Bowden, had in the 1750s and probably later also taken private pupils.[16] By 1787 the income from the James charity was being used to teach 12 girls, and the endowment continued to be so used until after 1835 when there were 21 girls, of whom a few were taught writing by the schoolmaster[17] and the rest taught to read and work by mistresses.[18]

By 1835 the parish had four day schools with a total of 97 pupils, and the James and Carew charities supported three, paying for 36 pupils.[19] A free Sunday school, supported by voluntary contributions and founded by 1825,[20] took 10 boys and 20 girls.[21] Two schools for girls continued to be supported by the James charity in the 1840s,[22] and in 1847 with a third dame school taught a total of 72 children; the Sunday school then had 49 children.[23] In 1851 there were 57 Sunday school children at morning and afternoon services at the parish church.[24] From 1854 the two charities supported the sole remaining school, continuing to clothe 15 boys and paying cash to the schoolmaster until 1882. The charities subsequently augmented school funds and in 1977 the income was spent on school prizes.[25]

In 1872 the day school was transferred from the upper floor of the church house to a new building on the southern edge of the village, and was thereafter linked with the National Society.[26] Average attendance was 75 in 1883 but fell to 55 in 1889. There were

69 children on the books in 1902 and numbers declined gradually to 49 in 1940. From 1951 children over 11 travelled to school in Williton. The number on the books fell to 37 in 1970 and from 1971 children left at the age of 9; there were 29 on the books in 1976.[27]

In 1789 John Tucker transferred his boarding school from Cannington to Crowcombe.[28] It may have occupied the cottage called Timewell and its neighbour, traditionally said to have been a private boarding school.

Brympton school, an independent boys' boarding school formerly at Brympton d'Evercy, occupied Crowcombe Court between 1974 and 1976.[29]

CHARITIES FOR THE POOR. In 1617 William Couch, a Crowcombe weaver, gave £60 to be lent out at interest to provide an income of 4d. a week each for four poor spinsters or widows.[30] By 1720 careless administration had reduced the income and from 1771 efforts were made to recover the capital. The overseers retrieved £50 and gave it to James Bernard, lord of Crowcombe Carew, who agreed to pay 4 per cent interest. The trust descended with the manor until 1833 when £50 was returned to the overseers and later deposited in a savings bank.[31] It has since been lost.

Elizabeth Carew of Stoodleigh (Devon) left £200 by will proved in 1669 for the benefit of the poor of Crowcombe. Land called Tuthill in Bishop's Lydeard was bought in 1673, the income to be divided between Stoodleigh and Crowcombe. By 1733 the Crowcombe income was converted to support a charity school for boys.[32]

William Gill of Flaxpool by will proved in 1725 left £2 to the overseers, the interest to be spent in buying bread for eight poor people at Easter.[33] For a time in the 1730s it was said to have been diverted for the charity school. Four widows received bread in 1938 but the charity has since been lost.[34]

Mary Anne Luxton, sister of T. G. W. Carew, by will proved in 1880 left £100, the interest to buy blankets for the six oldest deserving poor at Christmas. Elizabeth Carew (d. 1881) left c. £100 for the poor and Elizabeth Louisa Carew (d. 1887) left £100 to provide money or clothing for the six poorest parishioners. These charities have provided groceries, gifts, and a Christmas party but in 1977 were not distributed regularly.[35]

6 S.R.O., DD/X/SU.
7 Ibid. D/P/crow 13/2/1–2; *Char. Don.* H.C. 511 (1816), xvi.
8 *15th Rep. Com. Char.* p. 442, where, however, the identity of Dr. James is incorrect: *Alum. Oxon. 1500–1714; Alum. Cantab. to 1751.*
9 S.R.O., DD/CCH 61, accts. 1718–25.
10 Ibid. copy will.
11 Ibid. DD/TB 28. The master held a lease from Carew from 1728: ibid. DD/TB 7/2 and 24.
12 Ibid. DD/TB 29; *Char. Don.* H.C. 511 (1816), xvi.
13 S.R.O., DD/TB 29.
14 Ibid. 26.
15 Ibid. D/D/Vc 88.
16 Ibid. DD/TB 29, 32.
17 Ibid. DD/CCH 61; DD/TB 10/24; ibid. D/P/crow 18/3/1; *Educ. Enq. Abstract,* H.C. 62 (1835), xlii.
18 *15th Rep. Com. Char.* p. 442.
19 *Educ. Enq. Abstract,* H.C. 62 (1835), xlii.
20 *Ann. Rep. B. & W. Dioc. Assoc. S.P.C.K.* (1825–6).
21 *Educ. Enq. Abstract,* H.C. 62 (1835), xlii.
22 S.R.O., DD/CCH 8/1.
23 *Nat. Soc. Inquiry, 1846–7,* Som. 8–9.
24 P.R.O., HO 129/313/5/3/3.
25 S.R.O., DD/CCH 8/1–2; inf. from the Revd. J. Scammell, rector.
26 S.R.O., DD/CCH 61.
27 *Kelly's Dir. Som.* (1883, 1889); S.R.O., *Schs. Lists;* ibid. C/E 92; ibid. D/P/crow 23/5/6.
28 S.R.O., D/P/crow 23/2.
29 Brympton School, *Prospectus* (c. 1974); local inf.
30 S.R.O., D/P/crow 17/1/1.
31 Ibid. 4/1/1, 13/2/1–4, 23/2.
32 Ibid. DD/CCH 61; above, education.
33 S.R.O., D/P/crow 13/2/2, 23/2; *Taunton Archdeaconry Wills* (Brit. Rec. Soc. xlv), 211.
34 Above, education; S.R.O., D/P/crow 9/2/1.
35 Char. Com. files; inf. from the Revd. J. Scammell.

DODINGTON

THE ANCIENT parish of Dodington, probably so named after the Domesday occupier, Dodo,[36] lies on the north-eastern slope of the Quantocks west of Nether Stowey, almost entirely surrounded by detached parts of the parishes of Holford and Stringston. Irregular in shape, its north-west and south-east boundaries are marked by streams, its western by a road. The regularity of the boundaries on the Quantocks probably reflects the relatively modern formation of Dodington common, defined on the west by a pond called Wilmot's pool and on the south by a copse beneath Dowsborough hillfort. The ancient parish was estimated to be c. 585 a. in 1838.[37] Detached parts of Holford were added in 1884 and 1886 to give a total of 1,335 a. in 1891. The civil parish became part of the civil parish of Holford in 1933.[38]

From the northern boundary at Barnsworthy farm to the southern edge of Dowsborough copse 3 km. away, the land rises gradually at first from below 76 m. to 138 m. on the Bridgwater–Minehead road, and then steeply to c. 305 m. below Dowsborough. Most of the northern part is marl and gravel, though faulting at the foot of the scarp between the village and the main road revealed sandstone, slate, and limestone, which yielded copper ore in the 18th and 19th centuries. The higher land on the Quantocks to the south lies on Hangman Grits.[39]

Dodington village comprises the church, the former manor house known as Dodington Hall, and the former rectory house called Dodington House. It lies away from the Bridgwater–Minehead road, from which it is almost hidden by a spur of land. The growing use of the road from the late 17th century, confirmed by its adoption by the Minehead turnpike trust in 1765,[40] seems to have drawn settlement along the road near the Castle of Comfort inn and beside the Old Bowling Green; there were more houses there than in the village by 1791.[41] Barnsworthy Farm, mentioned in the late 13th century,[42] was probably always an isolated farmstead on the flatter land north of the village, beside the road linking Stringston with its land at Dowsborough.[43] Perry, probably the site of the Domesday mill, gave its name to a manor largely in Stogursey by the early 16th century, but the settlement there may have been shrinking by 1521[44] when several houses were reported to be ruinous.

There may have been open-field arable in the northern part of the parish, where a furlong was recorded c. 1200,[45] and a small piece of common pasture between Perry mill and Barnsworthy, called Furzegrove, survived until the mid 17th century or later.[46] Most of the common land lay on the Quantocks. Arable and grazing rights gave way to use only as a source of fuel by the mid 18th century, and from 1791 remaining common rights were bought out by the lord of the manor to increase the areas already used as coppice and plantation.[47] Inclosure and planting continued in the 19th century.[48] Duke's plantation and Sir Alick's plantation were named respectively after Richard Grenville (cr. duke of Buckingham and Chandos 1822) and Sir Alexander Fuller-Acland-Hood (d. 1892).[49] Some planting involved the diversion of roads across the commons.[50]

A victualler was licensed in 1689 and his family established the Castle of Comfort inn by 1713.[51] It continued as an inn until the 1880s,[52] but was thereafter known as the Castle Coffee Tavern, with refreshment rooms and later a post office. Between the two world wars it was a boarding house, and was sold as a guest house by Lord St. Audries in 1952.[53] In 1980 it was a private house.

The Dodington Rit was a festival held near the Castle of Comfort on the Sunday before Midsummer to find the first whortleberry of the season, when stalls were erected by the roadside.[54] The local name Walford's Gibbet records the site where the murderer John Walford was hanged at Dodington Green in 1789.[55]

There were 73 taxpayers in 1667.[56] The population of the parish was 71 in 1801, and rose to 113 in 1821, the last year of mining. After fluctuations in the 1830s and 1840s the total fell rapidly in the 1860s, though by 1881 it had recovered to 91. Thereafter there was a steady decline, but no separate figures for the ecclesiastical parish are available after 1911, when the total was 60. In 1931 the population of the civil parish was 74.[57]

Dodington gave its name to the family which held the manor from the 12th century or earlier and came to prominence in the 17th.[58]

MANOR. An estate known as Stawe, held in 1086 by Dodo in succession to Siwold, is identified as the later manor of *DODINGTON*.[59] The early name suggests a connexion with at least one of the other neighbouring estates called Stowey.[60] The name

[36] *V.C.H. Som.* i. 123. This article was completed in 1980.
[37] S.R.O., tithe award; ibid. Q/SR July 1788; San Marino (Calif.), Henry Huntington Libr., Stowe MSS., ST Map 107 (1765).
[38] *Census*, 1891; Youngs, *Local Admin. Units*, i. 424.
[39] Geol. Surv. Map 1″, drift, sheet 295 (1956 edn.); for mining, below.
[40] Below, Kilve, East Quantoxhead, introductions; 5 Geo. III, c. 93.
[41] Henry Huntington Libr., Stowe MSS., STT, box 20, manorial and local affairs, survey bk. 1713; ibid. ST Map 109 (1791); S.R.O., tithe award.
[42] N.R.A. list, Spencer-Bernard MS. R/4 (113).
[43] S.R.O., Q/SR July 1788.
[44] Below, local govt.; S.R.O., DD/AH 11/9, 11/10.
[45] Spencer-Bernard MS. R/1 (110).
[46] S.R.O., DD/AH 37/3, 37/12.
[47] Below, econ. hist.; Huntington Libr., Stowe MSS., ST Maps 106 (1764), 107 (1765), 108 (1784), 109 (1791).
[48] S.R.O., tithe award.
[49] W. L. Nichols, *The Quantocks and their Associations* (2nd edn. 1891), 50.   [50] S.R.O., Q/SR July 1788.
[51] Ibid. Q/RL; Huntington Libr., Stowe MSS., STT manorial and local affairs, box 20: survey bk. 1713.
[52] S.R.O., Q/RL; ibid. DD/AH 11/1, 37/15; Dyfed R.O., D/CAR 202; *P.O. Dir. Som.* (1875); *Kelly's Dir. Som.* (1883).
[53] *Kelly's Dir. Som.* (1889, 1902, 1914, 1919, 1939); S.R.O., DD/X/HUX 1.
[54] *Som. Co. Herald*, 18 Mar., 9 Apr. 1935.
[55] *S. & D. N. & Q.* xii. 17; *Western Flying Post*, 31 Aug. 1789.
[56] S.R.O., DD/WY 34.
[57] *V.C.H. Som.* ii. 351; *Kelly's Dir. Som.* (1921, 1935).
[58] Below, manor.
[59] *V.C.H. Som.* i. 523; *Proc. Som. Arch. Soc.* xcix and c. 43; *Domesday Bk. Som.* ed. C. and F. Thorn, 47.12.
[60] *Cal. Pat.* 1370–4, 193.

Dodington was used in the later 12th century when Henry II confirmed to Baldwin son of Harding 3 virgates of land which his father and his ancestors had held in Dodington of the order of St. John of Jerusalem.[61] The prior of the order of St. John was the overlord in 1444,[62] and the manor continued to be so held until the order was dissolved in 1540.[63] Thereafter Dodington was held as of the Hospitallers' former manor of Halse, in 1559 of William Hawley, and in 1620 of Sir Henry Hawley.[64]

Frodo of Preston, said to have been lord in Henry II's reign, may have held other land in the later parish. The terre tenant under him was Adam de Cunteville.[65] Adam's son William, succeeding to land at Dodington and Perry, became thereafter known as William of Dodington.[66] A Roger of Dodington was owner of land in Dodington in the late 12th century,[67] and was followed by another William.[68] By 1225 William had been succeeded by Roger of Dodington,[69] who was followed probably by his son William. Roger of Dodington, son of William and recorded in 1285–6,[70] was perhaps followed by Philip of Dodington.[71] Thomas of Dodington, son of Philip, is said to have died before 1361, and to have been followed by another Thomas.[72] A Thomas Dodington occurs in 1380 and survived until after 1415.[73] He was succeeded by his son John (d. 1444), and then by his grandson, also John.[74] A third John Dodington, married c. 1485,[75] may be the man who was knighted in 1505[76] and died in 1514.[77]

Sir John's son Richard (d. 1559) was followed by Richard's son John.[78] Under an agreement made in 1568 the manor passed on John's death in 1573 to his second son, George, who survived until 1620.[79] George's heir was his young grandson Francis Dodington, knighted by 1627, who for his ardent support of the royalist cause in the Civil War lost his estates in 1649.[80] The manor, with other family property, passed from the Treason Trustees to the Committee for Compounding, but in 1652 was formally conveyed to trustees for the benefit of John Dodington, Sir Francis's heir, himself a parliamentary sympathizer.[81] John was in control of the manor by 1653.[82] From 1660 the property was under a group of trustees led by Sir Richard Temple (d. 1697) of Stowe (Bucks.), John Dodington's brother-in-law.[83] John died c. 1673, and was succeeded by his son George.[84]

George Dodington, later of Eastbury (Dors.),[85] amassed a fortune in government service, but died childless in 1720, leaving as his heir his nephew, also George, son of his sister Alicia Bubb.[86] George Bubb, the politician and wit, who took the additional name Dodington in 1717, was created Lord Melcombe in 1761 and died without children in the following year.[87] Under his uncle's will his property, including Dodington, passed to Richard Grenville, Earl Temple, grandson of Sir Richard Temple and great-nephew of John Dodington. Richard, Earl Temple, was succeeded in 1779 by his nephew George Grenville (cr. marquess of Buckingham 1784) and in 1813 by George's son Richard, from 1822 duke of Buckingham and Chandos.[88] The duke sold the heavily mortgaged manor and adjoining properties to Sir Peregrine Fuller-Palmer-Acland in 1837.[89]

Sir Peregrine (d. 1871) was succeeded by his daughter Isabel (d. 1903), wife of Sir Alexander Fuller-Acland-Hood (d. 1892), and then by his grandson Alexander Acland-Hood (cr. Baron St. Audries 1911, d. 1917).[90] Alexander Peregrine, the 2nd baron, died in 1971, leaving as his heir his niece Elizabeth, later wife of Sir Michael D. I. Gass, K.C.M.G.,[91] lady of the manor in 1980.

The manor house, known in the 20th century as Dodington Hall, stands close beside the church. Although let as a farmhouse probably from the mid 17th century, much of the late medieval house is preserved, notably the open hall with a richly decorated roof, the archway into the oriel, and the plan of the screens passage and the parlour wing, where at least one of the beamed ceilings may be contemporary with the hall. Heraldic glass in the parlour wing dates from c. 1485.[92] Reconstruction took place in 1581, when the parlour wing was extended westward, the oriel was rebuilt to provide rooms on two floors, and most of the windows, including those in the hall, were renewed.[93] A large carved stone overmantel dated 1581 was put into the west wall of the hall. Alterations were made in the mid 18th century.[94] In the later 19th century the house was extensively restored, the service end to the east of the screen being completely rebuilt and extended. The mechanism of a water-driven spit is preserved in the cellar below the kitchen.

[61] S.R.S. xxv, pp. 184–5.
[62] P.R.O., C 139/113, no. 4.
[63] Knowles and Hadcock, Medieval Religious Houses (1971), 300.
[64] P.R.O. C 142/29, no. 8; C 142/119, no. 161; S.R.S. lxvii, p. 104.
[65] S.R.O., DD/AH 21/2: Thos. Palmer's hist., quoting a MS. owned by W. Simmonds of Bridgwater in 1712. Preston was Preston Bowyer in Milverton.
[66] S.R.O., DD/AH 21/2.
[67] S.R.S. xxv, p. 184; Spencer-Bernard MS. R/1 (110).
[68] S.R.O., DD/AH 21/2, quoting a charter then at Alfoxton.   [69] S.R.S. xi, p. 78.
[70] S.R.O., DD/AH 21/2, quoting an 'ancient charter'.
[71] Spencer-Bernard MS. R/4 (113). S.R.O., DD/AH 21/2 records Wm. son of Roger, 1306–17, and Philip 36 Edw. I to 1345.
[72] S.R.O., DD/AH 21/2, quoting an 'ancient charter'. Thomas Dodington occ. 1370: DD/AH 65/5.
[73] Spencer-Bernard MSS. R/5–7 (115, 119–20); S.R.O., DD/AH 37/1; Cal. Pat. 1385–9, 197.
[74] P.R.O., C 139/113, no. 4.
[75] S.R.O., DD/AH 21/2.
[76] Spencer-Bernard MSS. R/8–10 (125–7).
[77] P.R.O., C 142/29, no. 8.
[78] Ibid. C 142/119, no. 161.

[79] S.R.S. li, pp. 80–2; lxvii, p. 104; P.R.O., C 142/165, no. 162.
[80] P.R.O., CP 43/179, rot. 63; Cal. Cttee. for Compounding, i. 138–9.
[81] Cal. Cttee. for Compounding, iv. 2557; P.R.O., CP 25(2)/592/1652, Mich.; ibid. C 54/3681, no. 18.
[82] S.R.O., DD/AH 11/1.
[83] P.R.O., CP 25(2)/715/12 Chas. II Trin.
[84] Complete Peerage, viii, 640 n.; S.R.O., DD/AH 36/6–9; P.R.O., CP 25(2)/717/29 Chas. II Mich.   [85] D.N.B.
[86] S.R.O., DD/AH 11/2, copy will, where the sister's name is given as Alina. An abstr. of title (DD/AH 55/3) gives six sisters, including Alicia and Arabella, named in the will. Complete Peerage, viii. 640 names Mary as Dodington's only sister.
[87] Complete Peerage, viii. 640–1.
[88] Ibid. ii. 406–9; xii (1), 657–8; S.R.O., DD/AH 55/3.
[89] S.R.O., DD/AH 55/1.
[90] Burke, Peerage (1937), 2090–1.
[91] Who's Who (1980); local inf.
[92] C. Woodforde, Stained Glass in Som. (1946), 106. Glass now (1980) in the hall, dated from c. 1450, was in the chancel of the church until the 19th century: S.R.O., DD/AH 21/2; below, plate facing p. 93.
[93] Date on parlour window.
[94] S.R.O., DD/AH 11/5, plans.

ECONOMIC HISTORY. There were 3 plough-teams on the 3-virgate holding at Dodington in 1086. The demesne virgate had a team and there were 3 a. of meadow, 30 a. of pasture, and 3 a. of woodland. There were 3 serfs on the demesne, and 6 villeins and 2 bordars worked the rest of the land.[95] By the end of the 12th century open-field arable had evidently been established at Barnsworthy,[96] which was a tenant farm in the 13th century, and by 1380 included some manorial demesne.[97] By 1635 Barnsworthy's land extended into Stringston and amounted to some 60 a.,[98] though from 1654 the farm was divided.[99] It was reconstituted and extended early in the 18th century and by 1713 amounted to 163 a. The demesne farm at Dodington, occupied by successive lords of the manor until the mid 17th century, amounted to 158 a. in 1713. The two other main holdings in the manor in that year were Dodington Barton (223 a.) and Dyche farm (73 a.), both including land outside the parish. All were let at rack rents.[1]

Common rights in the parish included areas of pasture at Furzegrove, near Barnsworthy, and on the Quantocks, where the Barnsworthy tenant in 1654 could plough or graze cattle and cut heath and furze.[2] The tenant of Dodington farm in the 1750s could cut heath, furze, and fern for brewing and baking.[3] Wheat and barley seem to have been the principal crops in the late 17th century, with farmers owning only a few cows and sheep.[4] The parish, however, included a shop selling fabrics, haberdashery, tobacco, soap, candles, sugar, figs, and spice, the owner presumably taking advantage of the traffic on the developing route between Bridgwater and Minehead.[5] Farming covenants in the mid 18th century included the use of lime on all Bubb Dodington's property in the area and the stipulation that no more than 70 a. of Dodington farm were to be ploughed, half for wheat and peas, half for barley and oats.[6] There was already some consolidation of fields and holdings, and by 1774 Barnsworthy farm included part of the former Furzegrove common.[7]

Dodington (393 a.) and Barnsworthy (196 a.) farms were the two largest holdings on the marquess of Buckingham's estate by 1812, the latter 'greatly improved' by its first 'respectable' tenant.[8] Further improvements had already taken place on the Quantocks, where in 1791 Buckingham bought out the common rights of Durborough[9] and Dodington tenants, ex-cluding rights in existing woods and coppices[10] and the 'most distant' commons.[11] For some time before 1812 more than 100,000 trees were planted annually; in 1812 the whole of Buckingham's estate, including Holford commons, had 90 a. of coppice, 74 a. of forest trees, 106 a. of other plantations, and 40 a. in course of inclosure.[12] By 1838 nearly a fifth of the parish was under plantations. Arable land, amounting to 264 a., took nearly half the parish.[13]

Some reorganization of farms included the addition of land in Holford to Perry Mill farm in 1830.[14] By 1851 Dodington farm measured 350 a. and the tenant employed 25 labourers; Barnsworthy and Perry Mill farms were 205 a. and 135 a. respectively.[15] A gradual increase in the amount of grassland from the later 19th century continued in the 20th, accompanied by a contraction in population.

Mining for copper began in the parish before 1712,[16] and miners from Cornwall and Derbyshire were employed at various times in the early 18th century.[17] The lease of Dodington farm in 1755 reserved mining and quarrying on 'the downs' and elsewhere,[18] and an exploration lease of 1757 involved a copper-mine agent from Over Stowey and a Taunton tobacconist.[19] From the 1780s until 1802 ore was regularly mined and some was shipped through Combwich.[20] Work was abandoned by 1812 because the rector refused to come to terms for building a steam pumping engine on the glebe.[21] Miners were again employed regularly from 1817 under a scheme sponsored largely by Thomas Poole of Nether Stowey.[22] Work ceased in 1821 after heavy losses, though the prospect of success had been 'certain'.[23] Equipment was offered for sale in 1822, and the assay office, the counting house, and the house of the captain of the mines were among properties unsold in 1827.[24] The counting house and the remains of the engine house remained in 1980.

The mill on the estate in 1086[25] was probably at Perry where a fulling and a ruined grist mill stood in 1518.[26] A new fulling mill was built on a diversion of the mill stream before 1666.[27] By 1732 the property had been incorporated into Perry Mill Farm.[28]

LOCAL GOVERNMENT. Dodington and Halse, though widely separated geographically, formed a single tithing in 1569[29] and 1642,[30] presumably

[95] V.C.H. Som. i. 523.
[96] S.R.S. lxi, p. 3; Spencer-Bernard MSS. R/1, 4 (110, 113).
[97] Spencer-Bernard MSS. R/1, 4–5 (110, 113, 114); Cal. Inq. p.m. Hen. VII, p. 293.
[98] S.R.O., DD/AH 37/9, 66/2.
[99] Ibid. 37/12.
[1] Huntington Libr., Stowe MSS., STT box 20, survey.
[2] S.R.O., DD/AH 37/12.
[3] Ibid. 37/32.
[4] Ibid. DD/SP, inventories 1662, 1689.
[5] Ibid. inventory 1687.
[6] Ibid. DD/AH 37/12; cf. ibid. 37/22.
[7] Ibid. 37/12, 37/32. There is a survey of the whole estate for 1775 in Huntington Libr., Stowe MSS., STG box 49, and a map of 1764, ibid. Map 106.
[8] Huntington Libr., Stowe MSS., STG box 49, rental.
[9] Below, local govt.
[10] Huntington Libr., Stowe MSS., ST Maps 107 (1765) and 108 (1784). Coppices on the manor but in Over Stowey had been established by 1760: ibid. Stowe MSS., STT box 20.
[11] Huntington Libr., Stowe MSS., STG box 49, survey 1819; ibid. ST Map 109 (1791).
[12] Ibid. rental 1812.
[13] S.R.O., tithe award.
[14] Huntington Libr., Stowe MSS., STG box 50.
[15] P.R.O., HO 107/1920.
[16] S.R.O., D/P/b.lyd 13/3/3.
[17] J. Hamilton and J. F. Lawrence, Men and Mining on the Quantocks (1970), 29–31.
[18] S.R.O., DD/AH 37/22.
[19] Ibid. 37/3.
[20] Men and Mining on the Quantocks, 31–58.
[21] Huntington Libr., Stowe MSS., STG box 49, rental 1812.
[22] Men and Mining on the Quantocks, 31–58.
[23] Ibid. 58–68; S.R.O., DD/AH 14/7; Huntington Libr., Stowe MSS., STG box 49, rental 1812.
[24] Taunton Courier, 24 July 1822; S.R.O., DD/HWD 19.
[25] V.C.H. Som. i. 523.
[26] S.R.O., DD/AH 11/9, 11/10.
[27] Ibid. 12/12.
[28] Ibid. 37/3, 55/3.
[29] S.R.S. xx. 164–5.
[30] Som. Protestation Returns, ed. Howard and Stoate, 287–8.

because they had been associated, as they were in the 14th century,[31] as manors belonging to the Hospitallers.[32] By *c.* 1730 Preston Bowyer was considered part of Dodington,[33] and later in the century Barnsworthy was part of Durborough tithing in Stogursey and Perry Mill was in Holford tithing.[34]

By the early 16th century the two manors called Durborough Dodington and Perry Mill had jurisdiction within the parish.[35] The jurisdiction of Dodington manor, which in the 17th century included Dodington family holdings in St. Decumans, Holford, Fiddington, and Nether Stowey,[36] survived until 1819 or later,[37] and there are court papers for the period 1813–17.[38] A tithingman, two constables, and a hayward were appointed annually.[39] The manor of Durborough, probably a division of Durborough Dodington, survived until the early 19th century and included land on the Quantocks. Some land in the parish may also have been within the manor of Newhall in Holford.[40]

In 1840 it was reported that no vestry meetings had ever been held and that none were required. The sole churchwarden had then been in office for 'many' years.[41] The parish became part of the Williton poorlaw union in 1836, the Williton rural district in 1894, and the West Somerset district in 1974.[42]

CHURCH. There was a church at Dodington by the late 12th century. It was evidently then regarded as an independent living,[43] but by 1335 it was described as a chapelry, and was later dependent on Nether Stowey,[44] probably the source of its original foundation. By 1473 it was a rectory, and so remained, though it was joined with Holford in 1913.[45] In 1978 the united living of Dodington and Holford became part of the benefice of Quantoxhead.[46]

In the late 12th century Roger of Dodington gave the advowson to the order of St. John of Jerusalem.[47] By 1335 the Hospitallers were receiving a pension,[48] probably in lieu of rights which they had been obliged to resign, since before the end of the century the chaplain of Dodington was appointed by Goldcliff Priory (Mon.), as patron of Nether Stowey.[49] The priory's possessions passed to Tewkesbury Abbey, which was thought to have the rectory in 1463,[50] but ten years later John Dodington, as lord of the manor, presented to the living.[51] The patronage

was held by successive lords of the manor; from 1913 Lord St. Audries was joint patron of the united benefice,[52] and Lady Gass was a joint patron of the benefice of Quantoxhead from 1978.[53]

The rectory was valued at £5 6s. 8d. in 1535[54] and at £30 c. 1668 and 1705.[55] The net income was £120 in 1831,[56] about the same in 1851,[57] and £57 in 1913.[58] Tithes, with oblations and other casual receipts, were worth £4 13s. 2d. in 1535.[59] By 1705 hay tithes were payable as a modus of 1d. or 2d. an acre.[60] Tithes were commuted in 1838 for a rent charge of £90.[61] Glebe was worth 13s. 6d. in 1535,[62] and amounted to c. 20 a. in 1633.[63] By 1838 there were just over 18 a., which in 1868 and 1874 were exchanged for other land,[64] all of which was sold in 1920.[65]

The rectory house in 1633 comprised a hall, little parlour, buttery, and kitchen, with a single room and a small study above.[66] By 1815 its successor was a mere cottage having one room below and one above.[67] It was evidently rebuilt between 1831 and 1838 and was later extended.[68] The house was sold in 1920.[69] In 1980 it was known as Dodington House.

The church was served by curates from the 1560s.[70] Most rectors seem to have been resident in the 17th century;[71] Michael Pollard, rector 1659–67, was also rector of Holford.[72] Henry Castleman, rector 1714–18, was at the same time resident curate at Wedmore, and his successor, Benjamin Melliar, rector 1718–27, was from 1722 also vicar of Kilton and from 1723 rector of Bawdrip.[73] Curates were employed in the late 18th century.[74] In 1776 there were c. 12 regular communicants.[75] By 1815 the rector was an absentee serving Wembdon as curate and leaving Dodington to the care of a man who lived at Nether Stowey and who was curate of Holford. Services were then held every other Sunday.[76] The vicar of Stockland Bristol was serving the parish in 1827,[77] but from the 1830s there was a resident rector who by 1840 held services on alternate Sundays with quarterly celebrations of communion.[78] On Census Sunday 1851 the general congregation numbered 50, but the average was lower.[79] By 1870 two services, each with a sermon, were held each Sunday, with monthly celebrations.[80]

The church of *ALL SAINTS*, close to the former manor house, comprises a chancel with south chapel, nave with north porch, and west tower. The small nave may retain the 12th-century plan, the porch and the lower stages of the tower were added in the

[31] *Feud. Aids,* iv. 333.
[32] Above, manor.
[33] S.R.O., DD/AH 21/2.
[34] Ibid. Q/REl.
[35] Ibid. DD/AH 11/9, 11/10.
[36] Ibid. 11/1, 11/5, 14/7, 20/7, 37/11, 37/36.
[37] Huntington Libr., Stowe MSS., STG box 49, survey.
[38] S.R.O., DD/AH 14/14.
[39] Huntington Libr., Stowe MSS., STG box 49; S.R.O., DD/AH 14/4.
[40] Huntington Libr., Stowe MSS., STG box 49.
[41] S.R.O., D/D/V returns 1840.
[42] Youngs, *Local Admin. Units,* i. 424, 673, 675–6.
[43] *S.R.S.* xxv, p. 184.
[44] Ibid. ix, p. 239; *Cal. Pat.* 1370–4, 193.
[45] *S.R.S.* lii, p. 51; *Dioc. Dir.* (1913).
[46] S.R.O., D/P/dod 22/3/1.   [47] *S.R.S.* xxv, p. 184.
[48] Ibid. ix, p. 239: there spelled Bodyngdon.
[49] *Cal. Pat.* 1370–4, 193.
[50] St. George's Chapel, Windsor, MS. XV. 53. 81A.
[51] *S.R.S.* lii, p. 51.   [52] *Dioc. Dir.* (1913).
[53] S.R.O., D/P/dod 22/3/1.
[54] *Valor Eccl.* (Rec. Com.), i. 215.
[55] S.R.O., D/D/Vc 24; *Proc. Som. Arch. Soc.* cxii. 80.
[56] *Rep. Com. Eccl. Revenues,* pp. 136–7.
[57] P.R.O., HO 129/313/4/6/7.
[58] *Dioc. Dir.* (1913).
[59] *Valor Eccl.* (Rec. Com.), i. 215.
[60] *Proc. Som. Arch. Soc.* cxii. 80.
[61] S.R.O., tithe award.
[62] *Valor Eccl.* (Rec. Com.), i. 215.
[63] S.R.O., D/D/Rg 267.
[64] Ibid. tithe award; ibid. DD/AH 11/2.
[65] Ibid. tithe award, supplementary papers.
[66] Ibid. D/D/Rg 267.   [67] Ibid. D/D/B returns 1815.
[68] *Rep. Com. Eccl. Revenues,* pp. 137–7; S.R.O., tithe award.
[69] S.R.O., tithe award, supplementary papers.
[70] *S. & D. N. & Q.* xiii. 270; xxx. 90; S.R.O., D/P/dod 2/1/1.
[71] S.R.O., D/P/dod 2/1/1; *S.R.S.* xxiv. 273.
[72] *Som. Incumbents,* ed. Weaver, 356.
[73] *Alum. Oxon. 1500–1714.*
[74] S.R.O., D/P/dod 2/1/3.
[75] Ibid. D/D/Vc 88.
[76] Ibid. D/D/B returns 1815.
[77] Ibid. returns 1827.
[78] Ibid. D/D/V returns 1840.
[79] P.R.O., HO 129/313/4/6/7.
[80] S.R.O., D/D/V returns 1870.

15th century when the chancel was rebuilt. The nave was given new windows and a new roof in the 16th century. The chapel was built as a Dodington family pew in 1610.[81] The top stage of the tower was added or renewed in 1772.[82] Fragments of medieval glass remain in the east window of the chancel.[83]

There are four bells of 1870.[84] The plate is modern.[85] The registers begin in 1538, but pages between 1635 and 1651 have been cut out.[86]

NONCONFORMITY. None known.

EDUCATION. In 1847 a Sunday school for 9 boys and 6 girls was held in the church, and was supported by subscriptions.[87] It was still held in 1851,[88] but there was no day school, and from 1875 children attended school at Dyche in Stringston.[89] There was a private boarding school for girls in 1810,[90] and a school for boys was held at the rectory house in 1866.[91]

CHARITIES FOR THE POOR. None known.

ELWORTHY

THE PARISH of Elworthy lies on the eastern slopes of the Brendon Hills 7 km. north of Wiveliscombe, much of it within Exmoor National Park,[92] and the whole was probably once part of the minster estate of Stogumber.[93] With the addition of a small area of Stogumber in 1886 the present civil parish contains 716 ha. (1,768 a.).[94] The parish measures c. 5.5 km. from east to west, and lies in two irregular but compact parts joined by a narrow strip of land, the two parts perhaps representing the two Domesday estates of Elworthy and Willett. The western part stretches in a band about 1 km. wide from the plateau of the Brendons at 391 m. eastwards down the steep Elworthy combe to Elworthy village and the beginnings of the slope beyond, then south-east along the valley side to the tongue of Stogumber which almost divides the parish. The eastern part of the parish runs north-east from Willett Hill (274 m.), and then south-east across the gentler slopes of Tolland Down, including the village of Willett on the falling ground, and Willett House, Plash Farm, and Coleford Farm on the tributaries of the Doniford stream. The only natural boundary follows a stream south-west of Willett Hill, but the Brendon ridgeway marks part of the boundary in the west and some other boundaries are marked by minor roads.[95]

Brendon slate is the principal geological formation in the parish, with some small areas of sandstone south-east of Elworthy village and west of Willett and valley gravels in the east near Willett House.[96] There were small scattered quarries in the 19th century, and a limekiln north of Coleford Farm.[97]

On Elworthy common, 1.5 km. south-west of

Elworthy village, is a round cairn, probably the one opened in 1833, and a Bronze Age barrow was opened in Sparborough field at Willett in 1834.[98] Fields named Catborough and Great Burrow at Willett and Maunsberry, north-east of Elworthy village,[99] suggest further prehistoric sites.

There is only slight evidence, from the 16th century,[1] of open-field arable farming, and after 1831, when Elworthy common and Willett Hill were inclosed, there was no common pasture in the parish.[2] There were 90 a. of wood in 1086.[3] By 1840 there were 115 a. including plantations at Tilsey Farm above Elworthy combe, and on Willett Hill.[4] The tower on Willett Hill was built by 1782[5] 'at the expense of the neighbouring gentry' in the form of a ruined church, perhaps to serve as a 'steeple' for riders.[6] The parkland around Willett House had been created by 1840.[7] By 1905 the area of woodland had increased to 137 a.[8]

The former Willett farmhouse (replaced by Willett Farm, built in 1874) dates from the 15th century and was altered in the 1640s.[9] Plash Farm is of the 17th century or earlier, with 19th-century farm buildings. Elworthy Farm is of the 17th or early 18th century and also has a group of 19th-century buildings.

Elworthy village lies 500 m. north-west of the crossing of the Bampton–Hartrow road and the Wiveliscombe–Watchet road, both turnpiked in 1806.[10] Elworthy Cross House was a tollhouse belonging to the Wiveliscombe trust, with gates on each road except that leading to the village.[11] Save Penny Lane was the name given to a route between Brompton Ralph and Stogumber which skirted east of

[81] Date on E. gable. See also *Reliquary*, xiv. 188.
[82] Nichols, *The Quantocks*, 54.
[83] C. Woodforde, *Stained Glass in Som.*, 29.
[84] S.R.O., DD/SAS CH 16.
[85] *Proc. Som. Arch. Soc.* xlvii. 165.
[86] S.R.O., D/P/dod 2/1/1–3.
[87] Nat. Soc. *Inquiry, 1846–7*, Som., pp. 8–9.
[88] P.R.O., HO 129/313/4/6/7.
[89] *Kelly's Dir. Som.* (1883).
[90] S.R.O., T/PH/ay 1, June 1810.
[91] Ibid. DD/X/CNN.
[92] This article was completed in 1979.
[93] Below, Stogumber, intro.
[94] Youngs, *Local Admin. Units*, i. 425; *Census*, 1971.
[95] O.S. Map 1″, sheet 164 (1966 edn.).
[96] Geol. Surv. Map 1″, solid and drift, sheet 294 (1969 edn.).

[97] O.S. Map 1/25,000, ST 03, ST 13 (1962 edn.); S.R.O., tithe award.
[98] L. V. Grinsell, *Archaeology of Exmoor* (1970), 64–5.
[99] S.R.O., tithe award.
[1] *S.R.S.* ii. 46.
[2] S.R.O., Q/RDe 17.
[3] *V.C.H. Som.* i. 504.
[4] S.R.O., tithe award.
[5] *S.R.S.* lxxvi, Day and Masters map (1782).
[6] Collinson, *Hist. Som.* iii. 525.
[7] S.R.O., tithe award.
[8] Statistics supplied by the then Bd. of Agric. 1905.
[9] S.R.O., DD/V Wlr 9.2.
[10] Ibid. set of 1″ maps annotated by Sir Rob. Hall; 46 Geo. III, c. 152 (Local and Personal).
[11] S.R.O., tithe award.

Elworthy village and avoided the tollhouse. It was stopped in 1827.[12] The old road from Plash to Willett was closed in 1820, probably because it crossed the new park of Willett House.[13]

There were at least 62 adult males in the parish in 1641 and 244 people were listed for the 1667 subsidy.[14] By the 19th century the population had fallen considerably although there was a rise from 150 in 1801 to 216 in 1851. Between 1891 and 1901 the population fell sharply from 162 to 110 and between 1961 and 1971 it shrank still further from 82 to 62.[15]

MANORS. In 1086 William de Mohun held Elworthy except for 1 virgate which was retained by the king,[16] and the estate owed a rent to Dunster, the *caput* of William's honor, in 1777.[17]

Dunne possessed Elworthy T.R.E. and Dodeman in 1086.[18] During the 12th century it was held by the Elworthy family. In 1166 William of Elworthy held 4 fees of Dunster, two of which were probably Elworthy and Willett,[19] and Simon of Elworthy held a fee of Dunster in 1201 and 1202.[20] Philip of Elworthy was lord of the manor of *ELWORTHY* early in Henry III's reign,[21] and conveyed the estate with the service of one knight from Plash and Willett to William Malet of Bedgrave, in Weston Turville (Bucks.).[22] William's daughter Lucy married first Simon of Merriott of Hestercombe (d. after 1276), and secondly Thomas of Timworth.[23] Lucy had died by 1316 and the manor descended to her son Walter of Merriott, clerk (d. 1345).[24] Walter's heir was his nephew Simon of Merriott, who died before 1372.[25] The manor then passed to Margery (d. 1390), Simon's widow, and then to John, nephew of her second husband Thomas Willington. John, a lunatic, died in 1396, leaving as his heirs his two sisters, Margaret, wife of Sir John Wroth, and Isabel, wife of William Beaumont. Margaret received Elworthy.[26] Her son John died under age and his widow Joyce surrendered her dower.[27] The manor passed to John's sister Elizabeth (d. 1440), wife of Sir William Palton.[28] On Sir William's death in 1450 without issue Elizabeth's cousin, Thomas Beaumont, inherited Elworthy.[29]

William de Mohun also held Willett in 1086. T.R.E. and in 1086 it was held with Elworthy.[30] The manor of *WILLETT* continued to descend with Elworthy, except for a period during the 13th century when it was leased to the de la Plesse family,[31] until

1396 when it passed to William and Isabel Beaumont.[32] William was succeeded by his son Thomas who in 1450, the year before his death, inherited the manor of Elworthy.[33]

The manor of *PLASH* was mentioned in 1238 when it was held by Hugh de la Plesse.[34] Hugh was dead by 1248 and was possibly succeeded by Richard de la Plesse, who held a fee in Willett in the 1280s.[35] In 1303 Plash was held by Lucy of Merriott.[36] In 1396 the manor was in the king's hands on the death of John Willington and by 1424 it had been leased by Isabel Beaumont to William Squire.[37] From 1396 or earlier Plash was held with Willett, and the names were sometimes used interchangeably.[38]

On his death in 1451 Thomas Beaumont held all three manors and they descended in the Beaumont family until the end of the 16th century. Thomas's son William Beaumont (d. 1453) was succeeded by his brother Philip (d. 1473) after William's supposed son John had been declared a bastard in 1466, as the illegitimate son of William's wife Joan Courtenay and Sir Henry Bodrugan whom she later married. Philip allowed Joan and Sir Henry the use of the estates during her lifetime[39] and devised them to his half-brother Thomas Beaumont. In 1477, however, Thomas released the property to John Bodrugan or Beaumont who, with his reputed father, was attainted for involvement in Simnel's rebellion in 1496. The attainder was reversed after it was discovered that John had died before the rebellion. The manors of Elworthy, Plash, and Willett passed to John's son Henry (d. 1548) who called himself Beaumont,[40] to Henry's son Humphrey (d. 1572),[41] and to Humphrey's son Henry. The last Henry died without surviving issue in 1591 and the estates passed through his sister Elizabeth, wife of Robert Muttlebury, to her son Thomas.[42] In 1608 the property was forfeited temporarily because of Thomas Muttlebury's recusancy,[43] but he was lord of the manor of *ELWORTHY* or *ELWORTHY AND WILLETT* in 1634.[44] William Lacey (d. 1641) of Hartrow, in Stogumber, bought the estate c. 1635 and was succeeded by his grandson William Lacey (d. 1690),[45] by that William's son William (d. 1695),[46] and then by the latter's daughter Sarah, wife of Thomas Rich.[47] Sarah's son Thomas died in 1727 before his intended marriage to Margaret Hay, to whom he left his estate. On Margaret's death in 1753 the estate passed to her sister Mary (d. 1771) and then to the

[12] Ibid. Q/SR Mich. 1827.
[13] Ibid. Mich. 1820.
[14] *Som. Protestation Returns*, ed. Howard and Stoate, 159, 287; S.R.O., DD/WY 34.
[15] *Census*, 1801–1971.
[16] *V.C.H. Som.* i. 504. The virgate may be the land called Pirtochesworda in the Geld Inquest: ibid. i. 532; cf. *Domesday Bk. Som.* ed. C. and F. Thorn, p. 388.
[17] *S.R.S.* xxxiii, p. 351.
[18] *V.C.H. Som.* i. 504.
[19] *S.R.S.* extra ser. 179.
[20] *Pipe R.* 1201 (P.R.S. n.s. xiv), 34, 36; 1202 (P.R.S. n.s. xv), 91.
[21] B.L. Add. Ch. 4889.
[22] *S.R.S.* extra ser. 179.
[23] *S.R.S.* xxxiii, pp. 45, 53, 59; *Cal. Inq. p.m.* ii, pp. 178, 351; *Feud. Aids*, iv. 275, 304.
[24] *S.R.S.* xxxiii, pp. 70, 75; *Cal. Inq. p.m.* vii, p. 220; viii, p. 429.
[25] *S.R.S.* xvii. 184; extra ser. 36–7; *Feud. Aids*, iv. 347.
[26] *Cal. Fine R.* 1391–9, 198, 200, 203; 1399–1405, 31.
[27] *Cal. Close*, 1409–13, 382.

[28] *S.R.S.* xxii. 174; xxxiii, pp. 196, 209, 220; *Feud. Aids*, iv. 392, 407, 438.
[29] *S.R.S.* extra ser. 182.
[30] *V.C.H. Som.* i. 504.
[31] *S.R.S.* extra ser. 186; xxxiii, pp. 34, 49, 60.
[32] *S.R.S.* xxxiii, pp. 105, 109, 119.
[33] Ibid. pp. 192, 232; extra ser. 187–8.
[34] *S.R.S.* xxxiii, p. 34.
[35] *S.R.S.* xi, pp. 363, 365; xxxiii, pp. 49, 60; *Cal. Inq. p.m.* ii, pp. 178, 351.
[36] *Feud. Aids.* iv. 304.
[37] *Cal. Fine R.* 1391–9, 200; *Cal. Close*, 1422–9, 117.
[38] *Cal. Fine R.* 1391–9, 200.
[39] *S.R.S.* extra ser. 182; Devon R.O. 48/25/9/3, 5.
[40] *S.R.S.* extra ser. 184; xxxiii, p. 268.
[41] Ibid. xxxiii, p. 293; P.R.O., C 142/165, no. 155.
[42] *S.R.S.* extra ser. 185; xxxiii, p. 309.
[43] *Cal. S. P. Dom.* 1603–10, 403.
[44] S.R.O., DD/DR 9.
[45] P.R.O., C 142/462, no. 100; *S.R.S.* lxvii, pp. 32–3; extra ser. 185.
[46] S.R.O., DD/DR 32, 62.   [47] Ibid. DD/BR/fr 24.

Revd. Bickham Escott, son of their sister Sarah. A fourth sister Isabel had inherited land in Elworthy which had belonged to the Dodington family in the 17th century and on her death in 1772 her heirs were Bickham Escott and John Francis of Combe Florey.[48] Bickham Escott died in 1801 without male heirs and in 1811 a considerable estate, including Elworthy manor, was settled on his daughter Elizabeth who married Lt. Col. (later Gen.) Daniel Francis Blommart of Halse.[49] John Blommart (d. 1890) followed his father as lord of the manor and was succeeded by his sister Mary (d. 1910).[50] The estate was then or soon after divided, and no later claim to the lordship has been found. In 1979 the manor house belonged to Mr. E. W. Towler.

Willett House, built in or after 1816 by Richard Carver for Daniel Blommart,[51] is a square structure with a main south front of five bays and two storeys behind which there is in succession a lower service wing, a courtyard, stable, and coachhouse. A number of closes were destroyed to make a park of 40 a.[52] Later in the 19th century it was extended and in 1979 was mostly pasture with many specimen trees and an area of formal gardens south-east of the house. A capital messuage called Elworthy belonged in the late 16th century to the Muttlebury family,[53] and may be the precursor of the present Elworthy Farm.

A small estate at Coleford was held by Dodeman of William de Mohun in 1086 and had been held T.R.E. by Brictuin.[54] It was probably absorbed by Plash or Willett manor and is represented by the present Coleford farm.

ECONOMIC HISTORY. The Domesday estates together totalled 2 hides, of which 3 virgates were in demesne, but there were 170 a. of pasture, 90 a. of woodland, and, among the stock, 172 sheep. A recorded population of 20 villeins, 14 bordars, and 3 serfs, seems remarkably high.[55] Thereafter there is an almost total lack of evidence of economic activity until the 17th century.

Stock raising, principally of sheep, is recorded in 17th-century inventories. In 1640 a yeoman left sheep and lambs, a bull, cows and calves, horses, pigs, two cheese presses, and corn and malt.[56] In 1642 another yeoman had sheep, cattle, horses, pigs, and corn, and an inventory of 1648 shows a similar pattern with sheep, cattle, pigs, and corn.[57] A smallholder who died in 1646 kept bees, a cow, and two pigs,[58] in contrast with the wealthy yeoman Henry Sweeting, who in 1676 had many sheep, cattle, a horse, and various crops.[59] A farmer's livestock tended to be worth twice as much as his crops.

There is little evidence of clothmaking compared with the parishes to the north but Rack close lay

south of Willett Hill[60] and the parish supported a large population in the 17th century.[61] One poor weaver left looms worth only 10s.,[62] and other inventories contain only small amounts of wool and cloth.[63] In 1831 out of 36 families 30 were engaged in agriculture and only 4 in handicrafts.[64]

In 1840 the farms were few and large, in contrast to the many small holdings found in neighbouring parishes. The largest farm, Plash and Willett, measured 307 a., Elworthy farm had 202 a., and Higher Willett, Lower Willett, and Coleford farms were each over 100 a. Of the six other farms none was under 35 a. and four were over 60 a. Out of a total of 1,635 a., 1,215 a. were owned by the lord of the manor, Daniel Blommart.[65] The soil was said to produce average crops of wheat, oats, barley, potatoes, and turnips,[66] and in 1905 there were still 608 a. of arable land and 586 a. of grass.[67] By 1976 there were at least 700 a. of grass supporting 846 sheep and 510 cattle. Of the holdings returned, one was over 500 a., two were over 120 a., one over 75 a., and the rest between 5 a. and 50 a.[68]

There were two mills in 1086, one at Elworthy and one at Willett. The latter paid no rent but the mill at Elworthy was worth 4s.[69] One mill survived until 1630 or later[70] but by 1840 both mills had gone.[71]

LOCAL GOVERNMENT. The only known record of a manor court is a presentment to the court baron of Elworthy and Willett of 1682.[72] In 1556 the watch at Elworthy was concerned with firing beacons and other precautions against invasion.[73] There were two churchwardens and two sidesmen by 1613,[74] and there is a reference to a meeting of the vestry in 1738,[75] but no records of parish officers survive earlier than the 19th century. The vestry then nominated to the offices of overseer and surveyor, by 1836 there were two highway surveyors, and in 1858 four way-wardens. Road repairs were a major concern of the vestry in the 19th century, and in 1836 there was a scheme for payment to parishioners prepared to assist with the work. In 1832 a special meeting of the vestry was held to decide on precautions to be taken against a possible outbreak of cholera. A room in Tilsey Farm was to be equipped as a hospital, a nurse was appointed, and a board of health set up.[76]

There was a poorhouse in Cott Lane, in Elworthy combe, west of the village, by 1829.[77] In 1858, when it comprised four cottages, it was ordered to be sold, and it may have been demolished c. 1859.[78] The parish was part of the Williton poor-law union from 1836 and of the Williton rural district from 1894. Since 1974 it has formed part of West Somerset district.[79]

[48] Ibid. DD/CN 8/2.
[49] Ibid. DD/BR/gm 12.
[50] S.R.S. extra ser. 189.
[51] Dioc. Regy., Mun. Bk. iv. 150–2; S.R.O., T/PH/bscs, letter 13 Aug. 1818.
[52] S.R.O., tithe award.
[53] Cal. Proc. Chanc. Eliz. (Rec. Com.) i. 254.
[54] V.C.H. Som. i. 505.   [55] Ibid. i. 504–5.
[56] S.R.O., DD/SP, inventories 1635, 1640.
[57] Ibid. DD/SP, inventories 1642, 1648.
[58] Ibid. DD/SP, inventory 1646.
[59] Ibid. DD/SP, inventory 1676.   [60] Ibid. tithe award.
[61] Som. Protestation Returns, ed. Howard and Stoate, 159, 287; S.R.O., DD/WY 34.
[62] S.R.O., DD/SP, inventory 1686.
[63] Ibid. DD/SP, inventories 1642, 1646.
[64] Census, 1831.
[65] S.R.O., tithe award.   [66] Kelly's Dir. Som. (1883).
[67] Figures supplied by the then Bd. of Agric. 1905.
[68] Min. of Agric., Fisheries, and Food, agric. returns 1976.   [69] V.C.H. Som. i. 504.
[70] S.R.O., D/D/Ca 310.
[71] Ibid. tithe award.
[72] Ibid. DD/DR 62.
[73] Ibid. DD/WO 49/3.   [74] Ibid. D/D/Rg 341.
[75] Ibid. D/P/elw 2/1/1.
[76] Ibid. 9/1/1.
[77] Ibid. 4/1/1; ibid. tithe award.
[78] Ibid. D/P/elw 9/1/1.
[79] Youngs, Local Admin. Units, i. 675–6.

CHURCH. A church was mentioned in 1233.[80] The living was a rectory until 1969 when it became a chapelry within the parish of Monksilver, as part of the united benefice of Monksilver with Brompton Ralph, Nettlecombe, and, from 1977, Stogumber. In 1979 the church was declared redundant and vested in the Redundant Churches Fund.[81]

The advowson was quitclaimed in 1233 by William Malet to the Knights Hospitaller.[82] The prior presented to the benefice in 1509,[83] and presumably until the order was dissolved in 1540. In 1563 the advowson was granted by the Crown to Thomas Reve, William Revet, and William Hechins,[84] and by 1579 it was in the hands of William Lacey of Hartrow, thence descending with the manor to Margaret Hay. In 1727 she leased the advowson to David Yea and John Morley with the proviso that Morley's son Alexander, then rector, should be succeeded by one of his own sons.[85] Alexander died in 1731 when his sons were under age, and Yea presented a successor, but John Morley, one of the sons, was in 1746 presented by David Yea. In 1804 Sarah Escott, greatniece of Margaret Hay, sold the advowson to William Lock, who conveyed it to the Revd. Thomas Roe in 1820.[86] In 1835 the advowson was sold to Mrs. Clarkson, probably the mother of Christopher Clarkson, rector and patron from 1835 to 1844. In 1844 the advowson was conveyed in trust for John Eddy, rector and patron 1845–68.[87] In 1891 it was sold by trustees to Mrs. Simms, who transferred it to the rector, James Sanger, in 1897.[88] In 1919 the patronage was transferred as a free gift by Mrs. Somerset Gardner McTaggart, probably mother of the incoming rector of Monksilver with Elworthy, to the dean and canons of Windsor, patrons of Monksilver, pending the union of the two parishes.[89] The dean and canons became joint patrons of the united benefice.[90]

In 1291 the church was valued at £4 6s. 8d.,[91] in 1535 at £6 18s.,[92] and c. 1668 at c. £20.[93] In 1831 the average net income of the benefice was £244,[94] and in 1840 the tithes were commuted for a rent charge of £230 12s.[95]

In 1613 there were 69 a. of glebe both in the parish and in Stogumber,[96] and nearly 63 a. remained in 1840,[97] a small portion having been exchanged in 1831 during inclosure of the commons.[98] The glebe remained intact until 1910 but had been disposed of by 1931.[99]

There was a rectory house with garden, barn, and orchard in 1606,[1] and in 1698 it had 14 windows.[2] In 1827 the rector was said to be non-resident because the house was 'not in a fit state' although the curate lived in it[3] and it was declared fit in 1831.[4] A new house, in landscaped grounds, probably built c. 1838, was originally small and symmetrically planned with a south-west front of three bays. It was later extended, and has been a private house since c. 1919.

The first known rector, John de Massingham, instituted in 1310, was licensed to be absent for study from 1311 to 1313 and in 1314 to serve the prior of St. John of Jerusalem for a year.[5] John de Sutton, instituted in 1346, was licensed to follow the king's service for a year, but Walter de Chadelshounte, presented in 1349, was warned by the bishop in 1351 to take up residence.[6] William Dickes, rector 1589–1635, was accused in 1603 of setting up too many seats in the chancel.[7] John Selleck, rector 1643–5 and again from the 1660s until 1690, was ejected for loyalty to the king and was later involved in helping Charles II to escape. After the Restoration he became a canon of Wells and rector of Clifton Campville (Staffs.) and was responsible for ransoming English subjects held at Algiers in 1662.[8] Both Alexander Morley, 1712–31, and his son John, 1746–86, lived in the parish,[9] and Samuel Willis, 1786–1818, was also resident, but by 1815 took only weekday services because of 'infirmities of age'. Services on Sundays, Good Friday, and Christmas Day were taken by the rector of Sampford Brett.[10] Thomas Roe, rector 1818–35, was also rector of Brendon and was assisted in the parish by curates[11] including William Chilcott who also served as curate at Monksilver where he was later rector. In 1827 the curate lived in the rectory house and took services on Sundays.[12] Roe's successor from 1835 was resident and held two services with sermons and administered communion four times a year.[13] In 1851 30 people usually attended morning service and 60 the afternoon service. The 15 Sunday-school children attended both services.[14] Under Matthew Pierpoint, rector 1868–90, celebrations of communion were increased to once a month.[15] In 1951 monthly services were held at Willett.[16]

A church house was mentioned in 1636[17] but by 1727 it appears to have been used as a dwelling.[18]

A fraternity of St. Martin was mentioned in 1531 and 1536, and there were lights of St. Martin, St. Mary, St. Anthony, and All Souls.[19] A tenement, garden, and 1 a. of arable were given for a light in the church.[20]

[80] *S.R.S.* vi. 76.
[81] *Dioc. Dir.*
[82] *S.R.S.* vi. 76.
[83] *S.R.S.* i. 36; *Som. Incumbents*, ed. Weaver, 364–5.
[84] *Cal. Pat.* 1563–6, 13.
[85] *Som. Incumbents*, ed. Weaver, 364–5; S.R.O., DD/DR 9.
[86] St. George's Chapel, Windsor, MS. XVII. 34. 15–16.
[87] Ibid. MS. XVII. 34. 17–25; S.R.O., DD/CCH 2/3; DD/BR/py 62.
[88] St. George's Chapel, Windsor, MS. XVII. 34. 26, 31.
[89] Ibid. MS. XVII. 34. 33–4; S.R.O., D/P/mon 2/1/6.
[90] *Dioc. Dir.*
[91] *Tax. Eccl.* (Rec. Com.), 202.
[92] *Valor Eccl.* (Rec. Com.), i. 221.
[93] S.R.O., D/D/Vc 24.
[94] *Rep. Com. Eccl. Revenues*, pp. 136–7.
[95] S.R.O., tithe award.
[96] Ibid. D/D/Rg 341.
[97] Ibid. tithe award.
[98] Ibid. Q/RDe 17.
[99] *Kelly's Dir. Som.* (1910, 1931).
[1] Ibid. D/D/Rg 341.
[2] Ibid. D/P/elw 2/1/1.

[3] S.R.O., D/D/B returns 1827.
[4] *Rep. Com. Eccl. Revenues*, pp. 136–7.
[5] *S.R.S.* i. 43, 65, 74.
[6] *S.R.S.* x, pp. 528, 615, 662, 668.
[7] S.R.O., D/D/Ca 134, 160.
[8] *S.R.S.* lxxii, p. xxii; Lamb. Pal. Libr. MS. COMM. A/1/12, 16; A/8/55. Selleck was calling himself rector of Elworthy in 1660: Hist. MSS. Com. 2, *3rd Rep. Wells Cathedral*, p. 364; Hist. MSS. Com. 6, *7th Rep. House of Lords*, p. 108. John Hill, Selleck's curate in the 1630s (S.R.O. D/D/Rr 171), is said to have been ejected for failing to sign the covenant in *Alum. Oxon. 1500–1714*, but in 1662 in T. G. Crippen, *Nonconf. in Som.*
[9] S.R.O., D/P/elw 2/1/1–2.
[10] Ibid. D/D/B returns 1815.
[11] *Rep. Com. Eccl. Revenues*, pp. 136–7.
[12] S.R.O., D/D/B returns 1827.
[13] Ibid. D/D/V returns 1840, 1843.
[14] P.R.O., HO 129/313/5/6/8.
[15] S.R.O., D/D/V returns 1870. [16] Ibid. D/P/elw 9/3/3.
[17] Ibid. DD/DR 9. [18] Ibid. D/P/elw 2/1/1.
[19] *Wells Wills*, ed. Weaver, 80–1.
[20] *S.R.S.* ii. 46; xxvii, p. 63; *Cal. Pat.* 1549–51, 5.

The church of *ST. MARTIN* was so dedicated by 1531.[21] It stands on a steeply sloping site overlooking the village and has a chancel, nave with south organ chamber and vestry, and north porch, and battlemented west tower with external stair to the ringing chamber. The nave, which retains a lancet at the west end of the north wall, and the tower date from the 13th century, and the porch and the nave roof from the late 15th century. The chancel was rebuilt in 1695, and again in 1846, when the nave was also restored and reseated.[22] The organ chamber probably dates from 1846. The alabaster font is of the mid 17th century, evidently from Watchet. The altar rail and table are late 17th-century and there is some glass from the same period in the north-west window. The screen is a 19th-century creation incorporating a frieze dated 1632 and some 17th-century tracery with the arms and crest of the Lacey family.

There is a cup of 1573 by 'I.P.'.[23] Among the four bells one is medieval, from the Exeter foundry, and another is by Roger Semson of Ash Priors (1530–70).[24] The registers date from 1685 and are complete.[25]

NONCONFORMITY. The lord of the manor[26] and members of the Green family were presented for recusancy at various times between 1613 and 1665.[27] The Greens had estates in the parish until 1717 or later.[28] In 1776 there was said to be one papist.[29]

EDUCATION. There was no school in 1818[30] but 20 children were attending school daily in 1826, and in 1831 a free Sunday school was started with the same number of children.[31] In 1839 a school was built in Elworthy village in union with the National Society and supported by voluntary subscription.[32] In 1847 16 boys and 14 girls attended the day school, and 20 boys and 16 girls the Sunday school, which was also supported by school pence.[33] In 1870 and 1872 the vestry decided to raise a voluntary school rate and repair the school.[34] The school appears to have closed between 1875 and 1883 and another was opened in a cottage at Willett for 40 children.[35] In 1892 a National school opened in the old school house in Elworthy village for 30 children; 42 children were enrolled. Numbers fell sharply during the next three decades and by 1933 there were only 12 children attending the school. In 1937 it was closed and the children went to Monksilver and Williton.[36] Until 1951 the building was used for church purposes, and later the site was conveyed for a village hall. The hall closed *c.* 1965,[37] and in 1979 it was a private house.

CHARITIES FOR THE POOR. An estate at Willett consisting of a messuage, garden plot, and 1 a. of land, perhaps the endowment of a pre-Reformation light in the church, was held by trustees in 1676. The issues were payable to the churchwardens for the church, the poor, or other charitable purpose.[38] The property was exchanged for land in Elworthy village in 1831[39] but there is no further record of the charity.

HALSE

THE ANCIENT parish of Halse, which derives its name from the neck of land under which the village shelters,[40] was a detached part of Williton and Freemanors hundred. Roughly triangular in shape, it lies in the fertile vale of Taunton Deane, 1.75 km. east of the hundred boundary at Brompton Ralph, from which it was separated by Lydeard St. Lawrence and Fitzhead parishes.[41] In 1883 a detached part of Hillfarrance in the centre of Halse village and containing two houses was transferred to Halse, giving the parish an area of 534 ha. (1,320 a.).[42]

Halse is at the eastern end of a gently sloping sandstone ridge between two converging streams flowing down from the Brendons, which join just beyond the parish's south-eastern boundary. From the western limit at *c.* 95 m. the land falls away to the gravels and marls of the streams at *c.* 41 m. To the north, beyond the stream known as Halse water, a thin band of sandstone is overlain by Keuper Marl around the former hamlet of Stoford, and by less fertile conglomerate and Lower Marl as the parish narrows and the land rises to 169 m. at Common Down. Limekilns and quarries were worked at Common Down in the late 19th century.[43]

The parish boundary follows Halse water for a short distance on the east, a line which was the western boundary of Bishop's Lydeard by the late 10th century.[44] The boundary with Milverton and Fitzhead, on the open ground of the sandstone ridge, was the 9th-century limit of the manor of Taunton Deane,[45] and bears marks of regularity in an area of common-field cultivation. The division with Ash

[21] *Wells Wills*, ed. Weaver, 80–1.
[22] S.R.O., D/P/elw 2/1/1; 4/1/1; 9/1/1.
[23] *Proc. Som. Arch. Soc.* xlv. 165.
[24] S.R.O., DD/SAS CH 16.
[25] Ibid. D/P/elw 2/1/1–6.
[26] *S. & D. N. & Q.* v. 112.
[27] S.R.O., D/D/Ca 180, 235, 266, 274, 344; *Som. Protestation Returns*, ed. Howard and Stoate, 159.
[28] *Cal. Cttee. for Compounding*, iv. 3175; v. 3192; S.R.O., Q/RR recusants lands.
[29] S.R.O., D/D/Vc 88.
[30] *Educ. of Poor Digest*, H.C. 224 (1819), ix (2).
[31] *Ann. Rep. B. & W. Dioc. Assoc. S.P.C.K.* (1825–6); *Educ. Enq. Abstract*, H.C. 62 (1835), xlii.
[32] S.R.O., C/E 26; ibid. tithe award.
[33] Nat. Soc. *Inquiry, 1846–7*, Som. 8–9.

[34] S.R.O., D/P/elw 9/1/1.
[35] *P.O. Dir. Som.* (1875); *Kelly's Dir. Som.* (1883, 1889).
[36] S.R.O., C/E 8.
[37] Ibid. D/P/elw 9/3/3.
[38] Wilts. R.O. 754/101; above, church.
[39] S.R.O., Q/RDe 17; tithe award.
[40] Ekwall, *Eng. Place-Names* (1960), 203. This article was completed in 1981.
[41] S.R.O., tithe award.
[42] *Census*, 1891; S.R.O., tithe award. The small area, including Hillfarrance Cottages, was part of Hillfarrance manor by 1371: S.R.O., DD/AH 66/7.
[43] Geol. Surv. Map 1", drift, sheet 295 (1956 edn.); O.S. Map 6", Som. LIX. SE., LXIX. NE. (1887 edn.).
[44] G. B. Grundy, *Saxon Charters of Som.* 15–16.
[45] Ibid. 40.

Priors on the north-east may in the 13th century have been the small stream about 500 m. east of the present boundary, when Kerdon was part of Halse manor and Denbury was part of Halse parish.[46]

Halse village lies mostly on the eastern side of a curving street from which roads lead steeply westwards to the fields. To the east the grassland, crossed by a series of ditches, slopes down to Halse water. Houses front directly on the street and have long gardens and orchards behind. Halse cross stood at the centre of the village, its site remembered in 1711.[47] Beside it was the 'accustomed block' through which water flowed from a spring, perhaps the origin of the name of four 'block houses' whose tenants were responsible for the repair of the village stocks.[48] The water still emerges through a culvert into a stone trough. The church stands at the southern end of the village in a large rectangular plot whose size and prominence suggest pre-Christian occupation. The medieval manor house and the parsonage barn stood in an apparently detached position south-east of the village.[49]

The house called Lower Stoford, 1 km. north-east of the village, represents the hamlet of Stoford, established by the end of the 13th century at the 10th-century crossing-place of Halse water.[50] Northway, by the late 19th century a group of farms along the road from Wiveliscombe to Bishop's Lydeard, was in the early 18th century a single large farm called Nurthy, established by 1650 and also known as Cheeks.[51] The original farm site may be represented by the former Higher Northway Farm, from the 1920s known as Tugwell,[52] and if so the name Northway is likely to refer to the direct route, which survived in 1981 as a footpath, leading north from the village to Common Down. A medieval settlement called Oldelonde or Oddolonde has not been found.[53] The early 17th-century house called Halsewater, on the edge of the parish adjoining Ash Priors, and the late 17th-century house known as 'Old Ground' on Whitmoor,[54] show that settlement in Halse had long been partly scattered.

The sandstone plateau west of the village was the site of the main area of open-field cultivation, strips surviving in furlongs at least until the 1880s.[55] Field names such as Pavilands, Buccombe, and Ridgeditch of the 1840s recalled Pulverlong and Bovecombe of c. 1240 and Rygwoysdich of 1382.[56] The name Headland, on the boundary with Ash Priors near the quarries, may suggest another open-field site.[57] Meadow and pasture lay in a broad band beside Halse water across the centre of the parish and beside its tributary in the south. The tributary was used to feed ponds: by 1821 Holywell meadow changed its name to Bathing House meadow,[58] and a large fishpond was later built a little further downstream.[59] Halse water was diverted at several points to drive a mill and to water the meadows.[60] Common land by the time of inclosure in 1857 was confined to the high ground at Common Down and to wet pastures in the south at Whitmoor.[61]

The winding and often narrow and sunken roads of the parish were of local importance only, but the 14th-century name Rygwoysdich suggests the existence of a ridgeway, possibly the Greenway of 1507.[62] The road from Fitzhead through the village towards Ash Priors and Bishop's Lydeard became part of the Wiveliscombe turnpike trust network in 1806.[63]

In the 17th century farm houses ranged widely in size from one, probably at Northway, with five chambers over a hall with internal buttery, kitchen, parlour, and entry,[64] and another with six rooms above hall, kitchen, old and new butteries, entry passage, and dairy,[65] to one with only hall and kitchen with a single room over, probably the late medieval Blake's Farm.[66] The first may be the house known as Tugwell, which dates from the early 16th century or earlier, with additions of the early 17th century and later.[67] Stoford, formerly Stoford Farm, is a medieval building with an arch-braced hall roof. In the early 17th century a floor was inserted and the ceiling plastered and decorated with Tudor roses and oak leaves. Moulded plaster decoration is also found at Halsewater, a much more humble house with hall and kitchen only, at Rock Cottage, and at Blake's Farm.[68] Later building included Mount House and the extension of a farmhouse to create a small mansion for the Hancock family called Blake's House early in the 19th century.

Barns in the open fields were found by the late 17th century because space within the village was limited and several holdings had no farmhouses of their own. Manor farm barn incorporates jointed crucks.[69]

By 1691 there was an inn known as the King's Arms, occupying a house built in 1682.[70] It was owned by Philip Hancock, butcher, and by 1722 was known as the Butcher's Arms.[71] By 1738 its name had changed to the Red Lion, and by 1788 to the New Inn, though it almost certainly had a continuous history throughout the period, and in 1981 remained in business under the last name.[72] In the 1880s it was advertised as a 'family and commercial inn and posting house'.[73]

A 'Sociable Society' was founded in 1811 and met in the 19th century at the New Inn.[74] It was disbanded in 1931.[75]

The population in 1801 was 383. Between 1811 and 1881 it fluctuated above 400, and in 1861 was as high

[46] S.R.S. xxv, pp. 173, 175.
[47] S.R.O., DD/DV 12/3. Crosse tenement is recorded in 1675: Wilts. R.O. 473/176.
[48] S.R.O., DD/DV 2 (1675); ibid. DD/DV 12/3, sub annis 1711, 1716, 1720, 1732; below, local government.
[49] Below, manors.
[50] S.R.S. xxv, pp. 173–5.
[51] S.R.O., DD/DV 12/2 (rates 1650, 1653); ibid. Q/REl; Wilts. R.O. 437/170–1.
[52] S.R.O., DD/V; Devon R.O. 547B/P2695.
[53] S.R.S. iii. 185; xxv, pp. 185–6.
[54] S.R.O., DD/V.
[55] O.S. Map 6", Som. LXIX. NE. (1887 edn.). Hedges had been removed by the farmer before 1850: T. D. Acland and W. Sturge, Farming of Som. (1851), 36.
[56] S.R.O., tithe award; S.R.S. xxv, pp. 176, 187.
[57] S.R.O., tithe award.

[58] Wilts. R.O. 473/182, pencil endorsement on deeds of 1692.
[59] S.R.O., tithe award; O.S. Map 6", Som. LXIX. N.E. (1887 edn.).   [60] Below, econ. hist.
[61] S.R.O., Q/RDe 147; ibid. DD/DV 14.
[62] S.R.S. xxv, p. 187; S.R.O., DD/AH 11/9.
[63] 46 Geo. III, c. 52 (Local and Personal).
[64] S.R.O., DD/SP, inventory 1677.
[65] Ibid. DD/SP, inventory 1691.
[66] Ibid. DD/DV 5 (1677).   [67] Ibid. DD/V.
[68] Ibid.; local inf.   [69] S.R.O., DD/V.
[70] Wilts. R.O. 473/181.
[71] Ibid.; S.R.O., D/P/hal 4/1/2.
[72] S.R.O., D/P/hal 13/2/2, 3; ibid. Q/RL.
[73] Kelly's Dir. Som. (1889).
[74] Parish papers: articles 1866.
[75] Inf. from Mrs. May, Halse.

as 453. By 1891 the total had fallen to 352, and it continued to fall rapidly, reaching 276 in 1921 and 252 in 1931. After a recovery in the 1950s to 284 in 1961 the next two decades witnessed further decline, to 210 at 1980.[76]

Frederick North, Lord North, later earl of Guilford (d. 1792), statesman, was probably a temporary resident at Halse in 1786.[77]

MANORS AND OTHER ESTATES. Roger Arundel held *HALSE*, later known as *HALSE PRIORIS* or *HALSE ST. JOHN*,[78] of the Crown in 1086 in succession to Ailmar, the tenant in 1066, as part of his barony of Poorstock (Dors.).[79] Roger was succeeded by Robert Arundel, who in 1152 granted the manor to the order of St. John of Jerusalem. The grant was confirmed by Robert's son, Roger Arundel.[80] The manor remained in the hands of the Hospitallers as part of the preceptory of Buckland until 1540.[81] In 1374 Halse was said to be held in chief as of the manor of Hampstead Marshall (Berks.).[82]

In 1545 the Crown sold the former Hospitaller estate, including Halse, to William Hawley or Halley (d. 1567) of Buckland Priors in Durston, already farmer of the manor.[83] Hawley was followed successively by his sons Henry (d. 1573) and Gabriel or Geoffrey (d. 1603), and then by his grandson Sir Henry Hawley, son of his third son Francis.[84] Sir Henry died in 1623 leaving a son, also Henry, under age.[85] The manor was vested in trustees, holding on a nominal lease for 1,000 years, for the payment of Sir Henry's debts, and the unsold lands did not revert to his second but only surviving son, Francis (cr. Baron Hawley 1645), until 1639. Francis sold the manor to Thomas Wescombe of Halse in 1652.[86] In 1671 Wescombe assigned it to John Wescombe the elder, to be held in trust for members of the family, but after a suit in Chancery the manor was sold in 1688 to William Granger the younger of Milverton.[87]

Granger died c. 1714 and was followed by his only daughter Mary (d. 1733), wife from 1715 of Matthew Haviland of Langford Budville.[88] Matthew survived until 1738, when the lordship passed successively to his son, also Matthew (d. 1753), of Wellisford, in Langford Budville, and then to his daughter Mary (d. 1766), wife of William Webber, formerly of the Inner Temple.[89] In 1775 Webber sold the property

to George Prior, formerly of Whitechapel (Mdx.) and later of Sydenham (Kent), already owner of land in the parish.[90]

George Prior died in 1814 and was followed in turn by his sons William (d. c. 1826), John (d. 1852), and Edward (d. 1859), and then by his daughter Mary, wife of Richard Alexander of Corsham (Wilts.). Mary's son, Richard Alexander, who assumed the name Prior, died unmarried in 1902,[91] and his property passed through his sister Mary, wife of Sir Gabriel Goldney, Bt. (d. 1900), to Sir Gabriel Prior Goldney, C.V.O., C.B. (d. 1925). Sir Prior's heir was his great-nephew Hugh G. E. Dunsterville, son of Evelyn or Eveline, third daughter of Sir Prior's brother, Sir Frederick Goldney.[92] The property was put up for sale in 1939 and was divided, but the lordship was not included in the sale.[93]

The medieval manor house was described as 'destroyed and much wasted' in 1338, and by 1627 only its site survived.[94] The site was still known in the 1790s, when it formed part of a small farm at the south-eastern edge of the village. The field name Court meadow there suggests its proximity.[95]

A house called Halse House was standing by 1677, when it was part of the holding of Henry Gooding.[96] The estate, sometimes called the Combe House estate, descended to Samuel Gooding by 1716, and then to his daughter Sarah, wife of William Paige of Fremington (Devon).[97] The name Halse House was normally used by the end of the 18th century, and in 1781 the house belonged to John Hancock the elder, in whose family it remained until after 1833.[98] By 1840 it belonged to the lord of the manor, John Prior, who had occupied it as tenant since 1830.[99] The house, by then called Halse Manor, a farm, and cottages were bought in 1939 by Violet Bucknell of Crowcombe and, after use as a boarding school during the Second World War, the house was sold to the Ministry of Health in 1952.[1] In 1981 it was occupied by a hospital specializing in the psychiatric care of the elderly.

The house of 1677 had a four-roomed plan, a parlour, hall, buttery, and kitchen with four rooms above including a 'cross chamber'.[2] A symmetrical house facing south was added in the mid 18th century, for which garden works, probably including a brick Gothick garden house, were undertaken between 1758 and 1762.[3] Later in the century a drawing room was added in the north-west corner. The whole building was remodelled and extended in the early 20th century, when a service wing replaced the

[76] *V.C.H. Som.* ii. 351; *Census*, 1911–71; local inf.
[77] He purchased two seats in the parish church: S.R.O., D/P/hal 4/1/2.
[78] *Cal. Inq. Misc.* iii, p. 345; P.R.O., C 142/99, no. 28.
[79] *V.C.H. Som.* i. 493; Sanders, *Eng. Baronies*, 72.
[80] *S.R.S.* xxv, p. 171.
[81] *V.C.H. Som.* ii. 148–50. The preceptory was given to the prior of the Hospitallers in 1433: Knowles and Hadcock, *Medieval Religious Houses* (1971), 302.
[82] *Cal. Inq. Misc.* iii, p. 345.
[83] *L. & P. Hen. VIII*, xx (1), p. 125; below, econ. hist.; P.R.O., C 142/145, no. 18; *Som. Wills*, ed. Brown, vi. 69–70.
[84] P.R.O., C 142/145, no. 18; C 142/167, no. 84.
[85] Ibid. C 142/405, no. 46; *S.R.S.* lxvii, p. 23.
[86] S.R.O., DD/DV 1.
[87] Ibid. DD/DR 12; DD/DV 1; DD/SAS HV 15, 24.
[88] *A Chronicle of De Havilland . . .* (c. 1865), 103, 105–6; S.R.O., DD/DV 2, 12/3; DD/DR 12.

[89] *Chron. of De Havilland*, 103, 105–6; S.R.O., DD/DV 2, 12/4.
[90] S.R.O., DD/DV 2; Wilts. R.O. 473/177, 183, 328.
[91] S.R.O., DD/DV 12/1; DD/PD 76; *Proc. Som. Arch. Soc.* xlviii. 127; E. Green, *Bibliotheca Somersetensis*, iii. 159.
[92] Burke, *Peerage* (1910), 797–8; Burke, *Land. Gent.* (1937), 667.   [93] S.R.O., DD/X/LOV 13.
[94] *Knights Hospitallers in Eng.* (Camd. Soc. [1st ser.], lxv), 17; S.R.O., DD/DV 3.
[95] S.R.O., DD/DV 3; ibid. tithe award.
[96] Ibid. DD/SP, inventory 1677.
[97] Ibid. DD/BR/nsb 5; ibid. D/P/hal 13/2/2; ibid. Q/REl.   [98] Ibid. Q/REl.
[99] Ibid. tithe award; Wilts. R.O. 473/359, inventory.
[1] Deeds in possession of Som. Area Health Authority; local inf.
[2] S.R.O., DD/SP, inventory of Henry Gooding.
[3] Ibid. DD/WOA 3/1; Wilts. R.O. 473/359.

original house and canted bays were added to the front.[4] After 1831 a stable block replaced the garden house.[5] New buildings were added after 1952.

In 1548 John Barnehouse, who had been a free tenant of the manor of Halse since 1507 or earlier,[6] left half the manor of *HALSE ARUNDELL* to his two granddaughters, Mary and Elizabeth Southcote. The estate was held of William Hawley's manor of Halse St. John.[7] It may have derived its name from the family of William Arundell of Bagborough, who in 1568 sold lands in Halse and elsewhere to John Perry of Milverton.[8] John Perry, probably the same, and his son Robert in 1595 acquired from Ambrose Rowse and his wife Madeleine, probably as trustees, an estate called the manor of *HALSE*.[9] Four years later the Perrys, then of Halse, conveyed the estate to another trustee, Thomas Ridgeway of Torrwood (Devon), describing it as John's portion of Halse manor, lately the inheritance of Mary Ridgeway his mother, possibly granddaughter of John Barnehouse.[10]

In 1624 Robert Perry conveyed 'those parts of the manor of Halse alias Halse Arundell' lately held by Ambrose Rowse and Thomas Ridgeway to his sister Joan Jones of Stowey.[11] In 1681 Joan's son, Sir William, then of Gray's Inn, apparently sold the property to Abraham Hancock and Robert and George Comer of Halse, and any suggestion of manorial status was then and thereafter omitted.[12] Part of the land passed c. 1763 from William Scott to George Prior.[13]

Robert Arundel evidently included the rectory in his grant of the manor of Halse to the Hospitallers in 1152.[14] The property was thus included by the Crown in the sale to William Hawley in 1545, and by that time comprised the advowson of the vicarage and the great tithes.[15] Master Nicholas Halswell, esquire, presented to the living in 1556 and John Inglishe in 1562,[16] but by 1572 the property had come to John (later Sir John) Stawell.[17] The rectory descended in the Stawell family until the end of the 17th century, passing on the death of Sir John to his son, also John (d. 1604), and to his grandson Sir John Stawell, K.B. (d. 1662). From the last it descended to two sons, George (d. 1669) and Ralph Stawell (cr. Baron Stawell of Somerton 1683, d. 1689). Ralph's son John, Lord Stawell, died in 1692, leaving large debts.[18]

The Stawell estate was in the hands of trustees in 1696, and in the following year they sold the rectory to Richard Musgrave of Lyons Inn, London, later of West Monkton (d. 1727).[19] Two of Musgrave's

trustees presented to the living, one in 1720, another in 1744, and Thomas Musgrave of Old Cleeve presented in 1753, presumably after succeeding to the estate.[20] Thomas's heir was his sister Juliana, wife of Sir James Langham, Bt., of Cottesbrooke (Northants.). The Langham family retained the advowson, but offered the corn tithes for sale in 1795, when they were worth by composition nearly £160 and 'capable of great improvement'. The purchaser was Robert Uttermare Bullen of Taunton.[21]

Almost immediately Bullen began to sell the tithes of individual farms, but a substantial amount passed in 1801 to John Weech, in 1805 to John Donne, and by 1817 to Donne's son Richard (d. 1831).[22] John Hancock (d. 1852), who married Richard Donne's daughter Mary, was paying land tax on the estate in 1832, but by 1840 the remaining great tithes were held jointly by Anne, second wife of John Hancock, and by Elizabeth Donne, possibly Mary Donne's sister.[23] A tithe rent charge of £218 16s. 6d. was agreed in 1840,[24] and by 1867 the income had been transferred to the benefice.[25] The parsonage barn was retained by the Hancock family. John Hancock was succeeded by his son John Donne Hancock, and the latter by his son Richard Donne Hancock (d. 1912).[26] Richard's widow conveyed the barn to trustees for use as a village hall in 1929.[27]

In 1833 John Hancock, besides owning the rectorial tithes, was tenant of Halse farm, the mill, and the Combe estate; his cousin, Richard Murford Hancock, owned Combe House (later Halse Manor) and its land.[28] In 1840, after extensive sales to the Prior family, the Hancocks still owned 198 a. including Blake's farm and occupied a further 380 a. including Manor farm and Higher Blake's.[29] John Donne Hancock farmed 451 a. in 1851.[30] From his eldest son Richard the estate passed to George Arthur Donne Hancock, eldest son of Richard's brother George. G. A. D. Hancock sold the estate, comprising some 365 a. and Blake's House, to the Southwick Rochecourt Estates, of Fareham (Hants), in 1948, and in 1981 it was divided between three large farms.[31]

ECONOMIC HISTORY. The Domesday estate, assessed at 4 hides, had land for 7 ploughteams. The demesne farm, measuring 1 hide, had 2 teams, and 23 tenants with 3½ teams occupied the rest of the arable land. There were 8 a. of meadow, 12 a. of wood, and 20 a. of pasture, and the demesne farm supported 1 cow, 7 pigs, and 40 sheep.[32] Estates in

[4] By Sir Prior Goldney (d. 1925), whose initials appear in several places.
[5] Plate facing p. 125.
[6] S.R.O., DD/AH 11/9.
[7] P.R.O., C 142/99, no. 28.
[8] *S.R.S.* li, p. 77.
[9] P.R.O., CP 25(2)/207/37 Eliz. I East.
[10] S.R.O., DD/DV 8.
[11] Ibid. DD/DV 8; DD/SH (C/1165), box 16.
[12] Ibid. DD/DP 8/3; DD/DRd 7. For Sir William Jones see *D.N.B.*   [13] Wilts. R.O. 473/181, 328.
[14] *S.R.S.* xxv, p. 172.
[15] *L. & P. Hen.* VIII, xx (1), p. 125.
[16] *S.R.S.* lv, p. 145; *Som. Incumbents*, ed. Weaver, 372.
[17] *Som. Incumbents*, ed. Weaver, 372.
[18] G. D. Stawell, *A Quantock Family : hist. of the Stawell family, passim*; *Complete Peerage*, xii (1), 264–7; Hist. MSS. Com. 17, *14th Rep. VI, House of Lords, 1692–3*, p. 330.

[19] S.R.O., DD/DP 33/1; *Som. Wills*, ed. Brown, iii. 41–2.
[20] *Som. Wills*, ed. Brown, iii. 41; S.R.O., D/D/B reg. 25, f. 41; 27, ff. 5, 38v.
[21] S.R.O., T/PH/no 3; ibid. DD/DV 3; DD/NW 23.
[22] Ibid. DD/DV 3; DD/NW 23; ibid. Q/REl; ibid. D/P/hal 2/1/8.
[23] Ibid. Q/REl; ibid. tithe award; ibid. D/P/hal 2/1/5, 8.
[24] Ibid. tithe award.
[25] *Lond. Gaz.* 24 Dec. 1867, 7012.
[26] S.R.O., D/P/hal 2/1/5–6, 8–9; inf. from Mrs. R. Brayne-Baker, Uffculme.
[27] Char. Com. files.
[28] S.R.O., Q/REl.
[29] Ibid. tithe award.
[30] P.R.O., HO 107/1923.
[31] Inf. from Mrs. R. Brayne-Baker and Mr. H. G. Woodman, Halse.
[32] *V.C.H. Som.* i. 493.

GLATTING, OR HUNTING FOR CONGER EELS, *c.* 1920

RALEIGH'S CROSS SHEEP FAIR, 1983

HALSWAY MANOR, STOGUMBER, FROM THE SOUTH-WEST

KILVE COURT FROM THE EAST

the parish given to the Hospitallers in the late 13th century may derive from some of the Domesday tenant holdings; at least one estate, that of Richard of Stoford, included rents, reliefs, and wardships.[33] A late 13th-century grant by the Hospitallers at Stoford gave a life interest in 18 a. of arable subject only to a cash rent, limited suit of court, and a heriot, in return for marling and erecting suitable buildings.[34] By 1338 the demesne farm comprised 220 a. of arable, 80 a. of pasture, much of inferior quality, 18½ a. of meadow, and pasturage in moor and wood. Tenants' rents then amounted to £20 3s., but customary works were worth only 40s. and the manor house was in ruins.[35]

In 1501 John Verney of Fairfield, Stogursey, whose ancestor had held a small property in Halse in 1346,[36] took a 30-year lease of the whole of the Hospitallers' estate attached to the preceptory of Buckland, including Halse and two manors in Devon.[37] His two younger sons, John and George, were to succeed to his lease,[38] but they were replaced in 1508 by Edmund Mill of Wells and Anne his wife.[39] In 1516 Henry Thornton of Curry Mallet took a lease for 40 years,[40] a lease renewed for the same period in 1521.[41] In 1539 William Hawley succeeded Thornton, and as sitting tenant bought the estate from the Crown in 1545.[42]

On the death of Sir Henry Hawley in 1623 the estate was broken up because of his debts.[43] It passed first to trustees who subsequently sold land to raise money.[44] Already the parish had been divided into many small tenant farms, so that Sir Henry's widow in 1629 received six tenements totalling 212 a.[45] The Wescombe family, copyholders on the manor, in 1626 bought 3 small holdings and other closes, in all amounting to 128 a.;[46] John Perry, a prosperous yeoman and owner of the scattered estate known as Halse Arundell manor,[47] acquired c. 100 a. which later passed to the Haddridge family.[48] The site of the old capital messuage with 89 a. of largely customary land was bought by William Cox of Crewkerne, and part later passed to the Hancock family.[49] By the 1650s the parsonage was the most valuable single estate, though largely comprising the rectorial tithes. It was closely followed in value by that of Thomas Wescombe, worth £44 a year in 1653. Next came those of John Studdier (£20) and William Cade (£18), and after them three or four holdings worth between £12 and £14.[50]

Inventories and leases of the late 17th century suggest several substantial farms, perhaps the largest occupied by Henry Gooding (d. 1677), who had the Northway estate, Halse House, and land at Stoford.

The capital value of his personalty, including a lease at Ash Priors, was £2,154. The farm buildings at Northway included a substantial house, a malt mill, a wring house, chambers for cheese and apples, and a cider house. Crops were wheat, barley, and peas, and clover was grown in quantity. Stock included 7 milking cows, bullocks, oxen, calves, 14 'field' pigs, and two flocks totalling 162 sheep, together with the cash for others recently sold.[51] Richard Winter, Gooding's neighbour at Winter's farm, had a flock of 66 sheep, and in store 110 bu. of barley and 45 'shears' of wool.[52] Agnes Hancock (d. 1691), widow, left 96 sheep.[53]

Regular manuring was required in a lease of 1714, and grain crops were limited to two consecutive years, to be followed by fallow, peas, or vetch. A field called Waterletts in 1630[54] suggests irrigation which by 1840 had created 44 a. of water meadows and 33 a. of 'water pasture', fed by streams flowing from above the village to Halse water by means of a system of sluices.[55]

Four main holdings emerged during the 18th century, usually known as the Home estate (later essentially Manor farm), the Combe tenement or Halse House tenement (which included Northway farm), Blake's tenement, and a property which, in part at least, was the manor of Halse Arundell and included the mill.[56] By 1766 two men, John Hancock and George Prior, had begun to buy up parts of these holdings. The Hancocks had been prominent as butchers and farmers in the parish since the 17th century,[57] and were later to be well known as lawyers and maltsters at Wiveliscombe.[58] George Prior, the son of George Prior of Thurlbear, inherited land in Halse which represented part of Halse Arundell manor.[59] He bought the Home estate with the manor in 1775.[60] At his death in 1814 some of his property passed to his younger son Edward, but John, the elder, was by 1840 living in Halse House and owned 263 a. including Manor farm. Edward owned 226 a. The Hancocks owned or occupied 578 a.[61]

In 1803 John Hancock the younger had a farm with 134 a. under arable, nearly two thirds with wheat and nearly one third barley. His grassland supported 2,134 sheep, 23 young cattle, 5 cows, and 12 oxen.[62] Before 1814 Manor farm, then called Halse farm, comprised 186 a. of arable, 57 a. of meadow, 17 a. of pasture, and 15 a. of orchard.[63] Approximately the same proportions continued during the 19th century, grassland amounting to about a quarter of the arable acreage.[64] The parish was known for its wheat, barley, and root crops in the late 19th century,[65] and for the farming prowess of

[33] S.R.S. xxv, pp. 173–5.
[34] Ibid. pp. 174–5.
[35] Knights Hospitallers in Eng. 17.
[36] S.R.O., DD/AH 65/3.
[37] B.L. Lansd. MS. 200, f. 84 and v.
[38] S.R.S. xix. 103.
[39] B.L. Cott. MS. Claud. E. vi, f. 53v.–54.
[40] Ibid. 162v.–163v.
[41] P.R.O., LR 2/62, f. 87 and v.
[42] Ibid. f. 181 and v.; above, manors.
[43] P.R.O., C 142/405, no. 46.
[44] S.R.O., DD/DV 1; Wilts. R.O. 473/169.
[45] S.R.O., DD/DV 4; Wilts. R.O. 473/173.
[46] S.R.O., DD/DV 1.
[47] Wilts. R.O. 473/172; S.R.O., DD/SH (C/1165), boxes 16, 21, 24.
[48] Wilts. R.O. 473/169.
[49] Ibid. 473/171.

[50] S.R.O., DD/DV 12/2.
[51] Ibid. DD/SP, inventory 1677.
[52] Ibid. inventory 1677.
[53] Ibid. inventory 1691.
[54] Ibid. DD/DV 4.
[55] Ibid. tithe award.
[56] Ibid. Q/REl; ibid. DD/DV 12/2; ibid. D/P/hal 4/1/2–3, 13/2/2–3.
[57] Wilts. R.O. 473/181.
[58] e.g. S.R.O., DD/DV 3.
[59] Wilts. R.O. 473/327–8; above, manors.
[60] S.R.O., DD/DV 2; Wilts. R.O. 473/185.
[61] Wilts. R.O. 473/358; S.R.O., tithe award.
[62] S.R.O., DD/SF 3934.
[63] Wilts. R.O. 473/358.
[64] S.R.O., tithe award; statistics supplied by the then Bd. of Agric. 1905.
[65] Kelly's Dir. Som. (1883).

the Hancocks of Manor farm. J. D. Hancock employed 44 men, women, and boys on his 438 a. in 1851.[66] During the turnip season something like a gang system operated, and girls were brought in for bird scaring.[67] R. D. Hancock was a well known exhibitor of Devon cattle at the turn of the 20th century, while his neighbour, W. Greenaway, specialized in both Devon sheep and cattle.[68] By 1976 a gradual change in land use had increased grassland to about three fifths of the parish, shared between eight holdings, of which two were over 100 ha. One farm specialized in dairying, one in cattle and sheep, and one was a fruit farm.[69]

A clothier and two fullers were in business in the parish by 1631, and two Irish clothiers had property in the village until 1693.[70] A villager was reported in the manor court in 1706 and 1707 for building a dye house on the common.[71] In 1742 a complaint was made against pits for watering flax on Whitmoor common.[72]

MILL. There was a mill at Halse in 1086.[73] In 1630 it was let on long lease, and was occupied by members of the Blake and Crosse families in the 17th century.[74] By 1707 it had passed to the Risdons of Trull and Bradford on Tone.[75] Before 1761 it was acquired by William Scott, and passed from him to George Prior.[76] It descended with the Prior family estate until 1939.[77] The mill was rebuilt in 1801-2, when machinery was installed by Joseph Nation.[78] The mill, driven by a large overshot wheel, continued in use until c. 1948.[79]

MARKET. The prior of the Hospitallers was granted a Monday market at Halse in 1290.[80] No further trace of it has been found.

LOCAL GOVERNMENT. The tithings of Halse and Dodington were linked by the early 14th century because both were owned by the Hospitallers. They were regarded as a single tithing in 1569.[81] For the same reason Middleton farm in Huish Champflower and land in Skilgate, also belonging to the Hospitallers, were part of Halse tithing for land tax purposes until the early 19th century.[82] Dodington was claimed as part of Halse manor and its lord as a free suitor to the manor court as late as 1858, and the manorial rental included land in Skilgate, Bishop's Lydeard, Langford Budville, and Heathfield.[83] The

tithingman was chosen at the Halse manor court, and by the early 18th century the office was served in regular rotation by the holders of particular tenements.[84]

A draft of a session at Michaelmas 1507 and extracts from courts in 1530 and 1611 are the earliest manorial records to be found,[85] but a tenant at Stoford in the 1280s held land in return for suit twice a year.[86] The valuation of the manor in 1338 included pleas and perquisites worth 40s. a year.[87] The manor court at Halse continued until 1861 or later, and court papers and presentments survive for the periods 1705-12, 1716-98, 1804, 1806-30, 1837, and 1843-61.[88] By 1705 the court met only in October each year, normally at Halse and in 1837 at the New Inn, though in 1738 a session was adjourned to the Red Lion at Wiveliscombe. Meetings were held in the morning and were followed by a meal.[89]

In 1507 the officers of the court were two constables, a reeve, a tithingman, and an ale taster.[90] The constables survived until 1842. By the 19th century there were also a bailiff and a tithingman, from 1824 the former also serving as hayward and pound keeper. The three offices had been separated by 1861.[91] The court assumed jurisdiction over encroachments and nuisances, and in the early 16th century over assaults.[92] From the early 18th century it maintained the pound but disclaimed responsibility for the stocks and the cucking stool. The stocks, formerly the concern of the tithing, were from 1720 to be repaired by the tenants of four 'block houses' in the village. The cucking stool was reported out of repair in 1722 and was said to be quite demolished by 1738. The stocks survived until 1848 when the vicar objected to their further repair.[93]

In the mid 18th century the two wardens and two overseers were elected by a small group of parishioners known variously as the vestry, Halse Easter meeting, or Halse meeting.[94] The overseers, whose accounts date from 1638, spent their income from rates and parish land normally in small weekly payments and on occasional gifts of clothing. They also administered the charity money and the charity school.[95] By 1701 they had taken over the parish house, which the wardens had rented from 1627 or earlier, but that house and others acquired later in the century were not used to house the poor.[96] Parish paupers, wearing red badges from 1707,[97] were generously treated. The overseers awarded themselves £1 a year each for expenses from 1774 and employed a parish doctor from 1789.[98] In 1809 they severely limited the practice of taking parish

[66] P.R.O., HO 107/1923; T. D. Acland and W. Sturge, Farming of Som. 36.
[67] Rep. Com. Women and Children in Agric. [4202-I], pp. 121-2, H.C. (1868-9), xiii.
[68] V.C.H. Som. ii. 534, 536; Kelly's Dir. Som. (1914).
[69] Min. of Agric., Fisheries, and Food, agric. returns 1976.
[70] S.R.S. xxiv. 152, 165; S.R.O., DD/DV 2.
[71] S.R.O., DD/DV 12/3.
[72] Ibid. 12/4.   [73] V.C.H. Som. i. 443.
[74] S.R.O., DD/HLM 8; ibid. D/P/hal 4/1/2, 13/2/2.
[75] Ibid. DD/HLM 8; ibid. D/P/hal 4/1/2, 13/2/2; P.R.O., CP 25(2)/962/6 Anne Trin.
[76] S.R.O., DD/DV 12/2, poor rate 1761.
[77] Ibid. DD/X/LOV 13.
[78] Ibid. DD/DV 15; Wilts. R.O. 473/185 (duplicate accounts).   [79] Local inf.
[80] Cal. Chart. R. ii. 345.
[81] Feud. Aids, iv. 333; S.R.S. xx. 164-5; above, Dodington.

[82] S.R.O., Q/REl.
[83] Ibid. DD/DV 12/1, 13.
[84] Ibid. 12/2.
[85] Ibid. DD/AH 11/9; DD/WY 4/R2; DD/DV 4.
[86] S.R.S. xxv, pp. 174-5.
[87] Knights Hospitallers in Eng. 18.
[88] Presentments 1780-97, 1804, 1806-23, 1826-30 in the possession of Cdr. J. W. Endicott, Mill House, Halse; the remainder S.R.O., DD/DV 12/1-4.
[89] Ibid. DD/DV 12/4 (1775).
[90] Ibid. DD/AH 11/9.
[91] Ibid. DD/DV 12/1-4.
[92] Ibid. DD/AH 11/9; DD/DV 12/1-4.
[93] Ibid. DD/DV 12/1 (1848, 1861); 12/3 (1705, 1720, 1722, 1738).
[94] Ibid. D/P/hal 4/1/2 (1762-3), 4/1/3 (1809, 1814, 1818).
[95] Ibid. 13/2/1.
[96] Ibid. 4/1/1, 13/2/2.
[97] Ibid. 13/2/2.
[98] Ibid. 13/2/3.

apprentices.[99] There was a single poorhouse in the village by 1840,[1] its site in 1981 a garden east of the Old School House. The parish became part of the Taunton poor-law union in 1836, the Taunton rural district in 1894, and Taunton Deane district (later Borough) in 1974.[2]

CHURCH. Robert Arundel gave the church of Halse to the order of St. John of Jerusalem.[3] A chaplain was serving the parish c. 1159, and a vicarage had been ordained by c. 1188, perhaps at the time the original gift received episcopal confirmation.[4] The living was declared a rectory in 1867 on the transfer of the rectorial tithe rent charge to the benefice.[5] It remained a sole cure until 1933, when it was linked with Heathfield. About 1960 it became a united benefice with Heathfield, and for a time until 1975 was held with Ash Priors and Fitzhead. From 1975 the living, severed from Heathfield, was held with Ash Priors alone.[6]

The advowson of the vicarage in the Middle Ages was held by the priors of the order of St. John and in 1422 was exercised by the preceptor of Buckland as *locum tenens* for the prior.[7] From 1572, and possibly in 1556 and 1562, successive owners or occupiers of the rectory estate exercised the advowson.[8] The Langham family retained the patronage after the sale of the rectory estate in 1795,[9] and the advowson descended with the baronetcy until 1960 when Sir J. C. P. Langham transferred it to the bishop of Bath and Wells.[10]

The vicarage was valued at £10 in the 14th century and was not regularly taxed.[11] It was said to be worth only 10 marks in 1445,[12] was taxed at £6 in 1532,[13] and in 1535 was assessed at the same sum.[14] By c. 1668 the reputed value was £40.[15] The living was augmented in 1761–3 by grants of £50 from the patron, Thomas Musgrave, £50 from Mrs. Horner's and £100 from Mrs. Pincombe's trustees, and £200 from Queen Anne's Bounty. The same trustees gave the same sums, the vicar, Nicholas Spencer, £50, and the Bounty £200 in 1796–8, and in 1810 the Horner trustees added £200 to a parliamentary grant of £300.[16] In 1861 Queen Anne's Bounty increased the endowment by £150 to meet a further benefaction of £200 from the Horner trustees.[17] The net income in 1831 was £174.[18]

Tithes and oblations of the vicarage in 1535 were worth £5 18s. 4d. largely from wool, lambs, and personal offerings.[19] The tithes in 1613 were described as Easter oblations, tithe of lambs on St. Mark's day, of wool at shearing time, of grass of certain meadows, tithe corn from Hemplands, and the tithe of orchard fruit, later identified as pears, apples, and hops.[20] In 1840 the vicar was awarded £131 as a rent charge in lieu of vicarial tithe which since 1788 had been almost entirely subject to compositions.[21]

Vicarial glebe was worth only 20d. in 1535.[22] It amounted to 2 a. beside the vicarage house in 1571.[23] Land was purchased at Churchstanton (Devon) in 1763 with augmentation money, and more was held by the 1820s in Milverton and Heathfield.[24] Higher Willand farm, Churchstanton, was sold in 1916.[25]

In 1634 the vicarage house comprised a hall, parlour, and kitchen, with chambers over parlour and kitchen. Beside the house stood a milk-house, dovecot, barn, and stable, and nearby a herb garden.[26] The house was replaced by a stone building, presumably on the same site, in the later 19th century, and in 1964 by a brick house further west.[27]

The parish priest in 1316 was accused of various irregularities including clandestine weddings and doubtful acquisition of his orders.[28] Hugh Grobham, vicar 1457–64, was at the same time a brother of St. John's hospital, Bridgwater.[29] In 1532 there was a parish curate as well as the vicar.[30] The parish closely followed the liturgical changes of the Reformation, the cost being found from the proceeds of the Rood-mass ale and by collecting a due called 'hognceng' or hoggling money. The vicar, Thomas Cockes, contributed handsomely towards an English Bible c. 1546.[31] The south wall of the church contains painted extracts from the Prayer Book.[32] There were several complaints against Robert Harris, vicar 1601–44, for not preaching,[33] but in his time there were normally seven communion services each year, and the parish bought a cloth for the communion table and erected the royal arms in 1634 in due order.[34] Francis Nation, vicar from 1644, was deprived c. 1651, and is said to have taken a military command.[35]

During the 18th century the parish was served by resident vicars, and the fabric was regularly maintained.[36] Nicholas Spencer, vicar 1793–1840, nominally domestic chaplain to Earl Spencer and for a short time chaplain to the English factory and embassy at St. Petersburg, continued the tradition of residence. In 1815 there was a service with sermon

99 Ibid. 4/1/3.
1 Ibid. tithe award.
2 Youngs, *Local Admin. Units*, i. 427, 675–6.
3 *S.R.S.* xxv, pp. 171–2.
4 Ibid. pp. 177–8.
5 *Lond. Gaz.* 24 Dec. 1867, p. 7012.
6 *Dioc. Dir.*
7 *Som. Incumbents*, ed. Weaver, 372; *S.R.S.* xxx, p. 422.
8 Above, manors.
9 S.R.O., T/PH/no 3.
10 Inf. from Dioc. Regy.; Burke, *Peerage* (1970), 1535–6.
11 *S.R.S.* ix, pp. 224, 239–40, 423.
12 Ibid. xlix, p. 33.
13 S.R.O., D/D/Vc 20.
14 *Valor Eccl.* (Rec. Com.), i. 172.
15 S.R.O., D/D/Vc 24.
16 Ibid. DD/SF 3934; C. Hodgson, *Queen Anne's Bounty* (1845), pp. clxii, clxxviii, clxxxiv, ccxlii & *Suppl.* (1864), pp. l, lxii.
17 *Livings Augmented Q.A.B.* H.C. 122 (1867), liv.
18 *Rep. Com. Eccl. Revenues*, pp. 138–9.
19 *Valor Eccl.* (Rec. Com.), i. 172.

20 S.R.O., D/D/Rg 379.
21 Ibid. tithe award; ibid. DD/SF 3934.
22 *Valor Eccl.* (Rec. Com.), i. 172.
23 S.R.O., D/D/Rg 379.
24 Ibid. DD/SF 3934.
25 Ibid. D/P/hal 5/2/1.
26 Ibid. D/D/Rg 379.
27 Local inf.
28 *S.R.S.* i. 118.
29 Ibid. xlix, pp. 296, 409.
30 S.R.O., D/D/Vc 20.
31 Ibid. D/P/hal 4/1/4: TS. transcript, printed (not always accurately) in F. J. Montgomery, *Halse Village Notes* (priv. print 1902–3).
32 Possibly from the wedding service: *St. James Halse, Guide* (c. 1976).
33 S.R.O., D/D/Ca 151, 310.
34 Ibid. D/P/hal 4/1/1.
35 *Walker Revised*, ed. A. G. Matthews, 317.
36 S.R.O., D/P/hal 4/1/2. Money was raised in 1754 and 1759. A plaster roundel above the tower arch is dated 1758.

each Sunday.[37] By 1828 Spencer was also serving Ash Priors.[38] He bought a barrel organ for Halse in 1830.[39] Quarterly celebrations were usual until the 1840s, and by 1843 there was service twice a Sunday.[40] On Census Sunday 1851 attendances were 125 in the morning, including 35 from the Sunday school, and 180 in the afternoon, with 40 children.[41] By 1879 there were celebrations each month and at festivals.[42]

By 1548 a light was maintained in the church.[43] A church house had been built by c. 1559,[44] and it was still standing in 1789.[45]

In 1374 it was claimed that there had been a chantry in Halse church until twelve years earlier, and that it had been founded by Roger Arundel who had given the manor to the Hospitallers to support it. There appears to have been confusion of Roger with Robert Arundel, who not only gave the manor to the Hospitallers, but also granted land at Ash Priors for the use of Halse church, where his body was due to rest, to support a priest there.[46]

The church of *ST. JAMES*[47] stands on high ground at the south end of the village. It is built of local sandstone with Hamstone dressings and comprises a chancel with north chapel, nave with north aisle and south porch, and west tower. Until 1867 or later it was plastered and whitewashed externally.[48] The rear arch of the south door, the font, and a fragment of carved stone beneath the east window survive from the 12th-century church, which may have included the Arundel family chapel on the north side of the chancel, though the corbels in the present arch between chancel and chapel are of the 13th century. The plain tower has elements of 14th-century work and contains one, and formerly two, 15th-century bells from the Exeter foundry.[49] The north aisle was built c. 1546 by the mason John Harris.[50] The porch, which houses fragments of a late medieval cross, has large square-headed windows. The rood screen, once stretching across both nave and aisle, contains original work only across the nave. 'Old wooden work' above it was removed in 1803.[51] The north end of the screen was built c. 1903.[52] By 1771 there was a singing gallery in the aisle.[53] Additions in the 19th century included the glass of the east window of the chancel, incorporating panels made in Florence by artists from Bruges, one piece of which is dated 1548. The glass was given by the Revd. John Sanford to his wife's uncle, the vicar Nicholas Spencer.[54] A thorough restoration began in 1900, during which the chancel arch was replaced by a wooden rood

beam, the gallery was removed, the bench ends were designed and carved locally, and murals decorated aisle and chancel, all in the Arts and Crafts style.[55]

The plate includes a cup of 1723 given by Richard Musgrave, lay rector, and another of 1832 given by the vicar, Nicholas Spencer.[56] The registers date from 1558 and are complete.[57]

NONCONFORMITY. By 1845, and possibly by 1831,[58] there was a society of Bible Christians at Halse,[59] and a chapel was built in 1847. On Census Sunday 1851 there were 61 people at the afternoon service and 57 at the evening.[60] The chapel formed part of the Milverton and Taunton, later the Taunton, circuit, and became part of the United Methodist Church in 1926.[61] It closed in 1964.[62] The building was later converted to a garage.

EDUCATION. There was a school in the parish by 1603.[63] By 1750 six poor children were being taught at the expense of parish charities and a charity school continued until 1824 or later, tuition and a clothing allowance being given to children attending church and catechism.[64] The vestry appointed the master or mistress.[65] In 1818 there were 24 pupils.[66] A Sunday school was started in 1819,[67] and by 1832 was receiving the money formerly given to the charity school.[68] By 1835 three day schools, one a recently established National school, the others for 'very young' children, had 47 pupils between them. The Sunday school then had 56 children.[69] In 1847 the only day school was the parochial school with 44 children, including infants; 34 of those children also went to the Sunday school, which had a total of 58 pupils.[70] By 1851 there was also a Sunday school for c. 30 children at the Bible Christian chapel.[71]

In 1853 Edward Prior, lord of the manor, endowed the National school and gave a new building, completed in 1856.[72] The building was held on lease from his successors until 1939, when it was conveyed to the Diocesan Board of Finance.[73] In 1903 there were 66 children on the books.[74] By 1940 numbers had fallen by half, and from 1950 senior pupils were no longer taken. The school was closed in 1960 when there were only 14 children on the books.[75] In 1980 the school was a private house.

CHARITIES FOR THE POOR. About 1636

[37] S.R.O., DD/SF 3934, including Spencer's diaries; ibid. D/D/B returns 1815; M.I. in ch.
[38] S.R.O., DD/SF 3934; *Rep. Com. Eccl. Revenues*, pp. 138–9. [39] S.R.O., DD/SF 3934.
[40] Ibid. D/D/V returns 1840, 1843.
[41] P.R.O., HO 129/315/5/3/4.
[42] S.R.O., D/D/V returns 1870.
[43] *S.R.S.* ii. 32.
[44] S.R.O., D/P/hal 4/1/4.
[45] Ibid. D/P/hal 13/2/3.
[46] *Cal. Close*, 1374–7, 6; *S.R.S.* xxv, pp. 171–2.
[47] Collinson, *Hist. Som.* iii. 528.
[48] S.R.O., D/P/hal 4/1/3.
[49] Ibid. DD/SAS CH 16. The 4th was replaced in 1976 and in 1980 was exhibited in Exeter.
[50] Ibid. D/P/hal 4/1/4.
[51] Ibid. 4/1/3.
[52] *St. James Halse, Guide*.
[53] S.R.O., D/P/hal 4/1/2.
[54] *Proc. Som. Arch. Soc.* liv. i. 55; S.R.O., DD/SF 3934.
[55] S.R.O., D/P/hal 4/1/3; ibid. DD/SF 3934.

[56] *Proc. Som. Arch. Soc.* xlvi. 180.
[57] S.R.O., D/P/hal 2/1/1–6. [58] Char. Com. files.
[59] *Bible Christian Mag.* (1845); inf. from Mr. R. F. S. Thorne, district archivist.
[60] P.R.O., HO 129/315/5/3/5.
[61] Inf. from Mr. Thorne.
[62] Inf. from the Revd. I. Trigg.
[63] S.R.O., D/D/Ca 134.
[64] Ibid. D/P/hal 2/1/6, 13/2/2, 17/3/1, 17/3/4.
[65] Ibid. DD/SF 3934.
[66] *Educ. of Poor Digest*, H.C. 224 (1819), ix (2).
[67] *Educ. Enq. Abstract*, H.C. 62 (1835), xlii.
[68] S.R.O., D/P/hal 17/3/4.
[69] *Educ. Enq. Abstract*.
[70] Nat. Soc. *Inquiry, 1846–7*, Som. 10–11.
[71] P.R.O., HO 129/315/5/3/5.
[72] S.R.O., C/E 27; *P.O. Dir. Som.* (1861); datestone on building.
[73] S.R.O., C/E 27; DD/X/LOV 13; Char. Com. files.
[74] S.R.O., C/E 27.
[75] Ibid. C/E 63, log bks. 1904–60; ibid. *Schs. Lists*.

Christopher Norman of Heathfield gave £10 for the poor, the payment of interest secured on land already owned by the parish.[76] The income was distributed in cash at Christmas and Easter each year. By 1649 the capital had been augmented by a capital sum of £5, the accumulated rent paid for parish land.[77] The two charities were apparently absorbed in the endowment made by Edward Wescombe of London, merchant, member of a prominent local family, who before 1687 gave £200 for the benefit of the poor.[78] By 1721 the total income was £8 9s. 6d., and in the 1730s was distributed at Christmas and Easter.[79] By 1739 the capital was invested in an estate of c. 14 a. at Common Down, and by 1744 the income was £14 13s. 4d.[80] From 1756 the charity accounts were apparently separated from the overseers, and trustees seem to have controlled the original parish land and, by 1783, three cottages which had come to the parish in return for financial assistance to their owners. The trustees also supported the charity school. Until 1770 payments were made each Christmas, but thereafter throughout the year as needed.[81] Before 1786 Baker's charity had been founded with land near the church worth £4 10s. a year.[82] By 1826 it had been absorbed into the Wescombe and parish endowments, to which two more houses were added in 1805. The parish field was converted to garden allotments in 1831. The total income of the combined endowments was £42 10s. in 1826[83] and £52 in 1978.[84]

The sum of £50 was given to the parish before 1786 by George Tiffin, or Vivian, a former parish apprentice, half for the support of a school. An unsound title prevented the parish from claiming the bequest.[85]

By will proved 1859 Edward Prior of Halse House gave £100 for the poor. The annual income in 1965 was £2 9s. and in 1977 £2.44.[86]

Spiring Spurway Baker of Halse by will proved 1878 gave £200 for the poor. The income was distributed in coal between 1881 and 1886 and from 1887 in cash. In 1941 small sums totalling £5 4s. were given to 42 people.[87] The income in 1977 was £5.[88]

Lucilla Maria Spurway gave £50 by her will proved 1859. The income was normally administered with Edward Prior's charity, and was distributed in cash in May each year. In 1894 the sum of 4 guineas was shared between 64 parishioners. Nothing was given between 1944 and 1964 in order to allow cash to accumulate. The sum of £15 was given to 15 parishioners in 1973.[89] The income in 1977 was £1.20.[90]

Major-Gen. Nathaniel Thorn of Halse, by will proved 1857 left £300, the income to be used after repair of family tombstones to buy bread and clothing for distribution in April and December in church. In the 1950s the charity was paid by means of tickets at local shops. In 1977 the income was £7.48.[91]

The Halse Relief in Need Charity was formed in 1978 by the amalgamation of the surviving five charities, and its income, including investments after the sale of land at Common Down, amounted to c. £450 in 1980. It was available to people in need with longstanding connexions with the parish.[92]

HUISH CHAMPFLOWER

THE ANCIENT parish of Huish Champflower, its name in part signifying a cultivated area and in part its ownership in the 12th century by the Champflower family,[93] lay in two separate parts on the southern slopes of the Brendons, of which nearly one third was described as hills, woods, and waste in 1839.[94] The two parts together measured 2,909 a. in 1881, but when the detached area of Chipstable parish which divided them was added to Huish in 1884 the area increased to its present size of 1,349 ha. (3,334 a.).[95]

The southern portion of the ancient parish, which contains the village of Huish, occupies an irregular area rising to the west of the river Tone, including the valleys of two parallel streams. The southern boundary lies on Heydon Hill (c. 338 m.) above Huish moor, where rough common ground was shared with Chipstable until inclosure in 1845.[96] To the north the boundary with Clatworthy rises to 309 m. The western boundary follows a small stream.

The northern part of Huish lies on the steep slopes of the Brendons and is divided from the southern by the diamond-shaped portion of Chipstable comprising East Withy and Chitcombe. It is irregular in shape, its north-east and south-west boundaries marked by streams now running into Clatworthy reservoir, one of which, considered to be

[76] Ibid. D/D/Ca 310; ibid. D/P/hal 13/2/1.
[77] Ibid. D/P/hal 13/2/1.
[78] Ibid. DD/DV 1.
[79] Ibid. D/P/hal 13/2/2.
[80] 15th Rep. Com. Char. 448–9; S.R.O., D/P/hal 13/2/2 (1745–7).
[81] S.R.O., D/P/hal 17/3/1.
[82] Char. Don. H.C. 511 (1816), xvi.
[83] 15th Rep. Com. Char. 448–9; S.R.O., D/P/hal 17/3/4.
[84] Inf. from Mr. R. Lang, chmn. par. cncl.
[85] Char. Don.

[86] Char. Com. files; inf. from Mr. Lang.
[87] Char. Com. files; S.R.O., D/P/hal 17/3/3; DD/CH 53, will.
[88] Inf. from Mr. Lang.
[89] Char. Com. files; S.R.O., D/P/hal 17/3/2.
[90] Inf. from Mr. Lang.
[91] Char. Com. files; inf. from Mr. Lang.
[92] Inf. from Mr. R. G. Purves, clerk of the charity.
[93] Ekwall, Eng. Place-Names (1960), 256.
[94] S.R.O., tithe award.
[95] Census, 1881, 1891, 1971.
[96] Below.

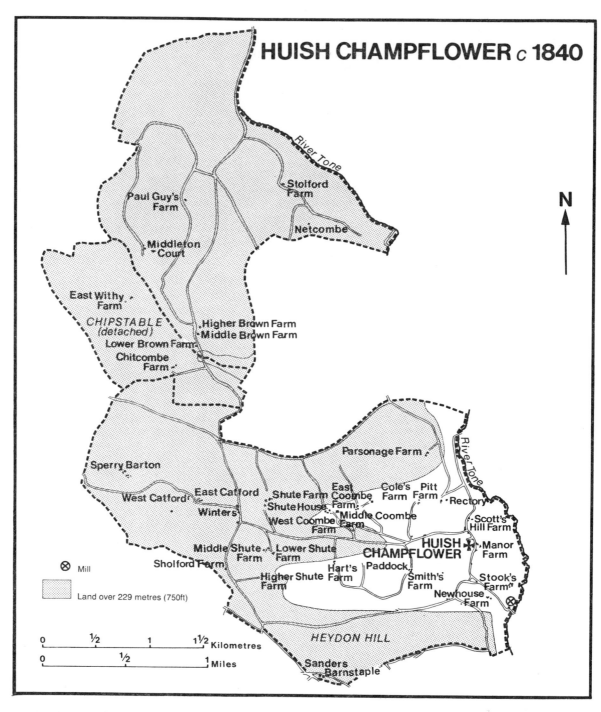

HUISH CHAMPFLOWER c 1840

N

⊗ Mill

Land over 229 metres (750ft)

0   ½   1   1½ Kilometres

0   ½   1 Miles

the headwater of the river Tone,[97] was disputed in 1231.[98] To the north-west the parish reaches the plateau of Brendon Hill (375 m.) and a ridge beyond at 396 m. The boundaries of the open ground on Brendon Hill are marked by the Bronze Age monolith known as Dun's Stone (Dinneston in 1187)[99] and by a stone known in the 12th century as Doleston.[1] Part of this northern section, an estate known as Middleton, probably became part of Huish parish when its tithes were granted to the chaplain of Huish in 1187.[2]

The parish measures nearly 7 km. from Heydon Hill in the south to Brendon Hill in the north. The northern part of the parish lies on slates, siltstones, and sandstones of the various beds of the Upper Devonian Morte Slates. In the south the Morte Slates continue southwards to Huish moor, where Pickwell Down beds are found beneath the ground rising to Heydon Hill.[3] Small, disused quarries are found throughout the parish.[4]

Three round barrows lie on or near the boundaries of the parish, one at the northern edge near the

[97] O.S. Map 1/25,000, ST 03 (1962 edn.).
[98] *Cal. Close*, 1227–31, 587.
[99] *S.R.S.* xxv, pp. 188–9; L. V. Grinsell, *Archaeology of Exmoor*, 41; *Som. Co. Herald, Notes and Queries*, 2 June 1929.

[1] *S.R.S.* xxv, pp. 188–9.
[2] Ibid. p. 189.
[3] Geol. Surv. Map 1″, solid and drift, sheet 294 (1969 edn.).
[4] O.S. Map 6″, Som. XLVII. SE. (1887 edn.).

Brendon ridgeway, and two on Heydon Hill.[5] Huish village is a small nucleated settlement including the church on sloping ground above the Tone in the south-east corner of the parish. Scattered farms were established elsewhere in the parish: Middleton (Middledon) is mentioned in 1187,[6] Stolford (Stoford) also in the late 12th century, and Sperry (Spareheghey) by 1306.[7] Other farms, probably of similar antiquity, such as Catford, Brown (formerly 'Bruneland'),[8] Shute, and Coombe, were subsequently divided, forming grouped holdings such as East and West Catford or Lower, Middle, and Higher Brown farms. In the early 19th century there were cottage encroachments on the edge of Huish moor,[9] at Winters beside the road between Shute and Catford,[10] and in the extreme south-west at Sanders Barnstaple, a name transferred from a small deserted farmstead in Raddington parish by 1822.[11] In contrast, farmsteads called Nuttons and Paul's Guys, both in the north part of the parish on the high ground, were merged into neighbouring holdings in the 19th century and lost their identity.[12]

No trace of open arable cultivation has been found in the parish. Brendon Hill and Huish moor were used as common pasture until inclosure in 1845 under an Act of 1842.[13] The road pattern which links the scattered farms includes two main north–south routes. One is above the valley of the Tone, through Huish village and crossing the river by Huish bridge. The other, a continuation of the wide route forming the Chipstable–Raddington boundary,[14] gives direct access to the Brendon ridge. An east–west route became prominent in the 18th century when the road from Wiveliscombe through Langley Marsh to the Watchet–Bampton road, entering Huish at Washbattle (formerly Maundown) bridge and passing through the village,[15] was turnpiked in 1786.[16] A new road across Huish moor was created in 1843 as part of the inclosure.[17]

Surviving farmhouses reveal building phases in the 16th and 17th centuries and remodelling in the 18th; at least one large house was built in the 19th century. The former West Catford Farm and the neighbouring Catford Farm both have 16th-century origins, the first decorated internally with good plaster work in the 1670s.[18] The former Middle Brown Farm, in 1981 used as a farm building, and West Coombe Farm were modest buildings of the 17th century, the latter remodelled in the 18th century.[19] Middleton Court, so called by 1807,[20] was

built probably for Thomas Gordon, formerly of Melton Mowbray (Leics.),[21] on the site of an earlier farm. It has a symmetrical five-bayed front with a steep pediment, the stone doorcase having an ogee head. Alterations were made in 1855 by Sir Walter Trevelyan,[22] when stables and farm buildings were probably added. Coombe End is a large, three-storeyed house of the late 19th century, with panelling said to have come from the medieval church at Upton.[23]

The Castle inn, built as a farmhouse c. 1821,[24] had become a public house by 1833 and an inn by 1840.[25]

There were 125 taxpayers in 1667.[26] The population rose sharply from 321 in 1801 to 454 in the decade before 1841. The high level was maintained until the 1860s, but was followed by a rapid fall to 226 by 1901. Since that date the level has varied little, and in 1971 was 213.[27]

MANORS. Ailric held the manor of *HUISH*, later *HUISH CHAMPFLOWER*, T.R.E., and Roger Arundel in 1086.[28] The overlordship of the manor descended, like that of Raddington,[29] with the barony of Poorstock (Dors.), passing to the Newburgh family.[30] In 1276 Henry de Newburgh granted land and fees, not specifically including Huish, to Queen Eleanor.[31] By colour of this grant the queen usurped other lands which had not been involved, including 2 knights' fees in Huish and Holford St. Mary (in Lydeard St. Lawrence).[32] In 1284–5 Henry's barony was described as held of the queen,[33] and in 1292 the terre tenants of Huish were said to hold of the king because of the feoffment to Queen Eleanor.[34] The fees in Huish and Holford St. Mary were declared c. 1305 to have been wrongfully taken by the queen when John de Newburgh claimed them,[35] but it is doubtful if they were recovered since John's son Robert (d. 1338)[36] alleged in 1326 that the 2 fees were in the hands of the king as Eleanor's heir.[37] The manor was said to be held of the king in chief by the terre tenant in 1339, but of Robert de Newburgh in 1333 and retrospectively in 1352, and of Robert's son Thomas in 1362 when it was said to be held of Winfrith Newburgh manor (Dors.).[38] In 1585 the manor was said to be held of the Crown.[39]

In 1166 Thomas de Champflower held 3 fees of Gerbert de Percy, lord of the barony of Poorstock, and was therefore probably the terre tenant of Huish.

[5] Grinsell, *Archaeology of Exmoor*, 146; *Proc. Som. Arch. Soc.* cxiii, suppl. 34.
[6] *S.R.S.* xxv, p. 189.
[7] S.R.O., DD/WY 5 F1/1.
[8] *S.R.S.* xxv, p. 84; above, hundred.
[9] S.R.O., tithe award.
[10] Ibid. D/D/Rm, box 2.
[11] Ibid. DD/HC 140, 145; *S.R.S.* lxxvi, Greenwood's map. It was called Saunderbastables in 1845: below, Raddington.
[12] S.R.O., tithe award; ibid. DD/HC 140.
[13] Ibid. DD/HC 140; 5 & 6 Vic. c. 7 (Local and Personal).   [14] Above, Chipstable, introduction.
[15] S.R.O., DD/SF 3126.
[16] 26 Geo. III, c. 135.
[17] S.R.O., DD/HC 140; ibid. Q/SR Mids. 1843.
[18] The date 1673 or 1675 appears in one bedroom and the royal arms in another; cf. S.R.O., DD/V Dulverton R.D.
[19] The date 1711 at West Coombe: S.R.O., DD/V Dulverton R.D.
[20] S.R.O., DD/HC 6E.

[21] Ibid. DD/WO 6/5.
[22] Datestone on house.
[23] Devon R.O. 547B/2444.
[24] *Taunton Courier*, 23 May 1821.
[25] S.R.O., D/P/h.c 2/1/4; ibid. tithe award.
[26] Ibid. DD/WY 34.
[27] *V.C.H. Som.* ii. 351; *Census*, 1911–71.
[28] *V.C.H. Som.* i. 493.
[29] Below.
[30] Sanders, *Eng. Baronies*, 72–3.
[31] *S.R.S.* vi. 381. The reference was unknown to Sanders.
[32] *Abbrev. Plac.* (Rec. Com.), 256.
[33] *Feud. Aids*, iv. 275.
[34] *Cal. Inq. p.m.* iii, pp. 95–6.
[35] *Abbrev. Plac.* (Rec. Com.), 256.
[36] *Cal. Inq. p.m.* viii, p. 93.
[37] *Cal. Mem. R.* 1326–7, p. 108.
[38] *Cal. Inq. p.m.* vii, pp. 361–2; viii, p. 162; ix, pp. 378–9; xi, pp. 258, 343; for Thos.'s parentage, ibid. viii, p. 93.
[39] P.R.O., C 142/257, no. 99.

He may have been succeeded by John de Champ-flower, who held a fee in 1196–7 and 1201–2 which Thomas had also held of the barony of Dunster.[40] Another Thomas de Champflower held 2 fees in Huish of Robert de Newburgh in 1212[41] and died c. 1222 leaving two daughters as heirs. After some dispute Huish was assigned as dower to Thomas's widow Nichole, then married to William Waleys or Walsh.[42] Nichole was still alive in 1243,[43] but had died probably by 1252 when Ralph Waleys, son of William, and his wife Joan, elder daughter of Thomas de Champflower, held an estate in Huish of Ralph's father.[44] Ralph and Joan in 1268 claimed land in Huish of the inheritance of Joan,[45] to whom alone the lordship of Huish was ascribed in 1274 and 1277.[46] By 1285 Joan had been succeeded by Nicholas Waleys,[47] probably her son, who died c. 1292 holding the manor and advowson of Huish jointly with his wife Margery.[48]

By 1303[49] the manor had passed to John Waleys (d. by 1333), whose son and heir Nicholas[50] had died c. 1339 leaving two infant daughters, Joan and Elizabeth, as heirs.[51] On the death of both daughters under age on the same day in 1350 the manor was divisible between Nicholas's two surviving sisters and the issue of two dead sisters,[52] subject to the dower of his mother Rose (d. 1361) and his widow Maud (d. 1359), who married as her second husband Walter Cancy.[53]

In 1393 Alice, one of the sisters of Nicholas Waleys and one of the heirs of another sister, Edith,[54] together with her second[55] husband, Williame Colne, made a settlement of two thirds of the manor.[56] By 1397 Alice had made a feoffment of those two thirds to Sir Hugh Courtenay[57] (d. 1425), of Haccombe (Devon). Sir Hugh's widow Maud (d. 1467) in 1428 and 1431 held part of Huish; in 1431 she was apparently living there and her estate was called the manor. Their son, Sir Hugh Courtenay (d. 1471) of Boconnoc (Cornw.),[58] was succeeded by his own son Edward, who was attainted and lost his estates in 1484 for his support of the duke of Buckingham against the king.[59] Huish manor was granted by Richard III in 1485 to John Verney.[60] Later that year Edward was created earl of Devon and regained his estates, but on his death in 1509 the earldom and

lands were forfeited because his son and heir, William, had previously been attainted. William, restored to favour and created earl of Devon in 1511, was succeeded in the same year by his son Henry, created marquess of Exeter in 1525 and attainted and executed in 1539.[61] Some of Henry's lands, including Huish, were granted in 1544 to John de Vere, earl of Oxford, who was immediately licensed to sell Huish to John Lucas.[62] Lucas was succeeded in 1556 by his son Thomas,[63] who in 1567 conveyed it to William Edney of London.[64] In the same year Edney was licensed to sell one third of the manor to Alexander Sydenham of Luxborough and the whole manor and advowson to Thomas Cappes of Jews, in Wiveliscombe.[65] Sydenham, who was apparently owner of the Brett share of Huish manor as mentioned below, bought from James and Nicholas Cappes in 1576 an estate described as half the manor.[66]

One part of Nicholas Waleys's estate passed to his sister Maud's son Simon Brett,[67] who was of age by 1355[68] and who unsuccessfully challenged Alice Colne's title to two thirds of Huish manor in 1393[69] and Sir Hugh Courtenay's in 1397 and 1404.[70] Simon's estate had passed by 1423 to William Brett of Brushford,[71] who was still alive in 1445.[72] In 1508 Alexander Brett sold c. 300 a. in Huish and the advowson or a share of it to William Nethway,[73] and John Nethway was licensed in 1548 to sell to John Norman, clerk, an estate which was said to comprise the manor and advowson of Huish Champflower.[74] Probably by virtue of acquiring that estate Alexander Sydenham presented a rector in 1561.[75]

Alexander Sydenham died in 1585 leaving an only daughter Elizabeth, wife of John (later Sir John) Poyntz of Iron Acton (Glos.).[76] Poyntz sold Huish in 1603 to Warwick (later Sir Warwick) Hele of Wembury (Devon).[77] Sir Warwick died in 1626 leaving as heir a nephew John (later Sir John) Hele still under age.[78] Sir John died between 1646[79] and 1648.[80] By 1663 the advowson and presumably the manor had passed to Sir John Stawell[81] of Bovey Tracy (Devon). Sir John died in 1670[82] leaving his son William to succeed as a minor.[83] William and two trustees held the estate in 1687.[84] By 1720 Samuel Crooke had acquired half the manor, evidently through his wife

[40] Red. Bk. Exch. (Rolls Ser.), i. 103, 216, 226.
[41] Bk. of Fees, i. 94.
[42] Cur. Reg. R. x. 281–2; xii, pp. 102–3, 235, 356; S.R.S. xi, pp. 87–8, which is wrong in suggesting that there were three daughters.
[43] S.R.S. xi, pp. 152–3, 171.
[44] Ibid. vi. 154–5; for Ralph's and Joan's parentage Cur. Reg. R. xii, pp. 102–3, 356.
[45] S.R.S. xxxvi. 35–6.
[46] Rot. Hund. (Rec. Com.), ii. 119, 138.
[47] Feud. Aids, iv. 275.
[48] Cal. Inq. p.m. iii, pp. 95–6.
[49] Feud. Aids, iv. 303.
[50] Cal. Inq. p.m. vii, pp. 361–2.
[51] Ibid. viii, p. 162.
[52] Ibid. ix, pp. 378–9.
[53] Ibid. x, p. 450; xi, p. 343. For the division of the estate ibid. xii, pp. 23–4; xiii, pp. 29–30; Cal. Close, 1364–8, 248; 1413–19, 173–4.
[54] Cal. Inq. p.m. xi, p. 258; Cal. Fine R. 1356–69, 243.
[55] Cal. Inq. p.m. xi, p. 343.
[56] S.R.S. xvii. 120–1.
[57] Sel. Cases in Chanc. (Selden Soc. x), p. 26.
[58] Feud. Aids, iv. 391, 440; Visit. Devon, ed. J. L. Vivian, 245; Wedgwood, Hist. Parl. Biogs. 229.
[59] Complete Peerage, iv. 328–9.
[60] Cal. Pat. 1476–85, 527.

[61] Complete Peerage, iv. 329–31.
[62] L. & P. Hen. VIII, xix (1), pp. 286, 383.
[63] P.R.O., C 142/107, no. 40.
[64] Ibid. CP 25(2)/204/9 Eliz. I East.; licence Cal. Pat. 1563–6, p. 403.
[65] Cal. Pat. 1566–9, pp. 79, 115. The Sydenhams had held land in Huish since 1438: S.R.S. xxii. 92.
[66] P.R.O., CP 25(2)/204/18 Eliz. I East.; ibid. C 66/1154, m. 5.
[67] Cal. Inq. p.m. ix, pp. 378–9; ibid. xi, pp. 258, 343.
[68] Cal. Close, 1354–60, 141.
[69] Ibid. 1392–6, 50.
[70] P.R.O., CP 40/519, Carte rot. 1; CP 40/573, rot. 133; Sel. Cases in Chanc. (Selden Soc. x), p. 26.
[71] S.R.O., DD/WY 4/T; cf. Feud. Aids, iv. 391, 440.
[72] Cal. Pat. 1441–6, 337.   [73] S.R.O., DD/AH 65/7.
[74] Cal. Pat. 1547–8, 268.
[75] Below, church.
[76] P.R.O., C 142/207, no. 99.
[77] Ibid. CP 25(2)/207/45 Eliz. I Hil.
[78] Ibid. C 142/423, no. 80.
[79] Cal. Cttee. for Compounding, i. 542.
[80] Visit. Devon, ed. J. L. Vivian, 464.
[81] Som. Incumbents, ed. Weaver, 379.
[82] G. D. Stawell, A Quantock family, 169.
[83] Som. Wills, ed. Brown, vi. 69.
[84] S.R.P., DD/WO 6/8.

Elizabeth, and in 1733 he conveyed half to John Cooke.[85] In the following year Cooke, then of Exeter, shared possession of Middleton farm with Barbara Taylor, also of Exeter.[86] An estate described as the manor and half the farm was sold by Cooke in 1752 to James Bryant of Withiel Florey.[87]

In or after 1774 Bryant was succeeded by his daughters, Amelia, wife of Thomas Stowell of Winsford, and Peggy, wife of John Bryant of Luxborough. The daughters in 1780 conveyed the lordship to Sir John Trevelyan of Nettlecombe. Sir John died in 1828, and was succeeded as lord of Huish by his second son, the Revd. Walter Trevelyan, under a settlement of 1788.[88] By 1831 the lordship comprised a few cottages and small chief rents.[89] The Trevelyan trustees disposed of the remaining chief rents later in the century,[90] but no sale of the lordship took place, and it is assumed that it passed on the death of Walter Trevelyan in 1830 successively to his son John (d. 1852), John's son Willoughby (d. 1867), and Willoughby's son Sir Walter John Trevelyan, Bt. (d. 1931). From 1891[91] the lordship was held by the successive owners of Nettlecombe manor.[92]

ECONOMIC HISTORY. In the mid 11th century Huish gelded for 2¾ hides but had land for 12 ploughteams. The demesne farm had 2 teams and was worked by 5 serfs. Twenty villeins and 6 bordars had 6 teams. The 20 a. of meadow were presumably near the village, beside the Tone and its tributary streams; there were 60 a. of woodland. The pasture, measuring a league by half a league, was perhaps the later common land on Huish moor and Heydon Hill. There was a flock of 100 sheep.[93]

The land in the northern part of the parish, more easily reached from the Brendon ridge, was being exploited by the late 12th century as independent estates. The Hospitallers acquired a holding there, based on the later Middleton farm, before 1187.[94] Stolford was also a separate farm by the late 12th century.[95] In 1306 William of Stolford granted his holding to Richard of Middleton in return for an annuity of 6 marks and an obligation to provide him with 1 bu. of pilcorn or rye every fortnight, 3s. in silver three times a year, 6 ells of russet cloth at Christmas, 4 ells of linen cloth and 5 lb. of wool at Pentecost, and pasture for 2 cows.[96] By the mid 15th century several other landowners had acquired pasture in the area.[97]

In the main part of the parish John Waleys's holding in 1333, which included land in Holford St.

Mary, comprised a capital messuage, 40 a. of arable, small parcels of meadow and of uncultivated hill ground, the rents of 10 free tenants, 6 customary tenants, and 4 cottagers, works worth 6d., and chevage worth 3d.[98] William Nethway's share of Huish manor in 1510 included 80 a. of pasture and 40 a. of furze and heath.[99] By that time the Courtenay demesne holding was let.[1]

The 10 freeholds of Huish manor recorded in 1333 may represent scattered separate farms, characteristic of the Brendons.[2] They probably included the ferling holding of Ingeram Brome by 1402[3] and the Knollys family's farms of East Coombe and Woodhouse established by 1515.[4] A farmer at Stolford in 1573 had the right to take timber from the 'out hedges' of his enclosed farm.[5] By the end of the 16th century both freehold and copyhold farms were often substantial. Shute farm measured 66 a. by 1546,[6] and by the end of the century farms were recorded with the following extents: Stolford 200 a., Sperry 75 a., Newhouse or Milland 67 a., West Catford 64 a., and Westcombe, perhaps the modern Coombe End, 36 a.[7] Newhouse and Catford were held for two centuries by the Marsh family, who had acquired the freehold of Catford by 1655.[8] Westcombe was held on a 99-year lease in 1599;[9] Coombe Tenement, later East Coombe or Coles's, now Coles's Farm, was apparently enfranchised by 1679.[10] Enfranchisement continued into the 19th century.[11]

A farmer at Stolford had rye, wool, heifers, and sheep in the late 16th century,[12] and at least three farms in the 17th century had a preponderance of sheep.[13] By the 18th century there was a marked distinction between the hill and the valley farms. The hill farms were usually larger, and were often owned by outside landowners. Brown, for instance, belonged to the Wyndhams, and passed to the Trevelyans in 1706;[14] Stolford was also Wyndham property, but was divided before the end of the century, and part had passed by 1833 to J. S. Fry, the Bristol chocolate manufacturer.[15] The Escotts of Carhampton occupied part of the divided Brown holding called Middle Brown by the mid 19th century,[16] and Sperry was held by the Davie family of Creedy Park (Devon) as part of their estate centred on Bittescombe in Upton.[17] By c. 1818 the Trevelyans had disposed of Lower Brown,[18] and by 1839 Higher and Lower Brown together formed a single farm of 226 a. Middleton was then 233 a.[19]

The southern farms were still small in the early 19th century with the exception of Sperry (215 a.),

[85] P.R.O., CP 25(2)/1056/6 Geo. I East.; CP 25(2)/1259/6 & 7 Geo. II Trin.
[86] S.R.O., DD/WO 6/5.
[87] Ibid. 6/7, 6/8.
[88] Ibid. 6/8.
[89] Ibid. 35/7.
[90] e.g. ibid. DD/HC 147.
[91] Burke, *Peerage* (1959), 2249-51, 2420.
[92] Below.   [93] *V.C.H. Som.* i. 493-4.
[94] *S.R.S.* xxv, pp. 188-9.
[95] S.R.O., DD/WY 5/F1/1.
[96] Ibid. DD/WY 6 I1/1,2; cf. DD/WY 5 F1/1-5; DD/WY 6 I1/3,4.
[97] Ibid. DD/WY 1 A21; 5 F1/6; 6 I1/4; 8 B2/19; *S.R.S.* xxii. 84, 92.
[98] P.R.O., C 135/35, no. 26.
[99] S.R.O., DD/AH 65/7.
[1] P.R.O., SC 6/Hen. VII/1099.
[2] Ibid. C 135/35, no. 26.
[3] B.L. Add. Ch. 64314.

[4] P.R.O., SC 6/Hen. VIII/6159, f. 40v.
[5] S.R.O., DD/WY 11/R3.
[6] P.R.O., STAC 3/1, no. 56.
[7] Ibid. C 142/409, no. 98; C 142/532, no. 235; S.R.O., DD/CCH 53/1; DD/PLE 59; DD/SF 3999.
[8] S.R.O., DD/CCH 53/1; DD/PLE 59, 67; P.R.O., C 142/532, no. 235.
[9] S.R.O., DD/SF 3999.
[10] Ibid. DD/SF 674, 955-7, 2728, 3904.
[11] *Taunton Courier*, 23 May 1821: Normans 'to be let in fee'.
[12] S.R.O., DD/WY 11/R3.
[13] Ibid. DD/SP, inventories 1666, 1677-8.
[14] Ibid. DD/WO 5/1-3, 6/1-2.
[15] Ibid. Q/REl.
[16] Ibid. DD/CCH 53/3; DD/WO 44/11, 12, 50/11, 12; ibid. Q/Rer.
[17] Ibid. Q/REl.
[18] Ibid.
[19] Ibid. tithe award.

though holdings at Catford and Shute had been joined to neighbours.[20] 'Summering' pasture was available for rent at Coombe farm in 1805[21] and by the 1820s a dairy had been established at Shute.[22] The inclosure of Huish moor apportioned some grassland to the southern farms,[23] though much of the area was wooded, contributing most of the total of 99 a. of woodland for the whole parish.[24] Two hill farms, Beverton and Tone, were formed on the inclosure of Brendon Hill in 1845.[25]

In 1839 there were 779 a. of arable, about a quarter of the whole parish.[26] By 1905 a third of the parish was under plough, and woodland had diminished.[27] Changes in ownership in the later 19th century included the attachment of Catford to the Ferguson-Davie holding of Bittescombe[28] and the creation of the Hancock estate based on Coombe House.[29] In the 1940s the break-up of the Trevelyan estate marked the end of large holdings in the parish.[30] By 1976 there were 29 separate farms, nearly all under grass, of which seven measured between 50 ha. and 199 ha. Four were dairy farms and eight were partly or entirely sheep farms.[31]

A fulling mill mentioned in the early 17th century and a woolcomber in 1705 are isolated evidence of the cloth industry in Huish.[32] Quarrying was carried on in the late 18th century,[33] and slates and tiles were produced by 1796.[34] Pit debris and a powder magazine, associated with the Raleigh's Cross iron workings, were within the northern boundary of Huish.[35]

There was a mill, presumably for corn, on the manor by 1086.[36] It remained part of the manorial estate until sold in 1687,[37] and by 1785 was known as Washbittle, later Washbottle or Washbrittle,[38] and in 1980 Washbattle. It ceased to grind soon after 1910.[39] There was another mill, probably at Brown, in 1572.[40]

LOCAL GOVERNMENT. By 1274 the lady of the manor took and kept strays, presumably by ancient custom.[41] The lordship in 1339 and the early 16th century included pleas of court sometimes from one and sometimes from two sessions a year,[42] but no manorial records have been found earlier than 1831. In that year the manorial rental included payments for a room to hold the court, the charges of the tithingman and the reeve for issuing notices, gifts to five poor men of the jury, and the costs of crying the

court twice. Two years later there were payments only for crying the court in church on two Sundays and to the tithingman for his 'attention to the commons'.[43]

Churchwardens' accounts from 1675 were occasionally signed in the late 17th century by two overseers and two or four sidesmen.[44] A decision of the parish in 1722 was witnessed by the rector and five parishioners, and a vestry continued to approve the wardens' accounts until at least the 1840s.[45] Highway surveyors were appointed in 1691 by the tithingman, a warden, and three householders. Wardens served in rotation according to their holdings,[46] and appointments of both wardens and overseers were recorded in the overseers' accounts dating from 1769. Payments, recorded separately as weekly, bastard, and extraordinary, were made in the parish by the late 18th century, and an agreement was made in 1797 with a Wiveliscombe doctor to attend the poor.[47] A pay table stood at the west end of the aisle in the parish church.[48] By 1831 the overseers were renting the former church house as a poorhouse.[49] One family was assisted to emigrate to Canada in 1830.[50] The parish became part of the Dulverton poor-law union in 1836. In 1894 the parish formed part of the Dulverton rural district, and in 1974 became part of the West Somerset district.[51]

CHURCH. There was a chaplain at Huish Champflower by 1187,[52] and a church is mentioned in 1226.[53] Until 1951 the living was a sole rectory. From that date it was held with Clatworthy, and from 1967 also with Chipstable and Raddington, the four becoming a united benefice in 1971.[54]

On the death of Thomas de Champflower the advowson of the living passed in 1226 to his daughters.[55] It evidently descended in a junior branch of the family until the death of the widow of Matthew Champflower c. 1297, when the Crown presented during the wardship of the heirs.[56] The advowson thereafter descended with the manor and, after its division, with that part held by the Courtenays between 1422 and 1525, although a share of the advowson seems to have been included in the Brett estate in 1508 when it passed to William Nethway.[57] John Nethway was licensed in 1548 to grant his right of presentation to John Norman, clerk.[58] Alexander Sydenham, later to acquire part of the manor and the

[20] Ibid.
[21] Ibid. DD/HC 1.
[22] Ibid. D/P/h.c 2/1/4.
[23] Ibid. DD/HC 140; ibid. Q/RDe 112.
[24] Ibid. tithe award.
[25] Ibid. Q/RDe 112; ibid. DD/WO 9/1.
[26] Ibid. tithe award.
[27] Statistics supplied by the then Bd. of Agric. 1905.
[28] Devon R.O. 48/24/3.
[29] Ibid. 547B/2073, 2444; S.R.O., DD/CCH 53/4, 59.
[30] S.R.O., DD/KW 1944/31, 1945/5.
[31] Min. of Agric., Fisheries, and Food, agric. returns 1976.   [32] S.R.O., D/D/Rg 345; ibid. DD/WO 6/4.
[33] Ibid. DD/WO 6/4.
[34] Ibid. DD/HC 85.
[35] O.S. Map 6", Som. XLVII.SE. (1887 edn.); S.R.O., DD/WO 15/13; DD/CCH 52/2; below, Nettlecombe.
[36] V.C.H. Som. i. 493.
[37] P.R.O., C 135/35, no. 26; ibid. CP 25(2)/795/2 Jas. II Mich.; Cal. Close, 1339–41, 645.
[38] S.R.O., DD/CCH 53/1; D/P/h.c 2/1/4; Kelly's Dir. Som. (1883).
[39] Kelly's Dir. Som. (1910).

[40] P.R.O., CP 25(2)/204/14 Eliz. I East.
[41] Rot. Hund. (Rec. Com.), ii. 119, 138.
[42] Cal. Close, 1339–41, 645; Cal. Inq. p.m. viii, p. 162; L. & P. Hen. VIII, ix, p. 479; P.R.O., SC 6/Hen. VII/1099; SC 6/Hen. VIII/6159, 6192.
[43] S.R.O., DD/WO 35/7.
[44] Ibid. D/P/h.c 4/1/1 (1675–1744); DD/HC 140 (1844–70).
[45] Ibid. D/P/h.c 4/1/1; DD/HC 140, 145.
[46] Ibid. D/P/h.c 4/1/1.
[47] Ibid. DD/HC 140 (1769–1814).
[48] Ibid. D/P/h.c 7/4/1.
[49] Ibid. DD/WO 35/7; below, church.
[50] S.R.O., D/P/h.c 2/1/4.
[51] Youngs, Local Admin. Units. i. 672–4, 676.
[52] S.R.S. xxv, p. 189.
[53] Cur. Reg. R. xii, p. 356.
[54] Inf. from Dioc. Regy.
[55] Cur. Reg. R. xii, p. 356.
[56] Cal. Pat. 1292–1301, 295; above, manors.
[57] S.R.S. xxx, p. 413; ibid. lv, p. 30; S.R.O., DD/AH 65/7.
[58] Cal. Pat. 1547–8, 268.

advowson which went with it, presented a rector in 1561, but his right to do so was successfully challenged shortly afterwards by Thomas Lucas, then in possession of the main manorial estate.[59]

Thereafter the advowson descended with the manor until the 1680s, but grants of the next presentation were made by the Heles, under which Philip Atherton of Bradford on Tone presented John Atherton in 1622, and Christopher Pitt, clerk, presented in 1637. The Crown presented in 1636 on Atherton's promotion to a bishopric.[60] In 1683 the Stawell trustees sold the advowson to Thomas Comens of Wiveliscombe, to hold in trust for the curate William Nichols. Comens, then of Huish, presented Nichols as rector in 1687. Robert, son of Thomas Comens, presented on Nichols's death in 1701, but in the following year, acting as Nichols's trustee, he sold the advowson to John Pym, clerk, of Litton Cheyney (Dors.). Pym presented in 1703, but in the next year he sold the advowson to trustees for the benefit of Samuel Taylor, the rector whom he had already presented.[61] In 1735 Taylor settled the property on his prospective son-in-law, William Willis of Selworthy, who became rector in 1743 on Taylor's death, at the presentation of Thomas Camplin and Thomas Willis, clerks.[62] William Willis, then of Luccombe, presented in 1757 and 1761, on the second occasion appointing his son William to the living.[63] Samuel Willis of Boxwell (Glos.), brother of the last, was patron by 1781, and two years later he sold his rights to Sir John Trevelyan.[64] The advowson then descended with the Trevelyan estate, and at least four members of the family held the living between 1803 and 1958: George Trevelyan, rector 1803–23, John Thomas Trevelyan, 1833–5, John Woodhouse, 1836–72, and Philip Woodhouse Perceval Hancock, 1915–58. In 1957 the advowson was transferred to the bishop of Bath and Wells.[65]

The living was valued at £5 6s. 8d. in 1291,[66] £13 9s. 4½d. net in 1535,[67] £130 c. 1668,[68] and £288 net in 1831.[69] The tithes were worth £11 6s. 8d. in 1535,[70] and a tithe rent charge of £254 6s. 9d. was agreed in 1841.[71] The glebe was valued at 51s. in 1535.[72] There were c. 119 a. of glebe by 1606,[73] 151½ a. by 1839,[74] and 200 a. in 1939.[75]

By 1606 the glebe house had a wainscotted hall and parlour, with six glazed windows. Among the adjoining buildings were a gatehouse, bakehouse, and dovecot.[76] The house was undergoing 'thorough'

repair in 1815,[77] and further work was done in 1836–8 creating a square, symmetrical house of three bays with shallow pitched roofs arranged around a central well, with older work to the west, the whole standing in ornamental grounds above a lake.[78] The house, destroyed by fire and rebuilt, with the help of parishioners, c. 1924,[79] was occupied by successive incumbents until c. 1972, when it was sold.[80] It had a private chapel in 1401.[81]

Thomas Payc, rector 1422 61, a lawyer and diocesan penitentiary, was licensed soon after his appointment to spend a year in the service of the patron, Sir Hugh Courtenay.[82] There was a parish chaplain in 1468.[83] John Tyler, rector 1525–61, seems to have survived all the Reformation changes,[84] but a chalice and ornaments could not be recovered in Mary's reign, and the walls of the church were painted with Biblical texts in the Protestant style, probably in Elizabeth's reign.[85] The present communion cup dates from 1573.[86] John Atherton, rector 1622–36, was accused of non-residence in 1630, the year when he became prebendary of Christ Church, Dublin. He held the rectory with the chancellorship of Killaloe and also of Dublin, and was promoted to the bishopric of Waterford and Lismore in 1636.[87] Chancel and parsonage house were then said to be in decay.[88] William Willis, rector 1743–57, was at the same time resident rector of Selworthy.[89] William, his son, served Huish in person from 1761 until the 1780s, but thereafter the parish was cared for by curates until the appointment as rector of William Darch in 1823.[90] George Trevelyan, rector 1803 23, was also rector of Nettlecombe, where he lived, and from 1817 archdeacon of Taunton.[91] His curate at Huish in 1815 was the resident rector of Clatworthy. Services were then held every Sunday, alternately morning and evening.[92] William Darch also held the living of Raddington, but by 1827 was taking prayers and preaching at Huish each Sunday, and holding evening services on alternate weeks.[93] By 1840 services were held twice every Sunday.[94] In 1851 the congregations on Census Sunday, considered 'about average', totalled 110 in the morning, including 32 from the Sunday school, and 190 in the afternoon, including 37 children.[95]

A church house, standing on the edge of the churchyard until after 1849,[96] was a two-storeyed building with a chimney and a tiled roof in the 17th century. It was then owned by the lord of the manor

[59] P.R.O., C 3/86/16; C 3/94/16.
[60] Som. Incumbents, ed. Weaver, 379.
[61] S.R.O., DD/WO 7/6.
[62] P.R.O., E 331/Bath and Wells/23; S.R.O., DD/WO 7/6.
[63] S.R.O., D/D/B reg. 27, f. 53; ibid. 28, f. 4.
[64] S.R.O., DD/WO 7/6.
[65] Inf. from Dioc. Regy.
[66] Tax. Eccl. (Rec. Com.), 198.
[67] Valor Eccl. (Rec. Com.), i. 222.
[68] S.R.O., D/D/Vc 24.
[69] Rep. Com. Eccl. Revenues, pp. 140–1.
[70] Valor Eccl. (Rec. Com.), i. 222.
[71] S.R.O., tithe award; ibid. D/P/h.c 3/1/1.
[72] Valor Eccl. (Rec. Com.), i. 222.
[73] S.R.O., D/D/Rg 345.
[74] Ibid. tithe award.
[75] Kelly's Dir. Som. (1939).
[76] S.R.O., D/D/Rg 345.
[77] Ibid. D/D/B returns 1815.
[78] Photograph, paintings, and inf. from Mrs. Hancock, Ford. The acct. bk. of work 1836–8 in S.R.O. DD/HC, formerly box 118, cannot be found.

[79] Inf. from Mrs. Hancock, and from Mr. R. K. Mulligan, owner of the house; S.R.O., DD/RI (C/1660), plans by L. G. Spiller.
[80] Dioc. Dir.
[81] S.R.O., D/D/B reg 3, f. 6; S.R.S. xxix, p. 31.
[82] S.R.S., xxx, pp. 413, 422; xlix, pp. 42, 57.
[83] Ibid. li, p. 28.
[84] Ibid. lv, p. 30; P.R.O., C 3/86/16; C 3/94/16.
[85] S.R.O., D/D/Ca 22, 27, 274.
[86] Proc. Som. Arch. Soc. xlv. 166.
[87] S.R.O., D/D/Ca 274; Alum. Oxon 1500–1714.
[88] S.R.O., D/D/Ca 310.
[89] C. E. H. Chadwyck Healey, Hist. W. Som. (1901), 225.
[90] S.R.O., D/P/h.c 2/1/2, 2/1/5; D/D/B reg. 33, f. 195.
[91] Ibid. D/D/B reg. 33, f. 4v.; Le Neve, Fasti, 1541–1857, Bath and Wells, 18.
[92] S.R.O., D/D/B returns 1815.
[93] Ibid. D/P/h.c 1/1/1; D/D/B returns 1827.
[94] Ibid. D/D/V returns 1840.
[95] P.R.O., HO 129/293/7/4/5.
[96] Taunton Castle, Braikenridge Colln., watercolour by W. W. Wheatley.[77]

and was let to the churchwardens.[97] By 1831 it was held by the overseers.[98]

The church of *ST. PETER*, so dedicated by 1535,[99] consists of chancel with north chapel, nave with north aisle and south porch, and west tower. A bequest was made in 1534 towards the new *ambulatorium*,[1] probably the aisle. Persistent local tradition maintains that the large six-light east window of the wide chancel chapel, with the remains of early 15th-century glass, evidently once a Jesse window, and probably also the arcade, were brought *c.* 1537 from the dissolved priory of Barlinch, near Dulverton.[2] The arcade is not characteristic of local work, and is thought to be an amalgam of 14th- and 15th-century features.[3] The remainder of the church seems to date from the 15th century, the tower containing a bell by Robert Norton of Exeter (1410–40).[4] The body of the wooden eagle lectern is also of the 15th century. A medieval screen, probably crossing the north aisle, is said to have been removed to Bicknoller in 1726.[5] A roodloft survived in 1683,[6] and a chancel screen was still in position in 1798.[7] Alterations elsewhere included the construction of the tower arch in 1703, a singing gallery in the aisle in 1713, a canopied, three-decker pulpit in 1717–18, and a singing gallery near the belfry *c.* 1795.[8] There were extensive repairs in 1846,[9] and the church is said to have been restored *c.* 1875–80, when the chancel arch was replaced.[10]

The registers date from 1559 and appear to be complete.[11]

Bequests to the fabric of All Saints made in 1534 and 1535[12] may refer to a separate building, possibly a chapel at Middleton founded by 1187.[13]

NONCONFORMITY. A family of Presbyterians was living in the parish in 1776.[14] In 1803 a house at Winters was licensed for worship by an unspecified denomination.[15]

EDUCATION. Clatworthy school in 1818 took

children from Huish,[16] but a church school was established at Huish by 1825.[17] A Sunday school was started in 1832. By 1835 there were two day schools with 37 pupils, whose parents paid fees, and the Sunday school had 79 pupils under one paid teacher.[18] By 1839 one school was held in a building on the glebe near Huish bridge,[19] between Huish and Clatworthy, known in 1847 as the Huish Champflower and Clatworthy village school, and in 1851 as Bridge School House.[20] This same school had 58 children attending by day in 1847, and another 25 attended in the evenings.[21] The other day school and the Sunday school seem to have closed.

About 1857 the school moved to a new building west of the village on the road to Catford, which the rector, John Woodhouse, had converted from a cottage.[22] The building was extensively altered in 1870 and again in 1898.[23] By 1903 the school and school house, held by trustees of Woodhouse's heir, the Revd. Frederick Hancock, were leased to the then rector for school use.[24] There were 40 children on the books.[25] It remained a voluntary school, but from 1950 took only children under the age of eleven. In that year there were 77 on the books.[26] Numbers fell rapidly, and the school was closed in 1963, children from the village travelling thereafter to school in Wiveliscombe.[27]

CHARITIES FOR THE POOR. By will dated 1781 Richard Marsh left £10, the interest to be paid at Easter to parishioners not receiving relief. The sum of £5 was also given for the same purpose by John Cruze or Cruwys before 1786.[28] The charities, their combined income totalling 15s. usually shared between 12 people, were paid until 1807. Thereafter, the capital seems to have been merged into the general parish stock.[29] A legacy of £1 a month given to the poor by Richard Darch was referred to in 1843, but no money had been received or distributed.[30]

KILTON

THE ANCIENT parish of Kilton took the first element of its name from Kilve Hill.[31] The main part of the parish lay between Kilve and Lilstock, and

was roughly **L**-shaped, its northern boundary marked by cliffs and a rocky foreshore *c.* 1 km. in length. From the south-western corner of the **L** a narrow

[97] S.R.O., D/P/h.c 4/1/1.
[98] Ibid. DD/WO 35/7.
[99] *Wells Wills*, ed. Weaver, 94.
[1] *Downside Rev.* xiv. 13.
[2] *Proc. Som. Arch. Soc.* xxix. 51; F. C. Eeles, *Som. Churches Near Dulverton* (Taunton 1928), 30–1; Taunton Castle, watercolour by W. W. Wheatley; below, plate facing p. 109.
[3] Pevsner, *South and West Som.* 201.
[4] S.R.O., DD/SAS CH 16.
[5] Above, Bicknoller, church.
[6] S.R.O., D/P/h.c 4/1/1.
[7] Ibid. 7/4/1.
[8] Ibid. D/D/Ca 438; D/P/h.c 4/1/1, 7/4/1; DD/HC 46.
[9] Ibid. DD/HC 140: churchwardens' accts. 1844–70.
[10] *Kelly's Dir. Som.* (1883).
[11] S.R.O., D/P/h.c 2/1/1–4.
[12] *Wells Wills*, ed. Weaver, 94; *Downside Rev.* xiv. 13.
[13] *S.R.S.* xxv, pp. 188–9; cf. S.R.O., D/D/B reg. 1, f. 117.
[14] S.R.O., D/D/Vc 88.
[15] Ibid. D/D/Rm, box 2.
[16] *Educ. of Poor Digest*, H.C. 223 (1819), ix (2).
[17] *Ann. Rep. B. & W. Dioc. Assoc. S.P.C.K.* (1825–6).
[18] *Educ. Enq. Abstract*, H.C. 62 (1835), xlii.
[19] *Nat. Soc. Inquiry, 1846–7*, Som. 10–11.
[20] S.R.O., tithe award; ibid. DD/HC 145; P.R.O., HO 107/1890.
[21] *Nat. Soc. Inquiry, 1846–7*, Som. 10–11.
[22] S.R.O., DD/HC 147; *Kelly's Dir. Som.* (1883).
[23] S.R.O., C/E 69, log bks.
[24] Ibid. C/E 27; Char. Com. files.
[25] S.R.O., C/E 27.
[26] Ibid. *Schs. Lists.*
[27] Ibid. C/E 69.
[28] *Char. Don.* H.C. 511 (1816), xvi; S.R.O., DD/HC 140: overseers' accts. 1769–1814.
[29] S.R.O., DD/HC 140: overseers' accts.
[30] Ibid. D/D/V returns 1843.
[31] Ekwall, *Eng. Place-Names* (1960), 276. This article was completed in 1978.

strip ran south for *c*. 3 km., first up the gentle incline towards Holford village, and then up the Quantock scarp to common land on Woodlands Hill. South-east of the main part of the parish, and divided from it by a narrow finger of Stringston parish, was a rectangular area known as Heathfield.[32] The parish, said to cover 1,691 a. in 1881, was altered for civil purposes in 1886 when the narrow southern strip was transferred to Holford and the detached area to Stringston. The remainder was joined with Lilstock to form an area of 1,689 a.[33] In 1933 Kilton-cum-Lilstock and Stringston were united to form the civil parish of Stringston.[34]

The boundary between Kilton and Lilstock had a regularity suggesting planned division, but was occasionally subject to disputes.[35] The southern boundary of the main part of the parish followed a former roadway linking Burton in Stogursey with the coast road through Kilve to Dunster. The western boundary with Kilve skirted Kilve Hill and was marked near Kilton Park wood by the bank and ditch of the medieval park, known as Deerleap. The southern strip was largely bounded on the west by a route along the coast from Nether Stowey, and was cut by a further east–west route known as Portway Lane,[36] which runs from Stogursey to Holford and thence over the Quantocks. The southern tip of the parish, on Woodlands Hill, included Shervage wood, a name perhaps suggesting its position on the boundary.[37] The regularity of the detached part of the parish at Heathfield was the result of arbitrary division in 1664.[38]

The main part of the parish lay on undulating ground, mostly on the Lower Lias, the village in the centre south and west of a stream, the church and former green[39] on rising ground to the north-east. Between the village and the coast the land falls to under 15 m. and then rises to the cliffs. Moorhouse farm and Woodlands occupy much of the narrow southern strip on valley gravel and Keuper Marl rising to over 122 m. Woodlands Hill, reaching to *c*. 224 m., is on the Hangman Grits of the northern Quantocks.[40] Around Moorhouse and Woodlands quarrying for stone and chalk left traces in field names, and a marl pit became a carp pond;[41] in 1495 a limekiln stood in the detached area at Heathfield.[42]

Kilton village lies on a road which runs from Lilstock and the shore to Holford and the Quantocks. Lanes fan outwards from it to the fields and to the coast road between Stogursey and Dunster. The village itself bears clear signs of shrinkage both at its eastern end, where the church and green stand in virtual isolation, and at its western end where the remains of house platforms were traceable in 1977.

There was a farm at Woodlands by 1346[43] and one at Moorhouse by 1378.[44] Plud Farm in the detached part of the parish also has medieval origins, and in the 16th century it was known as the Constable's House and was linked with Nether Stowey castle.[45] There is some evidence of a house, if not a more extensive settlement, at Shervage in 1402,[46] of a house at 'West Whittington' in 1589,[47] and of an isolated cottage at 'Wymellhead' in 1640.[48]

Open fields lay around Kilton village in the late Middle Ages, but strips were usually located by their furlongs rather than by the fields in which they lay.[49] Kilton Field and Sessons survived to the late 16th century,[50] and East and West fields were mentioned in the early 17th.[51] The two small areas of uninclosed arable that survived on the coast in the mid 19th century,[52] known since the late 17th century as East and West fields,[53] may have been created as part of a scheme for consolidation of holdings nearer the village.[54]

A park, later known as Kilton Park, was formed in the north-west corner of the parish by 1279,[55] but by the end of the 14th century it was divided into closes and part was ploughed.[56] It was sold as a single farm in 1710.[57] An arable field called Corn park in 1379 may have been part of the same park.[58] Cookeparke or Coxparke, south of Woodlands, may have been a medieval assart from Shervage wood.[59] Fields called Stone park, south of Moorhouse Farm, were probably so called when the grassland was improved in the 19th century.[60] Ancient woodland in Kilton Park and at Shervage survived in 1977.[61] The former measured *c*. 60 a. in the 17th century and *c*. 30 a. in the 20th.[62] Shervage covered *c*. 30 a. in the 17th century and in 1977 comprised oak standards.[63]

By the end of the 16th century most of the main farmhouses in the parish were of two storeys, but Woodlands Farm in 1588 had a hall, parlour, kitchen, and shop on the ground floor and only two chambers above. Outbuildings at Woodlands comprised a barn, shippon, milk house, buttery, apple house, wain house, and 'shelf' house.[64] Part of the late medieval hall remains, but it was probably ceiled by the early 17th century, and an overmantel on the first floor has decorated plasterwork bearing the symbols of the Five Wounds. A parallel north range was later added, and early in the 18th century a five-bayed block at the eastern end of both ranges, with a central staircase rising to the attic floor.

There was a licensed victualler in the parish in 1689 and an inn in 1726.[65]

John Sheppard, a tanner, created trouble in the parish, accusing several inhabitants in 1645 of having

[32] S.R.O., tithe award.
[33] *Census*, 1881, 1891.
[34] Youngs, *Local Admin. Units*, i. 429.
[35] e.g. S.R.O., DD/L P23/39 (1613).
[36] Ibid. tithe award.
[37] A. H. Smith, *Eng. Place-name Elements*, ii. 99.
[38] S.R.O., DD/AH 28/9.
[39] Ibid. tithe award.
[40] Geol. Surv. Map 1″, drift, sheet 295 (1956 edn.).
[41] S.R.O., tithe award; inf. from Mr. M. A. Aston.
[42] S.R.O., DD/L P23/16, P24/9.
[43] Ibid. P24, John de Mohun to Hugh of Kilve.
[44] Ibid. P24/3.
[45] Ibid. DD/AH 36/1.
[46] Ibid. DD/L P24/4.
[47] Ibid. P24/22, P25/36.
[48] Ibid. P25/40.

[49] Ibid. DD/AH 12/2; DD/L P24/2; P24 unnumbered deed, Geof. son of Hen. de Stauhill to Rob. de Radehull.
[50] Ibid. DD/L P24/16.   [51] Ibid. P24/16, P25/1.
[52] Ibid. tithe award.   [53] Ibid. DD/L 2/5/23, 26.
[54] Ibid. DD/L P24/16.
[55] *Cal. Inq. p.m.* ii. p. 175.
[56] S.R.O., DD/L P1/27, P3/12, P24/2–4, 7.
[57] Ibid. DD/AH 11/12, 12/11.
[58] Ibid. DD/L P3/11, P24/3.
[59] Ibid. DD/L P3/11, P24/10, P25/41; ibid. tithe award; inf. from Mr. Aston.
[60] S.R.O., tithe award; inf. from Mr. Aston.
[61] Inf. from Mr. Aston.
[62] S.R.O., DD/L 1/10/35A, 2/6/33.
[63] Ibid. DD/L P3/12, P25/31.
[64] Ibid. P24/16.
[65] Ibid. Q/RL.

NORTH-EASTERN PARISHES OF THE HUNDRED

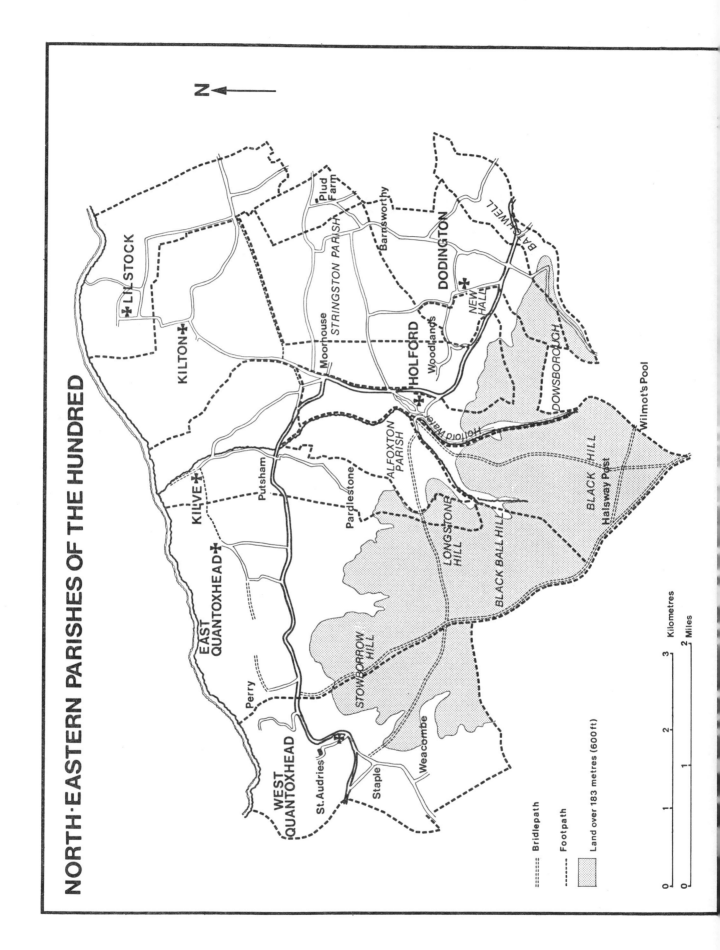

N

LILSTOCK

KILTON

KILVE

EAST QUANTOXHEAD

WEST QUANTOXHEAD

St. Audries

Perry

Staple

Weacombe

STOWBORROW HILL

Putsham

Pardlestone

ALFOXTON PARISH

Moorhouse
STRINGSTON PARISH

Plud Farm

Barnsworthy

HOLFORD

Woodlands

DODINGTON

NEW HALL

BAGBOROUGH

Holford Water

LONGSTONE HILL

BLACK BALL HILL

BLACK HILL

DOWSBOROUGH

Halsway Post

Wilmot's Pool

.... Bridlepath

- - - - - - - Footpath

Land over 183 metres (600ft)

Kilometres
0   1   2   3

Miles
0   1   2

90

royalist sympathies although they had declared themselves for parliament. He was in turn accused in 1647 of dishonest and disorderly behaviour.[66]

There were 102 taxpayers in 1667.[67] About 1791 there were 120 inhabitants and 22 houses.[68] By 1801 the number had fallen to 114, but thereafter the total rose almost every decade until 1851 when it was 181. Thereafter the number fell to 141 in 1881, 100 in 1891, and to 85 in 1901.[69]

MANOR AND OTHER ESTATES. King Alfred gave his estate at Kilton to his son Edward the Elder under his will dated 873 × 888.[70] Alward and Leuric held two manors 'in parage' T.R.E., but by 1086, as a single estate, *KILTON* had passed to William de Mohun (I) and descended with the barony of Dunster.[71] It was named as part of the barony in 1555.[72]

The estate passed in succession from William de Mohun (I), who died after 1090, to John Mohun (II), who died in 1279.[73] Kilton formed part of the dower of John's widow Eleanor,[74] later the wife of William Martin, Lord Martin (d. *c.* 1324), who remained in possession until after 1303.[75] John de Mohun (III) had succeeded his mother at Kilton by 1327, and died in 1330.[76] John de Mohun (V), his grandson, succeeded as a minor.[77] Settlements made in 1346 and 1369 gave John's wife Joan the disposal of the Mohun estates.[78] John died in 1375.[79] Between 1374 and 1376 Joan sold the reversion of Kilton and the other estates to Elizabeth Luttrell, but retained possession until her death in 1404.[80] John de Mohun's three daughters, however, seem to have laid claim to their father's estate: in 1402 the manor court at Kilton[81] was held in the name of the eldest daughter Elizabeth, widow of William, earl of Salisbury, of Edward, earl of Rutland and later duke of York, husband of the second daughter, Philippe, and 'others', presumably the heirs of Maud (d. 1400), the third daughter, formerly wife of Richard, Lord Strange of Knockin.[82]

Sir Hugh Luttrell, who succeeded his mother Elizabeth in 1395, took possession of the estates on Joan Mohun's death in 1404, and successfully established his claim against the Mohun heirs in 1405–6.[83] He remained in possession until his death in 1428.[84] He was succeeded by his son John, who

died in 1430, leaving Kilton as the dower of his widow Margaret, daughter of John, Lord Audley.[85] She survived until 1438 and then Kilton reverted to her son James, a minor until 1447.[86] He died after the battle of St. Alban's in 1461, when his estates were confiscated.[87]

In 1463 Kilton and other Luttrell property was granted to Sir William Herbert, Lord Herbert (cr. earl of Pembroke 1468), but on his death in 1469 his former Luttrell lands reverted to the Crown.[88] In 1472 Kilton and other properties passed to trustees for the benefit of Sir James Luttrell's widow, Elizabeth,[89] who seems to have retained them until 1485, when she exchanged Kilton and Minehead with Hugh, son and heir of Sir James.[90] In 1508 Sir Hugh Luttrell (d. 1521) settled Kilton on his second wife Walthean.[91] Her stepson, Sir Andrew Luttrell, was holding courts by 1533, and in 1537 was succeeded by his son Sir John (d. 1551).[92]

Sir John left as his heirs three daughters, all under age. His widow Mary held courts at Kilton in 1552,[93] but in 1554 she let half the manor to her husband's brother, Thomas Luttrell, who was called farmer of the manor.[94] Between 1560 and 1565 Thomas acquired the interests in Kilton of his nieces, and held courts in his own right between 1563 and 1566, and presumably until his death in 1571.[95] His widow Margaret and her second husband John Strode held the manor in right of the infant heir, George Luttrell, Thomas's son, until he came of age in 1581.[96] Margaret continued to have an interest until her death in 1588, but from 1584 courts were held by Mary, widow of Sir John Luttrell (d. 1551) who had later married James Godolphin.[97]

George Luttrell (d. 1629) settled Kilton on his eldest son Thomas in 1621.[98] Thomas died in 1644 and his widow Jane, joint holder of the manor, in 1668. George Luttrell, their son, was succeeded in 1655 by his brother Francis. Francis left three sons in 1666: Thomas died while still a minor in 1670; Francis died in 1690, leaving a son Tregonwell, who died under age and childless in 1703; and Col. Alexander Luttrell. Alexander was succeeded in 1711 by his son, also Alexander, then a minor. The son died in 1737 and left an only child, Margaret. She married her cousin Henry Fownes, who assumed the additional name Luttrell. Margaret died in 1766.[99]

[66] *Cal. S.P. Dom.* 1645–7, 395; 1648, 31–2; *Cal. Cttee. for Compounding,* 83.
[67] S.R.O., DD/WY 34.
[68] Collinson, *Hist. Som.* iii. 531.
[69] *V.C.H. Som.* ii. 351.
[70] H. P. R. Finberg, *Early Charters of Wessex,* p. 126.
[71] *V.C.H. Som.* i. 504; *S.R.S.* xxxiii, pp. xxiv, 2, 74, 133, 195, 198, 229–30, 274.
[72] *S.R.S.* xxxiii, p. 291.
[73] *Complete Peerage,* ix. 17 sqq.
[74] *Cal. Close,* 1272–9, 539–41; *Cal. Inq. p.m.* ii, p. 175.
[75] *Feud. Aids,* iv. 274, 303; *Proc. Som. Arch. Soc.* lxv. 22–5.   [76] *S.R.S.* iii. 165; *Cal. Inq. p.m.* vii, p. 218.
[77] Maxwell Lyte, *Dunster,* 43.
[78] *Cal. Pat.* 1345–8, 126; 1367–70, 293; Maxwell Lyte, *Dunster,* 46–53.
[79] *Cal. Inq. p.m.* xiv, p. 304.
[80] *Cal. Pat.* 1370–77, 26; *S.R.S.* xvii. 87, 89; Maxwell Lyte, *Dunster,* 53–8.
[81] S.R.O., DD/L P24/4.
[82] *Complete Peerage,* xi. 389–90; xii(1). 355–6; xii(2). 904.
[83] *Cal. Fine R.* 1399–1405, 302; *Cal. Pat.* 1405–8, 102; *Rot. Parl.* (Rec. Com.), iii. 577; Maxwell Lyte, *Dunster,* 83–6.

[84] P.R.O., C 139/33, no. 32.
[85] Ibid. C 139/51, no. 51; *Cal. Pat.* 1429–36, 99; *Cal. Close,* 1429–35, 75.
[86] Maxwell Lyte, *Dunster,* 118–19.
[87] P.R.O., C 140/5, no. 43.
[88] *Cal. Pat.* 1461–7, 231, 286, 336.
[89] Ibid. 1467–77, 330, 364, 522; Maxwell Lyte, *Dunster,* 125–6.
[90] *Cal. Inq. p.m. Hen. VII,* iii, p. 349.
[91] P.R.O., C 142/37, no. 116; C 142/106, no. 55.
[92] S.R.O., DD/L P3/11, P24/10, 13; *Cal. Pat.* 1550–3, 67–8; Maxwell Lyte, *Dunster,* 134–40, 162, 166.
[93] S.R.O., DD/L P3/11.
[94] Ibid. P3/11, P24/15.
[95] Ibid. P2/18, P3/11; P.R.O., C 142/159, no. 43; *Cal. Pat.* 1560–3, 186; 1563–6, p. 270; Maxwell Lyte, *Dunster,* 167.
[96] S.R.O., DD/L P3/11, P24/4, 16, 18. A second Margaret (d. 1580), joint holder of courts 1578–80, must be the aged widow of Sir Andrew Luttrell: ibid. DD/L P3/11, P24/16; Maxwell Lyte, *Dunster,* 140.
[97] S.R.O., DD/L P24/16; Maxwell Lyte, *Dunster,* 162.
[98] P.R.O., C 142/455, no. 82; Maxwell Lyte, *Dunster,* 176.
[99] Maxwell Lyte, *Dunster,* 185, 203–20, 228.

Henry Fownes Luttrell died in 1780 and was followed by his second son John Fownes (d. 1816) and by John's son, also John Fownes Luttrell. John died unmarried in 1857 and was succeeded by his brother Henry, also unmarried, who died in 1867. The heir was George, son of Francis Luttrell, brother of the two bachelors, who died in 1910. He was followed by his son Alexander (d. 1944), by Alexander's son Geoffrey (d. 1957), and by Geoffrey's son Lt.-Col. Geoffrey Walter Fownes Luttrell, lord of the manor in 1977 and lord-lieutenant of Somerset from 1978.[1]

The manor house at Kilton, standing near a tiled barn, stable, and oxhouse, included a hall and a great chamber in the late 14th century, but was not mentioned after 1381.[2] The manorial dovecot, established by 1329, survived until destroyed c. 1438.[3]

A building at Moorhouse, first recorded c. 1405, was described in 1455 as a capital messuage.[4] Two thirds of the estate was held by 1556 on a lease for 60 years and by 1590 was occupied by Edward and Philippe Stradling.[5] Thomas Symcocks (d. 1619), a London lawyer, left the lease to his wife Alice, but by 1656 the farm was in the lord's hand.[6] The farm was leased to the Palmers of Fairfield, Stogursey, from the early 18th century until 1763,[7] and was sold to Sir Peregrine Fuller-Palmer-Acland as a unit of 126 a., in 1870.[8] Moorhouse Farm is an early 16th-century house with a central hall, having a cross passage and kitchen at one end and at the other two smaller rooms in a short cross wing.

In 1235 a hide of land at Heathfield was sold by Ellis de Benington to Philip de Columbers (III).[9] Known thereafter as Heathfield Columbers, Little Heathfield, or Honibere Heathfield,[10] it was in the 17th century regarded as part of Honibere Lilstock manor within the parish of Kilton.[11] Heathfield descended through the Columbers and Tuchet families, and was held of the honor of Dunster until 1591.[12] By 1588 part of it came into the hands of Nicholas Luttrell (d. 1592)[13] and was thereafter merged with Honibere Lilstock. Another part was held in 1579 of Nether Stowey manor, and included the Constable's House. It was then owned by George Tuchet, Lord Audley, and was sold by his son, Sir Mervyn Tuchet, to John Prior the younger in 1615. John died in 1680 and the estate, including the house called variously Constable's House or Plud, passed to his elder son Robert, and on Robert's death to his grandson John, son of his second son, also John. John Prior of Kilton sold the estate, described as Plud and Constable's House, a second house, and 34 a. of land to Thomas Palmer of Fairfield in 1731.[14] Thomas died in 1734 leaving his estates to his wife Elizabeth (d. 1737).[15] She left them to Thomas's brother Peregrine (d. 1762), from whom they passed

to Arthur Acland (d. 1771), Elizabeth's nephew.[16] Arthur was followed by his son John (cr. Bt. 1818), who assumed the additional name Palmer in 1818. John's son Sir Peregrine Palmer-Acland (d. 1871) succeeded in 1831 and assumed the additional name Fuller in 1834.[17] Sir Peregrine's only daughter Isabel, wife of Sir Alexander Fuller-Acland-Hood (d. 1892), survived until 1903. Her eldest son Alexander (cr. Baron St. Audries 1911) died in 1917, and was followed by his son Alexander Peregrine, the 2nd baron, who died in 1971 leaving as his heir his niece Elizabeth, later wife of Sir Michael D. I. Gass, K.C.M.G.[18]

Plud Farm is a late medieval house, having originally a central hall with a cross passage and kitchen to the east. To the west the ground floor room has a panelled and decorated plaster ceiling dated 1622 and with the initials 'I.P.' for John Prior. The room above it has a decorated plaster ceiling and an overmantel depicting the sacrifice of Isaac, with the initials 'I.P.' and 'A.P.' and the date 1641.

William de Mohun (I) had granted the tithes of Kilton to Bath Priory by 1100, and by 1161 the monks had acquired tithes and land.[19] The ordination of a vicarage in 1283 gave the priory as appropriators of the rectory the great tithes of the whole parish except 'Lawndelond' and Heathfield.[20] The rectory was valued at 50s. in 1428,[21] and was farmed by John Luttrell for £4 in 1429–30.[22] The clear value was 56s. 4d. in 1535.[23]

The Luttrells were probably farmers of the rectory until 1539. At the Dissolution John Luttrell, second son of Sir Hugh, held the Kilton tithes as part of his lease of the site and estate of Dunster Priory.[24] John died in 1558 leaving his lease to his widow.[25] Thomas Luttrell was farmer of the rectory between 1561 and 1564, but the reversion was granted in 1563 to William Morgan and John Morris.[26] The descent of the estate has not been traced for a century, but by 1676 it seems to have been owned by Alexander Prior.[27] He was owner or occupier of land in Kilton until 1691 or later, but by 1711 his estate had passed to Col. Alexander Luttrell (d. 1711).[28] The rectory was devised by William Harrison (d. 1723) of Edmonton (Mdx.) to his three sisters, of whom Sarah brought it to her husband Thomas Hollier of East Greenwich (Kent). On Thomas's death in 1753 the rectory passed to his only daughter Elizabeth (d. 1788), wife of John Peryear of Lewisham (Kent), and then to her daughter Anna Margaretta, wife of William Griffiths of Camberwell (Surr.). Griffiths and his wife sold the rectory to John Acland in 1814.[29] Sir Peregrine Fuller-Palmer-Acland was awarded a tithe rent charge of £73 in 1842.[30]

[1] Burke, *Land. Gent.* (1952), 1595–7.
[2] S.R.O., DD/L P24/3.
[3] P.R.O., C 135/22, no. 11; S.R.O., DD/L P24/7.
[4] S.R.O., DD/L P24/7.
[5] Ibid. P24, deeds 1589–91; P25/43.
[6] Ibid. P3/12.
[7] Ibid. DD/L 2/6/27, 33.
[8] Ibid. DD/AH 12/11; Dyfed R.O., D/CAR 168, sale cat.   [9] *S.R.S.* vi. 96.
[10] *S.R.S.* xxxiii, pp. 49, 53, 109, 167.
[11] *S.R.S.* extra ser. 323.
[12] *S.R.S.* xxxiii, pp. 49, 307; S.R.O., DD/L P4/34; below, Nether Stowey, manor.
[13] *S.R.S.* extra ser. 335.
[14] S.R.O., DD/AH 16/4, 36/1.
[15] *Som. Wills*, ed. Brown, ii. 88–9.

[16] S.R.O., DD/AH 19/2.
[17] Burke, *Peerage* (1853), 9–10; ibid. (1949), 1760–1.
[18] *Who's Who.*
[19] *S.R.S.* vii (1), p. 61; vii (2), pp. 169–70.
[20] S.R.O., DD/AH 12/2.
[21] *Feud. Aids*, iv. 405.
[22] S.R.O., DD/L P24/7.
[23] *Valor Eccl.* (Rec. Com.), i. 220.
[24] *L. & P. Hen. VIII*, xv, p. 559; S.R.O., DD/L P16/8.
[25] S.R.O., DD/L P16/14; *S.R.S.* xxi. 212.
[26] S.R.O., DD/L 2/6/26; *Cal. Pat. 1560–3*, 591–2.
[27] P.R.O., CP 25(2)/717/27 Chas. II Trin.
[28] S.R.O., D/P/kln 4/1/2.
[29] Ibid. DD/AH 12/2.
[30] Ibid. tithe award.

KILTON CHURCH IN 1840

LILSTOCK CHURCH IN 1840

DODINGTON HALL FROM THE NORTH-WEST IN 1840

KILVE MANOR FROM THE SOUTH-EAST

The ruins of the eastern cross wing and chapel adjoin the surviving hall range

An estate at Woodlands, which may be traced to the holding of a knight Ralph in 1086[31] and may be the land of Hugh of Kilve in 1346,[32] was a freehold occupied by John Dodington by 1656.[33] It descended like Dodington manor, and by the end of the 18th century the marquess of Buckingham occupied both Lower and Higher Woodlands.[34] The Woodlands estate was sold by the duke of Buckingham to Sir Peregrine Fuller-Palmer-Acland in 1838.[35] Most of the land remained part of the Fairfield estate in 1977.[36]

A 'modern brick mansion', later Woodlands House, was built to the east of Woodlands Farm on the southern edge of the Woodlands estate by 1792, and was originally a building of four bays by three.[37] It was let to a Bristol surgeon with nearly 100 a. of land in 1810,[38] and was thereafter occupied by a succession of tenants until it was sold in 1947 to H. C. Daniel.[39]

ECONOMIC HISTORY. In 1086 Kilton gelded for 10½ hides, and there was land for 10 ploughs. There were 4 ploughteams on the demesne of 7½ hides and ⅓ virgate, and 5 teams on the tenants' land of 2 hides less ¼ virgate. The estate of the knight Ralph, said to be included in the main manor, was assessed at 1 hide, with 1 team for 3 virgates and 1 ferling on the demesne and 1 team on the 3 ferlings of the tenants. There were 60 a. of meadow, 60 a. of pasture, and 100 a. of wood on the main holding; 5 a. of meadow and 1 virgate of pasture belonged to Ralph's estate. Stock comprised 4 beasts, 10 swine, and 130 sheep on the main holding, and 4 beasts, 2 swine, 22 sheep, and 5 she-goats on Ralph's estate.[40]

By 1279 one free tenant, 25 villeins, and 3 cottars were contributing rents totalling well over £6, including customary payments of a rent called domescot (18d.) and a total of 700 eggs at Easter (8d.). Manual works were valued at £2 15s. 7½d. By 1330 the tenants comprised 6 freeholders, 18 *nativi*, and 6 *coterelli*, all paying cash rents and all performing services. Rents totalled £7 6s. and works were valued at £5 2s. 5¼d. The demesne farm in 1279 had 342 a. of arable, 34 a. of meadow, and 10 a. of pasture, the arable varying in value from 6d. an acre to just over 1d., with 242 a. of the best quality. By 1330 only 240 a. of arable were recorded, together with 31 a. of meadow, and unspecified areas of pasture. Grazing on Quantock had possibly replaced the low-quality arable of fifty years earlier. Herbage in the park mentioned in 1279 may have been represented by pasturage of 80 a. of woodland in 1330.[41]

There was little change in the size of the demesne farm until the end of the 14th century. During the period 1377–81 the arable crop was almost entirely wheat, grown in a three-year cycle, with very small areas of beans and peas and, in one year, barley. Stock comprised a herd of some 50 pigs and 25 cattle,

of which 17 were draught animals, in the first year only. The farm staff comprised 2 ploughmen, 2 drovers, and a swineherd. Manorial rents in the same four years rose from £8 12s. to £8 15s., including 'lardersilver' at Martinmas and Peter's Pence, to which were added small sums for the farm of demesne and bond land. A flock of 120 sheep introduced in 1380 indicates a change in the use of demesne pasture, and the increase in rents to £22 between 1381 and 1403 and to nearly £27 in 1406 is evidence that the demesne arable was probably let, and that cash was taking the place of labour in the economy. In 1377–8 the manorial tenants owed between them 891 works, of which more than a third were commuted for cash rents and others diverted for specific tasks other than hay and harvest works, such as fencing arable and pasture grounds, driving cattle, or repairing buildings. Cash was already being paid for haymaking and ploughing. There were 86 a. of wheat grown in that year. By 1403 the demesne arable was entirely let, one tenant holding as much as 54 a. Thereafter the only income from the demesne was from pasturage, underwood, and timber in the park.[42]

Changes in manorial income in the 15th century were solely the result of small variations in cash for the farm of the dovecot, timber sales, occasional levies of chevage, and perquisites of court. For most of the century the rental was over £28 and by the early 16th century the average net income was over £31. There was a notable contrast between the emergence of substantial tenant farms, often including former demesne, and the persistence of peasant status. A farm of 60 a. in 1447 was divided equally between neif and bord land; a holding called Holford Place and others at Woodlands commanded substantial fines.[43] By 1523 Moorhouse farm measured 100 a., another farm covered 97 a., there were two of over 80 a. and five more over 50 a.[44] One family, the Gouninghams, occupied c. 180 a. of land and held the rights over half the seaweed (or ore) gathered on the beach. An occupier of over 50 a. was Thomas Tailor alias Gregory, described as a neif. Chevage and marriage fines were regularly levied up to 1461–2 and six families were noted as neifs in 1448, with details of the place of residence of those outside the manor. Manumissions were granted in 1448 and 1497; reports of illegal residence elsewhere were made until 1498.[45]

The pattern of substantial farms continued in the late 16th and the 17th century, with an increasing acreage of wheat. From 1566, for example, John Chester held 110 a., of which 12 a. were meadow and the rest wheatlands, John Gouningham from 1547 held 83 a. of which all but 15 a. were wheatlands, and John Thorne from 1520 had 78 a. of which 75 a. were wheatlands. Another John Thorne, however, from 1565 had 113 a., of which 7 a. were meadow, 50 a. were wheat, and the rest ryelands[46] on a farm which evidently stretched to the top of the Quantocks

[31] V.C.H. Som. i. 504.
[32] S.R.O., DD/L P24, unnumbered deed, John de Mohun to Hugh of Kilve.
[33] Ibid. DD/L P3/12.
[34] Huntington Libr., Stowe MSS., ST Map 117; S.R.O., DD/AH 7/4, 11/5, 55/3.
[35] S.R.O., DD/AH 55/1. A previous sale in 1834 was abortive: ibid. DD/AH 16/3.
[36] Local inf.
[37] S.R.O., DD/MY 35; cf. ibid. DD/AH 7/4, 35/31.
[38] Ibid. DD/AH 7/4.
[39] Ibid. 2/6.
[40] V.C.H. Som. i. 504, 521.
[41] P.R.O., C 133/22, no. 1 (1279); C 135/22, no. 11 (1330).
[42] S.R.O., DD/L P24/3.
[43] Ibid. P1/17, 27, P2/9, P24/2, 4, 7–9.
[44] Ibid. P23/19.
[45] Ibid. P1/27; P24/7.
[46] Ibid. P3/11; P24/16.

where rye was being grown in 1504–5,[47] and where common was ploughed by 1606 for the cultivation of both rye and oats.[48] At least two farms, however, had dairies.[49]

By 1656 there were 23 copyholders for single lives, their farms ranging from 7 a. to c. 80 a., 7 small leaseholders, and 7 freeholders including Peregrine Palmer and John Dodington, holding respectively at Honibere Heathfield and Woodlands. Leaseholders were required to do suit of court, and enjoyed turf-cutting rights on the Quantocks.[50] By 1705 there were 30 holdings, two of just over 100 a. and four of c. 80 a.; nine were still copyholds on a single life, thirteen were leases for three lives, and four were in process of transfer from copyhold to leasehold. The common on Quantock was then used for pasturage, with rights to cut heath, furze, and turf. By the mid 18th century some further consolidation had taken place. All tenants were on leases for three lives, and one farm reached 160 a.[51] Improving clauses were introduced in leases at the same time, with such stipulations as the sowing of grass in barley.[52]

More radical rearrangement of the main Luttrell estate took place from 1796 onwards as the ancient tenements mostly centred on Kilton village were absorbed and let at rack rents, creating units to match the distinct holdings at Moorhouse and Woodlands. Thus Kilton farm of 534 a. was formed in 1815 out of at least twelve smaller units.[53] Moorhouse, already some 85 a. by the mid 17th century, was increased to c. 100 a. by 1680, and for c. 60 years in the 18th century was held on lease by the Palmers of Fairfield.[54] In 1842 it measured 84 a.[55] Two farms at Woodlands were let together by 1802 and became Woodlands farm in 1810.[56]

By the mid 19th century the pattern had changed little, though the Aclands increased their holdings by purchases from the duke of Buckingham and the Luttrells. They held Plud farm from 1731,[57] by 1767 occupied some 158 a. in the same general area nearest Fairfield, though not all in Kilton parish,[58] and added more in 1787.[59] By 1842 Sir Peregrine Acland held 380 a. in the parish, compared with the 847 a. of John Fownes Luttrell, 150 a. of John Govett, and 122 a. (the former Kilton Park) of Chester Jenkins.[60] By 1851 Kilton farm measured 592 a. and gave employment to 25 labourers, more than half the working population of the village.[61]

There was a significant change in land use. In 1842 there were 670 a. of arable, a considerable reduction from the amount in the 16th century, and the arable had been further reduced by 1905 when there were 428 a. in Kilton and Lilstock together. There was a corresponding increase in grassland,

which in 1842 still included 110 a. of common on the Quantocks and totalled 725 a. By 1905 the total for the two parishes was 1,177 a.[62] The balance in 1977 was strongly in favour of grass.

Woodland in the parish was managed by the late 14th century by the manor court. Underwood and thorn were regularly sold in the 15th century, and less often oak standards and stumps.[63] Wood at Shervage had been burnt for ash by 1504,[64] and Kilton wood was evidently replanted after ditching and fencing in 1596–7.[65] Customary tenants of the manor in the early 17th century could cut spar rods, faggots, and underwood except oak, ash, or crab apple, and could root up apple to plant in their orchards and take enough timber for repairs. Elm on their own holdings could be cut and sold.[66] Shervage was coppiced every 20 years by the mid 17th century.[67] In 1816–17 it comprised 46 oaks fit to be cut and 290 not then ready.[68]

From the early 16th century seaweed or ore from the foreshore was burnt for manuring. Four men were licensed to burn it from 1520 for a substantial rent, but from 1523 a quarter share was let with each of four of the tenant farms.[69] A lease of 1700 included half the seaweed along the coast and a fishpond, the silt from which was evidently used as manure.[70] Glatting or hunting conger was a common practice on the shore until the early years of the 20th century.[71]

Field names suggest that there was a windmill in the parish by 1516, and the name Windmill mead survived until 1753.[72]

LOCAL GOVERNMENT. Extracts and drafts of court rolls for the manor, which included small properties in Kilve and Stringston,[73] survive for 99 separate years between 1379 and 1680, including the periods 1399–1403, 1446–60, 1485–90, 1493–1504, 1590–99, and 1675–80.[74] There are presentments for the period 1739–79 and for 1782.[75] Courts leet seem normally to have been held twice a year at Hockday and Michaelmas, and courts were held at other times for entries and surrenders. After 1747 courts were held only once a year, in the autumn. In 1782 the court was held at Kilton in the afternoon, following a dinner. During the 14th and 15th centuries the courts administered the sale of wood and underwood. By the 18th century presentment of houses out of repair was the main concern of the court.

By 1377 the tenant who served as reeve was excused 54 works.[76] The office was taken in turn by 1775.[77] The tithingman was chosen each year at the Michaelmas court and the hayward at the Hockday

[47] Ibid. P24/9.
[48] Ibid. P25/46.
[49] Ibid. P24/16.
[50] Ibid. P3/12.
[51] Ibid. DD/L 2/6/33.
[52] Ibid. 2/6/28: lease 1723.
[53] Ibid. DD/L 2/6/29: leases 1796, 1815.
[54] Ibid. DD/L P3/12; DD/L 2/6/26, 27, 33.
[55] Ibid. tithe award.
[56] Ibid. DD/AH 7/4.
[57] Ibid. 16/4.
[58] Ibid. DD/AH bk. of maps 1767.
[59] Ibid. DD/AH 36/16.
[60] Ibid. tithe award.
[61] P.R.O., HO 107/1920.
[62] S.R.O., tithe award; statistics supplied by the then Bd. of Agric. 1905.

[63] S.R.O., DD/L P24/7: 76 oaks 1431–2, stumps 1448.
[64] Ibid. DD/L P24/9.
[65] Ibid. P24/19.
[66] Ibid. P25/46.
[67] Ibid. P3/12; P25/31.
[68] Ibid. DD/L I/10/35.
[69] Ibid. DD/L P3/11; P23/13, 16, 19; P24/10; V.C.H. Som. ii. 361.
[70] S.R.O., DD/L 2/6/26; inf. from Mr. M. A. Aston.
[71] V.C.H. Som. ii. 401.
[72] S.R.O., DD/L P23/19; DD/L 2/6/28.
[73] Ibid. DD/L P24/4, 7.
[74] Ibid. P23/16, 19, 39, 56, P24/2, 4–5, 7–10, 13–14, 16; P25/41.
[75] Ibid. DD/L 2/6/30.
[76] Ibid. DD/L P24/3.
[77] Ibid. DD/L 2/6/30.

court in the 15th century. The hayward by 1467 received half the profits from attachments.[78]

Two churchwardens were holding office according to their tenements by 1678, but by the 1840s there was only one warden. Two were again appointed from 1860.[79] In 1699 briefs were paid 'by consent of the major part of the parish',[80] but by 1843 the vestry had only three members.[81] Six members signed minutes in 1862.[82]

The former church house had become a poorhouse by 1656,[83] and was let to the overseers throughout the 18th century.[84] The parish was part of the Williton poor-law union from 1836, the Williton rural district from 1894, and the West Somerset district from 1974.[85]

CHURCH. Between 1090 and 1100 William de Mohun (I) gave the tithes of Kilton to the monastery of Bath.[86] A confirmation of the gift between 1138 and 1161 referred to the lands and tithes there.[87] There may have been an incumbent rector in the early 13th century, for Robert, prior of Bath 1198–1223, granted the messuage in Kilton where the priest's house used to be to John the parson for his life.[88] A vicar had been appointed by 1276,[89] and a vicarage was ordained in 1283.[90] The convent of Bath was patron until the Dissolution,[91] when the advowson passed to the Crown. In 1863 Henry Labouchere, Baron Taunton (d. 1869), bought the advowson from the Lord Chancellor, and in 1865 exchanged it for that of Over Stowey with the bishop of Bath and Wells. The bishop remained sole patron when Kilton was united with Lilstock in 1881, but became joint patron with Lord St. Audries after the union with Kilve in 1947.[92] When the benefice of Quantoxhead was formed in 1978 the bishop became patron jointly with Lady Gass and Lt.-Col. G. W. F. Luttrell.[93]

The vicarage was valued at £4 3s. 4d. in 1291 and at £7 6s. 9d. net in 1535.[94] The reputed value c. 1668 was £60,[95] and in 1831 was £189.[96] The living was augmented with £100 in 1859,[97] and the gross value after union with Lilstock was £238.[98]

Under the ordination of 1283 the vicar received the corn tithes of 'Lawnelond' and Heathfield and all the small tithes.[99] The tithes were worth £6 4s. 6d. in 1535.[1] By the 17th century the vicar still enjoyed

the small tithes, apparently payable as Easter dues and as oblations in wool, lambs, pigs, apples, and hops. Tithes of corn land and meadows came from the higher or southern part of the parish, including Heathfield.[2] In 1842 the vicar was awarded a tithe rent charge of £167 1s. 8d. in lieu of all tithes in the southern half of the parish.[3]

The vicar was assigned 63 a. of arable in the common fields and 2 a. of meadow for his horse in 1283.[4] The glebe was worth 33s. 4d. in 1341 and 33s. 8d. in 1535.[5] By 1571 the area was said to be just over 55 a.[6] and was reckoned at just over 49 a. in 1842.[7] There was no glebe in 1977.[8]

A house, perhaps that granted to John the parson by 1223,[9] was assigned to the vicar in 1283.[10] By 1626 the house comprised an entry, hall, kitchen, and buttery, with three rooms over, and farm buildings.[11] In 1815 the house was said to be unfit because it was old, mean, and neglected.[12] It was evidently rebuilt before 1831, when it was described as fit, and it was extended in 1859.[13] It was sold in 1960.[14] The house is of two storeys in local roughcast blue lias, and is irregular in plan.[15] It may incorporate part of the 17th-century building.

Lights and images were removed from the church in Edward VI's reign, and were not immediately replaced in 1554, and neglect of sermons was several times reported.[16] Annual church ales continued at least until 1636, the year when the royal arms were painted on the church wall and the communion table was railed.[17] Communion was celebrated in the 1630s five times a year with double services at Michaelmas and Christmas. By the 1670s there were usually only four celebrations, including one on Palm Sunday, though the vicar, Thomas Conway, was resident.[18] At his death in 1683 he possessed goods worth £165 including a pair of virginals.[19] In 1776 there were said to be 14 communicants.[20] Non-residence, in part due to neglect of the vicarage house in the 18th century, continued until c. 1859.[21] William Wollen, vicar from 1815, was already incumbent of Bridgwater and Chilton Trinity and combined all three until his death in 1844.[22] A curate living at Nether Stowey took two services a Sunday by 1827[23] but in 1840 there was no curate and only a single service.[24] In 1851 the incumbent of Dodington served as curate, and the general congregation averaged 30–50 with 15 from the Sunday

[78] Ibid. DD/L P24/7–8.
[79] Ibid. D/P/kln 4/1/1–3: accts. 1635–6, 1675–1736, 1843–1912. [80] Ibid. 4/1/2.
[81] Ibid. 4/1/3. [82] Ibid. 9/1/1.
[83] Ibid. DD/L P3/12; below, church.
[84] S.R.O., DD/L 2/6/33.
[85] Youngs, *Local Admin. Units*, i. 429, 673, 676.
[86] *S.R.S.* vii (1), p. 38; vii (2), pp. 169–70; Maxwell Lyte, *Dunster and its Lords*, 27–8.
[87] *S.R.S.* vii (1), p. 61.
[88] Ibid. vii (2), p. 14.
[89] Ibid. xli. 54.
[90] S.R.O., DD/AH 12/2: copy from Lincoln's Inn MS. 185, of an entry not included in printed calendar, *S.R.S.* vii (2).
[91] *Som. Incumbents*, ed. Weaver, 385.
[92] *Kelly's Dir. Som.* (1883); Order in Council 1 Apr. 1881; *Lond Gaz.* 10 Jan. 1865, 110; 6 Aug. 1940, 5; *Dioc. Dir.*
[93] *Dioc. Dir.*
[94] *Tax. Eccl.* (Rec. Com.), 198; *Valor Eccl.* (Rec. Com.), i. 215.
[95] S.R.O., D/D/Vc 24.
[96] *Rep. Com. Eccl. Revenues*, pp. 142–3.
[97] *Livings Augmented by Q. A. B.* H.C. 122 (1867), liv.

[98] *Dioc. Kal.* (1891).
[99] S.R.O., DD/AH 12/2.
[1] *Valor Eccl.* (Rec. Com.), i. 215.
[2] S.R.O., D/D/Rg 273.
[3] Ibid. tithe award.
[4] Ibid. DD/AH 12/2.
[5] E 179/169/14; *Valor Eccl.* (Rec. Com.), i. 215.
[6] S.R.O., D/D/Rg 273.
[7] Ibid. tithe award. [8] Local inf.
[9] Above. [10] S.R.O., DD/AH 12/2.
[11] Ibid. D/D/Rg 273.
[12] Ibid. D/D/B returns 1815.
[13] *Rep. Com. Eccl. Revenues*, pp. 142–3; S.R.O. DD/CC E 1337.
[14] Inf. from Dioc. Office.
[15] S.R.O., DD/CC E 1337 (plan).
[16] Ibid. D/D/Ca 22, 57, 151.
[17] Ibid. D/P/kln 4/1/1.
[18] Ibid. 4/1/1–2; *Som. Incumbents*, ed. Weaver, 385.
[19] S.R.O., DD/SP, inventory 1683.
[20] Ibid. D/D/Vc 88.
[21] Ibid. D/P/kln 2/1/1–4.
[22] *Alum. Oxon. 1715–1886*; S.R.O., D/D/B returns 1815.
[23] S.R.O., D/D/B returns 1827.
[24] Ibid. D/D/V returns 1840.

school.[25] From 1856 until union with Kilve in 1947 there were only two vicars, Samuel Shedden, 1856–91, and his son S. H. Shedden, 1891–1947.[26]

There was a church house by 1594.[27] In 1635–6 its loft was apparently converted to an upper chamber, possibly after the discontinuance of church ales earlier in the year.[28] By 1656 it was used as a poor-house.[29] It was still standing, on the edge of the churchyard, in 1843.[30]

The church of *ST. NICHOLAS* was so dedicated in 1533.[31] It stands on rising ground at the edge of the village, and comprises a chancel with north vestry, nave with south porch, and west tower. The lower parts of the tower and the chancel arch are of the 14th century and the plan of the nave and chancel is of that date or earlier. All the windows appear to have been renewed in the 15th or early 16th century.[32] It was extensively restored and partially rebuilt by John Norton between 1861 and 1864.[33] He added the top stage of the tower and replaced some of the chancel windows with lancets.[34] Box pews in chancel and nave were removed, but medieval fragments, incorporated in a later three-decker pulpit, were retained. The ornate late-medieval font retains traces of colour.[35] A barrel organ made in 1845 was purchased from Bishop's Hull in 1862.[36] After restoration it was placed in West Quantoxhead church in 1981.[37]

The four bells include the treble of *c.* 1350 from the Bristol foundry.[38] There is a cup and cover by 'I.P.' dated 1572–3.[39] The registers date from 1683 and are complete.[40]

NONCONFORMITY. None known.

EDUCATION. A day and a Sunday school were started in 1829 and by 1835 8 children attended during the week and 16 on Sundays. The schools were supported by the vicar of Kilton and a clerical neighbour.[41] By 1847 8 boys and 8 girls attended both during the week and on Sundays, and 2 girls attended on Sundays only, when the schools were said to be supported by subscriptions.[42] About 1860 a cottage in a terrace in the village was adapted as a school by the lord of the manor.[43] After improvements it was reconstituted as Kilton-cum-Lilstock National school in 1892,[44] supported by a voluntary rate, and in 1903 had 30 children on the books.[45] By 1920 numbers had fallen rapidly, and the school was closed in 1921.[46] In 1977 it was a private house.[47]

CHARITIES FOR THE POOR. James Houndrell of Kilton (d. 1673) gave £20 which was to be lent in four portions. Interest of 16s. was still paid in 1787,[48] but one portion was evidently lost soon afterwards. In 1826 it was intended to place the principal under the management of the vicar and church-wardens, but the holders of the three remaining portions distributed the interest themselves in the 1830s.[49] By 1870 the representatives of only one of the three holders were in a position to repay the principal, and the charity was thus considered to be lost.[50]

KILVE

THE ANCIENT parish of Kilve, which takes its name from the hill east of the village,[51] lies across the narrow band of country between the Quantocks and the Bristol Channel coast. From its shore, which attracted Wordsworth during his stay at Alfoxton but repelled Sir Walter Besant,[52] the ancient parish reached nearly 7 km. inland to the barren heights of the Quantocks, and formed two separate, but almost conjoined, areas covering 1,775 a.[53] In 1933 the southern part, covering 835 a., was transferred

for civil purposes to Holford, and the civil parish of Kilve measured 380 ha. in 1977.[54]

The northern part of the parish is an irregular area running in a narrow band from Longstone (290 m.) and Pardlestone hills down to a stream at Putsham. There the parish broadens, to 1.75 km. at its widest point, to embrace Kilve Hill (*c.* 110 m.), and continues north each side of the stream to a creek called Kilve Pill and a narrow shore line. The main boundaries to east and west are marked by wide

[25] P.R.O., HO 129/313/4/3/2.
[26] *Dioc. Kal.*; *Dioc. Dir.*
[27] S.R.O., DD/L P23/38.
[28] Ibid. D/P/kln 4/1/1.
[29] Ibid. DD/L P3/12.
[30] Ibid. D/D/V returns 1843.
[31] *Wells Wills*, ed. Weaver, 97.   [32] Plate facing p. 92.
[33] S.R.O., D/P/kln 6/1/1 (plans etc. 1861); E. Green, *Bibliotheca Somersetensis*, ii. 208 (consecration sermon). Pevsner, *South and West Som.* 210 says 1862.
[34] S.R.O., D/P/kln 4/1/2; Taunton Castle, Piggott Colln., drawing by J. Buckler, 1840.
[35] Font and canopy repainted 1635–6: S.R.O., D/P/kln 4/1/1.
[36] J. Speller, 'The Organs of Bishop's Hull Parish Church', *Musical Opinion*, xciii (Aug. 1970), 599–601.
[37] Inf. from the rector, the Revd. W. H. Minshull, who restored the instrument.

[38] S.R.O., DD/SAS CH 16/1.
[39] *Proc. Som. Arch. Soc.* xlvii. 166.
[40] S.R.O., D/P/kln 2/1/1–4.
[41] *Educ. Enq. Abstract*, H.C. 62 (1835), xlii.
[42] Nat. Soc. *Inquiry, 1846–7*, Som. 10–11.
[43] S.R.O., C/E 27; Char. Com. files.
[44] S.R.O., C/E box 11; Char. Com. files.
[45] S.R.O., C/E 27.
[46] Ibid. *Schs. Lists*; C/E box 11.
[47] Known as no. 11, Kilton.
[48] *Char. Don.* H.C. 511 (1816), xvi.
[49] *15th Rep. Com. Char*, p. 451; Char. Com. files.
[50] Char. Com. files.
[51] Ekwall, *Eng. Place-Names* (1960), 276. This article was completed in 1977.
[52] B. F. Cresswell, *The Quantock Hills* (1904), 62.
[53] S.R.O., tithe award.
[54] *Som. Review Order* (1933).

'freeboards or deerleaps'.[55] Most of the coastal area is on Lower Lias, with a band of shale along the stream and pockets of harder valley gravel. Attempts to extract oil from the shale c. 1923 have left standing remains near the beach.[56] The southern part of the parish, climbing up the wooded combes to the top of the Quantocks, lies on Keuper Marl and Hangman Grit.[57] Its boundaries are watercourses and, in the south, the line of the prehistoric ridgeway, marked at one point by Halsway Post or Cross.[58] In the southern area the land rises to c. 320 m. on Black Hill.

The coast road through Putsham forms the parish boundary east of the village. From it two roads run towards the coast, one over Kilve Hill, converge near the former rectory house, and lead past church and former manor house to the sea. Southwards from Putsham, Pardlestone lane to Higher Pardlestone[59] continues as a network of tracks, including part of the Great Road, across the top of the Quantocks. One of the tracks, known as the Hunting Path,[60] forms the parish boundary on Longstone Hill, and several converge in the extreme south at Crowcombe Park Gate.

Traces of early human activity include mesolithic flints, Bronze Age barrows on the Quantock ridgeway and on Hare Knap and Longstone hills, and a hoard of 3rd-century Roman coins from Putsham.[61] By the 11th century there were three areas of occupation: Pardlestone, relatively high on the Quantock slopes; Hill, in the lee of the hill from which it took its name; and Kilve, in the well watered country near the coast.[62]

It is uncertain whether the settlement by the church and medieval manor house later called Kilve Farm or Kilve Priory was ever the largest, though it lay on an ancient coastal route linking Watchet with Stogursey and perhaps with the Parrett passage at Combwich.[63] By 1280 the manor house had an adjoining park[64] which survived until 1441[65] and is traceable in fields called Great Lawn and Lawn Meadow west of the farm buildings.[66] Fishponds north of the house perhaps date from the time when the house itself was occupied by chantry priests in the 14th century.[67] The abandonment of the ancient coastal route and its replacement by the present road, evident by the 17th century,[68] encouraged the expansion of settlement at Putsham, the site of one of the Domesday mills, the name occurring by 1406.[69] By the late 18th century Putsham had certainly at-

tracted most of the population,[70] and a new manor house, Kilve Court, was built there between 1782 and 1785.[71] There was some scattered development on the wooded slopes above Pardlestone at the beginning of the 20th century[72] but most later building was confined to Putsham, and has included some ornate thatched cottages and local authority housing.

No evidence has been found of open-field farming in Kilve. Land use on the Quantocks may be suggested by the 200 oaks cut in Kilve wood c. 1242,[73] the grant of free warren in Kilve and Holford made in 1296,[74] and the valuation of heather in Kilve in 1441.[75] Woodland in 1821 measured 164 a. and was divided between Butterfly, Swinage, Frog, Ladies, Adder, Sturtcombe, and Somerton woods and Kenley quarry.[76] The name Somerton may recall the royal forest of Quantock other parts of which belonged to the royal manor of Somerton before the end of the 13th century.[77]

Kilve Pill, a 'creek for small boats', was condemned as dangerous by the port commissioners in 1559.[78] A limekiln was built at the head of the creek by 1769 to burn stone brought across the Bristol Channel from Wales.[79] The stony beach was a popular place for glatting or hunting conger eels until after the First World War.[80]

There was an inn at Kilve in 1689 and another in 1736.[81] Between 1822 and 1827 it was called the Chough and Anchor, and by 1841 the Hood Arms, its name in 1977.[82] There was a second inn in 1851.[83] A friendly society which met at the Hood Arms was disbanded c. 1911.[84] It was occasionally known as the Putsham club. The village hall, built by the rector in 1885, was later extended.[85]

There were 20 households in the parish in 1563,[86] 196 taxpayers in 1667,[87] and 30 dwellings c. 1790.[88] Between 1801 and 1821 the population rose from 176 to 263. From 260 in 1871 it fell rapidly, reaching 149 in 1901, but had more than doubled, to 365, by 1931. Within the next twenty years numbers had fallen to 286, but by 1971 had recovered to 317.[89]

MANORS. In 1086 the manor of *KILVE* comprised a main estate held by Roger de Courcelles in succession to Brictric, to which had been added two other manors, Hill and Pardlestone, held T.R.E. by Edwald and Parlo respectively.[90] Most of Roger's estates passed to the Malet family, and on the death of William Malet c. 1216 were divided between his

[55] S.R.O., tithe award.
[56] V. Waite, *Portrait of the Quantocks* (2nd edn. 1969), 68; B. Lawrence, *Quantock Country* (1952), 197; *Squibbs' History of Bridgwater* (1982), 123.
[57] Geol. Surv. Map 1", drift, sheet 295 (1907 edn.).
[58] S.R.O., DD/SAS (C/212), map 1825; ibid. tithe award.
[59] Pardlestone is from Parlo, the former tenant: *V.C.H. Som.* i. 488.
[60] S.R.O., tithe award.
[61] L. V. Grinsell, *Prehist. Sites in Quantock Country*, 12, 14; *V.C.H. Som.* i. 363.
[62] *V.C.H. Som.* i. 488.
[63] Below, East Quantoxhead, intro.
[64] *S.R.S.* xliv. 217.
[65] P.R.O., C 139/107, no. 32.
[66] S.R.O., tithe award.
[67] Below, manor.
[68] Below, East Quantoxhead, intro.
[69] Maxwell Lyte, *Dunster*, i. 98.
[70] Collinson, *Hist. Som.* iii. 532.
[71] S.R.O., DD/AH 13/1; DD/L 2/8/41.

[72] Ibid. DD/SAS (C/2401), 39; *Country Life*, 29 July 1911, 7*.
[73] *S.R.S.* xi, p. 209.
[74] *Cal. Chart. R.* i. 465.
[75] P.R.O., C 139/107, no. 32.
[76] S.R.O., D/P/kve 13/1/1.
[77] *Rot. Hund.* (Rec. Com.), ii. 121; *Proc. Som. Arch. Soc.* xlvi. 132.   [78] *S. & D. N. & Q.* xxx, p. 157.
[79] S.R.O., DD/L 2/8/44; cf. Old Cleeve, econ. hist.
[80] *V.C.H. Som.* ii. 401; Lawrence, *Quantock Country*, 199; local inf. including photos. in Hood Arms; cf. above, plate facing p. 76.
[81] S.R.O., Q/RL; Dyfed R.O., D/CAR 202.
[82] S.R.O., Q/RL; ibid. D/P/kve 4/1/1.
[83] P.R.O., HO 107/1920.
[84] M. Fuller, *West Country Friendly Socs.* 139.
[85] S.R.O., DD/X/PRD (C/2559).
[86] B.L. Harl. MS. 594, f. 55.
[87] S.R.O., DD/WY 34.
[88] Collinson, *Hist. Som.* iii. 532.
[89] *V.C.H. Som.* ii. 351; *Census*, 1911–71.
[90] *V.C.H. Som.* i. 488.

two daughters, Helewise, wife of Hugh Pointz (d. 1220), and Mabel, wife successively of Nicholas Avenel and Hugh de Vivonia (d. 1249).[91] In 1221 Kilve was adjudged to Avenel as husband of the elder daughter, and on his death in or before 1223 it passed to William de Forz (d. 1259), son of Hugh de Vivonia, and then to William's fourth daughter Cecily (d. 1320), wife of John de Beauchamp.[92] In 1284–5 she was said to hold the manor of the abbot of Glastonbury, of whom her main residence at Compton Dundon was held.[93] The overlordship continued in the Beauchamps and their successors, as trustees or lords of Dundon manor, until 1605.[94]

Robert son of William, who held Kilve at his death c. 1185–6, may have been the grandson of Robert de Pirou, a tenant under the Malets in Henry I's reign.[95] Robert son of William left three daughters and coheirs, of whom Joan married Henry Furneaux and inherited Kilve.[96] Henry died c. 1221 and was succeeded by his son, also Henry, probably a minor, whose possession was challenged by a second Nicholas Avenel, husband of another daughter of Robert son of William.[97] The dispute was continued by Matthew de Furneaux, probably the elder Henry's grandson, c. 1243,[98] and was settled when Matthew de Furneaux succeeded William Avenel, apparently heir of Nicholas, in 1253.[99] Matthew was dead by 1285,[1] and was succeeded by another Matthew, who settled the manor on his wife Maud in 1314[2] and died in 1316; Maud was still in possession in 1327, and probably in 1331.[3] Simon de Furneaux, the last Matthew's son or grandson, died in 1359, leaving an only daughter, Elizabeth, wife of John Blount.[4]

Elizabeth Blount, still in possession in 1386,[5] left an only daughter Alice, wife successively of Sir Richard Stafford and Sir Richard Stury. She held the manor in 1412 but died childless in 1414.[6] Her heirs were the descendants of the sisters of Simon de Furneaux, but by an arrangement made in 1421 Kilve and lands in Kilton and Holford were assigned as a third share of the estate to Ralph Bush and his wife Eleanor, widow of Sir John Chidiock and great-granddaughter of Eleanor Furneaux, the eldest sister.[7] Pending the settlement Ralph and Eleanor

sold what was then their quarter share in Kilve in 1419 to John Roger of Bryanston (Dors.), a merchant.[8]

John Roger or Rogers died in 1441 and was followed by his son, also John.[9] John the younger died in 1450, having settled Kilve on his wife Anne, later married to John, Lord Audley.[10] She died in 1498 and was succeeded by her son Henry Rogers (cr. K.B. 1501).[11] Sir Henry died c. 1506 and was followed by his son John (d. c. 1546) and his grandson, also John (d. 1565).[12] Richard Rogers, son and heir of the last,[13] was knighted in 1576 and died in 1605.[14] Sir John Rogers (d. 1613), son and eventual heir of Richard,[15] was followed in turn by his own sons Edward (d. 1624) and Richard. Richard was a minor,[16] and the manor was thus for some years in the hands of Sir Lewis Dyve of Bromham (Beds.), second husband of Howarda, Edward Roger's widow.[17]

Richard Rogers came of age in 1632, though his mother, after her second marriage known as Margaret Banastre (d. 1663), had jointure in Kilve, and he himself was described later as only tenant for life and as never having had possession of the manor.[18] He died in 1643 leaving two daughters, Elizabeth and Rogersa, in the guardianship of his mother and of Lancelot Lake.[19] Elizabeth married first Charles Cavendish, styled Viscount Mansfield (d. 1659), and second Charles Stuart, duke of Richmond and Lennox. She died in 1661,[20] and her half share was conveyed in 1662 to Sir John Rogers of Langton Long Blandford (Dors.), son of Richard Rogers, a younger brother of Sir John Rogers (d. 1613).[21] Rogersa, wife of Sir Henry Belasyse, K.B., died without issue.[22]

In 1664 Sir John Rogers divided his estate: the manor and most of the land was bought by John Cunditt, also of Langton Long Blandford.[23] Cunditt, then of Edmundsham (Dors.), was dead by 1679 when his executors presented to the living, and was succeeded by another John Cunditt, of Kilve, probably his son, who died in 1690, and by a third of the same name, probably a grandson, who survived until 1771.[24] The youngest John Cunditt sold his heavily mortgaged property in 1769 to Henry

[91] Ibid. 413; Sanders, *Eng. Baronies*, 38–9.
[92] *Cur. Reg. R.* x. 106–7, 229; *Pat. R.* 1216–25, 310; Sanders, *Eng. Baronies*, 39.
[93] *Feud. Aids*, iv. 275.
[94] P.R.O., C 139/107, no. 32; C 142/290, no. 127; *Cal. Inq. p.m. Hen. VII*, p. 107.
[95] *Pipe R.* 1188 (P.R.S. xxxviii), 164; *V.C.H. Wilts.* viii. 101; Collinson, *Hist. Som.* iii. 532.
[96] Collinson, *Hist. Som.* iii. 532, quoting 'ancient charter'.
[97] *Cur. Reg. R.* x. 106–7, 229; *Pat. R.* 1216–25, 310.
[98] *S.R.S.* xi, p. 209.
[99] Ibid. xxxv. 66; P.R.O., C 132/14, no. 13.
[1] *Feud. Aids*, iv. 275.
[2] *S.R.S.* xii. 47–8.
[3] Ibid. extra ser. 317; iii. 165; *Cal. Inq. p.m.* vii, p. 220.
[4] *Cal. Inq. p.m.* x, p. 395; *S.R.S.* xxxv. 98–9.
[5] *S.R.S.* lvii, p. 33.
[6] *Feud. Aids*, vi. 514; *Reg. Chichele* (Cant. & York Soc.), ii. 7–10, 678.
[7] *S. & D. N. & Q.* xvi. 281–5.
[8] Ibid. xxii. 180; *Feud. Aids*, iv. 439; *Coll. Top. et Gen.* i. 243.
[9] P.R.O., C 139/107, no. 32.

[10] *S.R.S.* extra ser. 319.
[11] *Cal. Close*, 1485–1500, p. 317; *Cal. Inq. p.m. Hen. VII*, ii, p. 107; P.R.O., C 142/13, no. 53.
[12] *Cal. Pat.* 1494–1509, 541; *S.R.S.* extra ser. 320.
[13] *Cal. Pat.* 1560–3, 584.
[14] *S.R.S.* extra ser. 321.
[15] P.R.O., C 142/290, no. 127; C 142/407/70; *S.R.S.* lxvii. 196; *Cat Anct. D.* vi, C 8001.
[16] P.R.O., C 142/407, no. 70.
[17] *S.R.S.* extra ser. 321; *Som. Incumbents*, ed. Weaver, 386.
[18] P.R.O., CP 25(2)/527/8 Chas. I Mich.; ibid. CP 43/199, rot. 111; *Cal. Cttee. for Compounding* iv. 2874.
[19] *Som. Incumbents*, ed. Weaver, 386.
[20] *Complete Peerage*, x. 835.
[21] B.L. Add. Ch. 5984; Hutchins, *Hist. Dors.* i. 250. Sir John was a claimant to the estate before 1652: *Cal. Cttee. for Compounding*, iv. 2874.
[22] Burke, *Extinct Peerage* (1831), 49. Hen. Belasyse married for a second time in Oct. 1662: *Complete Peerage*, ii. 90 n.
[23] S.R.O., DD/L 2/7/37.
[24] Ibid. DD/MDW 14, 20; DD/SF 962; M.I. in Kilve ch.

Sweeting, who died in 1785.[25] Henry's son John died in 1815, and his grandson John Hankey Sweeting of Kilve and Great Houghton (Northants.) in 1841. John Hankey Saumarez Sweeting of Chelmsford (Essex), son of J. H. Sweeting, sold the lordship to Edward Fownes Luttrell (d. 1865), second son of Col. Francis Luttrell.[26] From Edward Luttrell the lordship passed to his elder brother George, of Dunster, who conveyed it to Daniel Badcock in 1886. Badcock died in 1915 and the lordship has not been traced thereafter.[27]

A court, stable, and bakehouse were recorded in 1242-3.[28] The manor house became the residence of the college of priests founded under licence in 1329,[29] though the college ceased to exist probably in the late 14th century. The house was regarded as the capital messuage of the manor by 1441, though by the late 16th century it was let.[30] From the mid 17th century it was known as the 'old mansion' or Kilve Farm.[31] It evidently ceased to be a farmhouse when its land was linked with Parkhouse farm in the late 19th century, and has since been known as the Priory or Kilve Priory. By 1906 it was offered to holiday-makers as apartments.[32] In 1977 it was divided between Priory and Chantry cottages.

The two cottages comprise the hall range of a substantial medieval house. The two-storeyed eastern cross wing, largely ruined but dating from the late 13th century, is the former solar, having a contemporary first-floor chapel against its east wall. Late medieval additions, post-dating the college, project from the north-eastern corner.[33]

In 1862 Edward Fownes Luttrell (d. 1865) bought with the lordship of Kilve a house called Kilve Court at Putsham.[34] The house, where he had lived since the 1820s,[35] passed with the lordship to his brother George, and then to Daniel Badcock (d. 1915). Badcock's widow Mary sold the house in 1920 to Col. Joseph Cook-Hurle, who was succeeded on his death in 1930 by his widow Norah Lilian (d. 1960), a prominent member of Somerset County Council. Her son, Lt. Col. R. J. Cook-Hurle, sold Kilve Court in 1961 to the county council for use as a residential Youth (now Education) Centre.[36]

The 'neat new-built dwelling'[37] was erected by Henry Sweeting between 1782 and his death in 1785.[38] It has a principal front of five bays and three storeys. The central staircase and main rooms have contemporary decoration. There is a lower service wing in the rear, with modern accommodation for its use as a college.

In 1664 Sir John Rogers sold the southern part of his estate to John St. Albyn of Alfoxton. The property was described as the manor of KILVE AND HOLFORD, and included tenements in Putsham and Pardlestone.[39] During the 18th century, as

further lands were acquired, the estate was variously described as the manor of HOLFORD or of ALFOXTON,[40] and descended in the St. Albyn

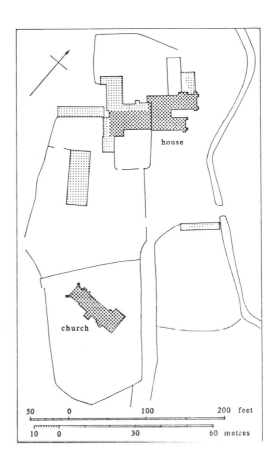

KILVE MANOR HOUSE

The darker stipple indicates the area of
medieval buildings.

family from John to his son Lancelot (d. 1708-9), and then to Lancelot's brother George (d. 1750).[41] The Revd. Lancelot (d. 1791) succeeded his elder brother John (d. 1768), George's heir,[42] and was

[25] S.R.O., DD/L 2/8/41; DD/AS 13/1; DD/SAS HV 68/6.
[26] Ibid. DD/SAS HV 68/6; deeds in possession of Somerset county council.
[27] Deeds in possession of Somerset C.C.
[28] S.R.S. xi, p. 209.
[29] Cal. Pat. 1327-30, 414.
[30] P.R.O., C 139/107, no. 32; ibid. C 3/247/42.
[31] S.R.O., DD/L 2/8/43.
[32] Kelly's Dir. Som. (1906).
[33] Plate facing p. 93.
[34] Deeds in possession of Somerset C.C.
[35] S.R.O., DD/SAS HV 68/6.
[36] Deeds in possession of Somerset C.C.
[37] Collinson, Hist. Som. iii. 532; above, plate facing p. 77.   [38] S.R.O., DD/AH 13/1; DD/L 2/8/41.
[39] Ibid. DD/L 2/7/37.
[40] Ibid. DD/MDW 14, 21.
[41] Som. Wills, ed. Brown, i. 87.
[42] Ibid. i. 85-7.

himself followed by his great-nephew, born Langley Gravenor, who assumed the name St. Albyn in 1806.[43] Langley St. Albyn's estate in 1839 amounted to 201 a. in Kilve and included Pardlestone farm and Higher and Middle Hill.[44] It passed to his son Lancelot, but was sold by the family in the 1890s.[45]

ECONOMIC HISTORY. In 1086 the three estates of Kilve, Hill, and Pardlestone amounted to 5 hides. The demesne farm at Kilve dominated that 2½-hide estate, leaving the tenants with only 5 ferlings between them; at Hill the home farm seems to have accounted for three-quarters of the holding, leaving the tenants with half a ploughteam; and at Pardlestone there was 1½ virgate in demesne and ½ virgate held by tenants. In all there were 23 a. of meadow, 38 a. of wood, and two substantial areas of pasture. No stock was recorded at Hill, but the other two demesne estates between them supported, besides 2 riding-horses, 9 beasts (*animalia*), 7 swine, 53 sheep, and 74 she-goats.[46]

Hill and Pardlestone, separately named estates until the mid 14th century,[47] have continued as distinct farms until the present. Common ownership, however, effectively unified the estate, and a verdict of 1223 on the value of the harvest of 200 a. of demesne corn evidently related to the whole property.[48] By 1441 the demesne farm measured 239 a., rents of free tenants were worth 69s., and of tenants at will 4s.[49] In 1327 the township was one of the more highly taxed in the district.[50]

Farming in the 16th and 17th centuries may have been largely arable: in 1535 the tithes of corn and hay produced £4 in comparison with only 24s. from wool and lambs.[51] An inventory of 1671 shows crops of wheat, barley, oats, beans, and peas, some 47 cattle, 3 mares, 'hogs of all sizes', geese and other poultry, and a threshing mill.[52] Covenants in a lease of Lower Hill in 1769 limited arable cropping to two years in succession and required lime or dung on all land ploughed for wheat, the lime to be provided from the lord's limekiln.[53] Similar terms, with a heavier use of lime, were agreed on the same farm in 1806.[54] The first lease was for 9 years at £24 for 34 a.; the second for 7, 10, or 14 years at £28. Common grazing and turbary were still claimed in respect of holdings in the parish in the 18th century either in general terms, or precisely as two days' cutting of turf.[55]

By 1664 the main holdings in the parish were Pardlestone, Middle and Lower Hill, Poorhouse, and Kilve farms.[56] By 1769 Kilve farm was the largest,

with c. 275 a., Poorhouse measured 53 a., and Lower Hill 35 a.[57] By 1839 Kilve farm was slightly smaller at 244 a., Poorhouse had increased to 118 a., and Pardlestone measured 102 a. There were four other holdings of between 40 a. and 70 a., together with 164 a. of woodland and some 617 a. of common.[58] Kilve farm claimed exclusive common on Black Hill.[59]

Poorhouse farm, which c. 1860 was renamed Parkhouse farm, then had equipment which included a water-powered threshing machine.[60] The balance of land use, slightly in favour of arable in 1839, had changed by 1905: there was then more grassland and slightly less wood.[61] In 1976 there were seven farm holdings in the civil parish, one of which specialized in dairying, another in cattle and sheep. Grassland had increased further in proportion to arable.[62]

In 1296 Matthew de Furneaux was granted a weekly market on Wednesdays and a fair on the eve, day, and morrow of St. Margaret's day (19–21 July).[63] No later evidence of either has been found.

Like its neighbours on the coast Kilve was a place for burning seaweed from the late 16th century onwards; in the 19th century the product was used either in bottle manufacture or for manure.[64] More distinctive was the tradition of clothmaking, certainly carried on from the beginning of the 17th century.[65] A fulling mill was in operation by 1636,[66] and in the 1660s there were at least 2 clothiers, 2 weavers, and 1 fuller in the village with business connexions in Melksham and Bradford-on-Avon (Wilts.),[67] and there were at least 3 fulling mills in the vicinity.[68] Clothiers and a serge maker occur during the 18th century,[69] and Richard Shurt the younger, from one of the leading clothing families, leased a fulling mill in 1732 with rights to rack cloth and to wash his own sheep in the washing pond each year.[70] From 1721 linen houses were built on the waste of the St. Albyn estate,[71] and a dyehouse on Shurt's tenement survived until after 1839.[72] There was a wool dealer in the parish in 1851.[73]

In 1676 a tailor died leaving goods in his shop worth £112.[74] By 1851 the craftsmen in the village included 4 carpenters, 3 shoemakers, 2 blacksmiths, a tailor, a tanner, and a mason. The village supported a draper's and grocer's shop.[75]

MILLS. There were two mills in 1086, one attached to Kilve manor, the other to Hill.[76] Both probably descended with Kilve manor, and by the 17th century they were corn mills, distinguished as Kilve

[43] *Alum. Oxon. 1715–1886.*
[44] S.R.O., tithe award.
[45] *Kelly's Dir. Som.* (1894, 1897).
[46] *V.C.H. Som.* i. 488.
[47] *Feud. Aids*, iv. 303, 346.
[48] *Cur. Reg. R.* xi, p. 160.
[49] P.R.O., C 139/107, no. 32.
[50] *S.R.S.* iii. 165–9.
[51] *Valor Eccl.* (Rec. Com.), i. 215.
[52] S.R.O., DD/SP, inventory of Wm. Kebby.
[53] Ibid. DD/L 2/8/44.   [54] Ibid. 2/8/41.
[55] Ibid. DD/MDW 14.
[56] Ibid. DD/L 2/7/37–9, 2/9/48.
[57] Ibid. 2/8/41.
[58] Ibid. tithe award.
[59] Ibid. DD/AH 18/4, 38/9.
[60] Ibid. DD/WY 140.
[61] Statistics supplied by the then Bd. of Agric. 1905.

[62] Min. of Agric., Fisheries, and Food, agric. returns 1976.
[63] *Cal. Chart R.* i. 465.
[64] *V.C.H. Som.* ii. 361.
[65] S.R.O., D/D/Ca 151; *S.R.S.* xxiv. 165; *Som. Wills*, ed. Brown, ii. 18.
[66] S.R.O., D/D/Ca 310.
[67] Ibid. DD/L 2/7/37–8.
[68] Below.
[69] S.R.O., DD/MDW 14; DD/L 2/8/40–1.
[70] Ibid. DD/MDW 14. A field called Rack close occurs in 1613: S.R.O., D/D/Rg 274.
[71] Ibid. DD/MDW 14.
[72] Ibid. DD/L 2/8/41; D/P/kve 13/1/1; ibid. tithe award.
[73] P.R.O., HO 107/1920.
[74] S.R.O., DD/SP, inventory 1676.
[75] P.R.O., HO 107/1920.
[76] *V.C.H. Som.* i. 488.

mill, closely associated with Kilve farm and probably, therefore, near the former manor house, and Nether mill at Putsham, so called in relation to a fulling mill a few yards upstream. Kilve mill was occupied by the tenant of the capital messuage in 1665, and occurs in 1697 but not thereafter.[77] Nether mill first occurs under that name in 1635[78] and was for some time held by the Sealy family.[79] By 1697 it formed part of a 20-a. holding[80] and by 1706 seems to have been occupied by the Shurt family, substantial clothiers, who renewed their lease in 1732.[81] It was then described as burnt down, but the property also included a fulling mill at the head of the millpond. The mill was evidently rebuilt, and was in use as a flour mill until c. 1906.[82]

Higher mill, a few yards upstream, probably originated as one of three fulling mills on the estate in 1664, though one and possibly two were probably in Holford parish.[83] The Mallet family occupied one by 1636 until after 1664[84] and Charles Mitchell, a clothier, held it in 1723.[85] This may have been the clothing mill belonging to John Wheddon in 1821.[86]

LOCAL GOVERNMENT. A court was being held for Kilve manor in 1671, and one for Kilve with Holford in 1684.[87] Suit to Kilve manor was required in 1684. Leases of land or houses from the St. Albyns in the 18th century required suit to Alfoxton or Holford manor.[88]

Two wardens, two overseers, and a tithingman occur in 1641,[89] and two wardens were chosen in the 18th and 19th centuries.[90] A meeting of the vestry in 1762 comprised the wardens, the curate, and three other inhabitants.[91]

Poorhouse Farm, recorded in 1664, may have been named after a parish poorhouse.[92] The parish became part of the Williton poor-law union in 1836, the Williton rural district in 1894, and the West Somerset district in 1974.[93]

CHURCH. A rector of Kilve was named between 1265 and 1273.[94] A single reference to the living as 'Mynsterculve' in 1436[95] might suggest an earlier foundation, but probably recalls the college or chantry, licensed in 1329.[96] Five chantry chaplains, one of whom was styled the minister,[97] were to cele-

brate daily in the parish church for the souls of Simon de Furneaux and his heirs. The college was to be supported by land in Kilve and Stringston and the advowsons of both churches.[98] Appointments to the chantry were made in 1332 and 1350, and the minister was named in 1369,[99] but the foundation probably ceased to function before the end of the 14th century, and certainly by 1411.[1] By 1433 the parish church had reverted to its original status, but the link with the chapel of Stringston had been revived by 1532.[2] The rectory of Kilve with Stringston remained a sole benefice until 1946, when it was linked with East Quantoxhead. In 1947 it was united with Kilton and Lilstock, and in 1977 was joined by West Quantoxhead, Holford, and Dodington to form the benefice of Quantoxhead in 1978.[3]

The advowson belonged to the lords of the manor until 1329, when Simon de Furneaux granted it to his newly established college of chantry priests.[4] The priests presented a rector in 1335,[5] but the patronage had reverted to the lord of the manor by 1411.[6] Successive lords or their trustees presented until the 16th century, but before 1570 Catherine, widow of John Rogers, gave the advowson to John Foster of Pylle, who devised it to his brother Robert, a clergyman.[7] In 1587 Sir Richard Rogers conveyed the patronage by lease or sale to John Kaines, but by 1626 it had reverted to the lords.[8] Margaret Banastre and Lancelot Lake presented in 1662 and Sir John Rogers in 1666, and the advowson passed to John Cunditt, the new lord of the manor, before his death in 1679.[9] Another John Cunditt, probably his son, sold the advowson to Balliol College, Oxford, in 1688.[10]

Balliol retained the advowson until 1893, when it was sold to the Revd. Herbert Sweet Escott, son of the then rector. From him it passed in quick succession to Mary Edith Greswell in 1894, and to the Revd. Herbert Price in 1895. Price sold it in 1906 to Frances Caroline James, wife of the then curate of Kilve, and her husband was given the living in 1910. Lord St. Audries bought the patronage in 1931, and from 1947 shared with the bishop of Bath and Wells the right of joint presentation to the united benefice. His niece, Lady Gass, retained his share in 1977.[11]

The church was worth £10 in 1291,[12] £9 16s. 6½d. net in 1535,[13] reputedly £100 c. 1668,[14] and £642 net in 1831.[15] The tithes were valued at £7 4s. in 1535,

[77] S.R.O., DD/L 2/7/37–8, 2/8/43; DD/SF 3943.
[78] Ibid. DD/L 2/7/36.
[79] Ibid. 2/8/43; DD/MDW 14; DD/SP, inventory 1666.
[80] Ibid. DD/L 2/7/38; DD/SF 3943.
[81] P.R.O., CP 43/492, rot. 70; S.R.O., DD/MDW 14.
[82] *Kelly's Dir. Som.* (1906).
[83] S.R.O., DD/L 2/7/37.
[84] Ibid. D/D/Ca 310; DD/L 2/7/37.
[85] Ibid. DD/L 2/7/37; DD/MDW 21.
[86] Ibid. D/P/kve 13/1/1.
[87] Ibid. DD/L 2/7/36; DD/MDW 14.
[88] Ibid. DD/MDW 14.
[89] *Som. Protestation Returns*, ed. Howard and Stoate, 162.
[90] S.R.O., DD/L 2/9/48; ibid. D/P/kve 4/1/1.
[91] Ibid. DD/L 2/9/48.
[92] Ibid. 2/7/37.
[93] Youngs, *Local Admin. Units*, i. 670, 673, 675–6.
[94] S.R.O., DD/L P22: Alex. Luttrell to Hen. de Furneaux, rector.
[95] *S.R.S.* xxxi, p. 198.
[96] *Cal. Pat.* 1327–30, 414.

[97] *S.R.S.* ix, pp. 111, 165, 250; x, p. 607; S.R.O., DD/L P32/2: John Spray, minister, to John and Joan Basing.
[98] *Cal. Pat.* 1327–30, 414.
[99] *S.R.S.* ix, p. 111; x, p. 607; S.R.O., DD/L P32/2.
[1] *S.R.S.* xxix, pp. 100–01.
[2] Ibid. xxxi, pp. 142–4; lv, p. 162; S.R.O., D/D/Vc 20.
[3] *Dioc. Dir.*
[4] *Cal. Pat.* 1327–30, 414.
[5] *S.R.S.* ix, p. 250.
[6] Ibid. xxxi, pp. 100–01.
[7] *Som. Incumbents*, ed. Weaver, 386; *Som. Wills*, ed. Brown, iii. 78–9.
[8] P.R.O., CP 25(2)/206/29 Eliz. I East.; *Som. Incumbents*, ed. Weaver, 386.
[9] *Som. Incumbents*, ed. Weaver, 386.
[10] S.R.O., DD/L 2/9/48.
[11] Ibid. DD/AH 36/22; *Dioc. Dir.*
[12] *Tax. Eccl.* (Rec. Com.), 198.
[13] *Valor Eccl.* (Rec. Com.), i. 215.
[14] S.R.O., D/D/Vc 24.
[15] *Rep. Com. Eccl. Revenues*, 142–3.

and in 1839 they were commuted to a rent charge of £211 10s.[16] In 1535 the glebe lands were worth £3 12s.,[17] and presumably included the lands of the former college in Kilve and Stringston. In 1613 there were some 63 a. of glebe in Kilve, 45 a. in Stringston, and 28 a. in Chilton Trinity.[18] There were nearly 60 a. in Kilve in 1839,[19] and 121 a. in all until sales in 1926–7 reduced the total to 78 a. for the whole benefice, with just over 13 a. in Kilve. Further sales reduced the total to just under 70 a. in 1948, with nearly 4 a. in Kilve and 45 a. in Stringston, the remainder in Wembdon and Cannington, perhaps the result of exchanges with Chilton.[20]

The large rectory house, regarded as adequate in the early 19th century,[21] was given up in favour of the glebe cottage in 1913, and was sold c. 1938.[22] Known as the Old Rectory, it stands in its own grounds south of the church. The symmetrical north and east fronts and most of the internal fittings appear to be of the early 19th century, but one room at the south-east corner has 18th-century decoration, and other rooms on the south side have thick internal walls, suggesting that an older building is incorporated. The present rectory house is in Putsham.

Disputes over the legal status of the benefice were said in 1433 to have led to the neglect of the parish.[23] In 1448 a new rector, whose understanding of scripture and letters was said to be 'very mediocre', was ordered to employ a chaplain for two years and to study grammar. 'Hardly any progress' had been made by the end of that period, but in 1451 he was found competent and given a further two years to study.[24] In 1554 the church lacked books and ornaments because of bad debts.[25] The rector was in 1577 reported for non-residence.[26]

At least seven of the rectors appointed by Balliol were members of the college, including Henry Farr Yeatman, D.D., rector 1784–96, and William Greswell, rector 1837–76.[27] Hay Sweet Escott, rector 1877–1910, came to the parish on retirement from the post of first headmaster of the Somersetshire College at Bath. He died as rector at the age of 94.[28] There were 10 regular communicants in 1776.[29] For most of the 19th century only one service was held at Kilve, alternately morning and afternoon or evening, with communion only five or six times a year.[30] In 1851 the average general congregation was 60 in the morning and 100 in the afternoon or evening, with 50 Sunday-school pupils.[31]

There was a light in the parish church, supported in 1548 by a rent charge of 6d. on land in the parish.[32]

The church of ST. MARY,[33] in local grey stone, comprises a chancel with north vestry, nave with south porch, and western tower. The vestry, added in memory of William Greswell (d. 1876),[34] occupies the site of an earlier building formerly linked to the chancel by an arcade, now of only 1½ bay, but suggesting that the chancel itself may have been longer, perhaps to provide a choir for the 14th-century college of chantry priests. The porch is also of the 14th century, but the chancel arch, windows, and nave roof indicate a rebuilding of the nave and chancel in the 15th century, when the addition of a screen[35] involved the creation of a shallow southern projection to house both the roodloft light and a pulpit. The font is probably 12th century, with a plain bowl and cable-moulded base. A plain window at the west end of the nave lit the gallery added c. 1771.[36] The tower may have been added as late as c. 1636. Before that time the bells, including one of c. 1500 from the Bristol foundry,[37] were in a separate, thatched building, open to damage by parishioners. The wardens in 1636 were ordered 'to build up some new room . . . adjoining to the west end of the church'.[38] There is some medieval glass in the chancel, and a wooden panel in the choir stalls is dated 1687.

The registers, with burials from 1539, baptisms from 1591, and marriages from 1632, have gaps from 1648 to 1665 but are thereafter complete.[39]

NONCONFORMITY. In 1782 a house at Putsham was licensed for use by Baptists.[40] A chapel for Independents was built next to the inn at Putsham in 1807 and was licensed in 1810.[41] It was served 'for many years' from Nether Stowey or Bridgwater, but was closed in 1888 in order not to oppose the 'earnest and godly' rector.[42] The chapel was sold in 1912.[43] Wesleyans, preaching at Putsham in the late 18th century, were enquiring about a preaching house in 1846, but the cause was given up in 1848.[44]

EDUCATION. By 1835 there was a day school for 20 children, supported equally by the rector and parents.[45] In 1847 25 boys and 28 girls attended each weekday and on Sundays, and an additional 23 boys and 19 girls on Sundays, and the schools were said to be principally supported by the rector.[46] From 1876 children from the parish attended the school at East Quantoxhead, on the road between the two villages, until its closure in 1971.[47]

[16] S.R.O., tithe award.
[17] Valor Eccl. (Rec. Com.), i. 215.
[18] S.R.O., D/D/Rg 274. There were 2 a. in Kilton, part of the Stringston holding.
[19] Ibid. tithe award.
[20] Ibid. D/P/kve 3/1/1–6.
[21] Ibid. D/D/B returns 1815.
[22] Ibid. D/P/kve 3/4/2–3.
[23] S.R.S. xxxi, pp. 142–4.
[24] Ibid. xlix, pp. 97, 149, 170.
[25] S.R.O., D/D/Ca 22.
[26] Ibid. 57.
[27] S.R.O., D/D/B reg. 32, f. 61v.; Alum. Oxon. 1715–1886.
[28] S.R.O., DD/X/PRD (C/2559).
[29] S.R.O., D/D/Vc 88.
[30] Ibid. D/D/B returns 1815, 1827; D/D/V returns 1840, 1843, 1870.
[31] S.R.O., HO 129/31 3/4/2/10.
[32] S.R.S. ii. 51, 225.
[33] Possibly earlier to St. Margaret, on whose feast the fair was held: above.
[34] M.I. in ch.
[35] Fragment in ch.
[36] S.R.O., DD/L 2/9/48.
[37] Ibid. DD/SAS CH 16/1.
[38] Ibid. D/D/Ca 310.
[39] Ibid. D/P/kve 2/1/1–8.
[40] Ibid. D/D/Rm I, p. 47.
[41] P.R.O., HO 129/313/4/2/11; S.R.O., D/D/Rm, box 2 Char. Com. files.
[42] Rep. Som. Cong. Union (1891).
[43] Char. Com. files.
[44] W. Symons, Early Methodism in W. Som. [c. 1894]; S.R.O., D/N/wsc 3/2/2.
[45] Educ. Enq. Abstract, H.C. 62 (1835), xlii.
[46] Nat. Soc. Inquiry, 1846–7, Som. 10–11.
[47] Below.

CHARITIES FOR THE POOR. By will dated 1643 Alexander Standfast of Kilve gave a rent charge of £1 on land in Lilstock, one third to be given to the unrelieved poor of Kilve.[48] Until *c.* 1820 the charge was regularly paid, but for a decade the tenant refused.[49] Money was still paid in 1871, but after 1879 the churchwardens, as trustees, were unable to prove their title and payments lapsed.[50]

James Houndrell, by will dated 1711, gave a sum of either £20 or £30 for 'poor old housekeepers'.[51]

The capital was lent out by the churchwardens, income amounting to £1 in 1786–7.[52] Capital and interest totalling £50 was invested in 1828 in Bridgwater market tolls, but interest was not paid for some years before 1874, when the market became insolvent. The charity received 7s. 6d. in the £, and invested it in stock. The sum of £1 each was paid to five recipients in 1956.[53] No distribution was made in 1977.[54]

LILSTOCK

THE ANCIENT parish of Lilstock, the *stoc* of Lylla and his people,[55] occupied a band of coastline 2 km. long and 1 km. in depth, from the eastern end of which a narrow strip less than 1 km. wide ran inland for 2.5 km. Its boundaries with Kilton and Stogursey were regular, but there were detached areas of Lilstock in Stogursey until 1811.[56] In 1881 the parish measured 1,160 a.[57] In 1886 the parish was amalgamated with part of Kilton to form the civil parish of Kilton-with-Lilstock.[58] In 1933 the parish of Stringston was added to create the civil parish of Stringston.[59]

The parish lay on Lower Lias with pockets of clay and limestone; limestone has been quarried and burned there.[60] The land is mostly below the 30-m. contour, and the coastal band is bisected by a stream which runs northwards almost to the coast and then turns east behind the pebble bank, where a harbour was formed in the 19th century.[61] Two open arable fields, east and west fields, occupied the coastal band, divided from each other by Upper or Goose common and Lower or Horse common, a marshy area beside the stream.[62] About area of common land were inclosed in 1811.[63] By 1886 the valley was used as a rifle range.[64]

Lilstock village clusters on the west side of the valley. The remains of its church lie at its southwestern edge, but further south are house platforms and a field called Castle Ditch, an indication of more extensive settlement.[65] Roman pottery has been found on the cliffs to the north-west.[66] There was a secondary settlement at Honibere, to the south-east of Lilstock village, by the 11th century. It was the site of a manor house,[67] and was still described as a

village in 1655,[68] but it is now represented only by Honibere Farm. The land around Honibere, south of Lilstock east field, seems to have been inclosed by the 12th century and may have originated in clearings in the wood and heathland which survived further south, in Kilton, into the 16th century.[69]

The village is served by a lane which leads from the road between Burton in Stogursey and Kilton. The straight section of the lane north from Honibere Farm was not fenced until after 1764[70] and its northern end, running east and then north into the village, was created early in the 19th century, probably after the passage of the Inclosure Act in 1803.[71]

About 1820 Sir John Acland built a boathouse on the beach near the stream,[72] and cross-channel trade grew up. Coal was brought from Wales for domestic use on the Acland estate and to fire the large limekiln on the cliff. Pit props were the main export.[73] A harbour was built around the stream where it ran almost parallel with the beach. By 1848 there were resident coastguards, and by 1855 a customs officer.[74] About 1860 a stone pier was built from the northern side of the harbour wall, with a wooden awning and a butler's pantry at its end.[75] By 1886 warehouses were standing under the cliff beside the southern harbour wall.[76] A plan for a ship canal from Seaton (Devon) to terminate at Lilstock was considered by the Board of Admiralty in 1888.[77] The harbour was apparently abandoned and the pier subsequently destroyed after the First World War.[78]

About 1832 Sir Peregrine Acland created a private road between his house at Fairfield and the cliff above the harbour, and built a wooden house there for his delicate only daughter.[79] A promenade along

[48] *Char. Don.* H.C. 511 (1816), xvi.
[49] *15th Rep. Com. Char.* (1826), pp. 450–1.
[50] *Dig. End. Char. 1869–71,* H.C. (1873), li; S.R.O., D/P/kve 17/1/1.
[51] *Char. Don.; 15th Rep. Com. Char.,* pp. 450–1.
[52] *Char. Don.*
[53] Char. Com. files; S.R.O., D/P/kve 17/2/1.
[54] Inf. from the rector, the Revd. W. H. Minshull.
[55] Ekwall, *Eng. Place-Names* (1960), 298. This article was completed in 1977 with additional material to 1980.
[56] S.R.O., Q/RDe 54.
[57] *Census,* 1881.
[58] *Local Govt. Bd. Order* 19,063.
[59] *Som. Review Order* 1933.
[60] O.S. Map 6″, Som. XXXVII. SW. NW. (1886 edn.); S.R.O., DD/AH 34/23.
[61] Below.
[62] Huntington Libr., Stowe MSS., ST Map 118 (1764); S.R.O., Q/RDe 54.
[63] S.R.O., Q/RDe 54.
[64] O.S. Map 6″, Som. XXXVII. NW. (1886 edn.).
[65] S.R.O., Q/RDe 54; inf. from Mr. T. Pearson.
[66] Local inf.
[67] Below, manors and other estates.
[68] S.R.O., DD/AH 36/5.
[69] Ibid. 28/9.
[70] Huntington Libr., Stowe MSS., ST Map 118.
[71] S.R.O., DD/AH 14/8; ibid. Q/RDe 54.
[72] Ibid. DD/AH 24/7.
[73] Local inf.; Wedlake, *Watchet,* 87.
[74] S.R.O., D/P/lk 2/1/5.
[75] *Som. Co. Herald,* 30 Dec. 1933. A man who worked on the building as a mortar boy d. 1930 aged 82: S.R.O., D/P/lk 2/1/4.
[76] O.S. Map 6″, Som. XXXVII. NW. (1886 edn.); above, plate facing p. 45.
[77] S.R.O., DD/AH 3/7.
[78] Inf. from Mr. L. S. Colchester, Wells.
[79] S.R.O., DD/AH 24/7; *Som. Co. Herald,* 30 Dec. 1933.

the cliff became a recreation for local gentry, and in the 1860s and 1870s pleasure steamers plied between Lilstock, Burnham, Ilfracombe (Devon), and Cardiff.[80] A naval bombing range was established off the coast west of the village in 1954.[81]

A beer house called the Limpet Shell was in business early in the 20th century.[82]

There were 11 households in the parish in 1563,[83] 65 taxpayers in 1667,[84] and 12 inhabited houses at the end of the 18th century.[85] The population was 56 in 1801. It fluctuated considerably during the century, rising to 91 in 1811 and 94 in 1881, but falling to 48 in 1841 and 58 in 1901.[86] Later figures for the population of Lilstock alone are not available, but in 1977 there were 5 inhabited houses.

MANORS AND OTHER ESTATE. In 1086 Ansger the cook held *LILSTOCK* of the Crown in succession to Bricsic.[87] Before 1107 William de Falaise gave part of the tithes of his demesne there to the monks of Lonlay (Orne).[88] William's lands, described as the barony of Stogursey, passed to his daughter Emme, and through her marriage to William de Curci descended to William de Curci (d. 1194). Alice, sister of the last, left two daughters, and by 1225 the barony was shared between them, Lilstock evidently passing to Joan, wife of Hugh de Neville of Essex (d. 1234). John, Hugh's son, died in 1246, and his grandson, also Hugh, in 1269. The latter was succeeded by his son John (d. 1282), and then by John's son, another Hugh, who came of age in 1298 and who died in 1335.[89] A fee at Lilstock was said in 1303 to be held of John de Neville,[90] but no further trace of Neville lordship is recorded.

The terre tenant of Lilstock in 1303 was John de Columbers, already occupier of Honibere and Heathfield in the parish.[91] John died in 1306[92] and Lilstock passed first to his son and heir Philip (d. 1342) and then to Stephen de Columbers, clerk, Philip's brother.[93] The land descended, like Honibere, in the Columbers family to the Audleys, and in 1428 was held by James, Lord Audley.[94] The manor, with Honibere and Stowey, was settled on James's great-grandson, John, Lord Audley, in 1535,[95] and from the mid 16th century was united with Honibere as the manor of *HONIBERE LILSTOCK*.[96]

In 1086 Anscetil the parker held *HONIBERE* of the Crown in succession to Alvric.[97] It may be identified with an estate called Bura, the second tithes of which Robert de Chandos gave to Goldcliff Priory (Mon.) in Henry I's reign.[98] Maud de Chandos, Robert's granddaughter, and lady of Nether Stowey, granted Honibere in Richard I's reign to Walter de Castello, probably for a term of years, since it was to be held as Goslan held it.[99] Honibere thereafter seems to have passed to the descendants of Maud de Chandos by her husband Philip de Columbers (d. 1186). Their son Philip (d. 1215) and their grandson, also Philip de Columbers (d. 1257), were followed by another Philip de Columbers, who died in 1262 holding a fee in Honibere.[1] The latter's widow, Egelina, held it in dower in 1297.[2] Egelina's second son, John de Columbers, died in 1306[3] and Honibere passed to John's second son Stephen, clerk, and then by 1337 to Stephen's elder brother Philip (d. 1342).[4] The manor then descended like Nether Stowey manor through the Audleys until the execution and forfeiture of James, Lord Audley, in 1497, when it was granted for life to John Arundell, knight of the body.[5] It was evidently recovered by James's son John, Lord Audley, in 1512, and was security for his debts to the Crown and the subject of litigation within the family.[6] In 1535 it was settled on John and his wife and their son George in tail,[7] but like Nether Stowey the manor passed in 1538-9 to Edward Seymour, earl of Hertford.[8]

After Seymour's attainder and death in 1552 the combined manor of Honibere Lilstock was granted by the Crown to John Dudley, duke of Northumberland,[9] and on his attainder in 1553 reverted to the Crown. It had been leased after Seymour's death to Hugh Benny; he was followed by 1560 by Nicholas Luttrell who, after disputes with undertenants, acquired the estate in fee in 1562.[10] Luttrell, a younger brother of Thomas Luttrell of Dunster, died in 1592 and was succeeded by his son Andrew, of Hartland (Devon).[11] Andrew settled it on his second son John, of Braunton (Devon), in 1611.[12] John died in 1617 but Elizabeth Luttrell, possibly his sister,[13] continued to occupy the house until her death in 1637.[14]

Under John Luttrell's will the manor was to be sold, and it had passed by 1635, the year of his death, to Sir Sampson Darell, himself descended from Margaret, wife of James, Lord Audley (d. 1497). Darell's heir in 1635 was his son Marmaduke, then a minor.[15] By 1650 the estate had passed to Sir

[80] *Som. Co. Herald*, 30 Dec. 1933; Wedlake, *Watchet*, 90.
[81] S.R.O., D/P/kve 17/7/2.
[82] Local inf.
[83] B.L. Harl. MS. 594, f. 55.
[84] S.R.O., DD/WY 34.
[85] Collinson, *Hist. Som.* iii. 533-4.
[86] *V.C.H. Som.* ii. 351.
[87] Ibid. i. 521.
[88] *S.R.S.* lxi, p. 1.
[89] Sanders, *Eng. Baronies*, 143.
[90] *Feud. Aids*, iv. 304.
[91] Ibid.; below.
[92] *Cal. Inq. p.m.* iv, p. 256.
[93] Ibid. viii, pp. 266-72; *Feud. Aids*, iv. 347.
[94] Below; *Feud. Aids*, iv. 392.
[95] 27 Hen. VIII, c. 31.
[96] *Cal. Pat.* 1553, 179.
[97] *V.C.H. Som.* i. 521.
[98] *Cal. Chart. R.* ii. 363; *S.R.S.* extra ser. 324-5.
[99] S.R.O., DD/AH 21/2: MS. of Thos. Palmer, quoting charter at Fairfield in 18th cent.
[1] Sanders, *Eng. Baronies*, 67; cf. *Cal. Inq. p.m.* i, p. 146, where the fee was said to be held of Hugh de Neville,

probably because Philip was Hugh's tenant at Lilstock.
[2] *Close R.* 1261-4, 89-90; *Cal. Inq. p.m.* ii, p. 133; *Feud. Aids*, iv. 275; *S.R.S.* extra ser. 327.
[3] *Cal. Inq. p.m.* iv, p. 256.
[4] *S.R.S.* xii. 192-3, 241.
[5] Below, Nether Stowey, manors and other estates; *Cal. Pat.* 1494-1509, 107.
[6] *L. & P. Hen. VIII*, iii(2), p. 1190; iv(3), pp. 3182-3; viii, p. 260.
[7] 27 Hen. VIII, c. 31.
[8] *Cal. Proc. Chanc. Eliz.* (Rec. Com.), i. 24; *S.R.S.* extra ser. 333.
[9] *Cal. Pat.* 1553, 179.
[10] P.R.O., REQ 2/25/164; *S.R.S.* xx. 177; *Cal. Pat.* 1560-3, 311.
[11] P.R.O., C 142/233, no. 109.
[12] Ibid. CP 25(2)/346/9 Jas. I. Trin.
[13] *Som. Wills*, ed. Brown, vi. 16; Maxwell Lyte, *Dunster*, 515.
[14] S.R.O., DD/SP, inventory 1637.
[15] P.R.O., C 142/486, no. 10; *Som. Wills*, ed. Brown, vi. 16.

Francis Dodington,[16] and it descended like Dodington manor.[17] In 1977 the owner was Lady Gass, niece of Lord St. Audries.

There was a capital messuage at Honibere in 1306.[18] According to charters surviving at Fairfield in the mid 18th century,[19] Philip de Columbers (d. 1342) granted a messuage and land which Agnes de Columbers had held to Eleanor, widow of John Amaury, and her sons in tail male. In 1488–9 John Amaury of Taunton conveyed land and a house called Honibere Court to John Verney (d. 1507) of Fairfield, and John's son Robert (d. 1546)[20] sold the estate to Humphrey Colles. Nicholas Luttrell is said to have bought the Colles holding, and to have made Honibere Court his residence in Edward VI's reign.[21] About 1610 Jane Luttrell granted to John Luttrell, grandson of Nicholas Luttrell, the greater part of the house and her land in return for an annuity and her maintenance there.[22] The house was still standing in 1729.[23] Its site is probably on or near the present Honibere Farm.

ECONOMIC HISTORY. Lilstock was assessed at 5 hides and Honibere at 1 in 1086; there were 2 ploughlands at Honibere, but the size of the arable at Lilstock was not recorded. Lilstock had a demesne farm of 3 ploughlands, and the tenants' holdings, occupied by 11 villeins and 7 bordars, measured 1¾ hide. There were two areas of woodland, but no meadow or pasture was recorded. The value of the estate had remained stable at 100s. since 1086. Honibere, farmed with 3 bordars and 1 serf, included 60 a. of pasture, but its value had been reduced from 20s. to 5s.[24] By 1306 the Columbers family occupied a demesne farm of 159 a. of arable and 24½ a. of meadow, described as at Honibere but probably the demesne of their entire holding in the parish. There were 16 customary tenants and 3 cottars.[25] In 1327 the parish was assessed at a higher figure than most of its neighbours, largely because of the stock of Alice de Columbers at the manor house.[26] By 1386 the Audley holding comprised a farm of 218 a. of arable, 55 a. of meadow, and 24s. 6d. rent.[27] By 1484–5 the whole estate was let for cash rents worth £21 18s. 6d.[28]

By the early 17th century the main survivals of medieval farming were the common pasture at Honibere Heathfield and the two open arable fields on the coast divided by marshes. The common pasture at Honibere, located in Kilton parish, included 30 a. for Lilstock tenants alone.[29] Three free tenants held by military service, including the Verneys of Fairfield, and heriots were payable on 13 tenements. About 1615 there were two farms of over

80 a., two of 70 a., two of c. 50 a., and one of 40 a., in all 11 separate holdings and 5 cottages. Thomas Engram was the most substantial tenant, with 88 a. by lease dating from 1562.[30] Apart from the common at Honibere Heathfield, tenants had oxen and bullock leazes ('shuts') in North Marsh and horse leazes in Rexway.[31] A tenant of 40 a. in 1683 had rights to cut fuel in Honibere wood for frith staves and spars like the other tenants of the manor and to take seaweed and fish. Those rights were not mentioned when the same farm was leased again in 1721.[32] A lease of a small farm in 1706 included a share in the seaweed and sea fishery.[33] The weirs to catch red mullet along the foreshore are survivals from the 19th century.[34]

Produce on which tithes were payable in 1633 included grain, seaweed, lambs, sheep, piglets, calves, horses, and milk.[35] Two tenants shared a flock of 22 sheep in 1637.[36] Holders of land in the late 17th century included a Stogursey yeoman, a clothier from Over Stowey, a fuller from Stogursey, a Dodington weaver, and a butcher, besides Lilstock yeomen and husbandmen. A Lilstock soapboiler, established at Honibere in 1692, undertook to dress his land with soap ashes, and agreed not to grow more than two grain crops without manuring.[37]

The number and size of farms remained largely static until the late 18th century, but the owners of Fairfield manor extended their holdings north and west of the house into the parish.[38] Elsewhere from 1780 onwards leases for lives were converted to 7- and 14-year leases, and several small and decayed holdings were consolidated.[39] Lilstock farm, a union of three ancient holdings, was let for 14 years, with penalties against growing flax or hemp and encouragement to sow clover or grass between two arable crops. Two further ancient holdings were added to the farm in 1786, and the whole was let in 1795 for 7 years.[40]

Under an Act of 1803 the common holdings in the two open fields and in the marshes which divided them were inclosed.[41] Lilstock farm was the largest to emerge, followed by the newly created Glebe (later Park) farm (83 a.), Bartlett's or Upper farm (65 a.), and Honibere (31 a.).[42] By 1824 some further reorganization had taken place, creating Manor farm from part of Lilstock farm and increasing the size of Upper (116 a.) and Honibere (99 a.) farms.[43] By 1851 there were four main farms, headed by Honibere (170 a.).[44] By the 1880s there were two principal holdings.[45] The land was fairly evenly divided between grassland and corn on the two farms which occupied the whole of Lilstock in 1977.

In 1488–9 John Amaury conveyed a mill at Honibere called Ameris mill to John Verney, and

[16] *Cal. Cttee. for Compounding*, iv. 2557.
[17] Above, Dodington, manor.
[18] *Cal. Inq. p.m.* iv, p. 256.
[19] S.R.O., DD/AH 21/2.
[20] *Vis. Som.* 1531, 1575, ed. F. W. Weaver, 83.
[21] S.R.O., DD/AH 21/2.
[22] Maxwell Lyte, *Dunster*, 518–19.
[23] S.R.O., DD/AH 8/5.   [24] *V.C.H. Som.* i. 521.
[25] *Cal. Inq. p.m.* iv, p. 256.
[26] *S.R.S.* iii. 122–3, 165–6.
[27] *Cal. Inq. p.m.* xvi, p. 73.
[28] P.R.O., SC 6/1116/2.
[29] S.R.O., DD/AH 14/7; *S.R.S.* extra ser. 323.
[30] S.R.O., DD/AH 14/7.
[31] e.g. ibid. 36/5, 12.

[32] Ibid. 36/12.
[33] Ibid. 36/14.
[34] *Proc. Som. Arch. Soc.* cxxiv. 134–5.
[35] S.R.O., D/D/Rg 276.
[36] Ibid. DD/SP, inventory of Ric. Coales 1637.
[37] Ibid. DD/AH 34/23, 36/4–5, 7–8, 12.
[38] P.R.O., SC 6/Hen. VII/1065; S.R.O., DD/AH 14/7, 36/2, 11, 16–17.
[39] S.R.O., DD/AH 36/9.
[40] Ibid. 36/20.
[41] Ibid. Q/RDe 54.
[42] Ibid. DD/AH 13/8.
[43] Ibid. 14/11, 36/21.
[44] P.R.O., HO 107/1920.
[45] *Kelly's Dir. Som.* (1884).

before 1546 Robert Verney sold it to Humphrey Colles.[46] A mill-house at Honibere was converted *c.* 1692 to a soap-boiling factory.[47]

LOCAL GOVERNMENT. No court rolls for the manors of Lilstock, Honibere, or Honibere Lilstock have been found, but the Audleys held courts twice a year in the 1490s for an estate called Honibere[48] and by the early 17th century the lord claimed to hold courts leet and baron with the royalty of felons', outlaws', and pirates' goods, deodands, and wrecks.[49] In 1824 courts were said to have been held regularly.[50] Suit of court was occasionally required of leasehold tenants.[51]

The tithing of Honibere comprised the whole parish of Lilstock and part of Fairfield in Stogursey.[52] No records of parish administration have been found, but two wardens and two overseers served in the 17th century.[53] The parish became part of the Williton poor-law union in 1836, of the Williton rural district in 1894, and of the West Somerset district in 1974.[54]

CHURCH. Between 1100 and 1107 William de Falaise gave to the monks of Lonlay (Orne) the church of Stogursey and the tithes of two thirds of his demesne in Lilstock.[55] The advowson of Lilstock was confirmed to Lonlay between 1161 and 1171, in practice a confirmation to the alien priory of Stogursey which had by then been established.[56] In 1251 the church was appropriated by the priory, and passed to Eton College on the dissolution of the house *c.* 1442.[57] The status of Lilstock was not clear from the 16th century, and the church was described variously as a chapel[58] and as a parish church,[59] the living as a rectory[60] and as a benefice consolidated or united with the vicarage of Stogursey.[61]

The monks of Stogursey appointed a chaplain under the appropriation of 1251,[62] but the vicar of Stogursey had to find one in 1465.[63] Eton College took responsibility soon afterwards,[64] but the vicar of Stogursey was paying the priest at Lilstock by 1535.[65] The living was usually served by curates appointed by the vicar of Stogursey in the late 18th and early 19th centuries.[66] In 1881 the chapelry of Lilstock was separated from Stogursey and annexed and united with Kilton.[67] From 1947 the united benefice was held with Kilve, Stringston, and East Quantoxhead, and from 1978 became part of the united benefice of Quantoxhead.[68]

No separate valuation of the living has been found until 1827, when it was said to be worth £105.[69] In 1851 the income was £97,[70] and in 1879 £85 12*s.*[71] The parochial chaplain was paid £6 in 1535[72] but in the 1570s he received for the cure only 6*s.* 8*d.*[73] In 1827 the curate had £50.[74]

Apart from a house and the churchyard there was no glebe in 1633, but tithes payable to the vicar of Stogursey included personal offerings of 1*d.* at first communion, thereafter 2*d.*, 3*d.* for a married couple, and 3½*d.* for a widow or widower.[75] Under the inclosure award of 1811 tithes on all but the Honibere estate were replaced by an allotment of 136 a. of land.[76] The Honibere tithes were commuted for a rent charge of £13 10*s.* in 1846.[77] By 1851 the value of the glebe was £84.[78] In 1881 just over 68 a. of glebe were transferred to the vicarage of Stogursey and some 10 a. of glebe in Stogursey and the tithe rent charge were transferred to the new benefice of Kilton-with-Lilstock.[79]

In 1557 the parsonage house needed repair.[80] In 1633 it comprised a porch, hall, and inner room, with lofts.[81] In 1715 the vicar was suspended, partly for not repairing the house.[82] Only part of a wall was standing in 1827.[83]

In 1554 the chancel needed repair and the nave windows were 'greatly ruined'.[84] In 1557 there was no priest.[85] By 1827 the parish was served by a curate who lived at Kilve and who also served Stringston.[86] By 1831 the vicar of Stogursey claimed to take part duty at Lilstock.[87] Services in the 19th century were held every Sunday, alternately morning and evening, with communion four times a year.[88] In 1881, on the annexation of the parish to Kilton, the church was demolished save for the chancel, which was rebuilt to serve as a mortuary chapel.[89] The chancel was declared redundant in 1980.[90]

Until *c.* 1492 the lord of the manor paid 6*d.* a year for candles and mass bread.[91] A church house is referred to *c.* 1615.[92]

The church of *ST. ANDREW*, so dedicated by

[46] S.R.O., DD/AH 21/2: Thomas Palmer's MS.
[47] Ibid. 34/23.
[48] P.R.O., SC 6/Hen. VII/1065.
[49] S.R.O., DD/AH 14/7. Stogursey Priory claimed wrecks in 1310: *Cal. Pat.* 1307-13, 254.
[50] S.R.O., DD/HC 81.
[51] Ibid. DD/AH 36/6 (1663), 36/19 (1740).
[52] *S.R.S.* extra ser. 323-4.
[53] *Som. Protestation Returns*, ed. Howard and Stoate, 163; Dwelly, *Dir. Som.* ii. 198.
[54] Youngs, *Local Admin. Units*, i. 430, 673, 675-6.
[55] *S.R.S.* lxi, pp. 1, 4-5, 7, 29.
[56] Ibid. pp. 5, 21, 48-9, 75; *Cal. Papal L.* i. 17.
[57] e.g. *S.R.S.* liv, pp. 69-70; B.L. Harl. MS. 594, f. 55; *S. & D. N. & Q.* xiii. 270.
[58] B.L. Harl. MS. 594, ff. 55, 60v.
[59] *S.R.S.* xxi. 23.
[60] S.R.O., D/D/Rg 276; ibid. DD/AH 14/7; ibid. D/P/lk 2/1/1.
[61] *S.R.S.* liv, pp. 69-70; S.R.O., D/D/B returns 1815.
[62] *S.R.S.* lxi, pp. 35-7.
[63] Ibid. p. 65.
[64] Ibid. p. 87.
[65] *Valor Eccl.* (Rec. Com.), i. 214.
[66] S.R.O., D/P/lk 2/1/2; ibid. D/D/B returns 1827; *Rep. Com. Eccl. Revenues*, pp. 152-3.
[67] S.R.O., D/P/lk 6/1/1: Order in Council 1 Apr. 1881.
[68] Ibid. D/P/hol 22/3/1.
[69] Ibid. D/D/B returns 1827.
[70] P.R.O., HO 129/313/4/4/3.
[71] S.R.O., DD/AH 14/7.
[72] *Valor Eccl.* (Rec. Com.), i. 214.
[73] *S. & D. N. & Q.* xiii. 270.
[74] S.R.O., D/D/B returns 1827.
[75] Ibid. D/D/Rg 276.
[76] Ibid. Q/RDe 54.
[77] Ibid. tithe award.
[78] P.R.O., HO 129/313/4/4/3.
[79] S.R.O., DD/AH 28/3; for an earlier (1879) plan, ibid. 14/7.
[80] Ibid. D/D/Ca 27.
[81] Ibid. D/D/Rg 276.
[82] H. R. Phipps, *Taunton Archdeaconry Probate Rec.* (TS. in S.R.O.), 74.
[83] S.R.O., D/D/B returns 1827.
[84] Ibid. D/D/Ca 22.
[85] Ibid. 27.
[86] Ibid. D/D/B returns 1827.
[87] *Rep. Com. Eccl. Revenues*, pp. 152-3.
[88] S.R.O., D/D/B returns 1827; D/D/V returns 1840, 1870.
[89] Ibid. D/P/lk 6/1/1.
[90] Inf. from Dioc. Office.
[91] P.R.O., SC 6/Hen. VII/1065.
[92] S.R.O., DD/AH 14/7.

1532,[93] consisted of chancel, nave with south porch, and embattled west tower. The east window was evidently of the 14th century, while those in the nave may have been inserted or have formed part of a rebuilding in the early 16th century.[94] A 12th-century font remained in the former chancel until its removal to Stogursey church in 1981.

There were said to be four bells in 1791, but only two survived in 1881.[95] A cup and cover by 'R.O.' of 1574 are at Kilton.[96] The registers begin in 1654; those for marriages end in 1869 and for baptisms in 1881. The last burial was in 1974.[97]

There were chaplains at Honibere in 1174.[98]

NONCONFORMITY. A Presbyterian teacher had 14 hearers in a house in the parish in 1669.[99]

EDUCATION. In 1577 John Culverwell was licensed to teach in the parish.[1]

CHARITIES FOR THE POOR. By will dated 1643 Alexander Standfast of Kilve charged land in Lilstock with 6s. 8d. to be paid to poor householders at Easter in the parishes of Kilve, Kilton, and Lilstock. Payment was refused by 1786–7, and the charity was lost.[2] A 'small benefaction' was 'duly applied' in 1840, but no further details are known.[3]

MONKSILVER

MONKSILVER lies on the eastern slopes of the Brendon Hills 2.5 km. west of Stogumber, and part of the parish, including the village, is within Exmoor National Park.[4] The parish may once have been part of the minster estate of Stogumber, and crops on two pieces of land were owed to the rector of Stogumber in 1249.[5] Until the 14th century the parish was called Silver, but thereafter it was called Silver Monachorum or Monksilver because of its ownership by Goldcliff Priory (Mon.).[6] The ancient parish included detached areas at Doniford, 3 km. southwest in Old Cleeve, and two parcels in Stogumber, at Horse or High Parks, 2.5 km. south, and at Silverdown, 1.5 km. south-east.[7] Stogumber absorbed Silverdown in 1883 and High Parks in 1884, and Doniford was added to Old Cleeve in 1884. The civil parish of Monksilver measured 317 ha. (783 a.) in 1971.[8]

A deep and narrow alluvial valley divides the parish. On each side of the stream the land rises over Leighland and Brendon Hill slates,[9] steeply at first to the north-east towards Merry Farm, more gradually to the west, reaching 122 m. at Birchanger and the Nettlecombe Park road. To the south the land is higher, reaching 281 m. at Colton Cross. Doniford, on the side of a steep combe, lies on the 335 m. contour, and High Parks even higher at 358 m.[10]

Monksilver village lies on the south-west side of the valley close to the southern boundary of the parish. It consists of a main street along the valley with a back lane, and two roads running south-west, one on each side of the church. The more southerly of the two roads was known as New Street in the 16th century. The village appears to have expanded at this period and a rental of 1561 records six dwellings in New Street.[11] Until the early 19th century there were also cottages along a lane running southwest to Bird's Hill. Twentieth-century development has taken place along the street north of the church.[12] Most of the houses date from the 16th, 17th, and 18th centuries.[13] Woodford Farm lies 1 km. northwest of Monksilver on the border with Nettlecombe.

Some open field arable survived, probably east of the village, in the 16th century,[14] but the glebe was entirely enclosed by 1606.[15] Wood and underwood were recorded in 1086;[16] there were c. 34 a. of woodland in 1841,[17] and c. 80 a. in 1976, forming part of the Combe Sydenham estate.[18] Field names indicate quarrying in the parish before 1841 when there was a large quarry open.[19] Copper may have been mined on the eastern outskirts of the parish at Beech Tree Cross.[20]

The main road through the parish along the valley was turnpiked in 1765 as part of the route from Taunton to Minehead over Ashbeer Hill in Stogumber. The diversion of traffic away from Stogumber to a more easterly route under the Quantocks was followed in 1806 by the adoption of the road through

[93] *Wells Wills*, ed. Weaver, 100.
[94] Plate facing p. 92.
[95] S.R.O., DD/SAS CH 16/1.
[96] *Proc. Som. Arch. Soc.* xlvii. 166–7.
[97] S.R.O., D/P/lk 2/1/1–6.
[98] *S.R.S.* lxi, p. 48.
[99] *Orig. Records of Early Nonconf.* ed. G. L. Turner, i. 9; ii. 1090.
[1] S.R.O., D/D/Ol 5.
[2] Holford ch., Charity bd.; *Char. Don.* H.C. 511 (1816), xvi; *Som. Co. Herald*, 21 July 1925.
[3] S.R.O., D/D/V returns 1840.
[4] This article was completed in 1979.
[5] *H.M.C. Wells*, i. 2–3; below, Stogumber.
[6] Below; Ekwall, *Eng. Place-Names* (1960), 314.
[7] S.R.O., tithe award. Horse Parks was also known as Broadridge before the late 18th cent.: S.R.O. DD/SAS BK 87.

[8] *Census*, 1891, 1971. Doniford is also known as Dorniford.
[9] Geol. Surv. Map 1″, solid and drift, sheet 294 (1969 edn.).
[10] O.S. Map 1/25,000, ST 03 (1962 edn.).
[11] St. George's Chapel, Windsor, MS. XV. M. 1.
[12] S.R.O., tithe award; O.S. Map 1″, sheet 75 (1809 edn.); ibid. 1/50,000, sheet 181 (1974 edn.).
[13] S.R.O., DD/V Wlr. 15.1. A house on the main street is dated 1609.
[14] Ibid. tithe award; St. George's Chapel, Windsor, MS. XV. M. 1.   [15] S.R.O., D/D/Rg 350.
[16] *V.C.H. Som.* i. 488, 512.
[17] S.R.O., tithe award.
[18] Min. of Agric., Fisheries, and Food, agric. returns 1976.   [19] S.R.O., tithe award.
[20] J. Hamilton and J. F. Lawrence, *Men and Mining in the Quantocks* (1970), 70.

Monksilver village as part of the Wiveliscombe turn-pike route to Watchet.[21] Minor roads from the village now lead to Birchanger, Sampford Brett, and Stogumber.

There were unlicensed victuallers in the parish in the 15th and 16th centuries and ale was sold in 1551.[22] There was an alehouse in the early 17th century.[23] A tippling house was recorded in 1665[24] and there were two licensed victuallers in the parish in 1736.[25] The Ram inn, established by 1675,[26] was called the Half Moon by 1785[27] and acquired its present name, the Notley Arms, between 1861 and 1866.[28] The Red Lion was mentioned in 1743.[29]

In 1554 there were apparently 63 householders.[30] There were at least 60 adult males in the parish in 1641 but only 82 subsidy payers were listed in 1667.[31] In 1801 the population was 260; it reached a peak of 322 in 1831 and then declined rapidly to 164 in 1881, 143 in 1901, and 87 in 1971.[32]

MANOR AND OTHER ESTATES. An estate called Silver was held by Alwi Banneson T.R.E. and in 1086 by Richard of Alfred d'Epaignes.[33] Robert de Chandos, who married Alfred's heir Isabel, gave what was described as the manor of *SILVER*, later *MONKSILVER*, as part of the foundation of his priory at Goldcliff (Mon.) in 1113.[34] The monks held the property, subject to the confiscations which alien priories suffered during the 14th century,[35] until 1441 when the priory and its lands were given to Tewkesbury Abbey.[36] In 1474 Tewkesbury exchanged the manor with the canons of Windsor[37] and the canons retained Monksilver until 1800; it was normally let on long leases, from 1567 until 1716 to the Sydenhams of Combe Sydenham.[38] The manor was sold to the Revd. George Notley in 1800,[39] and on his death in 1831 it passed to his son James Thomas Benedictus (d. 1851). James was followed by his son Marwood (d. 1903), then jointly by two of his grandsons, Montague and Marwood Notley (d. c. 1958). The descendants of Montague and Marwood Notley in 1979 were Miss V. A. Notley and Messrs. R. and P. M. Notley, all of Monksilver.[40]

There was a house called Court Hall, with associated buildings, and fields called Court field, Court moor, and Court berie in the 1460s. Court Hall was let to the manorial reeve in 1469.[41] The Trevelyans

held the house by 1515 and until 1567 or later.[42]

Two small estates, each called Silver, were held in 1066 by Brismar and Eldred and in 1086 by Alric and Eldred of Roger de Courcelles.[43] In the early 14th century John Brett held ¼ fee in Monksilver of the manor of Bicknoller, and another freeholder of Bicknoller held a tenement in Monksilver which he leased from Brett.[44] These estates may have originated in the Courcelles holdings in the parish and probably merged later into the Combe Sydenham estate, which was itself held of Bicknoller.[45]

The detached estate of High Parks formed part of the Combe Sydenham estate in the 17th and 18th centuries.[46] Doniford farm was mentioned in the 12th century when it was said to form, with Monksilver manor, part of the estates granted to Goldcliff Priory.[47] Afterwards Doniford was absorbed into Monksilver manor and was not recorded again until 1796.[48]

ECONOMIC HISTORY. In 1086 the three estates in Monksilver together had land for 12 ploughteams, of which three quarters were in Alfred d'Epaignes's manor. The demesne of that manor had 4 serfs and 2 teams, while the small demesnes of the other two estates appear to have had no teams though one included a serf. The agricultural tenants, 16 villeins and 9 bordars, had 9 teams. Only on the large demesne was there no excess of land over teams. In all, 11 a. of meadow and 238 a. of pasture were recorded. Each of the small estates had the same value, £1, in 1086 as in 1066, while the value of the large estate had increased from £3 to £4, notwithstanding an annual render of 18 sheep to the royal manor of Williton, newly exacted since 1066.[49]

In 1291 the prior of Goldcliff's estate in Monksilver was valued at £3 0s. 8d. a year.[50] In 1461, while Monksilver was in the hands of Tewkesbury Abbey, the income from the manor was £13 13s. 4d., and ten years later receipts totalled £17 2s. 7d.[51] During the 16th century the canons of Windsor had a gross income of about £11 a year.[52] In the early 17th century rents from Monksilver manor were £18 15s. 10½d. a year,[53] but in 1715 the annual value was said to be £654.[54] Sheep were of major importance during the 17th century, and arable crops included wheat, barley, oats, and peas.[55] There were several malthouses in the village.[56]

[21] S.R.O., set of 1″ maps annotated by Sir Rob. Hall; 5 Geo. III, c. 93; 46 Geo. III, c. 52 (Local and Personal).
[22] St. George's Chapel, Windsor, MSS. XV. 27. 28; XV. 27. 34; XV. M. 1.
[23] *S.R.S.* xxiv, p. 140; lxv, p. 65.
[24] S.R.O., Q/SR 107/26.   [25] Ibid. Q/RL.
[26] Ibid. DD/SP, inventory 1675.
[27] Ibid. DD/CCH 71; ibid. Q/RL; ibid. tithe award.
[28] *P.O. Dir. Som.* (1861, 1866).
[29] S.R.O., DD/SFR(w) 38.
[30] St. George's Chapel, Windsor, MS. XV. M. 1.
[31] *Som. Protestation Returns*, ed. Howard and Stoate, 163; S.R.O., DD/WY 34.   [32] *Census*, 1801–1971.
[33] *V.C.H. Som.* i. 512.
[34] *Reg. Regum Anglo-Norm.* ii, no. 1014; iii, no. 373; Knowles and Hadcock, *Medieval Religious Houses* (1971), 67.
[35] *S.R.S.* i. 2; *Abbrev. Rot. Orig.* (Rec. Com.) ii. 11, 18; *Cal. Fine R.* 1327–37, 86.
[36] *Cal. Chart. R.* 1257–1300, 362; *Cal. Papal Reg.* viii. 241–3.
[37] *Cal. Pat.* 1467–77, 461; St. George's Chapel, Windsor, MS. IV. B. 2, ff. 139–40.

[38] B.L. Harl. MS. 79, f. 23; St. George's Chapel, Windsor, MSS. XV. 27. 34, 37; XV. 50. 6.
[39] St. George's Chapel, Windsor, MS. XV. 50. 15.
[40] S.R.O., DD/CCH 3/4; local inf.
[41] St. George's Chapel, Windsor, MS. XV. 27. 28; 53. 81A.
[42] S.R.O., DD/WO 43/7; St. George's Chapel, Windsor, MS. XV. 27. 34.
[43] *V.C.H. Som.* i. 488.
[44] *H.M.C. Wells.* i. 348.
[45] G. F. Sydenham, *Hist. Sydenham Family*, 130.
[46] S.R.O., DD/CCH 72.
[47] *Reg. Regum Anglo-Norm.* iii, no. 373.
[48] St. George's Chapel, Windsor, MS. XV. 50. 10.
[49] *V.C.H. Som.* i. 436, 488, 512.
[50] *Tax. Eccl.* (Rec. Com.), 205.
[51] St. George's Chapel, Windsor, MS. XV. 53. 81A, 96.
[52] Ibid. XV. 3. 19; XV. M. 1.
[53] S.R.O., DD/SAS BK 87; St. George's Chapel, Windsor, MS. XI. M. 1.
[54] St. George's Chapel, Windsor, MS. XV. 50. 10.
[55] S.R.O., DD/SP, inventories 1646, 1679, 1684.
[56] Ibid. DD/CCH 71; ibid. tithe award.

COMBE SYDENHAM HALL, STOGUMBER, FROM THE SOUTH-WEST

NETTLECOMBE COURT AND CHURCH FROM THE SOUTH-WEST

MONKSILVER CHURCH

NETTLECOMBE CHURCH: THE FONT

HUISH CHAMPFLOWER CHURCH:
THE NORTH AISLE

In 1841 there were 13 farms under 50 a., 4 between 50 a. and 100 a., and only 3 over 100 a. including the hill farm of Doniford. Two farms had absorbed neighbouring holdings, and arable land accounted for about two thirds of the parish.[57] Ten years later the number of farms had been reduced, with the two largest employing a total of 17 men, although the farmer of Doniford employed only 1 man; one farmer employed men both on the land and in his shoemaking business.[58] By 1904 several holdings had been amalgamated by the Notley family and the parish specialized in barley, wheat, oats, and root vegetables.[59] In 1939 Birchanger and Burford's farms each contained over 150 a., the latter having increased from 41 a. in 1841.[60] In 1976 three dairy farms, all over 100 a., accounted for most of the land in the parish and less than one third of the land was under arable cultivation.[61]

Field names such as Rack close at Woodford suggest cloth making in the parish.[62] A dyehouse was mentioned c. 1524[63] and clothiers were recorded throughout the 16th and 17th centuries.[64] One man in the early 17th century had a 'spooling chamber' with weaving implements and wool, and another had 20 lb. of yarn.[65] In 1675 a clothworker possessed yarn, wool, racks, and pinions worth £53 15s., over half the total value of his goods. Early in the following century a clothier had raw and dressed cloth worth £22 together with yarn, pinions, and a clothier's rack.[66]

There were clockmakers in Monksilver in the late 17th and early 18th centuries.[67] In 1851 there were four drapers and grocers in the village, and other occupations included harness makers and straw-bonnet makers.[68]

MILL. In 1086 there was a mill at Monksilver.[69] In 1461 the mill paid £6 3s. 10¼d. rent.[70] It continued in use until after 1841,[71] but milling seems to have ceased by 1906.[72] The 19th-century mill and the house survive, but the wheel and machinery have been removed.

LOCAL GOVERNMENT. Monksilver formed part of the tithing of Preston Bowyer and Monksilver in Freemanors hundred in 1334 and in the 1560s,[73]

but by 1649 it was a separate tithing.[74] The manor court leet had jurisdiction both in the parish and over Rodhuish in Carhampton. There are court rolls for 1465–9, 1544, 1550–5, 1567–9, and 1707–14.[75] The court appears to have been held annually by the mid 15th century, and its officers were a bailiff, a constable, a tithingman, and a pound-keeper.[76] From the 16th century tithingmen served in rotation.[77]

The two churchwardens and two sidesmen also served in rotation.[78] Wardens' accounts were by 1610 approved by the minister and parishioners.[79] A vestry of four or five and the rector was meeting by 1755.[80] There were waywardens by the end of the 18th century,[81] and a poorhouse had been built by 1796.[82] Monksilver joined the Williton poor-law union in 1836. The parish was part of Williton rural district from 1894 and of the West Somerset district from 1974.[83]

CHURCH. The 12th-century window on the north side of the chancel predates the first reference to the church at Monksilver in 1291.[84] The patronage of the living, a rectory, descended with the manor until 1800, when the canons of Windsor, patrons since 1474, retained the advowson at the sale of the manor. The Sydenham family, lessees under the canons, presented between 1572 and 1711.[85] The benefice was united with Elworthy in 1921,[86] and in 1969 became part of the united benefice of Monksilver with Elworthy, Nettlecombe, and Brompton Ralph.[87]

In 1535 the rectory was worth £9 15s. 4d.,[88] and c. 1668 £80.[89] In 1831 the average net income was £230,[90] and in 1841 the tithes were commuted for a rent charge of £217 10s.[91]

In 1606 there were 34 a. of glebe in the parish and a share in meadow in St. Decumans.[92] In 1846 some glebe was sold as a site for the school,[93] and the rest was disposed of between 1906 and 1931.[94] The rectory house was said in 1594 to be in decay.[95] A new house was built, probably in 1838, in classical style.[96] It was sold and a new house was erected in the grounds c. 1968.[97]

Nicholas Foster appears to have held the rectory from 1546 to 1572 despite the ecclesiastical changes which affected most parishes in the period.[98] Timothy May, rector 1592–1619, and William

[57] Ibid. tithe award.
[58] P.R.O., HO 107/1920.
[59] S.R.O., DD/CCH 3/4; Kelly's Dir. Som. (1906).
[60] Kelly's Dir. Som. (1939); S.R.O., tithe award.
[61] Min. of Agric., Fisheries, and Food, agric. returns 1976.
[62] S.R.O., tithe award.
[63] Ibid. DD/WO 49.
[64] Som. Wills, ed. Brown, iii. 48; S.R.O., DD/WY 34; ibid. Q/SR 18/18.
[65] S.R.O., DD/SP, inventories 1635, 1637.
[66] Ibid. 1675, 1730.
[67] J. K. Bellchambers, Som. Clockmakers (Ant. Horological Soc. mon. 4, 1968), 72.
[68] P.R.O., HO 107/1920.
[69] V.C.H. Som. i. 512.
[70] St. George's Chapel, Windsor, MS. XV. 53. 81A.
[71] S.R.O., DD/SAS BK 87; ibid. tithe award.
[72] Kelly's Dir. Som. (1906).
[73] Subsidy of 1334, ed. R. E. Glasscock, 265; S.R.S. xx. 174.
[74] S.R.O., DD/SAS BK 87.
[75] St. George's Chapel, Windsor, MSS. XV. 27. 6, 28, 34, 37; XV. M. 1.
[76] Ibid. XV. 53. 81A; XV. 60. 62; S.R.O., DD/SAS BK 87; DD/CCH 71.

[77] S.R.O., D/P/mon 4/1/1; DD/SAS BK 87; DD/CCH 71; St. George's Chapel, Windsor, MS. XV. M. 1.
[78] S.R.O., D/D/Rg 350; D/P/mon 4/1/1.
[79] Ibid. D/P/mon 4/1/1.
[80] Ibid. 4/1/3.   [81] Ibid. DD/CCH 71.
[82] St. George's Chapel, Windsor, MS. XV. 50. 10; S.R.O., DD/CCH 71.
[83] Youngs, Local Admin. Units, i. 674–6.
[84] S.R.O., D/D/B reg. 1, f. 229.
[85] S.R.S. xiii. 56; lx, p. 83; Som. Incumbents, ed. Weaver, 402–3; St. George's Chapel, Windsor, MS. XV. 50. 15.
[86] St. George's Chapel, Windsor, Livings Bk. 99.
[87] Dioc. Dir. (1979).
[88] Valor Eccl. (Rec. Com.), i. 223.
[89] S.R.O., D/D/Vc 24.
[90] Rep. Com. Eccl. Revenues, pp. 146–7.
[91] S.R.O., tithe award.
[92] Ibid. D/D/Rg 350.
[93] St. George's Chapel, Windsor, MS. XV. 50. 11.
[94] Kelly's Dir. Som. (1906, 1931).
[95] S.R.O., D/D/Ca 98.
[96] Ibid. D/D/V returns 1840; St. George's Chapel, Windsor, MS. I. B. I.
[97] Inf. from the Revd. R. N. Swinburn.
[98] Som. Incumbents, ed. Weaver, 402; S. & D. N. & Q. xiv. 63.

Wilmott, rector 1621–42, were both accused of failing to preach every Sunday and for neglecting morning and evening prayers during the week.[99] In 1630 the churchwardens took a collection for an itinerant puritan preacher who visited the parish.[1] James Upton, rector 1712–49, a former fellow of King's College, Cambridge, and master at Eton, was master of Ilminster grammar school and then of Taunton.[2] William Walker, rector 1803–25, was also reader to Lincoln's Inn, and the parish was in the charge of a curate who also served Huish Champflower.[3] Walker's successor, Edward Coleridge, taught at Eton, and the parish shared a curate with Elworthy. Only one service was held each Sunday in 1827.[4] By 1840 there were two Sunday services and five celebrations of communion each year,[5] but there were monthly celebrations three years later.[6] Coleridge was succeeded by William Chilcott (1843-63), who had been resident curate since 1827. Under Chilcott the church was restored and the school built, and he was rural dean from 1844 until his death.[7] On Census Sunday 1851 morning service was attended by 52 people and the afternoon service by 105. Both services were also attended by 40 Sunday-school children.[8]

By 1561 the churchwardens were renting the church house from the lord of the manor;[9] it retained the name until 1786 but by 1707 it was used as a dwelling.[10] There was a brotherhood at Monksilver by 1530.[11]

The church of *ALL SAINTS*, so dedicated by 1449,[12] comprises chancel with south chapel, nave with south aisle and integral south porch, and west tower. The north wall of the chancel and possibly that of the nave are of the 12th century. The tower, and probably the porch, are of the 14th century but the porch was reconstructed in the 15th when the chancel was widened on the south side, the nave was rebuilt, and the elaborate south aisle and chapel were added. The south chapel, with a heavy statue bracket surviving, was probably that dedicated to St. Giles by 1530.[13] The roofs are probably of the 16th century with some later embellishment. The fittings include a medieval wooden pulpit approached by a stair in the north wall, a rood screen said to have been brought from elsewhere,[14] a medieval wooden lectern eagle, and many pews with carved bench ends, including a hunting scene. The font dates from the 15th century and there is an uninscribed late-medieval tomb chest reset under a recess in the north

wall. In the south chapel there is a medieval stone altar table. By the south door, which has medieval ironwork, there is a poor box dated 1634. A great yew in the churchyard is possibly that planted by the blacksmith in 1770.[15]

There are five bells including one by Roger Semson of Ash Priors (1530–70).[16] The registers date from 1653 and are complete.[17]

NONCONFORMITY. Houses were licensed for nonconformist meetings in 1672[18] and 1689,[19] and a Quaker lived in the parish in the 1690s.[20] In 1743 the Red Lion inn was licensed as a Quaker meeting house.[21]

Wesleyan Methodists were active in the parish in the 1890s and in 1897 the present chapel was built.[22] It was still in use in 1979. It is constructed of corrugated iron and stands on the edge of the village, just over the border in Stogumber parish.

EDUCATION. There was no school in 1818, and children attended a school in Nettlecombe.[23] Day and Sunday schools were started in 1825 with 45 children, financed by parental contributions. In 1832 a second day school was opened with 31 children.[24] By 1847, when a new school, united with the National Society, was built on the glebe,[25] the two day and Sunday schools between them took 58 boys and 31 girls.[26] The National school was enlarged in 1870 and was supported by a parish rate.[27] By 1949 there were only 20 children, and the school was closed two years later, the children having transferred to Williton.[28] The school buildings became a private house.

CHARITIES FOR THE POOR. In 1641 George Churcheys left £5 for the poor of the parish. By 1786 this sum was said to be part of £50 lent to the Minehead turnpike trust. James Withycombe, by will dated 1752, gave £10 to provide an annual distribution of bread to the poor.[29] The bread charity was distributed at Christmas until the 1960s by the rector and churchwardens together with coal provided under a bequest of Miss Joanna Gatchell in 1871.[30] Distributions of the charities were no longer made in 1979.[31]

[99] S.R.O., D/D/Ca 134, 151, 175, 235; *S.R.S.* xliii, p. 79.
[1] S.R.O., D/D/Ca 273.   [2] *D.N.B.*
[3] S.R.O., D/D/Bp; D/D/B returns 1815.
[4] *Rep. Com. Eccl. Revenues*, pp. 146–7; S.R.O., D/D/B returns 1827.
[5] S.R.O., D/D/V returns 1840.
[6] Ibid. 1843.
[7] St. George's Chapel, Windsor, MS. XV. 50. 15.
[8] P.R.O., HO 129/313/5/5/7.
[9] St. George's Chapel, Windsor, MS. XV. M. 1.
[10] S.R.O., DD/CCH 71; St. George's Chapel, Windsor, MS. XV. 27. 37.
[11] *Wells Wills*, ed. Weaver, 107.
[12] *S.R.S.* xlix, p. 118; above, plate facing p. 109.
[13] *Wells Wills*, ed. Weaver, 107.
[14] In 1717 the churchwardens paid for moving the screen: S.R.O., D/P/mon 4/1/3.
[15] S.R.O., D/P/mon 2/1/2.
[16] Ibid. DD/SAS CH 16/1.
[17] Ibid. D/P/mon 2/1/1-6.
[18] *Cal. S.P. Dom.* 1672-3, 178.
[19] S.R.O., Q/SR.
[20] *S.R.S.* lxxv, pp. 211, 217, 220, 225.
[21] S.R.O., DD/SFR(w) 38.
[22] *Wesleyan Methodist Church, Williton Circuit, Centenary Celebration Booklet* (1910); S.R.O., D/N/wsc 3/2/9, 3/2/22, 4/3/29.
[23] *Educ. of Poor Digest* H.C. 224 (1819), ix (2).
[24] *Educ. Enq. Abstract*, H.C. 62 (1835), xlii.
[25] St. George's Chapel, Windsor, MS. XV. 50. 11.
[26] Nat. Soc. *Inquiry, 1846–7*, Som. 12–13.
[27] *Kelly's Dir. Som.* (1906); S.R.O., D/P/mon 18/3/1.
[28] S.R.O., C/E box 15; ibid. *Schs. Lists.*
[29] *Char. Don.* H.C. 511 (1816), xvi.
[30] *Kelly's Dir. Som.* (1906); S.R.O., D/P/mon 9/3/1; Char. Com. files.
[31] Inf. from the Revd. R. N. Swinburn.

NETTLECOMBE

NETTLECOMBE parish occupies a ridge, called Raleigh's Down in the 18th century,[32] in the north-eastern part of the Brendons, within the bounds of the Exmoor National Park. It is irregular in shape. It stretches just over 3 km. from the Washford river at Roadwater in the west to the hamlet of Woodford, in the next valley to the east, and measures more than 6 km. from Torre hamlet in the north to Holcombe water on the high ground of the Brendon ridgeway in the south, where the boundary was confirmed after disputes in 1505.[33] Much of the parish lies above the 152 m. contour, and reaches 358 m. on the ridgeway. The land is nearly all steeply sloping, especially on the west above the Washford river. A detached part of Nettlecombe in Warmoor was transferred to St. Decumans in 1882. The ancient parish absorbed the detached areas of St. Decumans at Lower Hayne and Kingsdown in 1883, to give a total area of 1,243 ha. (3,073 a.).[34]

The parish lies mostly on slate, with small areas of pebble beds, sandstone, and limestone in the north and west, and alluvium along the valley between Woodford and Yard.[35] There was a quarry at Woodadvent, above the Washford river, in the 15th century[36] and others at Beggearn Huish, Colton, Woodford, Holcombe Water, Yard, and Rocky Lane near Torre in the 19th century.[37] In 1838 there were limekilns at Clitsome, Yea, and Woodavent farms.[38] Iron ore was mined in the 19th century.[39]

Nettlecombe village and its associated green[40] lay near the church and manor house in a sheltered valley on the eastern side of the parish, but its precise site has not been located. The village was removed in the course of improvements to the park: the poorhouse was replaced by one at Woodford c. 1780,[41] exchanges of glebe were made in 1790,[42] and the former rectory house was pulled down c. 1797. The village had been completely removed by 1800,[43] the tenants thereafter living mostly in the estate village of Woodford, just beyond the park gate, or elsewhere in the parish. Beggearn Huish, Woodadvent, and Lodhuish (later represented by Huish Barton) were Domesday settlements.[44] Woodford, Yard, and Torre had emerged as hamlets or farms by the 14th century, and grew in the 18th and 19th centuries when Nettlecombe village disappeared.[45] Colton was in existence by 1327,[46] and in 1515 com-

prised six tenements, but it seems to have become a single farm in the 19th century.[47] Woodadvent was similarly reduced by 1838. Roadside cottages were built before 1838 at Vemplett's Cross, Egypt, and Fair Cross, on the road from Woodadvent to Watchet.[48]

No evidence of common arable fields has been found, but common pasture on the Brendons, with small areas occasionally under plough, survived until 1778. Between 1780 and 1796 the area was inclosed, partly to be divided into small fields for grazing or arable, the rest shared between Colton and Holcombe Water farms as large tracts of rough grazing.[49]

A park north-east of the manor house was mentioned in 1532, and measured 80 a. in 1556.[50] A second park, south of the house, was created by Sir John Trevelyan (d. 1755), probably because the old park was low-lying and more suited to meadow than to pasture.[51] It was extended by his successors to cover c. 185 a.[52] Part of the park was landscaped by John Veitch in 1792.[53] There were evidently small parks at Woodadvent and between Slade and Yea farms beside the Washford river.[54]

In 1086 there were 50 a. of wood at Nettlecombe.[55] Timber from the park was regularly sold for ship-building, church repairs, and other purposes during the 19th century, and was shipped out of Watchet in 1591 to build a market house in Cornwall.[56] Sir John Trevelyan (d. 1846) had thousands of trees planted in the parish, including elm, larch, acacia, and black poplar, and in 1838 there were c. 175 a. of woodland.[57] In 1905 there were 177 a. of woodland and plantations.[58]

The Taunton–Minehead road enters the parish at Woodford and the Bampton–Watchet road at Nettlecombe Lodge, the two joining at Fair Cross where they leave the parish. Both roads were turnpiked by the Minehead trust in 1765.[59] In addition the Brendon ridgeway, turnpiked by the Wiveliscombe trust in 1806, forms part of the southern boundary of the parish.[60] The farms and settlements of the western part of the parish are linked by narrow lanes running between high banks. Most of these lanes derive their names from the farms or hamlets they serve, but the road from Fair Cross to Vemplett's Cross was known as Coal Carriers road in 1858.[61] The lane from Woodadvent to Nettlecombe church

[32] Collinson, *Hist. Som.* iii. 535. This article was completed in 1980.
[33] S.R.O., DD/WO 41/22.
[34] O.S. Map 1/50,000, sheet 181 (1974 edn.); *Census,* 1891.
[35] Geol. Surv. Map 1″, solid and drift, sheet 294 (1969 edn.).
[36] S.R.O., DD/WO 37/21.
[37] Ibid. D/P/net 4/1/2.
[38] Ibid. tithe award; ibid. DD/WY map of Nettlecombe 1843.
[39] Below.
[40] S.R.O., DD/WO 43/1.
[41] Ibid. 55/11.
[42] Ibid. D/D/Cf.
[43] Ibid. D/D/Bg 8; ibid. DD/WO 44/11; *S.R.S.* lxxvi, map 1782.
[44] *V.C.H. Som.* i. 488, 510, 532.
[45] S.R.O., DD/WO 38/3; *S.R.S.* iii. 167; vi. 249.
[46] *S.R.S.* iii. 167.
[47] S.R.O., DD/WO 42/24; ibid. tithe award; O.S. Map

1″, sheet 75 (1809 edn.); O.S. Map 6″, Som. LIX. NW., XLVIII. SW. (1887 edn.).
[48] S.R.O., DD/WO 43/1, 49/3; ibid. tithe award; *S.R.S.* iii. 336.
[49] Ibid. DD/WO 12/9, 15/6–7; DD/WO map 1796.
[50] Ibid. 43/1, 7; 49/2; *S.R.S.* xx. 180.
[51] S.R.O., tithe award; ibid. DD/WO 40/11; 55/4, 11; 56/11.
[52] Ibid. tithe award.
[53] Ibid. DD/WO 40/12, 51/15; M. Hadfield, R. Hailing, and L. Highton, *British Gardeners* (1980), 294.
[54] S.R.O., tithe award.
[55] *V.C.H. Som.* i. 438.
[56] Ibid. ii. 570; S.R.O., DD/WO 40/11, 54/11, 55/11.
[57] S.R.O., DD/WO 30/12; ibid. tithe award.
[58] Statistics supplied by the then Bd. of Agric. 1905.
[59] S.R.O., set of 1″ maps annotated by Sir Rob. Hall; 5 Geo. III, c. 93.
[60] 46 Geo. III, c. 52 (Local and Personal).
[61] S.R.O., DD/WO map of Nettlecombe 1859.

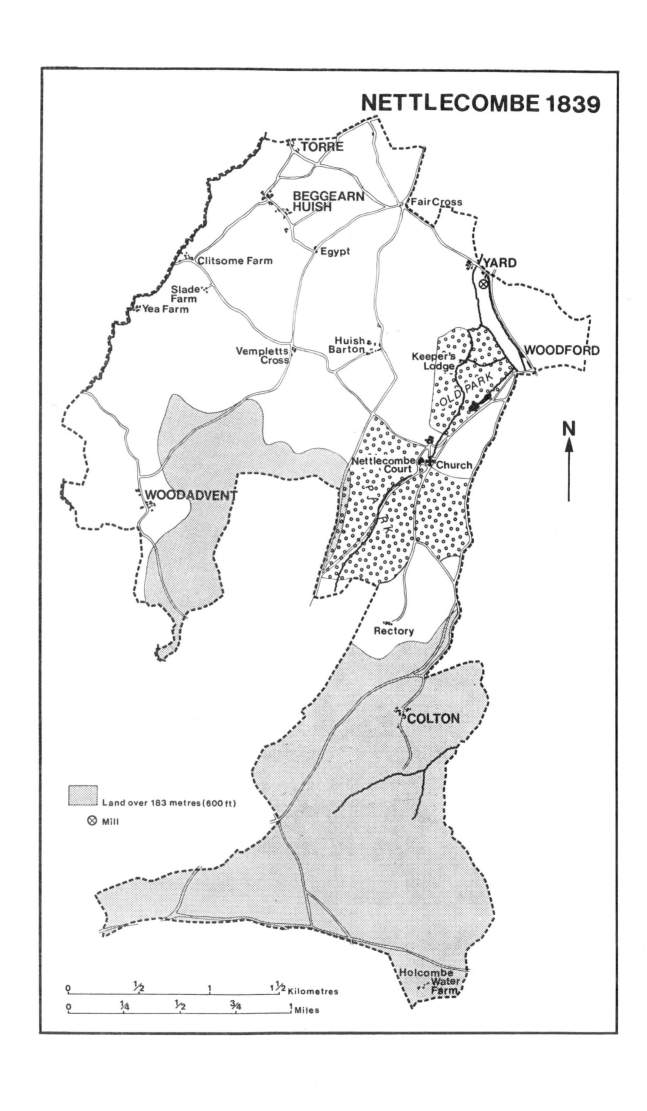

NETTLECOMBE 1839

TORRE

BEGGEARN
HUISH

Fair Cross

Egypt

Clitsome Farm

YARD

Slade
Farm

Yea Farm

Huish
Barton

Keeper's
Lodge

WOODFORD

Vempletts
Cross

OLD PARK

N

Nettlecombe
Court

Church

WOODADVENT

PARK

Rectory

COLTON

Land over 183 metres (600 ft)

⊗ Mill

Holcombe
Water
Farm

0   ½   1   1½ Kilometres

0   ¼   ½   ¾   1 Miles

was known as Liche Way in the 15th century.[62] In 1734 Sir John Trevelyan (d. 1755) obtained permission to enclose part of a highway to Nettlecombe church and provide an alternative route.[63] A road through the park from the lodge to the church was closed by 1838 and may have been the road which the earl of Egremont declared he would assist Sir John Trevelyan (d. 1846) to keep private in 1841.[64]

Raleigh's Cross, on the Brendon ridgeway, was said to have been built originally as a landmark for travellers near a dangerous bog north of the road. It marked the junction of five ways, only four of which remain, and it was mentioned as a marker in a view of the Nettlecombe manor boundary in 1425–6.[65] The cross was moved across the road on the orders of Sir Walter Calverley Trevelyan (d. 1879) to mark the boundary between the land of Trevelyan in Nettlecombe and of Carew in Clatworthy.[66] All that remains of the cross is a polygonal stump set in a square base beside the western entrance to the Raleigh's Cross Hotel.

In 1658 beer was being sold illegally in the parish.[67] An alehouse was recorded in 1661.[68] The inn at Yard was first mentioned in 1736 and by the end of the century it was known as the Hare and Hounds.[69] By 1822 a different building was used for the inn, following a change in the line of the road,[70] and in 1838 it formed part of the buildings at Yard Farm. The Trevelyan Arms at Yard was mentioned in 1840,[71] but no later record of a public house in the parish has been found. The Temperance Hall at Roadwater was built c. 1877 by Sir Walter Calverley Trevelyan, who encouraged temperance meetings in Nettlecombe Park and on Brendon Hill in the 1850s and 1860s attended by as many as 1,500 people.[72] The hall was a private house in 1980. There was a friendly society in Nettlecombe from 1807 until 1829 or later. The Nettlecombe Union and Friendly Society met at the Hare and Hounds inn or at Yard mill once a month, and held an annual feast on Whit Tuesday. In 1828 there were 180 members.[73]

There were at least 120 adult males in the parish in 1641.[74] The population during most of the 19th century was over 300 and reached a peak of 372 in 1821, but between 1871 and 1891 the total fell from 344 to 259, possibly caused partly by the closure of the iron mines. By 1961 the population had fallen still further to 201, but an increase in the next decade raised the figure to 247 in 1971.[75]

William Musgrave (d. 1721), physician and antiquary, was the youngest son of Richard Musgrave of Nettlecombe. He lived at Exeter and attended the Trevelyan family. He wrote several treatises on arthritis and four volumes of *Antiquitates Brittanno-Belgicae*.[76]

MANORS. *NETTLECOMBE* was held by Godwin son of Harold in 1066 and by the Crown in demesne in 1086.[77] By the 12th century it was held of the manor of Hampstead Marshall (Berks.), with which it remained until the end of the 14th century.[78] Between 1440 and 1563 the overlordship was said to belong to the heirs of Robert FitzPayn.[79]

No record of a terre tenancy has been found before the late 12th century when Henry II confirmed a grant of Nettlecombe made by John Marshall to Hugh de Ralegh.[80] Hugh appears to have had no son and gave the estate to his nephew Warin de Ralegh. Warin died before 1199 and was succeeded by his son Sir Warin who died before 1246.[81] Sir Warin de Ralegh, son of Sir Warin, died before 1280 and was followed by Sir Simon de Ralegh (d. c. 1284), probably his brother.[82] Simon was followed by his son John (d. before 1293) and then by Sir Simon de Ralegh (d. c. 1304), son or brother of John, who received a grant of free warren on his demesne at Nettlecombe in 1304. By this date Rowdon manor in Stogumber was held with this manor and the two were generally administered as a single unit known as the manor of *NETTLECOMBE AND ROW-DON*.[83] Sir Simon's successor was probably his second son John de Ralegh (d. 1340). John was succeeded by his son Sir John (d. 1372),[84] and Sir John by his eldest son John (d. c. 1403), and then by another son, Simon de Ralegh.[85] Simon died childless in 1440 and his heir was Thomas Whalesborough (d. 1481), son of his sister Joan.[86] Thomas's son Edmund died in his father's lifetime and the estates descended to Edmund's sister Elizabeth who had married John Trevelyan of Trevelyan in St. Veep (Cornw.).[87]

From John Trevelyan (d. 1492) the manor descended in the direct male line through Sir John (d. 1521), John (d. 1546),[88] John (d. 1563), and John (d. 1577) to John Trevelyan (d. 1623).[89] The last named was succeeded by his grandson George Trevelyan, a minor.[90] George compounded for his estates during the Interregnum and died in 1653.[91] His son George, created a baronet in 1661,[92] died in 1672 leaving a son John only a few months old.[93] John Trevelyan, M.P. for Somerset 1695–8

[62] Ibid. DD/WO 37/21.
[63] Ibid. 35/1.
[64] Ibid. 35/1, 40/11; ibid. tithe award.
[65] Ibid. DD/WO 41/9.
[66] *Proc. Som. Arch. Soc.* xxix. 47–8.
[67] *S.R.S.* xxviii. 363.
[68] S.R.O., Q/SR 104/4–5.
[69] Ibid. Q/RL; ibid. DD/WO 43/4.
[70] Ibid. DD/WY map of Yard 1822.
[71] Ibid. DD/WO 55/11; ibid. tithe award.
[72] Ibid. DD/WO 54/11, 55/11.
[73] Ibid. DD/HC 6E.
[74] *Som. Protestation Returns*, ed. Howard and Stoate, 164.
[75] *Census*, 1801–1971.
[76] *D.N.B.*; *Diary of a West Country Physician*, ed. E. Hobhouse, 66; *Som. Wills*, ed. Brown, i. 57, iii. 40–1.
[77] *V.C.H. Som.* i. 438.
[78] S.R.O., DD/WO 1.
[79] P.R.O., C 139/101, no. 67; C 140/80, no. 41; C 142/135, no. 11; S.R.O. DD/WO 11/5, 23/12.
[80] S.R.O., DD/WO 1; 62/9.
[81] Ibid. DD/WO 1; DD/AH 21/2.

[82] Ibid. DD/WO 1; DD/AH 21/2; *Cal. Pat.* 1364–7, 267, exemplifying a partition of 33 Hen. III, records Simon holding Nettlecombe in 1249.
[83] S.R.O., DD/WO 1; *Cal. Chart. R.* 1300–26, 44.
[84] S.R.O., DD/WO 1; 38/3; 61; *S.R.S.* iii. 76, 167; xii, 12, 159; xvii. 64; *Cal. Pat.* 1317–21, 86; *Cal. Inq. p.m.* x. p. 64.
[85] S.R.O., DD/WO 1; 38/3; *Cal. Inq. p.m.* xiii, p. 171; *Feud. Aids*, iv. 392, 438; *Cal. Pat.* 1399–1401, 498; *S.R.S.* xvi, pp. 146–7; xxii, pp. 176, 182, 186, 203.
[86] S.R.O., DD/WO 1; P.R.O., C 139/101, no. 67.
[87] S.R.O., DD/WO 1; 2; 24/1; P.R.O., C 140/80, no. 41; C 142/23, no. 7.
[88] P.R.O., C 142/37, no. 115; C 142/75, no. 75.
[89] S.R.O., DD/WO 2/4; 21/1; 61; P.R.O., C 142/135, no. 11; C 142/183, no. 47; CP 25(2)/207/38 Eliz. I. Trin.
[90] *Som. Wills*, ed. Brown, i. 41.
[91] *Cal. Cttee. for Compounding*, ii. 1077–8; *Som. Wills*, ed. Brown, i. 42.
[92] *Cal. S.P. Dom.* 1661–2, 137, 154.
[93] *Som. Wills*, ed. Brown, i. 42; S.R.O., DD/WO 16/7.

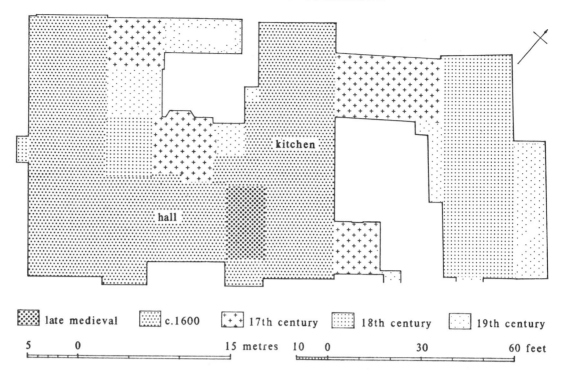

late medieval   c.1600   17th century   18th century   19th century

5   0   15 metres   10   0   30   60 feet

NETTLECOMBE COURT

and 1701, died in 1755 when his heir was his son, Sir George Trevelyan.[94] Sir George died in 1768, and the manor passed to his son Sir John (d. 1828), M.P. for Somerset 1780–96. John's son Sir John (d. 1846) succeeded in turn, and was followed by his own son, the naturalist Sir Walter Calverley Trevelyan.[95] Sir Walter died in 1879 without issue and his nephew Arthur Trevelyan (d. 1891) inherited the estates and title. Sir Arthur had five daughters but no son and the inheritance passed to Walter (later Sir Walter) John Trevelyan, a cousin. Sir Walter (d. 1931) left Nettlecombe to his daughter Joan (d. 1943), wife of Garnet Wolseley (d. 1967).[96] Joan's son John Wolseley was the owner in 1980.

Nettlecombe Court,[97] standing in its park close beside the parish church, is a complex house of red sandstone with Ham stone dressings. In 1525 a hall, eleven chambers, and five service rooms were mentioned in an inventory.[98] The oldest part of the house seems to be the south-east range, containing the hall and screens passage. The present hall, which was built in 1599 and still has its decorated plaster ceiling and overmantel,[99] narrows at the screens passage, an indication that it preserves there the width of an earlier building on the site, probably the hall which John Sydenham built of stone with a tiled roof under the terms of his lease of 1532. Sydenham's hall was to be built 'as the old hall now is' and of almost the same dimensions,[1] implying that the old hall, too, was in the same position, and not on the site of the kitchen range, which lies at right angles to the north-east end of the present hall.[2]

The kitchen range, which has a three-roomed plan, contained re-used medieval doorway mouldings, probably indicating, like the re-used mouldings in the range north-east of the kitchen range, the existence of a medieval service range and service court on the site.

The house as reconstructed by John Trevelyan c. 1600 probably had two courts, although that behind the hall and south-west of the kitchen range may not have been closed on the north-west. The two-storeyed porch to the screens passage lay close to the centre of the south-east front; the hall was between it and a three-storeyed parlour wing forming a south-west range. There was probably a staircase in the angle between the back door of the screens passage and the kitchen chimney stack.

George Trevelyan added the small three-storeyed block behind the hall fireplace c. 1641. The ground and first floor rooms of that block have elaborate plasterwork. Soon after he came of age in 1691 Sir John Trevelyan began to improve the principal rooms. Between 1703 and 1707[3] he altered the south-west range from three to two storeys and built a new staircase to serve the upper floor. He also panelled the hall and redecorated the rooms on the main front, beyond the screens passage, which had presumably been part of the service court. The alterations were probably completed by 1710 but the further room in the south-west range was still unfinished in 1749 and the staircase was not given its rococo decoration until 1753.[4] Sir John Trevelyan (d. 1828) completed the decoration of the south-west

[94] S.R.O., DD/WO 11/11, 50/7.
[95] Ibid. 4/5, 11/11, 21/3, 62/13.
[96] Ibid. 33/5; Burke, *Peerage* (1949), 2008.
[97] G. U. S. Corbett, 'Nettlecombe Court: the buildings', *Field Studies*, iii (2), 289–296; above, plate facing p. 108.
[98] S.R.O., DD/WO 49/2.

[99] The source for the overmantel was Clement Perret, *Exercitatio Alphabetica* (Antwerp, 1569), pl. xxii. Inf. from Mr. A. Wells-Cole.
[1] S.R.O., DD/WO 31/2.
[2] *Field Studies*, iii (2), 289.
[3] S.R.O., DD/WO 51/1.   [4] Ibid. 40/5, 51/5.

range in 1787–8, almost certainly replanning the interior.[5]

The kitchen court was reconstructed and much of the exterior was stuccoed to give it a uniform 'Tudor Gothic' appearance by Sir John Trevelyan (d. 1846).[6] The stable block, which stands north of the house, is dated 1792, and contains original 18th-century stable fittings and late 19th-century loose boxes. Further north lay extensive kitchen gardens including a range of terraced greenhouses. The park was landscaped in 1792.[7]

In 1963 Nettlecombe Court was the home of the preparatory department of St. Audries School for girls, West Quantoxhead.[8] Since 1967 the house has been used as the Leonard Wills Field Studies Centre.

An estate called Oda, later Woodadvent, was exempt from geld in 1084 and does not appear in the Domesday survey.[9] In 1284 WOOD or WOOD-ADVENT was held of Compton Dundon, like Kilve manor, and it remained in that overlordship until the end of the 16th century or later.[10]

In 1284 Robert Avenant held ½ fee at Woodadvent, probably as successor to Thomas Avenant (fl. 1242–3), and possibly as son of Thomas Avenant (fl. 1271–2).[11] The Avenants probably held the estate in succession to the Wood family, Robert son of Hugh of Woodadvent having held adjoining land c. 1200.[12] Richard Avenant held the fee in 1287.[13] At the beginning of the 14th century Woodadvent was held by William Burghland with unnamed co-heirs, and in 1327 by Thomas FitzUrse, who is said to have married Alice, daughter of Robert Avenant.[14] In 1335 Woodadvent was settled by Thomas Fitz-Urse on John de Ralegh and his three younger sons in reversion. The sons died without issue and Wood-advent reverted to John's eldest son, Sir John de Ralegh, and descended with Nettlecombe manor.[15]

A house at Woodadvent is referred to as the manor place in 1523. In 1619, described as a farm, it comprised a higher and lower hall, two entries, kitchen, buttery, six upper rooms, and several outbuildings.[16] The house and farm were rebuilt by Sir John Trevelyan (d. 1828).[17]

Huish, later Beggearn Huish, was held in 1066 by Merlesuain and in 1086 by Ralph Pagnell with Ralph de Reuilly as his undertenant.[18] It descended with Pagnell's manor of East Quantoxhead and was held of that manor until the 17th century or later.[19] In 1310–11 Andrew Luttrell granted the terre tenancy, presumably by way of confirmation, to Lucy, widow

of Thomas de Raleigh of Devon, his wife's cousin.[20] It probably descended through William de Raleigh (d. c. 1325) and his son Thomas to John de Raleigh who in 1362 held the estate, then described as the manor of *BEGGEARN HUISH* or *HUISH GAUNT*.[21] John died in 1376 and his daughter and heir Thomasia held the manor until her death in 1402 when her heir was her son John by her first husband, Sir John Chichester.[22] John Chichester succeeded c. 1406 and held the manor until his death in 1437.[23] He was followed by his son Richard (d. 1498) and then by his great-grandson John Chichester (d. 1536).[24] John was succeeded by his grandson Sir John Chichester (d. 1568) and Sir John by his son of the same name who died in 1586. The last Sir John was followed by his son Sir Robert who conveyed the manor to Richard Burton in 1604.[25]

Richard died in 1607 and his son and successor Nathaniel died without issue in 1632. Nathaniel's wife Julian (d. 1639) remarried and had a daughter, Eleanor Hobbes.[26] In 1656 the manor was probably held by trustees.[27] Richard Burton, great nephew of Richard Burton, and Eleanor Hobbes died without issue. In 1661 Richard's sister Martha Saddler and Anne, wife of Richard Mayfield, conveyed the manor in reversion to Aldred Seaman.[28] In 1666 Mary Thorne, aunt by marriage to Eleanor Hobbes, conveyed her interest to John Pratt of Thurloxton.[29] Seaman and Pratt mortgaged the manor in 1667 and in 1672 Pratt released his interest to Seaman.[30] Aldred Seaman and his son Aldred conveyed the manor to Lucy Luttrell in trust for Francis Luttrell of Dunster in 1679.[31] The manor was mortgaged to Sir William Wyndham in 1682 and after the death of Francis Luttrell, a debtor, in 1690 it was forfeited to Wyndham in whose family it descended like Orchard Wyndham to George Colville Wyndham (d. 1982). In 1980 it was the property of George's elder son William Wadham Wyndham.[32]

Another estate called Huish, later Lodhuish, was held in 1066 by Ulfgar and in 1086 by Roger de Courcelles with Bertram as his undertenant.[33] From Roger the lordship descended to the lords of Compton Dundon manor from which Lodhuish was held until the 15th century.[34] A mesne lordship was held by the lords of Kilve manor,[35] from whom in 1284 and 1286 Geoffrey of Huish held Lodhuish as terre tenant.[36] Geoffrey was probably succeeded by John of Lodhuish (fl. 1286–1334), who had licences for an oratory there in 1318 and 1334.[37] His successors

[5] Ibid. 40/10.
[6] *Proc. Som. Arch. Soc.* liv, i. 83.
[7] Above, introduction.
[8] Char. Com. files.   [9] *V.C.H. Som.* i. 436 n., 532.
[10] Above, Kilve, manor; *Feud. Aids*, iv. 275; S.R.O., DD/WO 42/25–6, 28.
[11] *Feud. Aids*, iv. 275; *S.R.S.* xi, p. 304; xxxiii, p. 44; B.L. Add. Ch. 40615.
[12] B.L. Add. Ch. 11162; cf. S.R.O., DD/AH 21/2.
[13] S.R.O., DD/WO 10/1; *S.R.S.* xxxv. 30.
[14] *S.R.S.* iii. 167; xxxv. 66; Collinson, *Hist. Som.* iii. 540.
[15] S.R.O., DD/WO 1; 11/1; 41; 61; *Cal. Inq. p.m.* viii, p. 322; *Feud. Aids*, iv. 392.
[16] S.R.O., DD/WO 43/1, 47/25.
[17] Ibid. 56/11.   [18] *V.C.H. Som.* i. 510.
[19] Below, E. Quantoxhead; *Cal. Inq. p.m. Hen. VII*, iii, p. 312; *Cal. Pat.* 1555–7, 468; P.R.O., C 142/295, no. 79.
[20] S.R.O., DD/AH 21/2; Collinson, *Hist. Som.* iii. 541.
[21] Devon R.O. 50/11/1/1; *Cal. Inq. p.m.* vi, p. 450.
[22] P.R.O., C 137/44, no. 36; S.R.O., DD/L P22/1, 3, 6, 8; *Cal. Inq. p.m.* xiv, p. 279.

[23] S.R.O., DD/L P22/4; *Feud. Aids*, iv. 392, 438; *S.R.S.* xxxiii, p. 253.
[24] S.R.O., DD/L P7/36; P24/8, 9; *S.R.S.* xxxiii, pp. 248, 273; P.R.O., C 142/58, no. 88; Devon R.O. 50/11/1/8x, 10.
[25] P.R.O., C 142/58, no. 88; C 142/151, no. 9; ibid. CP 25(2)/345/6 Jas. I East.; S.R.O., DD/WY 13/14.
[26] *S.R.S.* lxvii. 13, 116; S.R.O., DD/L P23/40; P.R.O., C 142/295, no. 79; C 142/467, no. 118; C 142/488, no. 53.
[27] *S.R.S.* xxviii. 322.   [28] S.R.O., DD/WY 13/14.
[29] Ibid. 13/14; DD/L 2/11/58.
[30] Ibid. DD/WY 13/14.   [31] Ibid. DD/L 2/11/58–9.
[32] Ibid. 2/11/57–8; DD/WY 25/25B, 58; below, St. Decumans.
[33] *V.C.H. Som.* i. 488.
[34] *Cal. Inq. p.m.* viii, p. 322; xi, p. 22; *Feud. Aids*, iv. 392.
[35] Above, Kilve; *Feud. Aids*, iv. 275; P.R.O., SC 6/1119/17; ibid. C 140/42, no. 51.
[36] *S.R.S.* iii. 6; xxxv. 29; *Feud. Aids*, iv. 275.
[37] *S.R.S.* i. 18; iii. 167; ix, p. 172; xii. 164; *Cal. Pat.* 1313–17, 152; S.R.O., DD/WO 1; 11/5.

were probably Geoffrey of Lodhuish (fl. 1342–51) and John of Lodhuish (fl. 1418).[38] In 1434 the manor of *LODHUISH* was held by Joan Huish,[39] but it came into the hands of the Hill family, probably by 1442, and was in the possession of Cecily Keriell, widow of John Hill, when she died in 1472.[40] The heir was her granddaughter Genevieve (d. 1480), wife of Sir William Say (d. 1529). They had no surviving issue and Lodhuish came into the possession of one of their heirs, John Waldegrave (d. 1543).[41] John was succeeded by his son Sir Edward (d. 1561), M.P. for Somerset 1554, by Edward's son Charles (d. 1632), and by Charles's son Sir Edward (d. 1647). In 1648 Lodhuish was settled on Sir Edward's son Sir Henry for life.[42] On Sir Henry's death in 1658 Lodhuish passed to his brother Sir Charles (d. 1684). Henry, Lord Waldegrave (d. 1689), succeeded his father Sir Charles and was followed by his son James, Lord Waldegrave.[43] James sold Lodhuish to Sir John Trevelyan in 1714[44] and it descended in the Trevelyan family with Nettlecombe manor.

Huish Barton is probably in origin a 16th-century house but it was largely rebuilt and extended northwards in the 17th century. In 1647 the tenant was required to spend £100 on repairs.[45] The north wing comprises a first-floor chamber of five bays with attics and basement. Over a fireplace is a plaster panel bearing the date 1698 and the monogram of the Musgraves who occupied the house for most of the 17th century. Among the adjoining farm buildings is a barn probably of the late 17th or early 18th century.[46]

ECONOMIC HISTORY. In 1086 the estates at Nettlecombe, Lodhuish, and Beggearn Huish together measured 5 hides, with land for 20 ploughs; $1\frac{5}{8}$ hide and 5 ploughs were in demesne. The demesnes were worked by 9 serfs, and 27 villeins and 12 bordars worked the remainder with 11 ploughs. There were 21 a. of meadow, 230 a. of pasture, and 50 a. of wood. The estate probably at Woodadvent may have measured $\frac{1}{2}$ hide. Apart from a riding horse at Nettlecombe the only estate livestock recorded was at Beggearn Huish which had 1 horse, 2 cattle, 1 pig, and 30 sheep.[47]

Beggearn Huish, Lodhuish, and Woodadvent continued as separate estates throughout the Middle Ages. Only from Nettlecombe and Rowdon manor is there information about medieval agriculture, and it is not always possible to distinguish what relates exclusively to Nettlecombe parish since Rowdon lay in Stogumber. By the late 14th century most services had been commuted, but in 1390 there were boon-workers on the Nettlecombe demesne who received

two sheep carcasses for food, and chevage was still paid by one man in 1401.[48] Cash rents, which accounted for about a third of manorial income in the early 1380s, grew with the inclusion of cash payments for commuted services and new rents, and by 1400 amounted to over two thirds of the whole income.[49]

The demesne farms at Nettlecombe and Rowdon were evidently worked together, sharing two ploughmen, two drovers, two shepherds, a reaper, a cowherd, a neatherd, and a dairy maid. During the last two decades of the 14th century the area under plough on the demesne varied from under 100 a. to over 200 a., and during the same period pasture on the Brendons in Nettlecombe parish was let on short leases for tillage.[50] The Nettlecombe demesne produced most of the rye and oats on the manor, oats accounting for about half the total in any one year, and producing cash sales reaching in 1386–7 a quarter of the manor's income excluding rents.[51] Up to 13 a. of waterleets lay at Nettlecombe where vetches and grain were sown.[52]

Stock on Nettlecombe barton at Michaelmas 1380 comprised 15 oxen, 37 young cattle, 4 horses, 59 pigs, and 34 sheep.[53] Twenty years later the whole manor employed a few more oxen, some of which had come from Wales, and the sheep flock had increased to 219.[54] The sheep flock had been much larger in 1373–4 when over 200 fleeces of wether wool, a large quantity of fleece wool, and 24 lb. of lambs' wool were sold. Three inspectors of carcasses employed on the manor in 1385 suggest widespread grazing both on the Brendons in Nettlecombe and on the high ground at Capton in Stogumber.[55]

Tenant farmers were paying in the 16th century to till land on the Brendons,[56] but sheep were still pastured there, both by outsiders and by local men.[57] The demesne estate at Nettlecombe was exploited and improved by John Trevelyan (d. 1623). Stock both from the village and from Clatworthy, Wiveliscombe, Stogumber, and Monksilver was allowed to graze in the park in return for cash rents,[58] and fruit trees were planted in the orchards.[59] The home farm supported horses, cattle, sheep, pigs, geese, turkeys, and ducks.[60] During the 1590s the dairy produced 4 gall. of butter a week in early summer as well as cheese.[61] Oats, followed by barley and rye, were the main arable crops in the early 17th century.[62]

By the end of the 17th century the barton at Nettlecombe employed as many as fourteen shearers, some indication of the size of the flock.[63] Common grazing still played an important part in the economy; there were 700 a. belonging to the manor in 1619, and by custom tenants at Colton, Chidgley, and Nettlecombe pastured as many sheep and cattle on the Brendons as they could winter on their own land.

---

[38] S.R.O., DD/WO 1.
[39] P.R.O., C 139/71, no. 36.
[40] Ibid. SC 6/1119/17; SC 6/977/11, 23; ibid. C 140/42, no. 51; below, Raddington, manor.
[41] *Cal. Inq. p.m. Hen. VII*, iii, p. 59; P.R.O., C 142/41, no. 35.
[42] S.R.O., DD/WY 12/C4.
[43] Ibid. 12/C4; DD/DP 33/7; DD/JL.
[44] Ibid. DD/WO 11/7.
[45] Ibid. DD/WG 13/1.
[46] Ibid. DD/V Wlr 16.1.
[47] *V.C.H. Som.* i. 436, 488, 510, 532; H. C. Darby and R. W. Finn, *Dom. Geog. SW. Eng.* 169. Some of this land was in other parishes.
[48] S.R.O., DD/WO 42/20, 23.
[49] Ibid. 42/7, 22–3.
[50] Ibid. 42/3–23.
[51] Ibid. 42/9.
[52] Ibid. 42/3–23; below, St. Decumans, econ. hist.
[53] S.R.O., DD/WO 42/3.
[54] Ibid. 42/22.
[55] Ibid. 38/3, 41/10.
[56] Ibid. 49/7.
[57] Ibid. 42/24, 29; 49/3, 7.
[58] Ibid. 49/3, 7.
[59] Ibid. 49/7.
[60] Ibid. 49/3.
[61] Ibid. 49/10.
[62] Ibid. 56/7.
[63] Ibid. 49/10.

They might also each till an acre there.[64] In 1721 a Nettlecombe tenant kept two flocks, one described as 'the small hill sheep'.[65]

By the early 18th century the Trevelyans possessed all estates in the parish except Beggearn Huish, which was split into several large freeholds, later known as Clitsome, Torre, and Slade.[66] Woodadvent, virtually a single farm, had been absorbed into Nettlecombe manor by 1598[67] and Lodhuish, later Huish Barton, another single farm, was acquired in 1714.[68] Within Nettlecombe manor itself there was a substantial leasehold farm at Yard, but most of the land belonged to the home farm. The annual value of Nettlecombe, Rowdon, and Woodadvent together was £2,452 8s. 10d. in 1773, of which just under half came from rack rents.[69] Farming of the home estate, not easily distinguished in surviving accounts from other family holdings, involved 15 labourers in 1753 with 17 shearers.[70] In the autumn of 1755 the stock at Nettlecombe included 19 horses, 1 bull, 14 plough cattle, 23 cows and young cattle, 297 sheep, and 29 pigs. There were also 20 a. of barley, 622 bu. of wheat, and 990 bu. of white and grey peas.[71] Recorded business in 1789 illustrates the range of activity: purchases of stock, including heifers from Stogumber fair, ewes and lambs, white clover, and rye seed; sales of corn, skins, bark, and game; wages for shearing, mowing, lifting potatoes, and picking apples; payments for collecting holly and whitethorn berries, beechnuts, and acorns.[72] In 1791 36 hogsheads of cider were made and in 1798 stock-keeping in the park produced c. £300.[73] In 1803 wheat, barley, and oats were grown at Huish Barton.[74]

By 1838 there were five farms over 250 a. in the parish, all on the Trevelyan estate. On the Brendons Colton farm (540 a.) and Holcombe Water (330 a.) had both been taken largely from the common land there between 1780 and 1796.[75] On the lower ground were Nettlecombe Barton (428 a.), Huish Barton (397 a.), and Woodadvent (278 a.). The largest farm at Beggearn Huish was 142 a., with smaller holdings at Yard (102 a.), Clitsome, Berryman's, and Torre (50 a.–100 a.). More than half the tithable area was under arable, with 370 a. of poor sheep pasture on the Brendons, and 349 a. of meadow and pasture. There were 430 a. of tithe-free land including woodland.[76]

Sir John Trevelyan (d. 1828) recorded that when he took over the Nettlecombe estate in 1768 the buildings were in a bad state of repair, including the farmhouse at Woodadvent which he rebuilt.[77] Cottages were provided for the bailiff, gardener, and gamekeeper, and pairs of cottages were built on the farms.[78] In 1821 there were 66 families, of whom 54 were engaged in agriculture, living in 59 houses.[79] There were 68 labourers recorded on nine farms in 1851,[80] and in the 1860s there were complaints that large numbers of workers came from outside the parish and threatened to overburden the poor rate.[81] By 1905 permanent grassland (1,137 a.) had increased in relation to arable (1,010 a.).[82] By 1976 less than a third of the land was under plough, but the size of holdings had not changed significantly from the 1830s, two farms having over 200 ha. (494 a.) and seven over 50 ha. (123 a.). One farm specialized in dairying and another in cereals, but most raised livestock.[83]

In 1606 a tanner bought bark from 10 a. of wood from Sir John Trevelyan for £10 and two dressed hides.[84] A weaver was at work in the parish in the same period,[85] and in 1669 a woodworker had a workshop with tools and a sawpit.[86] In 1689 a Nettlecombe gunsmith was employed to repair guttering at Bicknoller church.[87]

Iron ore deposits were found in the parish at Fair Cross and Beggearn Huish in 1843 and a mine was opened at Beggearn Huish then.[88] Mining was, however, concentrated at Colton, just north of the Brendon ridgeway, where possible 18th-century workings were found in the 1860s. In 1859 the Trevelyans leased mining rights at Colton pits in return for a minimum rent of £50 and a charge of 1s. for every ton of ore.[89] A new adit was opened by the Ebbw Vale Steel, Iron, and Coal Co. in 1865. In 1881 the Colton mine was worked on five levels, but the ore was still carried by horse and cart to Brendon Hill. The mines were closed in 1882 but reopened by the Somerset Mineral Syndicate in 1907.[90] A light railway was then constructed to carry ore to the mineral railway at Brendon Hill, and an incline with boiler and winding engine was installed to carry ore from Galloping Bottom up to the new line. A steam pump enabled working at lower levels and over 2,000 tons were mined in 1908, but a slump in the steel industry led to closure of the mines in 1909.[91]

There was a mill at Beggearn Huish in 1086.[92] There is no further record of the mill, which may have been on the Washford river. Corneford mill was mentioned in the 13th century in connexion with an estate at Slade but its site is unknown.[93] The mill at Yard, belonging to Nettlecombe manor, was perhaps the Hurd mill recorded as in need of repairs in 1373; Yard mill was mentioned in 1374–5, and in 1379–80 materials were purchased for its repair.[94] In 1381–2 it was farmed[95] but it was in hand in 1398–9.[96] The

[64] Ibid. 41/3; 43/1.
[65] Ibid. DD/SP, inventory 1721.
[66] Ibid. DD/L 2/15/81; DD/WY 13/14; 47/2/18.
[67] Ibid. DD/WO 42/28.
[68] Ibid. 11/7; DD/WG 13.
[69] Ibid. DD/WO 14/9.
[70] Ibid. 51/6.
[71] Ibid. 50/7.
[72] Ibid. DD/CCH 72.
[73] Ibid. DD/WO 51/13; DD/CCH 72.
[74] Ibid. DD/WO 11/3.
[75] Ibid. 12/9; map 1796.
[76] Ibid. tithe award. Nettlecombe barton and the glebe were not tithable.
[77] S.R.O., DD/WO 56/11.
[78] Ibid. 39/3.   [79] Census, 1821.
[80] P.R.O., HO 107/1920.
[81] S.R.O., DD/WO 58/4.

[82] Statistics supplied by the then Bd. of Agric. 1905.
[83] Min. of Agric., Fisheries, and Food, agric. returns 1976.
[84] S.R.O., DD/WO 11/2; S.R.S. xxiii. 310.
[85] H. R. Phipps, Taunton Archdeaconry Probate Rec. 33.
[86] S.R.O., DD/SP, inventory 1669.
[87] Ibid. D/P/bic 6/1/1.
[88] Ibid. DD/WY, map of Nettlecombe 1843.
[89] Ibid. DD/CCH 52/2.
[90] Sellick, W. Som. Mineral Rly. 11, 13, 46; S.R.O., DD/CCH 52/2.
[91] Sellick, W. Som. Mineral Rly. 72.
[92] V.C.H. Som. i. 510; H. C. Darby and R. W. Finn, Dom. Geog. SW. Eng. 412.
[93] S.R.O., DD/WO 62.
[94] Ibid. 41/6–7; 42/1, 3.
[95] Ibid. 42/5.
[96] Ibid. 42/19.

mill was let in 1755.[97] In 1872 the miller was also a corn, seed, and coal merchant.[98] Milling ceased after 1910[99] but the mill and its overshot wheel and machinery, including stones, survived in 1980.

In 1838 there were blade mills at Yard and on the Washford river on the site later occupied by the Temperance Hall;[1] the ruins of the former survived in 1980.

LOCAL GOVERNMENT. About 1225 Beggearn Huish and Lodhuish together formed one tithing but Maurice de Gaunt joined Beggearn Huish to the tithing of East Quantoxhead.[2] In the 17th century Beggearn Huish, Lodhuish, Nettlecombe, and Woodadvent were each a separate tithing.[3] By the 19th century Woodadvent and Nettlecombe tithings had been combined.[4]

Court rolls and books for Nettlecombe and Rowdon manor survive with a few gaps for the periods 1369–1449, 1476–1688, and 1759–67.[5] In 1276 Warin de Ralegh had gallows and assize of bread and of ale in Nettlecombe manor,[6] and in 1532 stocks were provided by the manor court.[7] There were three and occasionally four courts a year from the 14th to the 16th century, and during the 17th century courts met four times a year, two being views of frankpledge.[8] In the early 18th century courts were held in the church house.[9]

In the 14th century there were three inspectors of carcasses, one for Nettlecombe and two for Rowdon, four reeves, and a tithingman. By the early 15th century there were three reeves and a rent collector.[10] Later in the century only one reeve was appointed.[11] The court elected a constable, tithingman, and reeve during the 16th to 18th centuries.[12]

The court rolls of Woodadvent manor survive intermittently between 1380 and 1647. Courts met twice a year at Hocktide and Michaelmas. By the 16th century the bailiff of Nettlecombe manor was also responsible for Woodadvent.[13] Only one court roll, of 1682, is known for Beggearn Huish manor; a few rolls survive for the period 1594–1605 for Lodhuish.[14]

From the early 16th century there were two churchwardens, whose accounts survive for the period 1507–1617 and from 1705.[15] The wardens were helped in the 16th century by people called the four men, presumably sidesmen.[16] In the 18th cen-

tury churchwardens and overseers were elected according to a rota of property.[17] A vestry had been formed by 1756.[18]

There were four overseers of the poor by 1641 and until 1660, and then two.[19] The poorhouse, probably the former church house, was said to have been demolished c. 1780 when the paupers were moved to Woodford,[20] where a poorhouse given by Sir John Trevelyan (d. 1828) already stood.[21] It was divided into two-roomed cottages in 1834, the inmates paying rent to the overseers according to their means. In 1841 the house was sold.[22]

Two surveyors of the highways were appointed in 1660 but in 1691 they and the overseers contracted with a local man to maintain the highways for seven years for a payment of £7 a year, excluding the cost of landslips and fallen trees.[23] Surveyors' accounts date from 1756, and from 1788 separate accounts were kept for the parish and for turnpike roads.[24]

Nettlecombe became part of the Williton poor-law union in 1836 and was in the Williton rural district from 1894. Since 1974 it has been in the West Somerset district.[25]

CHURCH. There was probably a church in Nettlecombe by the late 12th century.[26] In 1327 the advowson of the rectory belonged to John de Ralegh and descended with Nettlecombe manor. The representatives of Garnet Wolseley, deceased, were patrons in 1980.[27] In 1968 Nettlecombe became part of a united benefice with Monksilver and Brompton Ralph, and since 1977 has been held in addition with Stogumber.[28]

The benefice was valued at £8 in 1291.[29] In 1535 it was worth £17 6s. 7d.[30] and its reputed value c. 1668 was £120.[31] The net income in 1831 was £445.[32] The tithes were assessed at over £12 6s. 8d. in 1535.[33] In 1613 moduses were payable on geese, hay, hops, apples, pears, honey, wax, and pigs, and 1d. was due from each garden and on the birth of every calf. Each person making a first communion had to pay 1½d.[34] In 1838 tithes were commuted for a rent charge of £480.[35] The glebe was worth 30s. in 1535[36] and at the end of the 16th century comprised c. 35 a. In 1613 and 1639 there was slightly more, including two closes in St. Decumans parish.[37] There were exchanges of glebe with the Trevelyans in 1790, 1797, 1838, and 1866, largely in order to

[97] Ibid. DD/MDW 24.
[98] Morris & Co. *Dir. Som.* (1872).
[99] *Kelly's Dir. Som.* (1889); local inf. The wheel is dated 1910.
[1] S.R.O., tithe award.
[2] *Rot. Hund.* (Rec. Com.), ii. 125.
[3] S.R.O., DD/MY 24; DD/WY 34.
[4] Ibid. Q/REl Williton.
[5] Ibid. DD/WO 41. This manor also covered a large part of Stogumber parish.
[6] *Rot. Hund.* (Rec. Com.), ii. 125, printing Calee for Ralee. Court field and Gallows close lay NW. of Nettlecombe Court in 1838: S.R.O., tithe award.
[7] S.R.O., DD/WO 49/2.
[8] Ibid. 41.
[9] Ibid. D/P/net 8/3/1.
[10] Ibid. DD/WO 41/10–12, 16.
[11] Ibid. 41/19.
[12] Ibid. 41/2, 24.
[13] Ibid. 42/26, 28.
[14] Ibid. DD/L 2/11/59; DD/WG 6/13, 16–17.
[15] Ibid. DD/WO 49/1, 9; ibid. D/P/net 4/1/2–3, 4/4/1.
[16] Ibid. DD/WO 49/9; ibid. D/P/net 4/4/1.

[17] Ibid. D/P/net 4/1/2, 13/2/2.
[18] Ibid. 4/1/2–3, 13/2/3.
[19] Ibid. 4/4/1, 13/2/1.
[20] Ibid. DD/WO 55/11.
[21] Ibid. D/P/net 4/1/3; 13/2/3; *Char. Don.* H.C. 511 (1816), xvi.
[22] S.R.O., DD/WO 9/1, 37/22, 55/11; ibid. D/P/net 13/2/4.
[23] Ibid. D/P/net 13/2/1, 14/7/1.
[24] Ibid. 14/5/1.
[25] Youngs, *Local Admin. Units,* i. 674–6.
[26] S.R.O., DD/WO 62/9.
[27] *S.R.S.* i. 255; *Dioc. Dir.*
[28] *Dioc. Dir.*
[29] *Tax. Eccl.* (Rec. Com.), 198.
[30] *Valor Eccl.* (Rec. Com.), i. 224.
[31] S.R.O., D/D/Vc 24.
[32] *Rep. Com. Eccl. Revenues,* pp. 146–7.
[33] *Valor Eccl.* (Rec. Com.), i. 224.
[34] S.R.O., D/D/Rg 351.
[35] Ibid. tithe award.
[36] *Valor Eccl.* (Rec. Com.), i. 224.
[37] S.R.O., D/D/Rg 351.

increase the size of the park.[38] In 1838 the glebe measured over 59 a.; it was sold in 1922.[39]

In 1577 the parsonage house was said to be in decay.[40] In 1613 the house had a court with two chambers to the north, a pumphouse, bakehouse, stable, barn, and stall.[41] By 1724 the house comprised kitchen, hall, parlour, brewhouse, larder, five chambers, nursery, garret, and study.[42] About 1797 the house was demolished and the site, with neighbouring glebe closes, exchanged for lands and a new parsonage house on the Lawn in Pooke wood south of Nettlecombe park.[43] The house, later known as Combe, was sold in 1922 and a new house between Woodford and Yard was bought.[44] After the last resident rector left in 1968 it was sold, and in 1980 was a guest house.

Andrew de Ralegh, rector 1316–27, studied at Oxford on his appointment.[45] John FitzHide, rector 1449–50, was required to study for four years and present himself to the bishop each year.[46] George Trevelyan, rector 1502–11, was later chaplain to Henry VIII.[47] William Cavell, rector 1511–54, also studied at Oxford in his early years as rector and was later a pluralist.[48] The chantries and numerous lights in the church at the end of Henry VIII's reign and the covert transfer of a medieval chalice to John Trevelyan when the chantries were dissolved contrast with the protestantism suggested in the failure of the wardens to restore the tabernacle and the figures of the rood in 1557.[49] Baldwin Hill, rector at the time, was living at Tallaton (Devon), and his successor, Henry Slocombe, was also non-resident.[50] Robert Gay, rector 1631–72, is supposed to have attacked Nettlecombe Court during the civil wars.[51]

During the 18th century there were resident rectors and both Christopher Haslam (1724–55) and John Rugge (1755–92) married into the Trevelyan family.[52] George Trevelyan, rector 1792–1827, was archdeacon of Taunton from 1817 until his death in 1827. He was usually resident although he spent part of each winter at Wells. Services at Nettlecombe were held twice on Sundays in the summer and once in winter.[53] George's brother Walter was rector from 1827 until his death in 1830 and was also a prebendary of Wells. Noel Ellison, rector 1831–51 and son-in-law of Sir John Trevelyan (d. 1846), was a pluralist and Nettlecombe was usually served by curates, two of whom also became Sir John's sons-in-law. By 1843 there were two services on Sundays and communion was celebrated seven or eight times a year.[54] In 1851 there were two services each Sunday

and the average attendance, excluding Sunday-school children, was 100 at the morning service and 70 in the afternoon.[55] In 1870 there were two services on Sundays and communion was celebrated weekly.[56] Hugh Willoughby Jermyn, rector 1858–70, later became bishop of Colombo and of Brechin.[57]

A church house was mentioned in 1519, and was used for church ales and wedding feasts. By 1617 it was let as separate dwellings.[58] The building was described in 1619 as having three rooms with a loft over.[59] It was used as a poorhouse by the 18th century.[60] The house may have been rebuilt, since in the late 18th century it was said to have been of two storeys with an external stone stair. It was demolished when the park was extended over the village site.[61]

Simon de Ralegh (d. 1440) gave land to establish a chantry in the chapel of St. John the Baptist in the parish church. A mortmain licence was granted in 1443 and the first chaplain, formerly rector of Nettlecombe, was appointed in 1453.[62] The chaplain, who had a house in the parish, celebrated mass daily.[63] In 1535 the net income was £7 4s. 8d.[64] and in 1549 the chantry was adequately supplied with plate and vestments.[65] After suppression its lands were granted to John Bellowe and Edward Streitbury;[66] the chaplain's house survived until 1768.[67]

An obit was founded by Simon de Ralegh (d. 1440) and another by Thomas Whalesborough. The latter, with property in Taunton, supported a priest. The estate was still held in 1547,[68] but is not recorded thereafter. There was a brotherhood of Our Lady by 1507 and lights of the High Cross, St. Nicholas, St. George, St. Anthony, St. Mary Magdalene, All Souls, Our Lady, Our Lady in the chancel, St. John the Baptist, and other lights described as Rood light and Christ light. An image of St. George was mentioned c. 1536.[69]

The church of the *BLESSED VIRGIN MARY*, so dedicated by 1440,[70] is built of local red sandstone and comprises chancel with north chapel and south organ chamber, clerestoried nave with north and south aisles, north porch, and west tower. The 14th-century rib-vaulted recesses in the south aisle contained not only the two surviving Ralegh effigies but also two wooden ones, assumed to be Ralegh wives, which were removed in the 19th century.[71] The aisle was probably the chapel which in 1440 was dedicated to St. John the Baptist.[72] Before the south chapel was rebuilt as an aisle the tower was built; it contains a bell of c. 1440.[73] The Devon style

[38] Ibid. D/D/Cf; D/D/Bg 8; ibid. D/P/net 3/1/1; ibid. tithe award.
[39] Ibid. tithe award; ibid. D/P/net 3/4/1.
[40] Ibid. D/D/Ca 57.
[41] Ibid. D/D/Rg 351.
[42] Ibid. DD/SP, inventory 1724.
[43] Ibid. D/D/Bg 8.
[44] Ibid. D/P/net 3/4/1–2; ibid. DD/CC E4874. Combe was bombed in 1942: ibid. DD/KW 146/58.
[45] S.R.S. i. 119.   [46] S.R.S. xlix, p. 129.
[47] S.R.S. liv, pp. 73, 95.
[48] S.R.S. xxi. 162; S.R.O., D/D/Vc 20.
[49] S.R.O., DD/WO 49/9; ibid. D/D/Ca 27; below.
[50] S. & D. N. & Q. xiv. 63.
[51] S.R.O., DD/WO 54/12; ibid. D/P/net 2/1/3.
[52] Ibid. D/P/net 2/1/4.
[53] Ibid. D/D/B returns 1815, 1827.
[54] Rep. Com. Eccl. Revenues, pp. 146–7; S.R.O., D/D/V returns 1840, 1843; ibid. D/P/net 2/1/4.
[55] P.R.O., HO 129/313/3/3/3.
[56] S.R.O., D/D/V returns 1870.

[57] Clergy Dir. (1900).
[58] S.R.O., DD/WO 49/1, 9; ibid. D/P/net 4/4/1.
[59] Ibid. DD/WO 43/1.   [60] Ibid. D/P/net 13/2/2.
[61] Ibid. DD/WO 55/11.
[62] S.R.S. extra ser. 370–1; xlix, pp. 216–20; Cal. Pat. 1441–6, 161; S.R.O., DD/WO 61.
[63] S.R.S. xlix, pp. 216–20; S.R.O., DD/WO 62/9.
[64] Valor Eccl. (Rec. Com.), i. 224.
[65] S.R.S. ii, pp. xxi, 48, 221; P.R.O., E 117/8; B.L. Harl. MS. 605, ff. 4–5; an inventory of chantry goods was made in 1545–6: Reliquary (1892) p. 3.
[66] Cal. Pat. 1548–9, 209–10; S.R.S. lxxvii, pp. 23–4.
[67] S.R.O., DD/WO 10/14, 44/12.
[68] S.R.S. ii. 48; xvi. 146–7; S.R.O., DD/WO 11/5; 49/1, 9.
[69] S.R.S. xix. 197–8; Wells Wills, ed. Weaver, 110; S.R.O., DD/WO 49/1.
[70] S.R.S. xvi. 146–7.
[71] Proc. Som. Arch. Soc. xxxi. 74.
[72] Above.
[73] S.R.O., DD/SAS CH 16.

capitals of the south arcade are copied in a different stone in the north arcade, which was formed when that aisle was built c. 1536.[74] The north chancel chapel of Our Lady and St. George, planned under the will of Sir John Trevelyan (d. 1521),[75] was being built between 1531 and 1534.[76]

The stair giving access to the pulpit formerly led to the rood loft, which was taken down in 1529–30 when the north nave wall was being demolished.[77] The loft was finally taken down in 1562.[78] The carved font, of East Anglian design, depicts the Seven Sacraments.[79] There are some bench ends dating from the late 16th century. The floor, paved in the earlier 18th century, includes some medieval titles in the south aisle. There was a singing loft in 1713.[80]

The church was restored by Richard Carver c. 1820.[81] More extensive work was done between 1858 and 1870 by C. E. Giles under the guidance of James Babbage, the Trevelyan agent, who claimed that the new clerestory made the church look two centuries older.[82] The church contains monuments to the Trevelyans and their servants.

The chalice and paten of 1479, the oldest dated church plate in the country, were in 1980 in the St. Nicholas Church Museum, Bristol; the church also possessed a flagon of Charles I's reign until c. 1956, when it was sold to pay for church restoration.[83] The registers date from 1540 and are complete except for a gap between 1646 and 1653.[84]

NONCONFORMITY. None known.

EDUCATION. In 1819 a school was established at Yard by the rector, George Trevelyan, which then took 120 poor children. Those whose parents could afford it paid 2d. a week. At the same time a Sunday

school was attended by 80 children.[85] The Sunday school, with an average attendance of 60 children, was still in existence in 1851.[86] In 1825–6 there were 130 children at the day school.[87] In 1835, out of a total of 107 at the school, 42 children were paid for by Sir John Trevelyan, his son Walter, and the rector; the rest were paid for by their parents.[88] The schools were said to be 'going on well' in 1846 when there were 96 children.[89] The Trevelyans continued their support, and occasional voluntary rates were levied.[90]

In 1903 Sir Walter John Trevelyan leased the premises to the rector and churchwardens at a peppercorn rent.[91] There were then 34 children on the books.[92] In 1931, after the senior pupils were transferred to Washford and Williton, only 29 remained. During the next decade numbers fell still further until in 1945 there were only 5 children on the books and the school was closed.[93] In 1980 the former school building was shared between a private house and the village hall. The schoolroom and teacher's house were designed by Richard Carver in 1819 for Sir John Trevelyan,[94] and are of colour-washed rubble with gables and traceried windows.

CHARITIES FOR THE POOR. Edward Milborne, rector 1579–1604, gave £10 to set the poor to work, and other bequests of unknown origin provided a further £30 capital.[95] In 1655 it was decided to use the money for the benefit of the second poor, and distributions of the interest were made until the early 19th century, augmented with blankets given by the Trevelyan family.[96] Between 1826 and 1894 the capital was held by the Trevelyans, who paid interest which was laid out in clothes by the churchwardens.[97] The charity has since been lost.[98]

EAST QUANTOXHEAD

THE PARISH of East Quantoxhead, known in the 13th century as Great Quantoxhead,[99] takes its name from its position on the headland of the Quantocks 'where seaward Quantock stands as Neptune he controld'.[1] The parish runs south from the low cliffs on the coast across a vigorously undulating coastal strip, and then up the scarp by ridge or combe to the top of the Quantocks, forming a wedge-shaped area 6.5 km. long and at most 3.5 km. wide. The whole

parish comprises 946 ha. (2,338 a.), of which slightly more than half is open land on the hills.[2]

Most of the boundaries of the parish on the high ground appear to follow tracks, notably the western limit, the prehistoric Quantock ridgeway, which was still in the late 17th century the road to Taunton.[3] To the east the boundary with Kilve runs for a short distance along Hodders Combe and is thereafter an arbitrary line, often disputed in the 17th century

[74] Wells Wills, ed. Weaver, 110; S.R.O., DD/WO 49/1.
[75] S.R.S. xix. 197–8.
[76] S.R.O., DD/WO 42/26, 49/2.
[77] Ibid. 49/1. [78] Ibid. 49/9.
[79] Pevsner, South and West Som. 254; above, plate facing p. 109.
[80] S.R.O., D/P/net 4/1/2.
[81] Ibid. DD/WO 35/1.
[82] Ibid. 55/11; ibid. D/P/net 8/3/2.
[83] Ibid. D/P/net 9/3/1.
[84] Ibid. 2/1/1–9.
[85] Educ. of Poor Digest, H.C. 224 (1819), ix (2).
[86] P.R.O., HO 129/313/3/3/3.
[87] Ann. Rep. B. & W. Dioc. Assoc. S.P.C.K. (1825–6).
[88] Educ. Enq. Abstract, H.C. 62 (1835), xlii.
[89] J. B. Clarke, Acct. of Church Educ. among Poor (1846); Nat. Soc. Inquiry, 1846–7, Som. 12–13.

[90] S.R.O., C/E 27; ibid. DD/CCH 45.
[91] Ibid. DD/CCH 2/2; Char. Com. files.
[92] S.R.O., C/E 27.
[93] Ibid. Schs. Lists; ibid. C/E 16; ibid. D/P/net 18/11/1.
[94] Ibid. D/P/net 18/11/1.
[95] Char. Don. H.C. 511 (1816), xvi; S.R.O., D/P/net 2/1/2.
[96] S.R.O., D/P/net 13/2/1, 17/1–3.
[97] 15th Rep. Com. Char. 452; Char. Com. files.
[98] Inf. from the Revd. N. Swinburn.
[99] S.R.S. xli, p. 15; Feud. Aids, iv. 275. This article was completed in 1978.
[1] M. Drayton, Poly-Olbion (1612).
[2] V.C.H. Som. i. 351.
[3] L. V. Grinsell, Prehist. Sites in Quantock Country, 20; map by George Withiel 1687 in the possession of Lt.-Col. G. W. F. Luttrell, Court House.

despite a 15-ft. strip and frequent boundary cairns. One heap of stones above Short Combe was then described as 'the place of parley' about an encroachment made by the lord of Kilve manor. Towards the coast Perry Gully formed the limit on the west, and a dispute there in the late 17th century was caused by the diversion of the watercourse into West Quantoxhead.[4]

Most of the land above the 76 m. contour is on Hangman Grit,[5] and rises to over 320 m. on Black Ball Hill (Balack Hill 1687) and Thorncombe Hill. By the end of the 17th century the high ground in the parish was divided by the Great Road from Nether Stowey to Watchet: to the south lay 472 a. of the lord's common; to the north were 692 a. of the tenants.[6] Between the scarp and the coast the parish is on Keuper marls, with an outcrop of Hangman Grit and substantial patches of valley gravels and limestone from Lower Lias and Rhaetic beds.[7] A limekiln was built near the coast in the north-east c. 1797,[8] and another there and one a little further west by 1839,[9] all to burn imported stone, though a fourth near the eastern boundary by 1886 presumably produced lime from stone dug nearby.[10] The coastal area is crossed by small streams one of which, presumably that flowing through East Quantoxhead village, was bridged by the late 13th century.[11]

The headland of the Quantocks is rich in Bronze Age burial mounds and twenty-six have been identified in the parish.[12] No early signs of occupation have been recognized on the coastal strip, but two mounds, one supporting a windmill in the 18th century,[13] had begun as burial cairns.[14] There were two main settlements in the Middle Ages, both on major watercourses running from the hills. East Quantoxhead village lies largely on a single street leading south from the manor house and the church, with a westward extension along what was later called West Street, Church Path or Lane, or Underway Lane,[15] leading to the second settlement, Perry. The lane ceased to be a through route during the 19th century, and the hamlet of Perry contracted at the same time, though it had once been divided into Higher and Lower Perry, and in the early 18th century had contained at least seven dwellings.[16] The main farm there in the 14th century had a house with a temporary oratory,[17] and a dovecot and an oxhouse are mentioned in 1407-8.[18]

East of the main village the road from Perry provided a direct link through Kilve to the Luttrell

property in Kilton until the late 17th century or later.[19] The route in the 1670s ran north to the coast before turning east, but claims for its repair in the manor court until 1723 suggest a more direct route beside East Wood.[20] There was also a road linking the village with Putsham, its course stopped in 1818.[21] The substantial number of travellers helped by the churchwardens in the early 17th century is evidence of the frequent use of roads through the parish.[22]

There were two, and possibly three, other medieval settlements. Combe is mentioned by 1273 and throughout the 14th century.[23] It had close links with an estate in Holford and may have been near the eastern boundary by Higher Pardlestone.[24] It was also probably near the contemporary hamlet called Domescombe, later Dennaryscombe (1394) and Dunscombe (1687), where the stream through Dun Combe or Denscombe emerges into the fields on the edge of the common.[25] The third possible settlement, perhaps representing an extension of the main village north of the manor house, seems to have lain in an area known as Plantesayssh (1407) or Plontesyaysshe (1495), the bounds of which included a field later called Plains.[26] The bounds themselves extended into the sea 'so far as the lord of the manor could ride on a horse pulling a "slegge" weighing 12 lb.'.[27] A new house was mentioned there in 1408.[28] No remains of any settlement have been found there, but closes adjoining the manor house called Town Place and Culverhays in the 17th century suggest that the present isolation of the house may have been the result of contraction of settlement.[29] In contrast, the spread of houses south of the village to Townsend, first traced in 1616,[30] and having a smithy by 1688,[31] is an indication of the growing use of the higher east–west route through the parish away from the original settlements, and the consequent decline of the road between East Quantoxhead village and Perry. Isolated cottages were built in the 18th century along steep lanes leading to the small inclosures on the edge of the common land.[32] The higher route was straightened and improved c. 1828.[33]

There is no evidence of open fields in the late 14th and the 15th century;[34] demesne pasture called West field, recorded in 1404, suggests conversion from arable,[35] but there remained a wide band of demesne arable and grassland in the centre of the parish in the late 17th century.[36] Field names of the 16th century and field patterns at Perry and south-east of East

[4] Map 1687; sketch of the same, S.R.O., DD/L 1/10/35A; ibid. 2/15/82, map of Perry.
[5] Geol. Surv. Map, 1″, drift, sheet 295 (1956 edn.).
[6] Map 1687.
[7] Geol. Surv. Map, 1″, drift, sheet 295 (1956 edn.).
[8] S.R.O., DD/L 2/14/75, lease Luttrell to Jenkins mentions kilns 'built or to be built', 1797.
[9] S.R.O., tithe award.
[10] O.S. Map 6″, Som. XXXVI. SE. (1886 edn.).
[11] Cal. Close, 1272-9, 24, refers to a bridge and to Ralph de Ponte. Philyce or Felyce bridge occurs in 1407: S.R.O., DD/L P22/5.
[12] Proc. Som. Arch. Soc. cxiii, suppl. 30-1.
[13] S.R.O., DD/L 2/15/82, map of Perry. There was a field called Stoneborowe in 1611: ibid. DD/L P23/38.
[14] Proc. Som. Arch. Soc. cxiii, suppl. 30-1.
[15] Map 1687; S.R.O., DD/L 2/15/77; O.S. Map 6″, Som. XXXVI. SE. (1886 edn.). [16] S.R.O., DD/L 2/15/82.
[17] S.R.S. x, p. 494.   [18] S.R.O., DD/L P22/5.
[19] Ibid. DD/L 1/10/35A.   [20] Ibid. 2/15/77.
[21] Ibid. Q/SR, Easter 1818.
[22] Ibid. D/P/qua.e 4/1/1, e.g. 1636.

[23] Cal. Close, 1272-9, 24; S.R.O., DD/L P22, deed, Gryme to Ralegh, 1375; S.R.S. iii. 165.
[24] S.R.O., DD/L P22, deeds, Coume to Holford, 1313, and Holford to Bozun, 1314.
[25] Ibid. DD/L P22/3; map 1687; Cal. Close, 1272-9, 24; S.R.S. iii. 165. The site of Domescombe is approximately ST 140419.
[26] S.R.O., DD/L P22/5, P23/16; ibid. tithe award.
[27] Ibid. DD/L P23/16.
[28] Ibid. P22/5.   [29] Map 1687.
[30] S.R.O., DD/L P23/41, Luttrell to Saunders.
[31] Ibid. DD/L 2/13/72, Luttrell to Pearce.
[32] e.g. S.R.O., DD/L 2/13/73, Luttrell to Chilcott, 1722, Yarde to Wythers, 1724. Newly inclosed ground at Townsend occurs in 1620: ibid. DD/L P23/43, Luttrell to Cockeslie. At least 40 plots had been formed from common by 1839: ibid. tithe award.
[33] 9 Geo. IV, c. 84 (Local and Personal); S.R.O., DD/L 2/15/82.
[34] The surviving account and ct. rolls are S.R.O., DD/L P22, P23.   [35] Ibid. DD/L P22/5.
[36] Map 1687.

Quantoxhead village at the same date suggest the division of fields into small closes.[37] Closes called Waterleets are recorded in 1273,[38] and the name survived above Perry in the 1550s.[39] In the 18th century the mill stream in the village was diverted at weekends to flood a meadow.[40] The stream's present course is man-made.

Knowle wood and Marshwood are found in the 13th century, Northwood and Morewood in the 15th,[41] though Northwood was partly cultivated in 1407–8.[42] Knowle wood, running up the scarp in the centre of the parish, covered twice its present area in the 1680s;[43] Northwood lay in the north-eastern tip bordering the cliffs, and was surrounded by a pale in the 1490s.[44] East wood, first so named in 1723, may be the later name for Marshwood.[45] Bircham wood was established between Sheppards and Slaughterhouse combes on the Quantocks by 1687.[46]

In 1412 a 6-a. farm was let on condition that a house of three bays was built within two years.[47] Most of the buildings in the village date from the 18th or 19th centuries, and include three terraces of thatched cottages. Nearly all stand on foundations occupied in the late 17th century.[48] Nos. 43 and 45 East Quantoxhead, at the extreme south end of the village street, is a late medieval house with former open hall, a first floor having been inserted c. 1600.[49]

A beer retailer is recorded in 1894.[50] The village hall was built in 1913 in memory of Mrs. Alice Luttrell. The hall included a library and baths.[51]

The population of the parish was 151 in 1667.[52] It was 262 in 1801 and rose only slightly during the earlier 19th century to 281, and then markedly to 339 in 1861. From that year there were losses each decade until 1911 (138) and then slight recoveries until the Second World War. In 1971 the population was 131.[53]

Sarah Biffin (1784–1850), the limbless painter of miniatures, was born in the parish.[54]

MANOR. The manor of *EAST QUANTOXHEAD* or *GREAT QUANTOXHEAD*[55] was held T.R.E. by Merlesuain. By 1086 it was owned by Ralph Pagnell, one of the two owners of the later barony of Hooton Pagnell (Yorks. W.R.). Ralph de Reuilly held the manor as his tenant.[56] Ralph Pagnell died between 1118 and 1124, and was followed by his

son William (d. c. 1146). Their estate, which also included Irnham manor (Lincs.), descended through William's daughter Alice (d. before 1181) to her daughter Avice, wife of Robert de Gaunt,[57] and then to their son Maurice (d. 1230).[58] Maurice de Gaunt died without issue, and his heir was Andrew Luttrell, son of Frethesant Pagnell, Ralph Pagnell's grandchild, by Geoffrey Luttrell (I) (d. 1216–17).[59]

Andrew Luttrell succeeded in 1232,[60] and his descendants have owned the property ever since. The manor was granted by Andrew to his second son Alexander,[61] and it was later said to be held of the senior branch of the family as of the manor or barony of Irnham.[62] The overlordship thus descended from Andrew Luttrell (d. 1265), through his son Sir Geoffrey (II) (d. c. 1270) to his grandson Robert (d. 1297); it was claimed in 1366 by Sir Andrew Luttrell,[63] and in 1493 was held by the heirs of Geoffrey Luttrell.[64]

Alexander Luttrell had died by June 1273, probably on crusade. His heir, Andrew, was a minor, and his widow received not only dower but held the remainder at farm. Andrew was still alive in 1310[65] but was probably dead by 1324.[66] The manor then passed in succession to his son Alexander (d. 1354), to Alexander's son Thomas (d. c. 1366), and to Thomas's son Sir John, K.B. (d. 1403).[67] Sir John was succeeded by his cousin, Sir Hugh Luttrell, owner of Dunster, on whose death in 1428 it passed to his son John (d. 1430). John's son and successor Sir James died of wounds after the second battle of St. Albans in 1461, and soon afterwards was attainted for his support of the Lancastrians.[68] Ten years earlier his wife Elizabeth had received the manor as part of her jointure, but her claims were over-ridden, and in 1463 the Luttrell estates were given to Sir William Herbert (cr. earl of Pembroke 1468).[69] Herbert was executed in 1469 and the manor reverted to the Crown during the minority of his heir, but from 1472 it was held by trustees, evidently for Elizabeth Luttrell's benefit.[70] By 1475 she had apparently regained her jointure.[71]

Elizabeth Luttrell died in 1493, leaving the manor to her son Sir Hugh, K.B. (d. 1521), who evidently lived there. His widow Walthean held it as her jointure until her death in the following year, having refused to be driven out by her son Andrew.[72] Andrew, who also lived on the manor, died in 1537, and his widow occupied the property until 1580. Meanwhile their son Sir John Luttrell died in 1551,

[37] S.R.O., DD/L P3/18; map 1687.
[38] Cal. Close, 1272–9, 24.
[39] S.R.O., DD/L P3/18.
[40] Ibid. DD/L 2/15/72, 78, 83.
[41] Cal. Close, 1272–9, 24; S.R.O., DD/L P22/5, 9, 12.
[42] S.R.O., DD/L P22/5.
[43] Map 1687.
[44] S.R.O., DD/L P23/16; DD/L 1/10/35A; ibid. tithe award.
[45] Ibid. DD/L 2/15/77. The route from Marshwood mead to Kilton is mentioned in 1690–1.
[46] Map 1687.
[47] S.R.O., DD/L P22/10.
[48] Map 1687.
[49] S.R.O., DD/V Wlr 8.1.
[50] Kelly's Dir. Som. (1894).
[51] Ibid. (1923).
[52] S.R.O., DD/WY 34.
[53] V.C.H. Som. ii. 351; Census, 1911–71.
[54] D.N.B.
[55] Feud. Aids, iv. 275; S.R.S. xli, p. 15; Rot. Hund. (Rec. Com.), ii. 125.
[56] V.C.H. Som. i. 510; Sanders, Eng. Baronies, 55.
[57] Son of Rob. FitzHarding, lord of Berkeley (Glos.).
[58] Sanders, Eng. Baronies, 55; Bk. of Fees, i. 83.
[59] Sanders, Eng. Baronies, 55; Cal. Inq. Misc. i, p. 8; Close R. 1227–31, 373, 437, 499, 504.
[60] Close R. 1231–4, 59.
[61] S.R.O., DD/L P22/1; Maxwell Lyte, Dunster, 66.
[62] Feud. Aids, iv. 275, 304.
[63] Maxwell Lyte, Dunster, 72–3.
[64] Cal. Inq. p.m. Hen. VII, iii, p. 349.
[65] Maxwell Lyte, Dunster, 66–7; Cal. Close, 1272–9, 24, 103; Rot. Hund. (Rec. Com.), ii. 125; S.R.S. xli, p. 15.
[66] Cal. Pat. 1321–4, 394, 444.
[67] Maxwell Lyte, Dunster, 72–4.
[68] Ibid. 122.
[69] Cal. Pat. 1461–7, 286, 366.
[70] Ibid. 1467–77, 330; Maxwell Lyte, Dunster, 125–6.
[71] Cal. Pat. 1467–77, 522.
[72] P.R.O., C 142/37, no. 116; C 142/106, no. 55; ibid. STAC 2/16, ff. 20–22; Cat. Anct. D. iii, A 5501, A 5505; Maxwell Lyte, Dunster, 135–7.

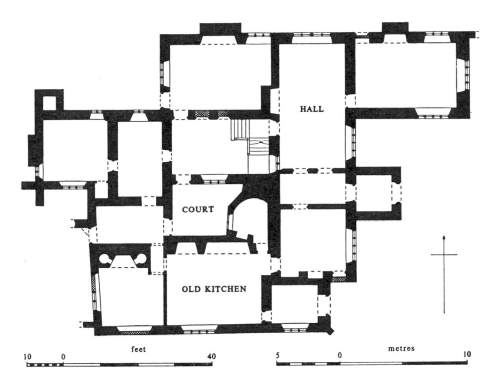

HALL

COURT

OLD KITCHEN

feet   metres
10   0   40   5   0   10

COURT HOUSE, EAST QUANTOXHEAD

leaving three daughters. Their uncle, Thomas Lut-trell (d. 1571), acquired their shares between 1560 and 1569,[73] and left the reversion to his son George.

George Luttrell died in 1629, leaving the manor in the hands of his widow Silvestra. She tyrannized her second husband, Sir Edmund Skory, and out-lived both her stepson Thomas Luttrell (d. 1644) and Thomas's son and heir George (d. 1655). The manor passed on her death after 1655 to George's brother Francis Luttrell (d. 1666).[74] It thereafter descended with the main Dunster estate like the manor of Kilton. The manor house was let to tenant farmers until Alexander Fownes Luttrell went to live there in 1888. His son Geoffrey lived at Dunster, but his grandson, Lt.-Col. G. W. F. Luttrell, lord-lieutenant of Somerset since 1978, lived at East Quantoxhead in 1980.[75]

The manor house, known as Court House from the 19th century,[76] stands on a knoll between the village and the sea, with the church and farm build-ings on its southern side. In 1273 the house was adjoined by two stone-roofed houses, one opposite the hall, and by farm buildings, a gatehouse, gardens, and fishponds.[77] A great chamber is referred to in 1403–4, a tile-covered 'loigge' in 1421–2, and a buttery garden in 1478–9.[78] In 1408–9 a carpenter made a 'stresschold' for the oriel door and a new 'enterclose' for the oriel.[79] The plan of this evidently substantial house cannot now be recognized in the

present building, but its strategic position, overlook-ing the Bristol Channel, might suggest that the form of the early building was determined as much by the requirements of defence as by domestic conventions.

The surviving medieval portions are an embattled four-storeyed tower and a wall adjacent to it at the south-east corner, and the short west range. The contemporary intervening buildings were removed or altered beyond recognition in a major rebuilding of the early 17th century.[80] This rebuilding appears to have taken place in two stages. The first provided a new south range with a northern return at its west end and a newel staircase at the east end of its north side. The stair turret is in the angle with the later hall range, which implies that the hall replaces an older building on its site. In the south range the principal room on the ground floor was the kitchen; on the first floor two rooms have plaster friezes and decorated overmantels, one of which is dated 1614. The second phase of rebuilding must have been separated from the first by only a few years and pro-vided the new or reconstructed range which now forms the north and east sides of the house and a well staircase in the angle between them. The east range contains the hall, the screens passage which is entered through a two-storeyed porch, and the study which is adjacent to the old kitchen (now the estate office) and may formerly have been a service room. The upper end of the hall extends to the north wall

[73] Cal. Pat. 1560–3, 86; 1563–6, p. 270; 1566–9, p. 301; P.R.O., C 142/159, no. 43; ibid. CP 25(2)/204/11 & 12 Eliz. I Mich.; Maxwell Lyte, Dunster, 140.

[74] P.R.O., C 142/455, no. 82; ibid. CP 40/2666, rot. 10; Maxwell Lyte, Dunster, 178–9.

[75] Proc. Som. Arch. Soc. xcii. 37; local inf.

[76] Below, local govt.   [77] Cal. Close, 1272–9, 24.

[78] S.R.O., DD/L P22/5, 9, 12; P23/15.

[79] Ibid. 22/5, memo. attached to roll.

[80] Sir Hugh Luttrell (d. 1521) has been claimed as a substantial builder there: Maxwell Lyte, Dunster, 132; below, plate facing p. 125.

of the house and the drawing room is in a wing which projects to the east. The decoration of the rooms in the hall and drawing room ranges is of the earlier 17th century, and one fireplace is dated 1629. Both stages of rebuilding were thus undertaken by George Luttrell (d. 1629), perhaps finished after his death by his widow; one room behind the kitchen was built by Francis Luttrell in 1689.[81]

East of the house is a walled forecourt, and gardens extend down the slopes east and south-east. To the north-east a long rectangular pond has been formed from a group of fishponds.

ECONOMIC HISTORY. The estate in 1086 measured 7 hides; it was one of those holdings where the ploughlands, 20 in number, far exceeded the number of teams, and where the value had fallen since the Confessor's time. The demesne farm of $5\frac{1}{4}$ hides may have been predominantly under grass or uncultivated moorland, since there were only 2 ploughteams there, while the tenants had 7 teams for their $1\frac{3}{4}$ hide.[82]

The demesne in 1273 included 112 a. of arable, 10 a. of meadow, 15 a. of several pasture, and 160 a. of common pasture on Quantock. There were 2 free tenants paying rent and 9 villein tenants. Some of the arable was described as in furlongs, while the size of other areas varied from a single unit of 45a. and 20 a. in two crofts, to a small piece of 2 a.[83] During the period 1402–33[84] the income from the manor averaged just over £41, and the sales of grain (mostly of wheat) and stock accounted for up to a third of the total. The demesne farm then included at least nine large arable inclosures, cropped in rotation; the extent of arable thus varied each year, averaging 132 a. Until 1433 sheep farming yielded usually between £4 and £5 from the sale of wool and skins, and the size of the flock[85] fluctuated, producing 644 fleeces in the best year, 1418–19, though only 18 fleeces came from reared lambs and most from wethers recently bought in Wales. Wool was sold either through the Luttrell estate surveyor or direct to purchasers, including a man from Stogursey.

The demesne farm in 1404 was staffed by a hayward, a shepherd, 4 ploughmen, 4 drovers, 2 grangers, and a dairy keeper. The dairy was mentioned infrequently: butter and cheese were produced from 11 cows in 1405–6, there were 9 cows in 1413, and the milking of 5 was sold in 1415–16. Other stock were usually few in number. Crops sown in 1405–6, reflecting the normal balance, were 104 a. of wheat, 15 a. of oats, and 24 a. divided between peas, barley, beans, and rye. Customary works were not of great significance. Services were owed according to the standard sizes of holdings: a 24-a. tenant in 1403, with an additional pasture holding, owed 2 days for ploughing and 2 for reaping, his harrowing was commuted for 1d., and he gave to the lord annually a bushel of wheat.[86] The theoretical total of works was 146 in 1402–3, but already by the 1380s cash rents had been introduced, and by 1412 all works were commuted for cash.[87]

The economy began to change in the early 1430s. The sheep flock was transferred permanently to Carhampton in 1431–2, and there was a slight decrease in demesne arable. By 1450 parts of the demesne were let, and all grain and stock were sent to the lord's household and not sold. More demesne was let in the next few years, producing over £5 in new rents; among other changes a small flock of sheep was again kept and, in 1457–8, customary works were revived. The total cash income after these changes averaged only just over £27, though the net value of the estate was probably greater than thirty years earlier.[88]

Tenant farms were reckoned by the late 14th century at 24 a., 12 a., or 6 a., and some were then being let for two lives.[89] In 1403 there were 14 holdings of 24 a., 3 of 12 a., 4 of 6 a., and there were 11 cottagers with 2 a. or 3 a.[90] Holdings like that of William Poulett called Tresouresplace in 1427–8,[91] or of John Pury, which united two customary holdings and some demesne,[92] show relatively frequent change of tenant and the engrossment of holdings. From the 1540s land was leased in relatively large units, and by the 1570s there were 8 holdings ranging in size between 40 a. and 124 a. Wheat still predominated as a crop in the 16th century, the wheatlands covering some 466 a. in the 1570s, while ryelands, probably on the hills, amounted to 55 a.[93] The legal status of tenants retained its traditional pattern, with 22 customary leases, a holding by widowhood, and 3 tenants at will in 1581.[94]

By the 1680s the demesne farm or barton, measuring 406 a., was followed in size by 4 farms of between 40 a. and 55 a. and by 11 more over 20 a. The total number of holdings, which included altogether 1,028 a. of inclosed land, was only nineteen.[95] The demesne farm was kept in hand throughout the 17th century, but for most of the 18th it was let for periods of 5, 10, or 14 years,[96] while the tenant farms were held at the beginning of the 18th century either by copyhold or leasehold for lives, on the same pattern as thirty years before.[97] Licences granted in the manor court from the 1670s onwards allowed customary tenants to let their holdings for seven years or more.[98] Leases for lives still continued on small holdings in 1834, but consolidation of larger ones was achieved, for example, at Perry under a 14-year lease in the 1790s.[99] By 1839, with a demesne farm slightly reduced in size to 381 a., there were three other substantial farms, Bakers (253 a.), Perry (196 a.), and Townsend (155 a.).[1] Those four holdings, known in 1978 as Court House, Court, Perry, and Townsend farms, continued the pattern in the 1970s.

Farming practice as revealed in covenants of the

[81] S.R.O., DD/L 2/15/85.
[82] V.C.H. Som. i. 510; H.C. Darby and R. W. Finn, Dom. Geog. SW. Eng. 156.
[83] Cal. Close, 1272–9, 24.
[84] S.R.O., DD/L P22/5–6, 9–10, 12.
[85] There were two flocks in 1412–13: S.R.O., DD/L P22/5.
[86] Ibid. P22/6.
[87] Ibid. P22/5–6.
[88] Ibid. P22/12, P23/13, 15.
[89] Ibid. P22/3.

[90] Ibid. P22/6.
[91] Ibid. P22/6, 12.
[92] Ibid. P22/12.
[93] Ibid. P3/18.
[94] Ibid. P23/24.
[95] Map 1687.
[96] S.R.O., DD/L 2/14/74, 2/15/82.
[97] Ibid. 2/15/77, 82.
[98] Ibid. 2/13/69.
[99] Ibid. 2/14/75.
[1] Ibid. tithe award.

CLATWORTHY RESERVOIR FROM THE NORTH, *c.* 1960

QUANTOCK LANDSCAPE

From the west, with Bicknoller village right of centre below the spur of Bicknoller Hill

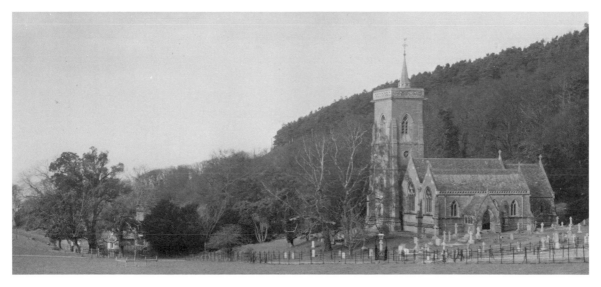

ST. AUDRIES, WEST QUANTOXHEAD: THE CHURCH AND PARK

HALSE MANOR FROM THE SOUTH-EAST IN 1831

EAST QUANTOXHEAD: COURT HOUSE FROM THE EAST

late 18th century was affected by national improvements; the growth of flax, hemp, and rape was discouraged, and turnips eaten by sheep were not regarded as a crop.[2] Lime was to be added in the usual precise quantities.[3] In 1839 there were 700 a. of arable and 273 a. of grass in the parish, with 1,135 a. of commonable land on the high ground.[4] By 1905 the land, excluding the higher parts of the parish, was almost equally divided between arable and grassland.[5] By 1976 arable had increased to about 60 per cent of the total.[6] Farming was almost the sole occupation in the parish by the mid 19th century, and the four main farms employed 52 men between them in 1851.[7] The stock on Court farm in 1853 included 315 sheep, 63 head of cattle including 16 oxen, and 5 colts.[8] Farming in the 1970s involved dairying, cattle, and sheep.[9]

The value of the commonable half of the parish is difficult to assess. General rights to graze and dig turf existed in the Middle Ages,[10] and the manor court supervized the repair of a common way there.[11] Unspecified areas of the common were noted as cultivated in 1454–5 and in the early 17th century, both probably on what was described as the lord's share of the common, in the 17th century for growing rye.[12] Unlicensed removal of furze, stones, and turf is recorded in the 16th and 17th centuries, and burning heath was prohibited in 1716.[13] In 1608 grazing on the northern part of the common was ordered to be restricted to customary tenants,[14] while the lord's share in the 1680s comprised pastures for wild bullocks.[15] The lord was responsible for all access gates,[16] and in 1724 he let a site for a cottage in Quantock Hill lane in return for maintaining the 'lord's bounds and banks' there. The new tenant was given 1,000 turves a year from 'the outer common called Lady's common'.[17] Common rights on the Quantocks were long established by the 18th century; for example a holding of 2 a. in the village had common for 20 sheep, 1 bullock or colt, and 2 days cut of turf by one man,[18] and the miller, with 4 a., could graze horses or cut turf.[19]

The beach and the sea contributed little to the income of the manor, but the lord used stones from the beach for building,[20] let certain fishing grounds, controlled the burning of seaweed, and until the end of the 18th century claimed wrecks.[21] Fishing from the ridge, an offshore bank, was let in the early 15th century,[22] but tenants could presumably fish from the shore, and until the 20th century used dogs to search for congers under the rocks.[23] The foreshore was let from the early 16th century for the collection and burning of seaweed. Surviving leases divided the coast into two or three areas and restricted burning to prevent smoke reaching the manor house.[24] The practice still continued in 1602.[25]

A clothing industry was established in the parish by the early 17th century. There was a dyehouse on the manor by 1611,[26] and by the 1670s it was held by the Shurt family, who were described as clothiers.[27] Two producers of serge were also there in the 17th century,[28] and cloth was racked in the village.[29] Clothiers, weavers, and tailors occur in small numbers throughout the 18th century, and include Philip Hellicar, formerly of Bicknoller, who had an interest in mining speculation in East Quantoxhead and later moved to Williton.[30] In the 1770s manor officers noted that courts should not be held in the village to clash with Wells fair, since the clothiers would be absent.[31] The industry evidently died out soon after 1800.

Search for copper ore in the parish, and also in Kilton, began shortly before 1713, and in the following year a mining lease granted to a London merchant and a group of local tradesmen refers to pits and mines already opened 'at Perry hill or Quantock'.[32] No further reference to mining has been found in the parish.

Six masons in the parish in 1851 probably worked at the quarries at West Quantoxhead, but the 3 carpenters and 3 blacksmiths found employment enough at home. There was then one shop.[33] By 1906 apartments were being offered to holiday makers, and by 1931 tea rooms had been opened.[34] The picturesque village was a popular attraction for visitors in the 1970s.

MILL. There was a mill on the demesne in 1086;[35] by 1341 it had two pairs of stones.[36] By the late 17th century it was usually let for periods of 7 years,[37] and by 1711 was held for a time by the tenant of the demesne farm.[38] In 1725 it was described as lately burnt, and the present mill house, a two-storeyed building of rubble with a thatched roof, is dated 1729.[39] The mill continued in operation as a flour mill until the early 1920s.[40]

[2] Ibid. DD/L 2/13/71.
[3] Ibid. 2/14/75, lease 1797.
[4] Ibid. tithe award.
[5] Statistics supplied by the then Bd. of Agric. 1905.
[6] Min. of Agric., Fisheries, and Food, agric. returns 1976.   [7] P.R.O., HO 107/1920.
[8] S.R.O., DD/WY 140.
[9] Min. of Agric., Fisheries, and Food, agric. returns 1976.
[10] S.R.O., DD/L P22, deeds, Luttrell to Bathe, 1340, Popham to Grove, 1379.
[11] Ibid. P22/6.
[12] Ibid. P22/12, P23/35.
[13] Ibid. P23/19, 35; 2/15/77.
[14] Ibid. P23/35.
[15] Map 1687.
[16] S.R.O., DD/L P23/56.
[17] Ibid. 2/13/73, Yarde to Wythers.
[18] Ibid. 2/13/73, Luttrell to Gribble, 1709.
[19] Ibid. 2/13/71, Luttrell to Popham, 1725.
[20] Ibid. P22/9, 1418–19.
[21] Ibid. 2/13/71, lease 1797.
[22] Ibid. P22/5, 10; V.C.H. Som. ii. 400.

[23] F. C. Gould, Natural Verses (1923); local inf.
[24] S.R.O., DD/L P23/19, 26, 26A, 35.
[25] Ibid. P23/35.
[26] Ibid. P23/38. A Dyehouse close occurs near Bullers fm. in 1839; ibid. tithe award.
[27] Ibid. DD/L P23/56 (1675, 1679); ibid. 2/7/37.
[28] Ibid. DD/SP, inventory of Jos. Conway 1678; DD/L 2/15/79.
[29] Ibid. DD/L 2/15/77 (1682). Rack mead and close occur in 1839: ibid. tithe award.
[30] Ibid. DD/L 2/13/73, 2/14/74, 2/15/83.
[31] Ibid. 2/15/77 (1770, 1772).
[32] Ibid. 2/13/71, 2/15/78, 83.
[33] P.R.O., HO 107/1920.
[34] Kelly's Dir. Som. (1906, 1931).
[35] V.C.H. Som. i. 510.
[36] S.R.O., DD/L P22, deed Alex. Luttrell to Rob. Pavely and John son of Rob. le Clerk.
[37] Ibid. DD/L 2/15/83.
[38] Ibid. 2/15/77, 82.
[39] Ibid. 2/13/71, 73. It bears the initials of Hugh Popham.
[40] Kelly's Dir. Som. (1910, 1923); local inf.

LOCAL GOVERNMENT. The tithing of East Quantoxhead, which included the manor of Beggearn Huish in Nettlecombe, was constituted in the time of Maurice de Gaunt (d. 1230).[41] There are rolls or extracts from courts held for East Quantoxhead manor for most years in the period 1382–1428, and for scattered sessions in 45 years between 1446 and 1592; for the periods 1593–1615 and 1675–80 the records are continuous.[42] Extracts, copies of presentments, and precepts survive for 1655 and for the periods 1682–1728, 1755–79, and 1820–90.[43] Courts were normally held twice a year and were usually described as leet or manor courts. The phrase 'view of frankpledge' was introduced by 1520 and was used regularly twice a year from the 1580s.[44] From 1691 until 1728 or later the Easter or Hockday court was discontinued, but it was revived again in the period 1755–9.[45] Thereafter annual courts, described in the 1760s as 'court leet and baron for the manor and borough', were normally held in late October.[46]

Sessions were held at the church house, the 'ancient and customary place', by 1722.[47] By 1772 the church house had become dilapidated, and in that year and in 1779 courts were held at the home of one of the court jurors. By 1865 and until 1886 sessions were held at the manor house, hence its name Court House, but from 1887, when Alexander Fownes Luttrell was preparing to take up permanent residence there, until 1890 or later, the court sat at Blanchflowers Farm.[48]

By the early 15th century the Michaelmas court was submitting names for the office of reeve, and itself appointed the hayward. The choice of tithingman seems also to have been made by the Michaelmas court by 1417. The reeve was probably no longer chosen by the court after the early 16th century, when the manor was administered with Kilton, but the court continued to appoint the tithingman and one or more haywards. The office of manor hayward is not found after 1604, and by the 1680s tenants served as tithingman in rotation or by deputy. The office continued until replaced by that of constable in 1842, and the constable served the precept on suitors until the 1870s. The office of pound keeper occurs between 1820 and 1890.

Like the court at Kilton, the manor court in the early 15th century seems to have been closely involved with the sale of grazing, stock, and produce, and regularly from 1408 for nearly 20 years included details of sales of wool and losses of sheep by disease.[49] The maintenance of watercourses and trespasses on common were regular concerns in the 15th and 16th centuries, and from the 17th the sur-vival of rights of way from the village to Kilve church and to the shore.[50] House and bridge repairs were frequently demanded from the 17th century. The court ordered the parish to provide a new pair of stocks in 1688,[51] and presented the tithing in 1708 for allowing the cucking stool and pillory to become damaged. The stocks were reported as out of repair in 1756.[52]

Parish accounts in 1605 were agreed by 6 men and 'all the rest',[53] and the rector, the wardens, the tithingman, and 7 others signed the appointment of highway surveyors in 1690.[54] In the 18th century nominations of wardens and overseers were made by the minister and between 2 and 6 people. There were normally two wardens, both nominated by the parish except between 1769 and 1799, and two overseers. There were two highway surveyors for some years after 1689. The office of overseer was held in rotation according to property qualifications.[55] The overseers regularly paid house rents and bought goods and clothing, and in the 1650s rented the church house, presumably for paupers.[56] In 1818 a house in the centre of the village was used as a poorhouse.[57] The parish became part of the Williton poor-law union in 1836, and joined Williton rural district in 1894 and the West Somerset district in 1974.[58]

CHURCH. There was a church at East Quantoxhead by 1259 when the advowson formed part of an estate bought by Henry de Gaunt for St. Mark's Hospital, Bristol. Possession was confirmed to the hospital in 1268,[59] but Andrew Luttrell (d. 1265) also claimed ownership, and gave the advowson to his second son Alexander.[60] The bishop of Bath and Wells appointed to the living in 1265 by authority of the King's council,[61] presumably before a settlement was reached. The Luttrells had established their claim by 1329[62] and thereafter the advowson descended with the manor. Trustees of James Luttrell appointed in 1442, Thomas Malet presented in 1484 in right of his wife Elizabeth, James Luttrell's widow, John Wyndham in 1543 as a trustee, and William Foster, clerk, in 1799 by grant of Francis Luttrell. The bishop appointed by lapse in 1766 and 1779.[63] The living was a sole rectory until 1975; it was held with Kilve and Kilton until 1978 and then became part of the benefice of Quantoxhead. Lt.-Col. G. W. F. Luttrell is one of three joint patrons of the benefice.[64]

The rectory was valued at £10 13s. 4d. in 1291[65] and at £10 0s. 4d. net in 1535.[66] The reputed value was £80 c. 1668,[67] and the net income was £325 in 1831.[68] The tithes in 1535 amounted to £8 16s. 4d.[69]

[41] Rot. Hund. (Rec. Com.), ii. 125.
[42] S.R.O., DD/L P3/18; P22/3, 6, 10, 12; P23/14–16, 19, 21, 24, 35, 38–9, 56 and unnumbered; P24/8–9.
[43] Ibid. DD/L 2/15/77.
[44] One session in 1469 was described as view of frankpledge and halmote: ibid. DD/L P23/15.
[45] Ibid. DD/L 2/6/31, 2/15/77.   [46] Ibid. 2/15/77.
[47] Ibid. 2/13/73.
[48] Ibid. 2/15/77.
[49] The same inf. is included in the bailiffs' accts.
[50] Above, intro.
[51] S.R.O., DD/L 2/15/77. The wardens had repaired stocks and cuckingstool in 1613: ibid. D/P/qua.e 4/1/1.
[52] Ibid. DD/L 2/15/77. The overseers had repaired them in 1729: ibid. D/P/qua.e 13/2/2.
[53] Ibid. D/P/qua.e 4/1/1.
[54] Ibid. 4/1/3.
[55] Ibid. 13/2/2.
[56] Ibid. 13/2/1; below, church.
[57] S.R.O., Q/SR, East. 1818.
[58] Youngs, Local Admin. Units, i. 435, 674, 676.
[59] Reg. Godfrey Giffard, ed. J. W. Willis Bund (Worcs. Hist. Soc.), i. 15.
[60] S.R.O., DD/L P22/1.
[61] S.R.S. xiii, p. 9.
[62] Ibid. i. 300.
[63] Ibid. xxxii, p. 279; lii, p. 127; Som. Incumbents, ed. Weaver, 423–4.
[64] Dioc. Dir.; S.R.O., D/P/qua.e 22/3/1.
[65] Tax. Eccl. (Rec. Com.), 198.
[66] Valor Eccl. (Rec. Com.), i. 215.
[67] S.R.O., D/D/Vc 24.
[68] Rep. Com. Eccl. Revenues, pp. 150–1.
[69] Valor Eccl. (Rec. Com.), i. 215.

and were commuted in 1839 to a rent charge of £265.[70] In 1630 the tithes included the right shoulder of every deer taken in the park, and were payable in kind on wool, lambs, calves, pigs, geese, apples, pears, hops, honey, and wax. There were moduses for hay from ancient meadow, milk, and first calves.[71] The glebe was worth 24s. in 1535,[72] and measured 27 a. in 1571 and apparently over 30 a. in 1630.[73] By 1839 the land was in a compact unit of just over 28 a.[74]

In 1635 the parsonage house included a hall and a great buttery with two chambers over it. Out-buildings comprised two barns, a stable, and a square house in the outer court gate. Many of the buildings were then dilapidated, and an additional wing on the house was unfinished.[75] That house stood until 1763, when it was virtually uninhabitable, and by 1799 there was said to be no house on the benefice.[76] A new house, designed by George Gale of Dunster,[77] was largely built between 1806 and 1810.[78] It was altered and extended in the 1830s or 1840s, and a verandah was added after 1880. The house was occupied by successive rectors until 1975, and was subsequently sold and renamed West House. The remains of the former house stand below the stable block.

Andrew Luttrell, presented as rector by his elder brother in 1329 before he was in major orders, was absent for study for at least two years, and in 1337 spent a year in his brother's service.[79] Richard Puldon, rector by 1366, surrendered to the Fleet prison in 1370 after outlawry for debt.[80] Richard Pynwyn, rector by 1440 and until 1442, was given three years leave of absence for medical treatment for his eyes.[81] The parish clerk was reported in 1612 as usually reading divine service when the minister was away, and at certain times also reading a homily.[82] William Bisse, rector 1634–77, escaped sequestration by the 'interest of a great man of the times', but his property was plundered 'several times'.[83] During the vacancy before his arrival the Laudian furnishings were installed,[84] but the communion rails were broken up in 1646 and the royal arms defaced in 1650.[85] The church was extensively repaired and decorated in 1698.[86]

During the later 18th century absentee rectors left most of the work to curates, partly for lack of a house.[87] At least two rectors, Leonard Herring (1763–6) and Laurence Luxton (1816–18), undertook to resign the living in favour of any member of the Luttrell family. Alexander Fownes Luttrell,

rector 1818–88, was presented on Luxton's resignation.[88] In 1776 there were nine regular communicants,[89] and the pattern of quarterly celebrations was unchanged from the 1600s until the 1870s or later.[90] Two Sunday services were normal during the 19th century, and on Census Sunday 1851 there were congregations of 27 in the morning and 120 in the afternoon, with 37 Sunday-school children at each service.[91]

By 1597 the church house, standing on the south side of the mill pond, was let by the lord of the manor.[92] In the 1650s it was occupied by the overseers and later by individual tenants, and by 1722 part was used for the manor court.[93] It was still standing in 1794, when it comprised three rooms on the ground floor, two occupied as shops, and a single room above.[94] It had been demolished by 1839.[95]

There was a light before the image of the Virgin from 1403,[96] and by 1548 there were other endowed lights.[97] Blessed bread and a candle were given to the church by the manor in 1427–8 in respect of a tenement then in hand.[98]

The church of *ST. MARY* comprises a chancel with north vestry, nave with south porch, and west tower, and stands close to the south side of Court House above the village. The vestry stands on the site of a larger north chancel aisle. An altar recently dedicated in 1329[99] and the surviving tower arch suggest an early 14th-century date for the origin of the present building. Foundations dug on the site in 1427–8 may have been connected with new work during refenestration.[1] The vestry was probably added during restoration in the 19th century. The rood screen may date from the late 14th century, and was formerly topped with a wide loft. The elaborate canopied tomb chest in the chancel, used as an Easter Sepulchre when the chancel aisle was standing, commemorates Hugh (d. 1521) and Andrew Luttrell (d. 1537). Andrew requested burial before the picture of Our Lady on the north side of the altar, and the window above was to be newly made.[2] The pulpit, reader's desk, communion rail, and benches date from the early 16th and the 17th century.[3]

The registers date from 1559 and are complete.[4]

NONCONFORMITY. There was one family of recusants in 1636, and it had been joined by Dame Silvestra Skory and a married couple by 1642. One recusant at least remained in the parish in 1654.[5]

---

[70] S.R.O., tithe award.
[71] Ibid. D/D/Rg 268.
[72] *Valor Eccl.* (Rec. Com.), i. 215.
[73] S.R.O., D/D/Rg 268.
[74] Ibid. tithe award.
[75] Ibid. D/D/Cd 81.
[76] Ibid. DD/L 2/1/3, 2/15/79.
[77] Ibid. 2/15/84, plans dated 1799, 1800, 1802.
[78] Ibid. 2/15/83–4; ibid. DD/HC 89.
[79] *S.R.S.* i. 300; ix, pp. 6, 20, 31, 64, 330.
[80] *Cal. Pat.* 1367–70, 360.
[81] *S.R.S.* xxxii, pp. 250–1, 279.
[82] S.R.O., D/D/Ca 175.
[83] *Walker Revised*, ed. A. G. Matthews.
[84] S.R.O., D/P/qua.e 4/1/1.
[85] Ibid. 4/1/2.
[86] Ibid. 4/1/3.
[87] Ibid. 2/1/4.
[88] Ibid. DD/L 2/13/69, 2/15/78.
[89] Ibid. D/D/Vc 88.

[90] Ibid. D/P/qua.e 4/1/1–5; ibid. D/D/B returns 1815, 1827; D/D/V returns 1840, 1870.
[91] P.R.O., HO 129/313/4/1/1.
[92] S.R.O., DD/L P23/46.
[93] Ibid. DD/L 2/13/72–3; ibid. D/P/qua.e 13/2/1.
[94] Ibid. DD/L 2/14/75.
[95] Ibid. tithe award.
[96] Ibid. DD/L P22/5, acct. 1402–3.
[97] *S.R.S.* ii. 51.   [98] S.R.O., DD/L P22/12.
[99] *S.R.S.* i. 300.
[1] S.R.O., DD/L P22/12.
[2] *S.R.S.* xxi. 41.
[3] The pulpit, made from fragments of early 16th-century panelling, may have been constructed in 1633, the date carved inside.
[4] S.R.O., DD/L 2/15/80 (register 1559–1653); ibid. D/P/qua.e 2/1/2–3.
[5] Ibid. D/D/Ca 310; *Som. Protestation Returns*, ed. Howard and Stoate, 289–90; *Cal. Cttee. for Compounding*, v. 3182.

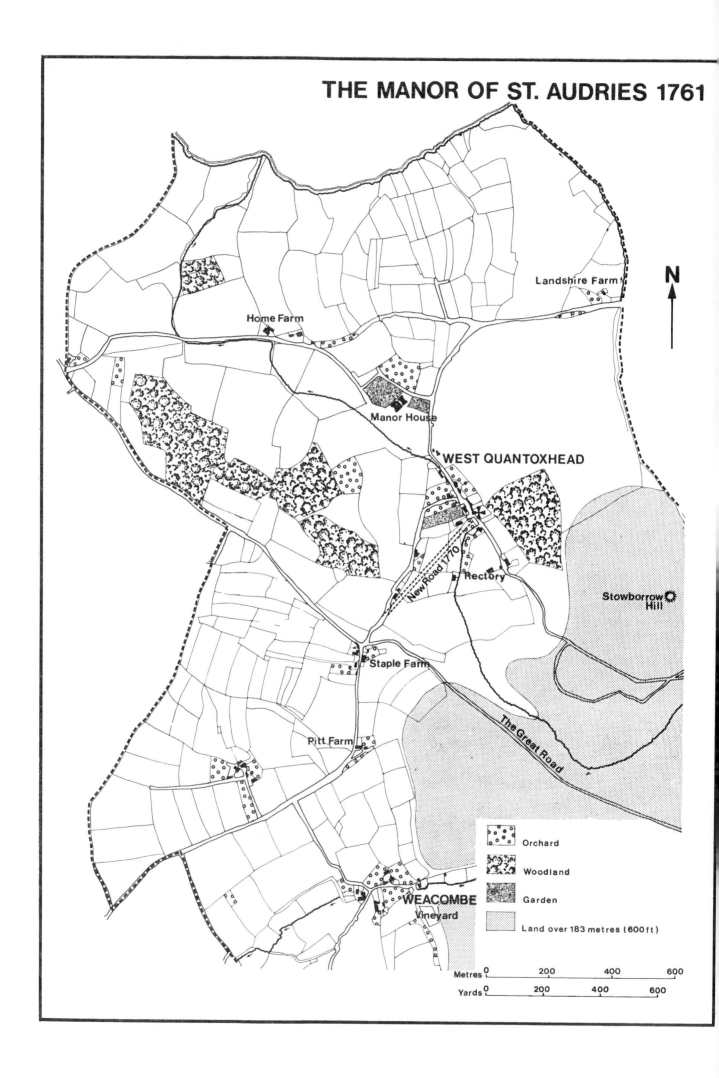

THE MANOR OF ST. AUDRIES 1761

N

Landshire Farm

Home Farm

Manor House

WEST QUANTOXHEAD

New Road 1770

Rectory

Stowborrow Hill

Staple Farm

The Great Road

Pitt Farm

WEACOMBE
Vineyard

Orchard

Woodland

Garden

Land over 183 metres (600 ft)

Metres 0   200   400   600

Yards 0   200   400   600

EDUCATION. There seems to have been a school in the parish in 1646.[6] A school established by 1819[7] had 60 children by 1825, of whom 50 attended on weekdays and all on Sundays.[8] The school was affiliated with the National Society by 1835,[9] and by 1839 was held in a building in the village street adjoining the cottage known in 1978 as no. 38 East Quantoxhead.[10] In 1846–7 there were 47 children on the books, of whom 33 attended both day and Sunday school and the remainder the Sunday school only. The school was largely supported by the rector, with parental contributions.[11] In 1876 G. F. Luttrell provided a new building on the road between East Quantoxhead and Kilve, to be shared between the two villages. Kilve and East Quantoxhead Council school, on its transfer to the county council in 1903, had 44 children on the books.[12] From 1930 only infants and juniors were taken. It was closed in 1971 and children have since attended school in Williton.[13]

CHARITIES FOR THE POOR. James Houndrell, possibly the benefactor to Kilton or his namesake at Kilve,[14] gave £20 to the second poor of East Quantoxhead, producing £1 a year.[15] The charity was said c. 1824 to have been augmented by a gift of £5 by a Mr. Pugsley at 'some distant period'.[16] William Hawkes (d. 1792) gave £100 and John Feltham (d. 1816) a similar sum.[17] In 1819 the capital, formerly in private hands, was invested to produce just over £10 a year, given in clothing at Christmas by the wardens.[18] In 1869–71 the income was £10 1s. 10d.[19] Alexander Fownes Luttrell, rector 1818–88, bequeathed £200 to the trustees of what was then known as the Parochial Charity,[20] and the annual income in 1891 was £15 14s. 10d.[21] In 1965 the charity was distributed between 11 recipients; in 1981 2 people received £7.50p. each.[22] Between 1700 and 1749 twenty people described as almsmen and almswomen were buried in the parish.[23]

WEST QUANTOXHEAD

THE PARISH of West Quantoxhead or St. Audries shares with East Quantoxhead the northern end of the Quantock ridge and the narrow coastal strip beyond.[24] Its 594 ha. (1,467 a.) extend nearly 3 km. from the coast to the top of Weacombe Hill, and it is between 1.5 km. and 2 km. wide. From Beacon Hill (310 m.) in the south-east, on the sandstone shales of the Quantocks, where Bronze Age barrows lie near the prehistoric ridgeway, the land falls gradually to the low cliffs of St. Audries bay in the north. Below the west-facing scarp, broken by the long and narrow Weacombe combe, the land levels out on gravels and marls.[25]

The main ancient settlement, the village of West Quantoxhead, lay at the head of a second, wider combe, sheltered from the east by Stowborrow Hill, where the land slopes to the coast over marls, shales, and limestone. A secondary Domesday settlement called Weacombe lay at the mouth of its combe. Landshire, in the north-east corner of the parish, seems to have emerged as a consolidated farm by the 14th century,[26] and Bidwell, north-west of Weacombe, occurs in the 13th century.[27] Quarries in the centre of the parish were extensively used in the 19th

century,[28] and lime was burned near the coast in the 17th century and dug at Landshire in the 18th.[29]

There were two ancient, roughly east-west routes through the parish: the coast road from Stogursey ran from Perry in East Quantoxhead to Rydon in St. Decumans, passing just north of the manor house, and the Great Road over the Quantocks from Nether Stowey to Watchet. A third route under the scarp ran northwards, linking Weacombe with the main village, crossing the Great Road at Staple, the centre of population since the 19th century.[30] The name Staple occurs in fields from the early 17th century, and the Staple highway is referred to in 1626.[31]

The village of West Quantoxhead thus lay between roughly parallel through routes, the manor house standing at the northern end of the village street. The extension of the park south and west of the house from the late 1820s had a profound effect on the parish, and particularly on its road system. The first stage was to straighten the road between Staple and the village in 1770.[32] The second was to divert the coast road to run further north from the manor house in 1815.[33] More significant was the replacement of that coast road by a route cut into the

[6] S.R.O., D/P/qua.e 4/1/2, opposite accts. for 1646.
[7] Educ. of Poor Digest, H.C. 224 (1819), ix(2).
[8] Ann. Rep. B. & W. Dioc. Assoc. S.P.C.K. (1825–6).
[9] Educ. Enq. Abstract, H.C. 62 (1835), xlii.
[10] S.R.O., tithe award.
[11] Nat. Soc. Inquiry, 1846–7, Som. 14–15.
[12] S.R.O., C/E 26.
[13] Ibid. Schs. Lists; ibid. D/P/qua.e 18/7/1–2, 4.
[14] Above, Kilve, Kilton, charities for the poor.
[15] Char. Don. H.C. 511 (1816), xvi. The gift was said c. 1824 to have been made 'above a century back': 15th Rep. Com. Char. p. 452; cf. printed copy of entries on former benefaction bd. (in ch.) where the date is 1610 and the benefaction £25.
[16] 15th Rep. Com. Char. p. 452; cf. Collinson, Hist. Som. iii. 501, which records a single charity; and cf. Char. Don., where Edm. Pugsley held some of the capital of the Houndrell char.
[17] 15th Rep. Com. Char. p. 452, but the name there is Hen. and not Wm. Hawkes; copy of benefaction bd.

[18] 15th Rep. Com. Char. p. 452.
[19] Digest Endowed Char. 1869–71, H.C. pp. 50–1 (1873), li.
[20] Char. Com. files.
[21] Digest Endowed Char. 1869–71.
[22] Inf. from Lt.-Col. G. W. F. Luttrell.
[23] S.R.O., D/P/qua.e 2/1/3.
[24] This article was completed in 1978.
[25] Geol. Surv. Map 1″, drift, sheet 295 (1956 edn.); Proc. Som. Arch. Soc. cxiii, suppl. 40–1; L. V. Grinsell, Prehist. Sites in Quantock Country, 4–5, 22.
[26] S.R.O., DD/DT; DD/WY 7/Z1c/8.
[27] S.R.S. xli. 200.
[28] S.R.O., DD/AH 22/5; P.R.O., HO 107/1920.
[29] S.R.S. xxviii. 357; S.R.O., DD/AH 40/2; P.R.O., HO 107/1920.
[30] S.R.O., DD/AH 40/1: map 1761.
[31] Ibid. D/D/Rg 365.
[32] Ibid. DD/AH 40/1.
[33] Ibid. Q/SR East. 1815.

rising ground east of the house which then followed the contour south and west in a gentle curve, cutting the village street between the church and the rectory house and joining the Great Road below Staple. The new route was formed by Act of Parliament of 1828 for adoption by the Minehead turnpike trust.[34] The village street thereafter gave access only to the manor house,[35] and its houses and cottages were gradually removed as tenants transferred to new homes at Staple. There were ten dwellings and other buildings there in 1761 and eight in 1835, a lease in 1783 having been conditional upon replacement of three dilapidated cottages by one dwelling. By 1840 there were only five dwellings, and by 1853 four, one having been removed to improve the view from the rectory house.[36] The park was thus gradually extended over the site of the village to the line of the turnpike road, and took its final form in the 1850s with a construction programme[37] involving the re-siting and rebuilding of the church (1854–6), almost alone at the main entrance to the park,[38] and the building of four lodges (Fairfield Lodge 1850, another by 1851).[39] The school was built at the edge of the park in 1857, and St. Audries or Home Farm was removed from its former site beside the coast road to a new one near the shore in 1855.[40] The whole park was surrounded by ornamental ironwork fencing and was linked to the deer park beyond the turnpike road by a bridge. The bridge was demolished just after the Second World War to permit the passage of double-deck buses.[41]

Traces of open fields survived in the 1830s northeast of the manor house, west of Staple, and southeast of Weacombe.[42] The grant of free warren to Philip de Cauntelo in 1267[43] was the origin of the later medieval warren on the slope of Stowborrow Hill (Conyger Hill in 1418),[44] which in the 19th century had become the deer park. A park was part of the demesne let to farm in 1418 and was described as 'opposite' the manor house.[45] The name Park mead survived for a field in front of the house in the 19th century.[46]

Inventories of the mid 17th century imply houses with two or three ground floor rooms, their halls with rooms above.[47] One house, described as new in 1757,[48] remains beside the line of the former coast road north of the manor house. The houses at Staple date from the 1830s and include Staple Farm, described as new in 1835.[49]

The butts in the village were mentioned in 1529,[50] and wrestling in 1575.[51] A victualler was licensed in 1736.[52] The Windmill Country Hotel, formerly Quantock Barns, was established in the 1930s;[53] its successor, also called the Windmill, was rebuilt after the Second World War. A small harbour, begun c. 1835,[54] was built to import coal for the estate.[55]

The population of the parish was 103 in 1665.[56] In 1801 there were 192 people, a total which fell slightly in the next decade, rose to 225 by 1821, and then fluctuated, increasing to 278 in 1881 but falling to 139 by 1921. By 1931 the total had increased to 184.[57] Thereafter more houses were built at Staple, and by 1971 the total population had risen to 452, including resident pupils at St. Audries School.[58]

The Rt. Revd. C. R. Alford, bishop of Victoria, Hong Kong, 1867–72, was born at West Quantoxhead rectory house in 1816.[59]

MANORS. An estate called Quantoxhead, measuring 3½ hides, was held in 1086 by William de Mohun (I) as part of a fee held T.R.E. by Elnod the reeve, a fee which included Brompton Ralph and Heathfield.[60] William died after 1090 and his son William (II) (d. c. 1155) granted the fee to an unknown tenant before the end of Henry I's reign.[61] By 1166 it was held of William (III) de Mohun (d. 1176) by Roger of Newburgh.[62] The manor of *LITTLE* or *WEST QUANTOXHEAD* or *ST. AUDRIES*[63] which was part of this fee continued to be held of the honor of Dunster until 1788.[64] Roger of Newburgh had died by 1201, and was followed after a minority by his son Robert.[65] Robert died c. 1246, and c. 1270 his son Henry quitclaimed his remaining rights to John de Mohun (I).[66]

Robert de Cauntelo, who held the estate in fee from the Newburghs before 1215, was followed by his son Simon. In 1229 Philip de Cauntelo, to whom Robert had subinfeudated it, defended his possession.[67] This Philip, or another of the same name, was still there in 1267 and 1280, but was dead by 1284.[68] About 1285 the property was divided into three parts, possibly for three Cauntelo heirs, though the manor was said to be held in fee by Eve, wife of John de Pavely, from whom two parts were held by William de Ramsey and William de Pavely.[69] William de Ramsey still held his share in 1292,[70] but he does not occur thereafter, and his part seems to

[34] 9 Geo. IV, c. 84 (Local and Personal).
[35] S.R.O., DD/AH 14/3: sale cat. map 1835. The road beyond the house was closed in 1839: ibid. Q/SR Epiph. 1839.
[36] Ibid. DD/AH 14/3, 39/3–4, 40/1–2; ibid. tithe award.
[37] Ibid. 62/1; *Proc. Som. Arch. Soc.* cxxi. 119–20.
[38] Plate facing p. 124; below, church.
[39] Datestone; P.R.O., HO 107/1920 (Williton Lodge).
[40] Date on wind vane over dovecot.
[41] Inf. from Mr. A. H. Jarvis, East Quantoxhead.
[42] S.R.O., DD/AH 14/3, 40/1.
[43] *Cal. Chart. R.* 1257–1300, 76.
[44] S.R.O., DD/L P22/5; DD/AH 14/3.
[45] Ibid. DD/L 2/15/86.
[46] Ibid. DD/AH 14/3.
[47] Ibid. DD/SP, inventories 1640, 1663/4, 1665.
[48] Ibid. DD/AH 38/6.
[49] Ibid. 14/3.
[50] *L. & P. Hen. VIII*, iv (3), p. 2708.
[51] *Cal. Pat.* 1472–5, p. 421.
[52] S.R.O., Q/RL.
[53] *Kelly's Dir. Som.* (1939).
[54] S.R.O., DD/AH 22/5.

[55] Wedlake, *Watchet*, 87; inf. from Mr. L. S. Colchester, Wells.
[56] S.R.O., DD/WY 34.
[57] *V.C.H. Som.* i. 351; *Census*, 1911–31.
[58] *Census*, 1951–71.
[59] *Som. Roll*, ed. A. L. Humphreys (1897).
[60] *V.C.H. Som.* i. 504.
[61] *S.R.S.* extra ser. 124; xxxiii, p. iv.
[62] Ibid. xxxiii, p. x.
[63] Little Quantoxhead 1215–85: *S.R.S.* extra ser. 125; *Feud. Aids*, iv. 275; West Quantoxhead 1332: *Cal. Close*, 1330–3, 481; St. Audries 1540 onwards: Leland, *Itin.* ed. Toulmin Smith, i. 164.
[64] *S.R.S.* xxxiii, pp. 351–2.
[65] Ibid. extra ser. 13, 15.
[66] S.R.O., DD/L P23: deed dated Friday before St. Peter in Cathedra *quinquagesimo quarto*, ? 54 Hen. III.
[67] *Rot. Litt. Claus.* (Rec. Com.), i. 237; *Cur. Reg. R.* xiii. 211, 410.
[68] *Cal. Chart. R.* 1257–1300, 76; *S.R.S.* xxxiii, pp. 47, 53.
[69] *Feud. Aids*, iv. 275; *Cal. Inq. p.m.* ii, p. 352.
[70] *Cal. Close*, 1288–96, 262.

have been divided between the two surviving heirs between 1303[71] and 1327. About 1292 Eve de Pavely married William de Welle or Welles and their son Roger atte Welle was in possession of half the manor by 1327.[72] He was still owner in 1346,[73] but probably not in 1349 when the advowson was exercised by trustees.[74] By 1378 the property had passed to Sir William Lucy, from whom the reversion was bought by Sir Baldwin Malet, to be settled on his son John and his prospective wife Joan, daughter of Sir John Hylle.[75] Lucy was evidently dead by 1382.[76]

John Malet, knighted by 1391,[77] died c. 1394, leaving his widow Joan and a daughter Eleanor, later wife of Sir Edward Hull.[78] Joan had a life interest in the property, described as half the manor and the advowson, and she married three times more. Her second husband, Simon Michell, occurs in 1402–3 and 1406–7, but was dead by 1409.[79] From 1410 until c. 1422 she was married to John Luttrell, and he was followed by William Cornu, who survived until 1442 or later.[80] A settlement made in 1425 established a life interest for Cornu, with remainder to Eleanor Hull.[81]

On Eleanor's death in 1460 the property passed to her father's half-brother Hugh Malet (d. 1465) and then to Hugh's son Thomas.[82] Thomas died in 1501, and was succeeded by his son Baldwin, later the king's solicitor.[83] Baldwin died in 1533, having bought out the Iver family's share of the other half of the manor.[84] His son Michael bought out the Jacob share and at his death in 1547 held the whole advowson.[85] Richard, Michael's son, was a minor at his father's death, and his step-grandmother, Baldwin's widow Anne Trevanion, had jointure in the manor.[86] Richard survived until 1614, and was succeeded by his son Arthur.[87]

Arthur Malet died in 1644, devising his estate to his so-called wife Joan, and then to Thomas Malet of Poyntington, great grandson of Baldwin Malet and a judge of the King's Bench. Sir Thomas succeeded in 1646 and died in 1665.[88] His son, Sir John, who lived for a time at West Quantoxhead, died in 1686.[89] Baldwin and William, Sir John's son and grandson, mortgaged their lands.[90] William Malet was dead by 1736 when the estate was owned by his brother Baldwin, then rector of Street, as heir at law of William's daughter Anne. Baldwin sold the property in 1736 to James Smith.[91]

Smith died in 1748 leaving West Quantoxhead to his daughter Lavinia, who sold it in 1764 to Robert Balch formerly of Bridgwater and probably lessee of the estate.[92] Balch died in 1779 and was followed by

his sons Robert Everard (d. 1799) and George (d. after 1810) and his daughter Christiana.[93] She died in 1824 leaving as her heir Henry Harvey. Harvey sold the manor in 1831 to the Revd. Elias Webb, who in 1835 divided the property, selling Weacombe farm and some 70 a. to Thomas Cridland Luxton, and some 1,186 a. with common rights on the Quantocks to Sir Peregrine Fuller-Palmer-Acland.[94]

Sir Peregrine (d. 1871) bought the estate for his daughter Isabel (d. 1903), wife of Sir Alexander Acland-Hood, Bt., and they lived there after their marriage in 1849. Their eldest son Alexander (cr. Baron St. Audries 1911) died in 1917, and his son Alexander Peregrine, the second baron, sold the estate, though not the lordship of the manor, in 1925 to W. A. Towler of Littleport (Cambs.).[95] The lordship is assumed to have descended on the death of the 2nd Lord St. Audries in 1971 to his niece Elizabeth Acland-Hood, later the wife of Sir Michael Gass, K.C.M.G. The estate was divided, the mansion and parkland passing in 1934 to the Misses L. and K. D. Townshend, and Staple and St. Audries farms to individual farmers.[96]

The manor house, known as St. Audries, is a large mansion in the Tudor style. It appears to be mostly of the mid and later 19th century, but at least in its plan it retains the outlines of a medieval house. That had a central hall range, whose smoke-blackened roof survived until c. 1870.[97] By the late 18th century[98] upper floors had been put into the hall range, and the principal elevations had new and symmetrically arranged windows. By 1835[99] the garden and park had been considerably improved, and elaborate Gothic porches had been added to the west and north fronts.[1] Between 1835 and 1870 the house was completely rebuilt or refaced. The first phase, under Richard Carver of Taunton, seems to have involved work on the dining room, and may have included the interior decoration of the rooms on the north side.[2] The second phase, in the early 1850s,[3] included a large service and stable court to the east, partly replacing earlier buildings. The north and south fronts were then refaced. About 1870 the hall range was rebuilt to provide a larger great hall; its cross wings were extended westwards, and an entrance tower was added. The architect for the last phase, and probably for the refacing work and the service additions, was John Norton of London, who was evidently at work on other parts of the estate in the 1850s. The latest work on the house, completed in 1870, provided a total of 42 bedrooms.[4]

Among the 19th-century garden improvements[5]

[71] Wm. de Welle had more than one co-parcener in 1303: *Feud. Aids*, iv. 304.
[72] *S.R.S.* iii. 166; *Cal. Inq. p.m.* vii, p. 220.
[73] *Feud. Aids*, iv. 346.
[74] *S.R.S.* x, p. 608.
[75] Ibid. xvii. 95, 112; lxviii, p. 121; S.R.O., DD/S/WH 43/4.   [76] *S.R.S.* xvii. 112.
[77] Ibid. lxviii, p. 128.
[78] Ibid. extra ser. 128; J. C. Wedgwood, *Hist. Parl., Biogs.* 481.
[79] *S.R.S.* xxxiii, pp. 114, 128, 135.
[80] Maxwell Lyte, *Dunster*, 111; *S.R.S.* xxxiii, p. 210.
[81] Wedgwood, *Hist. Parl., Biogs.*, 481.
[82] *S.R.S.* extra ser. 131.
[83] Ibid. xix. 10; xxxiii, p. 245; *Cal. Inq. p.m. Hen. VII*, ii, pp. 249–50.
[84] *S.R.S.* xxi. 17–18; below.
[85] *S.R.S.* extra ser. 132–3.
[86] Ibid. xxxiii, p. 294.
[87] P.R.O., C 145/519, no. 86.
[88] *D.N.B.*; *Cal. Cttee. for Compounding*, ii. 1512.
[89] *S.R.S.* extra ser. 135.
[90] *Cal. Treas. Papers*, 1702–7, 300, 346; S.R.O., DD/AH 38/1, 39/2.
[91] S.R.O., DD/AH 38/1, 40/2.
[92] Ibid. 16/7, 38/1.
[93] Ibid. 10/10, 39/1, 40/1.
[94] Ibid. 14/3, 16/2, 39/1, 40/1.
[95] *Som. Co. Herald*, 11 Oct. 1925; Devon R.O. 574B/P2570.   [96] Local inf.
[97] W. L. Nichols, *The Quantocks and their Associations* (2nd edn.), 59 n.
[98] Collinson, *Hist. Som.* iii, opp. p. 497.
[99] S.R.O., DD/AH 14/3.
[1] Taunton Castle, Tite Colln., sepia drawing 1835.
[2] S.R.O., DD/AH 22/5, 62/1.
[3] Ibid. 62/1.
[4] *The Architect*, 21 Sept. 1872, 156; rainwater heads dated 1870.
[5] S.R.O., DD/AH 14/3.

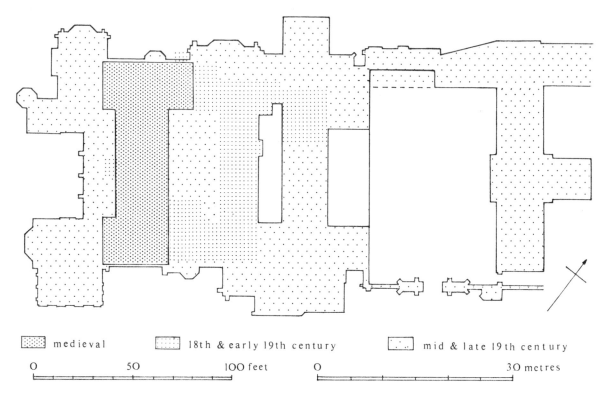

☒ medieval   ⬚ 18th & early 19th century   ⬚ mid & late 19th century

0   50   100 feet   0   30 metres

ST. AUDRIES

were a large orangery (later converted for use as a school chapel), a grotto decorated with shells on the formal terrace garden, a sea grotto[6] near the cascade on the cliffs, and a conservatory, later removed, on the south side of the house.

In 1285 William de Pavely's share in the manor evidently derived from his wife as one of the heirs of Philip de Cauntelo. Probably a son of the same name held it in 1327 and 1332,[7] but between then and the early 15th century the estate was divided between three coheirs, represented by the families of Pavely, Rivers (otherwise Iver or Court), and Lambrook. An Adam, son of Adam Pavely, occurs in 1361 and 1366,[8] and Joan, widow of Adam Pavely, occurs in in 1406. She was credited with half the manor until 1416, and by 1420 was succeeded by William Pavely.[9] John Pavely was returned with ¼ fee in 1430 and ⅓ of ½ fee in 1431.[10] He was followed between 1442 and 1447 by Henry Pavely, variously described as gentleman and franklin, occupier of Over Weacombe. The two estates thereafter descended together.[11]

The Rivers share of the estate was owned at his death in 1406 by John Rivers.[12] He was succeeded by his son William, who did homage for ¼ fee in 1413.[13] Under the name William Court he was still in occupation in 1430, though by 1442 his widow

Margaret Iver had succeeded him. She survived at least until 1447.[14] Richard Iver alias Court had a share in the advowson in 1475;[15] another Richard did homage in 1491, and David Iver, son of John Iver, was owner in 1504.[16] David was co-patron of the living in 1505,[17] and in 1515 conveyed all his property in the parish to trustees for sale to Sir Baldwin Malet.[18]

The second share was held in 1412 by John Lambrook (d. c. 1420), and then by another John in 1424. Eleanor, widow of John, occurs in 1429, and she was followed after 1432 by William Cloutsham, husband of her daughter Margaret. William occurs in 1447,[19] but in 1475 Margaret acted as co-patron of the living.[20] She died in 1491 and was succeeded by two daughters, Margaret Cloutsham and Elizabeth, wife successively of William Jacob and John FitzJames the younger.[21] Elizabeth acted without Margaret as co-patron in 1505[22] and died in 1510, when her heir was her son John Jacob.[23] John's half-brother, Aldred FitzJames, sold the estate in 1540 to John's widow's nephew Michael Malet[24] and thus the manor and advowson were reunited.

In 1086 an estate at *WEACOMBE* was held under Roger de Courcelles by Geoffrey and William in succession to three thegns.[25] The lordship descended like Kilve manor. It was held in 1303 by Matthew de

[6] Worked on in 1858: S.R.O., DD/AH 62/1.
[7] *Cal. Inq. p.m.* vii, p. 220; *Cal. Close,* 1330–3, 481.
[8] *S.R.S.* extra ser. 137; *Cal. Close,* 1364–8, 247; *Cal. Inq. Misc.* iii, p. 224.
[9] *S.R.S.* xxxiii, pp. 128, 136, 144, 161, 171.
[10] Ibid. p. 199; *Feud. Aids,* iv. 438.
[11] *Cal. Pat.* 1446–52, 115, 162; below.
[12] *S.R.S.* extra ser. 127.
[13] Ibid. 154. Wm. was called John elsewhere: ibid. 131, 136–7, 142, 147, 150.
[14] Ibid. 199, 210, 222.

[15] Ibid. lii, p. 58.
[16] S.R.O., DD/L P7/36; *S.R.S.* extra ser. 141.
[17] *S.R.S.* liv, p. 112.
[18] Ibid. extra ser. 141.
[19] *S.R.S.* xxxiii, pp. 149, 161, 172, 185, 199, 202, 220.
[20] Ibid. lii, p. 58.
[21] *Cal. Inq. p.m. Hen. VII,* i. p. 291.
[22] *S.R.S.* liv, p. 112.
[23] P.R.O., C 142/25, no. 41.
[24] Ibid. CP 40/1106, carte m. 17.
[25] *V.C.H. Som.* i. 489.

Furneaux of Cecily de Beauchamp as of Compton Dundon manor, and in 1346 formed part of the Kilve fee held by Simon de Furneaux. John Rogers (d. 1441) held it in 1428 in succession to Simon.[26] Henry Pavely occupied an estate called Over Weacombe by 1447,[27] and by 1455 had been succeeded by his two daughters Joan and Elizabeth. By 1459 Elizabeth was the sole heir. She probably married John Dobell, and her son Robert (d. c. 1531) was in 1520 holding an estate described as the manor of Over Weacombe.[28] Robert's son Giles sold it to George Harrison in 1552, and when George died in 1559 he left the capital messuage, subject to his widow's life interest, to his third son Alexander.[29] Alexander succeeded some time after 1581 and survived until 1622.[30] In 1606 his holding, which he then settled on his son Ames, included land at Weacombe held of George Luttrell, presumably part of the former Pavely estate.[31]

Ames was succeeded in 1622 by a young son Alexander (d. 1665).[32] Alexander's son Ames (d. 1690) was followed by Ames Harrison (d. 1731), whose daughter Frances (d. 1767) married Richard Cridland (d. 1757), an attorney of Combe Florey.[33] Thomas Cridland, younger son of Richard and also a lawyer, occupied Weacombe at his death in 1789.[34] The Weacombe estate, which included large holdings in Stogumber and elsewhere,[35] passed in trust to Thomas's sister Elizabeth and to his son, also Thomas (d. 1811).[36] By 1813 the estate was occupied by the Revd. Laurence Herd Luxton and his wife Frances, daughter of the elder Thomas Cridland.[37] Luxton was succeeded by his son Thomas Cridland Luxton, who bought some adjoining land from St. Audries manor in 1835.[38] Luxton held the estate until his death in 1850, when he was succeeded by his sister Frances (d. 1862), wife of Langley St. Albyn.[39] The St. Albyn crest appears in glass in the house and in stone on the lodge. Anne and Caroline, daughters of Frances, were owners in 1864,[40] but from 1865 the estate may have been let to a succession of tenants.[41] About 1871 it was acquired by the Revd. Ottiwell Sadler (d. 1899). His son Ottiwell Tennant Sadler (d. 1937) was succeeded by his niece Rachel, wife of William Territt Greswell (d. 1971). The owner in 1979 was Mr. A. J. Greswell.[42]

Weacombe Farm, an early 19th-century building, probably represents the capital messuage of the Harrison estate. Weacombe House[43] stands on a landscaped site c. 100 yards to the south-west of the capital messuage. The original building of the mid 18th century comprised a principal front of five bays and two storeys, the openings having heavily rusticated surrounds. Interior decorations are of high quality. A lower service wing on the east side was partly rebuilt in a similar style to the front in the later 18th century, and the staircase was renewed. Further additions were made in the 19th century which extended both the main accommodation and the kitchens. The principal front appears to have been originally roughcast, and was rendered in imitation of ashlar early in the 19th century, when a Tuscan porch was added to the main entrance.

ECONOMIC HISTORY. Two Domesday estates in the parish together measured 4½ hides. Two-thirds of the larger holding were in demesne, with 7 serfs and 3 ploughs, leaving the remainder to be farmed with 6 ploughs by 10 villeins and 4 bordars. Weacombe, measuring 1 hide, was shared by two tenants, with one bordar on the estate. Stock on the main holding included 200 sheep, and there was pasture measuring a league square, 16 a. of meadow, and 50 a. of wood.[44]

There were again 10 principal holdings on the main manor in 1407, comprising 5 free tenements and 5 farms of 24 a., their holders paying cash for rents and all services.[45] One of the free holdings was Landshire, possibly that occupied by William Poulett.[46] That farm perhaps originated in the 13th century or earlier from a rearrangement of holdings in the manor to consolidate the demesne. It remained in different ownership from the manor and was later divided between Higher and Lower Landshire until the late 18th century.

By the early 15th century most of the demesne was let. The income from fixed rents and court fees, normally about £8 5s., was increased by rents from demesne let as copyholds at will, bringing in c. £5 in 1417 and over £6 by 1435. The rector held a substantial share of the demesne and acted as receiver of the estate; the remainder was shared between 18 tenants, who held in addition to the closes mainly of grassland between the manor house and the coast, up to a total of 35 a. of arable on the hills for growing rye.[47] Individual holdings in the manor cannot be accurately assessed, though in 1418–19 the rector paid 29s. 5d. for his share of the demesne and c. 1422 John Holcombe paid 25s. 4d.[48] Eleanor Lambrook, also c. 1422, claimed to hold 6 messuages, 119 a. of land, 19 a. of meadow, and 20 a. of wood, her share of the whole manor.[49]

Seventeenth-century inventories suggest prosperous individual farmers whose holdings are traceable backwards for several generations. Michael Conibere (d. 1640) left property around Weacombe to the value of £327, a third of which was corn;[50] Henry Conibere (d. c. 1530) possessed a flock of at least 36 sheep.[51] Alexander Harrison (d. 1665) left

[26] Feud. Aids, iv. 303, 346, 392.
[27] Cal. Pat. 1446–52, 115, 162.
[28] S.R.S. extra ser. 138–9.
[29] P.R.O., C 142/119, no. 164.
[30] S.R.S. extra ser. 139; S.R.O., D/P/qua.w 2/1/1.
[31] P.R.O., C 142/535, no. 4.
[32] P.R.O., C 142/535, no. 4; S.R.O., D/P/qua.w 2/1/1; ibid. DD/SP, inventory 1665.
[33] C. E. H. Chadwyck Healey, Hist. W. Som. 149; S.R.O., DD/FS 70, marr. articles 1710; D/P/co.fl 2/1/2; Som. Wills, ed. Brown, iv. 78.
[34] S.R.O., D/P/qua.w 2/1/1, 4/1/1; D/P/co.fl 2/1/2; DD/GC 64; DD/DP 125, will of Thos. Cridland.
[35] Below, Stogumber, manors.
[36] S.R.O., D/P/qua.w 2/1/1, 4/1/1.
[37] Ibid. 4/1/1; DD/DP 125, will of Thos. Cridland; D/P/co.fl 2/1/2.   [38] Ibid. DD/AH 39/1; D/P/qua.w 4/1/1.
[39] Ibid. D/P/qua.w 4/1/1.
[40] Ibid. DD/AH 41/10; D/P/qua.w 4/1/1.
[41] Ibid. D/P/qua.w 4/1/1.
[42] P.O. Dir. Som. (1875); inf. from Mr. A. J. Greswell.
[43] Plate facing p. 60.   [44] V.C.H. Som. i. 489, 504.
[45] S.R.O., DD/L P22/5; ibid. 2/15/86.
[46] S.R.O., DD/DT; S. & D. N. & Q. xi. 212–13; see also S.R.O., DD/WY 7/Z1C/8.
[47] S.R.O., DD/L P22/12.
[48] Ibid. DD/L 2/15/86; DD/L P22/5.
[49] P.R.O., C 1/5, no. 45.
[50] S.R.O., DD/SP, inventories.
[51] Wells Wills, ed. Weaver, 136.

goods and stock worth £169 including 72 sheep.[52] The Conibere and Harrison holdings survived until the late 18th century, together with Lower Landshire, which was bought back into the manor in 1774,[53] after at least two centuries in the hands of the Popham family of Porlock.[54] The lord of the manor, the rector, and the Harrisons were the leading resident owners in the 1640s and 1667.[55] Inventories of the 17th century suggest flocks of sheep commonly over 50.[56] A weaver's shop occurs in 1581, a clothier and shearman in 1642, and a clothier in 1738.[57]

The extension of the park was probably begun by James Smith (d. 1748). His trustees leased to a Bicknoller clothier not only the house and farm but a nursery for fruit trees, a new orchard, and some newly inclosed land on the edge of the common.[58] By the 1780s the small tenant holdings outside the park were being consolidated into farms at Bidwell, Landshire, Staple, and Weacombe, a process which continued well into the next century, and in 1835 they measured 79 a., 96 a., 59 a., and 65 a. respectively.[59] Consolidation involved in 1817 a rearrangement of the glebe.[60] By 1851 the four main farms outside the park had merged into three, Landshire (100 a.), Staple (140 a.), and Weacombe (151 a.). Some further rearrangement of holdings took place at the time of the removal of the home farm to a site near the coast in 1855, and the main farming units in the 1880s were Weacombe, Staple, and Rydon farms, the latter afterwards known as St. Audries or Home farm.[61] In 1840 about a third of the parish comprised commonable land on the hills, and half was equally divided between arable and grass.[62] Some 370 a. of grassland were reported in 1905 compared with 264 a. of arable.[63] In 1976 there were three major farms, two heavily involved in dairying and one concentrating on cattle and sheep.[64]

The development of the park around the house was accompanied by the creation of the deer park on the rising ground to the south-east. Woodland east of the church by 1761 was extended towards the coast by 1817 over the former warren, and by 1835 comprised a deer park of 66 a.[65] It was extended southwards over Stowborrow Hill, and by c. 1900 covered 350 a., stocked with 120 fallow and 25 red deer.[66] Some 50 a. had been planted with ash, elm, and sycamore in the 1890s, and in 1905 the whole parish had some 140 a. of woodland.[67] The existence of common rights over the high ground in the south prevented planting on an extensive scale by the Forestry Commission in 1927,[68] though in 1976 nearly 18 ha. of wood remained in the parish, some

under the commission's control.[69]

Between 1836 and 1838 as many as 49 people were employed on improvements to the manor house and grounds, apart from the normal domestic and farm staff, the whole representing a significant contribution to the economy of the parish.[70] There were the usual village craftsmen – carpenter, tailor, cordwainer, blacksmith, baker, dressmakers, and straw-bonnet maker – in 1851.[71] A holiday camp, known in 1979 as St. Audries Bay Holiday Hamlet, was established on the coast below Landshire by 1935,[72] and the Home Farm Holiday Centre, at Home Farm, was developed in the 1970s.[73]

Field names Mill mead and Wood mill, occurring in 1761, suggest the site of a water mill west of Home Farm.[74] A water-driven mill was included in the new buildings at St. Audries Farm in 1855.[75]

LOCAL GOVERNMENT. Court rolls for West Quantoxhead manor have been found for single sessions in 1491 and 1493.[76] Four courts were held each year in the 1430s.[77] Leases of 1783 and 1785 mention suit of court, but no evidence of sessions has been found.[78] In both November 1491 and May 1493 a reeve and haywards were appointed.[79]

By the end of the 18th century the parish was administered by two wardens and two overseers, the latter serving by rotation in an eight-year cycle. A vestry, so named by 1786, nominated wardens and overseers by 1818. Overseers' accounts were signed by only three or four men in the 1780s, and wardens' accounts at first by the rector alone, and then in the 1820s also by the tenant farmers.[80]

The vestry in 1786 refused money to paupers not badged; by 1787 it was paying for inoculation, and in 1808 bought canvas for paupers to work. The church house was occupied as a poorhouse by 1785 until 1817 or later.[81] The wardens made new stocks in 1791. The parish became part of the Williton poor-law union in 1836, the Williton rural district in 1894, and the West Somerset district in 1974.[82]

CHURCH. A church had been established by 1265 when the bishop appointed a rector on the direction of the king's council during the Barons' War.[83] The rectory remained a sole benefice until 1977, and in 1978 it became part of the newly formed united benefice of Quantoxhead.[84]

The advowson was owned by the lords of the manor in the late 13th century and by the joint

[52] S.R.O., DD/SP, inventories.
[53] Ibid. DD/AH 40/1.
[54] Ibid. 38/5, 39/3, 40/1–2; *Som. Wills*, ed. Brown, ii. 14; *S.R.S.* xx. 175.
[55] *Som. Protestation Returns*, ed. Howard and Stoate, 290; S.R.O., DD/WY 34.
[56] S.R.O., DD/SP, inventories 1640, 1663, 1665; D/D/Rg 365.
[57] P.R.O., REQ 2/28, no. 93; S.R.O., DD/AH 40/2; DD/WO 15/11A.
[58] S.R.O., DD/AH 40/2.
[59] Ibid. 14/3.
[60] Ibid. 16/2, 21/12.
[61] *Kelly's Dir. Som.* (1883).
[62] S.R.O., tithe award.
[63] Statistics supplied by the then Bd. of Agric. 1905.
[64] Min. of Agric., Fisheries, and Food, agric. returns 1976.
[65] S.R.O., DD/AH 14/2, 3; 40/1.
[66] Ibid. 14/3, 39/1, 3; *V.C.H. Som.* ii. 569.
[67] *V.C.H. Som.* ii. 569; statistics supplied by the then Bd. of Agric. 1905.
[68] *Royal Com. on Land, Mins. of Evidence 49* (1947).
[69] Min. of Agric., Fisheries, and Food, agric. returns 1976.
[70] S.R.O., DD/AH 22/5.
[71] P.R.O., HO 107/1920.
[72] *Kelly's Dir. Som.* (1935); local inf.
[73] Local inf.
[74] S.R.O., DD/AH 40/1.
[75] Local inf.
[76] S.R.O., DD/L P23/16.
[77] Ibid. P22/12.
[78] Ibid. DD/AH 38/6.
[79] Ibid. DD/L P23/16.
[80] Ibid. D/P/qua.w 4/1/1, 13/2/1.
[81] Ibid. 13/2/1.
[82] Youngs, *Local Admin. Units*, i. 435, 674, 676.
[83] *S.R.S.* xiii, p. 9; ibid. extra ser. 106.
[84] *Dioc. Dir.*

owners, possibly acting alternately, at least until 1319.[85] Ownership remained divided until 1378 or later.[86] During the 15th and early 16th centuries the owners of one half of the manor, represented in 1434 by William Cornu, husband of Joan Malet, in 1491 by Thomas Malet, and in 1519 by Baldwin Malet, presented alternately with the owners of two shares of the other half of the manor.[87] Thereafter, until the 18th century, the Malets normally exercised patronage, though in 1559 the young Richard Malet was joined by his mother and her second husband; and in 1617 the patron was William Evans, lessee of the estate.[88] Malet trustees presented in 1733, and James Smith was patron in 1736.[89] Successive owners of the manor continued thereafter to be patrons until 1831, when Henry Harvey retained the advowson on selling the estate. He sold the patronage to the new owner, Sir Peregrine Fuller-Palmer-Acland, in 1836.[90] The property then descended in Sir Peregrine's family to Lady Gass, who in 1978 was joint patron of the benefice of Quantoxhead.[91]

The rectory was taxed at £4 6s. 4d. in 1291 and at £11 8s. 8d. in 1535.[92] In 1434 its poverty was noted.[93] It was by 1291 charged with a pension of 7s. to the priory of Stogursey, a charge which remained at least until 1569.[94] The living was worth c. £60 by 1668 and £232 net in 1831.[95]

The tithes amounted to £8 4s. in 1535.[96] They were redeemed for a rent charge of £227 2s. 6d. in 1840.[97] The glebe in 1341 was worth 30s., and 26s. 8d. in 1535.[98] It measured c. 35 a. in the early 17th century and in 1817, when the rector exchanged some 27 a. with Miss Balch.[99] In 1840 the total was just over 38 a.[1] In 1855 nearly 3 a. were sold to enlarge the churchyard, and a small exchange was made in 1875.[2] The tithe barn at Staple was sold in 1840.[3]

The rectory house was described as fit in 1835.[4] It was about to be improved in 1840, and was evidently then or later extended.[5] In 1977–8 it was sold. The house, in local stone, stands on rising ground overlooking the church and park.

No rector before 1519 is known to have been a graduate, though Robert Pavely, rector 1319–47, was licensed to study for a year at Oxford.[6] John Skelton, rector 1519 until after 1532, was a pluralist,[7] and curates served in the absence of rectors early in Elizabeth's reign.[8] Gawen Evans, rector from 1617, was removed c. 1647 when Silvester Harford was

intruded, but lived in the parish until his death in 1660.[9] Rectors were normally resident in the 18th century even though employing curates regularly.[10] There were c. 20 regular communicants in 1776.[11] Under Charles Alford, rector 1814–72, services were held twice each Sunday, and the communion was celebrated four times a year in 1843.[12] By 1870 there were two Sunday services and monthly celebrations.[13]

A church house occurs by 1757, and may be that given by John Jacob in 1518–19.[14] It was used as a poorhouse by 1785. It stood in the north-west corner of the churchyard, and was sold to Sir Peregrine F.P. Acland in 1843.[15]

By 1530 the church had a light of St. George, and five years later a mortuary light.[16]

The church of *ST. ETHELDREDA*, designed in a late 13th-century style by John Norton and built in 1854–6,[17] comprises chancel with north aisle, nave with north and south aisles and south porch, and north-west tower. It replaced a medieval church which had a chancel, said to have been rebuilt c. 1583,[18] a nave with south chapel and south porch, and a west tower. That building had details of the 13th and 14th centuries in the chancel and of the 15th century in the nave and tower.[19] Interior furnishings of the former church included a screen now at Exford, an elaborate three-decker pulpit, some plain late-medieval benches, and 18th-century box pews.[20] The church was galleried in 1787.[21] The new church was paid for by Sir Peregrine Acland and Sir Alexander Acland-Hood. The family arms occur in the decorative tiles in the chancel and initials in the pierced parapet of the tower. The church is richly decorated and includes piers of Babbacombe marble. The plain 12th-century font survives from the previous church.

There are five bells including two from the medieval Exeter foundry.[22] Registers from 1558 survive in a 17th-century copy, which appears to have no break during the Interregnum, when marriages by Justices of the Peace were recorded.[23]

NONCONFORMITY. A small Wesleyan society was formed in 1827, but it failed to find a permanent meeting-place 'independently of the Baptists', and services ceased. There were attempts to re-establish the group in 1835, and regular services were held

[85] *S.R.S.* i. 20.
[86] Ibid. xvii. 95, 112.
[87] Ibid. xxxii, p. 164; lii, pp. 58, 168; liv, p. 112; lv, p. 9.
[88] Ibid. lv, p. 156; P.R.O., CP 25(2)/346/10 Jas. I East.; *Som. Incumbents*, ed. Weaver, 425.
[89] *Som. Incumbents*, ed. Weaver, 425.
[90] S.R.O., DD/AH 13/4, 16/2, 40/1.
[91] *Dioc. Dir.*
[92] *Tax Eccl.* (Rec. Com.), 198; *Valor Eccl.* (Rec. Com.), i. 224.
[93] *S.R.S.* xxxii, p. 164.
[94] *Tax. Eccl.* (Rec. Com.), 198; *S.R.S.* lxi, pp. 66–9.
[95] S.R.O., D/D/Vc 24; *Rep. Com. Eccl. Revenues*, pp. 150–1.
[96] *Valor Eccl.* (Rec. Com.), i. 224.
[97] S.R.O., tithe award.
[98] P.R.O., E 179/169/14; *Valor Eccl.* (Rec. Com.), i. 224.
[99] S.R.O., D/D/Rg 365; ibid. DD/AH 21/12.
[1] Ibid. tithe award.
[2] Ibid. DD/AH 38/5, 39/3; ibid. D/P/qua.w 4/1/1.
[3] Ibid. DD/AH 40/1.
[4] *Rep. Com. Eccl. Revenues*, pp. 150–1.

[5] S.R.O., DD/AH 40/1.
[6] Ibid. D/D/B reg. 1, f. 189a.
[7] Ibid. D/D/Vc 20.
[8] *S. & D. N. & Q.* xiv. 63; D/D/Ca 57.
[9] *Walker Revised*, ed. A. G. Matthews; S.R.O., D/P/qua.w 2/1/1.
[10] S.R.O., D/D/Vc 88; ibid. D/P/qua.w 2/1/1–2, 4/1/1.
[11] Ibid. D/D/Vc 88.
[12] Ibid. D/D/V returns 1840, 1843.
[13] Ibid. 1870.
[14] *Char. Don.* H.C. 511 (1816), xvi; S.R.O., D/P/qua.w 4/1/1.
[15] S.R.O., D/P/qua.w 13/2/1; DD/AH 16/2.
[16] *Wells Wills*, ed. Weaver, 136.
[17] Faculty granted 1853: S.R.O., DD/AH 39/3; above, plate facing p. 124.
[18] Collinson, *Hist. Som.* iii. 496–7.
[19] Taunton Castle, Braikenridge Colln., water-colour W. W. Wheatley, 1845.
[20] Taunton Castle, Braikenridge Colln., water-colour by S. C. Tovey, 1845.
[21] S.R.O., D/P/qua.w 4/1/1.
[22] Ibid. DD/SAS CH 16/2.
[23] Ibid. D/P/qua.w 2/1/1–7.

between 1841 and 1844.[24] Summer services were arranged by Methodists at St. Audries Bay Holiday camp from 1956.[25]

EDUCATION. There was an unlicensed schoolmaster in the parish in 1623.[26] A school for *c.* 40 children had been founded by 1818,[27] and by 1825 there was a day school with 51 children and a Sunday school with 68.[28] By 1835 there were two day schools for a total of 30 children, one partly supported by subscribers including Sir Peregrine Acland who paid a mistress to teach 6 children. A Sunday school for 35 children was also supported by Sir Peregrine.[29] By 1846–7 'a day school had 30 children and a Sunday school 15.[30] A schoolroom, mentioned in 1829–30,[31] was replaced in 1857 by a new building given by Sir Alexander Acland-Hood, and possibly designed by John Norton, on a site just within the park below Staple.[32] West Quantoxhead Church of England school was given aided status when trans-

ferred to the county council in 1903, and it then had an average attendance of 42 children.[33] From 1928 seniors were no longer taken, and in 1962, when Doniford army camp was empty, the juniors and infants were transferred to Watchet and the school closed. The building was sold to St. Audries School in 1964.[34]

St. Audries boarding school for girls was established in the mansion in 1934 on its move from Weston-super-Mare. In 1944 it was vested in the National Society, together with an estate of 83 a. of park and woodland. In 1978 there were 250 pupils ranging in age from 8 to 18 years.[35]

CHARITY FOR THE POOR. By will dated 1756 a Dr. Lucas of Wells gave £30, interest to be paid at 5 per cent for the second poor. Until the 1820s the interest was distributed in cash on St. Thomas's Day in sums of 1s. or 2s., but none was paid by 1869.[36]

RADDINGTON

THE ANCIENT parish of Raddington lies on the southern edge of the Brendons 6 km. WSW. of Wiveliscombe, its southern boundary forming part of Somerset's boundary with Devon.[37] Roughly triangular in shape, the parish stretches north for 3 km. from the boundary ridge known as Shute Hill (*c.* 280 m.) to a point above Potter's Cross on Heydon Hill above 320 m. The western boundary with Bampton (Devon) is the river Batherm, flowing in a steep-sided valley, and the north-western follows a stream which rises on Heydon Hill and flows down a combe to join the Batherm at Blackwell. The eastern boundary, with Chipstable, is largely the course of a wide hollow way, known in the 19th century as Old Way, which runs from Old Bank[38] above Potter's Cross and continues southwards to an east-west route through Raddington village, and then as a bridle way passing the medieval settlement of Batscombe (recorded in 1408),[39] to the late 19th-century settlement of Higher Batscombe.[40] The whole parish measured 1,519 a. in 1901.[41]

Raddington lies in Devonian sandstone country,

divided between the largely slate Pilton Beds in the south and the predominantly sandstone Pickwell Down Beds.[42] There were small quarries and gravel pits by the late 19th century,[43] and a quarry had been opened at Batscombe by 1583.[44] Chubworthy, Little Wilscombe, Notwell, and Kingston Farms lie in dry combes which lead into a central watered valley and thence into Raddington Bottom, where the stream flows west into the river Batherm. The parish church stands isolated on a spur on the north side of Raddington Bottom, and the former rectory and manor houses and the mill stand on the edge of the meadows and one of the mill leats.[45] The meadows contrasted in the 15th and early 17th centuries with the bare or furze-covered surrounding hills, the whole parish before 1840 being almost entirely under grass.[46] There is no evidence of open arable cultivation; two 'great fields' of glebe known as Sanctuary,[47] and smaller closes[48] were established by the 16th century. There was extensive common on Heydon Hill, where closes were reported as open in 1602.[49]

[24] Ibid. D/N/wsc 3/2/2.
[25] Ibid. 3/2/9.
[26] Ibid. D/D/Ca 235.
[27] *Educ. of Poor Digest,* H.C. 224 (1819), ix(2).
[28] *Ann. Rep. B. & W. Dioc. Assoc. S.P.C.K.* (1825–6).
[29] *Educ. Enq. Abstract,* H.C. 62 (1835), xlii; S.R.O., DD/AH 22/5.
[30] *Nat. Soc. Inquiry,* 1846–7, Som. 14–15.
[31] S.R.O., D/P/qua.w 4/1/1.
[32] *P.O. Dir. Som.* (1861); Pevsner, *South and West Som.* 343.
[33] S.R.O., C/E 26; ibid. *Schs. Lists.*
[34] Ibid. *Schs. Lists;* Char. Com. files.
[35] Inf. from the Headmaster. It was founded as St. Faith's School in 1906.
[36] *15th Rep. Com. Char.* pp. 452–3; S.R.O., D/P/qua. w

13/2/1; *Digest Endowed Char. 1869–71,* H.C. pp. 50–1 (1873), li.
[37] This article was completed in 1980.
[38] S.R.O., tithe award.
[39] *S.R.S.* xxii. 27.
[40] O.S. Map 6″, Som. LXVIII. NE., SE. (1888 edn.).
[41] *V.C.H. Som.* ii. 351.
[42] Geol. Surv. 1″, solid and drift, sheet 294 (1969 edn.).
[43] O.S. Map 6″, Som. LXVIII. NE., SE. (1888 edn.).
[44] S.R.O., DD/SF 3137.
[45] Ibid. D/D/Rg 355.
[46] e.g. Broom close, Barren ground: S.R.O., D/D/Rg 355; cf. *S.R.S.* xv. 9; xxii. 198; S.R.O., tithe award.
[47] S.R.O., D/D/Rg 355.   [48] *S.R.S.* xxvii. 200–6.
[49] P.R.O., CP 25(2)/346/10 Jas. I Hil.; S.R.O., DD/WG 16/16; *S.R.S.* xxviii. 296.

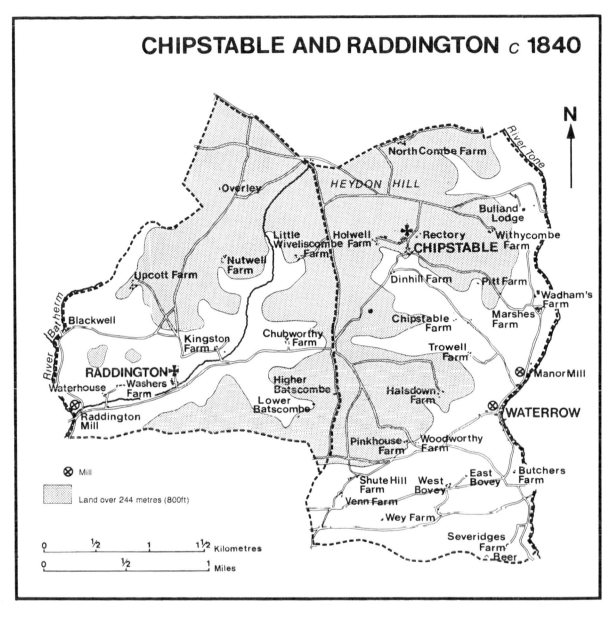

CHIPSTABLE AND RADDINGTON c 1840

N

⊗ Mill

Land over 244 metres (800ft)

0   ½   1   1½ Kilometres

0   ½   1 Miles

Some land was still common in 1719,[50] but the whole had been inclosed by 1795.[51] The farm attached to the capital messuage in 1652 included land called New Park and Coneygore.[52] The former survived until 1795.[53] By 1840 there were also traces of a park on the Blackwell estate.[54] Raddington wood was recorded in 1480.[55] Oak, ash, and blackthorn were growing at Batscombe by 1583.[56]

There was probably no nucleated village in the parish. Chubworthy, recorded in the mid 11th century,[57] Upcott (1198),[58] Batscombe (1408), and Nutwell (1409)[59] indicate scattered medieval settlement, and by the 1630s all the farmsteads surviving in the 1980s had been established.[60] In the 19th century some expansion of population led to the building of cottages in Raddington Bottom and the

creation of Higher and Lower Batscombe.[61] By the mid 20th century the medieval site of Batscombe had been abandoned.[62]

The scattered settlement pattern was dictated by the terrain and the consequent difficulty of communication between the deep valleys. An axial road known as Hill Lane, serving some of the farmsteads, runs south from Heydon Hill to a point north of the church, parallel with the eastern hollow way. Roads from Wiveliscombe crossed the parish from east to west, towards Dulverton along Heydon Hill, and towards Bampton through Raddington Bottom passing Chubworthy, the former manor house, and the mill. The second route was turnpiked by the Wiveliscombe trust in 1786, though the line was abandoned for a more southerly route, that now

[50] P.R.O., CP 25(2)/1056/6 Geo. I Mich.
[51] S.R.O., DD/SF 3346.
[52] Ibid. DD/WG 13/1, pp. 98–9.
[53] Ibid. DD/SF 3346.
[54] Ibid. tithe award.
[55] P.R.O., SC 6/977/23.
[56] S.R.O., DD/SF 3137.

[57] V.C.H. Som. i. 505.
[58] Cur. Reg. R. i. 65.
[59] S.R.S. xxii. 27.
[60] S.R.O., D/D/Rg 355.
[61] Ibid. tithe award; O.S. Map 6″, Som. LXVIII. NE., SE. (1888 edn.).
[62] O.S. Map 6″, ST 02 NW. (1963 edn.).

followed by the main road, in 1825.[63] North of the church Pitcombe Lane, linking Blackwell with Hill Lane, was abandoned in the 19th century.[64]

There were 92 payers of a subsidy in the parish in 1667.[65] The population was 105 in 1801, and it remained constant for three decades. By 1841 it had risen to 126, but thereafter it fell, reaching 86 in 1891 and 65 in 1921.[66]

MANORS. In 891 King Alfred gave to his companion Berthulph land in Raddington, free of the common dues,[67] in exchange for other property. Two thegns held an estate called Raddington T.R.E.; by 1086 it was occupied by Robert, who held the land of Roger Arundel.[68] The overlordship descended with the barony of Poorstock (Dors.) like that of Huish Champflower, passing from the Arundels to the Newburghs.[69] Henry de Newburgh in 1276 sold some of his property to Queen Eleanor,[70] but he was still lord of Raddington in 1284–5.[71] John de Newburgh, Henry's son, brought an unsuccessful action against the queen c. 1305 for an estate including 2 fees in Raddington and Upcott,[72] but his son Robert (d. 1338) recovered the fees soon after 1327.[73] In 1434 the manor of *RADDINGTON* was said to be held in socage as of Lodhuish manor in Nettlecombe,[74] and in 1529 the manor was said to have been so held in former times.[75]

Between 1196 and 1198 there were disputes over fees in Raddington involving William of Upcott and his wife Scolace, Isabel de Gatemore, and William de la Fenne and his wife Emme.[76] Thereafter no occupier is known until Robert of Raddington in 1284–5,[77] though Walter de la Fenne and Emme his wife conveyed the advowson to Alice de Luceles in 1262.[78] John of Raddington seems to have held the manor in the late 13th century[79] and had been followed by Robert of Raddington by 1332,[80] and by John of Raddington by 1361.[81] In 1369 the manor was settled on John and his wife Margaret.[82] John was dead by 1408, but his widow survived until after 1420;[83] Walter Hill had acquired the reversion in 1408 and had succeeded by 1423.[84]

The manor passed from Walter to John Hill (d. 1434), who held it in right of his wife Cecily, later

wife of Sir Thomas Keriell.[85] It remained in her possession until her death in 1472,[86] and then descended to Genevieve, wife of William Say, Cecily's granddaughter.[87] Genevieve died in 1480 but her husband continued to occupy her property, not without challenge, until his death in 1529.[88] Genevieve's estates were then divided between the grandchildren of her aunt Elizabeth Hill, namely John Waldegrave, heir of a half share through his mother Mabel, Elizabeth Hill's elder daughter, and the three children of Joan, her younger daughter: Ellen Babington, William Clopton the younger, and Thomas Hussey. John Waldegrave (d. 1543) acquired Ellen Babington's share,[89] but not certainly the other interests in Raddington, though later Waldegraves held the advowson undivided and called their estate the manor of Raddington. John Waldegrave was succeeded by his son Sir Edward (d. 1561)[90] and Edward by his son Sir Charles (d. 1632) of Cossey (Norf.).[91] In 1599 Sir Charles settled the manor on his heir Edward (kt. by 1607, Bt. 1643, d.1647).[92] Sir Henry Waldegrave (d. 1658), son of the last, was followed successively by his son Sir Charles (d. 1684), Charles's son Sir Henry (cr. Baron Waldegrave 1686, d. 1689), and Henry's son James (cr. Earl Waldegrave 1729). James sold the manor to Thomas Davys or Davis the younger of Milverton in 1718.[93]

Thomas Davys the younger in 1719 settled the manor on Thomas Davys the elder,[94] and a Thomas Davys of Milverton was patron in 1746 and 1749.[95] Another Thomas Davys, rector 1749–84, was probably both lord of the manor and patron, and was evidently succeeded in 1784 by his brothers Benjamin, of Raddington, James of Milverton, and George, also of Raddington. Both manor and advowson were conveyed to Simon Richards, clerk, in 1784.[96] No reference to the manor has been found after that date, though the Davys family were in occupation of a small property in the parish in 1980.[97]

The hall was recorded in 1086.[98] The capital messuage was known by the 17th century as Moorhouse, and in the 19th century by that name or as Washer's, the name of a 17th-century tenant family.[99] Washer's Farm, which bears traces of 17th-century

[63] 26 Geo. III, c. 135; 6 Geo. IV, c. 93 (Local and Personal).
[64] S.R.O., tithe award; O.S. Map 6″, Som. LXVIII. NE., SE. (1888 edn.).
[65] S.R.O., DD/WY 34.
[66] V.C.H. Som. ii. 351; Census, 1911–21.
[67] H. P. R. Finberg, Early Charters of Wessex, 127.
[68] V.C.H. Som. i. 495.
[69] Sanders, Eng. Baronies, 72–3.
[70] Cal. Mem. R. 1326–7, pp. 107–8; S.R.S. vi. 381.
[71] S.R.S. iii. 7; Feud. Aids, iv. 275. Sanders, Eng. Baronies, says Henry d. 1271.
[72] Abbrev. Plac. (Rec. Com.), 256.
[73] Cal. Mem. R. 1326–7, pp. 107–8.
[74] P.R.O., C 139/71, no. 36.
[75] Ibid. C 142/51, no. 35.
[76] Mem. R. 1207–8 (Pipe R. Soc. N.S. xxxi), 89; Feet of Fines (Pipe R. Soc. xxiv), 241; Rot. Cur. Reg. (Rec. Com.), i. 154; Cur. Reg. R. i. 65.
[77] Feud. Aids, iv. 275. Rob. occurs 1280: S.R.S. xliv. 4, 292.
[78] S.R.S. vi. 188.
[79] B.L. Harl. Ch. 55. B. 13.
[80] S.R.S. ix, p. 279. Rob. was alive 1332–5: S.R.S. xii. 160, 179–80.
[81] Ibid. ix, p. 753.

[82] P.R.O., E 211/494B; S.R.S. xiii. 46; see also ibid. xxii. 194.
[83] S.R.S. xxii. 27; xxx, p. 393.
[84] Ibid. xxii. 27; xxx, p. 434.
[85] P.R.O., C 139/71, no. 36.
[86] S.R.O., DD/WG 7; S.R.S. xxii. 95.
[87] Cat. Anct. D. ii, A 3222.
[88] P.R.O., C 1/594, no. 64; C 142/51, no. 35; E 210/ 10759; Cal. Inq. p.m. Hen. VII, iii, p. 59; L. & P. Hen. VIII, iv (1), p. 569.
[89] P.R.O., C 142/68, no. 54; C 1/406, no. 37; S.R.S. extra ser. 314–15.
[90] Collinson, Hist. Som. ii. 117; S. W. Bates Harbin, M.P.s for Som. 123.
[91] P.R.O., C 142/467, no. 173.
[92] Ibid.; Burke, Peerage (1949), 2005.
[93] S.R.O., Q/R enrolled deed 412.
[94] P.R.O., CP 25(2)/1056/6 Geo. I. Mich.
[95] Below, church.
[96] P.R.O., CP 25(2)/1197/24 Geo. III Hil.; S.R.O., D/D/B reg. 27, f. 18v.; ibid. 32, f. 62.
[97] Local inf.
[98] V.C.H. Som. i. 495.
[99] S.R.O., DD/WG 13/1, pp. 98–9; 13/4, p. 27; 13/5, pp. 55, 61; 13/6, p. 54; 16/16; ibid. Q/R, papists' estates, roll 3, rot. 19, 19d.; ibid. tithe award; P.R.O., HO 107/1921.

origin, was largely reconstructed after a fire in the late 19th century.[1] There was a dovecot at the farm in 1443.[2]

In 1086 Meinfrid and Robert held of William de Mohun an estate called Chubworthy (Cibewrde) in succession to two thegns, Seric and Uthret.[3] The property continued to be held of Dunster until 1777.[4]

In the 1270s Robert of Chubworthy, son and heir of Walter of Chubworthy, did homage for his holding, shortly afterwards reckoned as ½ fee.[5] A Robert of Chubworthy died in 1333 leaving Philip as his heir.[6] The succession is not clear thereafter. John Chubworthy occurs between 1378 and 1402, followed by Richard between 1403 and 1408, and then by John Chubworthy, possibly his brother, until c. 1420. William Chubworthy, who succeeded in 1420 and had died by 1421, left a son Geoffrey, a minor, who survived until 1446 or later. Geoffrey's heirs were two coheirs, one his sister Agnes, and by 1499 the property was divided between John Southey and John Sydenham.[7]

John Southey died in 1532, leaving a son Nicholas to succeed to an estate described as half the manor of *CHUBWORTHY*.[8] By 1563 John Southey had inherited half the barton place and lands of the manor and half an estate in Raddington called Rowlands.[9] By 1580 the estate had been sold to the Sydenhams, who already owned the other half through the marriage of John Sydenham of Bathealton to Agnes Chubworthy.[10] John Sydenham, perhaps their son, died in 1504, and was followed by his son Edward (d. 1543) and Edward by his son John (d. 1558).[11] John Sydenham was followed by his son and namesake, who died in 1580, and then by his grandson Humphrey Sydenham (d. 1625) of Dulverton.[12] Humphrey inherited the whole estate.[13]

In 1609 Humphrey Sydenham settled Chubworthy and half Rowlands as a marriage portion for his sister Susan, then betrothed to Martin Sanford.[14] On his death by 1647 Martin left the estate, perhaps to ensure him a share in the whole family inheritance, to his son William for 80 years.[15] William was still alive in 1663,[16] but early in the following year he had been succeeded by his nephew John Sanford (d. 1711).[17] John's son William (d. 1718) was succeeded in turn by William's son, also William (d. 1770), and then by the younger William's son John (d. 1779) and John's son William Ayshford (d. 1833).[18] Edward Ayshford Sanford, M.P. (1794–1871), son of the last, was followed by his son William Ayshford Sanford (1818–1902). The family continued to hold the estate until the early 20th century, when it was sold to a farmer.[19]

Chubworthy Farm, known as the Manor House in the early 20th century,[20] is a large 19th-century structure, with slightly earlier farm buildings.

ECONOMIC HISTORY. The two Domesday estates of Raddington and Chubworthy together amounted to 3 hides of arable, less than a quarter of the later parish, and there were 7 a. of meadow, 11 a. of wood, and 50 a. of pasture at Chubworthy and 4 furlongs by 3 furlongs of pasture at Raddington. Chubworthy was solely a demesne farm; Raddington's demesne was 1½ hide and ½ virgate. Together the demesnes were stocked with 128 sheep and 37 she-goats.[21]

Chubworthy continued as a separate estate, though parts were let by customary tenure and such holdings survived into the 1560s.[22] Batscombe emerged from it as a separate holding with land in adjoining Clayhanger (Devon) by 1467 and probably much earlier.[23] The division of Raddington into separate units is less clear. A virgate held by Reynamus of Raddington was mentioned in 1235.[24] By the 1440s the demesne was let and accounted for nearly two thirds of the rent income.[25] By 1480 the demesne had been reduced in size as tenancies of parts became permanent, while rent in lieu of customary services still survived.[26] The appearance of holdings at Upcott by 1198,[27] Nettlewell by 1327,[28] and Nutwell by 1408[29] suggests the establishment of separate farms, the first as its name shows a subsidiary settlement founded to exploit the higher and more marginal ground.

Grazing of cattle and sheep seems to have been an important part of the parish economy. Tithes of wool and lambs in 1535 amounted to only 40s., but a single copyhold tenement in 1537 supported at least 7 bullocks and about 140 sheep.[30] At least three generations of the Shercman family lived in the parish up to the same period.[31] Under a lease of Batscombe in 1583 the lord was obliged to provide timber for a barn with linhays at its ends to house cattle.[32] In the later 17th century clothiers from Bampton (Devon) and Stogumber leased grazing in the parish,[33] and inventories suggest continued stock raising. James Wipple (d. 1683), of Chubworthy, left sheep worth £42 and cattle worth £24; Susan Ballett (d. 1691), widow of John Ballett, rector 1669–85, had 33 sheep; and Richard Yeandle (d. 1732), probably of Upcott, had 160 sheep, and his dairy cows were the source for his 57 cheeses.[34] Identification of isolated farmsteads is clearer from

[1] Inf. from Mrs. J. P. E. Welch, Washer's Fm.
[2] P.R.O., SC 6/1119/17.
[3] *V.C.H. Som.* i. 505; *S.R.S.* extra ser. 214–18.
[4] *S.R.S.* xxxiii, p. 351.
[5] Ibid. extra ser. 214–15; *Cal. Inq. p.m.* ii, pp. 178, 352.
[6] *Cal. Inq. p.m.* vii, p. 355; *S.R.S.* extra ser. 215; *Cal. Fine R. 1327–37*, 412.
[7] *S.R.S.* extra ser. 215–17.
[8] P.R.O., E 150/925, no. 27.   [9] S.R.O., DD/SF 1020.
[10] P.R.O., C 142/191, no. 76; Collinson, *Hist. Som.* iii. 522.
[11] P.R.O., C 142/25, no. 23; C 142/68, no. 31; C 142/115, no. 52.
[12] S.R.O., DD/SAS HV 7/1.
[13] P.R.O., C 142/191, no. 76.
[14] S.R.O., DD/SF 4039.
[15] *Som. Wills*, ed. Brown, vi. 56.
[16] S.R.O., DD/SF 270.   [17] Ibid. 1737.
[18] Burke, *Land. Gent.* (1952), 2249–50; S.R.O., DD/SF

690–1, 1768, 3137, 3271, 3887, 4006; Devon R.O. 49/1/20/3.
[19] S.R.O., DD/SF 4525; *Kelly's Dir. Som.* (1910, 1914).
[20] *Kelly's Dir. Som.* (1910, 1919, 1927).
[21] *V.C.H. Som.* i. 495, 505.
[22] S.R.O., DD/SF 1020.
[23] Ibid. 4053; DD/L P33/4.   [24] *S.R.S.* vi. 94.
[25] P.R.O., SC 6/1119/17.
[26] Ibid. SC 6/977/11, 23. See also SC 6/1248/22; SC 6/Hen. VII/544, 548.
[27] *Cur. Reg. R.* i. 65. *S.R.S.* xxiv. 241 may suggest the origin of Reynamus's estate.
[28] *S.R.S.* iii. 168.   [29] Ibid. xxii. 27.
[30] *Valor Eccl.* (Rec. Com.), i. 221; *S.R.S.* xxvii. 201; S.R.O., D/D/Rg 355 (1634) mentions no tithe wool, only a modus on lambs.
[31] S.R.O., DD/SF 4053; *Wells Wills*, ed. Weaver, 137.
[32] S.R.O., DD/SF 3137.
[33] Ibid. DD/WG 13/4, p. 61; 13/5, p. 34; 13/6, p. 33.
[34] Ibid. DD/SP, inventories.

the 17th century. Chubworthy, reflecting its owner-ship, was divided into two separate farms in the 16th century, and one half was let with half a farm called Rowlands.[35] Rowlands, later known as Rowland farm, became a separate holding in 1689 and continued in being until the end of the 18th century, though in 1802 the house was found to be down, leaving only a barn and yards, the site surrounded by beech trees and called Sanden Barnstables.[36]

The Waldegrave estate[37] was by the mid 17th century divided between three farms and three areas of hill pasture.[38] The capital messuage, then known as Moorhouse, and the land attached to it measured *c.* 90 a., and comprised 18 small and three large closes let to Walter Simes of Romsey (Hants).[39] The other two farms were known as Skinners tenement, by the early 18th century Kingston farm,[40] and Waterhouses. The three other holdings, known as overlands or roofless tenements since they were pasture lands without dwellings, were known as Potter's Down (24 a.), East North Down (50 a.), and Court Down (70 a.).[41] The remaining farms in the parish which had been part of Raddington manor were known in the 17th century as Blackwell Cleeve and Upcott, and were owned by the Wood family and let to the Miltons and later to the Yeandles.[42]

Wheat, oats, barley, dredge, and peas were recorded in 17th- and 18th-century inventories,[43] and husbandry clauses in a 14-year lease of Chubworthy in 1698 required heavy dressings of dung and lime after a crop of peas and three crops of corn. By 1815 when Chubworthy and Batscombe were farmed together with land in Clayhanger on a 7-year lease, a planting covenant required a succession of wheat or oats, followed by a dressing of lime, and turnips or a 'white' crop of wheat, barley, or oats with clover or rye, so as not to have two 'white' crops together. Clover and evergrass were to be sown with the last crop of the tenancy.[44]

At the end of the 18th century there were nineteen separate holdings in the parish, largely in the hands of the families of Davys, Yeandle, Bruer, and Were.[45] By 1841 the Sanford farms of Chubworthy and Batscombe amounted to 317 a., followed in size by the 281 a. of John Yeandle's Upcott and Blackwell, and the 272 a. of the elder Thomas Davys at Washers, Waterhouse, Heydon, and elsewhere. Kingston farm and adjoining high pastures measured 211 a., and Notwell farm 157 a. Little Wilscombe farm measured just over 141 a.[46] By 1851 Chubworthy and Upcott were centres of farms of 400 a.,[47]

Kingston farm remained constant in size, but Littel Wilscombe had grown to 214 a. All the large, isolated farms had many living-in servants.[48]

Pasture ground, some of it described as furzy, accounted for more than half the parish in the early 1840s, and for nearly two-thirds in 1905.[49] By 1980 the land was almost entirely under grass for cattle and sheep.

The landowning pattern of the 19th century continued into the 20th. The Davie family, later Ferguson-Davie, of Bittescombe,[50] the Sanfords of Chipley Park, Langford Budville, and the Capels of Bulland Lodge, Chipstable, were still owners of much of the land until shortly after the First World War.[51]

There was a mill at Raddington in 1086 working exclusively for the manor house.[52] The mill, recorded in 1481 and 1616,[53] was known by 1662 as Brewer's mill.[54] By 1687 it was held with the adjoining tenement called Waterhouses.[55] Known in 1851 as Lower Mill, in distinction from Bittescombe mill to the north, in Upton parish, it was then occupied by a labourer.[56] Two millers were working in Raddington in 1906 and 1910, but milling had apparently been abandoned by 1914.[57]

LOCAL GOVERNMENT. Raddington formed a separate tithing in the 13th century,[58] but by the 1560s was linked with Chipstable.[59] Courts for Raddington manor were held once a year by the later 15th century.[60] There are court rolls for the years 1592, 1594, and 1600–4.[61] A manor court was held at Chubworthy in the late 15th century,[62] and suit of court by the owners of Batscombe was still demanded in 1609.[63]

No parish records have been found. A building in the churchyard was probably used as a poorhouse.[64] The parish became part of the Wellington poor-law union in 1836 and the Wellington rural district in 1894. It was absorbed into Chipstable civil parish in 1933. Chipstable civil parish became part of Taunton Deane district in 1974.[65]

CHURCH. There was a church at Raddington by 1262.[66] The living was a rectory, from 1929 united with Chipstable. In 1971 the parish was united with Chipstable and became a chapelry.[67]

Walter de la Fenne and his wife Emme conveyed the advowson to Alice de Luceles in 1262;[68] from

[35] Ibid. DD/SF 438, 1020, 1768, 1771, 3137, 3271.
[36] Ibid. 3137, 4006. Rowlands Barn survives at ST 033274. The name Sanders Barnstaple has been transferred to a group of houses in Chipstable: above, Chipstable.
[37] Above, manors.
[38] S.R.O., DD/WG 13/4, p. 5; ibid. Q/R, papists' estates, roll 3.
[39] Ibid. DD/WG 13/1, pp. 98–9.
[40] Ibid. DD/WO 11/7.
[41] Ibid. 11/7, 11/12.
[42] Ibid. DD/SF 657, 819, 970; DD/WO 31/10; DD/X/ET(C/252).
[43] Ibid. DD/SP, inventories 1691, 1732.
[44] Ibid. DD/SF 3137.
[45] Ibid. 3346.
[46] Ibid. tithe award.
[47] *Rep. Com. Children and Women in Agric.* [4202–1] p. 126, H.C. (1868–9), xiii.
[48] P.R.O., HO 107/1921.
[49] S.R.O., tithe award; statistics supplied by the then Bd. of Agric. 1905.

[50] G.E.C. *Baronetage*, ii. 143–5.
[51] *Kelly's Dir. Som.* (1914, 1919, 1923).
[52] *V.C.H. Som.* i. 495.
[53] P.R.O., SC 6/977/23; *S.R.S.* xxiii. 183.
[54] S.R.O., DD/WG 13/4, pp. 27, 34.
[55] Ibid. 13/5, p. 117; 13/9, p. 15.
[56] P.R.O., HO 107/1921.
[57] *Kelly's Dir. Som.* (1906, 1910, 1914).
[58] *S.R.S.* xi, pp. 43–4, 96.
[59] *Ibid.* xx. 165; *Som. Protestation Returns,* ed. Howard and Stoate, 168, 286.
[60] *S.R.S.* xxvii. 200–6; P.R.O., SC 6/1119/17. No perquisites were noted in 1472–3, 1480–1: ibid. SC 6/977/11, 23.
[61] S.R.O., DD/WG 16, nos. 12–13, 16–17.
[62] Ibid. DD/SF 438.   [63] Ibid.
[64] Ibid. tithe award.
[65] Youngs, *Local Admin. Units,* i. 435, 675–6.
[66] *S.R.S.* vi. 188.
[67] Youngs, *Local Admin. Units,* i. 435.
[68] *S.R.S.* vi. 188.

NETHER STOWEY: THE MARKET PLACE FROM ST. MARY'S STREET IN 1837

To the right of the octagonal market house are Lime Street and the sign of the new George inn; to the left
are the entrance to Castle Street and the colonnaded market house

NETHER STOWEY CASTLE FROM THE EAST

Castle Street and Castle Hill House are in the foreground

LEIGHLAND CHAPEL, OLD CLEEVE, IN 1849

RADDINGTON CHURCH

1336 the lords of Raddington were patrons until the end of the 15th century.[69] In 1494 James, Lord Audley, presented by grant of Sir William Say.[70] The Crown presented in 1570,[71] but thereafter for more than a century the Waldegraves, disbarred as Roman Catholics from exercising the patronage, appointed local people in their place for each turn. William Lypescomb, perhaps the retiring rector, was patron in 1587; in 1639 Priscilla Ballet, widow of the late rector, presented in right of her late husband, who was executor of Richard Hill, the Waldegrave grantee.[72] In 1662 John Baker of Withypool and Jane Ballet, the wife of the then rector, were given the next turn.[73] In 1670 Edward Milton and Andrew Bowden, both of Bampton (Devon), were granted the next presentation, which was exercised by Milton alone in 1685.[74] In the same year John and Francis Bluet of Holcombe Rogus (Devon) acquired the next presentation in trust for the widow of the last rector, John Ballet.[75] John Southey and Samuel Taylor, clerk, presented in 1709,[76] but in 1718 the advowson passed with the manor from the Waldegraves to the Davys family.[77]

Thomas Davys, rector 1749–84, was succeeded as patron by his brothers Benjamin, George, and James.[78] They conveyed both manor and advowson to Simon Richards, clerk.[79] By 1791 the advowson was held by Richard Darch of Huish Champflower, who presented his son William in 1807.[80] William succeeded his father as patron.[81] Walter Calverley Trevelyan of Wallington (Northumb.) presented in 1833, and in 1841 Edward Otto Trevelyan (d. 1880) of Stogumber, clerk, presented his brother John (d. 1844).[82] John Hayne of Fordington (Dors.) was patron by 1861,[83] and was succeeded by his son John, rector of Raddington 1845–79, and then by John's son Edward, rector 1879–92.[84] Edward Hayne was succeeded as patron in 1929[85] by the Revd. H. S. Briggs who, after the creation of the united benefice of Chipstable with Raddington in 1929 had one turn in three.[86] Briggs's share of the patronage was transferred to the bishop in 1962.[87]

The living was valued at £8 7s. 7d. net in 1535,[88] and £50 c. 1668,[89] at £91 net in 1831,[90] and at £200 in 1851.[91] Tithes were assessed at £7 14s. 3d. in 1535,[92] and personal offerings and compositions by 1634 included 2d. each year from every communicant, 4d. for churchings, 6d. for weddings, and payments for milk, young stock, goslings, and 'gardens

of pot herbs'.[93] In 1841 the rector was awarded a tithe rent charge of £143, and a further £10 when the glebe was let.[94]

The glebe, worth 20s. in 1535,[95] was reckoned to be c. 63 a. in 1634 and 1841.[96] The rectory house in 1634 had four rooms including buttery and kitchen, with five chambers over them, and a first-floor study over a detached fuel house apparently near the farm buildings.[97] The house was usually let with the glebe from the 18th century, and was sold in the 1930s.[98] The rectors in the 19th century had the right to use a room as a vestry, a right still retained in 1980.[99] The house, standing in Raddington Bottom and linked to the church by a steep footpath, was rebuilt in the 19th century.

In 1532 the parish was served by a resident rector and a stipendiary priest,[1] and there was a parochial guild of St. Catherine in 1534.[2] Rectors normally resided, including three successive generations of the Ballet family between 1594 and 1685 and Benjamin Hammett, rector 1709–46, whose first wife was a daughter of the last Ballet.[3] Rectors were non-resident by the late 18th century, John Cope Westcote (1784–91) also holding Hatch Beauchamp, Edward Webber (1791–1807) Bathealton, and William Darch (1807–33) Milverton and later Huish Champflower.[4] By 1815 there were prayers and a sermon each Sunday, and the parish was served by a curate who lived in Wellington and also served Chipstable and kept a grammar school. He was succeeded as curate by the rector's son.[5] By 1843 communion was celebrated seven or eight times a year.[6] At the afternoon service on Census Sunday 1851 there were 102 people including 21 Sunday-school children. The average congregation was said to be slightly higher for afternoon services, but was usually only 59 in the mornings.[7]

John Hayne, appointed rector in 1845, was already resident rector of Stawley. He was followed at Raddington by his son Edward, rector 1879–92, and then by another son, John Popham Hayne, who had already succeeded his father at Stawley in 1879. John held Raddington until 1929, but from 1908 he lived in Minehead, and Raddington was in the care of curates-in-charge, usually the rectors of Kittisford or Chipstable.[8]

The church of ST. MICHAEL, so dedicated by 1510,[9] occupies a remote site, approachable only on foot. It comprises a chancel, nave with south porch,

[69] Ibid. vi. 753; ix, p. 279; xiii. 46; xvii. 194, 211–12; xxx, pp. 393, 434; lii, pp. 14, 137, 147, 153; liv, p. 25; lv, p. 47.
[70] Ibid. lii, p. 198.
[71] Cal. Pat. 1569–72, p. 58.
[72] S.R.O., D/D/B reg. 20, p. 53; Som. Incumbents, ed. Weaver, 426. Hill was tenant of Chubworthy: S.R.O., DD/SF 438.
[73] S.R.O., DD/WG, 13/4, p. 22.
[74] Ibid. 13/5, p. 19; 13/6, p. 19; Som. Incumbents, ed. Weaver, 426.
[75] S.R.O., DD/WG 13/5, p. 163.
[76] Som. Incumbents, ed. Weaver, 426.
[77] P.R.O., CP 25(2)/1056/6 Geo. I Mich.; S.R.O., D/D/B reg. 27, ff. 15, 17, 18v.
[78] S.R.O., D/D/B reg. 32, f. 62.
[79] P.R.O., CP 25(2)/1197/24 Geo. III Hil.
[80] S.R.O., D/D/B reg. 32, f. 115; 33, f. 36v.
[81] Rep. Com. Eccl. Revenues, pp. 150–1.
[82] S.R.O., D/D/B reg. 34, f. 156; 35, f. 177v.
[83] P.O. Dir. Som. (1861).
[84] Ibid. (1875); Crockford.
[85] M.I. in Stawley church.
[86] Crockford; Dioc. Dir.

[87] Inf. from Dioc. Regy., Wells.
[88] Valor Eccl. (Rec. Com.), i. 221.
[89] S.R.O., D/D/Vc 24.
[90] Rep. Com. Eccl. Revenues, pp. 150–1.
[91] P.R.O., HO 129/314/1/4/6.
[92] Valor Eccl. (Rec. Com.), i. 221.
[93] S.R.O., D/D/Rg 355.
[94] Ibid. tithe award.
[95] Valor Eccl. (Rec. Com.), i. 221.
[96] S.R.O., D/D/Rg 355; ibid. tithe award.
[97] Ibid. D/D/Rg 355.
[98] Kelly's Dir. Som. (1931, 1939).
[99] Local inf.
[1] S.R.O., D/D/Vc 20.
[2] Wells Wills, ed. Weaver, 137.
[3] S. & D. N. & Q. xiv. 64; S.R.O., D/D/Rr, marr. 1706; E. Dwelly, Par. Rec. viii (1921), 118–19.
[4] S.R.O., D/D/B returns 1827; D/D/Bo; D/D/Br; D/D/Bp; Rep. Com. Eccl. Revenues, pp. 150–1.
[5] S.R.O., D/D/B returns 1815.
[6] Ibid. D/D/V returns 1843.
[7] P.R.O., HO 129/314/1/4/6.
[8] Dioc. Dir.; Crockford; Kelly's Dir. Som. (1919).
[9] S.R.S. xix. 140; cf. S.R.S. liv, p. 47; plate opposite.

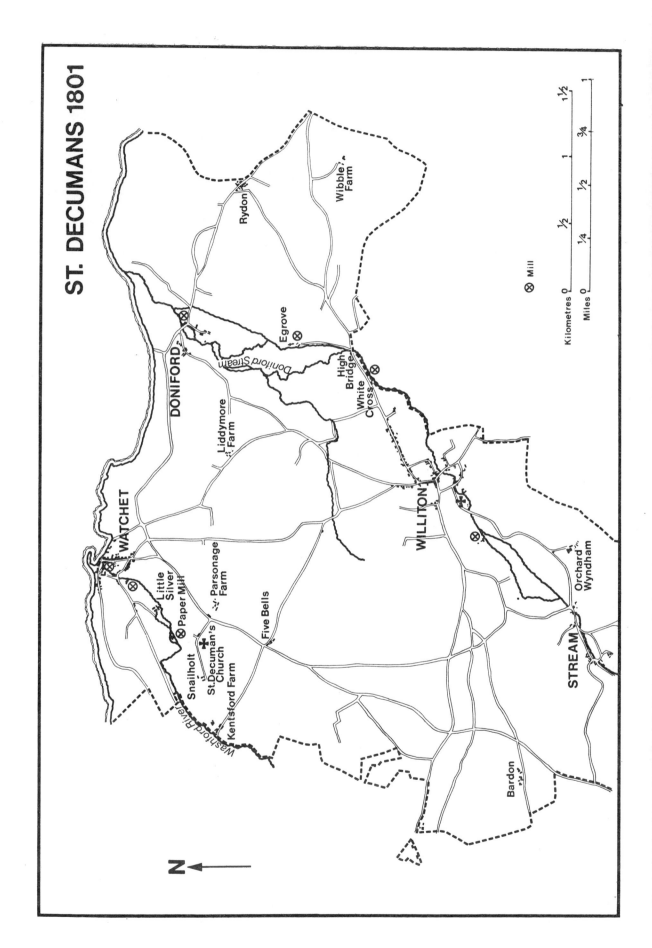

ST. DECUMANS 1801

Wibble Farm

Rydon

Egrove

DONIFORD

Doniford Stream

High Bridge

White Cross

Liddymore Farm

WILLITON

WATCHET

Little Silver

Paper Mill

Parsonage Farm

Five Bells

Snailholt

St. Decuman's Church

Kentsford Farm

Washford River

Orchard Wyndham

STREAM

Bardon

N

Kilometres 0   ½   1   1½
Miles 0   ¼   ½   ¾   1

⊗ Mill

142

and western tower. The whole building dates from the 14th century at the latest, its door including ironwork of the second half of the century,[10] and two of the four bells there until *c.* 1971 dated from the 1370s. One was then transferred to Odcombe.[11] The chancel screen below a plastered tympanum, retaining medieval paintwork under later colouring, is also thought to date from before 1400. Until the late 19th century the rood beam was in its original position west of the screen.[12] The font is of a 13th-century Purbeck type, and there are late medieval tiles on the floor. Carved bosses in the roof include a green man. The tower was evidently repaired or even rebuilt in 1675,[13] the reading desk bears the date 1713, and the royal arms were painted in 1852.

The plate includes a cup and cover of 1574 and a flagon of 1719.[14] The registers date from 1814, earlier ones from 1583 having been destroyed after 1914. There are transcripts from 1603.[15]

NONCONFORMITY.
A woman, first reported in 1630, was described in 1636 as an 'absolute' popish recusant.[16] The Waldegraves, lords and patrons of the rectory, were disbarred as papists from exercising their patronage from Elizabeth I's reign.[17]

EDUCATION.
A school was established apparently in the early 1840s, but in 1846 the 'most pleasing little school' was burnt down.[18] In 1847 the school had 7 boys and 14 girls attending on weekdays and Sundays and was supported by subscriptions and school pence.[19] A room adjoining the rectory house was used for a Sunday school by 1861, and by 1875 a National school was also held there.[20] By 1883 the children were taught at Chipstable or Skilgate.[21] The schoolroom was demolished during the First World War.[22]

CHARITIES FOR THE POOR.
The capital of two charities, one of unknown origin, the other founded by John Kemp at an uncertain date, totalled £3 1s. and was distributed by the overseers yearly at Easter. By will dated 1754 William Yeandle of Upton added a further £1 and in 1786 George Davys of Raddington left £4 for four labouring men every Easter. By 1826 the whole produced 8s. a year, and was given 'to such as appear to want it most'.[23] In 1840 the stock was said to have been divided among the poor 'many years ago',[24] but later in the century it was thought it had been spent to help pay the debt on the union workhouse.[25]

ST. DECUMANS

INCLUDING WATCHET AND WILLITON

THE PARISH of St. Decumans,[26] named after the patron saint of its church,[27] occupies the coastal plain at the mouth of a broad valley between the Quantocks and the Brendons. The former borough and market town of Watchet, on the coast in the north-west corner of the parish, and the large village of Williton, 2 km. south on the southern boundary, are the main settlements. The parish is roughly L-shaped,[28] occupying a band *c.* 2 km. wide which runs for 4 km. along the coast. At its western end it stretches southwards for 4.5 km. into the Brendons. A detached part of Nettlecombe in Warmoor, by the western boundary, was absorbed into St. Decumans in 1882 and part of Washford, beyond the western boundary and hitherto part of St. Decumans, was transferred with 7 houses and 34 people to Old

Cleeve in the same year. Three detached areas in the Brendons, part of the ancient parish, were transferred to other parishes, Hayne, now Lower Hayne, and Kingsdown (4 houses, 10 people) to Nettlecombe in 1883, and Timwood (1 house, 10 people) to Old Cleeve in 1886.[29] After those changes the parish measured 1,407 ha. (3,483 a.).[30] In 1902 the parish was divided between the urban district of Watchet and the civil parish of Williton. The two areas became constituent parishes in the West Somerset district in 1974.[31]

The boundaries of the ancient parish rarely followed natural features and interlocked with Old Cleeve between Washford and Kentsford[32] around an estate established there in the 10th century.[33] The eastern part of the parish lies on limestone, shale, and

[10] Dwelly, *Par. Rec.* viii. 108; S.R.O., DD/SAS CH 16.
[11] There were four bells until *c.* 1971 when the 2nd (1370–5) was transferred to Odcombe: inf. from Mr. G. Massey.
[12] *Proc. Som. Arch. Soc.* lii, pl. facing p. 59; W. Bligh Bond and B. Camm, *Roodscreens and Roodlofts*, 188.
[13] Tablet on S. side of tower.
[14] *Proc. Som. Arch. Soc.* xlv. 171.
[15] Dwelly, *Par. Rec.* viii. 108; *Inventory of Paroch. Doc.* ed. J. E. King (1938), 289; S.R.O., D/D/Rr.
[16] S.R.O., D/D/Ca 274, 310.
[17] Above, church.
[18] J. B. B. Clarke, *Acct. of Church Educ. among the Poor* (1846).
[19] Nat. Soc. *Inquiry 1846–7*, Som. 14–15.
[20] *P.O. Dir. Som.* (1861, 1875).

[21] *Kelly's Dir. Som.* (1883).
[22] Dwelly, *Par. Rec.* viii. 108.
[23] *Char. Don.* H.C. (1816), xvi; *15th Rep. Com. Char.* p. 453.
[24] S.R.O., D/D/V returns 1840.
[25] *Digest Endowed Char.* 1869–71, H.C. pp. 50–1 (1873), li.
[26] This article was completed in 1980, with additions in 1982.
[27] Below, church.
[28] S.R.O., tithe award.
[29] *Census*, 1891.
[30] Ibid. 1971.
[31] Below, local govt.
[32] S.R.O., tithe award.
[33] *Proc. Som. Arch. Soc.* xcviii. 122, 125.

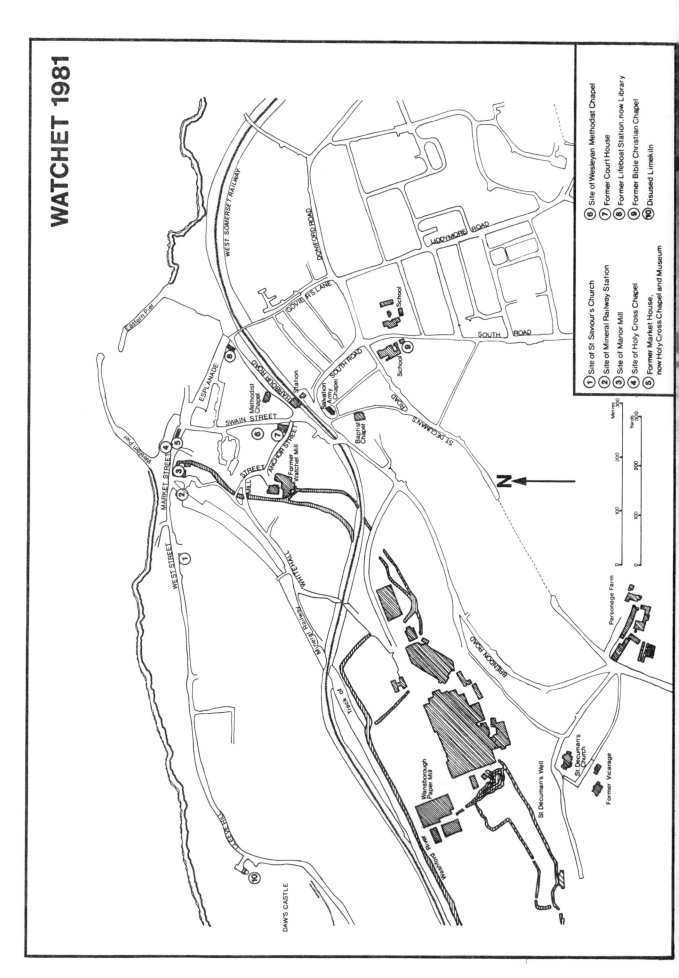

WATCHET 1981

Site of St Saviour's Church
Site of Mineral Railway Station
Site of Manor Mill
Site of Holy Cross Chapel
Former Market House,
now Holy Cross Chapel and Museum
Site of Wesleyan Methodist Chapel
Former Court House
Former Lifeboat Station, now Library
Former Bible Christian Chapel
Disused Limekiln

marl and slopes down from Rydon, on the eastern boundary, to the gravels of the Doniford stream. Further west, in the centre of the parish, is a limestone ridge rising to 75 m., which divides Watchet from Williton. North of the ridge the land slopes down to the coast and to the valley of the Washford river, and beyond the river rises steeply north-west to Cleeve Hill, the site of Daw's Castle.[34] The cliffs, largely of blue lias and marls with bands of harder limestone and gravels and rich in fossil remains,[35] have suffered severe erosion notably in Watchet and around the mouth of the Doniford stream. South of the limestone ridge, Williton lies on a broad band of marl, with gravels along the course of a stream flowing down from the Brendons. Further south the land rises over Upper Sandstone and Pebble Beds, and slate of the Upper Devonian to reach just over the 152 m. contour above Woodford in Nettlecombe.[36]

The parish was thus rich in building materials. Limestone was burnt in quantity from the later Middle Ages,[37] and sandstone was quarried south of Williton in the 19th century and probably before. Veins of alabaster in the cliff face were worked in the 17th century,[38] and lias for paving was taken below the high water mark.[39] There were attempts c. 1840 to find iron ore at Daw's Castle, iron and manganese at Stream quarry, and silver lead at Doniford.[40] Iron ore at Timwood was not actually reached when the Brendon mines were reopened in 1907.[41]

Palaeolithic, mesolithic, and neolithic flints have been found in quantity at Doniford, and three Bronze Age barrows, known as Graburrows,[42] survive at a site more familiarly known as Battlegore, north of Williton, where the discovery of weapons gave colour to the name.[43] The site was called Bytelgore[44] in the 14th century, probably a reference to the shape of a piece of land at the corner of an open field. A fourth round barrow, known as Bloody or Bleary Pate, near the parish boundary south-east of Rydon,[45] was known as Bleripate in the 16th century,[46] and the name is thus not Victorian.[47] A Romano-British site at Doniford was occupied in the 4th century.[48] Mother Shipton's Tomb in Black Down wood has been shown to be a copy of a Roman tomb found in Cumberland by the Wyndham family and was constructed in the late 18th or early 19th century.[49]

Celtic survival in the parish is suggested by the name Watchet, known in the 10th century as Waeced or Weced,[50] formed from two Welsh words meaning 'under the wood'.[51] The limestone ridge above Watchet was once covered in trees, as indicated by field names ending in 'grove',[52] and it retained some coppice in the late 17th century.[53] Celtic influence is also implied in the dedication of the church to the Welsh saint Decuman.[54] Williton (Willettun in 904)[55] appears to be named from the stream which passes through the hamlet of Stream and then flows close to the former manor house[56] and church. Both that stream and, by the 12th century, the Doniford stream[57] which it joins north-east of Williton, were called the Willet.[58] The Doniford stream at its mouth is known as the Swill river, and the tributary alternatively as the Guilly or Swilly.[59]

Apart from the main settlements of Watchet and Williton there were hamlets and farms scattered throughout the parish. Washford, Kentsford,[60] Doniford,[61] and an unidentified hamlet of Sualewecliffe[62] are recorded by name before the end of the 12th century. By the late 13th century there were houses or small farms at Little Silver in the Washford river valley,[63] Egrove (Hymgrave c. 1275),[64] and Wibble (Wybbehill);[65] at Bardon (Beredon)[66] on the ground rising towards the Brendons, Curlinch immediately west of Williton church;[67] at Culvercliffe, on the coast east of Watchet,[68] and at Huish.[69] Stream was established as a hamlet by 1314,[70] Rydon (Ridene) probably by 1327,[71] and there was a house or hamlet called 'la halle by Watchet' in the 1330s.[72] The last is not found after 1336, Sualewecliffe not after the 12th century, nor Huish after the 13th, and their sites have not been traced. Culvercliffe disappeared in the 15th century.[73] Orchard had emerged as a settlement by 1479,[74] and Snailholt (Snaylehole in 1528),[75] and Liddymore[76] were mentioned in the 16th century.

By the mid 17th century Doniford, Bardon, and Stream were the principal hamlets. In 1667 Stream comprised eight households,[77] and by 1714 it was in two parts, known as Higher and Lower Stream.[78] In 1801 Lower Stream had only one house,[79] and in 1851 Higher Stream comprised four farms and several cottages with a total population of 64.[80] Bardon, whose population of 113 in 1667 included

[34] Below.
[35] Wedlake, *Hist. Watchet*, 2–5.
[36] Geol. Surv. Map 1″, solid and drift, sheet 294 (1969 edn.), and drift, sheet 295 (1907 edn.).
[37] e.g. S.R.O., DD/CC 110079/18; DD/L P4/26A; 32/21, 27.
[38] Ibid. DD/WY 37/1.
[39] B.L. Add. MS. 33827, f. 44.
[40] S.R.O., DD/WY 154.
[41] Sellick, *W. Som. Mineral Rly.*, 75.
[42] *Proc. Som. Arch. Soc.* cxiii, suppl. 17. Gradborough in 1505: Winchester Coll. MS. 12864.
[43] Wedlake, *Watchet*, 5–14, 22–3; *Proc. Som. Arch. Soc.* cxiii, suppl. 3, 13, 41; J. Nightingale, *Beauties of Eng.* 13, pt. i. 578.   [44] S.R.O., DD/L P33/1 (1303).
[45] ST 10014212.
[46] S.R.O., DD/WY 47/2/23/1.
[47] *Proc. Som. Arch. Soc.* cxiii, suppl. 14.
[48] Wedlake, *Watchet*, 16–17; site O.S. Nat. Grid 09454336.   [49] *V.C.H. Som.* i. 365.
[50] *A.S. Chron.* (Rolls Ser.), i. 190–1; *Two Saxon Chrons.* ed. J. Earle and C. Plummer (1892), i. 99.
[51] Ekwall, *Eng. Place-Names* (1960), 500.
[52] S.R.O., tithe award.
[53] Ibid. DD/WY 65/36.
[54] Below, churches.
[55] *Cart. Sax.* ed. Birch, ii, p. 273.
[56] Below, Williton manor.
[57] *Proc. Som. Arch. Soc.* xcviii. 121.
[58] Ekwall, *Eng. Place-Names*, 519 suggests a possible British origin for the name; cf. S. M. Pearce, *Kingdom of Dumnonia* (Padstow, 1978), 195–7.
[59] Local inf.
[60] *Proc. Som. Arch. Soc.* xcviii. 122.
[61] *Chanc. R.* 1196 (P.R.S. N.S. vii), 199, 221.
[62] S.R.O., DD/L P33/1.
[63] Ibid. DD/L P33.   [64] Ibid.
[65] Ibid. DD/WY 19.
[66] Ibid. DD/L P33/1, 2.
[67] Ibid. DD/WY 10/O3/1; DD/L P33.
[68] Ibid. DD/L P32/2.
[69] Ibid. DD/L P33.
[70] *Cal. Pat.* 1313–17, 152; S.R.O., DD/L P33/1.
[71] *S.R.S.* iii. 182.   [72] S.R.O., DD/WY 19/Z2/8.
[73] Ibid. DD/L 2/7/36.
[74] Ibid. DD/WY 1.
[75] Ibid. 8/A2/2.
[76] Ibid. 9/W2/10.
[77] Ibid. 34.
[78] Ibid. 53/42; DD/L 2/19/109.
[79] Ibid. DD/WY, survey 1801.
[80] P.R.O., HO 107/1920.

some people living in Stogumber parish,[81] comprised only Bardon House and associated cottages in 1801.[82] In 1851 the population of Bardon was 9, but isolated cottages to the north at Shells (or Shelves) and Tomblands gave a total of 32 in that part of the parish.[83]

Apart from the expansion of Watchet and Williton, two other areas of growth in the 20th century were Five Bells and Doniford. The name Five Bells, used of a cottage in 1720,[84] was later given to the high ground at the junction of roads from Williton and Washford to Watchet, south-east of St. Decuman's church.[85] A few cottages beside the junction were joined in the 1930s by substantial detached houses. Doniford, which included cottages called Stoates Place in 1851,[86] had a summer camp site for the Territorials in the 1920s which continued in army use until the 1960s.[87] The camp site has since been developed as a holiday village.

Earthworks surviving on Cleeve Hill, near the boundary of Old Cleeve parish and known as Daw's Castle, were almost certainly[88] part of the *burh* of Watchet recorded in the Burghal Hidage.[89] The hill appears to have been occupied in Roman times and perhaps earlier,[90] and included the probable site of a minster church.[91] The defensive work, which may have been just over three furlongs in length,[92] was subsequently damaged by coastal erosion, lime workings,[93] and the adaptation of the area for a golf course.[94] The earthworks were known as 'le castell' *c.* 1537 when part of the hill was occupied by Thomas Dawe.[95]

A mint had probably been established in the *burh* in the late 10th century.[96] Old Cleeve manor had the third penny of the *burgherist* from four hundreds including Williton in 1086,[97] and it is possible that the *burh* of Watchet was the recipient of the tax.

The medieval town of Watchet, which succeeded the settlement on the headland, lay around the edge of a shallow bay, in a small area of level ground at the mouth of the Washford river, sheltered from the west by Cleeve Hill and from the east by the headland of Culvercliffe. At its heart was a large open space,[98] by the early 15th century known as Chipping Street and later as the market place or Market Street,[99] which was the site of the shambles,[1] the

Great Cross,[2] Holy Cross chapel,[3] the pillory,[4] and the 'tollestrig',[5] possibly a tolsey. At the west end the river was divided by an island to form east and west water.[6] A bridge spanned the river by the late 13th century.[7] Beyond west water, at the foot of Cleeve Hill, lay Bynneport or Byngeport, a name which perhaps signified an inner market or harbour, and which survived until the late 15th century.[8]

From the market place Culvercliffe Street ran eastwards along the shore. The street is mentioned from the 1270s until the mid 15th century.[9] By the 14th century there was a parallel street further south, known as Culver Street,[10] which survived into the 18th century, and is perhaps in part the modern Esplanade Lane.[11] During the 14th century the town spread inland with the formation of South Street (named between 1361 and 1385)[12] and Swine (later Swain) Street, the latter running from the eastern end of the market place to Lime Cross.[13] There may have been some building to the south-east, in an area known in the 14th century as Lourtegale,[14] where Glovers, later Govier's, Lane was recorded in 1438.[15] Culvercliffe Street seems to have disappeared when storms in the 1450s[16] swept away burgages and exposed the town to constant erosion.[17]

In the 16th century the town was protected by a weir or breakwater,[18] and by the quay which formed the northern side of the market place. The quay was rebuilt in the late 16th century.[19] The additional protection perhaps encouraged expansion or rebuilding at the western end of the market place. That end was called High Street by 1622,[20] a name which survived until 1743 or later.[21] New street names in the 18th century suggest infilling south of the market place, between the river and Swine Street: Silver Street by 1736,[22] Back Lane by *c.* 1725,[23] which later became Back Street and later still Anchor Street,[24] and Keck Alley Street by 1824.[25] By the 1850s the town had begun to expand westwards, in West Street,[26] but principally over the fields to the south and east, overlooking the harbour. Causeway Terrace was built in 1859,[27] Temple Villas and Temple Terrace were so called after the Bible Christian Chapel which was built on the town's edge in 1860.[28] Almyr and Wristland Terraces were named from the former open fields on

[81] S.R.O., DD/WY 34.
[82] Ibid. DD/WY, survey 1801.
[83] P.R.O., HO 107/1920.
[84] S.R.O., DD/WY 53/67.
[85] Ibid. DD/WY 29; also known as 'Groves of 5 bells': ibid. DD/WY 21.
[86] P.R.O., HO 107/1920.
[87] Wedlake, *Watchet*, 144–5.
[88] Inf. on excavations in 1982 from Dr. I. C. G. Burrow, county archaeologist.
[89] *A.-S. Charters*, ed. A. J. Robertson, 246–7; *Med. Archaeology*, viii. 74–88.
[90] Inf. from Mr. A. L. Wedlake, Watchet.
[91] Below, churches.
[92] *A.-S. Charters*, 246–7; *Med. Archaeology*, xiii. 90.
[93] S.R.O., DD/WY 196.
[94] Local inf.
[95] S.R.O., DD/WY 47/1/3.
[96] Wedlake, *Watchet*, 19–22.
[97] *V.C.H. Som.* i. 438; H. C. Darby and R. W. Finn, *Dom. Geog. of SW. Eng.* 198–9, 210.
[98] B.L. Add. Ch. 11172; S.R.O., DD/WY 6/N1/1.
[99] S.R.O., DD/L P32/11, 15; DD/WY 4/O2/19.
[1] Ibid. DD/WY 4/O2/5; DD/L P32/2, P33/9.
[2] B.L. Add. Ch. 11181.
[3] Below, churches.
[4] S.R.O., DD/WY 4/O2/1.

[5] Ibid. DD/L P32/11, P33/9; below, markets and fairs.
[6] S.R.O., DD/WY 4/O2/6, 7.
[7] Ibid. DD/L P32/5.
[8] Ibid. P32/5, 15.
[9] Ibid. DD/WY 4/O2/17, 4/R1/4, 22; DD/L P32/2, 20.
[10] Ibid. DD/L P32/2.
[11] Ibid. DD/WY 21 (1788).
[12] Ibid. 4/O2/11, 4/R1/6.
[13] Ibid. DD/L P32/2; DD/WY 8/T2/7; DD/WO 15/11D; Williton, Wyndham Estate Office, ct. bk. 1620–1727, *sub anno* 1621.
[14] B.L. Add. Ch. 11192; S.R.O., DD/WY 4/R1/4, 8, 9.
[15] S.R.O., DD/L P32/15.
[16] Below, econ. hist.
[17] S.R.O., DD/L P33/8; *S.R.S.* extra ser. 120.
[18] *L. & P. Hen. VIII*, xxi (2), p. 457.
[19] S.R.O., DD/WY 40.
[20] Ibid. 47/1/11.
[21] Ibid. 64/2, 12.
[22] Ibid. DD/WO 18/4.
[23] Ibid. 50/5.
[24] Ibid. DD/CCH 72.
[25] Ibid. DD/WO 15/11D.
[26] P.R.O., HO 107/1920.
[27] Datestone on building.
[28] Below, nonconf.

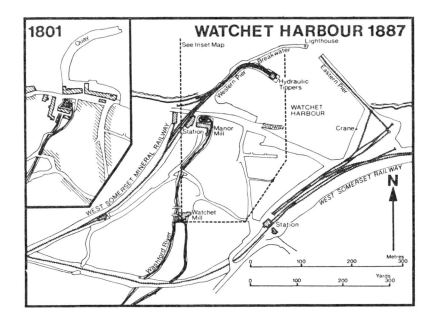

which they stood.[29] Detached villas on Cleeve Hill had been built by the 1880s,[30] but 20th-century building was principally to the south and east.

Meanwhile the creation of the harbour permitted some restoration of the ancient street pattern. The quay, damaged in the 1640s by storm,[31] was repaired in the 1660s by means of levies on imports of coal and salt[32] and by the issue of briefs.[33] The quay was said in the early 18th century[34] to be too low and not long enough to supply shelter, and it was seriously damaged c. 1797.[35] In 1807–8 it was extended with elm piles after suggestions that an eastern breakwater should be formed in place of the rocky beach. In 1838 George Rennie suggested an eastern breakwater as well as rebuilding and extending the pier which by 1801 had been constructed from the western end of the quay.[36] The works allowed the construction of the Esplanade in the 1840s.[37] Increasing business offered by the iron ore mines, deteriorating conditions in the harbour, and difficulties over ownership led to the appointment of harbour commissioners in 1857,[38] and under them the harbour was rebuilt by James Abernethy in 1861–2. The western pier was rebuilt and extended with a wooden breakwater and jetty, and an eastern quay and pier were added, thus enclosing a harbour capable of taking vessels up to 500 tons.[39] Much of the reclaimed land was used by the railways serving the quays.[40]

Surveys of Watchet from the mid 16th century described small town properties, normally two-storeyed, sometimes containing shops, and one having an outside stone stair to upper rooms, solars, and lofts.[41] A detailed covenant of 1517 specified the construction of a loft over a hall, which was to have windows and doors, and the insertion of a chimney.[42] Most of the earliest surviving buildings in the town are in Market and Swain streets, the main shopping area. They include no. 29 Swain Street, which dates from the later 17th century; Bank House, Swain Street, built c. 1735 in brick with stone dressings; the later 18th-century former court house and council offices; and the London inn. Earlier 19th-century building included the present West Somerset Hotel. There are at least two 18th-century houses on the Esplanade, and three cottages in Mill Street which date from the later 17th century. Building east and south-east of the harbour included the mid 19th-century Sea View Terrace.

There were at least five ale sellers in the town in the 1650s,[43] but the oldest named inn to be found was the Three Mariners, which was standing on the south side of the market place by 1657[44] and continued into the 18th century.[45] The Blue Anchor was mentioned in 1707[46] and survived until after 1807.[47] Three other inns in the earlier 18th century were the Black Boy (by 1711, washed away by 1738),[48] the White Hart (1743),[49] and the Bell (by 1744),[50] the last probably a new name for the former Three Mariners. In 1736 there were seven licensed houses in the parish as a whole,[51] and in 1755 eleven.[52] By 1787 there were eight inns in the town: the Greyhound, the George, the Ship, the Jolly Sailor, the Royal Oak, and the New Inn to add to the two earlier

[29] P.O. Dir. Som. (1861); Wedlake, Watchet, 135.
[30] O.S. Map 6″, Som. XXXVI. SW. (1887 edn.).
[31] S.R.O., DD/L 2/19/110.
[32] Ibid. DD/WY 40.
[33] Wedlake, Watchet, 83.
[34] S.R.O. DD/WY 40; Wedlake, Watchet, 84.
[35] S.R.O., DD/WY 40.
[36] Ibid.; Sellick, W. Som. Mineral Rly. 20–21.
[37] S.R.O., DD/WY 42, 158, 196; Sellick, W. Som. Mineral Rly. 21–2.
[38] 20 & 21 Vic. c. 141 (Local and Personal).
[39] S.R.O., Deposited Plans 252–3, 266; Sellick, W. Som. Mineral Rly. 22; above, frontispiece.

[40] Below.
[41] Ibid. DD/WY 47/1/3B; DD/L P32/96; DD/L 2/19/108; DD/WO 15/11B, 43/1.
[42] Ibid. DD/L P 32.
[43] Wyndham Estate Office, ct. bk. 1620–1727.
[44] S.R.O., DD/WY 46/2/27; DD/WY 176.
[45] Ibid. DD/WY 35; 47/2/18; 64/13.
[46] Ibid. DD/L 2/19/110.
[47] Ibid. DD/WY 35; 64/10; DD/WO 18/4.
[48] Ibid. DD/WO 5/5; 35.
[49] Ibid. DD/WY 64/2.
[50] Ibid. 29.
[51] Ibid. Q/RL.
[52] Dyfed R.O., D/CAR 202.

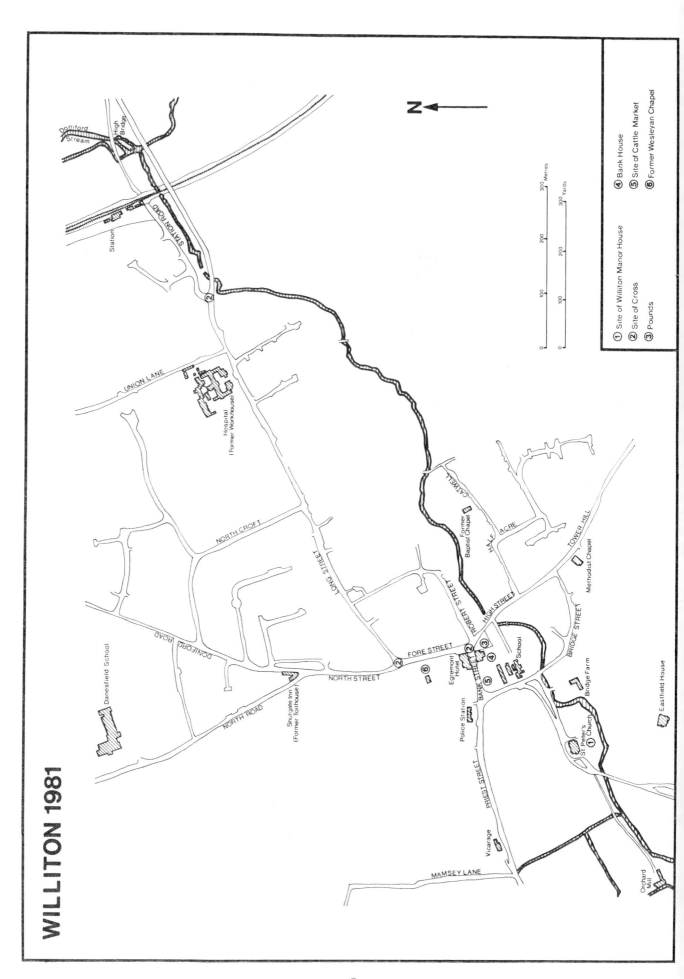

WILLITON 1981

N

Doniford Stream

High Bridge

Station

STATION ROAD

UNION LANE

Hospital (Former Workhouse)

NORTH CROFT

LONG STREET

Danesfield School

DONIFORD ROAD

NORTH ROAD

NORTH STREET

Shutgate Inn (Former Tollhouse)

⑥

Police Station

PRIEST STREET

Vicarage

MAMSEY LANE

FORE STREET

Egremont Hotel

② ③

④

⑤

BANK STREET

ROBERT STREET

HIGH STREET

School

St Peter's Church ①

Bridge Farm

BRIDGE STREET

Eastfield House

Orchard Mill

Former Baptist Chapel

CATWELL

HALF ACRE

TOWER HILL

Methodist Chapel

300 Metres
300 Yards
200
200
100
100
0
0

① Site of Williton Manor House   ④ Bank House
② Site of Cross   ⑤ Site of Cattle Market
③ Pounds   ⑥ Former Wesleyan Chapel

inns. The New Inn, the White Hart, the Ship, and the Jolly Sailor all stood on the quay, facing the north side of the market place and High Street.[53] By 1818 there survived only the Bell, the Greyhound, the Anchor (recorded in 1800), and the George. The London is first found in 1822, the Star in 1825,[54] and the Sailor's Delight in 1840.[55] The George had closed by 1841,[56] but the Greyhound survived until after 1861,[57] when business was transferred to the New Commercial, later the West Somerset Commercial (or Mossman's) Hotel.[58] The Wellington (1861) and the Railway (1866) survived for short periods, and by 1889 the Castle Temperance Hotel was established.[59] By 1894 the Anchor was offering accommodation for tourists.[60] The Bell, the London, the Anchor, the Star, and the West Somerset were the town's surviving historic inns in 1979.

The street pattern of Williton may have originated as a crossroads, the south-western quadrant thus formed including the manor house, the chapel, and a green. The name Bury, given to a field immediately north[61] of the chapel, and associated closes called Brodestrete, Lytellstrete, and Pleystrete, named together in the early 16th century,[62] indicate significant shrinkage at the west end of the village by that date, and the simple crossroads was already modified. The roads from east and west then joined the north-south road from Watchet at separate points, each marked by a cross.[63] The short street between them, possibly the Hokestrete mentioned in 1471,[64] was called High Street by 1621.[65] The eastern road was named Long Street in 1472–3[66] and the eastern limit of building along it was marked by White Cross. The western road was later named Priest Street because it passed beside the medieval priest's house; it became Bank Street after the building of a bank there c. 1860.[67] Other street names include Callis Street by 1750,[68] Shutgate Street (named after the toll house there) by 1766,[69] Bob Lane (later Robert Street) by 1816,[70] and Chapel Street by 1817.[71] Tower Hill, the south-eastern extension of the village, was so named by 1605.[72] In the 19th century there was cottage development south-west of the village centre at Catwell and Half Acre[73] and at the eastern end of Long Street, where the union workhouse and the railway station were built. There was extensive building after the Second World War to the north-east, off the Doniford road, and in the 1970s there was infilling among the scattered houses towards the eastern end of Long Street.

Much of the commercial centre of Williton dates from the later 19th century, but Long Street includes among its well spaced dwellings Honeysuckle Cottage, a small medieval hall-house. The house has traces of painting on the wattle and daub screen, and has a floor supported on high-quality medieval timbers but inserted in the 17th century. The dates 1607 and 1677 are on the outside wall.[74] In the same street is a row of three cottages dated 1624, and buildings of the 18th and earlier 19th centuries, ranging from roughcast and thatched cottages with access directly to the street, to the White House, an early 19th-century town house with angle pilasters and coved plaster eaves, set back behind a formal garden. There are 17th-century thatched and roughcast cottages in Bridge, Priest, Robert, and Shutgate streets.

The earliest known inn at Williton was the Pelican, established shortly before 1686.[75] In 1736 there were two inns, of which one was the Red Lion and the other perhaps the Coach and Horses, the second recorded in 1742.[76] By 1787 there were four: the Coach and Horses, the Red Lion, the New Inn, and the King's Arms.[77] By 1800 the Red Lion and the King's Arms had gone and the Wyndham Arms had been opened.[78] The Coach and Horses was pulled down c. 1830 and was replaced by the Wyndham (by 1861 the Egremont) Hotel, a larger establishment for the increasing business brought by the new turnpike road.[79] The Lamb, founded c. 1850, was renamed the Railway Hotel in 1858.[80] By 1866 the Masons' Arms, formerly a beer shop, occupied the former Shutgate toll house.[81]

Traces of open-field farming survived into the 19th century.[82] There was a park on Williton manor by 1321,[83] and an area called Stone Parks, near Battlegore, was mentioned in 1472–3.[84] Bathparks and Langpark were names of fields on Williton Regis manor in 1584.[85] The park at Orchard Wyndham existed in the early 18th century.[86] Field names suggest parks, or simply enclosures, on the western edge of Doniford, and adjoining Parsonage Farm and Stream, and warrens north of Parsonage Farm and north-west of Orchard Wyndham.[87]

Until the 19th century the main coastal route from Bridgwater entered the parish at Rydon and passed through Doniford to Watchet. From Watchet in the Middle Ages there were two parallel routes southwards to Williton,[88] known as Leechway and Liddymore lanes. They were closed in 1816.[89] The former took its name from the Leechway which linked Williton with Kentsford and Cleeve Hill.[90] From Watchet there were at least two other medieval routes, one serving the parish church, Snailholt, and Kentsford, leading to Cleeve Abbey,[91] the other

[53] S.R.O., DD/WY 35; ibid. survey 1801.
[54] Ibid. Q/RL.
[55] Wedlake, *Watchet*, 108–9.
[56] S.R.O., tithe award.
[57] *P.O. Dir. Som.* (1861).
[58] Ibid. (1866, 1875).
[59] Ibid. (1861, 1866); *Kelly's Dir. Som.* (1889).
[60] *Kelly's Dir. Som.* (1894).   [61] S.R.O., tithe award.
[62] Ibid. DD/L P33/2, 7, 8.
[63] H. Armstrong, *Parish of St. Peter, Williton* (1982), 32.
[64] S.R.O., DD/L P33/8.
[65] Wyndham Estate Office, ct. bk. 1620–1727.
[66] S.R.O., DD/L P33/8.
[67] P.R.O., HO 107/1920; S.R.O., DD/WY 158.
[68] S.R.O., DD/WY 97.
[69] Ibid. 50.
[70] Ibid. 97.
[71] Ibid. 158.
[72] Ibid. 47/1/10.
[73] P.R.O., HO 107/1920.

[74] *Proc. Som. Arch. Soc.* cxxiv. 137.
[75] S.R.O., DD/WY 55/4: 'now made a common inn'.
[76] Ibid. Q/RL; ibid. DD/WY 55/3; 97.
[77] Ibid. DD/WY 35.
[78] Ibid. Q/RL.
[79] Ibid. DD/WY, survey 1801; B.L. Add. MS. 33827, f. 42; *P.O. Dir. Som.* (1861).
[80] T. Hawkes, 'Williton', TS. of original notes c. 1903 ed. T. H. Andrew, in possession of Mr. D. Gliddon, Williton.   [81] *P.O. Dir.* (1861, 1866).
[82] Below, econ. hist.
[83] S.R.O., DD/L P32/1.
[84] Ibid. P33/8.
[85] Ibid. DD/WY 47/2/23/1.
[86] Below, manors (Orchard).
[87] S.R.O., tithe award.
[88] Ibid. DD/L P32/21.
[89] Ibid. DD/WY 158.
[90] Ibid. tithe award.
[91] Ibid. DD/L P32/7.

passing near the site of the old minster,[92] leading to Dunster, a route reported overgrown in 1472[93] and called the Greenway by the early 16th century.[94] The second route had a branch, probably that known as Old Lane in the 19th century,[95] which led to Little Silver.[96]

The principal local routes adopted by the Minehead turnpike trust in 1765 were the coastal route from Rydon through Watchet and over Cleeve Hill to Blue Anchor, and a road from Watchet southwards which divided at Five Bells, one branch passing south through Washford Cross and Fair Cross, the other south-east on the line of the Leechway through Williton to Tower Hill.[97] Until the early 19th century Williton was served from the south only by minor roads. One, through Stream, was itself probably a replacement for a more ancient route through Aller in Sampford Brett, abandoned in the 18th century during the emparkment of Orchard Wyndham.[98] The other linked the village over Tower Hill with Sampford Brett.

The turnpike road from Taunton came direct to Williton under an Act of 1807,[99] and in the next two decades improvements were made in existing routes.[1] A new line from West Quantoxhead c. 1829[2] brought traffic direct to Williton from Bridgwater, making Williton 'a great thoroughfare'.[3] From the 1930s onwards the route became of increasing importance, particularly to holiday traffic.

There were several bridges in the parish. Damsen Bridge (Damejonebrugge in 1465),[4] probably the bridge mentioned by the late 13th century,[5] carried the westerly route from Watchet. Cockle Bridge (mentioned 1659),[6] possibly crossed the Washford river further south. High Bridge (Heybrugge in 1438–9)[7] took a road east from Williton over the Doniford stream, probably to serve Egrove and Doniford. Fowl Bridge was built by 1492[8] to carry the Leechway over a stream at Battlegore. Little Bridge was standing at Doniford by 1515,[9] and the surviving structure of Kentsford bridge is probably of late medieval date.

After unsuccessful schemes to provide railway links between Watchet and Bridport (Dors.) and between Bridgwater and Minehead[10] the West Somerset Mineral Railway was founded in 1855 to carry iron ore from the Brendon Hill mines for shipment to South Wales. The track ran along the valley of the Washford river to a station at the south end of the western pier and loading facilities along the jetty. The line was in operation in 1856, but was not used for passenger traffic until 1865.[11] The West Somerset Railway was opened in 1862, linking the main Taunton–Exeter line with Watchet and providing a station at Williton and a terminus at Watchet with access to the eastern quay and pier. The line was continued to Minehead in 1874, following the mineral line up the Washford river valley to Washford.[12] The mineral railway survived the closure of the mines until 1898, was briefly reopened between 1907 and 1910, and was used to test automatic braking equipment until 1914.[13] The West Somerset Railway continued in operation until 1971, and was partially reopened in 1975 by a private company. The stations at Watchet and Williton were reopened in 1976.[14]

Friendly societies in the parish included a club at Williton by 1815 and the Social Order Benefit Society in 1820.[15] The Re-Union club was established at Watchet in 1849 and the Watchet United Sailors' Benefit Society in 1864. There were also branches of national friendly societies such as the Foresters, and various temperance societies. The United Sailors' Society, founded at Watchet in 1863, regularized a long-established pilotage system known at the Watchet Hobblers.[16] Local bands, theatricals at the West Somerset Hotel, the annual regatta, and a local custom called 'Caturn's Night' (25 November) were part of Watchet's social life in the late 19th century.[17] Williton acquired a reading room c. 1822, which became a school c. 1832.[18] Penny readings, musical entertainments, and recitations were held at the police station from the late 1850s, and a new reading room was built in 1867.[19] A newspaper called the West Somerset Free Press, founded at Williton in 1860, continued to be published in 1980.[20]

There were 63 taxed males in Watchet borough in 1378,[21] and 136 households in the whole ancient parish in 1563, including 60 in Williton chapelry.[22] The subsidy of 1667 recorded 503 inhabitants, comprising 167 at Watchet, 158 at Williton, 28 at Doniford, 21 at Stream, and 113 at Bardon, the last figure evidently including detached areas of the parish or manor stretching as far as the southern edge of Stogumber.[23] From 1801, when the total was 1,602, the population doubled in seventy years, and after a slight decline in the next two decades, reached 3,302 in 1901.[24] Watchet's population thereafter rose slowly, from 1,880 in 1901 to 1,936 in 1931, and to 2,597 in 1961, but in the next decade reached 2,900. Williton's fell in the first twenty years of the 20th century to 1,131 in 1921, rose slightly by 1931, but after the Second World War increased rapidly to 2,304 in 1961, and to 2,948 in 1971.[25]

During the Civil War, the Wyndham family was

[92] Ibid. DD/WY 4/O2/7.
[93] Ibid. 45/1/14/1.
[94] Ibid. DD/L P32.
[95] Ibid. tithe award.
[96] Ibid. DD/L P33/1.
[97] 5 Geo. III, c. 113.
[98] S.R.S. lxxvi: Day and Masters map, 1782; S.R.O., DD/WY 50.
[99] 47 Geo. III, c. 27 (Local and Personal).
[1] S.R.O., DD/WY 151; ibid. C/S 4, 15–18.
[2] 9 Geo. IV, c. 94 (Local and Personal).
[3] B.L. Add. MS. 33827, ff. 42–42v.
[4] S.R.O., DD/L P32/16.
[5] Above.
[6] Wyndham Estate Office, ct. bk. 1620–1727.
[7] S.R.O., DD/L P33/4.
[8] Ibid. P32/18.
[9] Ibid. P33.
[10] Wedlake, Watchet, 128–9.

[11] Sellick, W. Som. Mineral Rly. 19–20; S.R.O., DD/WY 149.
[12] E. T. Macdermot, Hist. G.W.R., rev. C. R. Clinker, ii. 87, 92.
[13] Sellick, W. Som. Mineral Rly. 47, 70–1, 78–9.
[14] J. A. Stanistreet, W. Som. Rly., Official Guide; J. A. Stanistreet and S. J. Edge, Stations and Buildings of W. Som. Rly.
[15] S.R.O., DD/WY 97; M. Fuller, West-Country Friendly Socs. 142; Hawkes, 'Williton'.
[16] Wedlake, Watchet, 119–22.   [17] Ibid. 124–5, 134.
[18] Hawkes, 'Williton'.
[19] S.R.O., DD/WY 196.
[20] L. E. J. Brooke, Som. Newspapers, 1725–1960, 84.
[21] P.R.O., E 179/169/31.
[22] B.L. Harl. MS. 594, f. 55.
[23] S.R.O., DD/WY 34.
[24] V.C.H. Som. ii. 351.
[25] Census.

divided in its allegiance: Sir William (d. 1683) accepted a baronetcy from Cromwell in 1658, and Orchard Wyndham was looted in June 1644 by the royalist Francis Wyndham, when it was in the possession of Sir John Wyndham, a parliamentary sympathizer.[26] Sir Edmund Wyndham of Kentsford was the royalist commander at Bridgwater.[27] The earl of Bedford's troops occupied 'the hill about Watchet' in 1642 when Hopton was occupying Minehead;[28] and a royalist ship, stranded by the tide in Watchet harbour, was taken by a troop of horse.[29] During Monmouth's rebellion in 1685 the parish sent six men to serve the king and another to carry arms to Taunton.[30] Twenty-six out of sixty muskets kept in the hall at Orchard Wyndham were 'taken away and lost' at the time.[31]

MANORS AND OTHER ESTATES. In 1086 Williton formed, with Carhampton and Cannington, a single estate, part of the royal demesne.[32] Williton passed between 1086 and 1107 to William de Falaise, who between 1100 and 1107 granted two thirds of the tithes there to the abbey of Lonlay (Orne).[33] The tithes passed to Stogursey Priory, Lonlay's cell, but are not later recorded. Sibyl de Falaise, possibly William's daughter,[34] married Baldwin de Boulers, and their daughter Maud married Richard FitzUrse (d. by 1158), lord of the barony of Bulwick (Northants.). Richard's son Reynold (d. 1172–5),[35] one of the murderers of Becket, divided the demesne manor of Williton in two halves.[36] The barony passed with his daughter Maud to the Courtenays, and King John granted the purparty which included the overlordship of Williton to Hubert de Burgh in 1216 and to William de Cauntelo in 1217. William was overlord of Williton in 1225.[37] On George de Cauntelo's death in 1273 the barony went to one coheir while the overlordship of Williton went to the other,[38] John de Hastings (d. 1313). From him it descended in the Hastings family, earls of Pembroke, being held as of Barwick manor.[39] That tenure was recorded in 1557 and 1629,[40] though in 1510 and 1524 Williton was said to be held of the earl of Northumberland.[41]

The manor of WILLITON, sometimes referred to as the manor of WILLITON AND WATCHET, was the half of the holding of Reynold FitzUrse which he granted c. 1172–5 to his half-brother Robert FitzUrse (occurs 1159–1202).[42] Robert was

succeeded by his son John, and John by his son Ralph FitzUrse (occurs 1243, d. by 1269).[43] John, son of Ralph, was in possession by 1273, but died c. 1280, leaving another Ralph, a minor, as his heir.[44] Ralph died c. 1321, and was followed by his son, also Ralph, a knight by 1335.[45] Sir Ralph died in 1350, holding Williton and the borough of Watchet jointly with his wife Maud, and leaving as heirs two daughters, Hawise, wife of Hugh Durburgh, and Joan, then unmarried.[46] Maud survived until 1388, when the heirs were James Durburgh, son of Hawise, and William and Joan Langdon, then under age, granddaughters of Joan.[47]

For the next two hundred years and more the manor was divided, the two estates being known as Williton Fulford and Williton Hadley. WILLITON FULFORD came into the Fulford family through the marriage of William Langdon with Henry Fulford. William's sister Joan is presumed to have died under age.[48] Sir Baldwin Fulford, son of William, attainted in 1461, was followed by his son Sir Thomas (d. 1490), and then by Thomas's sons Sir Humphrey (d. 1508) and William (d. 1517).[49] The estate passed through successive generations of Fulfords to Sir Francis Fulford, who sold what was described as the manors and lordships of Williton and Watchet to Sir John Wyndham in 1616.[50] The estate then descended like Orchard Wyndham manor.[51]

The later manor of WILLITON HADLEY descended to James Durburgh on the death of Maud FitzUrse in 1388.[52] James died in 1416 leaving a son John who died without issue and the estate passed to James's brother Ralph.[53] Ralph died in or after 1435,[54] and his Williton estate descended to his younger daughter Alice, wife of Alexander Hadley of London.[55] Alexander died in 1480 and was followed in the direct male line by John (d. by 1503), Richard (d. 1524), James (d. 1537), and Christopher Hadley (d. 1540).[56] Christopher's heir Arthur, who succeeded as a minor, married Eleanor, daughter of Sir John Wyndham, and died in 1558.[57] Eleanor, who married Thomas Carne or Kerne, retained dower in the manor, but Arthur's heir was his sister Margaret, wife successively of Thomas Luttrell and John Strode.[58] The estate descended in the Luttrell family until 1710, when it was sold by Alexander Luttrell to Sir William Wyndham.[59] It descended like Orchard Wyndham manor.

Reynold FitzUrse gave to his half-brother Robert

[26] H. A. Wyndham, A Family Hist. i (1939), 211–12, 258–9; Hist. MSS. Com. 3, 4th Rep. I, De la Warr, p. 296.
[27] D. Underdown, Som. in Civil War and Interregnum, 108–10, 185–6, 189–90.   [28] S.R.S. xviii. 18.
[29] S. & D. N. & Q. i. 227.
[30] S.R.O., DD/WY 37/8.
[31] Ibid. DD/WY 20, inventories 1683, 1697.
[32] V.C.H. Som. i. 435–6.
[33] S.R.S. lxi, p. 1.
[34] Ibid. pp. xx, 1; Sanders, Eng. Baronies, 22 n.
[35] Sanders, Eng. Baronies, 22.
[36] D.N.B.; below, Williton, Williton Temple.
[37] Sanders, Eng. Baronies, 23, 39–40; Cur. Reg. R. xii, p. 114.
[38] Sanders, Eng. Baronies, 23, 40.
[39] Cal. Inq. p.m. ii, pp. 17–18; v, p. 233; vi, p. 391; ix, p. 118; xiv, p. 155; xvi, pp. 260–1.
[40] P.R.O., C 142/114, no. 30; C 142/439, no. 53; Batten, Hist. Notes on S. Som. 9–10.
[41] P.R.O., C 142/25, no. 43; C 142/41, no. 36.
[42] S.R.O., DD/L P33; S.R.S. lxi, pp. 9–10.
[43] Proc. Som. Arch. Soc. lxviii. 97–8.

[44] S.R.O., DD/L P32/73; Cal. Inq. p.m. ii, p. 18; S.R.S. xli. 193; xliv. 139, 337–8; Proc. Som. Arch. Soc. lxviii. 99.
[45] S.R.O., DD/L P33/74; Proc. Som. Arch. Soc. lxviii. 100.
[46] Cal. Inq. p.m. ix, p. 390; Cal. Fine R. 1347–56, 257.
[47] Cal. Inq. p.m. xvi, pp. 260–1; Cal. Fine R. 1383–91, 301.
[48] S.R.S. xxii. 20–1, 173–4.
[49] Cal. Inq. p.m. Hen. VII, i, p. 270; P.R.O., C 142/25, no. 43; Burke, Land. Gent. (1914), 734.
[50] P.R.O., C 142/330, no. 93; S.R.O., DD/WY 1/80.
[51] Below.
[52] Cal. Inq. p.m. xvi, pp. 260–1.
[53] S.R.S. extra ser. 260–1.
[54] Ibid. xxii. 88.
[55] Ibid. extra ser. 263.
[56] P.R.O., C 140/76, no. 56; C 142/41, no. 36; C 142/114, no. 30; E 150/928, no. 15; S.R.S. extra ser. 263–4.
[57] P.R.O., C 142/115, no. 41; C 3/95/13.
[58] S.R.S. extra ser. 267; S.R.O., DD/WY 46/2/28/2.
[59] P.R.O., CP 25(2)/962/9 Anne East.

c. 1172–5 'a little house where he was accustomed to live'.[60] In 1321 Annora, widow of Ralph FitzUrse, was assigned as dower two barns and other buildings, and reference was then made to an old house and a lower court towards the water.[61] The division of the manor in 1388 involved a physical division of the house. One share was a chamber called 'lady chamber' with a privy, and a cellar below, with part of the hall including the porch as far as the service wing (which had a room called the 'gentleman chamber'), together with the eastern half of the barton next to the water and half the barn and the byre.[62] The two parts seem thereafter to have been regarded as two separate houses. The Hadley share of the house was held with a few acres in 1558[63] and by 1568 it seems to have been occupied by John Wyndham (d. 1572) and his wife Florence.[64] From 1578 it was let to Humphrey Wyndham, John's youngest brother,[65] who was still there in 1613.[66] From 1615, described as the 'capital messuage called the mansion house of Williton', it was let.[67]

The Fulford part of the house was let in the 15th century, and included a high chamber at the east end of the hall in 1454.[68] By 1605 it was let with half a ruined dovecot,[69] but a reversionary lease granted *c.* 1615 suggests that both parts were to be united in the occupation of the Dawe family.[70] The subsequent history of the house has not been traced, but it seems likely that the former manor house of Williton thus reverted to a single unit. It probably stood on the north side of the stream south-west of Williton chapel. There were buildings on the site in 1801.[71]

Before 1172 Reynold FitzUrse gave, or possibly sold, half his manor of Williton to the Knights Templar, perhaps to raise money to travel to Rome and the Holy Land to do penance for his part in the murder of Becket.[72] The estate passed to the Crown on the suppression of the Templars in 1312, and was given to the Knights Hospitaller in 1332.[73] On the dissolution of the Hospitallers in 1540 the estate again reverted to the Crown, but in 1544 it was granted to John (later Sir John) Leigh of London (d. *c.* 1563).[74] He settled it on his nephew, also John, but by 1567 some claim had passed to Edward FitzGarrett and his wife Agnes, Sir John Leigh's daughter.[75] John Leigh granted the manor to the Crown in 1572, but a 99-year sublease had been made in 1556 to Sir John Leigh's servant Richard Blount (d. 1575), of Coleman Street, London.[76]

Blount's widow Margaret, married successively to Jasper Fisher and Nicholas Saunders of Ewell (Surr.), retained the estate until 1584, and in the following year it passed to Blount's nephew, also Richard Blount, to whom the Crown granted a 1,000-year lease in 1575.[77] Sir John Wyndham occupied the estate as farmer from 1573,[78] and in 1602 he acquired the remainder of Blount's lease. In 1609 he purchased the freehold.[79] The estate, which until that date had usually been called the manor of *WILLITON TEMPLE*, was known in the 17th century as the manor of *WILLITON HOSPITAL*, and in the 18th as *WILLITON REGIS*.[80] It descended with Orchard in the Wyndham family, and Mr. G. C. Wyndham was owner at his death in 1982.

The capital messuage of the estate was let by 1505.[81] In 1612 it was held on lease with 68 a., and was described as lying by the highway and was associated with land called le Line.[82] Fields called Lines in the 19th century suggest that the site may be on or near the southern side of Bridge Street in Williton, leading to the green and the site of the other manor house.[83]

A fee held by William de Reigny (d. 1186–9) of Reynold FitzUrse in 1166 was evidently given by Reynold's father Richard (d. by 1158).[84] The fee was identified by 1196 as *DONIFORD*.[85] William's son or nephew John de Reigny was succeeded in 1222 by another John de Reigny,[86] who in 1225 held ½ fee in Doniford and Stogumber of William de Cauntelo as of the honor of Bulwick.[87] The overlordship descended with that of Williton until 1375 or later.[88] John de Reigny was succeeded apparently in 1246 by his grandson Sir William de Reigny,[89] whose heirs at his death in 1275 were his aunts and their heirs, namely Joan wife of Robert Grubbe, Joan wife of John de Locun, Alice wife of William le Pruz, Nicholas of Walton, and Elizabeth of Horsey; Joan Locun and Alice were jointly entitled to one of the quarter shares[90] in which the manor was later held.

Elizabeth of Horsey's share appears to have been held in 1316 by Walter of Rumton;[91] it was held by William of Horsey (d. 1327) in 1325, by Ralph of Horsey (d. 1354), and by Ralph's son John.[92] Eleanor Horsey was owner in 1375, Sir John Horsey in 1418, and by 1431 Henry Horsey of Clifton Maybank (Dors.).[93] Sir John Horsey of Clifton sold his estate in Doniford to John Wyndham in 1543.[94]

[60] S.R.O., DD/L P32–3.
[61] Ibid. P32/1.
[62] Ibid. P33/7.
[63] Ibid. P33/11.
[64] Ibid. P33/13.
[65] Ibid. P32.
[66] Ibid. P33/14.
[67] Ibid. DD/L 2/19/109.
[68] Ibid. DD/WY 10/D3.
[69] Ibid. 47/1/10.
[70] Ibid. 47/2/33/1, 47/3/43. Nicholas Dawe still occupied the house in 1653: DD/L P3/12.
[71] Wyndham Estate Office, survey 1621; S.R.O., DD/WY, survey 1801; Armstrong, *Parish of St. Peter, Williton*, 33.
[72] S.R.O., DD/L P32/3; *Chron. Rogeri de Hovedene* (Rolls Ser.), ii. 17; *Raccolta degli Storici Italiani*, ordinata de L. A. Muratori (1925), vii. 260–1; inf. from the Lord Sudeley and the suggestion of the late Dr. W. Urry, Oxford.
[73] *Cal. Close, 1330–3*, 514.
[74] *L. & P. Hen. VIII*, xix (1), p. 39; *Cal. Pat. 1563–6*, p. 167; P.R.O., E 318/708.
[75] *Cal. Pat. 1563–6*, pp. 167, 301; 1566–9, p. 45.
[76] S.R.O., DD/WY 9/W2/4; P.R.O., LR 6/17, no. 4.
[77] DD/WY 9/W2/3, 5, 7; 46/2/28/1–3; inf. from Dr. K. Wyndham. [78] Wyndham Estate Office, ct. bk.
[79] S.R.O., DD/WY 9/W2/13, 15.
[80] Ibid. DD/WY 45/1/9, 46/2/29; 97.
[81] Winchester Coll. MS. 12864.
[82] S.R.O., DD/WY 47/1/11.
[83] Ibid. tithe award.
[84] *Red Bk. Exch.* (Rolls Ser.), i. 334–5; S.R.O., DD/WY 9/W2/10; *S.R.S.* extra ser. 307.
[85] *Chanc. R.* 1196 (P.R.S. N.S. vii), 199, 221.
[86] *S.R.S.* extra ser. 307.
[87] *Cur. Reg. R.* xii, p. 114.
[88] *Cal. Inq. p.m.* ii, p. 95; v, p. 233; vi, p. 391; vii, p. 29; ix, p. 119; x, p. 160; xi, pp. 410–11.
[89] *S.R.S.* extra ser. 308.
[90] *Cal. Inq. p.m.* ii, pp. 94–5, 141.
[91] *Feud. Aids*, iv. 333.
[92] *Cal. Inq. p.m.* vi, p. 391; vii, p. 29; x, p. 160.
[93] Ibid. xiv, p. 155; S.R.O., DD/WO 10/3: Huish to Huish; *Feud. Aids*, iv. 439.
[94] *S.R.S.* li, pp. 18–19.

Nicholas of Walton (also called Nicholas of Barton after his manor in Winscombe)[95] retained his share in 1325,[96] and that quarter was settled on Stephen of Walton in 1338, with remainder to Alan and Isabel Walton.[97] Isabel survived until 1361 and was succeeded by her son John.[98] As John Barton he still held the estate in 1375,[99] but the family interest seems to have been leased by 1431.[1] John Huish (d. 1551–2) held a lease from John Walton which his cousin and heir Robert Walton afterwards confirmed.[2] The family's connexion with Doniford has not been traced further. John Grubbe was one of the lords of Doniford in 1316[3] and 1325.[4] His quarter share was settled in 1329 on his son John and on that John's wife Clemence,[5] who held it in 1375.[6] In 1431 it and the Waltons' quarter share were evidently those held by Henry North and William Allinscombe;[7] the Grubbes' share has not been traced thereafter. John Fraunceys in 1316 and 1325 held a quarter of the manor,[8] presumably as heir to Joan Locun and Alice le Pruz. His estate is said to have passed in 1369 to Oliver Huish, whose family had held land there by 1254.[9] The Huishes continued at Doniford until 1669, when Edward Huish died, but it seems likely that much of their land had already been sold by John Huish (d. 1649), Edward's brother, to the Wyndhams.[10] There were further sales c. 1672.[11]

In 1275 William de Reigny had a small hall, chamber, barn, stable, and dairy, all thatched, and a kitchen and granary roofed with stone, together with a chapel, used as a chantry served by the rector of Aisholt.[12] A mansion house was held by the Huish family by 1627,[13] and was acquired by the Wyndhams in 1669.[14] Known as Doniford Farm, it is a complex building. The present dwelling comprises on the south side of a courtyard a hall and parlour with a cross wing west of the hall and a kitchen at the rear of the parlour, the hall and parlour dating from c. 1500. North of the courtyard is a range with a smoke-blackened cruck roof which may have been an earlier house, later converted for use as the kitchen range of the present house.

An estate known as *HARTROW AND DONI-FORD* manor had emerged by 1527 as an extension of the Sydenhams' manor of Hartrow in Stogumber. It was divided between the sisters and heirs of John Sydenham (d. 1526), half passing to John and Elizabeth Wyndham and half to Thomas and Joan Bridges.[15] In 1549 Bridges sold his share to Sir John Wyndham and John Sydenham of Brympton.[16] In 1559 Sir John Wyndham conveyed his estate, de-

scribed as three parts of Hartrow and Doniford manor, to Joan Sweeting.[17] Joan's husband, William Lacey, acquired the Sydenhams' quarter share in 1563.[18] The land descended on William's death in 1607 to his son, also William (d. 1641), and then to his grandson William, son and heir of Thomas Lacey (d. 1626).[19] William died in 1690 leaving Doniford manor to his youngest son Arthur (d. c. 1729),[20] who probably sold the estate to discharge a mortgage. By 1730 it was owned by Sir John Trevelyan, and it descended in his family until exchanged with the earl of Egremont in 1804 and absorbed into the Wyndham estate.[21] It then comprised Court farm and some meadow and woodland.

Court Farm, Doniford, probably the manor house, has a cross-passage entry and three-roomed plan with extensive later additions. The former farm buildings were in 1980 converted for holiday accommodation.

An estate which in the late 15th century was known as the manor of *ORCHARD*[22] may be traced back to 1287 when Thomas of Orchard acquired lands called Orchard by exchange with Cleeve Abbey.[23] Thomas died in 1311 and was succeeded by his son John (d. c. 1360) and by John's daughter Joan, wife of John of Luccombe. Joan's daughter, also Joan, married Richard Popham of Alfoxton, who held lands in Watchet of the fee of Brompton Ralph in 1448.[24] Their daughter, a third Joan, married first John Sydenham (d. 1464), son of John Sydenham of Bathealton, and then John St. Aubyn.[25] In 1459–60 Orchard and other lands in St. Decumans, Crowcombe, Stogumber, and Dodington were settled on John and Joan and their son John Sydenham (d. 1521),[26] though in 1503 John St. Aubyn successfully claimed Alfoxton and other lands belonging to the Orchards.[27] John Sydenham was succeeded in 1521 by his grandson, also John Sydenham, who died in 1526 leaving as his heirs his two sisters, Elizabeth and Joan, subsequently married to John Wyndham and Thomas Bridges respectively.[28] Under an agreement of 1529 Wyndham acquired the Bridges' share, an estate which included the demesnes at Orchard, and lands at Curlinch, Snailholt, and elsewhere in St. Decumans, and at Cheddermarsh in Stogumber.[29] That purchase was the first stage in a process by which the Wyndham family became the dominant landowners in the parish within a century.

Sir John Wyndham survived until 1574, outliving his son, also John (d. 1572).[30] The younger John's son, another John (later Sir John), succeeded to the

[95] *Cal. Inq. p.m.* xi, pp. 410–11.
[96] Ibid. vi, p. 391.
[97] *S.R.S.* xii. 189.
[98] *Cal. Inq. p.m.* xi, pp. 410–11.
[99] Ibid. xiv, p. 155.
[1] *Feud. Aids*, iv. 439.
[2] *Som. Wills*, ed. Brown, i. 13.
[3] *Feud. Aids*, iv. 333.
[4] *Cal. Inq. p.m.* vi, p. 391.
[5] *S.R.S.* xii. 141.
[6] *Cal. Inq. p.m.* xiv, p. 155.
[7] *Feud. Aids*, iv. 439.
[8] Ibid. iv. 333; *Cal. Inq. p.m.* vi, p. 391.
[9] B.L. Add. MS. 33827, f. 68; *Cal. Inq. p.m.* xiv, p. 155; *S.R.S.* xii. 158.
[10] S.R.O., DD/WY 11/B4/13, 18.
[11] Ibid. 23/11.
[12] P.R.O., C 133/11, no. 11.
[13] Ibid. C 142/439, no. 53; *S.R.S.* lxvii, p. 27; S.R.O., DD/WY 11/B4/12.

[14] S.R.O., DD/WY 11/B4/16.
[15] P.R.O., CP 25(2)/51/366, 19 Hen. VIII Trin., Mich.
[16] S.R.O., DD/WY 1/40–3.
[17] P.R.O., CP 25(2)/204/1 Eliz. I East.
[18] Ibid. CP 25(2)/204/5 Eliz. I Hil.
[19] Ibid. C 142/462, no. 100; S.R.O., DD/DR 32; *S.R.S.* extra ser. 174–5; ibid. lxvii, p. 33.
[20] *S.R.S.* extra ser. 176.
[21] S.R.O., DD/WO 9/8, 44/12; DD/WY 158.
[22] P.R.O., C 140/28, no. 22.
[23] B.L. Add. MS. 33827, f. 61.
[24] S.R.O., DD/WY 1/A1, A4–5.
[25] B.L. Add. MS. 33827, ff. 61–3.
[26] S.R.O., DD/WY 1/A9, 1/A26, and unnumbered deed, quitclaim of Maud Wynston.
[27] P.R.O., C 142/37, no. 149; S.R.O., DD/WY 1/30–1, 33.
[28] P.R.O., C 142/45, no. 15; S.R.O., DD/WY 1/33.
[29] S.R.O., DD/WY 8/A2/3–4.
[30] Ibid. DD/WY 1/C.

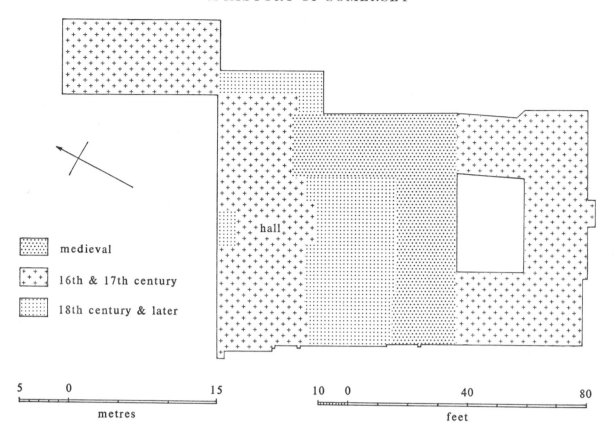

medieval

16th & 17th century

18th century & later

hall

5   0   15

metres

10   0   40   80

feet

ORCHARD WYNDHAM

family holdings in 1581.[31] He bought the Fulford and Hospital manors, and at his death in 1645 was followed by his second son John (d. 1649), and then by John's son William (cr. Bt. 1661, d. 1683). Sir William's son Edward (d. 1695) was followed by his son William (d. 1740), chancellor of the Exchequer under Queen Anne, and William's son Charles (d. 1763). Charles inherited from his uncle Algernon Seymour, duke of Somerset (d. 1750), the earldom of Egremont, estates in six counties, and a principal residence at Petworth (Suss.). George Wyndham, son of Charles and 3rd earl of Egremont, died unmarried in 1837, and was succeeded in the title and some of the estates, including Orchard Wyndham, by his nephew, George Francis. George Francis died without children in 1845, leaving the estate entailed, first for the benefit of his widow Jane (d. 1876) and then for a distant cousin, William Wyndham of Dinton (Wilts.). William died in 1914 and his son, also William, sold Dinton in 1916, thereafter making Orchard Wyndham his home. William Wyndham's charitable endowments, especially in the causes of local history, archaeology, and education, were assessed on his death in 1950 at £40,000. He died unmarried and was succeeded in the estates by his nephew George Colville Wyndham, the owner at his death in 1982.[32]

The house known as Orchard Wyndham lies in parkland 1 km. south-west of Williton. The house is arranged round two courtyards. One, on the south-east, is still open, the other now contains the main staircase. The central range was formerly a medieval open-hall house, and it retains a smoke-blackened cruck roof of three and a half bays. A two-storeyed cross wing with an arch-braced collar beam roof, probably of the 15th century, abuts the north-east end of the hall, but at the other end the line of the main roof is carried out to a gable above rooms on two floors, an arrangement which may be contemporary with the hall.

According to Leland John Sydenham (d. 1521) 'builded most part or almost all the good building of Orchard'[33] including a chapel licensed in 1499.[34] The new work included a second hall with cross wings to the north-west of the earlier house, with a short two-storeyed range running north-west from the end of the south-west cross wing, and a narrow range running back from the wing to the end of the earlier hall range. Other 16th- or early 17th-century buildings completed the south-east courtyard and housed, at least on the ground floor, the service rooms and offices. A 17th-century wing running north-west from the north corner of the house may have been stables. Early 17th-century moulded plaster ceilings survive at the east corner of the house, above the present kitchen, and in a first floor room, which has contemporary panelling, in the earliest cross wing. The room now used as a library, at the west corner of the house, and the room above it, were refitted in the late 17th century.

In the 18th century the narrow range joining the later cross wing to the earlier hall was removed, and

[31] Ibid. 1/D.
[32] Burke, *Land. Gent.* (1914), 2085–6; *West Som. Free Press,* 9 Dec. 1950; W. Rickford, 'Wyndham Family'

(TS. in Local Hist. Libr. Taunton).
[33] Leland, *Itin.* ed. Toulmin Smith, ii. 164; below, plate facing p. 156.   [34] S.R.O., DD/WY 7/Z1A/26.

the space occupied by it and the adjacent open court was filled by a new stair hall and drawing room. It is probable that by then both halls had upper floors and ceilings.[35] During the 19th century the north-east wing was refitted and brought into domestic use, and the front wall of the hall was carried out to the line of the ends of the cross wings. At about the same time the south-west wing was demolished and the north-east front of the house was refenestrated with mullioned and transomed windows. Further internal alterations resulted from the need to make provision for dressing rooms and bathrooms in the later 19th and early 20th century. Recent restoration has exposed a number of features including the roof of the second hall and a number of blocked windows and doorways.

In the 18th century a group of outbuildings, which may have been farm buildings, lay north-west of the house.[36] They were probably demolished early in the 19th century when new stabling and outbuildings were being erected south-east of the house. There was formerly a park centred on the valley south-west of the house. In the early 18th century it was being extended to include the small knoll of Black Down, where a wood was intersected by vistas.[37] The stream in the valley bottom was dammed to form ornamental ponds. The slope between them and the house was probably terraced in the 18th century and became an area of informal garden in the later 19th century.

An estate called *WATCHET*, held by Dodeman of William de Mohun in 1086,[38] has been identified with the later holding of *KENTSFORD*.[39] Between 1154 and 1189 land between St. Decuman's church and Kentsford, part of the estate and the fee of Ralph son of William, grandson of Durand de Mohun, was given to the abbey of Neath (Glam.).[40] Some of the Kentsford estate was later said to be in Watchet, in the fee of Nettlecombe, when another part was granted by Ralph before 1212 to John, son of Richard de Mohun, and then by John in fee to Roger the nephew and the heirs of Robert Fitz-Herbert.[41] Part of Durand's estate, including that granted to Neath, was considered part of Withycombe manor in 1520–1.[42] The continued interest of the Mohuns is reflected in Bruton Priory's claim to tithes there in 1238.[43] Kentsford was still held under the Luttrells, successors to the Mohuns, in 1555.[44]

Between 1154 and 1189 William de Staver confirmed to Neath Abbey a grant which his brother Gervase had made of land which their father had held of Ralph son of William.[45] By 1242 Hamon of

Basing held ¼ fee in Kentsford of Reynold Mohun.[46] Hamon made over the estate to his son William,[47] and by 1259 William had been succeeded by Ralph of Basing, who survived until soon after 1280.[48] Ralph was followed by John of Basing (I), whose successor in 1327 and 1330 was Jordan de Lovelinche, probably husband of John's widow.[49] Sir John Basing (II), son of John (I), died in 1337 leaving a son, John (III), a minor until 1340.[50] John (III) was still holding the estate in 1367 and probably in 1379,[51] and had been succeeded by his son Gilbert by 1393.[52] Gilbert died in 1436, leaving a young son Simon,[53] but under a settlement of 1416 the estate passed to Gilbert's daughter Eleanor and her husband John Kemmes. They conveyed it to Richard Luttrell, who in 1445 granted it back to them, to hold half in tail and half for lives, with reversion to Richard.[54] Richard's estate escheated to the overlord, Sir James Luttrell.[55] Eleanor, as a widow, settled her estate in 1450, apparently for the benefit of her daughters Jane and Edith.[56] Edith married first Richard Lood and secondly John Stalling, with whom in 1490 she held half of Kentsford in fee tail and received a grant of the other half for three lives from Sir Hugh Luttrell.[57] John and Edith, apparently alive in 1509, were succeeded by Edith's son Edward Lood, who claimed to hold the whole in fee tail and made a demise for lives.[58] The demise resulted in a Chancery suit which lasted until 1531 when it was decided in favour of Sir Andrew Luttrell.[59] About 1532 the estate seems to have passed, possibly by sale, to John (later Sir John) Wyndham and Sir John Sydenham, and Sir John Sydenham was in occupation of the capital messuage and some 80 a. at his death in 1557.[60] That estate was left to Sir John's widow Ursula, but then passed to John Wyndham (d. 1572). John was followed by his brother Edmund (d. 1616). Thomas (d. 1636), son of Edmund, was succeeded by his son, the royalist Sir Edmund (d. 1683).[61] Edmund Wyndham, son of the last, died in 1698 leaving no issue.[62] Kentsford passed to his uncle, Thomas Wyndham of Tale (d. 1713), and on Thomas's death was sold to William Blackford of Dunster (d. 1728). Another William, son of the last, died in 1731.[63] By 1748 Kentsford was occupied, if not owned, by Edward Dyke, and had passed by 1751 to Sir Thomas Acland (d. 1785). Sir Thomas paid rates on the estate until 1755,[64] but by 1794 it had come to the owners of Combe Sydenham manor.[65] In 1806 it was bought by the earl of Egremont and was absorbed into the Wyndham estates.[66]

[35] Ibid. DD/WY 20, inventories 1683, 1697.
[36] Painting at Orchard Wyndham.
[37] S.R.O., DD/WY 7/Z1N (maintenance of park 1740); DD/WY 50 (purchase of common rights on Black Down 1718).
[38] *V.C.H. Som.* i. 505.
[39] *S.R.S.* extra ser. 114.
[40] S.R.O., DD/L P32/2; *Rot. Chart.* (Rec. Com.), 174b.
[41] S.R.O., DD/L P33/2.
[42] Ibid. P32/4.
[43] *S.R.S.* vii, pt. 2, p. 32; viii, pp. 57–8.
[44] Ibid. xxxiii, p. 291.
[45] *Rot. Chart.* (Rec. Com.), 174b.
[46] *S.R.S.* vi. 110.
[47] S.R.O., DD/L P32/2.
[48] *S.R.S.* xxxiii, pp. 39, 48; *Cal. Inq. p.m.* ii, p. 178.
[49] *Cal. Inq. p.m.* ii, p. 352; *S.R.S.* iii. 182; xxxiii, pp. 54, 61, 73; ibid. extra ser. 116.

[50] *Cal. Inq. p.m.* viii, pp. 66, 92, 510; *Cal. Close, 1339–41*, 377–8; 1343–6, 97.
[51] S.R.O., DD/L P32/2; *S.R.S.* xxxiii, p. 89.
[52] S.R.O., DD/L P32/7.
[53] Ibid. P32/7, 11; P.R.O., C 139/87, no. 45.
[54] S.R.O., DD/L P32/15.
[55] *S.R.S.* xxxiii, p. lv; ibid. extra ser. 120; *Cal. Pat. 1461–7*, 286.
[56] S.R.O., DD/L P32/15; *S.R.S.* xxii. 107–8.
[57] *S.R.S.* extra ser. 120–1.
[58] Ibid. xxxiii, p. 262; ibid. extra ser. 120.
[59] Ibid. xxxiii, pp. 280–1; ibid. extra ser. 121.
[60] P.R.O., C 142/114, no. 23.
[61] *S.R.S.* xxi. 191; xxiii. 310; *Cal. S.P. Dom. 1629–31*, 363.   [62] Wyndham, *Family Hist.* ii (1950), 4.
[63] *S.R.S.* extra ser. 123.
[64] S.R.O., DD/WY 37/9.
[65] *S. & D. N. & Q.* xii, p. 243.
[66] Wyndham, *Family Hist.* ii. 5 n.

Kentsford Farm lies in a valley beside the Washford river on the extreme western edge of the parish. It is of two storeys with attics on an irregular **L**-shaped plan. The west wing, facing the river, may retain the plan of a late medieval house. It appears to have been largely rebuilt *c.* 1600 when it became the cross wing to a hall range running eastwards and entered by opposing doorways with a porch on the south. Further alterations seem to have taken place in the late 17th century when a kitchen fireplace was put into the south room of the cross wing, and the room beyond the entrance passage was made into a parlour. The cross wing includes a bedroom decorated with a moulded plaster ceiling. A carved fireplace formerly in a large attic room was removed to Orchard Wyndham.[67] Among the farm buildings is a stable of *c.* 1600. A medieval cross, probably to mark a parish boundary, is incorporated in a wall at the entrance to the farmyard.

About 1190 Simon Brett gave the church of St. Decuman as a prebend in Wells cathedral.[68] The *PREBEND* or *PARSONAGE* was farmed by 1434, the first known lessees being the vicar of Carhampton and William Everard of Aller in Carhampton.[69] William Bowerman was farmer in 1577, probably in succession to two members of the Clark family.[70] By 1586 it was let to Hugh Norris, the first of several generations of his family to occupy the estate until 1676, when the lease was assigned to Sir William Wyndham.[71] Thereafter successive members of the Wyndham family or their trustees held it on lease from the prebendaries until 1858 and the Wyndham trustees bought it from the Ecclesiastical Commissioners in 1862.[72]

The prebend comprised lands, including 23½ a. given by Robert FitzUrse, and the tithes of the parish.[73] The whole was valued at £23 6s. 8d. in 1291,[74] and more realistically at nearly £54 in 1321, but was reduced in that year by 8 marks to augment the vicarage.[75] In 1535 the net value was said to be £22 15s. 4d.[76] The lessee's net income from the estate in 1724 was £211 13s. 6¼d.[77] The net income was £1,212 14s., less the hay tithe, in 1805[78] and £1,190 19s. in 1822.[79] In 1844 the rent charge for the prebend was assessed at £526 7s.[80]

The prebendal glebe, known in the late 15th century as the 'sanctuary of St. Decuman',[81] amounted to *c.* 66 a. in 1613 and to just over 57 a. in 1841.[82] It was said to be worth 40s. in 1535,[83] but some forty years earlier a figure of £3 6s. 4d. was given.[84] Tithes

at the same time were worth nearly £25, and a little less in 1535.[85] Tithes in kind in the 1620s were collected by throwing aside every tenth sheaf of corn, or if not sheaved, every tenth 'ridge, swathe, wad, or otherwise'. No tithe was taken on green beans or peas grown for their owners' or the poor's use, and there was no tithe on raking or gleaning.[86] The tithes seem to have been sublet by the Wyndhams from the late 17th century;[87] in 1744 one tenant paid £90 for the Williton tithes for three years, and another paid £160 from 1747 for three years for the Watchet 'side'.[88]

The 'fair dwelling house' of the parsonage was mentioned in 1635–6.[89] Parsonage Farm is a two-storeyed, **L**-shaped building which appears to date from the late 18th century.

A small estate held by the Brett family in Culvercliffe passed like Sampford Brett manor to the Courtenays.[90] Described in 1377 as rent in Watchet and Williton,[91] in 1563 it was known as the manors of *CULVERSCLYFF AND WATCHET*,[92] and in 1611 as the manor of *CULVERCLIFFE WATCHET*.[93] The name survived in 1826,[94] but in 1846, when it was sold to Sir Peregrine Acland, the estate was reduced to two strips of land.[95]

A reputed manor of *WATCHET*, owned by Sir John Wyndham in 1598 and in the 17th century known as *WATCHET WITH THE MEMBERS*,[96] descended with Orchard Wyndham manor, and was not mentioned after 1729.[97]

Thomas, son and heir of Thomas of Halsway, owned an estate in Watchet *c.* 1275, and the heirs of John, son and heir of Thomas, succeeded *c.* 1295.[98] The estate descended with Halsway manor in Stogumber,[99] and was known as *WATCHET HAWEYE* in the early 14th century.[1] It was sold in 1637 with the Stradling family land in Halsway and elsewhere to James Cade of Wilton (d. 1640).[2] James, son of James Cade, was in possession in 1655,[3] and another James Cade had property in the town in 1718.[4]

In 1303 Matthew Furneaux (d. 1316) held a fee at *LITTLE SILVER* of Cecily Beauchamp as of Compton Dundon manor.[5] It descended with the manors of Kilve, Weacombe in West Quantoxhead, and Lodhuish in Nettlecombe to Simon Furneaux (d. 1358) and to Simon's heirs until it was sold in 1419 to John Roger or Rogers of Bryanston (Dors.). John was in possession in 1428[6] and his grandson Henry was holding Lodhuish in 1472,[7] but no later

[67] Local inf.
[68] *H.M.C. Wells*, i. 43, 45.
[69] S.R.O., DD/L P35/15.
[70] *Som. Incumbents*, ed. Weaver, 355.
[71] S.R.O., DD/WY 171; Orchard Wyndham, Wyndham MSS. 1/1, 11; *S.R.S.* xxviii. 126; lxxi, p. 20; *Som. Wills*, ed. Brown, ii. 107.
[72] S.R.O., D/D/Ppb; DD/WY 171; Midelney Manor, Trevilian MS. 385; Orchard Wyndham, Wyndham MSS. 1/12–18; *Lond. Gaz.* 25 Mar. 1862, p. 1612.
[73] *H.M.C. Wells*, i. 45; *Cart. St. Mark's Hospital* (Bristol Rec. Soc. xxi), p. 162.
[74] *Tax. Eccl.* (Rec. Com.), 200.
[75] *H.M.C. Wells*, i. 388–9.
[76] *Valor Eccl.* (Rec. Com.), i. 134.
[77] S.R.O., DD/WY 171; DD/CC 114110.
[78] Ibid. DD/CC 11086.
[79] Ibid. DD/WY 20.
[80] Ibid. tithe award.
[81] Ibid. DD/L P32/22.
[82] Ibid. D/D/Rg 356; DD/WY 171; tithe award.
[83] *Valor Eccl.* (Rec. Com.), i. 134.
[84] S.R.O., DD/L P32/22.

[85] Ibid.; *Valor Eccl.* (Rec. Com.), i. 134.
[86] S.R.O., DD/WY 171 (1629).
[87] Ibid. 53, 176.
[88] Ibid. 21.
[89] Ibid. D/D/Rg 356.
[90] Below, Sampford Brett.
[91] *Cal. Inq. p.m.* xiv, p. 307; *Cal. Fine R. 1413–22*, 115.
[92] Devon R.O. 248M/H7–8; P.R.O., CP 25(2)/259/5 Eliz. I East.
[93] P.R.O., C 142/331, no. 130.
[94] Ibid. CP 40/3938, rot. 182.
[95] S.R.O., DD/AH 5/3, 39/7.
[96] Ibid. DD/WY 46/2/27.
[97] Wyndham Estate Office, ct. bk. 1711–29.
[98] S.R.O., DD/L P32/2.
[99] Below, Stogumber, manors.
[1] *S.R.S.* xii. 117.
[2] P.R.O., CP 25(2)/480/13 Chas. I Mich.
[3] S.R.O., DD/WY 46/2/26/1.
[4] Wyndham Estate Office, ct. bk. 1620–1727.
[5] *Feud. Aids*, iv. 303; *S.R.S.* extra ser. 317.
[6] *Feud. Aids*, iv. 346, 392; above, Kilve, manors.
[7] P.R.O., C 140/42, no. 51.

ORCHARD WYNDHAM, ST. DECUMANS: THE HOUSE AND PARK IN THE 18TH CENTURY

The avenue leads north from the house towards the road from Stream to Williton; beyond the house is
the wooded Black Down

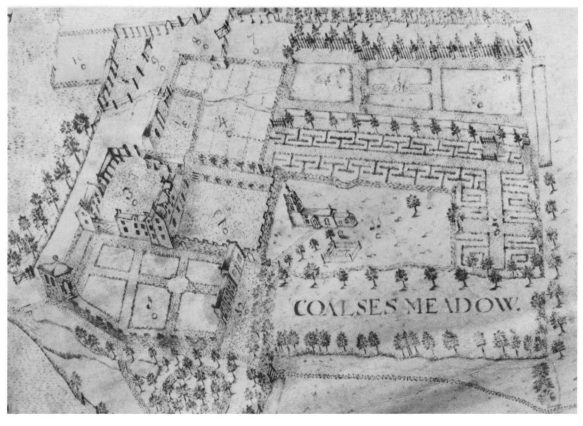

NETHER STOWEY: PART OF A MAP SHOWING STOWEY COURT AND CHURCH c. 1750

The map, with north at the top, depicts the courtyard with its raised walk between church and house,
the stable south of the court, the summer house, and the fishponds north of the church

WATCHET FROM THE EAST IN THE 18TH CENTURY

Cleeve Hill rises behind the quay and St. Decuman's church stands high on the left

WILLITON HOSPITAL, FORMERLY THE UNION WORKHOUSE, FROM THE SOUTH

reference to the fee at Little Silver has been found. There seem to have been at least two holdings called Little Silver by the end of the 15th century, one held by the Sydenhams of Orchard and another, following Lodhuish manor in Nettlecombe, held by the Waldegraves of Sudbury (Suff.).[8] A tenement called Little Silver was quitclaimed by Edward Waldegrave to John Wyndham in 1543,[9] but the Waldegrave holdings in Stream under Lodhuish manor were not sold to the Wyndhams until 1669.[10]

An estate at *BARDON*, held from the Hospitallers' manor of Williton by Robert Heythman by 1505,[11] passed to the Leigh family between 1589 and 1595.[12] A second estate there, held from Williton Fulford manor, was let to the Dawe family until the mid 17th century.[13] The two holdings were then combined under the Leighs, who remained tenants at the death of William Leigh in 1844.[14] The family continued their interest, purchasing the property from the Wyndham estate in 1919, but selling it in 1924 shortly before the death of Robert Kennaway Leigh.[15] From the mid 17th century[16] the Leighs practised as attorneys, and the legal practice was continued at the house in 1897.[17] Papers relating to the imprisonment and trial of Mary, Queen of Scots, and others were discovered in the house in 1834, brought there perhaps by the Scudamore[18] or Throckmorton families.

The south range of the house contains traces of a probably three-roomed plan with an added wing projecting forward from the western end. Additions were made to the north, partly around a courtyard, in the 18th and early 19th centuries.

In 962 King Edgar granted to Abingdon Abbey a vineyard near Watchet, with its vine growers and the land belonging to it.[19] No further trace of the estate has been found. The abbot of Cleeve had a burgage in Watchet c. 1383,[20] and at the Dissolution had small pieces of land in both Williton and Watchet.[21] In 1458 the canons of Barlinch held land in Doniford manor,[22] and the prioress of Buckland had land in Watchet by 1536.[23]

BOROUGH. In 1225 Watchet was independent of the hundred, and in 1243 was described as a borough.[24] It was owned by Sir Ralph FitzUrse at his death in 1350,[25] and descended with the manor of Williton, half passing to the Fulfords and half to the Hadleys on the division of the manor in 1388.[26] Thomas Fulford held half the borough at his death

in 1610,[27] and that half passed to Sir John Wyndham in 1616.[28] The other half was held by Richard Hadley in 1524[29] and evidently passed to the Luttrells in 1558.[30] In 1678 the chief rents of the borough were shared between Sir William Wyndham and Francis Luttrell,[31] but the borough was not mentioned separately from the manor of Williton Hadley when that estate was conveyed to Sir William Wyndham in 1710.[32]

Borough reeves were mentioned from 1293,[33] and in 1302 the borough was represented in parliament.[34] Watchet was taxed as a borough from 1306 onwards[35] and land was given to the 'community of the borough' in 1369.[36] There were 49 burgages c. 1383.[37] Burgesses were last mentioned in 1473.[38]

ECONOMIC HISTORY. Agriculture was of prime importance in the parish, but the port at Watchet supplied a wide hinterland, and the parish, and notably Watchet, was a centre for grain milling, fulling, and paper manufacture. In the 19th century Watchet was the port for shipping iron ore to South Wales, while Williton grew as a local government and commercial centre.

AGRICULTURE. In 1275 the demesne farm at Doniford measured 328 a., most of which was arable, with a small amount of pasture in severalty. The largest tenant held an estate reckoned as ⅕ fee, but 18 tenants, half of whom were freeholders, each had no more than 6 a. Villeins' works were valued at 21s. 3½d. out of a total net value of £10 15s.[39] The Templar estate was let for 16 marks a year from 1183[40] and in 1314 crops and stock there, worth £22 10s., included 42 cattle, small quantities of wheat, barley, oats, peas, and vetches, and 80 a. of corn still growing.[41] No further accounts or surveys have been found for any estate until 1399. By that date most of the demesne of Williton manor was let for the fourth of a six-year period and cash payments, including rents and commutations for mowing works, produced £26 16s. 10d. out of a total income of £28 14s. 3d. One tenant held both demesne and customary land for a rent of 39s. 8d.[42] By 1436 the Williton Hadley accounts consolidated demesne and assessed rents.[43] The income of Williton Hadley and Williton Fulford manors together was slightly higher in the late 15th century than a century earlier, in spite of the fall of income from Watchet borough which was shared between

[8] S.R.O., DD/WY 1; DD/WY 8/H2/1; *S.R.S.* xxii. 112, 123; above, Nettlecombe, manors.
[9] S.R.O., DD/WY 8/H2/1.
[10] Ibid. 12/C4.
[11] Winchester Coll. MS. 12864.
[12] S.R.O., DD/WY 9/W2/10; 47/1/11; C. Cotton, *Bardon Papers* (1907), 10.
[13] S.R.O., DD/WY 1/80; Wyndham Estate Office, survey bk. 1621.
[14] Cotton, *Bardon Papers*, 12.
[15] S.R.O., D/P/st.d 17/2/1; inf. from the owner, Mr. H. R. Heard.
[16] S.R.O., DD/WY 34.
[17] *Kelly's Dir. Som.* (1897).
[18] B.L. Eg. MS. 2124; *Bardon Papers* (Camd. Soc. 3rd ser. xvii). It was not then known that the Throckmortons owned property at Sampford Brett.
[19] H. P. R. Finberg, *Early Charters of Wessex*, p. 141.
[20] S.R.O., DD/L P32/20.
[21] P.R.O., SC 12/32, no. 5; SP 14/10A, no. 78.
[22] S.R.O., DD/WY 45/1/13.
[23] Ibid. 47/1/3.

[24] *S.R.S.* xi, pp. 36, 305.
[25] *Cal. Inq. p.m.* xi, p. 390.
[26] Above, Williton manor.
[27] P.R.O., C 142/330, no. 93.
[28] S.R.O., DD/WY 1/80.
[29] P.R.O., C 142/41, no. 36.
[30] Above, Williton Hadley manor.
[31] S.R.O., DD/L 2/19/110.
[32] P.R.O., CP 25(2)/962/9 Anne East.
[33] S.R.O., DD/L P23/2; DD/WY 4/O2/2; B.L. Add. Ch. 11175.
[34] *Members of Parl.* H.C. 69, p. 13 (1878), lxii.
[35] M. W. Beresford and H. P. R. Finberg, *Eng. Medieval Borough*, 159; *S. & D. N. & Q.* xxix, p. 12.
[36] S.R.O., DD/L P32/2.
[37] Ibid. DD/L P32/20.
[38] Ibid. DD/WY 45/1/14.
[39] P.R.O., C 133/11, no. 11.
[40] *Rec. of Templars in Eng.* ed. B. A. Lees, 62.
[41] P.R.O., E 142/111.
[42] S.R.O., DD/L P33/2.
[43] Ibid. P33/4.

L

them.[44] In comparison the rental of Williton Temple was £20 7s. 3½d.,[45] and the Sydenham holding was valued at £17 13s. 4d.[46]

There seem to have been separate groups of open fields for Williton, Watchet, and probably Doniford. An open field of Williton was referred to in 1288;[47] Gothangre field was recorded in the late 14th century,[48] Treagose, later Triggardes, field east of Williton in the late 16th century[49] and until 1683,[50] and North field in the 17th century.[51] All three were apparently small and close to Williton, and formed part of a larger group of 'crofts' and 'lands' of similar size, often divided into strips.[52] The fields of Watchet were mentioned from the late 13th century and included Wolfrecheslond field,[53] possibly later Wristland, Almscroft,[54] and Churchway field.[55] In 1801 the open fields survived in part as strips and landshares at Culvercliffe, on Cleeve Hill, and on the ridge south of the town.[56] Three small fields, Skurland,[57] Lilly, and Elm Stubbs,[58] remained at Doniford in the 18th century as remnants of open fields.[59] Elsewhere in the parish there were furlongs, lands, and crofts that contained strips and landshares ('lanskers') but did not make up fields or groups of fields that are now discernible,[60] unless the areas into which the whole parish was divided for tithe collection by the early 16th century represent such groups. There were 17 of those areas, including one each for Watchet, Bardon, and Orchard and three based on Stream.[61]

West of Williton streams flowing into Outmoor were evidently diverted by the late 14th century along man-made watercourses to form meadows called waterleets.[62] Additional water was diverted into Outmoor from below Orchard mill under Mamsey (formerly Martinsey)[63] Bridge, on the Williton–Washford road, and thence into Mamsey Course. The outflow north and north-east of Williton was similarly controlled, and the regulation of the water was the responsibility of the Williton manor court until the 1950s.[64] There were waterleets at Doniford by 1418.[65]

The largest estate in the parish in the 16th century, Williton Temple or Williton Regis, consisted of 1,075 a. of arable, 105 a. of meadow, 20 a. of wood or underwood, and common pasture, together with c. 260 a. of open hill land on the Brendons. There were tracts of 'barren' and 'very wild' arable at Bleripate and on the ridge between Williton and Watchet. In 1584 three leasehold tenants between them held the manor house; copyholds varied in size, the largest including 112 a. at Timwood, 50 a.

of 'wild common hill' at Kingsdown, 82 a. of inclosed land mostly near Williton, and 68 a. at 'Knapp'.[66] Small-scale exchanges and inclosure and improvements of marginal land are evident in the later 16th century during the tenure of the estate by the Wyndhams as lessees, but the total rent of £22 4s. 5½d. and the value of 12 harvest works compared unfavourably with the rent of £10 12s. 7½d. from the 320-a. Fulford estate in 1615.[67] The manor of Watchet, which comprised the borough and some surrounding land amounting to 217 a., produced in 1622 an income of £24 11s. 9d. and the value of 17 harvest days.[68]

By 1616 the Wyndhams were major landowners in the parish, having over 90 years acquired Orchard, Curlinch, Wibble,[69] Rydon, Snailholt, the estate of Watchet chapel,[70] Williton Regis, and Williton Fulford.[71] Tenant farms were largely unaffected by these changes. Most were under 60 a. and often changed hands, with the notable exceptions of the holdings of the Dawes and the Leighs at Bardon and of the Norrises at the Parsonage. The Dawes were tenants by 1581 and until 1653 or later,[72] the Leighs from the late 16th century until 1844,[73] and the Norrises from 1586 until 1676.[74]

In the later 17th century, when much of the arable land was still farmed in fields of an acre or less, wheat was the predominant crop, accounting for over 500 a. At the same time there were well over 300 a. of barley and smaller quantities of peas, beans, oats, dredge, and rye. By 1729, when a few strips had been consolidated, the acreage under beans had been doubled and the amount of oats and peas reduced. Stock and crops on Parsonage farm, probably the largest farm, comprised in 1744 a flock of 122 sheep, 18 adult pigs, horses worth £5, and bullocks worth £47 8s. There were five stacks of grain, mostly wheat, and some wheat and peas in the ground, the whole worth £296.[75]

By the end of the 18th century most of the parish had been consolidated into nucleated farms. Short-term leases often included improvement clauses, the Wyndham leases finally in a standard, printed form.[76] Wibble and Kentsford farms had been consolidated by the late 1730s,[77] Kentsford evidently combining the ancient estate with outlying grounds held in the 16th century by the farmer of the Parsonage.[78] A divided holding on the Luttrell estate in 1743, largely at Higher Stream but including a strip in the common field at Culvercliffe on the opposite side of the parish, was let for seven years with covenants to lime or manure all conversions

44 Ibid. P32/7, P33/9.
45 Winchester Coll. MS. 12864.
46 S.R.O., DD/WY 1/33.
47 Ibid. DD/L P33.
48 Ibid. DD/WY 4/O2.
49 Ibid. 47/2/23/1.
50 Ibid. 29.
51 Ibid. DD/TK 1/1; DD/WY 29.
52 e.g. Ibid. DD/L P32/2, P33; DD/WY 29, 50.
53 Ibid. DD/L P33/1.
54 Ibid. P33; Hadley and Hosyer to Vaghan.
55 Ibid. P32/22, P32: Luttrell to Wheddon 1663.
56 Ibid. DD/WY 47/2/23/1.
57 Ibid. 47/2/34.
58 Ibid. DD/WO 15/11C: 1722; DD/WY 60.
59 Ibid. DD/CCH 80; DD/WY 176.
60 Ibid. DD/WY 47/2/23/1.
61 Ibid. DD/L P32/22.
62 Ibid. P33/2, P33/22; Winchester Coll. MS. 12864.
63 S.R.O., DD/WY 21: deed 1759.

64 Wyndham Estate Office, ct. bk. 1843–1953, and papers including regulations for watering (1818) and map (1828).
65 S.R.O., DD/WO 10/3.
66 Ibid. DD/WY 47/2/23/1.
67 Ibid. 47/2/33/1; Wyndham Estate Office, survey bk. 1615–21.
68 S.R.O., DD/WY 47/1/11.
69 Ibid. 1/33.
70 Ibid. 1/D; below, churches.
71 Above, manors.
72 S.R.O., DD/WY 1/80, 47/1/5, 47/3/43; DD/L P3/12; Wyndham Estate Office, survey 1615–21; Som. Protestation Returns, ed. Howard and Stoate, 291.
73 Above, manors (Bardon).
74 Orchard Wyndham MSS. 1/1, 11.
75 S.R.O., DD/WY 29.
76 Ibid. e.g. DD/WY 20–1.
77 Ibid. 29.
78 Ibid. DD/L P32/63.

from grass to arable, which were to bear only three crops, of which one should be wheat. At the end of the lease 8 a. or more were to be left under clover.[79]

Between 1804 and 1815 Lord Egremont bought or exchanged land with the Trevelyans and the Escotts to acquire Kentsford, which his ancestors had occupied in the 17th century, Doniford Court and Wibble farms, and other small properties.[80] By 1841 the Wyndham estate comprised over 3,087 a., including many houses and cottages.[81] The only other landowners of consequence then were the Trevelyans, who owned some 200 a. in the detached parts of the parish at Kingsdown and Hayne. The Wyndhams continued to consolidate their holdings by exchange until 1846 or later[82] and by the mid 19th century their rent roll amounted to £3,380.[83]

By 1841 the farming units had achieved a stable pattern. The largest was Doniford farm (250 a.), followed by Rydon (163 a.), Snailholt (143 a.), Kentsford (131 a.), and Washford (123 a.). Several others, such as Bridge, Higher and Lower Stream, Egrove, and Wibble farms amounted to over 70 a. each. In the parish as a whole, arable was twice the area of grassland.[84] Within the next ten years there were slight re-arrangements of that pattern, notably the extension of Egrove to 156 a. and of Bridge farm (250 a.) to include the demesne lands of Orchard Wyndham, the merger of land in Old Cleeve with Kentsford and Washford farms, and the emergence of a dairy farm at Egrove. In 1851 119 men and 17 boys were regularly employed on the farms of the parish.[85] By the early 20th century the total acreage under grass had increased to 45 per cent of the parish.[86] Parts of the Wyndham estate were sold in 1918–19, 1952, and 1957, and in 1980 the estate totalled 2,289 a. including Aller farm in Sampford Brett.[87] The whole parish, rather more than half under grass, was divided between 12 farming units, six of them measuring over 100 ha. There were three specialist dairy farms, one mainly dairy, two breeding cattle and sheep, and one having mostly cereals.[88]

TRADE AND INDUSTRY. Watchet, as a 10th-century form of the name, Wecedport,[89] suggests, was by that time a commercial centre, but direct evidence of trading is not found until 1210, when Flemish merchants were arrested there.[90] In the 14th century there were business links with Cowbridge (Glam.),[91] and in the 15th with Bristol.[92] The port was said in 1458 to have been 'utterly destroyed' by storms,[93] and customs accounts of the later 15th century suggest that customable trade was no longer carried on at the port.[94] In 1559 the harbour was reputed to be unfit both for loading and unloading,[95] but coal and salt were imported;[96] in 1565 the port was reported as fit to accept small boats bringing wine, salt, victuals, wood, and coal.[97] In the 1560s a Watchet ship was involved in the wine trade between Bridgwater and La Rochelle,[98] and wine was coming to Watchet regularly by the late 1590s.[99] From the late 16th century Welsh cattle and sheep came through the port,[1] and in 1606 tolls were paid on 28 boat loads of coal, presumably from Wales, and 7 loads of salt.[2] There was also some traffic with Ireland.[3]

In 1630 a Bristol merchant was involved in buying the cargoes of two French salt ships at Watchet,[4] and a year later a bark with peas from Barnstaple was lying at the quay.[5] Demands for ship money in 1635 were met with the reply that the port was small, with little business save small barks coming from Wales with coal for lime burning.[6] A memorial of 1665, recalling the destruction of the port by storms early in the Civil War, referred to the import of coal, culm, iron, and salt,[7] and eight Watchet ships calling at Minehead in 1647 were evidently involved in trade in coal and iron with Wales.[8] In 1652–3 tolls were paid on 70 shiploads of coal, 72 of culm, and 6 of salt.[9] A similar rate of imports continued in the 1660s, including also small consignments of barley and malt.[10] The list of dues for imports and exports published in 1665 included Spanish and Gascon wine, fish from the North Atlantic, and cloth, wool, and livestock from Ireland and Wales.[11] In 1673 the port's eight ships were involved in bringing coal from Neath and London, taking peas to Barnstaple, and fish, grain, oxbows, and cloth to Bristol.[12] By the 1680s Watchet was the main importer of Welsh coal along the Somerset coast, leaving Minehead as the main port for cattle.[13] Among forty seamen recorded as living at Watchet in 1672 was one then absent 'upon Virginia voyage'.[14] Demands for a new slip in 1671 and for two in 1680 suggest growing business at Watchet.[15]

By the early 18th century Watchet ships still played a small part in the trade between Swansea and the Irish ports, but the port's main business was with Newton (Glam.) in coal, with occasional appearances of, for example, skins, oatmeal, and stockings.[16] Accounts of duty levied in the port show the developing pattern of trade in the 18th and 19th centuries. In 1709–10 Swansea, Tenby, and Neath between them sent 2,210 chalders of coal; in 1749–50 the figure was only slightly higher, at 2,749 chalders, but by 1828–9 some 4,075 chalders were

[79] Ibid. DD/L 2/19/109.
[80] Ibid. DD/WY 20; DD/WY, survey 1801.
[81] Ibid. tithe award.
[82] Ibid. DD/WY, survey 1801.
[83] Ibid. DD/WY 158.
[84] Ibid. tithe award.
[85] P.R.O., HO 107/1920.
[86] Statistics supplied by the then Bd. of Agric. 1905.
[87] Inf. from Mr. C. Connett, agent; S.R.O., DD/WY 149.
[88] Min. of Agric., Fisheries, and Food, agric. returns 1976.
[89] A.-S. Chron. (Rolls Ser.), i. 238–9; Two Saxon Chrons. ed. J. Earle and C. Plummer (1892), i. 125, 131.
[90] Pipe R. 1210 (P.R.S. N.S. xxvi), 74.
[91] S.R.O., DD/L P32/2.
[92] Cal. Pat. 1429–36, 10, 15.
[93] S.R.S. xlix, p. 304.
[94] P.R.O., E 122/26/9–11, 16.
[95] S. & D. N. & Q. xxx, p. 159.
[96] S.R.O., DD/WY 45/1/14.

[97] S. & D. N. & Q. xxx, p. 159.
[98] P.R.O., E 190/1081/4.
[99] Hist. MSS. Com. 80, Sackville, i, p. 84.
[1] Glam. Co. Hist. iv. 64.
[2] S.R.O., DD/L P32/76; DD/WY 23/11.
[3] S.R.S. xv. 24.
[4] Cal. S. P. Dom. 1629–31, 363.
[5] Ibid. 1631–3, 184.
[6] Ibid. 1635, 163.
[7] S.R.O., DD/L 2/19/110.
[8] F. Hancock, Minehead (1903), 311.
[9] S.R.O., DD/WY 46/2/26/1.
[10] Ibid. 46/2/26/1–2, 46/2/27; DD/L 2/19/110.
[11] Ibid. DD/WY 40.
[12] Wedlake, Watchet, 85.
[13] Glam. Co. Hist. iv. 356, 358–9.
[14] S.R.O., DD/WY 29.
[15] Williton, Wyndham Estate Office, Watchet Borough ct. bk. 1620–1727, sub annis 1671, 1680.
[16] Arch. Cambrensis, xcv (1940), 195, 198, 201.

brought in, largely then from Swansea and Newport, and only occasionally from Neath. Other imports in the early years of the 18th century included salt, wine, groceries, bottles, tobacco, iron, yarn, and Irish cloth, all from Bristol; roofing stones from Padstow (Cornw.); and occasional items such as butter and calfskins from Neath, flannel from Tenby, and wool and coal from Gloucester. In 1749–50 the rarer items included bricks from Bridgwater, and from Bristol furniture, clover seed, timber, and five swivel guns.[17]

Exports in 1709–10 comprised 547 qr. of corn, at least 38 packs of woollen cloth, 164 calves, 20 calfskins, kelp, and cider, all to Bristol. By 1749–50 corn and cloth exports had risen: 2,218 qr. of corn were sent to Bristol and 237 packs of cloth, together with small quantities of wood ash, oxbows, and paper. By 1828–9 17 ships were regularly using the port, mostly for the Bristol Channel trade but reaching as far as London, Liverpool, Newry (Co. Down), and Kircudbright. Watchet's exports then were principally corn (2,716 qr.), flour (531 tons), and paper (203 bales or bundles). Other commodities, on a much smaller scale, included Bridgwater bricks (171,000), timber, and two consignments of Welsh sheep.

In 1843 nine Watchet vessels were regularly trading with Bristol, Liverpool, Ireland, and the Welsh ports, bringing in coal, hides, and general merchandise and taking out corn, timber, flour, malt, and leather. There was also a limited passenger traffic to Bristol and, later, excursions in the Channel.[18] The port was radically altered by the opening of the iron-ore mines in the Brendons in 1853–5, and the development of the harbour as a terminal for shipping the ore to South Wales. Improvements in 1861–2, giving anchorage for vessels of up to 500 tons, made possible the export of over 40,000 tons annually between 1873 and 1878.[19] The closure of the mines in 1883 left the port dependent largely on imports of coal and grain and exports of flour and paper.[20] The import of Scandinavian wood pulp and of coal was the main trade in the earlier 20th century,[21] but during the Second World War business was restricted to the import of coal, wood pulp, and cattle feeding stuffs from the eastern coastal ports and the export of small quantities of scrap iron.[22] Coal, wood pulp, and esparto grass for the paper mills were brought in for a time after the war, but when the mills changed from coal to oil burning the losses to the port were serious until, from the late 1960s, timber was brought in from Russia and Scandinavia and other cargoes from Spain, Portugal, and Italy. Exports of motor parts and tractors from the Midlands to Spain and Portugal, which began in the 1950s,[23] expanded and in 1979 a transit depot for containers was established outside the town to handle the increased business.[24]

Natural resources exploited in the parish from the Middle Ages were limestone,[25] fish, and seaweed. Fish weirs were put up both off shore and at the mouths of the two rivers. One, belonging to Doniford manor, was valued at 2s. in 1275,[26] and there was another at the mouth of the Washford river by 1311.[27] In 1391 an offshore weir was held of the Crown by the township of Doniford, and one illegal weir in the Doniford stream stopped fish going upstream to spawn, while another diverted water through meadow land.[28] Three other weirs, described as three ponds with sea fishing and lying on the shore east of Watchet, were held by the Crown between 1398 and 1456.[29] The increased rent of Watchet borough in 1420–1 was partly accounted for by a weir in the sea and another at 'le Putt', and the tenant of Watchet manor mill was paying part of his rent in salmon by 1399.[30] The lord's weirs were still standing in 1476,[31] but stone was carried away from one to Wales in 1480.[32] In the late 16th century the profits of the borough included the income from two weirs, one described as in the 'fresh', the other 'a little below the quay head', together with a fishery and nets.[33] The three weirs were still standing in 1622, and then included one formerly belonging to Watchet chapel.[34] The miller at Little Silver still leased one weir in 1686.[35]

Ore-weed or seaweed was collected commercially along the shore at Doniford by the end of the 16th century, and a lease of 1572 included the 'ore marke' against a house and a place to dry the weed.[36] Tenants along the coast in the early 17th century could take the weed between their holdings and the low tide mark, and land was let as 'ore room' for drying or burning.[37] Tithes were claimed from c. 1600, but the parson or the farmer in fact levied half the sum claimed, provided the owners burnt the weed themselves.[38] Kelp, the ashes of the burnt weed, was exported to Bristol for the glass industry in the early 18th century,[39] but by 1847 the landing of the weed was considered in Watchet to be a nuisance.[40]

Fulling mills established by the early 14th century[41] seem to have made St. Decumans a centre of the cloth industry. Dyers, fullers, and weavers were found in Watchet before the 16th century,[42] and in the 17th century there were at least four fulling mills in the parish.[43] Williton clothiers like Aldred Bickham,[44] William Pyke,[45] and the Blinmans paid subsidies similar to those of prosperous tenant

[17] S.R.O., DD/WY 40: 'key duties' 1708–64, 1827–54.
[18] Wedlake, *Watchet*, 88–9, 105–6.
[19] Ibid. 127.
[20] S.R.O., D/U/wa 33/2/1–2: monthly tonnage returns 1865–1902.
[21] Ibid. 33/2/39: tonnage returns 1927–45; Wedlake, *Watchet*, 135, 137–8.
[22] S.R.O., DD/X/PSE; D/U/wa 33/2/3.
[23] Wedlake, *Watchet*, 142. [24] Local inf.
[25] Above, introduction.
[26] P.R.O., C 133/11, no. 11.
[27] S.R.O., DD/L P32/2.
[28] *Cal. Inq. Misc.* v, pp. 197–8; P.R.O., C 1/6, no. 265.
[29] S.R.O., DD/SAS PR 57.
[30] Ibid. DD/L P33/2, 3.
[31] Ibid. P32/27; DD/WY 45/1/14/1.
[32] Ibid. DD/WY 45/1/14/1.
[33] Ibid. DD/WY 40.
[34] Ibid. DD/WY 8/M2, 47/1/11; DD/WO 15/11B; cf. *Cal. Pat.* 1549–51, 135–6.
[35] S.R.O., DD/L P32/78; DD/WY 65/36.
[36] Ibid. DD/WY 11/B4/6.
[37] Ibid. 47/1/5, 11; 47/2/34; DD/WO 50/11; DD/L P32/78.
[38] Ibid. D/D/Rg 356.
[39] Ibid. DD/WY 40; *V.C.H. Som.* ii. 362.
[40] Williton, Wyndham Estate Office, Watchet Borough ct. bk.
[41] S.R.O., DD/WY 19.
[42] Maxwell Lyte, *Dunster*, i. 111; S.R.O., DD/L P32/2; DD/WY 45/1/14.
[43] Below, mills.
[44] *Som. Wills*, ed. Brown, iii. 87.
[45] S.R.O., DD/WY 51/11.

farmers, and Watchet clothiers such as the Wheddons and another branch of the Bickhams were not far behind.[46] In the later 17th century the leading manufacturers were the Slocombes of Little Silver and the Chapplyns of Egrove,[47] with business connexions in neighbouring parishes.[48] Cloth making continued in the 18th century, with Wheddons at Watchet and Pulmans at Doniford still in production, the latter until the later 19th century.[49]

Trade in Watchet in the early 19th century involved milling, malting, and the manufacture of paper, rope, soap, tallow, and mill puff, and dealing in coal, corn, earthenware, salt, alabaster, and timber.[50] By the 1840s there was a foundry at Watchet[51] which in 1851 employed four workers. Mariner or sailor was the commonest occupation in Watchet by the mid 19th century,[52] and in 1861 there were two shipowners, three marine store dealers, a ship builder, and a ship broker, as well as coastguards and a lifeboat station.[53] The Watchet Trading Co., the Brendon Hills Iron Ore Co., and the West Somerset Mineral Railway Co. had offices in the town. The improvement of the harbour after 1861–2 and the railway from Taunton led to considerable expansion of shipping, and to the beginning of a change in the port. By 1875 there were 21 master mariners, 10 ship owners, and 3 ship brokers, together with agents for sack companies and a bank.[54] In contrast, visitors were being encouraged by the appearance of two tourist hotels, refreshment rooms, and a widening variety of tradesmen, including a bookseller, a photographer, and a library agent.[55] A pleasure ground overlooking the harbour included a refreshment room, and a bathing place for ladies was established on a secluded beach.[56]

Williton remained the centre of an agricultural community, but its commercial life increased after the creation of the new road from Bridgwater and the establishment of the Union Workhouse. By 1851 it had a bank, and was the home of a physician, an architect, two land surveyors, an accountant, and a solicitor.[57] By 1861 the railway, a newspaper, another bank, an auctioneer, an omnibus proprietor, a post office, and the county court had brought many of the characteristics of a market town.[58] The Gliddon family moved from Watchet to manufacture prize kitchen ranges and agricultural machinery, but other industry was limited: an organ builder by 1866, an umbrella maker by 1875, a cycle manufacturer by 1897, and the English and American Artificial Teeth Company by 1902.[59] Essentially, Williton depended on its agricultural surroundings,

most of its working population in 1851 being craftsmen and labourers, many living in newly-expanding parts of the village at Half Acre and Shutgate Street. Agricultural depression at the end of the 19th century checked growth, but Williton remained an administrative centre for West Somerset, from 1894 the headquarters of a rural district and an outpost of county government.[60]

Williton continued its administrative role during the 20th century, becoming in 1974 the centre for much of the West Somerset District Council administration. The decline of the port at Watchet and its subsequent revival after the Second World War,[61] the reopening of the railway, and the expanding holiday camps on the coast between Doniford and Watchet boosted the economy of the parish as a whole, and Williton became by the late 1970s an important local shopping centre and tourist attraction.

MARKETS AND FAIRS. A market had been established at Watchet by 1222, when its existence was said to damage that at Dunster.[62] Shambles in the centre of the market place were mentioned in 1311.[63] They survived until c. 1805,[64] and were replaced in 1819–20 by the Market House.[65] The market was held on Saturdays by the earlier 17th century,[66] and apparently continued until the 1830s.[67] The two-storeyed stone Market House had open arches to the ground floor and an open stair at its west end to the upper floor. The ground floor was later converted to shops, and from 1979 housed a museum. The upper floor was used from the 1920s as a mission church, later known as Holy Cross Chapel.[68]

The prebendary of St. Decumans had a fair by 1244.[69] It was held on a site between the church and the prebendal house, later Parsonage Farm, in a field known in the 14th century as Twyfayrecroftes, and in the 19th as Fair close.[70] A fair house and horse shed on part of the site,[71] apparently so used in the 18th century and mentioned in 1841, was the former church house. The fair itself, held by 1767 on 24 August for cattle and all sorts of goods,[72] then belonged to the churchwardens, who let out poles and standings and in 1778 screened and brewed malt there. Income from the fair in the 18th century rose to a peak of £6 15s. in 1751, but by 1816 had been cut to one third.[73] The fair was discontinued in 1819.[74]

By 1767 a fair for hardware and toys was held at Williton on Trinity Monday,[75] and by 1792 there was also a fair at Watchet, held on 17 November.[76] The Williton fair survived until 1877;[77] the Watchet

[46] Som. Protestation Returns, ed. Howard and Stoate, 291–2.
[47] S.R.O., DD/WO 15/10; DD/WY 13/H4/1; 50; 51/1A, 4, 11; 55/35; DD/L 2/19/109; DD/TK 1/1; ibid. Q/SR 103/28.
[48] Ibid. DD/WY 55/35; DD/L 2/19/109.
[49] e.g. Ibid. DD/WY 50; 51/1–4; 176; DD/TK 1/1, 2; DD/WO 18/4; P.R.O., HO 107/1920.
[50] S.R.O., DD/WY 38B: rates 1820.
[51] Ibid. tithe award.
[52] P.R.O., HO 107/1920.
[53] P.O. Dir. Som. (1861).
[54] Ibid. (1875).
[55] Ibid. (1866, 1875); Kelly's Dir. Som. (1883).
[56] O.S. Map 1/2,500, Som. XXXVI. 13, 14 (1887 edn.).
[57] P.R.O., HO 107/1920.
[58] P.O. Dir. Som. (1861).
[59] Ibid. (1861, 1866, 1875); Kelly's Dir. Som. (1897, 1902).

[60] Ibid. (1919); below, local govt.
[61] Above.
[62] Rot. Litt. Claus. (Rec. Com.), i. 527.
[63] S.R.O., DD/L P32/2; DD/WY 4/O2/5.
[64] Wyndham Estate Office, Watchet ct. bk. 1728–present.
[65] S.R.O., DD/WY 21; 38/13.
[66] S.R.S. xv. 24.
[67] Lewis, Topog. Dict. Eng. (1848), iv. 434.
[68] Inf. from the vicar, the Revd. R. M. Barnett.
[69] S.R.S. xi, p. 325.
[70] Public Works in Medieval Law, ii (Selden Soc. xi), 138–40; S.R.O., tithe award.
[71] S.R.O., tithe award; Wedlake, Watchet, 111; below, churches.   [72] Bk. of Fairs (1767).
[73] S.R.O., DD/WY 37/2.
[74] Wedlake, Watchet, 124.
[75] Bk. of Fairs (1767).
[76] Owen, Bk. of Fairs (1792).
[77] S.R.O., D/P/bic 1/7/1.

fair, later transferred to 16 September, also survived for much of the 19th century, but by 1898 had almost vanished, its memory surviving as a 'lantern night' procession until the early 20th century.[78]

Cattle fairs or sales and new markets at Williton in the 19th century were established as the village developed as a local centre of trade and communications. By 1861 until the 1880s or later there were cattle fairs on the Friday before the last Saturday in April and the Tuesday before the first Wednesday in December.[79] By 1866 a market had been established on the second Monday in each month for sheep, pigs, and implements.[80] The cattle fair in the late 1880s was restricted to the second Monday in December, but markets were held twice a month in summer and monthly in winter.[81] That pattern continued until the Second World War, but the extra summer market was abandoned by 1910 and the date of the fair was altered to the first Thursday in December.[82] The market had ceased by 1948. Its site, next to Williton First School, was in 1979 occupied by an agricultural engineering firm.[83]

MILLS. There was a mill at Watchet in 1086.[84] By 1321 there were four mills, of which one was the manorial mill at Williton, later Egrove mill; one was probably the town mill at Watchet; one, held by John of Lodhuish, was probably at Stream; and the fourth was held by Edmund Martin, a tenant of Williton manor.[85]

Egrove mill was held by John FitzUrse c. 1275.[86] It descended with Williton manor and was shared in the 15th century between the Fulfords, the Hadleys, and the Hospitallers.[87] By 1489 it was occupied by the Torrington family, tenants until 1615 or later.[88] In 1617 Sir John Wyndham was accused of building two new mills near his manor of Williton, probably Orchard mills, taking the stones from Egrove and allowing that mill to decay.[89] In 1635 Robert Sweeting, a Sampford Brett clothier, agreed to build a fulling mill on the site. The mill was later let to the Chapplyn family, who had been fulling at Egrove since 1605.[90] In 1656 the mill was let to a West Quantoxhead clothier for 99 years.[91] It was still a fulling mill in 1712, but by 1721 it was occupied by John Rayner of Bristol as a paper mill.[92] The lease had passed by 1742 to a Bristol surgeon,[93] and paper making continued until 1847. William Wood of the Snailholt paper mills was apparently in charge of production in 1816.[94] Towards the end of the 19th

century a new wheel and stones were installed and it became a grist mill. The mill had an undershot wheel driven by a leat from the Doniford stream at Egrove Farm. The wheel was subsequently taken to Combe Sydenham.[95]

The town mill at Watchet, near the mouth of the Washford river, was shared between the Fulfords and the Hadleys in the 15th century.[96] The Fulford share was sold to Sir John Wyndham in 1616,[97] and the Hadley share came to the same family in 1710.[98] Milling continued until c. 1911.[99] The site was in 1979 occupied by a private house. The mill held in 1321 by John of Lodhuish[1] may have been the fulling mill at Stream mentioned in 1468[2] and 1472,[3] of which no later evidence has been found. A fulling mill established in Watchet by 1318[4] may be that held by Edmund Martin in 1321.[5] Known by 1378 as Brutcotes mill after the tenant,[6] and later as Little Silver,[7] it was let in 1381 with racks and the liberty to cut timber to maintain the weir.[8] The mill seems to have descended with the Hadley manor to the Luttrells, and was held by the Blinmans, the Slocomes, and the Wheddons in the 17th and 18th centuries.[9] In 1807 the mill passed to Richard Gimblett, another clothier,[10] but fulling was discontinued, probably soon after that date, although the mill may have been used for a time from 1824 to dress cloth made by the poor.[11] By 1832 the mill had been replaced by a new building further downstream, which was occupied by Thomas Stoate, a flour miller.[12] Stoate's mill, which had four pairs of stones and two powerful overshot wheels, was extended in 1847 and improved in the 1850s.[13] The Stoates, who also occupied the town mills, closed both after a fire at their new mills in 1911, transferring the business to Bristol. The building was reconstructed and occupied in 1916 by the Exmoor Paper Bag Company.[14] In 1979 it was in multiple occupation.

By 1587 a fulling and grist mill was held of the Wyndham estate by Silvester Bickham, and was still occupied by him in 1622.[15] By 1652 it was producing paper for John Saffyn of Cullompton (Devon) and it was described as at Snailholt,[16] site of the Wansbrough Paper Co's. mills in 1979. The mill continued to produce paper, and by 1727 the tenant was John Wood, the first of four generations of that family to work the mill until 1834.[17] By 1840 the mill was held jointly by John Wansbrough, James Date, and William Peach,[18] and the Wansbrough family

[78] Wedlake, *Watchet*, 123.
[79] *P.O. Dir. Som.* (1861); *Kelly's Dir. Som.* (1883).
[80] T. Hawkes, 'Williton', TS. of original notes c. 1903 ed. T. H. Andrew 1903, in possession of Mr. D. Gliddon, Williton.
[81] *Kelly's Dir. Som.* (1889).
[82] Ibid. (1910, 1939).
[83] Inf. from Mr. J. Hosegood, Barnstaple.
[84] *V.C.H. Som.* i. 505.
[85] *H.M.C. Wells*, i. 388.
[86] S.R.O., DD/L P33; *S.R.S.* xliv. 139.
[87] S.R.O., DD/L P33/2, 8, 9; Winchester Coll. MS. 12864.
[88] S.R.O., DD/L P33/9; DD/WY 47/3/43; Winchester Coll. MS. 12864.
[89] S.R.O., DD/WY 50.
[90] Ibid. 47/1/10; 55/35.
[91] Ibid. DD/L 2/19/109.
[92] Ibid. DD/WY 47/2/19.
[93] Ibid. 55/35.
[94] Wedlake, *Watchet*, 125.
[95] Local inf.

[96] P.R.O., C 142/41, no. 36; S.R.O., DD/L P32/25, P33/2, 9; DD/WY 10/E3/1.
[97] S.R.O., DD/WY 1/80.   [98] Above, manors.
[99] Wedlake, *Watchet*, 136.
[1] *H.M.C. Wells*, i. 388.
[2] P.R.O., C 140/28, no. 22.
[3] Ibid. C 140/42, no. 45.
[4] S.R.O., DD/WY 19.
[5] *H.M.C. Wells*, i. 388.
[6] P.R.O., C 131/26, no. 6.
[7] S.R.O., DD/WY 65/36.
[8] Ibid. DD/L P32/7.
[9] Ibid. P32/17, 55, 78; DD/L 2/19/108.
[10] Ibid. DD/WY 64/7, 65/36.
[11] Ibid. 37/3.
[12] Ibid. 151.
[13] Ibid. 21, 151, 196.
[14] Wedlake, *Watchet*, 136.
[15] S.R.O., DD/WY 47/1/11.
[16] Ibid. 12/E4.
[17] Ibid. 29, 37/2, 38/13, 65/38.
[18] *Co. Gaz. Dir.* (1840); S.R.O., tithe award.

continued in partnership with others until 1903.[19] The business was then bought by W. H. Reed and from 1910 formed part of the Reed and Smith group, from *c.* 1974 a public company known as Reed and Smith Holdings. In 1978 the company was taken over by St. Regis International of New York. About 1865, when 120 people were employed, the main power supply was a steam engine. The manufacture of paper bags began in 1886, and by the end of the 19th century the mill was the largest producer of its kind in the country. The work force of 280 in 1979 produced *c.* 1,500 tonnes a week, comprising brown paper for the cardboard box trade and glazed and wet strength papers for bags, envelopes, wallpapers, and wrappings, almost entirely from recycled materials.[20]

There was a grain mill at Doniford by 1275.[21] It descended with Doniford manor, and ownership was shared. By 1545 a fulling mill had been built there,[22] but a grist mill was still in use in 1623.[23] In the 18th and 19th centuries the Pulman family made cloth there,[24] and the mill was still in production in 1841. The buildings, standing by a leat fed by the Doniford stream, adjoining fields called Rack meadow,[25] included a miller's house, in 1979 comprising two houses called Swillbridge House and Ivy Cottage, and two mill buildings.

In 1617 Sir John Wyndham was said to have built recently two grist mills 'near his manor of Williton',[26] perhaps the origin of Orchard mills. The tenancy was taken in 1740 by John Morle of Stream on condition that he built a 'dry' for drying oats.[27] Richard Morle took the mills in 1771, and was followed by Thomas Leigh until 1845.[28] Milling continued until 1967.[29] In 1979 the mill was opened as a craft shop and museum.[30] The substantial main buildings are of the early 19th century. The overshot wheel is of iron and timber and the interior machinery of timber.

By 1735 a fulling mill was established at White Cross or Watering Place, at the end of Long Street, Williton. It was occupied by John Pulman from 1784, and by 1819 the buildings included dye houses, workshops, and napping, fulling, and rowing mills. About 1825 the mill was converted for use as a workhouse.[31]

LOCAL GOVERNMENT. Land in Watcet was held in the 14th and 15th centuries of the fee of

Brompton Ralph, and was described as in the hundred of Brompton Ralph.[32] By the late 13th century Culvercliffe was part of the fee of Sampford Brett.[33] That area was still part of Sampford manor in 1586,[34] and remained part of Sampford Brett tithing in the 17th century.[35]

Records of Watchet borough court date from 1273,[36] and survive thereafter for 1472–3,[37] 1476–7,[38] 1480–2,[39] 1490–2,[40] 1510–11, 1519,[41] 1558–60,[42] 1568–9,[43] 1571–6, 1583–4,[44] 1606,[45] and from 1620 to the present.[46] Sessions were held probably every three weeks during the 13th century,[47] at least seven times a year in the early 15th century,[48] and apparently every three weeks in 1621,[49] but in 1706 the frankpledge jury asked that the three-weekly court should be revived 'as formerly it hath been'. There is no trace of any revival of that court. The twice-yearly views of frankpledge at Easter and Michaelmas, interrupted by plague in 1646, were reduced to an annual meeting in October in 1651,[50] a pattern which continues to the present. Sessions, held in the court house and in the 18th century at the Bell inn,[51] were by the late 1970s held at the Downfield Hotel, Watchet.

In the late 13th century the borough reeve[52] presided at the court, supported by a group of good men, witnesses, and watchmen.[53] In 1476 the court officers were a reeve, two constables, two aletasters, and two breadweighers.[54] In 1573 there were also street keepers.[55] From the 1570s the reeve was normally known as the portreeve.[56] Holders of burgage property took office in rotation, but in the 1650s the office was frequently held by deputy, and a deputy served whenever it was the turn of the lord of the borough to serve. A water bailiff and two assistants were appointed from 1666 when the port was revived.[57]

Other officers, reflecting the changed function of the court and the growth of the town, included a scavenger in 1779, succeeded by four in 1813, eight in 1814, and nine in 1818.[58] Constables to serve in the whole parish were appointed by the vestry from 1842,[59] but a bellman or crier was elected in the court from 1841, and in 1979 there were also a recorder (clerk), a bailiff, a stock driver, and a pig driver.[60]

In 1273 the business of the court concerned the assize of ale and cases of debt and trespass.[61] By 1295 a pillory had been set up.[62] In the late 15th century the court had oversight of the common fields, made

19 Wedlake, *Watchet*, 126.
20 Inf. from Mr. G. Kneen, Wansbrough Paper Co. Ltd.
21 P.R.O., C 133/11, no. 11.
22 S.R.O., DD/WY 11/B4/4.
23 *S.R.S.* li, p. 25; S.R.O., DD/WY 11/B4/7.
24 Wedlake, *Watchet*, 69.
25 S.R.O., tithe award.
26 Ibid. DD/WY 50.
27 Ibid. 35.
28 Ibid. 21.
29 Inf. from Mr. R. W. Patten, Radstock.
30 Local inf.   31 S.R.O., DD/WY 51/4.
32 Ibid. DD/L P32: deeds 1307–55, 1472; DD/WY 19/Z2/8.
33 Ibid. DD/L P32/2, 7; DD/WY 4/O2/8, 6/N1/1.
34 Devon R.O. 248M/M7–8.
35 S.R.O., DD/WY 34.
36 Ibid. DD/L P32/5.
37 Ibid. DD/WY 45/1/14/1.
38 Ibid. DD/L P32/17.
39 Ibid. DD/WY 45/1/14/1.
40 Ibid. DD/L P32/8.
41 Ibid. P32/27.

42 Ibid. DD/WY 45/1/8, 45/1/14/1.
43 MS. in possession of (1978) R. C. Hatchwell, Little Somerford, Wilts.
44 S.R.O., DD/WY 45/1/10, 45/1/14/1.
45 Ibid. DD/L P32/76.
46 Wyndham Estate Office, ct. bks. and presentments; ct. rolls and papers in S.R.O., DD/WY 29; 40; 44/1/1A; 44/2/2–3; 44/3/4; 46/2/26–7; and in Wyndham Estate Office.   47 S.R.O., DD/L P32/5.
48 Ibid. P32/7.
49 Wyndham Estate Office, survey 1621.
50 Ibid. jury presentments.
51 Wedlake, *Watchet*, 73–4.
52 S.R.O., DD/L P32/2.
53 Ibid. P32/5.
54 Ibid. P32/17.   55 Ibid. DD/WY 45/1/10.
56 Ibid. DD/L P37/76; DD/WY 42/2/26–7.
57 Wyndham Estate Office, ct. bk. 1620–1727.
58 Ibid. ct. bk. 1728–present.
59 Below.
60 Wyndham Estate Office, ct. bk. 1728–present.
61 S.R.O., DD/L P32/5.
62 Ibid. DD/WY 4/O2/1.

orders for the repair of roads, and levied fines for breaches of the peace and of the assizes. All private brewing in the 1480s was forbidden when either the reeve or the churchwardens held an ale.[63] From the 1620s the court recorded changes in the ownership of borough properties and attempted, with apparently little success, to control ale selling. In 1623 it reported the stocks, pillory, and ducking stool to be out of repair, and frequently made orders against dangerous buildings.[64] Later presentments included those of nuisances created by a railway in 1837, by loading seaweed in 1838, and by lodging houses in 1852.[65] The court in 1980 possessed a bailiff's staff, dated 1722, a punch bowl and ladle, handcuffs, and a set of weights and measures.

Court rolls for Doniford survive for 1419, 1448–9, 1458, and 1461–2,[66] and copies for 1545[67] and 1669.[68] A tithingman was mentioned in 1462.[69]

For Williton Hadley manor there are court rolls for 1445–51, 1478–9, 1482–4, 1511, 1515,[70] 1579,[71] 1604–15,[72] 1681–3, and 1685–9,[73] and notes on rolls 1364–1492.[74] The manor retained its identity after its purchase in 1710 by Sir William Wyndham. Court sessions, held at the same time as the other Wyndham courts, were recorded separately until 1747, and court papers survive for the periods 1742–7 and from 1757 until the merger of the three Wyndham courts in 1766.[75] The name Williton Hadley survived in the general court books of the Wyndham manors until 1953.[76]

From the 15th century the court met usually twice a year and appointed a reeve and, by rotation, a tithingman. By 1745 there were a reeve and two constables. The court tried to prevent the playing of tennis against the chapel at Williton in 1445–6,[77] and in 1511[78] presented two men for hunting rabbits in the lord's warren. A copyholder convicted of high treason for supporting the duke of Monmouth was in 1685 adjudged by the court to have forfeited his estate.[79]

Court books or rolls for Williton, Williton Hospital, or Williton Regis, survive for 1505,[80] 1549,[81] 1556–63, 1565–84,[82] 1585–9,[83] 1625–40,[84] 1651–5, 1657,[85] and 1663–1740,[86] and court papers from 1741 until business was finally merged with the other Wyndham courts in 1766.[87] The name was retained as part of the title of the estate court between 1843

and 1953.[88] By the 16th century there were two court sessions a year, and there were a tithingman, a reeve, and a constable. There were later two constables. The court heard cases of debt, stray, and trespass, and in 1577 confiscated the goods of a felon.[89] With Williton Fulford and Williton Hadley manors it was jointly responsible for the maintenance of the ducking stool or 'shilvingstole'.[90] The manor court owned a crow net which in 1628 was reported missing.[91] In 1676 the court appointed a beadle and two constables, the beadle to serve for parts of Williton tithing in Stogumber and Doniford.[92]

Rolls of the manor court of Williton Fulford survive for 1473–4,[93] 1568–9,[94] 1573–7, 1587,[95] 1625–40,[96] 1651–5,[97] and 1658.[98] Court books cover the period 1665–1740, and court papers from 1741.[99] The name survived in the general court books of the Wyndham manors until 1953.[1] Sessions from the mid 17th century were held on the same day as the court of Williton Regis. Officers in the 16th century were a tithingman and a reeve, the former serving by rotation.[2]

By 1743 the three manors of Hadley, Regis, and Fulford in practice merged their activities, but retained separate records for some years. By 1744 all shared the same tithingman and constables, and the jury was common to each court, held annually in October. By 1766, when court records for all three manors were consolidated, two inspectors of weights and measures were appointed. A bailiff to impound cattle was recorded in 1803, and a hayward by 1842.[3] In 1842 a constable was appointed for the whole parish by the vestry.[4] Aletasters were recorded from 1843, and the court continued until 1953, its main practical concern being the watering of the meadows.[5] From the 1740s the courts, whether jointly or severally, were responsible for the stocks,[6] and retained the right to confiscate a felon's leasehold as late as 1813. By the late 1830s the court met at the Wyndham (from 1842 the Egremont) Hotel in Williton. Sessions in the later 19th century became in practice the annual rent days, when requests for repairs might be made.[7]

Extracts from court records for the manor of Watchet survive for 1598–9 and 1603–4,[8] and books for 1651–5,[9] 1658, 1662–3,[10] and 1676–1729.[11] No officers are mentioned, but the jurisdiction covered

63 Ibid. DD/L P32/17; DD/WY 45/1/14.
64 Wyndham Estate Office, ct. bk. 1620–1727.
65 Ibid. ct. bk. 1728–present.
66 S.R.O., DD/WY 45/1/13.
67 Ibid. 47/1/1/3B.
68 Ibid. 47/2/34.
69 Ibid. 45/1/13.
70 Ibid. DD/L P33/4, 8–9.
71 Ibid. DD/WY 46/2/28/2.
72 Ibid. DD/L P33/14.
73 Ibid. DD/L 2/19/110; DD/WY 46/3/61.
74 Ibid. DD/L P33/1.
75 Ibid. DD/WY 97.
76 Wyndham Estate Office, ct. bks.
77 S.R.O., DD/L P33/4.
78 Ibid. DD/L P33.
79 Ibid. DD/L 2/19/110.
80 Winchester Coll. MS. 12864.
81 Wyndham Estate Office.
82 S.R.O., DD/WY 45/1/8, 46/2/28/1–3.
83 Ibid. 46/2/28/4; Wyndham Estate Office.
84 S.R.O., DD/WY 44/1/1A, 44/2/2, 3, 44/3/4, 45/1/7/9, 46/2/29.
85 Ibid. 46/2/26/1, 2.
86 Ibid. 46/2/26/2; Wyndham Estate Office, ct. bks. 1665–76, 1676–1710, 1711–29, 1730–40.

87 S.R.O., DD/WY 97.
88 Wyndham Estate Office, ct. bks.
89 S.R.O., DD/WY 46/2/28/1.
90 Ibid. 46/2/28/2.
91 Ibid. 46/2/29.
92 Wyndham Estate Office, ct. bk. 1676–1710.
93 S.R.O., DD/WY 45/1/11.
94 MS. (1978) in possession of R. C. Hatchwell, Little Somerford, Wilts.
95 S.R.O., DD/WY 45/1/10.
96 Ibid. 44/1/1A, 44/2/2, 3, 45/1/9, 46/2/29.
97 Ibid. 46/2/26/1.
98 Ibid. 46/2/26/2.
99 Wyndham Estate Office; S.R.O., DD/WY 97.
1 Wyndham Estate Office, ct. bk. 1843–1953.
2 S.R.O., DD/WY 45/1/10, sub anno 1573.
3 Ibid. DD/WY 97.
4 Below.
5 Williton, Wyndham Estate Office, ct. bk.
6 S.R.O., DD/WY 97, sub annis 1742, 1745, 1776, 1784.
7 Williton, Wyndham Estate Office, ct. bk.; S.R.O., DD/WY 97.
8 S.R.O., DD/WY 46/2/27.
9 Ibid. 46/2/26.
10 Ibid. 46/2/27.
11 Williton, Wyndham Estate Office.

Watchet 'with its members'. Business was largely concerned with property transfers, and the court is likely to have merged with the borough court in the 18th century.

The prebendary of St. Decumans had peculiar jurisdiction throughout the parish in spiritual and testamentary matters. Wills proved by his official survive from 1348.[12] The last probate session was held at Wells in 1850. Visitations on behalf of the prebendary in the 17th and 18th centuries were held in the parish church, and involved the three or four retiring wardens, the new wardens, four (later two) assistants or sidemen, and a jury. One session was adjourned to the parsonage house. Presentments involved moral offences, the state of the vicarage house, and the failure of the prebendary to preach his customary two sermons each year.[13]

By the end of the 16th century the churchwardens of St. Decumans administered the parish in two parts, the Williton side and the Watchet side. Their records survive only from the mid 18th century, when their income derived from land, rates, the profits of St. Decuman's fair, 'lantere' money, and the rent of the Watchet church house. They contributed to the maintenance of Williton chapel as well as supporting the fabric and services of the parish church.[14] The parish vestry usually numbered eight men in the later 18th century, but on occasions the number was doubled. In 1815 the curate appointed one warden, and fifteen vestry members nominated the other. A select vestry, comprising in 1821 a warden, two overseers, and 21 members, met monthly in the earlier 19th century, alternating between the Market House in Watchet and the New Inn or the vestry room at Watering Place, both in Williton.[15]

The two chapel wardens at Williton, later supported by two sidemen, administered charitable funds in Williton through a committee of four by 1613, maintained their own services, raised money through church ales, and from 1634 collected a separate church rate.[16]

Records of the overseers begin in 1638. At that time there were four overseers, their income from parish rates supplemented by the interest from charitable bequests. There was a regular policy of out-relief in the form of house rents, clothing, and cash grants, with occasional extra relief in time of plague (1646–7) or for special medical care (1650–1).[17] A poorhouse, formerly the Williton church house and sometimes referred to as the almshouse or the 'four poor folks' house', was rented from 1630.[18] A workhouse was established at Watchet c. 1730,[19] and one at Williton by 1748.[20] Following a proposal in 1821 by a general parish meeting the

Watchet church house was converted for the use of the poor.[21] A proposal to reopen the Little Silver cloth mills in 1824 to dress cloth made by the poor was superseded by the acquisition of a house and mill at Watering Place as a workhouse in 1825. In 1828–9 it was in full use, stocked with raw materials, spinning turns, and other machinery.[22]

The Williton poor-law union was formed in 1836,[23] and the union workhouse, later known as Townsend House, in Long Street, Williton, was built in 1838–40 to the designs of William Moffatt.[24] Its chapel was licensed in 1838.[25] In 1979 it was used as a hospital. The vestry, meeting either at the Egremont Hotel in Williton or at the West Somerset (or Mossman's) Hotel in Watchet, appointed parish constables from 1842.[26] A police station and court house were built at Williton in 1857.[27] A fire service was established in the parish in 1855–6,[28] public lighting in 1867,[29] and a water undertaking in 1889.[30] The rural district of Williton was formed in 1894,[31] and St. Decumans parish council was created.[32] In 1902, after extensive damage to Watchet harbour, Watchet urban district was formed to replace the harbour commissioners, with jurisdiction over the town and its immediate surroundings.[33] The remainder of the ancient parish became the separate civil parish of Williton.[34] In 1974 the West Somerset district replaced both Watchet urban and Williton rural districts,[35] and the two civil parishes were thereafter represented by a town and parish council respectively.

CHURCHES. The church of St. Decuman was probably Celtic in origin, its dedication to a Welsh saint and its coastal site according closely with similar foundations in West Somerset, North Devon, and Cornwall.[36] Its original site seems to have been on the headland in or close to the Saxon *burh*: burials were discovered in the ramparts of the *burh*,[37] and a nearby field was called Old Minster.[38] The site was evidently abandoned in favour of another on the opposite side of the Washford river valley in face of coastal erosion, the move giving rise to a local feast of the translation of St. Decuman.[39] The present building has no features datable from before the later 13th century.

The name Old Minster suggests that the church was a minster in origin, and still in the mid 12th century it had a dean and at least one dependent chapel.[40] About 1190 Simon Brett gave the church, which included land given by Robert FitzUrse c. 1175, to Bishop Reginald, to form a prebend in Wells Cathedral.[41] In 1203 Sir Walter de Andelys, claiming to be patron of the prebendal church,

[12] S.R.O., DD/WY 19/Z2/9, 27. The official's seal depicts St. Decuman seated on a raft.
[13] S.R.O., D/D/Ppb; copies in ibid. D/P/will 23/6.
[14] Ibid. DD/WY 37/2, accts. 1746–1816.
[15] Ibid. 37/3, 5: mins. and accts. 1821–9.
[16] Ibid. 37/1: accts. 1590–1713.
[17] Ibid. 37/7–9; 38/10–12, 15; 39/16–20: accts. 1638–1831.
[18] Ibid. 37/1, 7.
[19] Ibid. 27.
[20] Ibid. 37/9.
[21] Ibid. 37/3; below, churches.
[22] S.R.O., DD/WY 39/28, 51/2.
[23] Youngs, *Local Admin. Units*, i. 673–4.
[24] Inf. from Mr. R. Lillford, County Planning Office, Taunton; above, plate facing p. 157.
[25] S.R.O., Dioc. Muniment bk. V, f. 14 and v.
[26] Ibid. D/R/wil 9/5/1.
[27] Date on building.
[28] S.R.O., DD/WY 158; DD/AH 63/5.
[29] Ibid. DD/WY 196; Wedlake, *Watchet*, 133; T. Hawkes, 'Williton', TS. of original notes c. 1903 ed. T. H. Andrew, in possession of Mr. D. Gliddon, Williton.
[30] S.R.O., D/R/wil 9/5/1.
[31] Youngs, *Local Admin. Units*, i. 675.
[32] S.R.O., D/R/wil 9/6/1.
[33] Ibid. D/U/wa 33/3/5.
[34] Youngs, *Local Admin. Units*, i. 436.
[35] Ibid. i. 676.
[36] Pearce, *Kingdom of Dumnonia*, 122–38.
[37] Inf. from Dr. I. C. G. Burrow, county archaeologist.
[38] S.R.O., DD/WY, survey 1801.
[39] Ibid. DD/WY 9/W2, notarial instrument 1512.
[40] H.M.C. *Wells*, i. 45; *S.R.S.* lxi, p. 47.
[41] H.M.C. *Wells*, i. 43, 45; above, manors.

presumably in succession to Brett, sued Bishop Reginald's successor Savaric for the right to appoint a prebendary,[42] and then sued the occupant, William of Wrotham.[43] A vicarage was ordained before 1245.[44] Successive prebendaries appointed vicars until 1554, and thereafter the patronage was exercised by the lessees of the prebend or their assigns until 1858.[45] The bishop was patron in 1859,[46] but trustees for the Wyndhams presented in 1884.[47] William Wyndham transferred the advowson to the bishop c. 1916.[48]

The vicarage was taxed at £4 13s. 4d. in 1291.[49] In 1321 it was said to be worth £6 4s. 6½d., and was increased to £11 1s. 2d. from the prebendal estate.[50] The vicarage was again augmented, from prebendal tithes, in 1464, and was still exempt from taxation because of poverty in 1468.[51] It was worth only £10 10s. 4d. net in 1535.[52] The reputed value was £40 c. 1668,[53] and by 1697 was being increased by £20 a year from the prebendal estate.[54] The net income in 1831 averaged £134.[55] By 1851 the sum had increased to £250 gross.[56]

Before the augmentation of 1321 the vicarage was endowed with tithes of calves, pigs, foals, geese, eggs, flax, and hemp, and of four mills and five dovecots. The additional tithes then given were those of milk, butter, wool, lambs, and honey, and all the small tithes of Doniford, together with the tithe hay of the free tenants of Doniford and the tithe of grain and beans in curtilages cultivated by hand.[57] The tithe of cheese and apples in the whole parish was added in 1464.[58] Tithes, with the altar offerings, amounted to £15 7s. in 1535.[59] By the 1630s the vicar claimed tithes of wool, lambs, pears, apples, hops, honey, and wax, and also the tithes of orchards and gardens. Cash was received for cows and calves. The tithe hay from Doniford was still paid according to custom, with other unspecified small tithes; and 1d. an acre was also received from New or Land meadow, but only in the first year after it was returned to grass.[60] In 1841 the tithes were commuted for a rent charge of £230.[61]

The vicarage had no land until St. Decumans Acre was given to it in 1321;[62] a further 11 a. were added in 1464.[63] The whole was worth 10s. in 1535.[64] There were 14 a. in 1635–6,[65] 12 a. in 1851,[66] and c. 6 a. in 1979.[67]

A vicarage house was mentioned in 1321.[68] In 1786 the house was in bad repair and uninhabited.[69] It was said in 1797 to be 'totally ruinated' and at various times thereafter to be either non-existent or ruinous.[70] In 1833 a new house was built in the grounds of the old, on the south side of the churchyard.[71] The new house was in turn replaced by a house further east in 1977.[72]

Among the medieval clergy was one who retained the living after promising to enter the community of Bridgwater Hospital before 1245.[73] Another, admitted in 1461, was found to be ill educated, and had to study successfully for a year or resign.[74] Alexander Browne was deprived in 1554, probably for being married.[75] Robert Parsons held the living without any apparent break from 1643 until 1662.[76] George Knyfton, vicar 1762–98, lived in Minehead for the whole of his vicariate and kept a school there. In 1777 he let the income of the living to the curate for forty years.[77] Henry Poole, vicar 1798–1835, was also vicar of Cannington until 1804. He resigned St. Decumans in favour of his son, Robert, who died in office in 1884.[78]

There were c. 12 regular communicants in 1776.[79] Services in 1815 were held once each Sunday, alternately morning and afternoon; the then non-resident vicar employed a curate who was also rector of West Quantoxhead.[80] Attendance on Census Sunday 1851 was 225 in the morning and 425 in the afternoon, including at each service the 75-strong Sunday school.[81] By 1870 the resident vicar was preaching two sermons each Sunday but celebrating communion only four times a year.[82]

By 1348 there were lights in the church before altars or statues of Our Lady, St. Nicholas, St. Peter, St. James, and the High Cross, and there was a statue of St. Decuman.[83] Then and in 1403 there was a parish chaplain.[84]

There was a church house by 1519.[85] It stood at the east end of the churchyard, beside the road to the church, and seems by the 18th century to have been used as a fair house.[86] After 1821 it was converted into a poorhouse,[87] and was still standing in 1841.[88] Its site was later incorporated into the churchyard extension.

The church of *ST. DECUMAN*, so dedicated by 1189,[89] stands in an isolated position above Watchet, its tall tower a landmark for miles in every direction.

[42] *Cur. Reg. R.* ii. 179, where he is named Audley; but cf. below, Stogumber, manors.
[43] *Sel. Canterbury Cases* (Selden Soc. xcv), 11–14.
[44] *H.M.C. Wells*, i. 122.
[45] *Som. Incumbents*, ed. Weaver, 354–5; *Som. Wills*, ed. Brown, ii. 107; S.R.O., D/D/B reg. 32, f. 119; reg. 34, f. 183v; Orchard Wyndham MSS. 1/1, 11, 17.
[46] *Clergy List* (1859).
[47] *Dioc. Kal.*
[48] *Dioc. Dir.*
[49] *Tax. Eccl.* (Rec. Com.), 198, 200.
[50] S.R.O., DD/CC 110025/11, printed in *H.M.C. Wells*, i. 388–9. [51] *S.R.S.* xlix, p. 408.
[52] *Valor Eccl.* (Rec. Com.), i. 223.
[53] S.R.O., D/D/Vc 24.
[54] Ibid. DD/WY 20.
[55] *Rep. Com. Eccl. Revenues*, pp. 136–7.
[56] P.R.O., HO 129/313/3/5/8.
[57] *H.M.C. Wells*, i. 388–9.
[58] *S.R.S.* xlix, p. 425.
[59] *Valor Eccl.* (Rec. Com.), i. 223.
[60] S.R.O., D/D/Rg 356.
[61] Ibid. tithe award.
[62] *H.M.C. Wells*, i. 388–9.
[63] *S.R.S.* xlix, p. 425.
[64] *Valor Eccl.* (Rec. Com.), i. 223.
[65] S.R.O., D/D/Rg 356.

[66] P.R.O., HO 129/313/3/5/8.
[67] Inf. from the vicar, the Revd. R. M. Barnett.
[68] *H.M.C. Wells*, i. 388–9.
[69] S.R.O., D/D/Ppb.
[70] Ibid. D/D/Ppb; D/D/B returns 1815, 1827; *Rep. Com. Eccl. Revenues*, pp. 136–7.
[71] S.R.O., DD/WY 20; B.L. Add. MS. 33827, f. 52v.
[72] Inf. from the vicar.
[73] *H.M.C. Wells*, i. 122.
[74] *S.R.S.* xlix, p. 358.
[75] Ibid. lv, p. 123.
[76] *Som. Incumbents*, ed. Weaver, 355; S.R.O., DD/WY 37/7.
[77] S.R.O., DD/WY 21; ibid. D/P/will 23/6.
[78] Ibid. D/D/B reg. 32, f. 159; reg. 34, f. 183v; St. Decumans ch., memorial E. window.
[79] S.R.O., D/D/Vc 88.
[80] Ibid. D/D/B returns 1815.
[81] P.R.O., HO 129/313/3/5/8.
[82] S.R.O., D/D/V returns 1870.
[83] Ibid. DD/WY 19/Z2/9.
[84] Ibid. 19/Z2/9, 27.
[85] Ibid. DD/L P32/27.
[86] Ibid. tithe award.
[87] Ibid. DD/WY 37/3.
[88] Ibid. tithe award.
[89] *Rot. Chart.* (Rec. Com.), 174b.

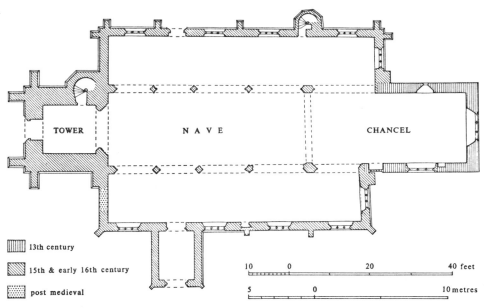

THE CHURCH OF ST. DECUMAN

It has a chancel with north and south chapels, nave with north and south aisles and south porch, and a west tower. The only part of the church to have survived rebuilding in the 15th or early 16th century is the chancel, which is unusually wide and long and dates from the later 13th century. The sequence of the building of the rest of the church is uncertain, but the arcades of four bays are of at least three different dates, and their irregularity may suggest the former existence of a central tower, still there when the aisles were first formed.[90] The eastern bay of the south aisle appears to have been used as a chapel before the building of the south chancel chapel. The north aisle and chapel are of one date, later than the tower. New work in the building was referred to in 1498.[91] The waggon roofs, contemporary with the rebuilding, have decorated wall plates and angel supports.

Tiles in the chancel and north aisle, formerly at the east end of the south aisle, were made in the 13th century, probably at Cleeve Abbey.[92] The late medieval octagonal font has angel-bust supports. Crudely carved figures in niches in the north arcade include St. George and St. Anthony.[93] The screens, the oldest dating from before 1500, survive from a more complicated arrangement which included a rood loft with entrances at both ends and parcloses forming chapels in the aisles and perhaps also in the nave. The communion table and pulpit are of the early 17th century and the contemporary communion rails were originally arranged on three sides of the altar. The Wyndham pew (1688), formerly in the chancel, stands in the north chapel with tombs and monuments of the Wyndham family dating from 1572 and an earlier slab commemorating one of the

Sydenhams, owners of Orchard.[94] The most remarkable tomb, until the demolition of the stone canopy, was that of Sir John Wyndham (d. 1574), which was in an 'Elizabethan form of Gothic'.[95] The monument to John Wyndham (d. 1645) and his wife is probably by Nicholas Stone.[96] The churchyard cross dates from the mid 15th century, and the tower bears a figure which may be a representation of St. Decuman.

The church has six bells, including one probably by the Exeter founder Robert Norton (1422–61), one each by the Somerset founders William Purdue (1668) and Robert Austen (1671), and two by E. and W. Evans of Chepstow (Gwent) (1723).[97] The plate includes an Elizabethan cup with later stem and foot, a cup of 1634 by 'R.C.', and two patens, one of 1634 by 'I.M.'.[98] The registers begin in 1602, but lack baptisms 1636–49, marriages 1653–63 and 1678–1704, and burials 1646–53.[99]

The chapel of the *HOLY CROSS* at Watchet was probably in existence in the early 14th century.[1] After 1369 land was given to support a chantry chaplain there to pray for the FitzUrse family,[2] and rent for wax for a candle before a representation of the holy cross was given in 1448.[3] By 1525 the chapel owned a tenement called 'le bruhowsse' and 7 a. of land.[4] Considered to be a chantry, the chapel was dissolved in 1548, and its two bells and ornaments were sold.[5] The whole property, including a messuage called the Roodhouse and a fishery called Roodweir, passed through the hands of George Payne of Hutton and then of William Moryce of Chipping Ongar (Essex), and was bought by John Wyndham in 1552.[6] The chapel was still standing in 1673,[7] and probably in 1701, but by 1830 it was in ruins, 'for many years part converted'.[8] The site,

[90] F. C. Eeles, *St. Decuman's* (1932), 8–9.
[91] *S.R.S.* xvi. 363.   [92] Eeles, *St. Decuman's*, 21.
[93] S.R.O., DD/WY 19/Z2/9.
[94] Eeles, *St. Decuman's*, 32. There seem to be no grounds for the date 1513 there given.
[95] Ibid. 25–6. Some fragments were at Orchard Wyndham in 1979.   [96] *Proc. Som. Arch. Soc.* xcii. 88–92.
[97] Eeles, *St. Decuman's*, 23–4.
[98] *Proc. Som. Arch. Soc.* xlv. 172–3.

[99] S.R.O., D/P/st.d 2/1/1–25.
[1] *H.M.C. Wells*, i. 388–9.
[2] S.R.O., DD/L P32/2.
[3] Ibid. DD/WY 8/T2/2.
[4] Ibid. 4/R1/15.
[5] *S.R.S.* ii. 47; P.R.O., E 117/12, no. 21.
[6] *Cal. Pat.* 1549–51, 135–6; S.R.O., DD/WY 8/M2.
[7] S.R.O., DD/WY 35.
[8] Ibid. 64/20.

between Market Street and the harbour,[9] was occupied in 1979 by the London inn.

Before 1202 Robert FitzUrse granted his right in the advowson of Williton chapel to the church of St. Decuman.[10] The chapel, which had a resident chaplain, had no burial ground, and attendance at the mother church was required at festivals,[11] specified in 1412 as the Ascension and the dedication and translation of St. Decuman.[12] Chaplains, after 1784 called perpetual curates or vicars, were appointed by successive vicars of St. Decumans.[13]

The chaplain was paid £5 6s. 8d. a year by the vicar of St. Decumans in 1535,[14] and had a house and 1 a. of land given with the chapel by Robert FitzUrse.[15] The living was augmented between 1784 and 1792 by Queen Anne's Bounty, and land was bought at Winsford.[16] By 1792 the vicar of St. Decumans paid a further £5 to a curate to serve the chapel twice a Sunday.[17] Two further augmentations in 1810 and 1813 totalling £1,400 were used to buy land at Hockworthy (Devon), but all the glebe was sold in 1847 and the proceeds invested, producing an income of £55 in 1851.[18] Further endowments from the Common Fund in 1882 provided a total income of £236 a year.[19]

The medieval priest's house stood at the west end of Williton, north of the road to Washford.[20] It was rebuilt in 1623,[21] but by 1827 was described as a 'poor cottage' and by 1835 was 'unfit'.[22] By 1851 the perpetual curate was living at Eastfield, on the south side of the village.[23] The present vicarage house, west of the site of the priest's house, was built in 1907.[24]

The fabric and services at Williton were maintained in the late 16th century from the proceeds of brewing ale at Whitsun revels or chapel ales. Other income was from rent of the church house from 1630, from rates by 1634, and from charges for encroachment on the unfenced chapel yard. Laudian furniture was introduced in 1634 and 1637, and chapel ales continued until 1641. They were revived between 1662 and 1688.[25] Thomas Vickary, curate by 1610 and until 1647 or later, was followed by a succession of temporary ministers in the next decade, and the priest's house was let.[26] It was let again from 1765 by the vicar of St. Decumans, the beginning of years of neglect of the chapel, which was served until 1792 by a curate who rented both St. Decumans and Williton from an absentee vicar.[27]

Charles Poole, perpetual curate by 1800 and until 1840, and brother of the vicar of St. Decumans, was so unpopular that the fulfilment of his promise in 1807 to live in Williton was strongly discouraged. In 1814 he declared that he would serve the chapel every three weeks, and that if he came once a fortnight it would be an act of grace.[28]

There was a church house at Williton by 1491.[29] By 1584 it was handed over by the tenants from Whitsun eve for a month to allow the chapel wardens to brew and sell ale.[30] The house was rebuilt in 1591 to provide a kitchen, hall, and solar. It was rebuilt again in 1629–30 and was then let to the overseers as a poorhouse.[31]

The church, formerly the chapel, of ST. PETER was dedicated by the early 14th century to All Saints.[32] The chapel wardens still presented their accounts near All Saints' day until the early 18th century.[33] The building has a chancel with north vestry and south chapel, a nave with north and south aisles and shallow north porch, and a western porch and bellcot. Its core is a medieval building of nave and chancel whose east and west walls survive. The south aisle, added in 1810–12, incorporates the late medieval windows of the original south wall of the nave.[34] The building was heavily restored and the north aisle and vestry added in 1856–9 by C. E. Giles.[35] A wooden bellcot was replaced by one in stone in 1896.[36] The Lady chapel on the south side of the chancel was added in 1932.[37] The alabaster font was bought in 1666.[38] There are two bells.[39] The plate includes a cup and cover of 1574 by J. Ions of Exeter and a secular plate of 1679.[40] Separate registers of baptisms begin in 1792 and of marriages in 1829.[41]

The mission church of ST. SAVIOUR, Watchet, formerly an iron church on Brendon Hill, had been re-erected by 1887 on the south side of West Street. Its site in 1980 was occupied by nos. 13 and 14 West Street.[42] In the 1920s it was succeeded by the Mission, later known as the chapel of HOLY CROSS, which occupied the first floor of the Market House. The chapel was restored in 1979.[43]

NONCONFORMITY. Silvester Huish of Doniford was reported as a recusant 1593–6,[44] and Henry Pyke, his family, and household were similarly described in 1642.[45]

9 Ibid. DD/WY, survey 1801.
10 H.M.C. Wells, i. 45.
11 Hist. MSS. Com. 15, 10th Rep. VI, Luttrell, p. 72.
12 S.R.O., DD/WY 9/W2.
13 e.g. ibid. DD/WY 21, 36; Clergy List; Dioc. Dir.
14 Valor Eccl. (Rec. Com.), i. 223.
15 H.M.C. Wells, i. 45.
16 S.R.O., D/D/Ppb; B.L. Add. MS. 33827, f. 73v.
17 S.R.O., DD/WY 36.
18 B.L. Add. MS. 33827, f. 73v.; S.R.O., D/D/Ppb; P.R.O., H.O. 129/313/3/5/7.
19 Lond. Gaz. 8 Dec. 1882, p. 6255.
20 S.R.O., tithe award; Armstrong, Parish of Williton, St. Peter (1982), 32.
21 S.R.O., DD/WY 37/1.
22 Ibid. D/D/V returns 1827; Rep. Com. Eccl. Revenues, pp. 158–9.
23 P.R.O., H.O. 129/313/3/5/7.
24 Armstrong, Williton, 15.
25 S.R.O., DD/WY 37/1: accts. 1590–1713; ibid. D/D/Ca 57.
26 Ibid. DD/WY 37/1; S.R.S. xxviii. 342; for a list of ministers see Armstrong, Williton, 28–30.

27 S.R.O., DD/WY 37/2.
28 Ibid. 36.
29 Ibid. DD/L P32/2.
30 Ibid. DD/WY 46/2/28/3: 7 Sept. 1594.
31 Ibid. 37/1.
32 Ibid. DD/L P33/1.
33 Ibid. DD/WY 37/1.
34 Ibid. 36; ibid. D/D/B returns 1815.
35 Ibid. D/P/will 8/2/2; 9/1/1.
36 Ibid. 8/2/1.
37 Kelly's Dir. Som. (1939).
38 S.R.O., DD/WY 37/1; S.R.S. xxviii. 343.
39 Ibid. DD/SAS CH 16.
40 Proc. Som. Arch. Soc. xlv. 176.
41 S.R.O., D/P/will 2/1/1–11.
42 O.S. Map 1/2,500, Som. XXVI. 13 (1887 edn.); Dioc. Kal.; above, Old Cleeve.
43 Dioc. Dir.; inf. from the vicar.
44 Recusant Rolls, 1593–4 (Catholic Rec. Soc. 57), 138; 1594–6 (Catholic Rec. Soc. 61), 82; S. & D. N. & Q. v. 114.
45 Som. Protestation Returns, ed. Howard and Stoate, 176, 291.

Protestant nonconformity was introduced to Watchet *c.* 1766[46] by Lady Huntingdon's preachers, and one addressed 'some hundreds' in 1771, claiming to have 'totally conquered' the people.[47] Preaching by student ministers continued there and at Williton,[48] and cottages and land were purchased at Watchet. The congregation changed its allegiance and the property was left by the purchaser's widow to a group of Particular Baptists, who were formally constituted as a church in 1808.[49] The chapel was built in 1824 and is still in use.[50] It is a simple building with a curved pediment above arched gallery windows, and stands prominently above the town. In 1851 morning and evening services were held on one Sunday and an afternoon service on the next, alternating with the chapel at Williton. On Census Sunday afternoon the Watchet congregation was 85, with 31 Sunday-school children.[51] The minister from Watchet was holding meetings in Robert Street, Williton, by 1813.[52] After difficulty over a lease from the Wyndham estate, a site was acquired from the Aclands at Catwell, and a chapel was opened in 1844.[53] Services there on Census Sunday 1851 were attended by 70 adults in the morning and 72 in the evening.[54] Ten years later Watchet and Williton chapels between them had 67 members.[55] Services at Williton were discontinued in 1919.[56] From 1883 a disused railway carriage at Doniford was used as a mission room. It was closed *c.* 1920.[57]

The house of John Date at Watchet was licensed for worship in 1803, the application for licence supported by Date himself, and by John and Mary Stoate and John Wood, members of three families prominent both in local Methodism and in the business life of Watchet.[58] Stoate moved to Williton in 1806 and his house, on the site of the present bank opposite the Egremont Hotel, was used for worship from 1810.[59] A class was formed at Williton in 1820 and another at Watchet in 1824, the latter soon to become the largest in the circuit.[60] The Williton class may at first have met in a building opposite Stoate's house,[61] but a chapel was built in 1820 in an alley off the west side of Fore Street.[62] In 1851 the average congregation was 120 in the morning and 140 in the evening, with 52 Sunday-school pupils in addition.[63] The chapel was replaced in 1883 by the present building at the bottom of Tower Hill, to which were added a minister's house and schoolrooms.[64] Membership in 1903 was 76 and in 1959

was 89.[65] A chapel was built off Swain Street, Watchet, in 1824 after earlier meetings had been held in a barn.[66] It remained in use until 1871[67] when the present building was erected in Station (now Harbour) Road. In 1903 four services were held each week, with an open-air service every Sunday evening in summer. Membership was 71 in 1903 and 85 in 1959.[68] A Wesleyan preaching place at Doniford was established in 1835, but it was given up in 1844.[69] In the 1860s there were Methodist meetings at the paper mills in Watchet during the ownership of John Wansbrough,[70] and the former Anglican chapel at Brendon Hill was brought to the mills *c.* 1883 but was later transferred to West Street.[71] Methodist meetings were held at High Bridge between 1874 and 1877.[72]

Bible Christians were established at Watchet in 1859, and opened a chapel, called the Temple after its Grecian style, in 1860 on the southern edge of the town, near new terraced houses.[73] The cause duly became part of the United Methodist movement, and services continued to be held there until 1962.[74] The building was later incorporated into St. Decumans C. of E. school.

The Salvation Army came to Watchet in 1882, and was formally established in 1884.[75] Until 1928 they occupied the former Methodist chapel in Swain Street, then known as Castle Hall, and later moved to their present premises near the railway station.[76]

EDUCATION. In 1575 Thomas Blinman, newly appointed curate of Williton, was licensed to teach boys there.[77] Robert Parsons the younger, possibly minister of the parish 1643–62, began teaching at a grammar school in St. Decumans in 1636;[78] between 1645 and 1660 George Wotton, ejected vicar of Bridgwater, taught at Williton.[79] There was a schoolroom near Williton chapel by 1791,[80] and a school was kept in the priest's house in Williton in 1802.[81] Another school, on Lancasterian lines, was opened in Williton in 1811. It was supported by subscriptions and was intended for children of labouring men 'with no apparent prospect of education whether in the parish or not', as well as for fee-paying pupils of any religious persuasion. Known as the Free School of Williton, it survived until 1821, when it closed because of the reluctance of the poor to attend.[82]

[46] Watchet Baptist Ch., min. bk. 1808–79, including 'Memoir . . . by the first pastor Joseph Tyso'.
[47] W. Symons, *Early Methodism in W. Som.* [*c.* 1894], 62.
[48] 'Memoir by Tyso'; Symons, *Early Methodism*, 4.
[49] 'Memoir by Tyso'; *Western Baptist Assoc. Letters, 1769–1823*.
[50] Date on building.
[51] P.R.O., HO 129/313/3/5/11.
[52] Watchet Baptist Ch., min. bk. 1808–79; T. Hawkes, 'Williton', TS. of original notes *c.* 1903 ed. T. H. Andrew, in possession of Mr. D. Gliddon, Williton; F. N. Cox, *Williton in Other Days* (1927), 8.
[53] Symons, *Early Methodism*, 53.
[54] Watchet Baptist Ch., min. bk. 1808–79; S.R.O., DD/AH 16/2, 39/6; P.R.O., HO 129/313/3/5/11.
[55] Watchet Bapt. Ch., min. bk. 1808–79.
[56] Ibid. 1901–49.
[57] *Baptist Handbk.* (1885, 1919, 1921); Watchet Bapt. Ch., min. bk. 1901–49; local inf.
[58] S.R.O., D/D/Rm 2; Symons, *Early Methodism*, 68.
[59] Symons, *Early Methodism*, 53; *Williton Methodist Ch., Centenary Booklet* (1910).
[60] Symons, *Early Methodism*, 17.
[61] Ibid. 53.

[62] T. Hawkes, 'Williton', 14; Symons, *Early Methodism*, 53; N. V. Allen, *Churches and Chapels of Exmoor* (1974), 88.
[63] P.R.O., HO 129/313/3/5/11.
[64] Hawkes, 'Williton', 15.
[65] S.R.O., D/N/wsc 3/2/9.
[66] Symons, *Early Methodism*, 63–4.
[67] Date on building.
[68] S.R.O., D/N/wsc 3/2/9.
[69] Ibid. 3/2/2.
[70] Inf. from Dr. A. W. G. Court, Washford, and Mr. G. Kneen, Wansborough Paper Co. Ltd.
[71] Inf. from Dr. Court.
[72] S.R.O., D/N/wsc 3/2/4.
[73] Wedlake, *Watchet*, 116.
[74] Inf. from Dr. Court.
[75] Wedlake, *Watchet*, 116–17.
[76] Allen, *Churches and Chapels of Exmoor*, 86.
[77] S.R.O., D/D/Ol 4.
[78] Ibid. D/D/subscription bk. 1.
[79] *Walker Revised*, ed. A. G. Matthews, 321–2.
[80] S.R.O., DD/WY 55/37.
[81] Hawkes, 'Williton', 14B.
[82] S.R.O., DD/WY 39/32; 68.

By 1818 there was a 'good' Sunday school in the parish 'tolerably well attended' by 80 boys and girls, and there were four day schools in Williton, together taking 46 children.[83] A Methodist Sunday school was started at Williton in 1822 and another at Watchet in 1825,[84] and in 1826 a Methodist established a day and boarding school at Watchet.[85] By 1835 there were eight day schools and four Sunday schools in the parish. Three of the day schools (100 pupils) were for the children of tradesmen and farmers, the remainder (100 pupils) were to teach poor children to read and write. The Sunday schools between them took 335 children: two were Methodist, one Baptist, one Church of England.[86] The 'diocesan' school at Williton, founded by 1841 and united to a diocesan board, was described as 'very good' in 1846, and was almost entirely supported by the curate there. It had a total of 75 day pupils and 156 on Sundays.[87]

In 1851 there were at least five schools: a Wesleyan Sunday school and a boys' boarding school at Sea View Terrace, both in Watchet, a day school and the Baptist Sunday school at Williton,[88] and a school in the workhouse.[89] During the 1860s a new day school was opened at Watchet and another at Williton, but the latter seems to have closed by 1866. The 'diocesan' school at Williton was later affiliated to the National Society, and new buildings were opened in 1872. The Watchet day school may have become the undenominational school opened in 1869–70. A new Church of England school at Watchet was built in 1873.[90]

In 1903 the two schools in Watchet and the National school at Williton were absorbed into the county council system. The undenominational school at Watchet became a council school, and then had an average attendance of 125 boys and girls and 39 infants. The Watchet National school, then regarded as two separate establishments for 'mixed' pupils and infants, assumed aided status, and had 135 boys and girls and 100 infants on its books.[91] The Williton school was slightly smaller, with 116 boys and girls and 80 infants.[92] All three schools were retained when a secondary modern school was built at Williton in 1957, with controlled status, for pupils over eleven years.[93] The Watchet National school was known from 1959 as St. Decumans C. of E. school. Further reorganization in 1971 converted Williton secondary school into a middle school, subsequently known as Danesfield, for pupils in the 9–13 age range, and converted the three contributing schools at Watchet and Williton into first schools.[94]

There were several private schools in the parish from the later 19th century. In 1861 there was a girls' school at Temple Place, Watchet, which continued until 1875.[95] By 1889 the Misses Green had established a school for girls at Stream which was still in being in 1910; and there were two other similar, but short lived, ventures, one at Williton and one at Watchet, by 1897.[96] In the 1920s and 1930s there were two private schools at Watchet known as Westcliff and St. Decumans, and from c. 1932 until 1945 there was a boys' school called St. Decumans on Tower Hill, Williton.[97] From c. 1927 there was a school for girls in Williton, later known as Beaconwood Private School, which survived until c. 1939.[98] Buckland School, St. Decumans Road, Watchet, founded in 1955, is a private day school for boys and girls.[99]

CHARITIES FOR THE POOR. By 1583 the churchwardens and sidemen of St. Decumans held c. 15 a. of land and other property, the income applied to the repair of the parish church, the maintenance of soldiers in Ireland or elsewhere, support of the poor, or payment of charges on the parish.[1] The estate almost certainly had been held by the pre-Reformation churchwardens,[2] and some of it had been given for masses under the will of William Klerc in 1403.[3] By 1787 the income was £6 4s. 10d.[4] Part of the estate, called the Poor's Land, c. 12 a. in 1841,[5] was gradually converted into stock, and by 1901 the St. Decumans charity, as it was called, comprised the stock, just over 6 a. of land, 10 houses and cottages, and a printing office, as well as the stock of charities described below. There was a net income of £103 from real property and £33 9s. 4d. from investments, and 168 people received blankets.[6] By 1977 all but one cottage had been sold, and investments produced an income of c. £1,100, applied to the repair of the parish church and in distributions to the old, the widowed, and the infirm of Williton and Watchet.[7] In 1939 coal vouchers replaced blankets, and grocery vouchers were given in the 1970s, in 1979 each worth £3.[8]

By 1638 the churchwardens administered the income of six other charities:[9] £100 given by James Huish of London (d. 1590),[10] £5 by a Mr. Jones, £15 by Thomas Heyman, 26s. 8d. by the rector of Calverleigh (Devon), £20 by Eleanor, daughter of Sir John Wyndham (d. 1574) and wife of Thomas Carne,[11] and £10 by Edmund Wyndham of Aller (d. 1627). Part of the capital was lent at interest, and by 1677 the income, not certainly including the

[83] *Educ. of Poor Digest*, H.C. 224 (1819), ix (2).
[84] *Williton Methodist Ch., Centenary Booklet* (1910).
[85] Symons, *Early Methodism*, 64.
[86] *Educ. Enq. Abstract*, H.C. 62 (1835), xlii.
[87] J. B. B. Clarke, *Account of Church Educ. among Poor* (1946); Nat. Soc. *Inquiry, 1846–7*, Som. pp. 8–9.
[88] P.R.O., HO 129/313/4/2/10, separate note numbered 59; Wedlake, *Watchet*, 118; Watchet Baptist Ch., min. bk. 1808–79.
[89] P.R.O., HO 107/1920.
[90] *P.O. Dir. Som.* (1861, 1866); S.R.O., C/E 28.
[91] S.R.O., C/E 28; ibid. *Schs. Lists.*
[92] Ibid. C/E 28.
[93] Ibid. *Schs. Lists.* Williton school had become controlled by 1950.
[94] Ibid. *Schs. Lists.*
[95] *P.O. Dir. Som.* (1861, 1875).
[96] *Kelly's Dir. Som.* (1889, 1897, 1910).
[97] Inf. from Dr. A. W. G. Court, Washford.
[98] *Kelly's Dir. Som.* (1927, 1939).
[99] *Som. Co. Gaz.*, 1 Aug. 1980.
[1] St. Decumans char., deeds in possession of Mr. A. L. Wedlake, Watchet.
[2] S.R.O., DD/L P32/2, 18.
[3] Ibid. DD/WY 19/Z2/27.
[4] *Char. Don.* H.C. 511 (1816), xvi.
[5] S.R.O., tithe award.
[6] Ibid. D/P/st.d 17/3/1.
[7] St. Decumans char., papers in possession of the clerk, Mr. R. S. J. Bryant, Williton.
[8] St. Decumans char., min. bk. 1921–79, in possession of the clerk.
[9] S.R.O., DD/WY 37/7.
[10] *Proc. Som. Arch. Soc.* xliii. 30.
[11] *Som. Wills*, ed. Brown, vi. 108; S.R.O., DD/WY 46/2/28/2.

Poor's Land, amounted to £35 2s.[12] 'Public money' in 1706 amounted to capital of £610 producing £20 10s., distributed to the second poor partly at need and partly at Christmas and Easter at St. Decumans church or Williton chapel.[13] In 1787 three of the charities, then of unknown origin, survived, with a combined capital of £602 17s., together with a bequest of £50 from Mary Smith.[14] By 1826 stock from all sources produced £28 15s. 4d.,[15] and by 1901 had evidently become part of the investments of St. Decumans charity.[16]

By will proved in 1935 Mary Huxtable Sutton of Minehead gave four houses and £1,100 to the trustees of St. Decumans charity to establish and endow almshouses, the money to build small houses for needy labouring men or women, the existing houses for those not of the labouring class. A pension charity was established from the sale proceeds of two of the houses in 1937, but no other houses were built, and in 1975 the accumulated funds of the two charities were combined to form the Mary Huxtable Sutton Relief-in-Need charity, payable to any living within six miles of Watchet not under 55 years.[17] In 1979 the trustees agreed to a maximum annual distribution of £200 to all recipients.[18]

A nursing association for the sick poor of Williton and Sampford Brett was founded c. 1932, supported by an endowment and payments from all but pensioners and those in receipt of parish relief. In 1932 William Wyndham of Orchard Wyndham gave £800 for the sick of Williton. After the establishment of the National Health Service in 1948 the funds were combined,[19] and in 1980 were regularly distributed in grocery vouchers in the two parishes.[20]

SAMPFORD BRETT

THE PARISH of Sampford Brett,[21] which probably takes its main name from a ford where the Doniford stream flows between outcrops of Upper Sandstone,[22] lies immediately south-east of Williton but may have been part of an estate centred on Stogumber.[23] East of the stream, on undulating Keuper marls, lies Torweston, sheltering under Castle Hill (81 m.). Sampford Brett village, at the heart of a second manor, lies 1 km. south-west, on the west bank of the Doniford stream, its southern boundary interlocking with Stogumber. Aller Farm lies 1.5 km. south-west of Sampford village on a tongue of land running up the Leighland Slate outliers of the Brendons, reaching 158 m. above Woodford in Nettlecombe.[24] The boundary between Aller and Stogumber is marked by a stream which probably watered the alders which gave the settlement its name. The parish also included a detached area 3 km. south-east of Sampford village, called Cagley or Kagley in the 14th century[25] and later Wayshill.[26] In 1883 Cagley was transferred to Stogumber, which had entirely surrounded it. In 1885 Lower Weacombe, including 31 people in 5 houses, was transferred from Stogumber to Sampford Brett civil parish.[27] In 1971 the parish measured 466 ha. (1,151 a.).[28]

Sampford village lies in a shallow valley formed by the Sampford stream flowing from Aller Farm. It comprises a single wide street with the church at its eastern end, the street having been widened by 1891[29] apparently to provide an improved view of the church from the estate cottages built by the Acland-Hoods among the surviving cottages of the 17th century or earlier.[30] There was a short lane running south from the church to serve the mill. From the 1930s onwards houses were built beside the main road north of the village as part of the development of Tower Hill in Williton, and other houses were built later on the northern boundary at Catwell.

There may have been some open-field arable south of Sampford Brett village,[31] but the glebe in the north-west was in closes by 1606.[32] Common meadow in Molland mead and Sampford moor in the extreme north of the parish survived until the early 19th century,[33] and by 1841 only two landshares remained.[34]

By the end of the 18th century the ford which gave its name to the village, perhaps forming a crossing from Woolston in Bicknoller near a field called the Green in Sampford,[35] had lost its significance in the local road pattern.[36] The main road through the parish, crossing the village street towards its western end, was part of a north-south route between Williton and Stogumber. The route was itself cut, north of the village, by the road from Tower Hill in Williton to Bicknoller.[37] In 1807 that road became part of the new turnpike route from Williton to

[12] S.R.O., DD/WY 37/7.
[13] Ibid. 38/12.
[14] Char. Don. H.C. 511 (1816), xvi.
[15] 15th Rep. Com. Char. p. 443.
[16] S.R.O., D/P/st.d 17/3/1.
[17] St. Decumans char., papers.
[18] Ibid. min. bk.
[19] Char. Com. files.
[20] Inf. from the Revd. A. H. Loveluck, vicar of Williton.
[21] This article was completed in 1979.
[22] Geol. Surv. Map 1", drift, sheet 295 (1956 edn.).
[23] Below, Stogumber.
[24] Geol. Surv. Map 1", solid and drift, sheet 294 (1969 edn.).
[25] Cal. Pat. 1313–17, 414.

[26] S.R.O., tithe award; O.S. Map 1", sheet 164 (1966 edn.).
[27] Census, 1891.
[28] Ibid. 1971.
[29] S.R.O., tithe award; O.S. Map 6", Som. XLVIII. NW. (1891 edn.).
[30] S.R.O., DD/V Wlr.
[31] Ibid. tithe award.
[32] Ibid. D/D/Rg 357.
[33] Ibid. DD/WO 9/9; DD/WO map 1796; DD/AH 38/8.
[34] Ibid. tithe award.
[35] Ibid.
[36] S.R.S. lxxvi, map 1782.
[37] S.R.O., DD/WY 151.

Taunton.[38] The West Somerset Railway, opened in 1862, was cut through the parish from the foot of Castle Hill across Sampford moor.[39]

There was a licensed victualler in the parish in 1736.[40]

Twelve people were assessed for tax in 1327, and Sampford Brett was probably the chief settlement; only one taxpayer was recorded for Torweston.[41] At least 66 adult males lived in the parish in 1641,[42] and 108 people were listed in the subsidy returns of 1667.[43] In 1801 the population was 180; it reached a peak of 280 in 1861, but fell to 158 in 1901.[44] Since 1931 the built-up area of Williton has extended into the parish at Tower Hill and Catwell. In 1951 the population was 221, by 1961 it was 255, and in 1971 there were 291 people in the parish.[45]

MANORS AND OTHER ESTATES. In 1066 *SAMPFORD* was held by Alnod and in 1086 by Hugh d'Avranches, earl of Chester, with William as his undertenant.[46] In the early 13th century it may, along with Torweston, have been reckoned part of the honor of Dunster,[47] but in 1284–5 it remained part of the barony of Chester, of which it was held in mesne lordship by the heirs of Roger of Kingston.[48] Roger had c. 1225 held the mesne lordship,[49] which has not otherwise been traced. By 1377 both Sampford and Torweston, which had long been held by the same undertenants, were part of the honor of Dunster,[50] in which they were described as a single manor in the late 15th century. Sampford was recorded under the same overlordship in 1777.[51] The Brett family, which gave the parish its distinguishing name, may have had the undertenancy of Sampford by 1197, when Simon Brett was holding 2 knights' fees, evidently of the honor of Dunster.[52] John Brett died before 1225 holding Sampford and leaving a minor as heir,[53] and later in the 13th century the Bretts held both Sampford and Torweston,[54] which thereafter descended together.

TORWESTON, held in 1066 by Lefsin, was in 1086 held by William de Mohun with Hugh as undertenant.[55] The overlordship remained as part of the Mohuns' honor of Dunster until 1777 or later.[56] Of that honor Simon Brito or Brett in 1166 held ½ knight's fee, apparently Torweston. It was presumably his son Simon Brett who held 2 knights' fees, possibly representing both Torweston and Sampford, in 1197; in the early 12th century he held them of the honor of Dunster.[57] By 1280 Sir William

Brett held both Sampford and Torweston, and he was still alive in 1294.[58] His heir was his son Adam, but in 1303 his widow Emme held Sampford and a younger son, Lawrence, was in temporary possession of Torweston.[59] In 1306 Adam Brett received the grant of a market and fair in his manor of Sampford and of free warren in his demesnes of Torweston.[60] He was succeeded before 1327 by John Brett,[61] presumably his son, who held Torweston in 1331.[62] William Brett, John's brother, held both manors by 1337, but part of Torweston was still held in dower by Adam Brett's widow, Alice, and her second husband Edmund of Sampford.[63] William and Alice continued in possession until 1359, when they sold the two manors and the dower lands to Hugh Courtenay, earl of Devon, and his wife Margaret.[64]

The earl died in 1377 and his widow in 1391, and the manors passed to their fourth son, Sir Philip Courtenay (d. 1406). Sir Philip's heir was his eldest son Richard,[65] bishop of Norwich 1413–15. The bishop died in 1415 leaving as his heir his nephew Philip (later Sir Philip) Courtenay of Powderham (Devon), then a minor.[66] Philip's second son, Sir Philip Courtenay of Molland (Devon), succeeded in 1463.[67] Sir Philip died in 1489, and his son and heir John in 1509.[68] John's son, Philip, a minor, came of age in 1516, and survived until 1547, when his heir was his son Robert.[69] Robert died in 1583 and was followed by his son Philip (d. 1611) and by Philip's second son Charles (d. 1612).[70] Charles's son and heir, John, was an infant who came of age c. 1629.[71] He died in 1660 and was followed in direct male line by John (d. 1684), John (d. 1724), and John Courtenay (d. 1732).[72]

Margaret, widow of the last John Courtenay, held the estate until her death in 1743, and it passed to John's sister Elizabeth, wife of John Chichester of Arlington (Devon). Elizabeth died in 1763 leaving the manors to her granddaughter Anna Maria Paston, wife of George Throckmorton (d. 1767) of Coughton (Warws.).[73] Anna died in 1791, and was followed by her second son George, who assumed the additional surname and arms of Courtenay before succeeding his elder brother as the 6th baronet in 1819.[74] Sir George died in 1826 and was succeeded at Sampford and Torweston by his nephew Robert George Throckmorton, of Buckland (Berks.), who himself succeeded to the baronetcy in 1840.[75] In 1846 Sir Robert sold the estate to Sir Peregrine Acland, Bt.[76] It was settled on Sir Peregrine's

[38] 47 Geo. III, c. 27 (Local and Personal).
[39] E. T. Macdermot, *Hist. G. W. R.* (1964), ii. 87.
[40] S.R.O., Q/RL.
[41] *S.R.S.* iii. 167.
[42] *Som. Protestation Returns*, ed. Howard and Stoate, 168. [43] S.R.O., DD/WY 34.
[44] *V.C.H. Som.* ii. 351.
[45] *Census*, 1911–71.
[46] *V.C.H. Som.* i. 473.
[47] Below.
[48] *Feud. Aids*, iv. 275.
[49] *S.R.S.* xi, p. 79.
[50] *Cal. Inq. p.m.* xiv, p. 307.
[51] *S.R.S.* xxxiii, pp. 239, 352.
[52] *Red Bk. Exch.* (Rolls Ser.), i. 103, 168.
[53] *S.R.S.* xi, p. 79.
[54] Ibid. extra ser. 145.
[55] *V.C.H. Som.* i. 505.
[56] *S.R.S.* xxxiii, p. 352.
[57] *Red Bk. Exch.* (Rolls Ser.), i. 103, 168, 226.
[58] *S.R.S.* extra ser. 145.

[59] S.R.O., DD/WO 11/6; *Feud. Aids*, iv. 304.
[60] *Cal. Chart. R.* 1300–26, 71.
[61] *S.R.S.* i. 275, where Adam is named Alan.
[62] *Cal. Inq. p. m.* vii, p. 220; *S.R.S.* xxxiii, p. 75.
[63] *S.R.S.* xii. 187–8.
[64] Ibid. xvii. 41–2.
[65] *Cal. Inq. p.m.* xiv, p. 307; P.R.O., C 136/69, no. 16; C 137/55, no. 51.
[66] *Cal. Fine R.* 1413–22, 115; P.R.O., C 138/16, no. 6.
[67] P.R.O., C 140/10, no. 29.
[68] *Cal. Inq. p.m. Hen. VII*, i, p. 223; P.R.O., C 142/25, no. 29.
[69] P.R.O., C 142/85, no. 51.
[70] Ibid. C 142/203, no. 50; *S.R.S.* lxvii, pp. 168–9.
[71] *S.R.S.* xxxiii, pp. 333–4.
[72] Ibid. extra ser. 161.
[73] Ibid. xxxiii, pp. 350, 352–3; Burke, *Peerage* (1949), 1986.
[74] Burke, *Peerage* (1949), 1986–7; S.R.O., DD/AH 39/6.
[75] Burke, *Peerage* (1949), 1987; S.R.O., DD/AH 38/8.
[76] S.R.O., DD/AH 5/3, 39/6.

daughter, Isabel, on her marriage in 1849 to Sir Alexander Hood, Bt.[77] The land was sold by Sir Alexander's grandson, Lord St. Audries, between 1924 and 1931 to William Wyndham and Sir Walter Trevelyan, but the lordship of the manors was not included in the sale.[78]

In 1316 Adam Brett had licence to crenellate his dwelling at Torweston.[79] This may have given rise to the field names Back Castle and Castle Coppice which lay on the south and west slopes of Castle Hill in the 19th century, but quarrying may account for stones said to have been found in the wood on the hilltop.[80] Torweston Barton was the name given in the mid 18th century to the farmhouse which stood in the garden of the present Torweston Farm.[81] The latter is a large, late 19th-century house, with a two-storeyed cider house, office, coach house, and stables beyond. To the north, on lower ground, is an extensive group of contemporary farm buildings ranged around two open yards.[82] The central range contains a mill driven by water supplied by two small ponds.

The manor of *ALLER* was held, like Sampford, of Hugh d'Avranches, earl of Chester, in 1086, but there is no further trace of overlordship. Ednod held the estate in 1066 and William in 1086.[83] In Richard I's reign it was held by William St. Stephen, probably in right of his wife Sibyl de Aure or Aller.[84] William was succeeded by his son Robert.[85] William son of William St. Stephen sold Aller to Godfrey of Sowy, whose son Richard sold it to Sir Maurice le Botiller (fl. 1262–80).[86] The estate probably descended through Ellis Butler to Sir John Ralegh (d. 1372) who married Ellis's daughter Maud.[87] By 1372 the estate was held by Robert Brice and his wife and was known as *ALLER BUTLER*.[88] They were still alive in 1389.[89] It is possible that the Brice family continued to hold the estate, and that it was divided in 1507 between Elizabeth, wife of John Frank, and Margaret, wife of Humphrey Trevelyan, as heirs of Thomas Brice.[90]

One half passed to John Frank's daughter Elizabeth and then to her son John Sydenham of Dulverton, who in 1558 bought the other half from John Trevelyan, son of Humphrey and Margaret.[91] John Sydenham sold Aller to John Trevelyan of Nettlecombe in 1568,[92] and the estate was settled in the same year on his son, also John Trevelyan.[93]

Except for a brief period between 1574 and 1581, when it was held by the Slocombes of Bristol by purchase,[94] Aller descended in the Trevelyan family until 1804 when it was conveyed to the earl of Egremont as part of an exchange of property.[95] During the early 17th century Aller was occupied by four unmarried Wyndham brothers.[96]

There was a chapel and possibly a house at Aller before 1197.[97] In 1507, when John Frank and his wife and Humphrey Trevelyan and his wife divided Aller between them, the house comprised a hall, kitchen, buttery, parlour, bakehouse, larder, and dairy, each with chambers over. There were also old and new barns, a shippen, and stables.[98] The present house incorporates one smoke-blackened cruck blade probably of the 16th century but the building, which has a short main range with a cross wing at the west end, now appears to be mainly of the 17th century, the main range having been heightened and the whole roof renewed early in the 18th century. The roof was recased and slated and much of the interior of the house refitted in the early 19th century, and additions were made later in the century. Behind the house a detached building appears to have been reconstructed in the later 19th century from a two-storeyed domestic building of the 16th or 17th century which had the kitchen at its west end. The farm buildings, which are mainly of the 19th and 20th centuries, include a long range which has a shouldered doorway of the 16th century and was at some time extended westwards. It formerly had a cruck roof of nine bays. Its east end was converted into a mill in the 19th century but the wheel, all the internal floors, and the upper part of the crucks have been removed.[99]

In Richard I's reign William St. Stephen confirmed his ancestors' gift to Stogursey Priory of the tithe of the demesne at Aller. In 1239 the tithes were given to the rector of Sampford Brett in return for an annual payment.[1] The payment continued to be made to Eton College, successors to Stogursey,[2] and the college also owned some land called Monkland which had been granted by Sibyl de Aure in Richard I's reign.[3] In 1806 the Merchant Venturers of Bristol, tenants of the college, assigned the lease to Lord Egremont's trustees, who then bought the reversion.[4]

ECONOMIC HISTORY. In 1086 the estates later forming the parish of Sampford Brett together measured 4 hides; there was land for 10 ploughs of which $2\frac{1}{2}$ hides and 4 ploughs were in demesne. There were $25\frac{1}{2}$ a. of meadow, 47 a. of pasture, and 102 a. of woodland. The stock comprised 17 beasts, 6 swine, and 188 sheep. Two serfs worked on the demesne and there were 7 bordars and 14 villeins.[5]

In 1585 3s. 11d. was received in assized rents from the free tenants of the manor of Sampford Brett and £30 5s. 4d. from the customary and copyhold tenants.[6] In the early 17th century at least two farmers had possessions and stock worth c. £300, both with mixed farms, although corn was the most valuable crop.[7]

In the early 19th century Aller and Torweston

77 Ibid. 16/2; above, West Quantoxhead, manors.
78 S.R.O., DD/AH 39/7; *Kelly's Dir. Som.* (1931).
79 *Cal. Pat.* 1313–17, 480.
80 S.R.O., tithe award; local inf.
81 S.R.O., DD/TK 2/3, lease 1766; local inf.
82 The date '[18]86' appears on one of the buildings.
83 *V.C.H. Som.* i. 473.
84 *S.R.S.* lxi, pp. 10–11.
85 *Feet of Fines*, 1196–7 (P.R.S. xx), p. 72.
86 *S.R.S.* vi. 208; xliv. 82–3.
87 S.R.O., DD/WO 1/MTD III/7A.
88 Ibid. 11/6.
89 Ibid. 1/MTD VIII/4A, 5A.
90 Ibid. 10/8, 11/6, 38/1; *Visit. Cornw.* 1620 (Harl. Soc. ix), 242.
91 *S.R.S.* extra ser. 232; S.R.O., DD/WO 10/8, 11/6.

92 S.R.O., DD/WO 10/9.
93 Ibid. 2/2.
94 Ibid. 10/8, 10/10.
95 Ibid. 2/1–2, 6; 9/8–9; 55/3.
96 Ibid. 10/10.
97 *S.R.S.* lxi, pp. 10–11.
98 S.R.O., DD/WO 10/8.
99 Inf. from Mr. B. A. Robertson, Aller Fm.
1 *S.R.S.* lxi, pp. 10–12, 34.
2 Ibid. pp. 38–9, 66–7, 68–9; *Valor Eccl.* (Rec. Com.), i. 224.
3 *S.R.S.* lxi, pp. 11–12.
4 Ibid. p. 74; S.R.O., DD/WY 151.
5 *V.C.H. Som.* i. 473, 505.
6 Devon R.O. 248M/M 7.
7 S.R.O., DD/SP, inventories 1639 and 1640.

were the largest farms. In 1804 Aller farm with *c.* 200 a. was valued at over £5,300 and the timber at *c.* £400.[8] Torweston, a farm of 357 a., was held from 1832 on a 14-year lease at £520 a year, with an additional charge of £50 an acre for breaking meadow and pasture or mowing new meadows. The lessee was required to convert a barn into a dairy and a dairyman's house, with cow-pens and pigsties.[9] The parish was said *c.* 1833 to produce good corn, vegetables, and cider.[10] In 1846, when Sir Peregrine Acland bought Torweston and most of the parish, the main crops were wheat, barley, and vetches.[11] In 1869 the lessee of Torweston paid his workers 10*s.* a week together with turnips and straw.[12] In 1906 the chief crops were wheat, barley, mangolds, potatoes, and turnips.[13] By 1976 most of the parish was under grass, with farms specializing in dairying and stock rearing.[14]

The field names Rack close and Rack meadow[15] indicate the presence of cloth making. John Hudforde (d. 1579), a Sampford weaver, had lands in St. Decumans parish, kept two servants, and owned among other goods a pair of virginals.[16] Clothiers and weavers are found in the 17th century,[17] and in 1704 Torweston mill was taken over for fulling by a Dunster mercer.[18] Gloving was also practised by the 17th century, and in 1687 the miller's possessions included leather, bark, and tools in his tanhouse.[19]

In 1306 Adam Brett was granted a weekly market at Sampford on Mondays with a yearly fair there for three days at the feast of St. George (23 April), but there is no evidence that either was ever held.[20]

In 1086 there were mills at Sampford and Torweston.[21] Sampford mill was mentioned in 1586;[22] in the 1660s it was held by John Strange, and during the 18th century was often known as Strange's mill.[23] The mill continued in production in 1923 but by 1931 had become Sampford Mill farm.[24] The mill building, leat, and iron undershot wheel survived in 1979.

Torweston mill was mentioned in 1674. About 1704 it was burnt down but was rebuilt as a grist mill with a fuller's stock adjoining.[25] It was part of Torweston farm and was leased with the farm in the 18th and 19th centuries.[26] Its site lies under the track of the railway, opened in 1862.

A third grist mill, Providence mills, had been established by 1831 and probably by 1826. It stood on the eastern edge of the village on the Doniford stream. Milling seems to have ceased after 1864.[27]

The mill was a private house in 1979.

There was a leather mill at Catwell in 1818.[28]

LOCAL GOVERNMENT. In the 14th century there were separate tithings of Sampford Brett, which included Sampford and Culvercliffe in St. Decumans, and Torweston, which may have included the Aller estate.[29] The two tithings continued into the 17th century.[30] No manorial records have been found. The tenant of Sampford mill was required to serve the office of tithingman in his turn in 1785.[31] Manor courts were held at Torweston in 1766.[32] A house called Court House, in Sampford village, was described as newly built in 1796.[33] It was called Court Place in 1979.

By 1641 the parish had two churchwardens and two overseers,[34] and by 1681 two highway surveyors.[35] All were elected from tenants in rotation at parish meetings until the mid 18th century, when the minister began appointing one churchwarden.[36] In 1840 one man was said to be sole warden and overseer.[37]

The overseers gave money in weekly relief and for provisions and clothing; extraordinary payments included thatching a cottage and bounties for information against sellers of illegal cider.[38] The former church house was occupied by the overseers by 1699,[39] probably for use as a poorhouse. The same building probably continued to house the poor until the 19th century.[40] In 1840 it comprised four dwellings, and was then sold to the earl of Egremont.[41] The parish became part of the Williton poor-law union in 1836, and was in the Williton rural district from 1894 and the West Somerset district from 1974.[42]

CHURCH. The church was mentioned in 1239[43] and the benefice was a sole rectory until 1978, when it became part of a united benefice with Bicknoller and Crowcombe.[44] The living was in the gift of the lords of Sampford manor, but the bishop collated by lapse in 1317,[45] the Crown presented during a minority in the 1420s,[46] and John Chichester and his wife, again during a minority, in 1510;[47] an attempt by George Luttrell to present as chief lord in 1619 was unsuccessful.[48] In 1628 the advowson seems to have been bought by Martin Webber, apparently for one turn; he presented a relative.[49] In 1765

[8] Ibid. DD/WO 9/8; DD/WY 158.
[9] Ibid. DD/TK 2/4.
[10] B.L. Add. MS. 33827, f. 150.
[11] S.R.O., DD/AH 16/2.
[12] *Rep. Com. Children and Women in Agric.* [4202-I], p. 124, H.C. (1868–9), xiii.
[13] *Kelly's Dir. Som.* (1906).
[14] Min. of Agric., Fisheries, and Food, agric. returns 1976.
[15] Ibid. tithe award; ibid. DD/AH 16/2.
[16] Ibid. DD/WY 9/C3/5.
[17] Ibid. DD/WY 34, 50; DD/TK 1/1; ibid. D/P/sa. b 2/1/2.
[18] Ibid. DD/TK 1/1.
[19] Ibid. D/P/sa. b 2/1/2; DD/WY 34; DD/SP, inventory 1687.
[20] *Cal. Chart. R. 1300–26*, 71.
[21] *V.C.H. Som.* i. 473, 505.
[22] Devon R.O. 248M/M 8.
[23] S.R.O., DD/WY 34; DD/TK 1/2, 2/3.
[24] *Kelly's Dir. Som.* (1923, 1931).
[25] S.R.O., DD/TK 1/1; D/P/sa. b 13/2/1–2.
[26] Ibid. DD/TK 2/3–4.

[27] Ibid. DD/AH 39/6.
[28] Ibid. DD/WY 51; above, St. Decumans, econ. hist.
[29] *S.R.S.* iii. 137.
[30] S.R.O., DD/WY 34.
[31] Ibid. DD/AH 39/6.
[32] Ibid. DD/TK 2/4.
[33] Ibid. DD/AH 39/6.
[34] *Som. Protestation Returns,* ed. Howard and Stoate, 168. [35] S.R.O., D/P/sa. b 13/2/1.
[36] Ibid. 4/4/1, 13/2/1, 13/2/3.
[37] Ibid. DD/AH 38/8.
[38] Ibid. D/P/sa. b 13/2/1, 13/2/3.
[39] Ibid. 13/2/2.
[40] Ibid. 4/1/1, 13/2/2; DD/WY 154.
[41] Ibid. DD/WY 143; DD/AH 38/8.
[42] Youngs, *Local Admin. Units,* i. 675–6.
[43] *S.R.S.* lxi, p. 34.
[44] *Dioc. Dir.*
[45] *S.R.S.* i. 167.
[46] Ibid. xxx, pp. 397, 413, 415, 435.
[47] Ibid. liv, p. 144.
[48] Ibid. xxxiii, p. 319.
[49] *Som. Incumbents,* ed. Weaver, 428.

Humphrey Tanner, rector 1740–80, held a lease of the advowson for three lives.[50] In 1780 it was inherited by Nicholas Tanner, who presented his brother Thomas.[51] On Thomas's death the advowson reverted to the lord of the manor, and Henry Tripp of Orchard Wyndham acquired it. He presented his nephew Charles.[52] During the early 20th century the advowson was owned by Owen Howard Owen, grandson of Charles Tripp. It had passed by 1953 to J. O. Howard Tripp, and in 1961 to the bishop of Bath and Wells.[53] The bishop is joint patron of the united benefice.[54]

In 1535 the rectory was worth £7 19s. 7d. net,[55] and c. £80 c. 1668.[56] By 1831 the average net income was £358 a year, increasing to £400 in 1851.[57] From 1239 the rector paid 7s. a year to Stogursey Priory for the tithes of Aller.[58] In 1534 the rector's oblations and tithes were valued at £7 5s. 6d.[59] Between 1830 and 1835 tithes averaged c. £265 a year. In 1841 they were commuted for a rent charge of £310.[60] In 1606 the glebe measured 33½ a., together with shares in common meadows.[61] In 1841 there were nearly 38 a.[62] Most of the glebe was sold in 1919–20.[63]

The former rectory house, known since 1978 as the Old Rectory, was until partial demolition of the south and west wings in 1903[64] built around a courtyard. On the east side was the original medieval building, with its kitchen at the south end, a central hall which survives with an arch-braced roof of four bays, and a parlour to the north. The parlour end was extended westward in the mid 16th century, the ground floor room having a ceiling divided by moulded and carved beams, and further extensions were made at various times to enclose a courtyard on the west side of the hall. There was some remodelling in the 18th century,[65] and the house was extensively refitted in the early 19th century when the functions of the rooms north and south of the hall were reversed. An inventory of c. 1839 indicates a substantial house with marble chimney pieces in the principal rooms and a servants' hall.[66] The house was sold in 1978.[67]

In 1315 the rector was deprived of his benefice and the church was put in the care of a chaplain.[68] There was some opposition to the reintroduction of the mass in Mary's reign.[69] William Webber, presented in 1628, apparently retained the living during the Interregnum and died in 1659. During the 18th century three celebrations of the communion were normally held each year, and in 1776 there were said to be 12 communicants.[70] In 1815 services with sermons were held alternately morning and after-

noon, but by 1827 there were two services each Sunday.[71] An evening sermon had been added during the summer months by 1843, and by 1851 there were three services throughout the year. Congregations on Census Sunday 1851 were 'about average', with 144 in the morning, 90 in the afternoon, and 169 in the evening, together with 45, 40, and 20 Sunday-school pupils.[72] From 1740 to 1830 three members of the Tanner family were rectors successively, and four members of the Tripp family held the living for a total of sixty years between 1830 and 1917.[73]

A church house was mentioned in 1585,[74] and the name continued in use until 1820,[75] but from 1699 or earlier it probably had been occupied as a poorhouse.[76] There were endowed lights in the church before 1547.[77]

The church of *ST. GEORGE* was probably so dedicated by 1306 when Adam Brett was granted a fair at the feast of St. George.[78] It comprises chancel with south vestry, nave with north transeptal chapel, south organ chamber, and tower, and west porch. At its restoration the church was described as being of 'a very early character, Anglo-Norman' with lancet windows in the south wall of the chancel.[79] The north transept dates from c. 1300, and the tower is probably of the 15th century. Between 1835 and 1843 the chancel, vestry, and west end of the nave were completely rebuilt and the west porch and organ chamber added. The interior was replastered throughout and the rear arches in the chancel were given moulded plaster hoods. The old roofs were replaced in both nave and chancel. The base of the font may be a medieval bowl inverted. The bench ends incorporate early 16th-century carved panels and some early 17th-century work, probably set in their present position during the 19th century when much other carved work, some of it old and some in antique style, was introduced. Amongst the fittings a 17th-century communion table is used as a side table. There is a late 13th-century effigy in the vestry. It formerly lay in the north chapel,[80] and possibly commemorates Sir William Brett (fl. 1280–94).

The plate includes cup and cover by 'I.P.' dated 1573.[81] The registers date from 1629 and are largely complete.[82] There are five bells.[83]

There was a chapel of ease at Aller before 1197.[84]

NONCONFORMITY. Two recusant families, the Martins and the Escotts, were presented between 1636 and 1665.[85]

Before 1827 a Wesleyan Methodist 'Sunday place'

[50] S.R.O., D/P/sa. b 23/2; ibid. DD/TK 1/2.
[51] Ibid. D/P/sa. b 2/1/3.
[52] Ibid. DD/WY 154; ibid. D/P/sa. b 23/2.
[53] *Kelly's Dir. Som.* (1906); *Crockford.*
[54] *Dioc. Dir.*
[55] *Valor Eccl.* (Rec. Com.), i. 224.
[56] S.R.O., D/D/Vc 24.
[57] *Rep. Com. Eccl. Revenues*, pp. 150–1; P.R.O., HO 129/313/3/6/12.
[58] *S.R.S.* lxi, p. 34.
[59] P.R.O., E 179/169/14; *Valor Eccl.* (Rec. Com.), i. 224.
[60] S.R.O., DD/WY 151; ibid. tithe award.
[61] Ibid. D/D/Rg 357.
[62] Ibid. tithe award.
[63] Ibid. D/P/sa. b 3/1/1–3.   [64] Ibid. 3/4/1.
[65] Ibid. 2/1/3.   [66] Ibid. DD/WY 154.
[67] *Som. Co. Gazette*, 6 Oct. 1978.
[68] *S.R.S.* i. 100–3.

[69] S.R.O., D/D/Ca 27.
[70] Ibid. D/P/sa. b 4/1/1; ibid. D/D/Vc 93.
[71] Ibid. D/D/B returns 1815, 1827.
[72] Ibid. D/D/V returns 1843; P.R.O., HO 129/313/3/6/12.
[73] S.R.O., D/P/sa. b 23/2.
[74] Devon R.O. 248M/M 7.   [75] S.R.O., DD/AH 39/6.
[76] Above, local govt.   [77] *S.R.S.* ii. 45, 222.
[78] *Cal. Chart. R.* 1300–26, 71.
[79] B.L. Add. MS. 33827, f. 154. Some of the arcading stands in the garden of the Old Rectory.
[80] B.L. Add. MS. 33827, f. 154.
[81] *Proc. Som. Arch. Soc.* xlv. 173; S.R.O., D/P/sa. b 5/2/1.
[82] S.R.O., D/P/sa. b 2/1/1–7.
[83] Ibid. DD/SAS CH 16/2.
[84] *S.R.S.* lxi, pp. 10–11.
[85] Ibid. D/D/Ca 310, 344; *Som. Protestation Returns*, ed. Howard and Stoate, 290.

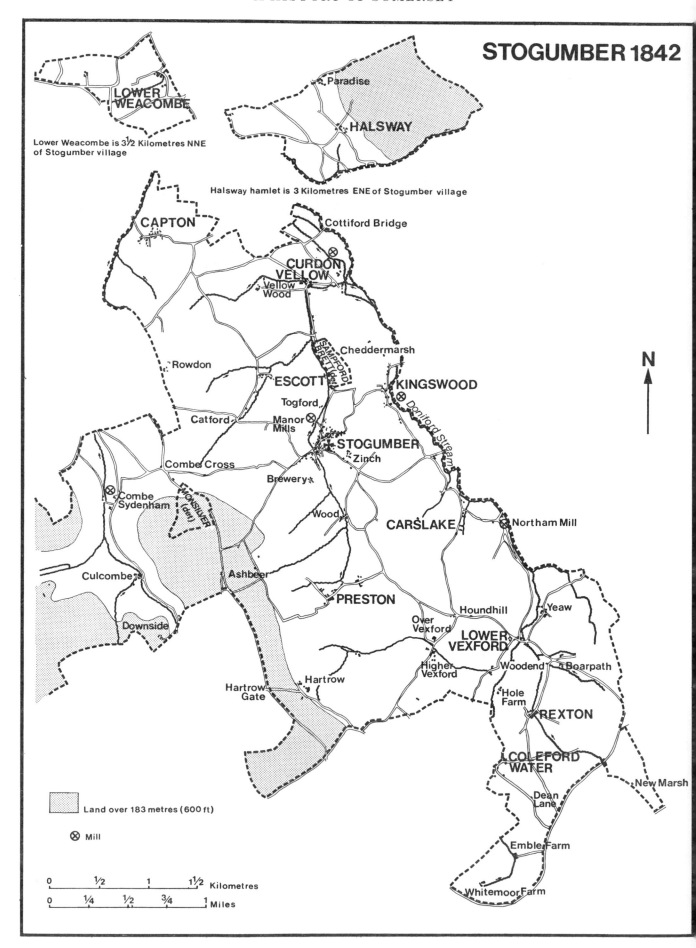

STOGUMBER 1842

LOWER WEACOMBE

Lower Weacombe is 3½ Kilometres NNE of Stogumber village

Paradise

HALSWAY

Halsway hamlet is 3 Kilometres ENE of Stogumber village

CAPTON

Cottiford Bridge

CURDON VELLOW

Vellow Wood

Cheddermarsh

SAMPFORD BRETT (det)

Rowdon

ESCOTT

KINGSWOOD

Togford

Catford

Manor Mills

STOGUMBER

Zinch

Doniford Stream

N

Combe Cross

Brewery

Combe Sydenham

MONKSILVER (det)

Wood

CARSLAKE

Northam Mill

Culcombe

Ashbeer

PRESTON

Houndhill

Yeaw

Over Vexford

LOWER VEXFORD

Downside

Higher Vexford

Woodend

Boarpath

Hartrow

Hole Farm

Hartrow Gate

TREXTON

COLEFORD WATER

New Marsh

Dean Lane

Land over 183 metres (600 ft)

⊗ Mill

Emble Farm

Whitemoor Farm

0   ½   1   1½   Kilometres
0   ¼   ½   ¾   1 Miles

had been established, but it was given up in that year.[86] Services were suggested again in 1835 and established on Sundays in 1841, but were given up in 1844 because the farmers supported the chapel at Williton.[87]

EDUCATION. There was a reading school in 1818, supported by subscription, with 15 pupils.[88] In 1835 a day school was attended by 15 children supported by their parents,[89] but it seems to have gone by 1847, when there were only Sunday schools.[90] St. George's National school was built in 1867 by Sir Alexander Acland-Hood for 100 children,[91] and in 1872 the vestry approved a voluntary rate for its support.[92] In 1903 there were 64 children on the books and the school was also used for evening classes, Sunday school, and confirmation classes.[93] In 1924 the owner, Lord St. Audries, gave notice to quit, but money was raised to buy the buildings.[94] By 1933 there were only 8 children and the school had closed by April 1934.[95] In 1979 it was a private house, still bearing Sir Alexander's arms.

CHARITIES FOR THE POOR. Lettice Webber (d. 1669), probably widow of the rector, William Webber, gave £10 to the poor of the parish. The interest was distributed each year by 1672.[96] In 1786 there were two other charity distributions from a sum of £6 given by William Cogan, rector 1660–89, and a further gift of £24 from an unknown donor.[97] By 1826 a total of £40, known as the Poor's money, was in the hands of a man who paid interest which was laid out in canvas for the deserving poor at an annual meeting.[98] In 1871 Joanna Gatchell left £180 for a coal distribution each Christmas to the poor of the parish.[99] The Poor's money was lost after 1894 and distributions of the coal charity were no longer made in 1979.[1]

STOGUMBER

STOGUMBER is a large, roughly triangular, parish stretching 7 km. in each direction in the valley between the Quantocks and the Brendons.[2] The name Stogumber, introduced by the early 13th century,[3] implies ownership of a place named Stoke by a lord of whom no post-Conquest trace has been found. The Domesday name, Warverdinestoch,[4] perhaps includes a variant of the same name, indicating a pre-Conquest owner called Warver (perhaps Warner) or Gomer. The boundaries between Stogumber and its neighbours on all sides suggest the earlier existence of a larger unit reaching as far east as the Quantock ridgeway and embracing the later parishes of Bicknoller and Crowcombe in the east, Elworthy in the south, Monksilver in the west, and Sampford Brett in the north. Ecclesiastical links between the wealthy church of Stogumber, its chapel of Bicknoller, and the churches of Monksilver and Elworthy suggest the existence of a minster at Stogumber.[5] Bicknoller, while still technically a chapelry, had achieved effective independence by the end of the Middle Ages.[6] Halsway was transferred to Bicknoller and Lower Weacombe to Sampford Brett in 1885, a small area was joined with Elworthy in 1886, and the small detached parts of Sampford Brett and Monksilver in Stogumber were in 1883 and 1884 absorbed. The civil parish thereafter measured 2,165 ha. (5,349 a.).[7]

Most of the parish lies on land rising gently westwards from the Doniford stream which marks its eastern boundary. In the west, between Monksilver and Elworthy, the land reaches 229 m. at Ashbeer, falls steeply into a valley which includes the settlements of Combe Sydenham and Culcombe, and then rises again steeply up an irregular valley into the Brendons, reaching 381 m.[8] The higher, western half of the parish lies on slate, giving way to Lower Sandstone, conglomerate, and marls towards the eastern boundary, with gravel along the valleys. In the extreme north around Capton and Vellow are pebble beds and Upper Sandstone.[9] Stone was quarried at Capton and Vellow, and also near the southern boundary at Coleford Water. Lime was burnt at Kingswood, beside the Doniford stream.[10] A general mining lease was granted in 1757 for exploration at Boarpath, on the heath land in the extreme south-east corner of the parish, but no trace of workings has been found.[11]

The earliest settlements in the parish were established largely beside streams which crossed the valley floor and fed the Doniford stream. Stogumber and its dependent settlement Preston (priest tun) were presumably pre-Conquest in origin, and both lie above the same stream flowing north to Vellow. Hartrow, Vexford, Coleford, and Embelle, on a network of streams further south, were all recorded in the mid 11th century, together with Halsway on the Quantock scarp, Combe Sydenham in a valley to the west, and Capton[12] on high ground overlooking

[86] S.R.O., D/N/wsc 3/2/2.
[87] Ibid. 3/2/2; 3/3/1–4.
[88] Educ. of Poor Digest, H.C. 224 (1819), ix (2).
[89] Educ. Enq. Abstract, H.C. 62 (1835), xlii.
[90] Nat. Soc. Inquiry, 1846–7, Som. 14–15.
[91] S.R.O., DD/AH 40/8.
[92] Ibid. D/P/sa. b 9/1/1, 18/3/1.
[93] Ibid. C/E, box 28.
[94] Ibid. D/P/sa. b 18/7/1; Char. Com. files.
[95] S.R.O., D/P/sa. b 18/7/1; ibid. Schs. Lists.
[96] Ibid. D/P/sa. b 13/2/1.
[97] Char. Don. H.C. 511 (1816), xvi.
[98] 15th Rep. Com. Char. p. 453; Char. Com. files.
[99] Char. Com. files.

[1] Inf. from Mrs. Collins, Woolston, Bicknoller.
[2] This article was completed in 1979.
[3] Cur. Reg. R. vii. 113.
[4] V.C.H. Som. i. 432.
[5] Below, church.
[6] Above.
[7] Census, 1891, 1901. Census, 1891, refers wrongly to Weston or Torweston.
[8] O.S. Map 1/50,000, sheet 181 (1974 edn.).
[9] Geol. Surv. Map 1", drift, sheet 295 (1956 edn.).
[10] S.R.O., D/D/Ca 274; ibid. DD/WO 14/8, 41/26; DD/WO, map 1796; ibid. tithe award.
[11] Ibid. DD/TB 26.
[12] V.C.H. Som. i. 438, 471, 488, 505.

the coastal plain in the north, where there are traces of possible Iron Age occupation.[13] Place names such as Curdon, associated with a so-called Iron Age camp known in 1578 as 'dead man's burial',[14] Catford, and Escott suggest the early development of secondary settlements.

By the 13th century the more marginal land was being settled or cultivated at Boarpath and Yeaw in the south-east, at Cheddermarsh and Carslake near the Doniford stream, and on the higher ground at Goodley, on the Brendon slopes above Combe, and Rowdon, the 'rough hill', an extension of the old farm at Capton.[15] Further settlements appeared in the latter Middle Ages including Rexton, near the southern border, by the late 14th century,[16] Fenne (later Downside) and Culcombe on the Brendon slopes by the mid 15th century,[17] and Kingswood and Northam perhaps later.[18] Lower Weacombe was recorded in the 16th century.[19] Cottages were built on the edge of Charlwood common, south of Vellow; there were 3 in 1556, 12 in 1619, and more in the 1630s, the last adjoining Vellow hamlet, the remainder perhaps beside the road between Vellow and Stogumber village at Kingswood.[20]

Most of the secondary settlements survive only as isolated farmsteads, or groups of two or three farms, but a few are substantial hamlets. Goodley and Hartrow are deserted, the former a single ruined building in forest land, the latter an isolated mansion near a hamlet which survived into the late 16th century.[21] Halsway and Combe Sydenham evolved as mansions with attendant cottages. Vellow, part of the Trevelyan family holding, has the appearance of an estate village of the 19th century, while Capton is virtually unchanged from the 1840s and includes cottages dating from the 16th century. Preston, which had eight farms in 1791,[22] was reduced to two farms and some cottages by 1979. Stogumber village lies principally on a slope where three roads converge to cross a stream. The church stands on a prominent site beside the middle of these roads, south of the market place, with the medieval vicarage house on its west and the probable former capital messuage of the rectory on the south-east. The former rectory estate, the lands of the probable Saxon minster, seems to have been concentrated in the area north and east of the church. The village expanded south-east of the church to Zinch (sentes, thorns) in the medieval period,[23] and later south-west across the stream. New building in the 1970s was again concentrated at Zinch.

There are references to open arable fields at the principal settlements in the parish. Furlongs or strips survived at Rowdon in the early 14th century,[24] at Carslake in the early 18th century,[25] and at Over Vexford, Rexton, and south of Stogumber village towards Preston in the 19th.[26] There were considerable areas of common pasture. Charlwood, shared between tenants of Rowdon and Cheddermarsh, was reduced to 30 a. because of cottage encroachment by 1724,[27] and was inclosed between 1796 and 1840.[28] Heathfield, on the south-eastern edge of the parish, was shared between Embelle, Boarpath, and Rexton. Emmel Heathfield was inclosed and known as New Marsh by 1636,[29] Rexton's share was called Rexton Gorths or Gorse by 1801.[30] Both areas were under woodland and furze in 1979. In the 16th century tenants of a farm in Elworthy had rights to pasture sheep on Hartrow Hill.[31] Capton tenants had pasture on Capton Down,[32] part of which was inclosed by the 17th century,[33] the rest by 1796.[34] The tenants of Halsway manor had common pasture over 200 a. on Quantock Hill or Higher Halsway Common,[35] an area which remained open in 1979.

Place and field names suggest extensive ancient woodland, notably in the northern half of the parish, but reference to the name Vellow (felly, meadow in newly-cultivated land)[36] by 1307[37] and common pasture at Charlwood by 1523[38] indicate medieval clearance. Woodland 4 furlongs by 2 furlongs and a further 71 a. were recorded in Domesday.[39] By 1840 there were 280 a. of wood, and a similar extent was recorded in 1905.[40] In 1976 there were over 300 a. of woodland.[41]

A park was recorded at Rowdon in 1307 and 1442,[42] and there were probably others on the rectory manor[43] and at Hartrow in the 16th century.[44] A park was established at Combe Sydenham by the 17th century[45] and in 1911 it had 13 a. stocked with red and fallow deer.[46] A new park was mentioned at Hartrow in 1816.[47]

In the late 17th century there were two main routes through the parish, both of which presumably had medieval origins. The route from Bridgwater to Barnstaple,[48] following part of the southern boundary of the parish and probably also forming part of the Saxon 'herpath' from beyond the Quantocks to the Brendon ridgeway,[49] forded a stream at Coleford Water, an 11th-century crossing place,[50] and proceeded through Hartrow to the parish boundary. The second route, from Taunton and Crowcombe,

[13] L. V. Grinsell, *Archaeology of Exmoor*, 204.
[14] S.R.O., DD/WO 41/3; Pevsner, *South and West Som.* 299; Grinsell, *Archaeology of Exmoor*, 201.
[15] S.R.O., DD/WO 1; DD/WY 6/K1; *H.M.C. Wells*, ii. 569; *Cal. Close, 1330–3*, 514.
[16] S.R.O., DD/WO 41/8.
[17] *Cal. Pat. 1452–61*, 184; S.R.O., DD/L P36/5.
[18] S.R.O., DD/L P35/8; DD/CC 110002.
[19] *Cal. Proc. Chanc. Eliz.* (Rec. Com.), i. 243.
[20] S.R.O., DD/WO 12/4, 14/3, 15/1, 43/1, 43/7.
[21] Ibid. DD/WY 47/1.
[22] Ibid. tithe award; Collinson, *Hist. Som.* iii. 546; G. F. Sydenham, *Hist. Sydenham Fam.* (priv. print. 1928), 130.   [23] S.R.O., DD/L P35/2.
[24] Ibid. DD/WO 47/1.
[25] Ibid. DD/TB, map of Stogumber *c.* 1724.
[26] Ibid. tithe award.
[27] Ibid. DD/WO 35/2.
[28] Ibid. DD/WO, map 1796; ibid. tithe award.
[29] Ibid. DD/TB 12/1 and boxes 25–6.
[30] Ibid. DD/WY, survey bk. 1801; DD/DR 68; DD/L P3/18.

[31] Ibid. DD/DR 62.
[32] Ibid. DD/WO 41/1, 7; 42/24.
[33] Ibid. 43/1.
[34] Ibid. DD/WO, map 1796.
[35] Ibid. tithe award.
[36] Ekwall, *Eng. Place-Names* (1960), 169.
[37] S.R.O., DD/WO 47/1.
[38] Ibid. 44/25.
[39] *V.C.H. Som.* i. 438, 471, 488, 505.
[40] S.R.O., tithe award; statistics supplied by the then Bd. of Agric. 1905.
[41] Min. of Agric., Fisheries, and Food, agric. returns 1976.
[42] S.R.O., DD/WO 41/19, 47/1.
[43] Ibid. DD/CC 131921/4, 13.
[44] Ibid. DD/DR 25, 62.
[45] *S.R.S.* lxvii, p. 65.
[46] *V.C.H. Som.* ii. 570.
[47] S.R.O., Q/SR 1816 East.; ibid. tithe award.
[48] J. Ogilby, *Britannia* (1675).
[49] S.R.O., DD/X/BOA.
[50] *V.C.H. Som.* i. 488.

passed through Stogumber village towards Watchet and Minehead, a route probably used by the military authorities in 1686.[51] Minor routes within the parish linked the many hamlets and farms, creating a network of lanes into Stogumber village and two parallel routes, one in the east along the Doniford stream, the other under the ridge above Hartrow through Ashbeer and Combe Cross to Stream in St. Decumans and thence to Watchet. In 1765 the Ashbeer route as far south as Hartrow Gate, west of Hartrow House, was adopted by the Minehead Turnpike trust,[52] and in 1778 the Taunton trust extended its routes from Lydeard St. Lawrence to the same place.[53] The Ashbeer route was abandoned in 1806 when the turnpike road was made through Combe Sydenham to Monksilver and beyond,[54] and the highways through the Hartrow estate were subsequently closed in 1816 and 1863.[55] The new road from Crowcombe through Bicknoller to Williton in 1807 further reduced the traffic through Stogumber, leaving the village isolated from main routes.[56]

There was a 'drinkhouse' at Vellow in 1619,[57] and probably another on the Minehead road in 1631.[58] An alehouse was suppressed in 1641,[59] but others survived; in 1656 it was ordered that no more alehouses in the parish should be licensed.[60] The Red Lion was established as an inn by 1668, the Swan by 1680, and the Ram or Black Ram by 1684,[61] giving a total of 29 beds and room for 15 horses in 1686.[62] There were three other inns or alehouses in the village in the 18th century: the Wine Hoop was established by 1723,[63] the White Horse by 1748,[64] and the Dragon by 1752.[65] There were also three inns on the developing Taunton–Minehead route: the Black Dog at Higher Ashbeer by 1729,[66] the Fleur de Luce at Combe Cross by 1759,[67] and the Rose and Crown at Coleford Water by 1800.[68] By 1755 there were five licensed alehouses in the parish,[69] but only three survived by 1800: the Swan and the White Horse in the village, and the Rose and Crown at Coleford Water. The last closed c. 1840.[70] The Swan closed c. 1912[71] and only the White Horse survived in 1979, having been extended in the 19th century to include the former market house and a skittle alley dated 1868.

In 1623 people were presented for playing bowls and tennis in the churchyard on Sunday,[72] and in 1840 an orchard at Capton farm was called the Skittle Alley.[73] A Stogumber and Crowcombe friendly society existed between 1803 and 1822.[74] In 1828 the Stogumber Union Society was formed; it

met monthly in the club room at the White Horse and held an annual feast.[75] In 1873 the society had 52 members.[76]

There were 133 households in the parish in 1563[77] and 339 men signed the Protestation in 1641.[78] In 1801 the population was 1,285 and rose to 1,456 in 1851 after which it declined. There was a fall from 1,242 in 1871 to 1,098 in 1891 and to 898 in 1901. By 1961 the population of the civil parish was only 568 but it rose slightly to 617 in 1971.[79]

There was some resistance to ship money in Stogumber in 1637.[80] In September 1642 royalists were quartered in the village on their way to Minehead.[81] Several local people suffered for their loyalty to the king, including Francis Dodington of Combe Sydenham, whose estates were confiscated, and Hugh Gore, Crown purveyor and servant of the duke of York.[82] In 1685 three men were hanged at Stogumber for their part in the Monmouth rebellion.[83]

Robert Dashwood of Stogumber (d. 1610) founded a family which produced two lines of baronets and several aldermen of London. Among his grandsons, born in Stogumber, were George (1617–82), brewer and alderman of London, John (1620–83), alderman of London, and Francis (1603–83).[84] Isaac Gilling, Presbyterian minister and author, and schoolmaster at Newton Abbot (Devon) was born in Stogumber c. 1662. Floyer Sydenham of Combe Sydenham (1710–87), barrister and scholar, published a translation of Plato.[85] The cricketer Jack White, captain of the Somerset team 1927–31 and of England 1929, was born in Stogumber.[86]

In 1632 Richard Tucker of Stogumber and a man from Brompton Ralph bought an estate in New Somersetshire which they called Stogummer (now Falmouth, Maine, U.S.A.).[87]

MANORS AND OTHER ESTATES. There were nine separate estates in Stogumber recorded in Domesday. The Crown had 1 hide at Capton in demesne, one of the king's clerks had the estate of the church, reckoned as 2 hides, Roger de Courcelles had a total of 2 7/16 hides in Coleford, Embelle, Halsway, and Vexford, and William de Mohun had 2 hides at Hartrow and Combe, later Combe Sydenham.[88] The recorded total of land[89] and the position of the known holdings suggests the exclusion from Domesday of a large area in the centre of the parish including Preston, possibly a large part of an estate which had supported the probable minster

[51] P.R.O., WO 30/48.
[52] 5 Geo. III, c. 93.
[53] 18 Geo. III, c. 97.
[54] 46 Geo. III, c. 52 (Local and Personal).
[55] S.R.O., Q/SR East. 1816; ibid. DD/CCH 80.
[56] 47 Geo. III, c. 27 (Local and Personal).
[57] S.R.O., DD/WO 43/1. An alehouse, possibly the same, was recorded in 1629: ibid. D/D/Ca 266.
[58] *S.R.S.* lxv, pp. 12–13.   [59] Ibid. lxxi, p. 4.
[60] Ibid. xxviii. 320.
[61] S.R.O., D/P/stogm 13/2/1.
[62] P.R.O., WO 30/48.
[63] It was burnt down and rebuilt 1740–5: S.R.O., D/P/stogm 13/2/3; ibid. DD/CC 111701.
[64] Ibid. D/P/stogm 13/2/1.
[65] Ibid. DD/BR/py 112; DD/CCH 5/2.
[66] B.L. Add. Ch. 57599.
[67] S.R.O., DD/CCHg 9.
[68] Ibid. Q/RL.
[69] Dyfed R.O., D/CAR/202.
[70] S.R.O., Q/RL.

[71] *Kelly's Dir. Som.* (1910, 1914).
[72] *S.R.S.* xliii, pp. 82–3, 117–18.
[73] S.R.O., tithe award.
[74] Ibid. DD/TB 32; DD/HC 6E.
[75] Ibid. Q/RSf.
[76] M. Fuller, *West-Country Friendly Socs.* 152.
[77] B.L. Harl. MS. 594, f. 155.
[78] *Som. Protestation Returns*, ed. Howard and Stoate, 169.
[79] *Census*, 1801–1971.
[80] *Cal. S.P. Dom.* 1637, 279.
[81] *S.R.S.* xviii. 18.
[82] *Cal. Cttee. for Compounding*, ii. 1256–7, 1594.
[83] R. Locke, *The Western Rebellion* (1782), 9.
[84] Burke, *Peerage* (1949), 550–1.
[85] *D.N.B.*
[86] S.R.O., D/P/stogm 23/4; *Wisden Cricketers' Almanack*, ed. J. Woodcock (1981), 247.
[87] S.R.O., D/P/stogm 23/4.
[88] *V.C.H. Som.* i. 438, 471, 488, 505.
[89] For the Mohun estate at Coleford, above, Elworthy.

at Stogumber before the Conquest, an estate which later became the two distinct manors of Stogumber Rectory and Stogumber.

The 2 hides belonging to the church were held in 1066 by Alvric and in 1086 by the king's clerk Richer de Andelys or Richer of Stoke.[90] While the advowson apparently descended in the Andelys family,[91] the land presumably supported successive rectors until the death or cession of the last rector between 1276 and 1291.[92] Thereafter the chapter of Wells appropriated the estate,[93] to which more land in Bicknoller was added in 1330 by grant of Hamelin de Godele.[94] The estate, known as the manor of *STOGUMBER RECTORY* or *STOGUMBER GODELEY RECTORY*,[95] was held by the chapter until 1857, when it was transferred to the Ecclesiastical (later Church) Commissioners. The estate was farmed to individual members of the chapter between 1302 and 1332[96] but later to laymen. Richard Hartrow was farmer by 1452,[97] followed in 1514 by Richard Biccombe of Crowcombe,[98] and then by members of the Hill family.[99] The Saffins and then the Sydenhams were lessees in the 17th century,[1] and Sir Philip Sydenham sold his interest to George Musgrave in 1711.[2] The Sanford family were lessees from 1751 until 1865 or later.[3] Part of the holding, amounting to c. 110 a. in 1840, was sold by the Ecclesiastical Commissioners to Langley St. Albyn in 1868.[4] No later reference to the manor has been found.

Hall Place, later Hall Farm, was probably the site of the capital messuage of the manor. The buildings included a dovecot by 1439,[5] and the construction of a barn was ordered in 1506.[6] In 1650 the barn was a stone building of nine bays with a thatched roof.[7] The present barn, on the south-eastern edge of the churchyard, is of seven bays with a jointed cruck roof, and probably dates from the later 17th century.

The estate held by the Andelys family in the later 13th century and probably part of the land of the former minster can be traced with certainty only from Robert de Andelys who held *STOGUMBER* in 1284-5.[8] It seems likely, however, that Robert was successor to Walter de Andelys, who was in possession of the advowson of Stogumber in 1214,[9] to John de Andelys from whom several men held land in 1225,[10] and to Walter de Andelys, son of John,[11] who had land in Stogumber and the advowson in 1259.[12]

In 1284-5 Robert de Andelys held Stogumber of Henry de Lacy, earl of Lincoln, who was tenant in chief[13] in right of his wife Margaret. Their daughter Alice, countess of Lincoln and Salisbury and widow of Thomas earl of Lancaster, granted her lordship of Stogumber to Hugh le Despenser, earl of Winchester, who also acquired her lordship of Trowbridge (Wilts.).[14] Stogumber was said to be held of the lordship of Trowbridge in 1352[15] and 1468.[16]

John de Andelys held ½ fee in Stogumber of the earl of Lincoln in 1303. In 1316 an estate called Doniford and Stogumber was attributed to four men who may have been trustees. In 1346 John Durburgh held the ½ fee in Stogumber which John de Andelys had held,[17] and at his death in 1352 had an estate in Stogumber and Preston. His son Sir Hugh[18] held the estate and was succeeded between 1372 and 1378[19] by his son James.[20] In 1393 the manor was held by John Dunster (d. by 1396). John Rivers, Dunster's heir,[21] sold it in 1396, subject to a life interest of Elizabeth, wife of Thomas Dodington, to Simon and Henry Sydenham, sons of Richard Sydenham of Combe Sydenham.[22] Simon, later bishop of Chichester, and his brother Henry, may have been in possession by 1417.[23] Henry died before 1427 and Simon in 1438. Simon's heir was his nephew John (d. 1468).[24] The manor then descended like Combe Sydenham until 1557 when it passed to John (d. before 1617), brother of Sir George Sydenham of Combe Sydenham. John was succeeded by his son, also John (d. 1625),[25] whose sons John and Ralph conveyed the manor to John Boys and his son John in 1626.[26]

John Boys, probably the younger, was dead by 1656.[27] By 1708 half the estate was owned by John Doble,[28] and he or a namesake were in possession in 1739.[29] By 1749 Doble had been succeeded by Joseph Ware,[30] and by 1770 by John Doble Ware.[31] The other half of the estate was probably held by the Treble family between 1717 and 1786 or later,[32] and both parts may have come to Thomas Cridland (d. 1789) and his grandson Thomas Cridland Luxton (d. 1844). Luxton's estate passed to his sister Frances (d. 1862), wife of Langley St. Albyn, and then to her two daughters, Anne, wife of Birt Jenner, and Caroline (d. 1870) wife of William Wait. Anne's son, Birt St. Albyn Jenner, mortgaged his reversionary share in 1882 and in 1895 William White took over the mortgage, having already acquired the other

[90] *V.C.H. Som.* i. 471, 532.
[91] Below, church.
[92] *H.M.C. Wells,* i. 376; ii. 568; *Rot. Hund.* (Rec. Com.), ii. 121.
[93] *H.M.C. Wells,* i. 376, 458.
[94] Ibid. 225.
[95] S.R.O., DD/CC 131923/1.
[96] *H.M.C. Wells,* i. 169-70, 192-3, 207, 222, 230.
[97] S.R.O., DD/CC 110079/22-4.
[98] *H.M.C. Wells,* ii. 236.
[99] S.R.O., DD/CC 11739; *L. & P. Hen. VIII,* ix, p. 34.
[1] S.R.O., DD/CC 111714; 131910A/3; 131925A/6, 11, 13; 131926/1-8; *S.R.S.* lxvii, p. 66; *H.M.C. Wells,* ii. 713; *Cal. Cttee. for Compounding,* ii. 1275.
[2] S.R.O., DD/DP 33/10; DD/JL 93; DD/SAS FA 179.
[3] Ibid. DD/CC 110003, 110007, 110012, 110022-3; DD/SAS C/432 16; DD/SF 694, 1719, 3348.
[4] Ibid. tithe award; ibid. DD/CCH 72.
[5] *H.M.C. Wells,* i. 520; S.R.O., DD/CC 110079/18.
[6] *H.M.C. Wells,* ii. 199.
[7] S.R.O., DD/CC 110001/1.
[8] *Feud. Aids,* iv. 275.
[9] *Cur. Reg. R.* vii. 113.
[10] *S.R.S.* xi, p. 64.
[11] *Cur. Reg. R.* xii, pp. 263, 389.
[12] *S.R.S.* vi. 182.
[13] *Feud. Aids,* iv. 275.
[14] *V.C.H. Wilts.* vii. 128; *Cal. Pat.* 1324-7, 102.
[15] *Cal. Inq. p.m.* x, p. 17.
[16] P.R.O., C 140/28, no. 22.
[17] *Feud. Aids,* iv. 304, 333, 346.
[18] *Cal. Inq. p.m.* x, p. 17.
[19] S.R.O., DD/L P36/5; *Cal. Inq. p.m.* xiii, p. 171.
[20] Hist. MSS. Com. 15, *10th Rep. VI, Luttrell,* p. 75.
[21] S.R.O., DD/WO 41/12.
[22] *S.R.S.* xvii, pp. 167, 170.   [23] Ibid. xxii. 53.
[24] G. F. Sydenham, *Hist. Sydenham Fam.* 103; *S.R.S.* xxxiii, p. 221; P.R.O., C 140/28, no. 22.
[25] P.R.O., C 142/114, no. 23; CP 25(2)/207/38 Eliz. I Trin.; *S.R.S.* lxvii, p. 149; below.
[26] P.R.O., CP 25(2)/479/1 Chas. I Hil.
[27] *Som. Wills,* ed. Brown, v. 69.
[28] P.R.O., CP 25(2)/962/7 Anne East.
[29] Ibid. CP 25(2)/1195/12 Geo. II East.
[30] Ibid. CP 25(2)/1197/23 Geo. II Hil.
[31] S.R.O., DD/AH 11/6; P.R.O., CP 25(2)/1398/10 Geo. III East.
[32] B.L. Add. Ch. 57598-9; S.R.O., DD/CCH 71-2.

share from Caroline's five daughters.[33] Part of the Stogumber manor estate, comprising 724 a. of land scattered widely in the parish, was sold in 1896. Marwood Notley of Combe Sydenham bought most of the estate, but no later reference to the manor has been found.

The manor of *CAPTON* was held in 1066 by Earl Harold and in 1086 was royal demesne.[34] It was occupied by the Raleghs of Nettlecombe by the late 13th century and the two estates may have been linked much earlier. By the 1280s the Raleghs' land extended south from Capton and the estate was thereafter known as the manor of *ROWDON*.[35] The manor descended like Nettlecombe manor in the Ralegh and Trevelyan families, but has not been found referred to as a manor after 1823.[36]

There was a manor house at Rowdon, with an oratory, by 1334,[37] and a 'manor place' was still standing in 1515.[38] Rowdon Farm dates largely from the 19th century.

An estate called *COMBE* was held in 1066 by Ailmer, and in 1086 by Turgis of William de Mohun.[39] It was later regarded as held of Bicknoller manor, and Reynold Mohun was recorded as overlord in the 13th century.[40] Usually described as a capital messuage, but occasionally as a manor, it was known from the late 14th century as *COMBE SYDENHAM*.[41]

Richard of Combe was probably occupier of the land c. 1240[42] and William of Combe was mentioned in 1325.[43] In 1367 Nicholas Orchard may have held an estate called Combe Allen, which was sold in the same year to Richard Sydenham, justice of Common Pleas.[44] Richard Sydenham died in 1403 and was succeeded by his son Henry (d. before 1427) and Henry by his son John (d. 1468).[45] The estate was held by John's widow Joan (d. 1472).[46] Their grandson John Sydenham (d. 1542) settled it on his son Henry (d. c. 1519) and Henry's wife Eleanor (d. 1539). In 1544, after John's death, it was said that Eleanor had an interest in the estate.[47] John was succeeded by his son Sir John (d. 1557) who devised Combe Sydenham to his son Sir George (d. 1597).[48] Sir George was followed by his only surviving child Elizabeth, wife of Sir William Courtenay, and on her death in 1598 by his nephew Sir John Sydenham (d. 1625).[49] Sir John was succeeded by his son John (d. 1627). The latter's son Sir John Sydenham, Bt., died in 1643 before attaining his majority and was succeeded by his son John Posthumous Sydenham.[50] Sir John's mother Alice, who married Sir Francis

Dodington, occupied Combe Sydenham from 1627[51] until its confiscation in or before 1651.[52] In 1653 Combe Sydenham was bought by John Ware,[53] but was later restored to Sir John Posthumous Sydenham (d. 1696).[54] In 1693 Sir John sold the entire estate to George Musgrave[55] (d. 1721) and it passed in the direct male line to George (d. 1724), George (d. 1742), and Thomas.[56] In 1765, the year before he died, Thomas Musgrave gave Combe Sydenham to his sister Juliana, who later married Sir James Langham, Bt.[57] In 1796, after her husband's death, Juliana sold the estate to George Notley of Chillington.[58] In 1800 part of Combe Sydenham was settled on Mary Marwood before her marriage to George Notley. Mary died in 1829 leaving her share to her husband.[59] The estate descended with the neighbouring manor of Monksilver in the Notley family until the death of Marwood Notley in 1903[60] when it passed to his youngest son Marwood (d. c. 1958). Marwood's daughter sold the estate to E. C. Campbell-Voullaire c. 1958.[61] The owner in 1979 was Mr. W. A. C. Theed.

Combe Sydenham Hall lies in a valley bottom, on a narrow site between the Elworthy–Monksilver road and a stream. Fragments incorporated in the west wing of the present building, including remains of a medieval tiled floor, suggest that by the early 16th century it was of substantial size and quality. Sir George Sydenham, whose initials and the date 1580 appear on the porch, remodelled the house and was probably responsible for extending it to enclose a roughly square court on the north side of the hall range. Further work was carried out, probably by Sir Francis Dodington in the 1630s or 1640s, by which time there were large stair turrets in the southern angles of the court. The south front contained a ground-floor hall and principal chambers, with perhaps a gallery at attic level, while other principal rooms were on the first floor of the west front. By the early 19th century the north and most of the east range of the court had been demolished.[62] The west range was then partly refitted, a new staircase being put into the base of the western tower, and the roofs and most of the windows renewed. New stables and coach house were built north-east of the house.

By the early 16th century there was a walled yard a short distance south from the house; it had an embattled gateway on the east side and a gatehouse range with central gateway surmounted by a tower on the north. The south side of the gatehouse tower

[33] S.R.O., DD/AH 41/10; DD/WO 9/9.
[34] *V.C.H. Som.* i. 438.
[35] S.R.O., DD/WO 1.
[36] Ibid. 61/5; above, Nettlecombe.
[37] *S.R.S.* ix. p. 172.
[38] S.R.O., DD/WO 42/24.
[39] *V.C.H. Som.* i. 505.   [40] *S.R.S.* xv. 27–8.
[41] S.R.O., DD/CC 110074; P.R.O., C 142/70, no. 9; C 142/160, no. 145; *S.R.S.* lxvii, p. 65.
[42] *S.R.S.* xv. 27–8.   [43] Ibid. i. 240.
[44] B.L. Add. Ch. 11165; P.R.O., E 210/6114; Sydenham, *Hist. Sydenham Fam.* 103, 434.
[45] Sydenham, *Hist. Sydenham Fam.* 103; *S.R.S.* xxxiii, p. 221.
[46] Sydenham, *Hist. Sydenham Fam.* 112; P.R.O., C 140/42, no. 45.
[47] P.R.O., C 142/70, no. 9; Sydenham, *Hist. Sydenham Fam.* 115.
[48] *S.R.S.* xxi, pp. 190–2; Sydenham, *Hist. Sydenham Fam.* 117–24, 126; P.R.O., C 142/70, no. 9.

[49] P.R.O., C 142/260, no. 145.
[50] *S.R.S.* lxvii, p. 65; P.R.O., C 142/525, no. 61; *Cal. Cttee. for Compounding*, ii. 1256–7.
[51] *Cal. S.P. Dom.* 1629–31, 486; 1631–3, 39; S.R.O., DD/CC 110074.
[52] *Cal. Cttee. for Compounding*, ii. 1256–7.
[53] Ibid. iv. 2558.
[54] S.R.O., DD/SF 3116; DD/SAS HV 7; DD/SAS C/432 16; DD/CCH 72, 74.
[55] Ibid. DD/DP 33/4A, 10; DD/CCH 72, 73; P.R.O., CP 25(2)/869/6 Wm. & Mary East.
[56] S.R.O., DD/SAS FA 179.
[57] Ibid. DD/SAS C/432 16; DD/CCH 72, 73.
[58] Ibid. DD/CCH 73, 74; ibid. T/PH/no 2.
[59] Ibid. DD/CCH 74, 77.
[60] Ibid. 3/4.
[61] *Kelly's Dir. Som.* (1906, 1939); Char. Com. files; inf. from Miss V. A. Notley.
[62] B.L. Add. MS. 36381; Sydenham, *Hist. Sydenham Fam.* facing p. 346; above, plate facing p. 108.

was reconstructed during the 20th century and much of the yard boundary wall was removed.

HARTROW was held in 1066 by Ulwold and in 1086 by Roger de Lisieux of William de Mohun, in whose honor of Dunster it remained until 1627 or later.[63] In 1194 Richard de Lisieux's heir was under age,[64] and in 1198 Alexander de Lisieux,[65] who was alive in 1202,[66] paid relief on his father's land. By 1243 Richard Vynar owned the estate,[67] and he or a namesake, in occupation in 1280, was apparently dead by 1284.[68] Richard de Windsor claimed to hold a fee at Hartrow in 1285.[69] William Hartrow was holding the fee by 1330, and in 1395 Robert, son of Walter Hartrow (fl. 1346–66).[70] Robert died in 1402 and in 1406 the fee was held by Joan Hartrow, probably Robert's second wife or daughter.[71] In 1422 William Crocker and his wife Joan, possibly the Joan of 1406, conveyed the estate to Richard Hartrow who was active locally in 1462.[72] In 1475 John Sydenham of Orchard held the fee at Hartrow and by 1499 his son John was in possession.[73] The younger John died in 1521 and the manor passed to his grandson, also John Sydenham.[74]

John Sydenham died in 1526 and in the following year an estate known as Hartrow and Doniford manor was divided between his two sisters and their husbands, John (later Sir John) Wyndham and Thomas Bridges. Almost immediately Wyndham and Sir John Sydenham of Combe jointly bought Bridges's share.[75] Sydenham died in 1557 leaving his quarter share to his son, also John.[76] Wyndham sold his three quarters in 1559 to Joan Sweeting, widow, who shortly afterwards married William Lacey.[77] Lacey bought the remaining share from John Sydenham in 1563.[78]

William Lacey was succeeded in 1607 by his son, also William.[79] William the younger died in 1641 when his heir was his grandson, William Lacey.[80] William died in 1690 and Hartrow passed with Elworthy manor to his eldest son, also William Lacey.[81] It descended with Elworthy until 1799 when Bickham Escott left it to his three daughters. They shared as tenants in common until 1811 when Mary, wife of Thomas Sweet Escott, took Hartrow.[82] After a family dispute in 1854 Mary leased the estate to her granddaughter, Anna Sweet Escott. Anna succeeded on her grandmother's death two years later,[83] and died in 1872, when her heir was her cousin, the Revd. William Sweet Escott (d. 1913). William's son, the Revd. W. S. Sweet Escott, sold

the property in 1914 to his cousin, the Revd. E. H. Sweet Escott,[84] who left the house c. 1936; the land was later bought by Mr. C. Thomas and farmed from Higher Vexford.[85]

A house at Hartrow was said to have been built c. 1580 by William Lacey, and fragments may be incorporated in a late 18th-century wing on the northwestern side of the present house.[86] South of the wing is a hall, said to have been built in 1817. About 1830 the main part of the house was replaced by a building with symmetrical elevations on the south and east and an open court to the north. Gothick additions were made in the 19th century, when fittings and decorations in medieval styles were introduced into the great hall, then converted for use as a chapel.

Two estates at Vexford were held in 1066 by Domne and Brismar and in 1086 by Alric and Roger as part of the fee of Roger de Courcelles.[87] The overlordship has not been traced later, except that in 1493 Over Vexford was said to be held of the heir of Geoffrey Luttrell of Irnham (Lincs.).[88] In the late 12th century an estate at Vexford was given by Henry Lovesgift to the Hospitallers of Buckland in Durston,[89] no further trace of whose ownership has been discovered. William Franklin of Over Vexford, recorded in 1242–3,[90] was followed by one of the same name, mentioned as of Vexford in 1279.[91] The latter conveyed to Richard de la Roche in 1309 land which passed in 1318 to Richard's son Simon as the manor of *OVER VEXFORD*. Simon was still alive in 1320.[92] John Roche held Vexford in 1381,[93] and he or a namesake in 1392 conveyed to John Luttrell (d. 1403) in trust lands there and elsewhere in the parish.[94] John (later Sir John) Luttrell (d. 1430) had an interest in land at Over Vexford by 1418,[95] and he conveyed the reversion of the manor after his own death to Thomas and Joan Trow. Thomas and Joan granted the manor in 1431 to Richard Luttrell, and on Richard's death trustees settled it in 1453 on James (later Sir James) Luttrell.[96]

Sir James Luttrell's estates, confiscated in 1462, were granted in the following year to Sir William Herbert, and were retained by him until his death in 1469.[97] During that period claims to ownership were made by John Roche, illegitimate son of John Roche (fl. 1392).[98] Sir James Luttrell's widow Elizabeth, later wife of Humphrey Audley, regained her first husband's estates in 1475[99] and died in 1493.[1] She was succeeded by her son Hugh Luttrell (d. 1521), and the manor then descended like Kilton

[63] *V.C.H. Som.* i. 505; *S.R.S.* xxxiii, p. 332.
[64] *S.R.S.* extra ser. 172.
[65] Ibid.; xxxiii, p. 10.
[66] Ibid. extra ser. 172–3.
[67] Ibid. xi, p. 159.
[68] Ibid. xxxiii, pp. 49, 53.
[69] Ibid. p. 60.
[70] Ibid. p. 72; extra ser. 173; S.R.O., DD/L P32/1.
[71] *S.R.S.* extra ser. 173; xxxiii, pp. 115, 128.
[72] S.R.O., DD/DR 25; *Cal. Close*, 1461–8, 147–8.
[73] *S.R.S.* xxxiii, pp. 232, 270.
[74] S.R.O., DD/WY 1/33; *S.R.S.* extra ser. 173.
[75] *S.R.S.* xxxiii, p. 284; S.R.O., DD/WY 1B.
[76] *S.R.S.* xxi, p. 191; P.R.O., C 142/114, no. 23.
[77] *S.R.S.* extra ser. 174; P.R.O., CP 25(2)/204/1 Eliz. I. East.
[78] P.R.O., CP 25(2)/204/5 Eliz. I. Hil.
[79] *Som. Wills*, ed. Brown, i. 33; *Cal. S.P. Dom.* 1631–3, 94.
[80] *S.R.S.* lxvii, p. 32; P.R.O., C 142/462, no. 100.
[81] *S.R.S.* extra ser. 176.

[82] S.R.O., DD/CCH 80; above, Elworthy.
[83] S.R.O., DD/CCH 80.
[84] *S.R.S.* extra ser. 178; *Crockford*; *Kelly's Dir. Som.* (1910, 1931).
[85] S.R.O., Q/R elect. reg.; inf. from Mr. Thomas.
[86] *Proc. Som. Arch. Soc.* xxix. 44.
[87] *V.C.H. Som.* i. 488.
[88] *Cal. Inq. p.m. Hen. VII*, iii, p. 349.
[89] *S.R.S.* xxv, p. 73.
[90] Ibid. xi, p. 146.
[91] Ibid. xli, p. 199.
[92] S.R.O., DD/L P32/1, P35/1.
[93] Ibid. DD/S/WH 43/14.
[94] Ibid. DD/L P35/2.
[95] *S.R.S.* xxii, p. 54.
[96] S.R.O., DD/L P35/4, 24; *S.R.S.* xxii, p. 115.
[97] *Cal. Pat.* 1461–7, 286, 366.
[98] *Cal. Close*, 1461–8, 147–8; *Cal. Pat.* 1467–77, 193–4, 200.
[99] *Cal. Pat.* 1467–77, 522.
[1] *Cal. Inq. p.m. Hen. VII*, iii, p. 349.

manor until 1709, when Alexander Luttrell sold Over Vexford to Sir William Wyndham.[2] It thereafter descended like Orchard Wyndham until 1864, when it was bought by Anna Sweet Escott and added to the Hartrow estates.[3]

Luke Lovesgift occupied land at Vexford in the late 12th century.[4] A man of the same name held land at Lower Vexford in 1242–3.[5] Either may have been the Luke of Vexford who previously held land which by 1291 was owned by Barlinch Priory.[6] The estate passed to the Crown at the dissolution of the priory in 1536[7] and as the manor of *VEXFORD* it was sold to Sir William Stourton in 1544.[8] In the same year Stourton sold it to John Sweeting (d. 1550) and his son John.[9] John the younger died in 1556 leaving a son, also John, a minor.[10] In 1623 John Sweeting settled his estate on his son John, a London clothmaker, who died in the same year leaving his kinsman John Vellacot as his heir.[11]

Ownership has not been traced thereafter until 1784 when the holding was divided: by 1791 part was held by the Revd. Simon Richards, part by Thomas Slocombe of Tirhill in Bishop's Lydeard.[12] Richards's son, the Revd. Simon Slocombe Richards, appears to have held the whole estate by 1840.[13] He died in 1853 and was succeeded by his grandson John Simon Richards; in 1859 John sold the estate to Langley St. Albyn. In 1871 St. Albyn gave it to his grandson Birt St. Albyn Jenner and it was sold with Stogumber manor.[14]

In 1086 Roger de Courcelles held *HALSWAY* with Alric, the owner in 1066, as his undertenant.[15] Like Kilve manor the estate was held of the barony of Compton Dundon, having passed through the Malet, Avenel, and Beauchamp families. The overlordship was last recorded in 1535.[16] Thomas of Halsway held a fee in 1166.[17] Matthew de Furneaux and Nicholas Avenel were in dispute over Halsway wood in 1243, when the latter denied selling it to Thomas of Halsway.[18] Thomas's son, Thomas, certainly occupied Halsway c. 1275, and in 1284–5 the vill was held by John of Halsway, the younger Thomas's son. John died before 1295,[19] and in 1303 John of Penbrigg was returned as a holder of ½ fee in Halsway and Coleford.[20] John's eventual heir was Joan, daughter of Thomas Halsway (fl. 1297), possibly John's brother. She married Peter Stradling (d. before 1314), of Berne (later Switzerland), and their son Sir Edward[21] did homage for Halsway manor, a 'great' knight's fee, in 1337.[22] The manor descended from Sir Edward (d. c. 1363) in the direct

male line to Sir Edward (d. 1394), Sir William (d. c. 1407), Sir Edward (d. 1453) who married Joan, daughter of Henry Beaufort, later bishop of Winchester and cardinal, Henry (d. 1476), Thomas (d. 1480), Edward (d. 1535),[23] Thomas (d. 1571), and Edward (d. 1602). Sir John Stradling (d. 1637), kinsman of the last, was the next owner, but his widow Elizabeth, her son Edward, and Edward's wife Mary sold the manor and other lands to James Cade of Wilton, Taunton, in 1637.[24]

James Cade (d. 1640) was followed by his son James (d. 1655).[25] The latter's son, also James (d. 1702), was followed by his son, another James Cade (d. c. 1741). In 1733 Cade sold part of the estate to Richard Hembrow of Bicknoller, and by the time of his death most of his property was either sold or heavily mortaged.[26] He was succeeded by his fifth son Charles (d. 1775) and then by another son, Nathaniel, a Bristol joiner. In 1787 Nathaniel sold the manor to William Snow of Porlock, one of the main creditors.[27] Snow held it until 1806 or later[28] but by 1817 it was owned by Mary Stoate of Porlock. In 1829 she left Halsway in trust for James Crang, lessee since 1817.[29] Crang (d. 1846) was succeeded by his son James (d. 1847), and the younger James by his son, also James Crang.[30] In 1875 the estate was bought from Crang by Charles Rowcliffe (d. 1877), of Cagley Court, in Sampford Brett. Rowcliffe was succeeded by his brother William, and William in 1900 by his son, also William.[31] William Rowcliffe sold the estate in 1914; the house passed through several hands until 1965 when it was bought by the English Folk Dance and Song Society. In 1979 it was used by the Society as a residential study centre.[32]

A medieval house, which included a chapel by 1415,[33] survived into the 19th century, and parts may remain in the much altered fabric. The house in the early 19th century had battlemented porches, probably of the 16th century, at both ends of the principal south-west front in addition to a similar porch close to the centre and a large lateral chimney stack in the hall.[34] Charles Rowcliffe after 1875 demolished and rebuilt at least some of the original work, and enlarged the house to the north and north-east in a 16th-century style. The interior was extensively altered between 1924 and 1938 by the then owner W. N. Mitchell and woodwork was introduced from elsewhere: the hall panelling and other features from Cock's House, Quay Side, Newcastle-upon-Tyne, the hall mantelpiece from the Albright-Hussey

[2] S.R.O., DD/WY 13/14; P.R.O., CP 25(2)/962/9 Anne East.; above, Kilton.
[3] S.R.O., DD/CCH 77; above, St. Decumans.
[4] *S.R.S.* xxv, p. 73.
[5] Ibid. xi, p. 146.
[6] Dugdale, *Mon.* vi. 385; *Tax. Eccl.* (Rec. Com.), 205.
[7] P.R.O., SC 6/Hen. VIII/3127.
[8] *L. & P. Hen. VIII*, xix (1), pp. 40, 85.
[9] P.R.O., C 142/97, no. 115.
[10] Ibid. C 142/110, no. 157; *Cal. Pat.* 1555–7, 526.
[11] P.R.O., C 142/519, no. 66.
[12] Collinson, *Hist. Som.* iii. 547; P.R.O., CP 25(2)/1400/ 24 Geo. III. Trin.
[13] S.R.O., tithe award; ibid. DD/CCH 2/5.
[14] Ibid. DD/AH 41/10; DD/CCH 62.
[15] *V.C.H. Som.* i. 488.
[16] *Feud. Aids*, iv. 275, 303; P.R.O., C 142/57, no. 68; above, Kilve.
[17] *Red Bk. Exch.* (Rolls Ser.), i. 227.
[18] *S.R.S.* xi, p. 209. Thomas de Haweie (fl. 1225) may be the same man: *S.R.S.* xi, pp. 44–5.

[19] *Feud. Aids*, iv. 275; S.R.O., DD/L P32/2.
[20] *Feud. Aids*, iv. 303.
[21] *Trans. Glam. Hist. Soc.* vii (1963), 15–47.
[22] *S.R.S.* xxxv. 85; cf. *Feud. Aids*, iv. 546.
[23] P.R.O., C 142/57, no. 68; S.R.O., T/PH/win; *Trans. Glam. Hist. Soc.* vii. 20–32.
[24] *Cal. Pat.* 1554–5, 146; P.R.O., CP 25(2)/480/13 Chas. I. Mich.; *Glam. Historian*, ix (1973), 11–28.
[25] *Som. Wills*, ed. Brown, iii. 9.
[26] S.R.O., DD/CCH 5/2; 57; 58; DD/HLM 12; DD/CH 81/1, 83/1; DD/TB 11/3; 29; 31; DD/DP 128.
[27] Ibid. DD/CCH 57, 64.
[28] Ibid. Q/REl Williton.
[29] Ibid. DD/CCH 64.
[30] Ibid. tithe award; ibid. D/P/stogm 2/1/12.
[31] Ibid. DD/CCH 42; DD/X/WD; *Proc. Som. Arch. Soc.* liv. 68–73.
[32] S.R.O., DD/X/WD; DD/CCH 58; local inf.
[33] *S.R.S.* xxix. 223.
[34] B.L. Add. MSS. 36382, f. 5; 36439, f. 340; cf. J. G. Marks, *Life and Letters of Frederick Walker* (1896), 153.

family of Shropshire, and the dining-room panelling from Standish Hall (Lancs.).[35] A stone gateway, since demolished, bearing crests with griffin supports was the subject of a painting by Frederick Walker.[36]

COLEFORD was held by Alric in 1066 and he continued to hold it, like Halsway, under Roger de Courcelles in 1086.[37] It formed part of the Halsway fee until 1428,[38] but has not been traced thereafter.

EMBELLE was held in 1066 by Ulgar and under Roger de Courcelles by Alric in 1086.[39] By 1424 it formed part of Thorncombe manor in Bicknoller, and so remained probably until the 17th century.[40] It thereafter descended as a freehold estate called Embelle farm.[41]

By 1280 a holding at *REXTON* was regarded as three separate freeholds of Woodadvent manor in Nettlecombe.[42] It was still so held in 1619.[43] Each part descended separately, one from James Luttrell in 1453 becoming part of Over Vexford,[44] one from the Gilbert family of Woolavington in the 15th century and Erasmus Pym in 1556 to the Laceys of Hartrow by 1619,[45] and one from the Sydenhams to the Wyndhams by 1556.[46] By 1841 the second and third parts were owned by Daniel Blommart of Willet in Elworthy.[47]

Three houses survive at Rexton, the most southerly, known as Rexton Farm Cottage, dating from the 16th century. A hall and slightly later kitchen survive. In 1980 the house was under extensive restoration and a screen south of the hall and remains of crucks had been removed.[48]

In 1294–5 an estate at Boarpath was granted by Robert of Tetton to Simon of Crowcombe.[49] It descended like Crowcombe Biccombe manor,[50] and in 1615, when it included New Marsh and common on Heathfield, it was described as the manor of *BOARPATH*.[51] It continued to be held with Crowcombe into the 20th century.[52]

In 1460 an estate at *CHEDDERMARSH* was settled on John and Joan Sydenham by William Gore.[53] After Joan's death in 1498 it passed to her son John Sydenham (d. 1521).[54] John's son John died a minor in 1526 leaving two sisters one of whom married John (later Sir John) Wyndham. Wyndham purchased the other sister's share in 1529, and the holding descended like Orchard Wyndham.[55] By 1610 Sir John's grandson, Sir John Wyndham, had added to this estate lands at Escott, Cottiford, and Combe Cross, formerly all in Thorncombe manor, Bicknoller,[56] creating an estate sometimes known as Stogumber manor.[57] In 1804 Cheddermarsh and

Escott were given to Sir John Trevelyan as part of an exchange, but Combe Cross was retained to form part of the Wyndhams' estate of Stogumber and Over Vexford in 1851.[58]

ECONOMIC HISTORY. Nine estates in Stogumber were mentioned in 1086, their recorded size suggesting that at least a third of the later parish was not under cultivation. Capton was the largest estate, with land for 5 ploughs, followed by Hartrow and the church estate with 4 ploughlands each, and Halsway and Combe with 3 each; the remaining estates were smaller. Halsway had 400 a. of pasture, presumably on the Quantocks, and Hartrow 100 a., but Combe, with the Brendons rising behind it, was credited with only 50 a. The two holdings at Vexford had 51 a. of woodland between them, and Combe had wood measuring 4 furlongs by 2 furlongs. Capton, Coleford, Combe, Halsway, Hartrow, and Vexford supported sheep.[59]

By the end of the 13th century more intensive exploitation of the land had produced several small freeholds and led to the extension of the Domesday estate at Capton. Holdings at Boarpath and Yeaw, probably carved from the less fertile land in the south-east, were mentioned in 1269,[60] and the former was held with Crowcombe Biccombe manor from 1294–5.[61] Carslake, perhaps once part of neighbouring Over Vexford, belonged to the Bolevill family by 1274.[62] Goodley, on the Brendon slopes above Combe and a property of the Templars before their suppression in 1312, was evidently another settlement on less productive land, but it still survived as a hamlet in 1597.[63]

The extension of Capton manor in the north was the work of the Ralegh family of Nettlecombe. By the 1280s the farm centre had moved south from Capton to Rowdon.[64] Ancient woodland south-east of Capton was cleared around Vellow before 1307,[65] and new acquisitions were made by the Raleghs at Maderknoll and Curdon, between Vellow and the Doniford stream, in 1293 and at Cottiford, a little further north, in 1316.[66]

By 1307 Rowdon manor was being improved by regular marling, and customary services included not only making hay and the harvest in the fields but carting duties from the Brendons when corn was sown there, and maintenance of earth banks, taking grain to 'Baghtrip' (?Bawdrip), Watchet, and Dunster, and bringing herring and salt from Lyme (Dors.) and Exeter.[67]

[35] S.R.O., DD/X/WD; above, plate facing p. 77.
[36] Marks, *Life and Letters of Frederick Walker*, 156, 167–8, and plate facing 174.
[37] *V.C.H. Som.* i. 488.
[38] *Feud. Aids*, iv. 303, 346, 392.
[39] *V.C.H. Som.* i. 488.
[40] S.R.O., DD/WY 4T; 7/Z1C/21; DD/BR/py 16; P.R.O., CP 25(2)/207/35 Eliz. I. Hil.
[41] S.R.O., DD/CC 110774; ibid. tithe award.
[42] Ibid. DD/WO 41/8; 43/1, 7.
[43] Ibid. 43/1.
[44] *S.R.S.* xxii. 115; S.R.O., DD/WO 43/1, 7; DD/DR 25, 68.
[45] S.R.O., DD/BW 38; DD/WO 43/1, 7; DD/DR 25; DD/CCH 80; *S.R.S.* xxii, p. 97; lvii, p. 41.
[46] S.R.O., DD/WY 1A; 1/33; DD/WO 43/1, 7; *S.R.S.* xxii, pp. 112, 123.
[47] S.R.O., DD/WY 153.
[48] S.R.O., DD/V Wlr 23.4.
[49] *S. & D. N. & Q.* vi. 160.

[50] Above, Crowcombe, manors.
[51] S.R.O., DD/TB 25.
[52] Dyfed R.O., D/CAR 36.
[53] *S.R.S.* xxii, pp. 112, 123; S.R.O., DD/WY 1A.
[54] *S.R.S.* xvi. 365; S.R.O., DD/WY 1/33.
[55] S.R.O., DD/WY 8/A2; 60; above, St. Decumans.
[56] S.R.O., DD/WY 8/V2; 47/2; 48.
[57] Ibid. DD/WY 115; 143; DD/WY Survey Bk. 1801; DD/CCH 74.
[58] Ibid. DD/WY 143, 152; DD/WO 9/8.
[59] *V.C.H. Som.* i. 438, 471, 488, 505, 570.
[60] Ibid. DD/WY 6/Ki.
[61] Above, Crowcombe, manors.
[62] S.R.O., DD/L P3/11; *Cal. Close, 1272–9*, 126.
[63] Ibid. 1330–3, 514; Sydenham, *Hist. Sydenham Fam.* 130.
[64] S.R.O., DD/WO 1.
[65] Ibid. 47/1.
[66] Ibid. 1.
[67] Ibid. 47/1.

By the end of the 14th century Rowdon and Nettlecombe were administered as a single farm. The granary at Rowdon, stocked with barley, oats, rye, wheat, and malt, indicated where most of the arable of the manor of Nettlecombe and Rowdon lay, but there were cowhouses and a slaughterhouse suggesting both dairying and stock raising.[68] Tenants at Curdon supplied both plough shares and shoes for ploughteams until the early 15th century.[69] Higher Vexford Farm and Yeaw Farm, both built as farmhouses by the 16th century, indicate continued economic activity on both prime and marginal land.

By the 16th century the Trevelyan estate covered as much as a third of the parish, and included further land at Vellow acquired in 1520.[70] More was to be added at Togford, formerly part of Stogumber manor, in the early 18th century.[71] Separate farms at Rowdon and Vellow Wood had emerged by the 16th century and the former was let in 1598 to Robert Dashwood, a member of a family which engrossed holdings on the estate.[72] The Dashwoods lived at Vellow Wood, which they held by 1612, for c. 150 years.[73] Elsewhere on the estate after 1659 Charlwood common, shared between the tenants of Rowdon and Cheddermarsh, was no longer broken for tillage for three years in every ten.[74] By 1724 only rights for Cheddermarsh tenants survived on the 30-a. common, and it was said to be insufficient for stocking with sheep seven in every ten years. Sir John Trevelyan then hoped to buy out the rights and let the whole for a substantial rack rent.[75] The common, however, survived until after 1796.[76] The Trevelyans also established water meadows at Curdon in the 17th century and at Togford in the 18th.[77]

In 1641, of the 29 taxpayers in Halsway tithing only 12 paid tax of 5s. or less but in Stogumber tithing 34 out of 44 taxpayers paid 5s. or less, suggesting a large number of small holdings in the centre of the parish.[78] Elsewhere in the parish several small freehold farms can be traced. The two 19th-century farms at Lower Weacombe probably originated in the 16th-century holdings of the Dodington and Saffin families.[79] The Slocombes held an estate at Carslake from 1551[80] until 1679 when they sold it to John Carew of Crowcombe.[81] Before 1619 the Slocombes had added c. 50 a. at Houndwell to their estate.[82] Northam comprised a capital messuage and 140 a. in 1662; by 1782 the holding had been enlarged to include land in Kingswood, Houndhill, and Carslake.[83] The break-up of the Halsway estate in the 18th century led to the creation of freehold farms including Cusdon's, held by the Hembrow family in the 18th and 19th centuries, Paradise, and Little Halsway.[84]

Several 17th-century farmers had goods worth over £100. One woman left oxen worth £30, cattle and pigs, 64 cheeses, and 4 gallons of butter. Another woman, whose inventory totalled over £350, kept cattle, horses, sheep, pigs, and poultry in addition to growing corn. A wealthy yeoman in 1640 had a library full of books, a small armoury, and corn worth £30.[85] In 1731 one farmer's goods were worth c. £750 and included a cased clock and virginals.[86] Wheat and barley seem to have been the principal crops; flax was grown on a small scale from 1665,[87] and hops and apples were produced at Vellow.[88]

During the 19th century there was a move to larger farms and several pairs of farms were formed, such as Hartrow and Higher Vexford, Embelle and Whitemoor, and Wood and Lower Preston.[89] Some farmhouses were improved in the 17th and 18th centuries. Yeaw Farm was enlarged in the 17th and the early 19th century and Higher Vexford Farm received a substantial addition in the 18th century including a new staircase and principal rooms.

In 1828 three men, including the lessor's son James Notley, became partners in farming Combe Sydenham farm on a 7-year lease from George Notley. James was to invest half the capital needed to stock the 700-a. farm for which the rent was £525 a year.[90] Arable land in the north of the parish was said to be worth 36s. an acre in 1835 but Sir John Trevelyan let it to his cottagers for 18s. an acre. He was said to be a fair landlord who let his cottages with large gardens at reasonable rents, and there were a number of allotments on the Trevelyan estates.[91] In 1840 there were 6 holdings of over 200 a.: Vellow Wood, Capton, Escott, and Wood with Lower Preston had between 200 a. and 300 a., the Hartrow and Higher Vexford farm was 358 a., and Combe Sydenham farm was 638 a. There were 12 farms of between 100 a. and 200 a., 12 between 50 a. and 100 a., and 22 between 10 a. and 50 a.[92] In 1851 the Combe Sydenham farm employed 30 labourers. A total of 92 men worked on 7 farms of over 150 a. and a further 45 on 10 farms with between 50 and 150 a.[93] After the addition of Over Vexford with a 100 a. during the 1860s the Hartrow estate produced average rents, after deductions, of over £1,000 a year.[94] As a result of amalgamation and increased prosperity, many farmhouses, including Rowdon and Embelle, were rebuilt during the 19th century while others, like Boarpath, on merged holdings were abandoned.

In 1840 there were 3,727 a. of arable and 1,506 a. of pasture,[95] and in 1861 the parish produced crops of wheat, barley, beans, mangolds, potatoes, and turnips.[96] In 1905 arable accounted for 2,570 a., grass 2,247 a., and woodland 265 a.[97] In 1976 at least

[68] Ibid. 42/2, 6.
[69] Ibid. 1.
[70] Ibid.
[71] Ibid. 1; 35/3; DD/SAS BK 87.
[72] Ibid. DD/WO 12/4; 13/2, 6, 7; 14/6.
[73] Ibid. 14/5.
[74] Tillage was paid for at 3s. 4d. an a. in 1598: ibid. 42/28.
[75] S.R.O., DD/WO 35/2, 42/24–9; ibid. Q/SR 102/57.
[76] Ibid. DD/WO map 1796; ibid. tithe award.
[77] Ibid. DD/WO 13/8, 35/3.
[78] Som. Protestation Returns, ed. Howard and Stoate, 292–3.
[79] P.R.O., C 142/242, no. 7; S.R.O., DD/BR/py 112; Cal. Proc. Chanc. Eliz. (Rec. Com.), i. 117, 243.
[80] P.R.O., C 142/278, no. 155; S.R.O., DD/TB 5/6.
[81] S.R.O., DD/TB 5/6.

[82] Ibid. 5/6; 36.
[83] Ibid. DD/AH 13/1; DD/TB 6/4, 5.
[84] Ibid. DD/CH 83/1; DD/DP 128; DD/TB 29; ibid. tithe award.
[85] Ibid. DD/SP, inventories 1639, 1640.
[86] Ibid. inventory 1731.
[87] Ibid. DD/SAS PD 57; DD/WY 152.
[88] Ibid. DD/WO 14/3.
[89] Ibid. tithe award.
[90] Devon R.O. 337B/101/27.
[91] S.R.O., tithe award; V.C.H. Som. ii. 330.
[92] S.R.O., tithe award.
[93] P.R.O., HO 107/1920.
[94] S.R.O., DD/CCH 80.
[95] Ibid. tithe award.
[96] P.O. Dir. Som. (1861).
[97] Statistics supplied by the then Bd. of Agric. 1905.

2,085 a. were under grass, 1,626 a. were arable, and 80 a. were under fruit and horticultural crops.[98] In the west the rough hill pasture on the Combe Sydenham estate was planted with trees in the late 1970s, and the estate was run as commercial woodland. There was also a trout farm on the estate in 1980.

Cloth making was concentrated largely in the hamlets along the Doniford stream and its tributaries where fulling mills were recorded from the 15th century.[99] There was a fuller at Vexford in 1243.[1] Weavers, fullers, dyers, and clothiers were prominent in the parish in the 16th and 17th centuries, including members of the Sweeting and Dashwood families.[2] Individual craftsmen were clearly prosperous. A weaver died in 1636 leaving looms, two reeling machines, cloth, yarn, flock, and wool worth £22.[3] Another seems to have finished his own cloth, for he owned not only weaving equipment but also two racks, shears, a brass furnace, and a supply of wool and cloth.[4] There were five fulling mills in the parish between the 15th and 18th centuries, and field names indicate racks at Capton, Stogumber village, Downside, Over Vexford, Lower Vexford, and Northam.[5] Dyeing was carried out in the 16th century at Vellow and Boarpath,[6] and later at Carslake.[7] Three combers in the parish were supplied by a serge weaver from Lydeard St. Lawrence in 1696 with wool already dyed.[8]

Henry Sweeting (d. 1685) had a shop selling a wide variety of imported cloth and haberdashery as well as tobacco, paper, sugar, canary seed, currants, soap, and glasses.[9] Other 17th-century and later occupations included tanning at Vellow,[10] gloving,[11] hat making,[12] and malting.[13] In 1821 out of 243 families 158 were engaged in trade and manufacture.[14] In 1851 there were a draper and a fellmonger in the parish as well as a milliner, dressmakers, shoemakers, building workers, several retailers, and professional men. Other trades included those of a carrier and a veterinary surgeon.[15] There was a smithy at Curdon by 1370[16] and others at Carslake and Capton in the late 18th and the 19th century.[17] A blacksmith's shop at Vellow, worked by five smiths in 1851, was converted to a pottery c. 1961.[18]

A brewery was established south of Stogumber village early in the 19th century using the reputedly

medicinal water from a spring called Harry Hill's well. Its product was sold throughout the country.[19] In 1851 the brewery employed labourers, coopers, a clerk, a manager, and at least one travelling salesman.[20] Brewing probably ceased c. 1910 but malting continued until 1923 or later.[21] Most of the buildings were demolished in 1973 but the small mineral water plant was still standing in 1975.[22]

MARKET AND FAIRS. In 1613 a road from Ashbeer to Stogumber was known as Market Way and in the village there was a shambles from which Sir John Sydenham received 70s. rent in 1614.[23] Sir John was said to have bought a Saturday market from the Crown in 1615, possibly because an earlier market had lapsed.[24] There was a clerk of the market in the 1630s and in 1637 the rent was £13.[25] In the late 17th century the market attracted produce from as far as Kilve and Kilton.[26] The market was still held in 1861 but was discontinued shortly afterwards.[27]

The market hall was built north of the church c. 1800 and comprised an arched area below and an assembly room over.[28] After 1840,[29] and probably in the 1860s when the market was abandoned, the building was incorporated into the White Horse inn.

From 1615 Sir John Sydenham held two fairs in the village, on the feasts of St. Peter ad Vincula (1 August) and St. Mark (25 April).[30] Until 1695 the fairs were said to be held from the Crown on a lease for lives[31] but were later held with Stogumber manor.[32] The spring fair for cattle continued until after 1861.[33] Bullocks and sheep were sold at the summer fair, which probably ceased soon after the mid 18th century.[34]

MILLS. There were two corn mills in 1086, one at Combe, the other at Hartrow.[35] The Combe mill was probably working in 1367[36] and certainly in 1613.[37] A new overshot mill was built c. 1794. Grinding had ceased by the 1880s,[38] but the building remained in 1979. Hartrow mill was not mentioned after 1086 but the name Mill meadow and a pond retained for ornamental purposes in the 19th century suggest the site of a later mill on the estate.[39]

There were two corn mills at Curdon:[40] one, mentioned in 1325, served the tenants at Capton,

98 Min. of Agric., Fisheries, and Food, agric. returns 1976. 99 Below, mills.
1 S.R.S. xi, p. 305.
2 S.R.O., DD/WO 14/6, 15/1; DD/WY 60; S.R.S. xxi, pp. 121-2; xxviii, p. 325.
3 S.R.O., DD/SP, inventory 1636.
4 Ibid. inventory 1693.
5 Ibid. DD/WO 43/1; DD/SAS BK 87; DD/L P35/8; ibid. tithe award; P.R.O., C 142/110, no. 157.
6 S.R.O., DD/WO 14/6; DD/TB 24; ibid. tithe award.
7 Ibid. DD/TB map c. 1724; ibid. map and survey 1797; ibid. tithe award.
8 Ibid. Q/SR 201/13.
9 Ibid. DD/SP, inventory 1685.
10 Ibid. DD/WO 14/3, 6; DD/SP, inventories 1634, 1664, 1685; ibid. tithe award.
11 Ibid. Q/SR 159/13, 161/5, 181/10.
12 E. Dwelly, Hearth Tax Exemptions, ii. 202-3; S.R.O., DD/SP, inventory, 1672.
13 S.R.O., DD/WO 14/3, 43/1; DD/CCH 62; ibid. tithe award.
14 Census, 1821.
15 P.R.O., HO 107/1920.
16 S.R.O., DD/WO 1.
17 Ibid. DD/WO 43/4; ibid. tithe award.
18 Ibid. DD/WO 43/4, 44/11; P.R.O., HO 107/1920; inf. from Mr. D. Winkley, Vellow.

19 S.R.O., DD/BR/lw 6; D/P/stogm 13/1/3; ibid. tithe award; Co. Gaz. Dir. (1840); F. & P. Hawtin, 'Stogumber Brewery', Som. Ind. Arch. Soc. Jnl. ii. 15-19.
20 P.R.O., HO 107/1920.
21 S.R.O., DD/X/MMN 10, 11.
22 Inf. from Mrs. M. Miles, Durston.
23 S.R.O., D/D/Rg 341; ibid. DD/SAS BK 87.
24 Ibid. Q/SR 23/18; S.R.S. xv. 27; lxvii, p. 66.
25 S.R.O., D/P/bic 13/2/4; DD/SAS BK 87.
26 Ibid. D/P/stogm 13/2/1; ibid. Q/SR 11/89-90, 189/1.
27 P.O. Dir. Som. (1861, 1866).
28 S.R.O., DD/CCH 6/2.
29 Ibid. tithe award.
30 S.R.S. lxvii, p. 66; Sydenham, Hist. Sydenham Fam. 138.
31 S.R.O., T/PH/rhs.
32 P.R.O., CP 25(2)/962/7 Anne East.
33 S.R.O., DD/CCH 72; P.O. Dir. Som. (1861).
34 Book of Fairs (1767); Collinson, Hist. Som. iii. 545.
35 V.C.H. Som. i. 505.
36 B.L. Add. Ch. 11165.
37 S.R.O., DD/SAS BK 87; S.R.S. lxvii, p. 65.
38 S.R.O., T/PH/no 2; ibid. tithe award; Kelly's Dir. Som. (1883).
39 S.R.O., tithe award.
40 Ibid. DD/SAS BK 87.

Escott, and Curdon.[41] Both mills appear to have been in use in 1392 and 1416.[42] One, held of Rowdon manor and called Curdon mills, was worked until 1840 or later.[43] It stood on a branch of the Doniford stream and in 1979 was a private house. The other mill was held of Stogumber manor.[44] That mill still existed in 1796, when it was worked by the Curdon miller, but it had gone out of use as a corn mill by 1840.[45] A fulling mill was attached to it between 1660 and c. 1778 and it was used as a sawmill in 1872.[46] Manor mill in Stogumber village, possibly in use by 1389,[47] was worked until 1889 or later but had probably ceased when the manor estates were sold in 1896.[48] The building, immediately north-west of the village, was in ruins in 1979, but it appears to have had an overshot wheel. The mill pond could be traced in neighbouring gardens. Kingswood mill was mentioned in 1613.[49] It went out of use between 1910 and 1914[50] and in 1979 was a private house. A corn mill at Northam by 1652[51] was still in use in 1848,[52] but it had ceased milling by 1866.[53] It stood on the Doniford stream and in 1979 was a private house. There may have been a mill at Escott before 1840.[54]

There was a fulling mill at Lower Vexford by 1537.[55] It stood north of the hamlet and was probably driven by the stream running from Willett.[56] It may have been the fulling mill rated between 1770 and 1806.[57] There was another in Over Vexford manor in the 16th century, possibly at Northam where a fulling mill was recorded in 1568.[58] A fulling mill was attached to the Stogumber manor mill at Curdon between 1660 and c. 1778.[59] The Cockesmill recorded in a Stogumber manor survey of 1613 may be the fulling mill recorded in 1636.[60] It was in use in 1695[61] and may have been the mill near Downside rated in 1770 and 1806,[62] which had gone by 1840.[63]

LOCAL GOVERNMENT. Stogumber (sometimes Preston and Stogumber) and Halsway tithings lay wholly within the parish.[64] The Trevelyan estates in the north formed part of Nettlecombe tithing, Combe Sydenham and Escott were considered part of Bicknoller tithing, Hartrow and Vexford part of Elworthy tithing, Ashbeer, Boarpath, Carslake, and Yeaw part of Williton tithing, and Rexton part of Woodadvent tithing, which had been absorbed into

Nettlecombe tithing by the 19th century.[65] Kilve and Dunwear tithings were said to include parts of the parish in 1670.[66]

No court rolls have been found for Stogumber manor but courts were still held in the 17th century.[67] Court rolls for the rectory manor survive for most of the years between 1469 and 1640 and between 1660 and 1668, and courts normally met twice a year.[68] In 1681 they were held in the almshouses but during the 19th century they met at Wells solely for the admission of tenants.[69] No court rolls have been found for Halsway but courts were held by the 14th and until the late 17th century[70] probably ceasing in the early 18th century.[71] Courts were held twice a year for Hartrow manor in the 16th century and were still being held in 1759,[72] but court rolls have been discovered only for the years 1562–3 and 1668.[73] The courts for Over Vexford manor met twice a year in the 15th century and chose a steward and reeve.[74] Records survive intermittently from the 14th to the 17th centuries.[75] The Wyndham estates in Stogumber were administered by a court sitting at Escott, but only one roll for 1636 has been discovered.[76] Rowdon manor was administered with Nettlecombe manor,[77] Boarpath with Crowcombe Biccombe,[78] and Combe Sydenham with Bicknoller manor.[79]

By the early 17th century two churchwardens and four overseers[80] were chosen by means of a property rota, half the officers coming from the west side of the parish and half from the east. By 1671 the retiring churchwardens were regularly elected way-wardens for the coming year.[81] A salaried assistant overseer was appointed in 1827, and in 1839 there was a paid highway surveyor.[82]

A vestry of 13 people met during the late 18th century and supervised the election of parish officers.[83] A select vestry of 20 people, meeting fortnightly by 1834, had perhaps ceased to meet by 1836 and was ordered to be restored.[84] The vestry met between 1852 and 1880 at the White Horse but the Easter vestry was held in the church.[85]

Poor relief in the 17th century included payment for funerals, removals, house rent, nursing, apprenticeships, clothing, shoes, and items of food.[86] The overseers had contracts with a surgeon (1741) and a carpenter (1749), the latter to make coffins. In 1752 they paid for a wooden leg.[87]

[41] Ibid. DD/WO 1.
[42] Ibid. 41/12. In 1394 tolls were prescribed for a mill at Curdon: ibid. DD/WO 1.
[43] Ibid. 42/25, 43/1; ibid. tithe award.
[44] Ibid. DD/WO 43/1.
[45] Ibid. 13/1, 44/11; ibid. tithe award.
[46] Morris & Co. Dir. Som. (1872).
[47] P.R.O., C131/37, no. 11.
[48] S.R.O., DD/CCH 62; Kelly's Dir. Som. (1889).
[49] S.R.O., DD/SAS BK 87.
[50] Kelly's Dir. Som. (1910, 1914).
[51] S.R.O., DD/L 2/19/109.
[52] Ibid. tithe award; ibid. DD/AH 13/1; DD/TB 6/5.
[53] P.O. Dir. Som. (1866).
[54] S.R.O., tithe award.
[55] P.R.O., SC 6/Hen. VIII/3127; ibid. C 142/110, no. 157.
[56] S.R.O., tithe award.
[57] Ibid. D/P/stogm 4/1/1.
[58] Ibid. DD/L P35/8; P36/4.
[59] Ibid. DD/WO 13/1, 44/11.
[60] Ibid. DD/SAS BK 87.
[61] Ibid. T/PH/rhs.
[62] Ibid. D/P/stogm 4/1/1–2.
[63] Ibid. tithe award.

[64] S.R.S. xx. 170; S.R.O., DD/TB 16/12; ibid. Q/REl Williton.
[65] S.R.O., DD/WY 34; ibid. Q/REl Williton; Som. Protestation Returns, ed. Howard and Stoate, 292–3.
[66] E. Dwelly, Hearth Tax Exemptions, ii. 202–3.
[67] S.R.O., DD/SAS BK 87.
[68] Ibid. DD/CC 111694–8, 131907–927, 174895.
[69] S.R.S. lxxii. 90; S.R.O., DD/CC 174895.
[70] S.R.O., DD/TB 12/1; 23; 28.
[71] Ibid. DD/HLM 12; DD/CCH 64.
[72] Ibid. DD/DR 25; DD/TB 6/4.
[73] Ibid. DD/DR 62.
[74] Ibid. DD/L P23/15, 16; P35/5, 8.
[75] Ibid. P3/18; P35/15, 20; DD/WY 46/3.
[76] Ibid. DD/WY 47/2; 48; 60; DD/CCH 74.
[77] Above, Nettlecombe.   [78] Above, Crowcombe.
[79] Above, Bicknoller.
[80] S.R.O., D/P/stogm 4/1/3; 13/2/7.
[81] Ibid. 13/2/1.
[82] Ibid. 13/8/1, 14/1/1.
[83] Ibid. 4/1/2, 9/1/1.
[84] Ibid. 9/1/3, 13/8/1.
[85] Ibid. 4/1/2.
[86] Ibid. 13/2/1, 7.
[87] Ibid. 13/2/3.

In 1752 the overseers agreed to pay the product of five poor rates each year to establish and maintain a workhouse. The house opened with 8 people, some of whom were paid for spinning.[88] In 1769 there were 25 residents including children who were taught at parish expense.[89] In 1834 the workhouse held 25 people, and a further 3 families lived in other houses owned by the parish. Outdoor relief was paid for the fourth and every subsequent child. During the year 481 people received relief, most of whom were infirm, disabled, or children under 9 years.[90] The parish became part of the Williton poor-law union in 1836[91] and the workhouse had been given up by 1840.[92] The cottages were retained until 1865.[93]

Stogumber formed part of Williton rural district from 1894 and in 1974 became part of the West Somerset district.[94]

CHURCH. The church of Stogumber, known in 1086 as the church of St. Mary of Warverdinestoch, had been supported by a large estate, suggesting that it had been a minster.[95] The possible extent of the area served by the church may be indicated by renders of grain due to the rectory in the 13th century from Monksilver[96] and Syndercombe in Clatworthy, the second referred to as churchscot,[97] and by the payment of tithe to the rectory in 1841 from Willett in Elworthy;[98] Bicknoller, moreover, remained a chapelry of Stogumber in the early 19th century.[99] The church and its estate were held by an individual owner in 1066 and by one of the king's clerks, Richer de Andelys, in 1086. Part of that estate formed the later rectory;[1] a rector was recorded in 1249[2] and there was presumably a rectory by 1214 when Walter de Andelys had the advowson.[3] Another Walter de Andelys gave the advowson in 1259 to William of Bitton, bishop of Bath and Wells (d. 1264), who gave it to the dean and chapter of Wells. Under a licence of 1271 the chapter appropriated the church[4] between 1274 and 1291, and a vicarage had been ordained by 1291.[5] The living remained a vicarage in the patronage of the chapter, occasional presentations being made by individual members who farmed the rectory,[6] until 1977, when it became a curacy-in-charge held with the united benefice of Monksilver with Brompton Ralph and Nettlecombe.[7]

The vicarage was assessed at £11 13s. 4d. in 1291, more than any other in the area.[8] It was valued at £18 2s. in 1535,[9] £80 in c. 1668,[10] and £239 net by 1831.[11] The value of the living was augmented to £300 in 1882.[12] In 1535 tithes of wool and lambs were valued at £9 2s. and personal tithes and casualties were worth £7 13s. 4d.[13] In 1840 the vicarial tithes were commuted for a tithe rent charge of £325 5s.[14] The vicarial glebe was valued at £1 6s. 8d. in 1535.[15] In 1571 the glebe comprised 5 gardens, 2 orchards, and the herbage of the churchyard, and in 1626 and 1840 there were 2 houses, including the vicarage house.[16]

The former vicarage house, north-west of the church, has a medieval east–west range of three rooms, including a three-bayed former open hall with partially surviving arch-braced roof. In 1736 there were a pantry, parlour, and study with four chambers above.[17] By that time the hall was ceiled and the fireplace added. A range was built on the west side of the house in the early 19th century.

Hugh Roper, instituted in 1476, was apparently still resident vicar in 1534.[18] Edward Lokton, vicar from 1536, was deprived in 1554 and replaced by James Bonde, S.T.P., a canon of Wells and later archdeacon of Bath.[19] Lokton was restored under Elizabeth but he does not seem to have been resident.[20] Richard Phelps was vicar for 40 years from 1581. Shortly after John Baynham began his 58-year incumbency in 1631[21] the puritan Anthony Scrope preached at Stogumber in 1633.[22] The parish registers include many of Baynham's comments and also entries omitted during the period of civil registration.[23] A successor commented on his wealth.[24] Richard Lux, resident vicar 1722–36, had plate and other valuables worth over £20, but his few books were worth less than £2.[25] John Turner, vicar 1761–1817 and archdeacon of Taunton 1780–1817, was non-resident because he was principal surrogate to the bishop's court at Wells. His resident curate held two services each Sunday.[26] The next vicar, James Talman, was resident chaplain at Bromley College (Kent), and his successor, George Trevelyan (vicar 1820–71), was absent because of mental illness.[27] Trevelyan's brother Edward Otto Trevelyan was resident curate until 1869.[28]

There were 432 communicants and 15 monthly and festal celebrations in 1842, and 75 people were confirmed in 1844.[29] In 1851 about 150 people attended morning service and 300 came in the afternoon. In addition the 60 Sunday-school children attended both services.[30] By 1868 the number of communicants had dropped to 115 but the number

[88] Ibid. 9/1/1, 13/2/3.
[89] Ibid. 13/2/4.
[90] Ibid. 13/8/1.
[91] Youngs, *Local Admin. Units*, i. 674.
[92] S.R.O., tithe award.
[93] Ibid. D/P/stogm 4/1/2; ibid. DD/CC 111693.
[94] Youngs, *Local Admin. Units*, i. 675–6.
[95] *V.C.H. Som.* i. 471, 532.
[96] *H.M.C. Wells*, i. 2–3.
[97] Ibid. ii. 573.
[98] S.R.O., Elworthy tithe award.
[99] Above, Bicknoller.
[1] Above, manors.
[2] *H.M.C. Wells*, i. 2–3.
[3] *Cur. Reg. R.* vii. 113.
[4] *H.M.C. Wells*, i. 2, 376; ii. 568.
[5] *Rot. Hund.* (Rec. Com.), ii. 121; *Tax Eccl.* (Rec. Com.), 198.
[6] *Som. Incumbents*, ed. Weaver, 444–5.
[7] *Dioc. Dir.*
[8] *Tax. Eccl.* (Rec. Com.), 198.
[9] *Valor Eccl.* (Rec. Com.), i. 222.
[10] S.R.O., D/D/Vc 24.
[11] *Rep. Com. Eccl. Revenues*, pp. 152–3.
[12] S.R.O., D/P/stogm 1/2/1.
[13] *Valor Eccl.* (Rec. Com.), i. 222.
[14] S.R.O., tithe award.
[15] *Valor Eccl.* (Rec. Com.), i. 222.
[16] S.R.O., D/D/Rg 360; ibid. tithe award.
[17] Ibid. DD/SP, inventory 1736.
[18] *Som. Incumbents*, ed. Weaver, 445; *Wells Wills*, ed. Weaver, 152.
[19] S.R.O., D/D/Rg 360; below.
[20] S.R.O., D/D/Ca 18; *S.R.S.* lv, p. 127.
[21] *Som. Incumbents*, ed. Weaver, 445.
[22] S.R.O., D/D/Ca 256.
[23] Ibid. D/P/stogm 2/1/1–2.
[24] Ibid. 2/1/2; *Som. Wills*, ed. Brown, iii. 111.
[25] S.R.O., DD/SP, inventory 1736.
[26] Ibid. D/D/B returns 1815.
[27] Ibid. D/P/stogm 1/1/1, 1/6/1.
[28] Ibid. 1/1/1, 2/1/6.
[29] Ibid. 23/2; ibid. D/D/V returns 1843.
[30] P.R.O., HO 129/313/5/4/4.

of celebrations had risen to 25, and two years later they were held weekly. In 1870 there were two sermons on Sundays.[31] E. A. Couch, vicar 1908–44, wrote a parish magazine, including notes on parish history, between 1910 and 1940. He set up a branch of the Temperance Movement and Band of Hope, kept a parish library, and held cottage services at Higher Vexford, Lower Vexford, Capton, Rexton, and Halsway.[32]

A church house was leased to the churchwardens from the rectory manor by the early 14th century.[33] It was said to have been burned c. 1616,[34] but it almost certainly survives as the two-storeyed building south of the former vicarage house. It has a jointed cruck roof and contains a large kitchen fireplace with evidence of later brewing activities. The building seems to have been incorporated into the glebe after the fire and to have become a kitchen and stable for the vicarage by 1626.[35]

In 1505 a stone image of the Holy Trinity was given to the church.[36] In the 1530s there were lights of the Blessed Virgin Mary, St. Anthony, St. George, St. Christopher, a 'dead' light,[37] and a light or statue of St. Michael,[38] some of which may later have been endowed.[39] By 1547 there was a rood light[40] and a fraternity of the Blessed Virgin Mary, formerly known as the brotherhood of the church.[41]

The church of *ST. MARY*, in a prominent position in the centre of the village, is built of sandstone with limestone dressings. It comprises chancel with north and south aisles, aisled nave with porches to north and south, and a south-west tower. The lower stages of the tower and the western bay of the south nave aisle are of the late 13th or early 14th century and, with the possible exception of the east end of the chancel, are all that survived extensive rebuilding and enlargement in the 15th century. The elaborate south chancel aisle, then owned by the Sydenham family, may have been the first addition, followed by the rebuilding of two bays of the south aisle of the nave, the construction of the north nave aisle, the north porch, the rood stair, the Halsway aisle north of the chancel, and the top stage and turret stair of the tower.

The stone pulpit and font are contemporary with the rebuilding and extension, but the bench ends probably belong to the 16th century. Monuments in the church include the elaborate tomb of Sir George Sydenham (d. 1597) and memorials to successive owners of the Combe Sydenham, Halsway, and Hartrow estates. A west gallery was erected in 1726 because of the 'multitude of persons' attending the church.[42] During the 19th century the fabric of the church was neglected,[43] and the lessees of the rectory

spent less than £1 a year on repairs in 1849, out of their total tithe receipts of over £740.[44] The Halsway aisle was also neglected by the owners and was said to have been ruinous in 1873.[45] The church was restored between 1873 and 1875 by J. D. Sedding. The chancel walls and roof were painted in the style of William Morris by Edward Jones, vicar 1871–1907.[46]

There are six bells including one by Thomas Pennington of Exeter dated 1624 and another by Thomas Purdue dated 1687.[47] The plate includes a chalice of 1615[48] and a paten and flagon of 1733.[49] The registers date from 1559 with gaps 1646–53 and 1712–17.[50]

There was a chapel at Hartrow, described in the early 18th century as a chapel of ease long since demolished.[51] It evidently stood on Hartrow Hill, and had been converted to a cottage by 1562.[52] The chapel was endowed with every third crop from land in Elworthy including Coleford farm, an endowment still paid to the rectory estate in 1801.[53] Tithes due to the rectory from fields at Willett in Elworthy in 1841[54] may represent the same payment.

The chapel of Our Lady Sweetwell at Vellow was licensed for mass and other services in 1542. It adjoined the house of John Hawkins[55] and was probably served by Hawkin's son John. In his will of 1547 Hawkins the elder provided that if mass was no longer said in the chapel then the furnishings should be bestowed for the good of his soul and the bells should be given to the parish church.[56] The chapel became part of the adjoining house, but was still known as the chapel of Sweetwell or Vellow as late as the 18th century.[57] Traces of the chapel remain in Sweetwell Cottage.

NONCONFORMITY. Two people were presented for recusancy in 1636.[58] By 1669 there were two groups of nonconformists.[59] A Presbyterian meeting house was licensed in 1672 and licences for unspecified congregations were issued in 1704 and 1713. By 1718 there were 170 Presbyterian members, but soon afterwards they seem to have transferred their allegiance to the Baptists.[60] Baptist preachers and teachers at Stogumber and Dunster had been supported from 1690 by an endowment given by Jane Prowse of Croydon in Old Cleeve.[61] A congregation was established by 1718.[62] A chapel was built c. 1726.[63] There was a resident minister c. 1799.[64] The chapel seated 200 and attendance on Census Sunday 1851 was 79 in the morning, 74 in the afternoon, and 90 in the evening.[65] The chapel was rebuilt in 1869[66] and was in use in 1979. There

[31] S.R.O., D/P/stogm 23/2; ibid. D/D/V returns 1870.
[32] Ibid. D/P/stogm 23/4.
[33] H.M.C. Wells, i. 520–1.
[34] S.R.O., D/D/Ca 310.
[35] Ibid. D/D/Rg 360.   [36] S.R.S. xix. 83.
[37] Wells Wills, ed. Weaver, 152.
[38] Ibid. 154.
[39] S.R.S. ii. 45; lxxvii, p. 70; Cal. Pat. 1549–51, 274.
[40] Som. Co. Herald, 28 Oct. 1922, transcript of will.
[41] Wells Wills, ed. Weaver, 152, 154; Som. Co. Herald, 28 Oct. 1922.
[42] S.R.O., D/P/stogm 6/1/1.
[43] Ibid. D/D/V returns 1843.
[44] Ibid. DD/SF 1719.
[45] Ibid. D/P/stogm 21/1/7.
[46] Ibid. 6/1/2, 21/1/7, 23/4; ibid. D/D/Cf 73/7.
[47] Ibid. DD/SAS CH 16/2.
[48] Ibid. D/P/stogm 2/1/1.
[49] Proc. Som. Arch. Soc. xlv. 174.
[50] S.R.O., D/P/stogm 2/1/1–15.
[51] P.R.O., E 134/8 Geo. I East./2.
[52] S.R.O., DD/DR 62.   [53] Ibid. DD/CC 111711.
[54] Ibid. Elworthy tithe award.
[55] Ibid. DD/WO 25/6.
[56] Som. Co. Herald, 28 Oct. 1922.
[57] S.R.O., DD/WO 14/4, 15/3, 43/7.
[58] Ibid. D/D/Ca 310.
[59] Ibid. D/P/stogm 2/1/2.
[60] Orig. Records of Early Nonconf. ed. G. L. Turner, i. 569; S.R.O., Q/RR.
[61] Char. Com. files.
[62] Dr. Williams's Libr. Evans MS.
[63] S.R.O., Q/RR; ibid. T/PH/pro 68.
[64] Western Bap. Assoc. Letters 1769–1823.
[65] P.R.O., HO 129/313/5/4/6.
[66] Lond. Gaz. 28 Sep. 1869, 5251.

is a register of births for the period 1810–36.[67] The congregation used hymn tunes by Joel Thorne of Stogumber published in *Pentecostal Hymns* (1906).[68] In 1792 a room at Carslake was licensed, probably for use by Baptists.[69]

Houses used by Methodists were licensed in 1753 and 1754.[70] In 1840 a building in the grounds of Capton House was converted for use as a chapel[71] and in 1843 Kingswood was taken into the Williton Wesleyan circuit for services on alternate Sundays.[72] A house was licensed there in 1844,[73] and a small chapel was built in 1848 but in 1855 it was abandoned.[74] Methodist services were revived in the 1860s,[75] possibly at Capton, where services in private houses were held regularly from 1868 until 1916.[76] Services were held at Vellow in 1886–7.[77]

A Congregationalist village evangelist held occasional meetings at Rexton and Coleford Water in the late 19th century.[78]

EDUCATION. There was an unlicensed schoolmaster in 1629.[79] Pauper children were being taught at parish expense in 1769, possibly in the workhouse.[80] The Baptist minister is said to have established a school in the late 18th century, and it certainly existed in 1803, occupying a building attached to the chapel.[81] By 1818 it taught 30 boys from the poorer classes. It was supported by voluntary contributions and was said to be 'well watched over'.[82] In 1840 it was taking both day and boarding pupils, but seems to have closed shortly afterwards.[83]

A church school was founded c. 1802 and by 1812 had 70 children.[84] It was said to be badly superintended in 1818,[85] and in 1825 had 58 children on weekdays and Sundays.[86] It was succeeded by a National school, founded in 1833, which by 1840 occupied a site near Zinch, and in 1846 had 103 children.[87] The buildings were enlarged in 1871 and by 1902 there were 5 teachers and 118 children on

the books.[88] Numbers fluctuated over the following decades as neighbouring village schools closed. From 1971 the school became a First School for children in the 5–9 age range, older children travelling to Williton.[89]

A private boarding and day school was kept between 1840 and 1852,[90] and a school for girls between 1859 and 1872.[91]

CHARITIES FOR THE POOR. Sir George Sydenham (d. 1597) gave six cottages for as many poor widows, supported by an annual rent charge of £15 on the Combe Sydenham estate.[92] In 1910 the owner of the estate was required to nominate the occupants and to pay 1s. a week to each.[93] In 1939 the houses were sold and interest on the proceeds given to two or three aged widows.[94] In 1979 the one recipient of the charity was a former employee of the Combe Sydenham estate.[95] The early 17th-century building, converted to a single dwelling after 1939, stands south-west of the church in the village street.

Cash bequests to the poor of Stogumber, notably by Lady Sydenham (d. ?1654), William Lacey (d. 1607), George Trevelyan (d. 1653), John Sweeting (d. ?1646), and George Huish, totalling £210, were used in 1658 to buy a rent charge of £10.[96] John Blake of Lower Weacombe, by will dated 1716, left £100 to provide clothing for the poor. In 1722 the money, together with nearly £200 from other charitable bequests, was used to buy land at Bishop's Lydeard, the income to be used to provide clothing and blankets for the respectable poor who attempted to live independently of the parish.[97] Both charities, with the addition of a gift of £90 by Mrs. Ann Ling, by will proved 1890, provided for the distribution of £40 a year in clothing and blankets until 1939 or later.[98] More recent distributions have been made in cash and vouchers. The rent charge bought in 1658 was redeemed in 1975 for £80.[99]

NETHER STOWEY

NETHER STOWEY is a small parish beneath the north-east slope of the Quantocks about 5 km. from the coast and 10 km. west of Bridgwater.[1] It had a castle, a borough, and a market and fair. The ancient parish included detached areas at Radlet, in Spaxton

parish, and Godsmoor, in Cannington parish.[2] The land at Radlet was transferred to Spaxton in 1880 and in 1886 Stowey Rocks (11 people in 2 houses in 1891) was transferred from Over to Nether Stowey. In 1971 the civil parish measured 446 ha. (1,103 a.).[3]

[67] S.R.O., T/PH/pro 68.
[68] *Som. Co. Herald*, 3 Jun. 1922.
[69] S.R.O., D/D/Rm, box 1, p. 107; ibid. T/PH/pro 68.
[70] Ibid. Q/RR.
[71] A. G. Pointon, *Methodists in W. Som.* (1982), 24.
[72] S.R.O., D/N/wsc 3/2/2.
[73] Ibid. 3/3/2; ibid. D/D/Rm, box 2.
[74] Ibid. D/N/wsc 3/2/2; P.R.O., HO 129/313/5/4/5.
[75] W. Symons, *Early Methodism in West Som. and the Lorna Doone Country* (c. 1898), 61.
[76] S.R.O., D/N/wsc 3/2/2, 4, 9; *Wesleyan Methodist Church, Williton Circuit, Centenary Celebration Booklet* (1910). [77] S.R.O., D/N/wsc 3/2/4.
[78] *Rep. Som. Cong. Union* (1896).
[79] S.R.O., D/D/Ca 266.
[80] Ibid. D/P/stogm 13/2/4.
[81] Inf. from Mr. J. C. Duddridge.
[82] *Educ. of Poor Digest*, H.C. 244 (1819), ix (2).
[83] *Co. Gaz. Dir.* (1840); S.R.O., tithe award.
[84] *Western Flying Post*, 5 Oct. 1812, cited in *Som. Co. Herald*, 15 Jul. 1944.
[85] *Educ. of Poor Digest*, H.C. 224 (1819), ix (2).

[86] *Ann. Rep. B. & W. Dioc. Assoc. S.P.C.K.* (1825–6).
[87] *Educ. Enq. Abstract*, H.C. 62 (1835), xlii; *Co. Gaz. Dir.* (1840); Nat. Soc. *Inquiry, 1846–7*, Som. 16–17.
[88] *Kelly's Dir. Som.* (1906); S.R.O., DD/EDS (C/1404); ibid. D/P/stogm 18/7/2; ibid. C/E 28; Char. Com. files.
[89] S.R.O., *Schs. Lists*; ibid. C/E S/211.
[90] *Co. Gaz. Dir.* (1840); *Slater's Dir. Som.* (1852–3); S.R.O., tithe award: P.R.O., H.O. 107/1920.
[91] *P.O. Dir. Som.* (1859); Morris & Co., *Dir. Som.* (1872).
[92] *15th Rep. Com. Char.* 456; S.R.O., D/D/Ca 151.
[93] *Kelly's Dir. Som.* (1910); Char. Com. files.
[94] *Kelly's Dir. Som.* (1939).
[95] Inf. from Miss J. E. May, parish clerk.
[96] S.R.O., D/P/stogm 17/1/1.
[97] Ibid.; *Char. Don.* H.C. 511 (1816), xvi; *15th Rep. Com. Char.* 454.
[98] S.R.O., D/P/stogm 17/5/1; *Kelly's Dir. Som.* (1939).
[99] Char. Com. files; inf. from Miss May.
[1] This article was completed in 1981.
[2] S.R.O. tithe award; ibid. DD/BR/ely.
[3] *Census*, 1881, 1891.

It is roughly trapezoid in shape and measures 2 km. in each direction. The south-eastern boundary follows the Stowey stream.[4]

Most of the land is below the 91 m. contour, but the village lies at the western end of the parish where the land rises gradually to 137 m. Castle Hill rises to 110 m. in the west and Pinnacle Hill to 97 m. to the north-east.[5] Much of the parish lies on Keuper marl with a broad band of gravel along the stream. Castle Hill is composed of Ilfracombe slates and grits and the extreme southern edge of the parish lies on sandstone.[6] Marl was dug in the Middle Ages and quarries were established by the mid 18th century.[7] In 1758 and 1759 licences were granted for mining on land in the west end of the parish near Bincombe.[8] The Stowey stream flows down from Bincombe and formerly powered a mill, supplied a tannery, and ran along St. Mary's Street providing the village with water. From 1887 the supply came from springs in the grounds of Castle Hill House.[9]

The name Stowey derives from the 'stone way', part of the Anglo-Saxon 'herpath' or military road which crossed the river Parrett at Combwich and ran through Over Stowey parish and across the Quantocks to Exmoor.[10] The alternative names of Nether and Market Stowey, the latter used in 1795,[11] distinguish it from Over Stowey. East of the village lay a settlement called Budley,[12] where the way from Stowey to Fiddington crossed an ancient route between Spaxton and Stogursey. The township, whose church may have been adopted by Nether Stowey,[13] was still in existence in the 13th century and the name continued to be used for land in the eastern end of the parish until the 16th century.[14] That part of the parish suffered further depopulation in the 19th century and several farms, cottages, and a mill have been lost since 1839.[15]

Strips of land surviving south and west of the village in 1839 and still visible in 1981 were probably the remains of the medieval North and South fields.[16] A small piece of common at Redburrow, west of the village, had been divided by the mid 18th century between the manor farm and the glebe.[17] In 1839 the parish had less than 10 a. of woodland;[18] none was recorded in 1905[19] and less than 1 ha. in 1976.[20]

A park was mentioned in 1222;[21] in 1248 Philip de Columbers was granted a park with free warren in his demesnes.[22] The park was stocked with deer in 1295,[23] and in the 16th century or earlier was divided between the red deer park and the fallow deer park.[24] The two together were said to be 3 miles in circumference in 1569.[25] By 1620 the red deer park (172 a.) had been divided into closes and by the 18th century the entire park had been converted into fields.[26] The park covered a rectangular area stretching from the northern to the southern boundary of the parish between the village on the west and the former Spaxton–Stogursey road on the east. There were deer leaps on the north and west sides.[27]

The Bridgwater–Watchet road was turnpiked by the Bridgwater trust as far as the middle of St. Mary's Street in 1759[28] and westward beyond that point by the Minehead trust when it was enlarged in 1765.[29] A tollhouse survives in St. Mary's Street. Ancient routes to Fiddington and Stogursey are followed by modern footpaths, the first described in 1807 as the former market road to Bridgwater.[30] Other roads lead to Stogursey from the north end of Lime Street, and to Taunton from South Lane. The course of the main road east of the village has been altered many times since the 18th century, and in 1968 a bypass was built north-east of the village.[31] Plans in the 1880s and 1899 to build railways through Nether Stowey were abandoned.[32]

The village forms a Y of three main streets: St. Mary's Street (Fore Street in 1851) to the east, leading to the church, and Lime Street, so named by 1591, were part of the Bridgwater–Watchet road until the bypass was built in 1968, and Castle Street, recorded in 1477, led to the castle at the west end of the village.[33] The junction of the three streets formed the market place where the medieval high cross probably stood and there was later a market house. The west end of St. Mary's Street was known as High Street in 1547 and the borough street in 1647.[34] Part of the village may have been a planted settlement, for a borough had been established by 1225.[35] Burgage plots had been laid out in the centre of the village by the early 14th century,[36] the burgesses holding small paddocks and orchards along the edges of the adjoining open fields.[37]

Leland described Stowey as 'a poor village'.[38] No. 30 Castle Street survives from the later Middle Ages;[39] most of the remaining houses in the central area, forming terraces of two-storeyed buildings opening directly on the street, have fronts of the 18th

[4] O.S. Map 1/25,000, ST 13, 14, 23, 24 (1959, 1962 edn.).
[5] Ibid. 1/50,000, sheets 181–2 (1974 edn.).
[6] Geol. Surv. Map 1", drift, sheet 295 (1956 edn.).
[7] S.R.O., DD/SAS (C/1207); DD/AH 65/2, 66/11; ibid. tithe award; Mrs. Henry Sandford, *Thomas Poole and his Friends* (1888), 171.
[8] S.R.O., DD/X/HEA; J. Hamilton and J. Lawrence, *Men and Mining in the Quantocks* (1970), *passim*; Collinson, *Hist. Som.* iii. 550.   [9] S.R.O., DD/PLE 100.
[10] Ibid. DD/X/BOA; Ekwall, *Eng. Place-Names*, 427.
[11] S.R.O., D/D/Rm 1.
[12] *Proc. Som. Arch. Soc.* cxxv. 125–6.
[13] Below, church.
[14] *V.C.H. Som.* i. 462; *Cal. Pat. 1292–1301*, 450; *S.R.S.* xvii, p. 121; P.R.O., C 142/142, no. 132; *Proc. Som. Arch. Soc.* cxxv. 125–6.
[15] S.R.O., tithe award; O.S. Map 1", sheet 75 (1809 edn.); O.S. Map 1/25,000, ST 24 (1959 edn.); *Som. Co. Herald*, 28 Oct. 1966.
[16] S.R.O., tithe award; ibid. DD/AH 65/4, 8; O.S. Map 1/25,000, ST 13 (1962 edn.).
[17] Ibid. D/P/n. sty 3/1/2; ibid. DD/SAS (C/1207).
[18] Ibid. tithe award.
[19] Statistics supplied by the then Bd. of Agric. 1905.

[20] Min. of Agric., Fisheries, and Food, agric. returns 1976.
[21] *S.R.S.* lvii. 26.
[22] *Cal. Chart. R. 1226–57*, 330.
[23] *Cal. Close, 1288–96*, 467.
[24] P.R.O., C 143/423, no. 11; Leland, *Itin.* ed. Toulmin Smith, i. 164.
[25] *S.R.S.* xx. 180.
[26] S.R.O., DD/NW 67; DD/AH 37/3; DD/SAS (C/1207).
[27] Ibid. tithe award.
[28] 32 Geo. II, c. 40.
[29] 5 Geo. III, c. 93.
[30] S.R.O., DD/AH 24/6.
[31] Ibid. DD/SAS (C/1207); ibid. tithe award; M. A. Aston and R. H. Leach, *Historic Towns in Som.* 110.
[32] S.R.O., DD/X/HEA; DD/AH 17/13, 22/13; ibid. Q/RUp 521.
[33] Ibid. DD/AH 37/4, 65/8; P.R.O., HO 107/1924.
[34] S.R.O., D/P/stogs 17/7/1, 15.
[35] Below, borough.
[36] *Cal. Inq. p.m.* iv, p. 256.
[37] S.R.O., DD/AH 65/2, 4; B.L. Add. Ch. 12966–72.
[38] Leland, *Itin.* ed. Toulmin Smith, i. 164.
[39] S.R.O., DD/V Bwr 22.1.

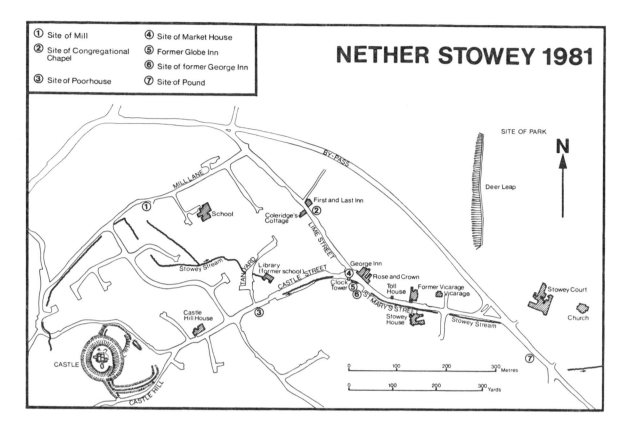

① Site of Mill	④ Site of Market House
② Site of Congregational Chapel	⑤ Former Globe Inn
	⑥ Site of former George Inn
③ Site of Poorhouse	⑦ Site of Pound

NETHER STOWEY 1981

or early 19th century in various materials including brick, roughcast, and stucco. The largest houses are in the wide centre sections of Castle and St. Mary's streets. Thomas Poole's house in Castle Street is a seven-bayed house of the 18th century, and there are several houses of similar date in St. Mary's Street including one of six bays.[40] In the centre of the village is the former Globe inn, now the Clock House, an early 19th-century stucco building with a flat-topped portico. The clock tower which dominates the central area was built in 1897 and restored in 1969.[41] Lime Street consists of small terraced houses with the remains of courts. There are several old cottages interspersed with later houses on Castle Hill. Castle Hill House, one of the few detached houses in the village, has a south range of the 17th century. It was remodelled c. 1800 when new windows were put in and additions, including a staircase hall, were made on the north side of the house. A coach house was built to the north-east in the mid 19th century. The west end of the house was demolished in the mid 20th century and a single-storeyed extension has been built on its site. Stowey House, formerly Stowey Farm,[42] at the east end of St. Mary's Street is a large E-shaped 16th-century house. Residential development in the 1960s and 1970s has taken place in the north-west and in the south.

The George inn mentioned in 1616[43] was a building of the 16th century or earlier on the south side of St. Mary's Street, and had a bowling green and a fives wall.[44] It had closed by 1781 and was rebuilt in 1843 as a private house, which retained a yard of decorated cobbling.[45] A new George inn had opened by 1804, probably on its present site; in 1899 and 1906 it had assembly rooms where theatrical entertainments were given.[46] The Crown, from 1687 the Rose and Crown, also existed in the early 17th century, when the poet John Taylor (1580–1653) complained of its bad service.[47] The George and the Rose and Crown were both in business at the centre of the village in 1981. The Swan was recorded from 1647 to 1740, but by 1743 it had been renamed the Globe.[48] It was the meeting place of the Dean's peculiar court and of the local magistrates, and closed c. 1850;[49] the building survives as the Clock House. The Globe's name was transferred c. 1894 to a public house in Castle Street which closed c. 1964.[50] The Three Mariners was named in 1691 and closed c. 1786.[51] The First and Last, first recorded by name in 1871,[52] was still in business in 1981 at the north end of Lime Street.[53] Coleridge's Cottage, opposite the First and Last, was a public house for a time, and the Bakers Arms was recorded in Castle Street in 1871 and 1881.[54]

A friendly society for working women was founded

[40] Ibid. DD/AH 66/27.
[41] Pevsner, *South and West Som.* 252; plaque on tower.
[42] Described as a capital messuage in 1620 and 1732: S.R.O., DD/NW 67; DD/AH 16/7.   [43] Ibid. DD/DT.
[44] Ibid. DD/AH 66/27; Taunton Castle, Pigott Colln.
[45] S.R.O., Q/REl Williton.
[46] Ibid. Q/RL; *Kelly's Dir. Som.* (1899, 1906).
[47] Devon R.O. 49/9/54/41; *D.N.B.*; *Som. Co. Herald*, 7 Feb. 1925.
[48] S.R.O., D/P/stogs 17/7/15; ibid. Q/SR 104; ibid. DD/BR/py 115; D/D/Pd 1.

[49] Ibid. Q/REl Williton; Q/RL; ibid. D/D/Bg 69; D/D/Pd 1; P.R.O., HO 107/1924; J. R. Hamilton and J. Lawrence, *Men and Mining in the Quantocks*, 24.
[50] S.R.O., D/D/Bg 69; Q/R elect. reg.; *Kelly's Dir. Som.* (1894).
[51] S.R.O., Q/REl Williton; ibid. DD/AH 19/4.
[52] Ibid. Q/RL.
[53] P.R.O., RG 10/2380.
[54] B. Lawrence, *Quantock Country* (1952), 172; Taunton Castle, Tite Colln.; P.R.O., RG 10/2380; RG 11/2371.

c. 1807 by Thomas Poole.[55] The society was wound up *c.* 1975 but the annual service and procession survive.[56] The Nether Stowey friendly society was established in 1839 and met in the Rose and Crown. The society was dissolved in 1912.[57] Poole also started the Stowey Book Society in 1793.[58] Until 1899 or later the Mutual Improvement Society maintained coffee and reading rooms.[59]

In 1377 there were 63 taxpayers in Nether Stowey.[60] There were 226 people recorded in the borough in 1667 with a further 131 in Bincombe tithing, part of which was in Nether Stowey parish.[61] In 1791 there were 106 houses in the village[62] and in 1801 the population of the parish was 586. The population rose rapidly during the early 19th century and reached a peak of 876 in 1861. By 1901 numbers had fallen to 581 but the total rose sharply from 688 in 1961 to 1,031 in 1971.[63]

Some inhabitants were involved in Lord Audley's rebellion in 1497 and were heavily fined.[64] Local men including members of the Walker family suffered for their loyalty to the king.[65]

Robert Parsons, the Jesuit, was born in Nether Stowey in 1546, the son of a blacksmith, and was assisted in his education by the vicar, John Hayward.[66] Thomas Poole (1765–1837), a self-educated tanner, was not only responsible for setting up the school and other local institutions, but also gathered around him at Stowey a circle of literary and scientific visitors including Samuel Taylor Coleridge, who lived for a while in Lime Street, the Wordsworths, Sir Humphry Davy, Robert Southey, Charles Lamb, and Thomas Wedgwood.[67] Samuel Grose (1791–1866), designer of a steam pumping engine, was born in Nether Stowey while his father was managing the Dodington copper mines.[68]

MANOR AND OTHER ESTATE. In 1066 Earl Harold, Alwi Banneson, and two thegns, Oswerd and Ailward, shared the estate called Stowey, but in 1086 the whole was held by Alfred d'Epaignes. Oswerd and Ailward continued as Alfred's undertenants, but Alwi's land was held by Robert and Herbert.[69] Alfred's daughter Isabel married Robert de Chandos (d. 1120) and was followed by her son Walter (d. by 1156) and Walter's daughter Maud, wife of Philip de Columbers (I) (d. *c.* 1185). Maud was returned in 1212 as holding *STOWEY* of the

king in chief as the head of an honor of 10 fees.[70]

Maud was succeeded in the manor of *NETHER STOWEY* by her son Philip de Columbers (II) (d. *c.* 1216), her grandson Philip (III) (d. 1257), and her great-grandson Philip (IV) (d. 1262).[71] When Philip died his estates, including Stowey, passed successively to his eldest son Philip (V) Columbers (d. 1277), and to his second son John (d. 1306).[72] John was succeeded by his son Philip (VI) (d. 1342), whose wife's sister, Joan Martin, married Nicholas Audley, Lord Audley. Philip made Joan's son, James Audley, Lord Audley, his eventual successor by settling his estates on his wife, Eleanor (d. 1343), and her heirs.[73] James, Lord Audley, died in 1386 and was succeeded by his son Nicholas (d. 1391), and then by Nicholas's wife Elizabeth.[74] Elizabeth was followed on her death in 1400 by two heirs, Nicholas's sister Margaret (d. 1411), wife of Sir Roger Hillary, and John Tuchet (d. 1408), later Lord Audley, grandson of another sister, Joan.[75]

Margaret was childless and Lord Audley's son James (d. 1459) succeeded to the whole estate.[76] James was followed by his son John (d. 1490) and John's son James, Lord Audley (d. 1497).[77] James was executed in 1497 and the escheated manor was leased to Sir Richard Pudsey (d. 1499) and later to John Bourchier, Lord Fitzwarren, brother-in-law of the attainted Lord Audley.[78] In 1512 John Tuchet (d. 1557), son of James, was restored to his father's land and title and in 1535 he settled Nether Stowey on himself and his wife with remainder to his son George and George's son Henry.[79] John Tuchet the younger, John's half-brother, claimed the estate under his father's settlement of 1492.[80] His claims passed to his brother James who sold the estate to Edward Seymour, earl of Hertford, later duke of Somerset, in 1538.[81] Audley was forced to give up the manor because of Somerset's 'great power' and the duke continued to hold Nether Stowey until his attainder in 1552.[82] Humphrey Colles leased the estate from the Crown in 1552 but in the same year the manor was granted to Sir Edward Seymour, eldest son of the duke of Somerset.[83] It reverted to the Crown by exchange in 1553, and was immediately granted back to Lord Audley.[84] Audley was succeeded in 1557 by his son George (d. 1560) and George by his son Henry (d. 1563).[85] Henry was followed by his son George, earl of Castlehaven (d. 1617), and George's son Mervyn, earl of

[55] Sandford, *Thos. Poole*, 188; S.R.O., DD/AH 63/7.
[56] *Som. Co. Herald*, 24 Jun. 1966; inf. from Mr. A. Tyler, Nether Stowey.
[57] M. Fuller, *West-Country Friendly Socs.* 138.
[58] Sandford, *Thos. Poole*, 44.
[59] *P.O. Dir. Som.* (1861); *Kelly's Dir. Som.* (1883, 1899).
[60] *S. & D. N. & Q.* xxix. 12.
[61] S.R.O., DD/WY 34.
[62] Collinson, *Hist. Som.* iii. 550.
[63] *Census*, 1801–1971.
[64] B.L. Royal MS. 14 B. vii.
[65] *Cal. Cttee. for Compounding*, ii. 1430; iv. 3091.
[66] *D.N.B.*
[67] Ibid.; Sandford, *Thos. Poole, passim.*
[68] *Som. Co. Herald*, 19 Nov. 1942.
[69] *V.C.H. Som.* i. 512–13; *Proc. Som. Arch. Soc.* cxxv. 124–5; *Dom. Bk. Som.* ed. C. and F. Thorn (1980), 364–5.
[70] Sanders, *Eng. Baronies*, 67; *Red Bk. Exch.* (Rolls Ser.), i. 63, 231; *Bk. of Fees*, i. 83.
[71] Sanders, *Eng. Baronies*, 67; *Cal. Inq. p.m.* i, pp. 145–6; S.R.O., DD/AH 60/10.
[72] *Cal. Inq. p.m.* i, pp. 145–6; ii, p. 133; iv, p. 256; *Close R.* 1261–4, 89–90; *Feud. Aids*, iv. 274.
[73] *Feud. Aids*, iv. 346; Sanders, *Eng. Baronies*, 67; *Cal.*

Pat. 1317–21, 335; 1334–8, 347; *S.R.S.* xiv, p. 163; xxii. 79; *Cal. Inq. p.m.* viii, pp. 268, 271–2; *Cal. Close*, 1343–6, 35. Philip's brother Stephen renounced his claim: *S.R.S.* extra ser. 328.
[74] *Cal. Inq. p.m.* xvi, pp. 73–4, 433; *Cal. Close*, 1385–9, 72; 1389–92, 396.
[75] *Cal. Pat.* 1391–6, 272, 369; *S.R.S.* extra ser. 329–30; xvii. 209; P.R.O., C 137/26, no. 56.
[76] *S.R.S.* extra ser. 330; *Cal. Pat.* 1401–5, 104; *Cal. Close*, 1405–9, 333; 1409–13, 160–1; P.R.O., C 136/84, no. 67; C 137/73, no. 47; C 137/84, no. 36.
[77] *Cal. Inq. p.m. Hen. VII*, i, p. 247.
[78] P.R.O., C 142/14, no. 69; *Cal. Inq. p.m. Hen. VII*, iii, p. 445; *L. & P. Hen. VIII*, i (1), pp. 121, 163; *Cal. Pat.* 1494–1509, 201, 229, 276; *S.R.S.* xxi, p. 26.
[79] 3 Hen. VIII, c. 17; 27 Hen. VIII, c. 31.
[80] *L. & P. Hen. VIII*, viii, p. 60; *Cal. S.P. Dom.* 1601–3, 533.
[81] P.R.O., C 54/417, no. 10.
[82] *S.R.S.* extra ser. 333; P.R.O., E 318/1929.
[83] P.R.O., E 315/224/211; E 318/1929.
[84] Ibid. E 318/1394; E 318/1930.
[85] Ibid. C 142/114, no. 55; C 142/128, no. 65; C 142/140, no. 159; ibid. WARD 9/450; *Cal. S.P. Dom.* 1601–3, 533.

Castlehaven. Mervyn sold the lordship to Angel Grey in 1627 after disposing of some of the land.[86]

Angel Grey was succeeded by his son George (d. by 1676) and George's daughter Christiana (d. 1747), wife of Edward Topp. Christiana's daughter and heir Susanna married Robert Everard of Spaxton. In 1745 Everard settled the manor on Robert Balch (d. 1779) of Bridgwater, husband of Everard's daughter and heir Susanna.[87] Balch was succeeded by his sons Robert Everard (d. 1799) and George (d. 1814), and by his daughter Christiana (d. 1824).[88] Christiana devised the estate to Henry Harvey who in 1838 sold some land and the lordship to Sir Peregrine Acland and the remaining land to Henry Labouchere, later Lord Taunton, whose estate, centred on Over Stowey, was afterwards called the manor of Over and Nether Stowey.[89] The lordship of Nether Stowey descended in the Acland-Hood family but was not mentioned when the estate was dispersed in 1952.[90]

Stowey Court lies east of the village beside the church. Leland referred in 1542 to 'a goodly manor place of the Lord Audley's standing exceedingly pleasantly'. The house was being enlarged in stone when Audley was executed in 1497.[91] It was leased by the Crown to Lord Fitzwarren in 1510 and to Humphrey Colles in 1552.[92] It is supposed to have suffered by fire during the Civil War when it was used as a royal garrison.[93] All that survives of the late medieval house is some of the walling of the courtyard between the house and the church, and two gateways in its southern side. The southern part of the present house was built probably in the later 16th century[94] and has a main east-west range of two storeys with attics and a short cross wing. The entrance was on the north side, and in the angle between the ranges on the south side there was a stair turret. Adjacent to, but not aligned with, the west end of the main range a row of cottages incorporates part of another 16th-century domestic building which may be older than the main house.

In the 18th century several rooms were redecorated and a kitchen block was built a short distance north of the cross wing. Additions at various times in the 19th century converted the intervening space into an entrance hall and made other service rooms. In the mid 20th century the house was divided into two dwellings and in 1981 a major restoration was beginning.

The outbuildings include a 16th-century stable just outside the south-east corner of the courtyard,

and a two-storeyed brick summer house of the mid 18th century. The layout of the 18th century gardens can still be traced and the raised walk, which forms the north side of the courtyard, and three large fish-ponds survive.

Two estates, called Bodeslege and Lege, may both represent a later holding called *BUDLEY*. The first was held by Winegod the priest in 1066 and by Roger de Courcelles from Glastonbury Abbey in 1086.[95] The Glastonbury lordship is not mentioned again. Lege was held by Dunn in 1066 but in 1086 by Alfred d'Epaignes and of him by Hugh.[96] During the 12th century Roger de Paris gave 1 a. of land at Budley to the church of Stowey, a gift confirmed by Maud de Chandos, lady of the manor of Nether Stowey.[97] Matthew de Paris appears to have had property at Budley in 1299,[98] and a Matthew Paris was described as of Budley before 1443.[99]

Edward Walker (d. 1565) held property in East Budley, probably including Roobies farm, and he is said to have had a lease of the castle and part of the park c. 1528.[1] He was succeeded by his son John (d. before 1635), John's son Edward (d. 1636), and Edward's son John (d. 1658).[2] A younger brother of John, Sir Edward (1612–77), was secretary to Charles I and Charles II, Garter King of Arms, and an author.[3] John Walker was followed by his son Edward (d. 1682) and Edward's son John.[4] John died without issue in 1718 leaving his estates to his widow Elizabeth.[5] She survived until 1739 when Roobies passed for his life to her late husband's cousin Sir Hugh Clopton of Stratford-on-Avon (Warws.), and on his death in 1752 to his nephew Edward Clopton of Clopton (Warws.).[6] Edward (d. 1753) was succeeded by his daughter Frances who, with her husband John Parthewicke, sold the estate to Robert Everard Balch in 1758.[7] The farm descended with the manor of Nether Stowey until 1952 when Roobies was sold to the tenant.[8]

Roobies Farm, formerly known as Rowbart's or Rowbear, was described as a capital messuage in 1774.[9] The house is of the 17th century, but has since been greatly altered.

CASTLE. The castle at Nether Stowey, on a steep outlier of the Quantocks west of the village, was built probably in the early 12th century. It was the *caput* of an honor of 10 fees which descended with the manor and was recorded until 1624.[10] Plud Farm in Kilton, held of Nether Stowey manor, was called

[86] P.R.O., CP 25(2)/345/7 Jas. I. Trin.; CP 25(2)/479/3 Chas. I Mich.; S.R.O., DD/SAS (C/96) 5; DD/AH 20/5; DD/X/GV; DD/NW 67; Cal. S.P. Dom. 1611–18, 451.
[87] P.R.O., CP 25(2)/593/1657 Mich.; S.R.O., DD/AH 16/7; DD/SAS(C/96)5; Hist. MSS. Com. 17, *14th Rep. VI*, H.L. p. 56; *Visit. Dorset, 1623* (Harl. Soc. xx), 48; *Addenda to Visit. Dorset, 1623*, ed. F. T. Colby and S. P. Rylands, 29; M. I. in Nether Stowey ch.
[88] S.R.O., DD/AH 16/7.
[89] Ibid. 3/2, 16/3, 19/2; Burke, *Land. Gent.* (1914), 1764.
[90] S.R.O., DD/X/HUX; DD/AH 51/7; above, West Quantoxhead.
[91] Leland, *Itin.* ed. Toulmin Smith, i. 164; S.R.O., DD/AH 21/2.
[92] *L. & P. Hen. VIII*, i (1), p. 163; *Som. Wills*, ed. Brown, i. 33; P.R.O., E 315/224/211.
[93] S.R.O., D/P/n. sty 2/1/1.
[94] Plate facing p. 156, which seems to misrepresent some features. A datestone (1588) is reset on the 19th-century doorway and may be original.
[95] *V.C.H. Som.* i. 462; *Proc. Som. Arch. Soc.* cxxv. 125–6. [96] *V.C.H. Som.* i. 513.

[97] *H.M.C. Wells*, i. 432.
[98] *Cal. Pat.* 1292–1301, 450. Matt. Paris was taxed in Bincombe tithing in 1327: *S.R.S.* iii. 165.
[99] *Cal. Close*, 1441–7, 155.
[1] P.R.O., C 142/142, no. 132; S.R.O., DD/AH 21/2.
[2] *Som. Wills*, ed. Brown, iii. 23–4; *S.R.S.* xx. 168; P.R.O., C 142/142, no. 132; S.R.O., DD/SF 4008; ibid. D/P/n. sty 2/1/1. [3] *D.N.B.*
[4] *Cal. Cttee. for Compounding*, iv. 3091; S.R.O., DD/DT; DD/WY 34; DD/AH 16/7, 19/4, 21/3.
[5] MSS. in possession of Mr. and Mrs. M. Hill, Farm Estate, Fiddington: will, John Walker.
[6] *Som. Wills*, ed. Brown, v. 80; S.R.O., DD/AH 16/7, 20/5, 34/12; MSS. in possession of Mr. and Mrs. M. Hill: pedigree.
[7] MSS. in possession of Mr. and Mrs. Hill: will, Edw. Clopton; S.R.O., DD/AH 16/7. Owners of the estate were required to maintain the Walker tombs at Nether Stowey.
[8] S.R.O., DD/AH 16/7; DD/X/HUX.
[9] Ibid. DD/AH 16/7.
[10] *Red Bk. Exch.* (Rolls Ser.), i. 231; *Proc. Som. Arch. Soc.* cxxv. 124–5; P.R.O., C 142/509, no. 190.

the Constable's House until the late 16th century and may have been connected with the constable of the castle.[11] The castle had been abandoned by 1485 when the site was let for pasture.[12]

The castle comprises a motte and two baileys. On the motte are the foundations of a small rectangular stone keep with inner dividing walls and a smaller outbuilding, possibly an entrance. The steep baileys, a triangular one on the east and another on the north-east, are divided by a ditch, but the surrounding banks and ditches have been partly quarried away.[13] The site slopes very steeply to the north and west. It was known as Castle Hill or Old Castle in 1620 when it was sold to Charles Steynings of Holnicote in Selworthy.[14]

BOROUGH. A borough was established possibly in 1157-8 when Philip de Columbers (I) paid 10s. *de uno burgriht*; by 1225 the borough answered separately at the eyre.[15] It was described as a free borough in 1274, when the lord's steward was accused of offences infringing the borough charter, referred to as ancient, including seizure of burgages.[16] The lord in 1280 claimed assize of bread and of ale in the borough time out of mind, and in 1306 the barony of Nether Stowey included 26 burgages.[17] In 1485 the borough produced an income from burgage rents worth over £4, pasture of the castle, lardersilver, and court profits, but no tolls.[18] A free burgage was held as of the manor in 1501.[19]

The extent of the borough in the Middle Ages is uncertain but probably coincided with the later borough tithing which covered the north-western part of the parish.[20] By the 18th century the borough included the village, the mill, Castle Hill, the glebe and other lands in the north-west, Blindwell and other lands along the Taunton road, and Portery meadow in Over Stowey parish. The borough was still a separate tithing in the mid 19th century.[21]

ECONOMIC HISTORY. The western part of the later parish of Nether Stowey was included in a group of Domesday estates called Stowey, of which one became the parish of Dodington[22] and others extended into Over Stowey parish.[23] The eastern part of Nether Stowey parish may have been the Domesday estates of Budley and Lege.[24] The total

demesne holding of the Stowey estates excluding Dodington amounted to nearly 7 hides with 4½ ploughteams in comparison with just over 1¼ hide occupied by 14 villeins and 11 bordars with 3 ploughs. Budley and Lege had no demesne holdings, 9 bordars sharing the land. The Stowey estates together included 100 a. of pasture and extensive woodland on the Quantocks.

Land holdings in the two open arable fields were partially consolidated by the 15th century[25] and the demesne was farmed by 1492.[26] The income of the manor was £30 19s. 10d. from agricultural rents in 1485.[27] From the later Middle Ages there was probably a concentration on cloth production and there is very little surviving evidence for farming. A flax pit was recorded in 1513, a dyehouse in 1517, and a tucker's rack in 1571.[28] During the late 16th and early 17th century weavers, clothiers, clothworkers, fullers, shearmen, and mercers worked in the village.[29] Racks were standing east of the castle by the 18th century,[30] when serge was being woven in the parish,[31] and silk was manufactured in the 19th century.[32]

Potters in 1275 paid 20s. for the right to work in Nether Stowey.[33] A kiln and potsherds of the 13th century were found in Portery field, south of the castle in Over Stowey parish, in 1969.[34] By the early 17th century a potter held land beside the Stogursey road,[35] and a kiln in use between c. 1550 and 1620 was discovered in 1968.[36]

A slaughterhouse in operation by 1593[37] produced meat for the market and skins for local tanners and glovers.[38] The Poole family was tanning from at least the early 18th century[39] and Thomas Poole (d. 1837) extended his father's tannery and built a bark-house and mill north of Castle Street.[40] There were at least four glovers at work in the 17th century.[41] Candlemaking and malting were also practised in the 18th century,[42] and there were three malthouses in 1839.[43]

By the 17th century the commercial importance of the market attracted business from Aisholt and Stogursey.[44] A mob converged on the village in a dispute over corn in 1795[45] and there was unrest over corn prices in 1801 involving a hundred people from Stowey. The magistrates ordered the overseers of the parishes in the area to provide a stock of food for the poor. Some farmers agreed to reduce their prices but there were accusations that grain was being

[11] S.R.O., DD/AH 36/1.
[12] P.R.O., SC 6/1116/3; SC 6/Hen. VII/1065; S.R.O., DD/AH 11/9-10.
[13] V.C.H. Som. ii. 515; O.S. Map 1/2,500, ST 1839 (1975 edn.); above, plate facing p. 140.
[14] S.R.O., DD/NW 67.
[15] Pipe R. 1156-8 (Rec. Com.), 98, 121; S.R.S. xi, p. 52.
[16] Rot. Hund. (Rec. Com.), ii. 127.
[17] Plac. de Quo Warr. (Rec. Com.), 690; Cal. Inq. p.m. iv, p. 256.
[18] P.R.O., SC 6/1116/2.
[19] Cal. Inq. p.m. Hen. VII, ii, p. 399.
[20] S.R.O., DD/BR/py 115; DD/AH 65/4, 7; P.R.O., SC 6/1116/2.
[21] S.R.O., Q/REl Williton; ibid. DD/TB 12/9.
[22] Above, Dodington.
[23] V.C.H. Som. i. 512-13.
[24] Ibid. i. 462, 513; Proc. Som. Arch. Soc. cxxv. 124-6.
[25] S.R.O., DD/AH 65/2, 4; B.L. Add. Ch. 12966-72.
[26] P.R.O., SC 6/Hen. VII/1065.
[27] Ibid. SC 6/1116/2.
[28] S.R.O., DD/AH 11/9, 11/10; ibid. D/P/n. sty 3/1/4.
[29] Ibid. DD/SAS(C/96); DD/SX 47/1-6; DD/AH 19/3, 37/8; ibid. Q/SR 106/32, 112/112; Devon R.O. 49/9/54/

[39]-41; Som. Wills, ed. Brown, iii. 78; S.R.S. lxv, pp. 38-9.
[30] S.R.O., DD/AH 66/27; ibid. tithe award.
[31] Ibid. DD/AH 35/18.
[32] Ibid. 63/6; ibid. D/P/n. sty 9/1/1; Robson's Dir. (1839).
[33] Rot. Hund. (Rec. Com.), ii. 127.
[34] Med. Archaeology, xv. 177; Aston and Leach, Historic Towns in Som. 110-14; S.R.O., tithe award, Over Stowey.
[35] S.R.O., DD/SAS (C/96).
[36] Aston and Leach, Historic Towns in Som. 110-14; Donyatt Research Group, Interim Report (1970); inf. from Mr. T. Pearson, Newcastle-upon-Tyne.
[37] S.R.O., DD/DT.
[38] Ibid. DD/AH 19/3; DD/WO 17/3.
[39] Ibid. DD/SAS (C/96).
[40] Sandford, Thos. Poole, 171; S.R.O., tithe award. The barkhouse was later converted to a dwelling.
[41] S.R.S. lxv, pp. 38-9; S.R.O., Q/SR 118/94.
[42] S.R.O., DD/AH 34/12, 35/20.
[43] Ibid. tithe award.
[44] S.R.S. lxv, pp. 38-9; S.R.O., Q/SR 104/34, 106/32, 143/6, 193/8.
[45] J. R. Hamilton and J. Lawrence, Men and Mining in the Quantocks, 23.

withheld from the market.[46] It was not easy for labourers to produce their own food; during the 1830s potato ground was let out by farmers at £8–£10 per acre. Wages, however, were slightly higher than average and piecework enabled men to earn up to 18s. a week in summer.[47]

In 1839 only half the farmland was arable and the rearing of cattle was clearly important.[48] The Stowey and Spaxton Cattle Plague Association was formed in the late 19th century.[49] The largest holdings in 1839 were Court farm (424 a.), Roobies farm (176 a.), Stowey farm (104 a. besides land in Over Stowey), and the glebe (51 a.). A further 8 holdings measured between 20 a. and 45 a., 19 between 3 a. and 20 a., and the remainder under 3 a.[50] In 1851 the tenants of Court and Stowey farms employed 30 and 15 labourers respectively. The remaining farmers had fewer than 5 employees.[51] In 1905 there were 612 a. of grass and 469 a. of arable.[52] By 1976 at least 367 ha. (880 a.) were under grass, and livestock included nearly 1,000 cattle, 1,485 pigs, and 1,375 sheep. Holdings remained small: only two measured over 50 ha. (120 a.), and specialized in dairying and rearing livestock.[53]

Clocks and watches were made at Nether Stowey during the late 18th and the 19th century. James Cole (d. 1808) made a clock for Enmore church and his sons James and Thomas were to become internationally renowned clock and watch makers, most of their work being done in London.[54] James Cole the younger made the Nether Stowey school clock in 1813 when he was only 15 years old. Watch making was continued by the Thristle family and Edward Browning.[55] Other tradesmen in the early 19th century included apothecaries and chemists, and in 1818 a surgeon's practice in the parish was sold.[56]

Of 155 families in the parish in 1821 there were 66 employed in agriculture and 72 in trade.[57] In 1851 the largest groups of non-agricultural workers were in the building trade and in the manufacture of clothing and shoes. There were also leatherworkers including a saddler, shopkeepers, blacksmiths, a silk throwster, a confectioner, a cooper, maltsters, a tallow chandler, and a straw-bonnet maker. Professional men included a surgeon, a solicitor, and an excise officer. Although the market had ceased by the late 19th century the retailers and craftsmen probably continued to serve the surrounding villages.[58] The increase in population in the 1960s and 1970s

has ensured the survival of a variety of shops and services in the village.

The Quantock Savings Bank was established in Nether Stowey in 1817 with agents in neighbouring parishes. It closed in 1884.[59] The building was an antique shop in 1981.

MARKET AND FAIR. In 1304 John de Columbers received a grant of a market on Tuesdays and a yearly fair on 7 and 8 September.[60] There were shambles south of the market place in 1608 and in the 1680s and 1690s sheep, corn, meat, and manufactured articles could be bought.[61] In 1713 the lord of the manor received 15s. from market rents.[62] A market house was built in the centre of the village, probably on the site of the medieval high cross, before the mid 18th century.[63] In 1791 it was an octagonal building with eight columns around a central stone pillar topped by a clock, a sundial, and a bell in a wooden belfry. The sundial was said to have been placed on the building by Sir Humphry Davy (1778–1829).[64] Another market house with a colonnade of seven bays was built over the pavement south of the market place c. 1810.[65] Both buildings were demolished in the late 19th century.[66] A market house and tolls were offered for sale with the manor in 1828 but did not form part of the conveyances to Sir Peregrine Acland and Henry Labouchere in 1838.[67] Tuesday and Saturday were market days in 1830 but the market had been discontinued by 1839.[68]

The fair, which existed in the late 17th century,[69] was held in the later 18th and the 19th century on 18 September.[70] In 1936 it was said to have had a long and uneventful history and to have ceased a generation earlier, probably before 1888.[71]

MILLS. In 1086 a mill on Alfred d'Epaigne's estate at Stowey paid 4d.,[72] and in 1275 the burgesses complained that their horses were taken when going to a mill outside the vill.[73] The manor mill was farmed for 20s. in 1485.[74] By 1560 there were two corn mills on the manor.[75] In 1620 Stowey mill was sold by Mervyn, earl of Castlehaven, to Charles Steynings with the mansion house later known as Stowey Farm.[76] A mill, possibly Stowey mill, was described as the town mill in 1691.[77] The mill appears to have been reconveyed to the lord of the manor before 1703. By 1760 it was ruinous and was let to a mill carpenter who was to repair it within

[46] Ibid. 23–4; S.R.O., DD/AH 59/12.
[47] V.C.H. Som. ii. 329–30.
[48] S.R.O., tithe award.
[49] Ibid. DD/X/HEA.
[50] Ibid. tithe award.
[51] P.R.O., HO 107/1924.
[52] Statistics supplied by the then Bd. of Agric. 1905.
[53] Min. of Agric., Fisheries, and Food, agric. returns 1976.
[54] S.R.O., DD/X/TYL 1; DD/AH 20/7.
[55] Ibid. DD/PLE 100; Robson's Dir. (1852–3); P.O. Dir. Som. (1875); Kelly's Dir. Som. (1883); P.R.O., HO 107/1924.
[56] S.R.O., DD/AH 19/1; 37/11; DD/BR/gd 11; ibid. tithe award; Robson's Dir. (1839).
[57] Census, 1821.
[58] P.R.O., HO 107/924.
[59] S.R.O., D/D/Bg 67; ibid. Q/R; P.O. Dir. Som. (1861, 1875); Kelly's Dir. Som. (1883); inf. from Mr. G. King, Lime St., Nether Stowey.
[60] Cal. Chart. R. 1300–26, 45.
[61] S.R.O., Q/SR 14/8, 118/95, 138/53, 143/5, 173/9, 193/8, 214/14; ibid. D/P/stogs 17/7/15.

[62] Ibid. DD/SAS PD 64.
[63] Ibid. DD/AH 65/4, 66/27.
[64] Collinson, Hist. Som. iii. 550; Som. Co. Herald, 7 May 1938; Taunton Castle, Pigott Colln.
[65] Plate facing p. 140; S.R.O., Q/REl Williton.
[66] Som. Co. Herald, 7 May 1938.
[67] S.R.O., DD/AH 3/2, 14/11.
[68] Pigott's Dir. Som. (1830); Robson's Dir. (1839).
[69] S.R.O., Q/SR 135/21.
[70] Owen, New Book of Fairs (1792); P.O. Dir. Som. (1861).
[71] Proc. Som. Arch. Soc. lxxxii. 147; Collinson, Hist. Som. iii. 550; Royal Com. on Market Rights and Tolls (1889).
[72] V.C.H. Som. i. 512–13.
[73] Rot. Hund. (Rec. Com.), ii. 127.
[74] P.R.O., SC 6/1116/2.
[75] Ibid. C 142/128, no. 65.
[76] S.R.O., DD/SOG 987; DD/BR/nf 1; DD/NW 67; deed in possession of J. S. Cox, St. Peter Port, Guernsey, 1969.
[77] S.R.O., DD/AH 19/4.

three years.[78] The mill lay on the Stowey stream north of the castle and was in use in 1839.[79] Milling ceased between 1872 and 1875,[80] and the site was occupied by a farmyard in 1981. A fragment of wall, the sluices, and the site of the mill pond survive. The pond was fed from a higher pond by the castle and both have been filled in. There was a mill on the Stowey stream in the east end of the parish in 1839 but milling had ceased by 1851 and no other trace has been found.[81]

LOCAL GOVERNMENT. The government of the parish was divided until the 19th century between the manor and the borough. By the early 16th century manor courts were held twice a year, and records survive from 1507 to 1522. The officers were a bailiff and an elected tithingman.[82] Borough courts were held twice a year in the late 15th and early 16th century. The borough was administered by a bailiff, a reeve, two constables, two aletasters, and two weighers of bread.[83] By the 18th century borough and manor jurisdictions were probably united.[84] Manor courts were held until c. 1842 but no records have been found.[85]

The parish was divided between two tithings, the borough in the west and the detached part of Bincombe in the east including Court farm and the parks, part of Stowey farm, Budley, and Roobies farm and its neighbours.[86]

By the 19th century the two constables were elected by the vestry.[87] Stocks were kept at the market place in the early 19th century[88] and the lockup was demolished between 1938 and 1948 to make way for a bus shelter.[89]

There were two churchwardens and two sidesmen in 1613.[90] The vestry employed an assistant overseer in 1825. There was a poorhouse by 1784; it stood at the west end of the village and was occupied by three families in 1839.[91] It was still known as the parish house in 1863 though not then owned by the parish.[92] Nether Stowey formed part of the Bridgwater poor-law union and from 1894 was part of the Bridgwater rural district. Since 1974 it has been in Sedgemoor district.[93]

CHURCH. A Domesday estate held by Winegod the priest[94] may be identified with the former settlement of Budley, east of the present church of Stowey.[95] The ownership of the estate by a priest,[96] the existence later of one and perhaps two dependent chapels, Dodington[97] and St. Michael's by the castle,[98] and claims to tithes in Otterhampton,[99] are characteristics of minster status. It was known by 1189 as the church of Stowey.[1] The living remained a sole cure until 1973, when it was united with the rectory of Over Stowey.[2]

Robert de Chandos (d. 1120) gave the second tithe (redecima) of his demesne at Stowey to Goldcliff Priory (Mon.)[3] which he founded in 1113 and which he later gave to the Norman abbey of Bec-Hellouin (Eure).[4] Walter de Chandos (d. c. 1166), Robert's son, gave 1 or 2 carucates of land in Stowey to Goldcliff.[5] Walter's daughter Maud de Chandos gave the church to Wells cathedral, a gift confirmed by the bishop, by the King in 1189, and by the pope in 1190.[6] Goldcliff Priory seems to have challenged Maud's gift, in 1201 beginning a plea against her concerning unspecified land in Somerset,[7] and she was witness to a compromise whereby the cathedral acknowledged the priory's right to the church in return for an annual pension of £2 to the cathedral.[8] Maud's agreement strongly suggests that the gift of Robert de Chandos had included the church as well as the tithes on his demesne. The pension was paid until 1560[9] or later, and Nether Stowey remained in the peculiar jurisdiction of the dean of Wells.[10]

Goldcliff's claim against Wells cathedral was successful in respect of tithes and second tithes, but it had to return to Philip de Columbers (III) in 1222 the land which Walter de Chandos had granted.[11] The possessions of Goldcliff Priory, as an alien house, were granted in 1441 to Tewkesbury Abbey (Glos.)[12] which, notwithstanding grants of 1451 and 1467 to Eton College (Bucks.),[13] remained in possession[14] until 1475, when they were granted to St. George's Chapel, Windsor (Berks.).[15] St. George's retained Nether Stowey rectory until 1719[16] or later. The rectory passed into the hands of the vicar of Nether Stowey, who was paying the land tax on it in 1766.[17] The rectory was commonly let at farm after 1335;[18] in 1462 the vicar, as tenant, held the corn and hay tithes of the parish, all the tithes of Dodington, tithes of wood and grazing in Lord Audley's park, and a barn and some land.[19] In 1562 the rectory was leased to Robert Dudley, earl of Leicester,[20] who in 1567 assigned the lease to George

[78] Ibid. DD/SX 47/7.
[79] Ibid. tithe award.
[80] Morris & Co. Dir. Som. (1872); P.O. Dir. Som. (1875).
[81] S.R.O., tithe award; P.R.O., HO 107/1924.
[82] Ibid. DD/AH 11/9–10; P.R.O., SC 6/Hen. VII/1065.
[83] P.R.O., SC 6/1116/2; SC 6/Hen. VII/1065; S.R.O., DD/AH 11/9–10, 65/2.
[84] S.R.O., DD/SAS PD 64.
[85] Pigott's Dir. Som. (1842).
[86] E. Dwelly, Hearth Tax Exemptions, ii. 198; Q/REl Williton.
[87] S.R.O., D/P/n. sty 9/1/1.
[88] Taunton Castle, Pigott Colln.
[89] Som. Co. Herald, 19 Jan. 1929, 4 June 1938; plaque on bus shelter.
[90] S.R.O., D/P/n. sty 3/1/1.
[91] Ibid. Q/REl Williton; ibid. D/P/n. sty 9/1/1; ibid. tithe award.
[92] Ibid. DD/AH 5/1.
[93] Youngs, Local Admin. Units, i. 438, 673, 676.
[94] V.C.H. Som. i. 462.
[95] Proc. Som. Arch. Soc. cxxv. 125.
[96] Cf. V.C.H. Som. iv. 191.

[97] Above, Dodington, church.
[98] Below.
[99] H.M.C. Wells, i. 40.   [1] Ibid. i. 41.
[2] Dioc. Dir.   [3] Dugdale, Mon. vi. 1022.
[4] D. Knowles and R. N. Hadcock, Medieval Relig. Hos. 67.
[5] Reg. Regum Anglo-Norm. iii, no. 373; Dugdale, Mon. vi. 1022.
[6] H.M.C. Wells, i. 41, 309, 435–6.
[7] Cur. Reg. R. ii. 40.
[8] H.M.C. Wells, i. 40.
[9] Ibid. 284.
[10] Tax. Eccl. (Rec. Com.), 199; V.C.H. Som. ii. 67.
[11] S.R.S. lvii. 26–7.
[12] Cal. Pat. 1441–6, 29; cf. Knowles and Hadcock, Medieval Relig. Hos. 67.
[13] Cal. Pat. 1446–52, 457; 1467–77, 48.
[14] St. George's Chapel, MS. XV. 53. 81A.
[15] Cal. Pat. 1467–77, 551.
[16] St. George's Chapel, MS. XV. 50. 3.
[17] S.R.O., Q/REl Williton.
[18] S.R.S. ix, p. 253; cf. ibid. i. 130.
[19] St. George's Chapel, MS. XV. 53. 81A.
[20] B.L. Harl. Ch. 79 F 23.

Sydenham of Combe Sydenham in Stogumber. The Sydenhams, who held the freehold during the Interregnum,[21] continued as lessees until 1716.[22]

An incumbent rector was recorded in the late 12th century,[23] and presumably the rectory was not appropriated when Maud de Chandos granted the church to Wells cathedral. Goldcliff Priory had evidently appropriated it by 1222 when it held the church, the tithes, and the second tithes.[24] A vicarage had been established by 1311, when the priory presented a vicar.[25] Later in the 14th century the Crown presented when the priory was in its hands because of the war with France,[26] and Tewkesbury Abbey presented in 1462, 1468, and 1473.[27] The Sydenhams presented vicars up to 1716 as lessees of the dean and canons of Windsor,[28] who presented at every vacancy from 1722,[29] and from 1973 were alternate patrons of the united benefice.[30]

In 1535 the vicarage was valued at £5 2s. 7d. net.[31] About 1668 it was assessed at c. £100,[32] and by the early 19th century was worth £400 a year.[33] In 1831 the net value was £334,[34] and was £455 in 1871.[35]

By 1535 the tithes said to belong to the vicarage were worth £5 9s. 3d.[36] The tithes of the parish, with moduses on ancient meadow and gardens and on cattle, all held by the vicar, were commuted for £300 in 1839.[37]

In 1535 land was worth 40s. to the vicarage.[38] By 1571 there were 52 a. attached to the living, more than half of which was let to Edward Walker.[39] By 1725 there were c. 63 a. of glebe,[40] the extra land probably former rectorial glebe. Some was sold in 1799[41] and in 1839 there were 51 a.[42] More had been sold by 1911, and in 1939 there were 47 a.[43]

The vicarage house was mentioned in 1461.[44] The site included a barn, garden, and orchard in 1571 and a hopyard in 1613.[45] The present Old Vicarage includes two rooms from a substantial late 17th-century building, one bearing the date 1681.[46] The house probably extended further south and southeast, and was of three-roomed plan with a detached kitchen.[47] Additions had been made by 1753[48] and a further block survives to the east close to the southern end, built in the late 18th century. In 1815 it was said to be a 'very good' house,[49] but further altera-

tions and additions were made in the early 19th century, probably for Benjamin Pope, including a new staircase hall and drawing room in the angle between the older buildings. By 1872, however, the house was thought inadequate. It was replaced in 1957 by a new house erected in the grounds.[50]

Paul Bushe, rector 1574–87, was non-resident and the parish was served by a curate.[51] Gregory Syndercombe, 1631–59, was ousted from his benefice in 1648 by Edward Bernard but bought back the living for £200 although Bernard kept a large part of the glebe.[52] Most of the 18th- and early 19th-century vicars were canons of Windsor and did not live in the parish.[53] Joseph Hunt, 1716–22, resigned to become master of Balliol College, Oxford.[54] During the 1720s communion was celebrated seven times a year and collections were taken for the poor or for the provision of books.[55] Henry William Majendie, vicar 1790–3, was later bishop of Chester (1800–9) and of Exeter (1809–30). His successor John Fisher, tutor to Edward Augustus, duke of Kent, and to Princess Charlotte, was later bishop of Exeter.[56] Fisher's successors William Langford (1796–1801) and Edward Northey (1801–20) were pluralists, and Langford was also a master at Eton.[57] John Keate, vicar 1820–4, was headmaster of Eton,[58] but during the early 19th century there were two services on Sunday taken by a resident curate.[59] Benjamin Pope, vicar 1824–71, was conduct at Eton;[60] he held two other livings and a minor canonry at Windsor in 1831, at a time when there was no curate in the parish.[61]

A church house was mentioned in 1691.[62]

The church of ST. MARY, so dedicated in the late 12th century,[63] comprises a chancel with north vestry, nave with north and south aisles and south porch, and western tower. The medieval church was a small building, with a nave of three bays, its last additions evidently dating from the 14th century.[64] The roodloft and screen survived until the 18th century.[65] A gallery was added before 1642.[66] Before 1722 the chancel was ceiled and wainscotted, and a vestry was built on its north side.[67] An attempt to enlarge the church in 1791 failed, but a long transept was built on the north side of the nave in 1814.[68]

[21] Lamb. Pal. MS. 917, f. 175.
[22] St. George's Chapel, MS. XV. 50. 3.
[23] H.M.C. Wells, i. 40.
[24] Above.
[25] S.R.S. i. 46.
[26] e.g. ibid. x, pp. 449, 513, 630.
[27] Ibid. xlix, p. 375; lii, pp. 16, 49.
[28] e.g. St. George's Chapel, MS. XV. 50. 6K.
[29] Ibid. Livings Bk. I. B.1*.
[30] Dioc. Dir.
[31] Valor Eccl. (Rec. Com.), i. 216.
[32] S.R.O., D/D/Vc 24.
[33] St. George's Chapel, MS. Livings Bk. I. B. 1*.
[34] Rep. Com. Eccl. Revenues, pp. 154–5.
[35] St. George's Chapel, MS. XVII. 35. 5.
[36] Valor Eccl. (Rec. Com.), i. 216.
[37] S.R.O., tithe award.
[38] Valor Eccl. (Rec. Com.), i. 216.
[39] S.R.O., D/P/n. sty 3/1/4. [40] Ibid. 3/1/2
[41] St. George's Chapel, MS. Livings Bk. I. B. 1*.
[42] S.R.O., tithe award. The introduction to the award gives only 47 a.
[43] St. George's Chapel, MS. III. F. 10; S.R.O., D/P/n. sty 3/1/3; Kelly's Dir. Som. (1939).
[44] St. George's Chapel, MS. XV. 53. 81A.
[45] S.R.O., D/P/n. sty 3/1/1, 3/1/4; ibid. D/D/Rg 278.
[46] On plaster heart with the inscription W & M G[riffin].
[47] Ibid. D/P/n. sty 3/1/2.

[48] Ibid. DD/AH 66/27.
[49] Ibid. D/D/B returns 1815.
[50] St. George's Chapel, MS. XVII. 35. 5; S.R.O., D/P/n. sty 9/3/3; inf. from the Revd. R. Parker, Nether Stowey.
[51] S.R.O., D/D/Ca 57.
[52] Calamy Revised, ed. A. G. Matthews, 556; Walker Revised, ed. A. G. Matthews, 320; S.R.O., D/P/n. sty 2/1/1.
[53] S.R.O., D/D/Bo; D/D/Bp; D/D/Pd 2; D/D/B returns, 1815, 1827. [54] D.N.B.
[55] S.R.O., D/P/n. sty 2/1/2–3. [56] D.N.B.
[57] St. George's Chapel, MS. Livings Bk. I. B. 1*; S.R.O., D/D/B returns 1815.
[58] D.N.B.
[59] S.R.O., D/D/B returns 1815, 1827.
[60] Ibid. D/D/B returns 1827.
[61] St. George's Chapel, MS. XVII. 35. 5; Rep. Com. Eccl. Revenues, pp. 154–5.
[62] S.R.O., DD/BR/py 115.
[63] H.M.C. Wells, i. 432.
[64] Taunton Castle, Pigott Colln.; S.R.O., DD/SAS (C/2402) 49.
[65] S.R.O., D/P/n. sty 2/1/1.
[66] Som. Wills, ed. Brown, ii. 102; S.R.O., D/P/n. sty 2/1/1.
[67] S.R.O., D/P/n. sty 2/1/1.
[68] St. George's Chapel, MSS. Livings Bk. I. B. 1*; XVII. 35. 5; S.R.O., D/D/B returns 1815; D/D/Pd 1.

Pressure for a further extension resulted in the complete rebuilding of the church with the exception of the tower in 1849–51, probably to the designs of C. E. Giles.[69] The church was extensively refitted in the 1950s and 1960s.[70] Two representations of mitres, set on brackets in the chancel, commemorate the two vicars who became bishops. The carved royal arms are of Queen Anne.[71]

There are six bells of which five date from the 18th century. They were recast in 1914, when the treble was added, and restored in 1953.[72] The registers date from 1640 and are complete. A note of 1720 on the earliest register declares that an older volume was burnt at the 'great house' during the civil war.[73]

A church dedicated to *ST. MICHAEL* is said to have stood near the castle, which was known as St. Michael's Hill in 1620.[74] A piece of masonry that was possibly a 12th-century cushion capital was discovered on a site south of the castle called Smith's close.[75]

NONCONFORMITY. Ten recusants were reported in 1591, and in 1613 the Walker family were said to have been recusants for 12 years.[76] In 1641 three men refused to sign the Protestation and five recusants, including the Walker family, paid the higher subsidy.[77]

In 1669 a nonconformist teacher had 18 hearers, and in 1672 a house was used for Presbyterian meetings.[78] Another house was licensed for worship in 1689 and in 1731 there was a newly erected Presbyterian meeting house.[79] A house, probably in Castle Street, was described as a meeting house from 1784 to 1793.[80] The Cornish miners working in Dodington included several Methodists, notably the Grose family.[81] Samuel Grose supported an application for a licence granted in 1795, and another supporter was Robert Williams, who occupied the Independent meeting house in 1806. Licences were issued for other houses in 1792 and 1819.[82] The latter may have been for the Methodists who had eight members in Nether Stowey c. 1818. Services appear to have ceased by 1823.[83]

The Congregational chapel for 200 was built in 1807 on the site of two cottages in the yard of a house, later to become the manse, at the north end of Lime Street. It was conveyed to trustees in 1808.

The trust property included the chapel and house and a second house described as a former meeting house.[84] The chapel continued in use until c. 1974, but was then closed and in 1980 was demolished.[85]

A Baptist minister was resident in the village in 1851.[86]

EDUCATION. A Sunday school was begun in the parish c. 1789 and was endowed with £100 under the will of Richard Stephens, vicar 1753–90.[87] In 1792 a 'school of industry' was attached to the Sunday school.[88] Further endowments were made in 1794, 1809, and 1845.[89] In 1826 up to 50 poor children attended the Sunday school and in 1835 there were 120.[90]

In 1812 a schoolroom, similar to that designed by Richard Carver for Nettlecombe in 1819, was built by Thomas Poole and in the following year a day school was opened; it soon had 118 children with two teachers.[91] The school was maintained by subscriptions and fees. In 1826 the school taught reading, writing, and arithmetic to 130 children including some from neighbouring parishes, and by 1835 there was a separate infant school.[92] The school was united with the National Society by 1847, when there were three separate buildings, though only two paid teachers, with 112 children attending daily.[93] There were 55 children and 38 infants on the register in 1903, though by 1912 numbers were falling.[94] An evening school was begun in 1917 and in 1925 an extension provided accommodation for a total of 130 children. In spite of the removal of senior pupils in 1957 numbers continued to rise with the increasing population of the parish.[95] A new school was built among new houses west of the village in 1979. The old schoolroom became a public library, museum, and exhibition centre in 1980.[96]

In 1792 a private boarding school was kept by the curate where boys were taught Latin, Greek, English, and geography for £20 a year, and for an additional fee might learn arithmetic, writing, and dancing.[97] In 1795 a French émigré priest was teaching French in the village.[98] A day school started in 1826 had 25 children in 1835 but there are no further references to it.[99] An academy for both sexes was kept by a Miss Brown in 1840 and there was a ladies' boarding school in St. Mary's Street during the 1870s.[1]

[69] St. George's Chapel, MS. XVII. 35. 5; S.R.O., D/P/n. sty 8/1/1, 9/1/1–2. Wm. Shewbrook of Taunton was the builder: plaque in church.
[70] S.R.O., D/P/n. sty 6/1/1.
[71] *Proc. Som. Arch. Soc.* lxxxiv, suppl. 2, 46.
[72] S.R.O., D/P/n. sty 6/1/1; DD/SAS CH 16/2.
[73] Ibid. D/P/n. sty 2/1/1–12.
[74] Ibid. DD/NW 67. The antiquarian Thos. Palmer refers to a rental of 1362, now lost: ibid. DD/AH 21/2.
[75] Inf. from Dr. I. Burrow, county archaeologist.
[76] *S. & D. N. & Q.* v. 114; S.R.O., D/D/Ca 180.
[77] *Som. Protestation Returns*, ed. Howard and Stoate, 172, 288–9.
[78] *Calamy Revised*, ed. A. G. Matthews; *Orig. Records of Early Nonconf.* ed. G. L. Turner, i. 9, 322.
[79] S.R.O., Q/RR meeting house lics.
[80] Ibid. Q/REl Williton.
[81] Hamilton and Lawrence, *Men and Mining in the Quantocks*, 7.   [82] S.R.O., D/D/Rm, box 2.
[83] W. Symons, *Early Methodism in West Som.* (London, 1893), 17, 115.
[84] S.R.O., DD/SAS (C/1207); ibid. D/D/Rm, box 2; *Cong. Year Bk.* (1900); deed in possession of Mrs. Hill, the Manse, Nether Stowey.
[85] New College, London, MSS. 322/17/1–3, 343/10, 372/10, 372/1/3; *Rep. Som. Cong. Union* (1896); *Kelly's Dir. Som.* (1906, 1910); deed in possession of Mrs. Hill; inf. from Mr. Trout, Nether Stowey.
[86] P.R.O., HO 107/1924.
[87] Sandford, *Thos. Poole*, 28; *15th Rep. Com. Char.* p. 458.   [88] Sandford, *Thos. Poole*, 58.
[89] *15th Rep. Com. Char.* p. 459; Char. Com. files; S.R.O., D/P/n. sty 3/1/1.
[90] *15th Rep. Com. Char.* p. 458; *Educ. Enq. Abstract*, H.C. 62 (1835), xlii.
[91] Sandford, *Thos. Poole*, 266–7; above, Nettlecombe, education.
[92] *Educ. of Poor Digest*, H.C. 224 (1819), ix(2); *Ann. Rep. B. & W. Assoc. S.P.C.K.* (1825–6); *15th Rep. Com. Char.* p. 458; *Educ. Enq. Abstract*, H.C. 62 (1835), xlii.
[93] Nat. Soc. *Inquiry, 1846–7*, Som. 12–13.
[94] S.R.O., C/E 27; ibid. D/P/n. sty 18/7/1.
[95] Ibid. D/P/n. sty 18/7/1; ibid. *Schs. Lists.*
[96] Ibid. DD/EDS 1721.
[97] Sandford, *Thos. Poole*, 26.   [98] Ibid. 44, 162.
[99] *Educ. Enq. Abstract* H.C. 62 (1835), xlii.
[1] *Co. Gazette Dir.* (1840); P.R.O., RG 10/2380; *P.O. Dir. Som.* (1875); Morris & Co. *Dir. Som.* (1872).

CHARITIES FOR THE POOR. John Hodges of East Quantoxhead (d. 1703) gave half the rents of two tenements in Cannington, for the term of a lease, to 12 poor people in Nether Stowey.[2]

In 1708 a sum of £100, comprising gifts by Charles Steynings, a Mr. Dyer, Jane Walker, and her sister Mary Marshal, and a donation from the parish, was used to purchase Budley meadow for the benefit of the poor. A rent of £6 was originally received for the poor but from 1811 a large part of the income, probably representing the proceeds of the parish donation, was diverted to parish funds.[3] In 1868 the charity was distributed to widows and orphans and in 1870 the meadow, then known as Poor's meadow, was given to Sir Peregrine Acland in exchange for land in South Lane.[4] By 1899, when the Budley charity became part of the Nether Stowey United Charities, the income from the land was £13 8s.[5]

By will dated 1709 Joseph Cooke, rector of Spaxton, left £3 a year from land in Stogursey to be distributed in bread to the respectable church-going poor of Nether Stowey for 1,000 years. The charity continued to be distributed throughout the 19th century.[6] Thomas Landsey left £100 to the parishes of Over and Nether Stowey under his will dated 1801, the income to be divided equally between the poor of both places. In the 1860s the money was given to widows and orphans.[7] By 1865 Landsey's charity was worth £166, of which Nether Stowey had a half share. Sums of £109 and £106 given to the poor by Francis Poole (d. 1832) and Elizabeth Sykes (d. 1863) were distributed in coal in 1911. Those charities were united with the Budley charity in 1899.[8]

A coal charity distributed in the 1860s was probably based on subscriptions.[9] Jenkin Buller's endowment of 1794 for the poor men's club was converted to a coal charity in 1913.[10] The Mary Stanley Sick Poor Fund, begun c. 1920, is used to send gifts to people in hospital. The Nether Stowey United Charities and Jenkin Buller's charity are distributed in cards and gifts to the elderly every second Christmas.[11]

[2] Collinson, *Hist. Som.* iii. 554; S.R.O., D/P/qua. e 2/1/3.
[3] *Char. Don.* H.C. 551 (1816), xvi; *15th Rep. Com. Char.* p. 457.
[4] S.R.O., D/P/n. sty 9/1/2, 17/7/1; ibid. DD/AH 18/5.
[5] Ibid. D/P/n. sty 3/1/3; Char. Com. files; Char. Com. reg.

[6] S.R.O., D/P/n. sty 2/1/3; *15th Rep. Com. Char.* p. 456.
[7] *15th Rep. Com. Char.* p. 458; S.R.O., D/P/n. sty 9/1/2.
[8] S.R.O., D/P/n. sty 2/1/7, 3/1/3, 17/2/1; Char. Com. files; Char. Com. reg.
[9] S.R.O., D/P/n. sty 17/2/1. [10] Char. Com. files.
[11] Ibid.; inf. from Mr. C. D. A. Brown, Nether Stowey.

INDEX